Dedication

We would like to dedicate the **Fifth Edition**
of *Hotel Management and Operations* to
all of the students who have touched our lives.
You have done so in more ways than
you can ever imagine.

M. J. O. and D. G. R.

HOTEL
MANAGEMENT
and OPERATIONS

FIFTH EDITION

Edited by

MICHAEL J. O'FALLON, PH.D.
Hospitality and Tourism Management
James Madison University

DENNEY G. RUTHERFORD, PH.D.
Endowed Chair Emeritus
School of Hospitality Business Management
Washington State University

WILEY

JOHN WILEY & SONS, INC.

Published by John Wiley & Sons, Inc., Hoboken, New Jersey.

Published simultaneously in Canada.

No part of this publication may be reproduced, stored in a retrieval system, or transmitted in any form or by any means, electronic, mechanical, photocopying, recording, scanning, or otherwise, except as permitted under Section 107 or 108 of the 1976 United States Copyright Act, without either the prior written permission of the Publisher, or authorization through payment of the appropriate per-copy fee to the Copyright Clearance Center, Inc., 222 Rosewood Drive, Danvers, MA 01923, 978-750-8400, fax 978-646-8600, or on the Web at www.copyright.com. Requests to the Publisher for permission should be addressed to the Permissions Department, John Wiley & Sons, Inc., 111 River Street, Hoboken, NJ 07030, 201-748-6011, fax 201-748-6008, or online at http://www.wiley.com/go/permissions.

Limit of Liability/Disclaimer of Warranty: While the publisher and author have used their best efforts in preparing this book, they make no representations or warranties with respect to the accuracy or completeness of the contents of this book and specifically disclaim any implied warranties of merchantability or fitness for a particular purpose. No warranty may be created or extended by sales representatives or written sales materials. The advice and strategies contained herein may not be suitable for your situation. You should consult with a professional where appropriate. Neither the publisher nor author shall be liable for any loss of profit or any other commercial damages, including but not limited to special, incidental, consequential, or other damages.

For general information on our other products and services, or technical support, please contact our Customer Care Department within the United States at 800-762-2974, outside the United States at 317-572-3993 or fax 317-572-4002.

Wiley also publishes its books in a variety of electronic formats. Some content that appears in print may not be available in electronic books.

For more information about Wiley products, visit our Web site at http://www.wiley.com.

Evaluation copies are provided to qualified academics and professionals for review purposes only, for use in their courses during the next academic year. These copies are licensed and may not be sold or transferred to a third party. Upon completion of the review period, please return the evaluation copy to Wiley. Return instructions and a free of charge return shipping label are available at www.wiley.com/go/returnlabel. Outside of the United States, please contact your local representative.

Library of Congress Cataloging-in-Publication Data

Hotel management operations / edited by Michael J. O'Fallon, Denney G. Rutherford. — 5th ed.
    p. cm.
  Includes bibliographical references and index.
  ISBN 978-0-470-17714-3 (pbk.)
  1. Hotel management. I. Rutherford, Denney G., 1942-   II. O'Fallon, Michael J.
  TX911.3.M27H663 2009
  647.94'068—dc22

                                     2009033114

Printed in the United States of America

10 9 8 7 6 5 4 3 2 1

CONTENTS

v

CHAPTER 7 MARKETING AND ASSOCIATED ACTIVITIES 306

CHAPTER 8 FINANCIAL CONTROL AND INFORMATION MANAGEMENT 371

CHAPTER 9 HUMAN RESOURCES POLICY MANAGEMENT 433

INDEX 487

PREFACE

As Denney would tell you, the **First Edition** of this textbook project was originally born out of a range of frustrations. While there are many outstanding textbooks in the hotel management field that deal with significant portions of operations, particularly housekeeping, front office, and food and beverage, there are very few that try to treat, in a balanced and in-depth way, each department in the hotel. One frustration was that some texts that dealt with these departments spent an inordinate amount of time focused on one aspect of the hotel operations—usually either front of the house, food and beverage, or marketing. Other departments, for better or worse, were treated as minor players. Consequently, students and readers of such texts were given only a cursory introduction to the intricacies of these "minor" departments, their management, their people, and their interactive functions in the overall hotel organization.

Another frustration he encountered was using the material available at the time to promote critical thinking among students of hotel administration. Critical thinking refers to that process whereby students are exposed to a number of different viewpoints within a theoretical structure. Then, from analysis of those viewpoints, they become better able to synthesize a viewpoint about hotel operations that will enable them to intelligently approach whatever practical situations they may find themselves confronted with in the "real world."

There is a conventional wisdom that goes, "something may be okay in theory, but it doesn't work in practice." Like economist Milton Friedman, we reject that statement. If theory doesn't work in practice, it is lousy theory. It is a professor's responsibility to guide students in understanding that theory (in the word of Friedman) explains, predicts, or controls, and does this in different ways given different variables in different organizations. This is another example of frustration that subsequent editions have been designed to further address.

NEW TO THE EDITION

In this **Fifth Edition** of *Hotel Management and Operations*, the reader will find new articles that were added for three primary reasons. First, new articles pertaining to recent trends in the lodging industry are included. This includes those covering topics such as spas, yield management techniques, unexpected events that have occurred in recent years, and changes in the food and beverage industry. Second, a few articles were added that are a little more accessible for those readers who may be in their first or second year in a hospitality program (e.g., "Face Recognition and Name Recall"). In addition, a few of these articles provide insight into ways in which students of hospitality programs, and new lodging professionals, can be successful in this industry. Finally, many of the "A Day in the Life" and similar readings are from industry professionals who are new contributors to this edition. All of them bring new insights into a fast-changing, rapid-paced, industry.

As we went about planning and designing the **Fifth Edition** of *Hotel Management and Operations*, we felt the need to continually remind ourselves of the lessons of the frustrations listed previously. We wanted to make sure the original idea behind this book did not get lost. By helping the reader gain an appreciation of what a variety of observers, thinkers, researchers, and commentators think about a topic, in this case, a hotel department, a student or hotel professional can feel better prepared to find ways to apply theory in a practical setting or situation. In the final analysis, it is up to you to make the best use of *Hotel Management and Operations, Fifth Edition* because, as we state above, none of us knows it all. Good luck; it is our pleasure to do this work for you.

A NOTE FROM DENNEY

As we put this last edition, with my involvement, to bed, I was struck by the fact that this book project has been ongoing for over 20 years. During that time, I have learned an awful lot about myself, my colleagues and peers, and the great graduates from our School of Hospitality Business Management program. This education has been, for the most part, pleasant and gratifying. During the course of these years, I have had the privilege to watch our students develop their careers in the hotel business to the point where they became contributors to various editions of the book. I think I can be excused for being very proud of them.

My coauthor, Professor O'Fallon, was an undergraduate student of mine in the mid 1990s. He actually used a rough draft of the **Second Edition** (it was a copy of the typed manuscript, and weighed about 22 pounds) as a student in our Hotel Ops class. That he has developed into a professor himself is, I suppose, the most gratifying experience for an old guy like me. He now has more than 20 years to grow and develop this project, and I have every expectation that he will succeed in making it better with each edition.

My partner and wife, Sandy Sweeney, continues to work as I enjoy retirement. Her support and encouragement over the years has been a critical factor in any success I have enjoyed as an author. She should be given equal credit as a coauthor. In the past, at the conclusion of every edition, we were moving. Not now. We will be in Port Townsend, Washington, for the duration and invite anyone visiting the area to contact us through the university.

To my former students, I salute you. To my friends and colleagues in I-CHRIE and at other universities around the world, it has been my privilege to share this time with you. To my coauthors on various research projects, you made me better and I thank you. To Washington State University, the College of Business and the School of Hospitality Business Management, I value the opportunities you have provided me beyond description; Terry, Rom, and Eric, you were especially valuable.

Goodbye for now; may you always have a high REVPAR.

CONTRIBUTORS

JE'ANNA ABBOTT, Professor, Attorney, and Spec's Charitable Foundation Professor in Social Responsibility, Conrad N. Hilton College of Hotel and Restaurant Management, University of Houston

HOLLEIGH ALEXANDER, Spa Director, The Ritz-Carlton Club, Aspen Highlands

PETER ANDERSON, ISHC, Anderson and Associates

MARIO ARNALDO, Adjunct, Travel Industry Management, Hawaii Pacific University

MARK BEATTIE, Director of Distributive Learning, Gonzaga University

CHERYLYNN BECKER, Associate Professor, Tourism Management, The University of Southern Mississippi

RICH BENNINGER, CMP, Vice President, Sales and Marketing at Clear Span Tents, Las Vegas, Nevada

SHERIE BREZINA, Director and Associate Professor, Resort and Hospitality Management, Florida Gulf Coast University

PAUL CHAPPELLE, CRME, Regional Revenue Manager, Red Lion Hotels Corporation

BETH G. CHUNG-HERRERA, Associate Professor, College of Business, San Diego State University

FELIPE G. COFIÑO, Director of Human Resources, Hyatt Regency Bethesda

MARK CONKLIN, Area Vice President, Western Europe, Marriott Hotels, Resorts, and Suites, Frankfort, Germany

CARY C. COUNTRYMAN, Associate Professor, Hospitality and Tourism Management, Brigham Young University-Hawaii

MELISSA DALLAS, Department Head and Professor, Hospitality and Restaurant Administration, Missouri State University

AGNES L. DEFRANCO, Professor, Conrad N. Hilton College of Hotel and Restaurant Management, University of Houston

JOHN DEW, Executive Consultant, Bellevue, Washington

GARRY DICKOVER, General Manager, Courtyard Convention Center, Las Vegas, Nevada

NICHOLAS R. DIMEGLIO, Vice President, Ritz-Carlton Club Operations

MICHAEL J. DRAEGER, Controller, Dayton Depot Casino, Dayton, Nevada

TOM DUPAR, Principal, Dupar Dynamics, Bellevue, Washington

CATHY A. ENZ, Louis G. Shaeneman Professor of Innovation and Dynamic Management, Cornell University School of Hotel Administration

C. LEE EVANS, Director of Purchasing, The Oasis Resort; Casa Blanca Spa and Golf and Virgin River Hotel and Casino

EMILIO FABICO, Walt Disney World, Orlando, Florida

GIL FRIED, Chair Sports Management/Hospitality and Tourism Management Department, University of New Haven

JACINTA GAU, Assistant Professor, Department of Criminal Justice, Washington State University

AJAY GHEI, Senior Human Resources Officer, The World Bank Group

ROBYN GRAFF, Catering/Convention Service Manager, Hyatt Regency Washington on Capitol Hill

BIANCA GROHMANN, Associate Professor of Marketing, John Molson School of Business, Concordia University

SHARON K. HODGE, Assistant Professor, Love School of Business, Elon University

EARL D. HONEYCUTT JR., Professor, Love School of Business, Elon University

PAUL IACOVINO, Vice President, Marketing— Asia Pacific, Four Seasons Hotels and Resorts

THOMAS JONES, Associate Professor, Harrah Hotel College, University of Nevada, Las Vegas

CHRISTINE KAY, Principle Associate, Christine Kay & Associates

JOHN LAGAZO, Interim Executive Director at Midland County Convention and Visitors Bureau, Midland, Michigan

MELENIE J. LANKAU, Associate Professor, Terry College of Business, University of Georgia

STEPHEN M. LEBRUTO, Associate Dean, Rosen College of Hospitality Management, University of Central Florida

JENNIFER LUCAS, Director of Education and Development, Loews Hotels

VALENTINO LUCIANI, Past Instructor, University of Nevada, Las Vegas

MELIH MADANOGLU, Assistant Professor, Resort and Hospitality Management, Florida Gulf Coast University

VINCENT P. MAGNINI, Assistant Professor, Hospitality and Tourism Management, Pamplin College of Business, Virginia Tech University

CHRIS E. MCGOEY, CPP, CSP, CAM, Crime Doctor, Los Angeles, California

OLIVER MEINZER, Resident Manager, Newport Beach Marriott Suites

SILVIA MILLA, Graduate of the Conrad N. Hilton College of Hotel and Restaurant Management, University of Houston

ELISA MONCARZ, Professor, School of Hospitality and Tourism Management, Florida International University

SUSAN V. MORRIS, Principal, The NewHeight Group

GLEN B. MOUNTS, FMA, Director of Engineering, Marriott Newport Beach Hotel & Spa

SUZANNE K. MURRMANN, Professor, Hospitality and Tourism Management, Pamplin College of Business, Virginia Tech University

ARTHUR E. NATHAN, New Product Thought Leader, Mellon HR Solutions

EDDYSTONE C. NEBEL, III, Purdue University, Emeritus

PETER O'CONNOR, Professor, France's Institute de Management Hotelier International, Essec Business School, France

WILLIAM J. QUAIN, Florida International University, School of Hospitality Management

CLINTON L. RAPPOLE, Professor Emeritus, Conrad N. Hilton College of Hotel and Restaurant Management, University of Houston

LOUIS B. RICHMOND, Founder and CEO, Richmond Public Relations

CARL D. RIEGEL, Professor, Hospitality and Restaurant Administration, Missouri State University

MICHAEL RILEY, Professor, School of Management, University of Surrey

RAYMOND S. SCHMIDGALL, Professor, Hilton Hotels Professor of Hospitality Financial Management, School of Hospitality Business, Michigan State University

MARGARET SHAW, University of Guelph, School of Hotel and Food Administration

SUSAN B. SHERIDAN, Owner, Taughannock Farms Inn, Trumansburg, New York

PATTI J. SHOCK, Professor, Director of Distance Learning, Harrah Hotel College, University of Nevada, Las Vegas

STOWE SHOEMAKER, Associate Dean of Research and Donald Hubbs Professorship, Conrad N. Hilton College of Hotel and Restaurant Management, University of Houston

JUDY A. SIGUAW, Professor, Cornell University School of Hotel Administration

MARTA SINCLAIR, Lecturer, Griffith Business School, Griffith University

CARL SINCLAIR, Griffith University

ERIC R. SPANGENBERG, Dean, College of Business, Washington State University

JOHN M. STEFANELLI, Professor, Harrah Hotel College, University of Nevada, Las Vegas

ROBERT W. STRATE, National Aeronautics and Space Administration

NANCY SWANGER, Associate Professor, School of Hospitality and Business Management, Washington State University

J. BRUCE TRACEY, Associate Professor, Academic Area Director, Cornell University School of Hotel Administration

TOM UNDERWOOD, General Manager, Richmond Marriott Downtown (White Lodging)

TANYA VENEGAS, Executive Director of HFTP Research Institute, Conrad N. Hilton College of Hotel and Restaurant Management, University of Houston

FLETCH WALLER, Principal, FCW Consulting, Seattle, Washington

ACKNOWLEDGMENTS

As any author or editor of a published piece of material can attest, the project is never completed by a single individual. This book, in particular, was completed through the knowledge, creativity, and ingenuity of many individuals. It would be a huge mistake on our part if we didn't take a moment to thank those individuals who helped put this together. However, as Denney has mentioned in the past, while it has been a team effort, all of its flaws, and there probably are more than a few, are solely our responsibility.

First of all, the authors of the various pieces included here who knowingly or unknowingly have contributed their thoughts, research, ideas, opinions, and expertise to this exercise in critical thinking about hotel departmental operations deserve recognition. Without the rich mixture of interest and talent extant in the hospitality profession and its educational establishment today, this collection of readings would not have been possible. It is our great good fortune that our friends, colleagues, and former students could devote the time they did to contribute to this project. Our badgering, cajoling, begging, and bribing aside, Denney and I think we're all still friends.

We particularly want to salute those who crafted "custom" pieces for this edition and those professionals who contributed "Day in the Life" and "As I See It" pieces. They have made this edition a richer and more user-friendly book. They also add a view of the real world that is invaluable. To each and every one of you, thank you for your contributions, especially on such last minute notice as I was notoriously known to give.

The support and encouragement of our colleagues, at both Washington State University and James Madison University were critical. In particular, we thank the past director of the School of Hospitality Business Management program at WSU, Terry Umbreit, and a plethora of students who all contributed to the success of this project with advice, counsel, and suggestions.

Mary Cassells, our editor at Wiley, provided much-needed support throughout the entire process. As she can verify, I wasn't exactly the easiest individual to work with. However, she continued to be punctual with responses to my naïve questions, and was very patient with me, particularly when things didn't go as planned.

We both owe a great deal to our wives, Sandy Sweeney and Lisa O'Fallon. To Sandy, Denney thanks you for always being there for him. He loves you more than you will ever know. To Lisa, my wife, you are the backbone of our family. Thank you so much for your patience through this entire process. In particular, I truly appreciate your role as my editor and sounding board. I love you dearly.

I would also like to thank my children, Mikaela, Samantha, and Hannah, for your unconditional love. I knew that I could always come home from a rough day at work, look at your faces, and forget everything that happened that day. You brighten my day, and I am so proud to be your dad.

To my parents, Jim and Elaine O'Fallon, thank you for being the greatest parents I know. I hope to be half the parents you were to me, to my children. I love you. To my sister, Christy Fitzgerald, and brothers, Ryan and Andy O'Fallon, thank you for always challenging me. I love you all.

Finally, I would personally like to thank you, Denney, for the encouragement and assistance that you gave, and continue to give, me. My curiosity for learning began back in 1994 when I took your hotel operations course as a sophomore at Washington State University. At that point in my life, I never would have thought that I would end up in higher education. I can honestly say that if it weren't for you, I wouldn't be here today. I am truly honored to be a part of this project with you. Thank you, my colleague and friend.

Michael J. O'Fallon
Harrisonburg, Virginia

Denney G. Rutherford
Port Townsend, Washington

OVERVIEW

1.1 INTRODUCTION

The vast majority of research articles and essays in this book deal with one or more aspects of what has been called the art and science of modern hotel management. It should be noted that the word modern can be loaded with the potential for much misunderstanding. Hotels are changing and will continue to change. As a result, the techniques of management of modern hotels must adapt to changing circumstances. Subsequent sections of this book are designed to help the student and practitioner discover information, methods, and techniques for dealing with these changing circumstances.

✦ INFLUENCES

Like many other American businesses, hotels have been affected by shifts in emphasis in the country's living patterns. People and industry have moved from the so-called rust belt to the sun belt. The hotel business has been active in reborn and reconstructed central cities. The explosion of technology and information-based companies has concentrated human endeavor in technological corridors in California, Massachusetts, Washington, Texas, and North Carolina, to name a few such places. It can be safely said that where jobs are and major concentrations of economic activity occur, hotels will follow.

Among other current and ongoing influencers of hotel design, construction, marketing, and operation are the following. Note: This list is neither exhaustive nor exclusive.

- *Demographics* play a major role and will continue to be influential in the foreseeable future. As the baby boom generation and its children mature, the population of the country will for many years be older, healthier, and better educated than previous generations. These facts will present new challenges and opportunities to all business managers.

- *Technology*—in the form of computers, communication, personal devices, and laborsaving mechanical equipment—has had and will have a major effect on the way in which hotels are managed and operated. The speed with which information is accumulated, stored, manipulated, and transferred is such that today most travelers expect that the hotel rooms they rent will allow them to be as productive as they are in the office or at home. Increasingly, with portable computing, personal data assistants (PDAs), wireless communication, and virtually everything somehow connected to the Internet, hotels must provide services and access that allow guests a seamless transition from the business, travel, or home environment to that of the hotel. Increasingly, entertainment must be fused with communication and productive processes.

- The concept of *market segmentation,* or ever-increasingly finely tuned market definitions, will dictate hotel structures and organizations. In addition, management tactics designed to address those market segments have become even more important to the management of hospitality service businesses. With the increased power in the information and data manipulation realm, hotels have available to them ever-expanding databases about guests and are creating new products to attract those markets.

- One of the effects of the aging demographic is the emergence of *vacation resorts*—a modern incarnation of the time-share properties of several decades ago. Because these are being developed and operated by name hotel companies and are marketed to the affluent, healthy, well-educated population segment, resort managers have had to absorb new managerial realities.

- The well-documented change in the complexion of the *national economy* from one that emphasizes goods and, to a lesser extent natural resources, to one that emphasizes services has kindled new ideas about the way in which we manage the design and delivery of these services. Hotels, restaurants, and travel services are now seen as unique entities that dictate special kinds of managerial techniques and strategies.

- Changes in people's *travel patterns* have altered the way we manage our hotel properties. Deregulation of the airlines has driven a change in the way millions of people travel each year, given the hub-and-spoke design of airline services. Many hotel companies are now locating major hotel properties adjacent to hub air transport facilities, taking advantage of the fact that business travelers may not need to travel to a central business district (CBD) to accomplish their purpose in a given area. Meetings and conferences can now be scheduled within a 5-minute limousine ride from the air terminal, and the business traveler can be headed for his or her next destination before the day is over without having to stay overnight in a CBD hotel.

- New *patterns of investment* in hotel facilities have emerged in the last two decades, and more attention is now paid to achieving optimum return on investment. Because people from outside the hotel industry are now participating in its financial structuring, hotel operations are no longer dependent on the vision of a single entrepreneur. Managers now must design tactics and strategies to achieve heretofore unanticipated financial goals. The same trend has also altered the complexion of management and organization of the modern hotel.

This is especially true of publicly owned hotel firms, where Wall Street stock analysts heavily influence stock prices through expectations of quarterly revenues and profits. This puts pressure on hotel companies and their operations managers to perform, on a quarterly basis, in a way contrary to many managers' instincts.

Most of the foregoing issues and influences still operate (to a greater or lesser extent) on the organizational structures and strategies of the modern hotel. Since the last edition of this book, however, other phenomena of an economic, cultural, and social nature have come to the fore, complicating our view of hotel management. This furthers the argument that the hotel industry is a part of the greater economy and at the mercy of elements often completely out of its control.

The cyclical nature of the U.S. and international economies has recently affected significantly hotels' ability to respond to changing circumstances. In early 1993, for instance, employment growth was stagnant, corporate profits were low, the expansion of the gross national product (GNP) was only a marginal percentage above previous years, and travel in most segments was down because of corporate restructuring, downsizing, or reorganizing. Vast layoffs in the hundreds of thousands had been announced every month. While fuel prices continued to be relatively stable, consumer spending patterns and high employment growth had not materialized, particularly in light of corporate layoffs and the ongoing nervousness of consumers about whether or not their financial wherewithal was safe.

Now consider early 2000, when the third edition of this book was being written. Unemployment was at an all-time low, the Dow Jones Industrial Average was between 10,000 and 11,000, hotel occupancies had stabilized nationally in excess of 70 percent, and the federal government was running a surplus for the first time in the memory of most.

Then what happened? The terrorist attacks in New York and Washington, DC, in 2001 changed the face of all business and travel. Major airlines were (and still are) in bankruptcy; hotels were struggling to achieve profitable occupancies; business travel was down; the high-tech stock market bubble burst; the country was (and still is) at war in a number of locations; security made travel more difficult, if not actually annoying; and people were nervous. Combine this with an imbalance of trade, the outsourcing of jobs, and the largest federal deficits in history, and the face of the economy is challenging. This translates directly to an effect not only on business travel but on personal and recreational travel as well. Finding ways to operate profitably in such an environment is the job of the next generation of hotel operators.

Although there were still a few issues stemming from 9/11, as the economy improved in the mid-2000s, so did the hotel business. In fact, the hotel industry hit an all-time high in total revenue in 2004 at $113.7 billion (Smith Travel Research). However, that was short-lived. With the crash of the housing market, analysts are predicting the economy in the year 2008/2009 to be in its worst shape in history since the Great Depression. As a result, hotels are seeing all-time low occupancy percentages, leading to low revenue and profit levels. Unfortunately, many major hotel organizations have been forced, once again, to lay off individuals, causing managers to pick up duties that used to be assigned to other management positions. This has forced a change in the structure of an organization and how management leads its employees.

In preceding editions, a prediction was made that cultural diversity would play a role in the management and organizational structure of the modern hotel in the United States. As surely as living patterns, economic cycles, and market segmentation have influenced the hotel industry, so would the change in ethnicity of the workforce. The cultural backgrounds that an increasingly diversified workforce would bring to hotel operations may be seen as a problem, or a challenge, or both. To most operators, it would be seen as an opportunity to demonstrate to an increasingly diverse clientele that hotel companies are committed to hiring and training a workforce structure that mirrors society. We see no reason to change that prediction now; if anything, acculturation of the hospitality business will accelerate.

The legal and regulatory environments are becoming increasingly important to all business managers, and hotel operators are no exception. Increasingly, operators must be aware of and alert to realms of risk that can engender lawsuits against them. Several articles and essays in this edition highlight these threats to hotels and their guests. It should be noted that present-day security concerns also have significantly affected the ways in which hotels are operated. Awareness of the risk environment and the regulatory realm are factors that affect a hotel's ability to compete in the early part of the twenty-first century. Essays and articles in the security section and the human resources section address this issue.

✦ INTRODUCTORY READINGS

We have attempted in this edition to present new and (sometimes) different takes on the hotel business. This section is also used to explore ideas that are new to the management process, and that—who knows?—may never completely catch on. Rather than focus exclusively on the operations of the major chains, the readings here are from the perspectives of operators, leaders, and experts such as regional operators, major industry consultants, and independent branded hotels.

John Dew, former president of Inn Ventures, a regional hotel management and development company that has built and operated many Marriott products, in addition to a proprietary hotel product, provides an insider's view of the steps needed to bring a hotel from conception to construction and operation. This unique view of hotel operations connects the concept of hotel development with the realities of day-to-day operation. It should help aspiring managers understand how the intricacies of the development process may influence the marketing and management of the hotel.

Because new construction of hotels diminished greatly after 9/11 but firms still needed to grow, rebranding existing properties generated a lot of growth activity. Rebranding is a complicated process that must be accomplished within critical time frames to coincide with marketing, financial, and operational variables. Tom Dupar is a seasoned veteran at this fascinating and important activity and has participated in rebranding operations around the world. His essay on the intricacies of rebranding was a mainstay in the previous edition of this book. Today's economic circumstances are different, and Dupar's business has changed its focus to opening new major projects. His piece serves as a useful companion to that of John Dew, and the two should be read together, with an eye toward comparing Dew's smaller project focus and Dupar's large projects.

As technology has rapidly changed the way hotels do business, the article written by O'Connor on online pricing is timely. It is not uncommon to get the answer, "I do" from a computer-savvy guest when he or she is asked, "who books your hotel reservations?" The question addressed by O'Connor relates to the distribution channels (e.g., Expedia.com, the hotel's own website, etc.) most likely used by a guest to make a hotel reservation. Interestingly enough, price quotes across channels may differ.

As Kim and Kim report, "65 percent of hotel guests tend to switch lodging brands across different parent hotel companies on their next stay" (2007:61). This tends to suggest that customer loyalty may be a thing of the past. As a result, hotel companies are looking for ways to distinguish themselves from their competitors. The articles remaining in this chapter (most of which are new to this edition) address this issue.

Drawing from the psychology literature, Magnini and Honeycutt discuss ways in which a hotel associate can recall a guest's name and face from a recent interaction. Given the importance of guest satisfaction, a guest who is addressed by their first name when approached by a hotel associate may feel more comfortable in the hotel, resulting in that guest becoming a loyal customer. As the authors state, remembering a name of a guest is a difficult task as it is the third step in a three-step process. Upon reading this article, the reader will have a better understanding of the process associated with a guest/associate interaction. In addition, techniques for remembering faces and names are discussed.

Perhaps proving the axiom that "everything old is new again," the concept of health and wellness spas as a hotel and resort product has enjoyed a resurgence. Once the province of high-end hotels and resorts, a spa in which guests can be pampered has been added to the service mix in many more modest hotels and resorts. While the big-name spas at five-star properties still set the standard for pampering and pricing, the comfort of personal service in less lavish spas seems to appeal to the modern traveler as well. Peter Anderson's overview of the spa industry provides insights into this fascinating service product.

The importance of spas, not only to a guest as described by Anderson, but to hotels and resorts, is examined in the article written by Madanoglu and Brezina. Moving beyond the idea that spas are a luxury to have in a hotel, the authors argue that they are now a necessity. A hotel with a spa may be able to significantly increase the revenue of the hotel. In fact, in a technique developed by the authors based on previously published information, a hotel with a spa may produce $3,500,000 a year more in revenue than a hotel without a spa. In addition, the authors discuss techniques that hotel operators can use to increase spa revenues.

In moving away from the theoretical perspectives of the previous two articles on spas, Holleigh Alexander, spa director at the Ritz-Carlton Club, Aspen Highlands, does a phenomenal job of explaining what it is like to manage a spa on a daily basis. Similarly to the message set forth by other articles in this book, Alexander explains that her primary goal is to "create memorable experiences." In order to make this occur for the guest, she is always on the move, whether that means she is examining financials, having one-on-one meetings with her supervisors, or promoting Ritz kids' activities. Inspiringly, Alexander describes what she does, and what it takes to be a spa director, as she sees it.

At the end of this section are a number of suggested readings for the reader who would like to gain more in-depth knowledge about the hospitality industry as a whole. In particular, the books by Hilton and Jarman look closely at the intermachinations of the establishment by two early pioneers of the industry, one of whom, Conrad Hilton, lives on in an international, publicly traded company operated by one of his sons. E. M. Statler's contributions to the modern hotel business are legendary in that he is generally credited with founding and operating the first commercial hotel that recognized the realities of the early business traveler at the beginning of the twentieth century. The suggested articles are drawn from recently published historic overviews of the hotel side of the hospitality industry in the United States. They also highlight other major forces in the development of the modern hotel business.

1.2 THE HOTEL DEVELOPMENT PROCESS John Dew

✦ INTRODUCTION

The bulldozers are working and a construction crane is being erected on that vacant lot you pass each day going to and from home. The sign on the fence states that a new hotel is being built with a planned opening date of spring 2007. If you have ever wondered just how that hotel was created, you may have wondered about some or all of the following questions:

- How did someone select that particular vacant lot?

- Who actually creates a new hotel?

- Who owns it?

- Where did they get the money to build it?

- How long does the process take from idea to grand opening day?

- Who selects the architect, the engineers, and the interior designer?

- Who manages the myriad details that go into the development of a new hotel?

- Who will manage the hotel once it's open?

We hope to address these and other questions you may have in this chapter.

✦ THE DEVELOPMENT COMPANY

The developer is the entrepreneur, the risk taker, who originates the idea for the hotel. Depending on the business structure selected, the developer often puts his or her personal wealth at risk when engaging in a hotel project. The developer, along with a small staff of people, networks with commercial real estate agents on the lookout for a suitable hotel site. Depending on the type of hotel to be developed, a site of at least 2 to 4 acres is required (for comparison, an acre is roughly the size of a football field). This property must be zoned by the city for a hotel, be visible from a freeway or major street arterial, and have city approval for such construction activities as curb cuts, left-hand turn lanes, and delivery truck access. Commercial realtors offer sites for the developer's consideration that include maps, aerial photos, and proof of hotel zoning.

Sometimes the developer views potential sites by driving around the neighborhood within 5 miles of the site or touring multiple sites by helicopter, noting where the potential guests live and work and where potential competing hotels are located.

The price per square foot of land is considered. The higher the cost of land, the higher the rates the hotel will need to charge. Is the price too high for the average daily rate (ADR) in this particular market? Is it too low? Or is it acceptable? This is determined when the hotel's financial pro forma budget document is created.

✦ THE FEASIBILITY STUDY

When the developer selects a site, a feasibility study is often commissioned to obtain an analysis of the site by an objective third party. Companies offer hotel feasibility studies for a fee and are experts in a particular market, or developers may use the consulting group of one of the major public accounting firms.

The company retained to do the feasibility study can spend up to several months gathering detailed data to see if, in their opinion, it makes economic sense to build the hotel. Their conclusion offers an objective third-party opinion as to whether the project is feasible, hence the term

feasibility study. Generally, the feasibility study considers, evaluates, and makes recommendations about the project based on the following variables:

The Site

- Proper zoning
- Size in square feet/acres
- Visibility from arterials/freeways
- Traffic counts/patterns
- Accessibility from streets, freeways, airports, train stations, etc.
- Proximity to where potential guests live, travel, or work
- Barriers that discourage competition coming into the market, if any
- How adjacent property and businesses are utilized
- Master area development plans
- Local permitting process and the degree of difficulty for that particular city
- Impact fees charged by the city

The Economy of the Area

- Major employers, government agencies
- Business trends for each employer/agency
- Hotel needs and the demand for each
- Leisure travel demand in the area
- Nearby tourist attractions
- Visitor counts
- Conventions, trade shows, and meetings history

The Hotel Market

- The competitors, both existing and planned
- Historical occupancy of hotels in the area

- Historical average rate
- Proprietary data on area travel

Identification of Which Hotel Market Segment to Serve

- Full service
- Limited service
- Extended stay
- Luxury
- Midprice
- Economy
- Budget

Selection of Appropriate Hotel Design

- High-rise
- Midrise
- Garden apartment style
- Hybrid design

Selection of Appropriate Hotel Brand

- Franchised (Marriott, Sheraton, Hyatt, etc.)
- Licensed (Best Western, Guest Suites, etc.)
- Independent
- Independent with strategic market affiliation (Luxury Hotels of America, Historic Hotels of America, etc.)

Ten-year Projection

- Occupancy projection by year
- ADR by year
- Estimated cash generated for debt
- Estimated cash generated for distribution to investors

- Estimated cash-on-cash return (after-tax income divided by equity invested)
- Overall projected yield
- Projected internal rate of return
- Net present value of the project over each of the next ten years

Once the feasibility study is completed, the developer is prepared to move forward with the project. Often, at this stage of the process, the developer purchases an option on the land to tie it up until the remaining development steps can be completed and to prevent the competition from purchasing it.

✦ CREATION OF THE OWNERSHIP ENTITY

An ownership entity (note that this is different than and separate from the development company) must be created to hold title to the land—and the hotel, once it's built. Considering the limitation of liability to the investors, tax consequences, estate implications for the investors, and potential requirements of the mortgage lender, a business structure is selected, normally in one of the following forms:

- Limited liability company (LLC)
- Limited partnership (LP)
- S corporation (formerly known as a *Sub-S corporation*)
- C corporation

✦ THE DEVELOPMENT AGREEMENT

The newly formed entity now enters into a development contract with the development company to take the project to completion. The development company charges a fee, approximately 3 percent of the total project cost, for this service. The agreement generally covers such variables as:

- Selection of architect/engineers
- Selection and supervision of a general contractor
- Processing all building and occupancy permits
- Raising all the equity money from investors
- Securing a construction mortgage loan
- Selecting a franchise company
- Securing the franchise
- Selecting an interior designer that meets the franchise company's requirements
- Purchasing all opening furniture, fixtures, equipment
- Selecting a management company to operate the hotel
- Liability for cost overruns

✦ SELECTING A FRANCHISE

Depending on the type of hotel to be built (based on the feasibility study), the developer recommends a franchise company to the hotel owner. A major consideration is the best franchise brand for the market segment to be served. Each franchise company has different franchise fees, royalty fees, and marketing/miscellaneous fees as part of its agreement structure with the operating company. Consideration must also be given to the brands already represented in the target market that may be available for franchise. The franchise company is approached and a franchise is requested, with the feasibility study offered as backup for the request.

The next step is for the franchise company to conduct an impact study of the market.

This considers such matters as possible negative impact on existing hotels that carry the franchiser's flag. If the impact is judged to be insignificant, a franchise is usually granted to the ownership entity for a one-time fee of about $400 per room, depending on the franchise selected, with continuing royalty and marketing fees, usually based on a percentage of hotel revenue.

✦ SELECTING AN ARCHITECT

Because the final product of this process is a building that the operator has to run as a hotel, the architect's experience in designing hotels, his or her experience with the prototypical drawings of the franchise selected, the fee, and his or her on-time record must be considered. Architects' fees can run up to 5 percent of the total project cost but are often negotiated down, if the project is big enough. The firm's experience and record on similar projects are critical. The architect does not have to operate the hotel when it is completed. The developer wants the architect to design a hotel that will be easy to operate and maintain.

✦ SELECTING A GENERAL CONTRACTOR

Major considerations are the quality and reliability record of the general contractor and the firm's use of and relationships with the many subcontractors needed for a project as complex as a hotel. Again, experience in building the hotel type is important. It is hoped that the general contractor has learned from any mistakes made in building similar hotels. The general contractor and architect often bid the project as a team; this helps the developer determine the final cost. Often, up to a 10 percent contingency cost that allows for unforeseen circumstances is built into the project bidding process.

✦ FINANCING THE PROJECT

The following variables must be determined to qualify for financing:

- The cost of the land

- Design and construction cost of the building

- The cost of furniture, fixtures, equipment, and opening supplies

- Pre-opening marketing and labor costs

- A six-month operating capital cash reserve

The sum of these constitutes the total cost of the project for purposes of securing financing.

With this information, the ten-year operating pro forma budget is updated to reflect actual costs. It's now time to go to the money markets for construction financing. The terms and conditions of a construction loan can vary widely, depending on the individual lender. Important terms that can affect the cost of the loan include:

- Personal guarantees by developers and/or equity partners/investors

- Loan origination fees

- Interest rate

- Required loan-to-value ratio

- Terms of repayment

- A requirement that interest/taxes be held in reserve

- Required debt service coverage ratios

- Length of the construction loan; length and costs of extensions

These are only a few of the considerations that must be analyzed when selecting a lender. The developer, on behalf of the owning entity, then approaches a number of lending institutions. The lending institutions analyze the deal and offer a proposed term sheet that answers all of the borrowers' questions. This allows the borrowers to select the lending institution with which they wish to work. The lender then commissions an appraisal of the project by an independent appraisal company such as Hospitality Valuation Services (HVS). Based on the appraisal, the lender issues a loan commitment for the project that usually offers up to 60 percent of the project's cost. The balance must be raised as equity from investors.

✦ RAISING THE EQUITY INVESTMENT FUNDS

With the bank committed to about 60 percent of the cost, the remaining 40 percent must be raised in equity commitments by investors. To pursue these, the developer prepares an offering solicitation document that meets current securities and exchange laws. The nature of this document depends on the type of business entity that was formed. For limited partnerships or limited liability companies, a private placement offering circular and project description is prepared. For S or C corporations, stock offerings are prepared for sale consistent with applicable federal and state securities laws.

The developer now contacts money sources that have risk capital available to invest. These can include:

- Individual investors

- Private asset managers

- Opportunity fund managers

- Venture capital fund managers

These potential investment sources are offered the opportunity to invest in the hotel. Based on their study and evaluation of the reports, documents, and studies detailed above, they decide whether or not to offer funding to the developer.

Once the loan is secured, the equity raised, and the building permit issued by the city, the land purchase option is exercised and the purchase is completed. Then the 12–16-month construction process begins. If the architect's plans work as intended; if the general contractor has no problems with subcontractors, unions, or permits; if all the furnishings, fixtures, and equipment arrive on time; if the weather cooperates; and if the employment market is such that human resources are sufficient to open a hotel, then congratulations! The hotel will open on time.

✦ SELECTING THE MANAGEMENT COMPANY

Often even before the construction activity commences, the owning entity selects an appropriate management company to manage the pre-opening, marketing and sales, selection and training of the opening staff, preparation of the operating budget, and day-to-day operations once the hotel is opened. Management companies charge 3–5 percent of revenue for this service. In recent years, management companies have charged 3–4 percent of revenue and 2–3 percent of gross operating profit, so they can be measured and evaluated on both sales and profitability.

The franchise company may offer to provide management services to franchisees. Marriott International, Inc., for example, manages about 50 percent of all hotels that carry the Marriott flag under 20-year contracts. Independent management companies manage the remaining hotels under long-term management contracts of up to 10 years' duration, often with several 5-year renewal options.

✦ CONCLUSION

This is a largely linear explanation of the complicated process that a developer goes through in order to create a hotel. It has been described in a step-by-step process, but in reality, many of the steps are carried out concurrently to save time (and money). Nevertheless, the hotel development process takes about 3 years from original conception to first guest. It is important to remember that during the initial stages of the process, the developer can have as much as $1 million (U.S.) or more at risk in the process before a final go/no-go decision is reached. Only after the project is approved and all financing is in place can the developer start to recover upfront costs and collect development fees.

Hotel development and its component parts of hotel feasibility studies, hotel appraisal, hotel real estate finance, and hotel management are all among the career opportunities available to hotel and restaurant administration graduates.

✦ PUTTING IT ALL TOGETHER— THE STORY OF AN EXTENDED-STAY HOTEL DEVELOPMENT PROJECT

The City Development Commission in a Pacific Northwest community purchased a 1.55-acre parcel of riverfront land in the downtown area. The land was previously contaminated with industrial pollutants that made the parcel unsafe for habitation and construction. The City Development Commission used state, local, and federal grants to have the land decontaminated, created a master plan for the area, and then offered the parcel for sale and development.

The City Development Commission issued a request for proposal (RFP) that outlined the asking price of $2,076,240 ($30/sq. ft.) for the land and the design requirements set down by the commission for a building that would fit the intended look and feel of the area. The RFP was sent to many major hotel companies and commercial real estate brokers, asking prospective buyers to submit a purchase price bid along with a statement of the buyer's development history and ability to develop a hotel of the type envisioned by the commission. It listed a closing date by which all bids had to be submitted.

An area commercial real estate broker contacted a hotel development and management company with a long history of developing and managing extended-stay hotels in the Pacific Northwest, including a property located in a similar setting to that being offered for sale. The commercial realtor offered to represent the developer in negotiations with the City Development Commission, which would be paying the real estate commission on the sale. An agreement was reached with the commercial real estate broker to represent the buyer to the seller, and the developer went to work preparing a proposal.

The developer conducted a feasibility study to see all of the conditions in the marketplace that would be encouraging or discouraging to the development project. Studies were conducted to estimate how many room-nights were

being sold within a five-mile radius, how many extended-stay room-nights were available in the market, how many hotel rooms existed, and how many were being planned over the following 5 years. From this, the developer was able to estimate the number of extended-stay room-nights available needed to produce an 82 percent occupancy with an average daily room rate of $141 when the hotel achieved stabilization 3 years after opening. That provided the basis for a 10-year revenue estimate.

The developer proposed a nine-floor, 258-suite extended-stay hotel with an indoor pool, spa, and exercise facility, a guest laundry, offices, meeting facilities, and a three-floor parking garage with parking for 193 automobiles, all at a total cost of $38 million, or $147,286 per suite.

The $38 million construction budget was broken down as follows:

Land	6.0%
Construction	66.0%
Office Equipment	1.4%
Furniture, Fixtures, Equipment	7.4%
Architecture/Engineering	2.8%
Permits/Fees/Environmental	2.8%
Appraisal/Legal/Tax/Insurance	1.3%
Pre-Opening Expenses	1.3%
Construction Loan Fee	1.1%
Developer Fee	2.8%
Construction Interest	2.8%
Working Capital	2.1%
Contingency	2.2%
Total	100%

The opening date for the hotel was projected at 27 months from the date of proposal acceptance.

The City Development Commission awarded the project to the developer, and work began.

First, an ownership limited liability company (LLC) was formed as the ownership entity that would hold title to the hotel.

The LLC, in turn, entered into a development and construction management agreement with the development company to manage the arrangements for financing and construction of the hotel.

The developer, as agent for the ownership LLC, also entered into a hotel management contract with a management company to manage the pre-opening marketing, pre-opening hiring and training, and the day-to-day operation of the hotel once it was opened. The arrangements called for the management company to be paid 3 percent of revenue and 2 percent of the net operating income for management services.

The ownership LLC then contacted a major hotel company and applied for a franchise to allow the development and operation of an extended-stay hotel. A 20-year franchise was granted with a fee of $400 per suite or, $102,800. This was to be followed by a 5 percent royalty and a 3 percent advertising fee once the hotel was open and operating.

The developer, acting as agent for the owner, prepared a private placement memorandum document seeking investments from accredited investors. These investors were primarily defined as people with a net worth of $1 million, or those with an income in excess of $200,000 over the previous 2 years and expecting an income in excess of $200,000 in the current year. (Note: Additional entities may also be defined as accredited investors by the Securities and Exchange Commission.)

The private placement memorandum offered $100,000 units of ownership to accredited investors, guaranteeing a 9 percent priority return on the investment and a combined 50 percent ownership in the hotel. A group of initial investors retained the other 50 percent in exchange for putting the project together. This effort was successful in raising 40 percent of the total cost of the hotel in anticipation that a lender would provide the remaining 60 percent in the form of a construction loan. In addition to the priority return, investors could expect to participate in any future capital gain realized should the hotel be sold.

The development company, continuing to function as agent for the owner, then sought a commercial bank to provide 3-year construction financing for the project. As $22,800,000, or 60 percent, of the $38 million development cost was to be borrowed, only major banks were considered as prospective lenders. The size of the construction loan was above the lending limits of most small regional banks. After a pre-construction appraisal by a third-party appraisal firm chosen by the lender confirmed the value at $38 million upon completion of construction, and for an origination fee of $400,000, a three-year construction loan was secured. The terms allowed the developer, as agent for the owner, to draw down the loan every 30 days after providing proof that funds had been properly disbursed in the construction process. The loan documents set an interest rate and also required that the ownership LLC seek a permanent mortgage prior to the 3-year expiration date on the construction loan.

The development company then negotiated with and selected a general contractor with significant hotel construction experience who acted on behalf of the developer, as agent for the owner. The general contractor then selected design-build subcontractors and an interior designer to select colors, fabrics, furniture, fixtures, and equipment to meet the hotel franchise design requirements.

Building permits were applied for, and the building design was presented to the City Development Commission for its approval, along with other groups with a stake in the appearance of the finished building in relation to the area and neighborhood. With all of these approvals in place, construction commenced, and the hotel opened 2 years later.

✦ POSTSCRIPT

Three years after the hotel opened, the ownership LLC had the obligation to secure permanent financing on the hotel to replace the construction loan. The September 11, 2001, terrorist attacks on the World Trade Center and the Pentagon slowed travel throughout the United States. As a result, the hotel did not achieve the projected occupancy or average daily rate during the 3-year construction loan period. An appraisal that was primarily based on the hotel's trailing 12-month net operating income produced a value about $2 million below the original construction cost. The bank that had provided the construction loan notified the owners that they did not wish to provide permanent financing under these circumstances. The owners were forced to conduct a search for a new mortgage bank. They were able to find a mortgage, but only after buying down the loan by $2 million to bring the loan-to-value ratio back to 40 percent equity and a loan at 60 percent of the appraised. This illustrates the risk that developers face when entering into a hotel project.

However, as hotel values historically peak and decline on about a 10-year cycle, the owners look forward to the option of selling the hotel on the next peak, which will allow them to capture the original projected return through capital appreciation. Hotel development and ownership is a high-risk, high-reward enterprise.

1.3 THE ART AND SCIENCE OF OPENING A HOTEL Tom Dupar

If you ever have the chance to be involved with opening a hotel, jump at the opportunity. Opening a hotel is one of the most rewarding jobs in the hospitality industry despite its frustrating and exhausting aspects.

Walk into any hotel, anywhere, and look around. Everything you see, hear, and feel, every detail, involved many people and countless decisions. I have been an operations project manager (OPM) since 1989 and have opened over 40 three-, four-, and five-star hotels around the world. From Guam to Malta, Berlin to St. Louis, each project has been unique, each project has been the same, and each has been professionally rewarding.

The OPM is the third person hired, after the general manager and the director of marketing. The role of an OPM is to pull together the visions of the architect, interior designer, owner, operator, and others. When these visions are successfully melded, the hotel guest is satisfied, the owner makes money, and the architect and interior designer can add the project to their list of successful accomplishments.

The OPM oversees the following aspects of a project:

- Reviewing blueprints and specifications for the entire building
- Assisting with the creation of a model room
- Developing the pre-opening staff plan
- Developing and managing the pre-opening budget
- Developing the operational supplies and equipment budget (OS&E)
- Overseeing the purchasing, warehousing, delivery, and installation of the OS&E
- Developing the interior graphics package
- Coordinating the installation of third-party vendors

✦ BLUEPRINTS

The OPM's responsibilities start with the architectural blueprints. The focus is to ensure a good flow for guests, staff, and goods.

The bellperson bag storage room should be located between the porte cochere (entry) and the elevators and contain 1 square foot of space for each guest room.

If valet parking is offered, ensure that a convenient cashier's station is located near the porte cochere. Arrange for a key rack to hold the keys for each valet parking stall.

Given a 10,000-square-foot ballroom, the catering department can sell functions for 800 for dinner. This requires eighty 6-foot round tables, 800 chairs, a dais for the head table, a dance floor, and staging for the band. If sold for a 700-guest all-day meeting, the classroom setup requires 1400 linear feet of narrow tables and 700 chairs. A short theater meeting setup for 1000 requires 1000 chairs, a podium, staging, and audio visual equipment. The same space accommodates a cocktail reception for 1400 guests; this requires cocktail tables, portable bars, buffet stations, and so on. This all boils down to ensuring ample storage space for equipment not being used—at least 1500 square feet.

Moving goods from the back of the house to the front requires careful planning to ensure that precious labor dollars are used efficiently. Are the rollaway beds, cribs, and high chairs stored near an elevator for quick delivery? The housekeepers' closets should be centrally located on guest room floors to cut down on access time. A 6-foot, 2-cubic-yard garbage cart will not work if the elevator is only 5 feet deep.

If ice machines are offered for guest self-service, they must produce an ample supply (10 pounds per room per 24-hour period) for the number of guest rooms on that floor or floors. The ice machine room requires the proper utilities, including electricity, plumbing, lighting, and HVAC. Don't forget the sign on the outside of the room, which must meet Americans with Disabilities Act (ADA) standards!

✦ MODEL ROOM

Build a typical king and double/double guest room close to the site, so you can review every single item in them. Are ample electrical and telecom outlets placed exactly where the TV, lamps, clock radio, minibar, coffeemaker, hair dryer, Internet access, and telephones are located so the cords are hidden? Are spare outlets offered for guest use (computer, iron, etc.)? Is the closet rod hung so that the ironing board organizer and ironing board fit in the closet? Is the thermostat location convenient for guest access?

Are the case goods (dresser, nightstands, headboards, chairs, etc.), designed for commercial heavy-duty use? Will they hold up to abusive use? Do they have sharp corners that will snag guest clothing? Does the bedskirt hang ½ inch off the floor? Do the bedside lamps give off enough lumens so that guests can read in bed? Does the room meet or exceed every operator brand standard?

These model rooms serve as sales tools for the sales and marketing staff selling group rooms up to 3 years before opening.

✦ PRE-OPENING STAFF PLAN

The pre-opening staffing begins with an organizational chart with all positions. Once the titles and staff counts by position are finalized, then spreadsheets are created to include the position titles, start dates, pay rates, bonus, transfer allowances, and number of full-time equivalents (FTEs) for all positions.

The pre-opening staff plan is a comprehensive document that states who is hired, when they start, how much they are paid, and whether or not they are allocated a relocation allowance and benefit costs. Each of these pieces is used to build the pre-opening staff plan budget. If hiring has already begun and the opening date changes, the budget must be amended. Hiring a position that does not conform to the plan, such as bringing on a renowned chef one month earlier than planned, also requires that the budget be modified.

✦ PRE-OPENING BUDGET

The OPM develops and manages the pre-opening budget. This budget typically consists of three major categories; labor cost (40 percent), sales and marketing efforts (40 percent), and miscellaneous (20 percent).

The labor cost is taken directly from the pre-opening staff plan.

Sales and marketing activities comprise advertising, collateral, public relations, and travel to see clients.

Rounding out the budget are all of the miscellaneous items. These include office space rental before moving into the hotel, utilities (power, water, Internet, and telephone), human resources recruitment (ads, headhunters, drug testing, etc.), training materials, association dues, and licenses and permits (business, liquor, sales tax collection, etc.).

If the hotel opening date is delayed for any reason, the pre-opening budget is affected. Additional costs include labor, office rent, utilities, and marketing efforts. If the opening date changes within three weeks of the original plan, major costs are encountered, as most of the staff is already hired.

✦ OPERATIONAL SUPPLIES AND EQUIPMENT (OS&E)

The largest and most complex aspect of the OPM's responsibility is specifying, quantifying, and budgeting for the operational supplies and equipment (OS&E) list. This budget typically pencils out to $8,000 to $10,000 per guest room for a typical four-star property. The list of goods typically exceeds 2500 line items. Add a little more for a full-service resort; deduct a little for an in-city business hotel.

The OS&E comprises all of the items that are not nailed down, with the exception of the furniture, fixtures, and equipment (FF&E). The FF&E is typically specified and ordered by the interior designer.

Typical guest room items include bedding (frames, box springs, mattresses, mattress pads, sheets, pillows, pillowcases, towels, etc.), clock radios, hangers, laundry bags, laundry tickets, iron, ironing board, ironing board organizer, luggage rack, guest amenities (soap, shampoo, lotion, etc.), hair dryer, shower curtains, and shower curtain hooks.

Housekeeping equipment includes vacuums (guest room and wide-area units), carpet shampooers, carpet extractors, housekeeper carts, laundry bins, garbage trucks, valet delivery carts, and shelving, to name a few of many items. Housekeeping must also keep an inventory of guest request items, including humidifiers, dehumidifiers, cribs, high chairs, rollaway beds, bedboards, spare pillows, towels, amenities, refrigerators, laundry soap, and so on.

Food and beverage front-of-the-house items include flatware (knives, forks, and spoons), hollowware (serving trays, serving utensils, chafing dishes, sugar bowls and sauce boats, punch bowls), glassware, table linens, napkins, skirting, salt and pepper shakers, china, plate covers, espresso machines, menu covers, and the list goes on and on.

Banquet items include all of the above plus tables, chairs, staging, staging steps and railings, dance floors, carts, carving boards, ice carving trays, flags, podiums, portable bars, ice bins, pianos, and tray jack stands.

The largest purchase order—typically over 100 pages long—is for a full-service kitchen and includes everything a chef needs to produce the menus being sold at the hotel. Every utensil, pot, pan, dish, and glass rack, warewashing chemicals, mops and buckets, specialty items (roller-docker, anyone?) must be reviewed by the chef, purchased, and delivered the day before the chef starts burning in the kitchen.

On the hotel administration side, the OPM specifies the office desks, chairs, cork and dry-erase boards, conference tables, filing cabinets, safes, bullet-proof window for the general cashier's office, fax machines, copiers, currency and coin trays, and a set of flags for the exterior flagpoles.

One of the largest and most complicated purchase orders is for staff uniforms. My recent Kona, Hawaii, project uniform purchase order was 68 pages long. The invoices covered over 100 pages!

Before quantifying uniform needs, many questions are asked. Do we need summer and winter uniforms? Will the uniforms be laundered by the hotel or the hotel associates? How many extra servers are needed for a capacity dinner function in the ballrooms? Is the intent to have a large percentage of part-time staff? Which uniforms need custom embroidery (restaurants, culinary, engineering, etc.)? What percentage of spare uniforms are needed in reserve?

Once these questions are answered, the selection process begins. Operations and the interior designer review the look and feel of the options available. Each position (housekeeper, bellperson, etc.) or similar position (front desk clerk/concierge) has different requirements. Housekeepers and bellpersons require durable uniforms that breathe and can handle lots of bending and stretching. The uniforms of the culinary and engineering staffs are often stained and must hold up to numerous launderings.

The uniform order is placed 90 to 120 days *before the first uniformed staff is hired*. To quantify the sizes required, a typical bell chart sizing curve is used for the particular country or region of the hotel. The uniforms are delivered and sorted prior to the individual fitting process. On the line staff's second day on the job, each individual is measured for uniforms. An army of seamstresses then takes the pants, jackets, and dresses and alters each piece for each associate. The fitted uniforms are issued a few days before opening day.

✦ PURCHASING, WAREHOUSING, DELIVERY, AND INSTALLATION OF THE OS&E

In an ideal process, the 500 purchase orders are issued beginning 6 months prior to opening. Each order is tracked to ensure it is delivered to the proper location on the desired date. Most goods are delivered to a local warehouse and pulled for delivery to the site as the general contractor completes construction and turns over areas. Some goods are shipped directly to the site to eliminate double handling. These large orders include bed sets (twenty-one 40-foot shipping containers for the Kona project), televisions (3 containers), banquet chairs (2 containers), banquet tables (3 containers), and guest room safes (1 container). The linen order for guest rooms and F&B are shipped to an off-site laundry facility for initial washing.

Once the goods are on site, they are typically staged in the largest ballroom for unpacking and distribution. The unpacking process requires a plethora of workers. For example, each clock radio must be unpacked, the electrical twist tie removed, the 9-volt battery installed, and the time set. Then the unit is placed in a guest room on the nightstand. For the 525-room Kona project, this task required two people for three 8-hour days. Once they completed this task, they spent the next five working days installing the 7000 shower curtain hooks, 525 shower curtains, and 525 shower liners. Then they unboxed 30,000 glasses and placed them in glass racks for washing. These kinds of tasks must be carried out for each of the 2500 line items.

Once receiving and distribution begins onsite, another element comes to the forefront: garbage. During the 5-week Kona installation process, over 3 tons of packing material were generated *every day!* Making friends with the local waste-hauling service is a priority.

✦ INTERIOR GRAPHICS PACKAGE

The project manager reviews the interior graphics package for errors and omissions. This package includes every sign needed to direct guests and staff in front and back of the house areas. The recent Kona project included 1600 signs, 98 percent of which were one of a kind. The text must be correct, the directional arrows must point the correct way, and most are required to include raised Braille text, per the ADA.

The OPM works with the marketing department to develop the identity for the unique areas within a property. These include the restaurants, bars, pools, spa, and retail areas. These logos are incorporated into the signage package, collateral material (cocktail napkins, menus, check presenters, etc.), and uniforms.

✦ THIRD-PARTY VENDORS

Many third-party vendors must have access to the property prior to its opening. The project manager schedules and directs all of these vendors, including the soft-drink vendor (who installs soda guns for the bars and vending machines for the guest floors), the coffee company (which must install and test equipment), the pay-per-view TV vendor (who must connect every television in the building and test the signal strength), the warewashing chemical vendor (who must install and calibrate the dishwashing machines), and the office furniture installer (who must assemble all office equipment). Among the other vendors are those dealing in copier services, postage machines, telephones, fitness center equipment, security systems, and first aid supplies.

These vendors are constantly informed when they can install their equipment based on the general contractor's completion dates. When the construction schedule changes, vendors must be updated so they show up when the area they need access to is ready.

✦ HUMAN RESOURCES

The OPM assists the human resources (HR) personnel during the last two months of pre-opening so that they have all of the tools they need to recruit and hire the staff. On average, the HR department interviews at least five applicants for every position. This works out to over 1000 applicants for a typical 300-room four-star hotel. This process is referred to as the *mass hire*.

The mass hire is typically conducted over a 2- or 3-day period 6 weeks before opening. To interview this many job seekers, HR requires office space, reception space for up to 200 at one time, rest rooms, and break rooms for the interviewers. The OPM coordinates all of these details so that the operations team can focus on the recruitment.

Once the offer letters are accepted, all line associates start work about three weeks out. The first few days on the job are dedicated to group training, operational philosophies, code of conduct, and other general policies. On day three, divisional training takes place. In the second week of training, the staff is broken out into departmental or job-specific duties.

Departmental training includes teaching staff to make beds, clean a room, cook every menu item, the most efficient route to each guest room, and what to tell the guest en route to the room.

✦ OPENING DAY

The activity during the last 72 hours before the opening ceremonies is chaotic. This is the time that all hands are on deck. Sixteen-hour days are the norm. Rooms are cleaned. Housekeeping closets are stocked. Liquor and food storerooms are filled. The general contractor completes all small details such as paint touch-ups. Artwork and furnishings are installed in the public areas. Rehearsals are conducted for all aspects of the operation, including serving test meals and cocktails, guest check-ins and check-outs, and even such easy-to-overlook activities as valet parking and vacuuming the pool.

As soon as the general manger cuts the ceremonial ribbon, the OPM knows what kind of job has been done. The next step is to find the next project and do it all again!

1.4 ON-LINE PRICING: AN ANALYSIS OF HOTEL COMPANY PRACTICES Peter O'Connor

The importance of electronic hotel-distribution routes has grown substantially in recent years. According to statistics quoted in the Horwath Worldwide Hotel Industry Studies, direct reservations fell from approximately 39 percent in 1995 to 33 percent in 1999, with the shift in sales going almost exclusively to electronic channels (O'Connor, 2001, 70–93). While hotels continue to make extensive use of travel-agent-oriented global distribution systems (GDSs), consumer adoption of the Internet as a reliable and secure commerce medium has prompted a change in the way in which hotel rooms are being distributed.

The Internet has dramatically changed the way people communicate, research information, and buy goods and services. Travel products in particular have proven to be suitable for sale online. The typical Internet user—an affluent, frequent traveler who spends more than the average on leisure and entertainment—is an attractive market for travel suppliers (NFO Plog Research, 2000). Furthermore, from a consumer's perspective purchasing travel products online has, in many instances, become faster, easier, and more convenient than contacting a travel agent or telephoning a supplier directly. As a result, online travel-related revenues are forecast to grow sharply. For example, according to a report by Jupiter Media Metrix, online travel sales will more than triple in the next five years—from US$18 billion in 2002 to US$64 billion in 2007 (Jupiter Media Metrix, 2001).

Booking volumes are also forecast to climb. The Travel Industry Association of America (TIAA) estimated that by the end of 2002 between 6 percent and 10 percent of all travel reservations originated on the web (TIAA, 1998). If Jupiter's 2007 prediction comes true, travel will be the biggest selling online product, with a volume nearly double that of the current leading product, PC hardware (Forrester Research).

Price is key to selling successfully online. Studies by Internet analysts Gomez and PhoCusWright, and also a study by TIAA, all identified price as being one of the key motivating factors that encourages consumers to purchase travel online (Gomez.com, 2000; PhoCuSWright, 2001; TIAA, 2001). For example, the PhoCusWright study found that competitive pricing is the best way to attract customers (Pastore, 2001). When travelers who haven't bought online were asked what would encourage them to do so, 64 percent said that saving money would make them more interested. No other benefit—whether saving time, getting bonus loyalty-club points, more control, or obtaining better information—came close to this level of response.

✦ HOTEL PRICING ON THE WEB

Yesawich, Pepperdine, and Brown found in a 2000 study that almost six out of ten leisure travelers now actively seek the "lowest possible price" for travel services (Yesawich, Pepperdine, and Brown, 2000). Similarly, a 2001 Forrester

Research study found that 66 percent of all buyers had used an online discount in the previous 12 months to buy travel online (Forrester Research, 2001), and a study by the Joint Hospitality Industry Congress found a real expectation among consumers that Internet prices would be lower than those available in the "bricks and mortar" world (Joint Hospitality Industry Congress, 2000).

Such a perception has developed for several reasons. First, many of the best-known Internet retailers (such as, for example, Amazon.com) initially competed with traditional outlets based, to a large extent, on price. Second, savvy consumers are aware that web-based distribution costs are lower than those of other channels (Nua, 1998). As Jack Geddes, Radisson Hotels Worldwide's managing director, sales and marketing Asia, has pointed out: "Consumers now understand that suppliers are cutting costs through this channel and expect savings to be passed on to them, as well as being

rewarded for making the booking themselves" (Muqbil, 1998). Such expectations are being reinforced by the budget-airline sector, which offers substantial discounts for online bookings. Companies such as EasyJet, RyanAir, and Buzz estimate that by avoiding telesales and travel agents, they can achieve savings of up to 30 percent—which they pass on to customers in the form of lower fares (Cooke, 2000). Similar or even greater levels of savings can be made by hotel companies, as can be seen from the internal Accor figures in Table 1.1, which show how an 80- to 90-percent savings in transaction charges can be achieved by selling directly to the consumer online. Finally, many hotels (and airlines) use the web to sell last-minute deals—packages at relatively low prices but with short lead times. While such promotions can help dispose of unsold inventory, they have also resulted in the public's associating rooms sold over the Internet with lower prices.

Table 1.1 Reservation Cost By Distribution Channel

ROUTE		TRANSACTION FFF					TOTAL COST
	Customer	Traditional Travel agent	GDS	Switch	CRS	Hotel	
Traditional route		$5.90	$3.20	$0.20	$4.20		$13.50
	Customer	Online travel agent	GDS	Switch	CRS	Hotel	
Online intermediary route		$3.00	$3.20	$0.20	$4.20		$10.60
	Customer	Hotel company website				Hotel	
Direct online route		$1.50					$1.50

Source: Dresdner Kleinwort Benson/Accor, quoted in *Travel and Tourism Intelligence, The International Hotel Industry: Corporate Strategies and Global Opportunities* (London: Economic Intelligence Unit, 2001).

These factors have combined to make consumers associate online booking with good value, which in the consumer's mind translates into low prices. However, in the case of hotel brands' own web sites, industry practice frequently seems to be the opposite of theory. In a 1999 survey, for instance, a colleague and I found that rates obtained from the web site were usually substantially higher than those obtained by contacting the central reservations office (O'Connor and Horan, 1999). That study was limited, however, in that it focused only on direct sales over hotel chains' own branded web sites. Electronic distribution is rapidly evolving for hotels, and a large number of other online consumer-focused channels are now available, with most chains using multiple routes to reach the consumer (Castleberry et al., 1998, 19–24).

The availability of numerous points of sale poses some interesting questions. Foremost among these is: Is there consistency between the room availability and prices being offered over each of the channels? Unlike in the physical world, where a potential customer would have to telephone or visit several suppliers, comparison shopping on the web can generally be accomplished relatively quickly. Research has shown that consumers shopping for travel online almost always check more than one site before purchasing. According to Jupiter Media Metrix (2001), just 10 percent of would-be guests visit only one site to book a hotel room, another 43 percent visit two or three sites, and 22 percent visit four or more sites. Because they check prices in several places, online purchasers have become increasingly intolerant of inconsistent information, and may react unfavorably to a firm's disparate rates by booking with the company's competitor. Two related questions, then, are:

1. If rates are not consistent across channels, is any one route consistently cheaper?
2. Is the company's approach to pricing logical from both the consumer's and the hotel's perspective?

In this section, I seek to answer those questions.

✦ METHODOLOGY AND LIMITATIONS OF THE STUDY

Previous studies of hotels' Internet use have been limited. Murphy et al. (1996, 70–82) focused on rating the content of hotel web sites, while Van Hoof and Combrink (1998, 46–54) attempted to measure managers' perceptions of and attitudes toward the Internet. Web-reservations facilities were investigated in detail in the co-authored paper that I mentioned above (O'Connor and Horan, 1999). However, the issue of pricing over several distribution channels does not appear to have been the subject of extensive systematic research to date. The objective of this study, therefore, was to analyze the room rates being offered to consumers over multiple electronic distribution channels.

An exhaustive analysis of the rates being offered by all hotels would be virtually impossible. Those rates are constantly in flux, as hoteliers project occupancy rates and open or close rate classes accordingly (according to yield-management principles). I believe, however, that major international hotel chains' electronic-distribution activities are indicative of industry patterns, because research has shown that large companies are most active on the web—perhaps because their size often gives them an advantage in terms of technical expertise and financial resources. As a result, I decided to focus this study on the behavior of the top-50 international hotel brands. While this strategy means that the findings are not representative of the industry as a whole (and, therefore, not generally applicable), it does allow establishment of an accurate benchmark of trends as they currently stand. The companies were chosen based on the ranking of the top-50 hotel brands published in *Hotels* magazine in July 2000. Two of those companies (Disney and Club Med) were removed from the listing because they operate resorts and distribute their rooms largely as part of packages, which means that their products are not directly comparable to the rest of the industry. Furthermore, another three companies neither offered online reservations on their own web site nor were they listed on any of the other channels studied. Thus, the results discussed below reflect the findings from the 45 hotel brands for which consistent data could be found.

Five major types of electronic business-to-consumer distribution channels were identified from the literature, and leading examples of each category were selected for inclusion in the study. In addition to a chain's own web site (e.g., www.marriott.com), these comprised channels that draw their data and reservations engine from the GDS (i.e., Expedia and Travelocity); those that are based on the databases and reservation engine of the switch companies (namely, Travelweb); and pure web-based channels with an inventory and reservations database that is maintained online (i.e., WorldRes). While not collectively exhaustive, these represent the majority of hotel-reservation sites. Omitted from the study were the auction-style web sites, such as Priceline.com, which are not comparable to typical booking approaches.

As another point of comparison, I incorporated voice channels into the study by analyzing the rates offered by the toll-free number to the central reservations service (CRS). Data were collected by repeatedly offering to reserve a standard double room for specified dates in a selected property from each of the brands using each of the distribution channels discussed above. Where the product requested was available on the system, both the number of rates displayed and the lowest rate available were recorded for analysis. To help ensure consistency, I ignored rates not available to the general public (e.g., corporate, military, AARP, and AAA), and analyzed only those rates that could be booked by a "normal" customer. After checking the web sites, I telephoned the hotel company's CRS to request the same booking. In that case, I recorded only the first rate quoted by the agent, and I did not ask for a lower rate (nor did I record any subsequent offers after I demurred from making a reservation). Although better rates could probably be achieved by haggling, I decided that negotiating would leave no systematic way of consistently determining the lowest rate, depending as it does on the caller's persistence. The above process was repeated for five sets of alternative dates to reduce the possibility of error due to system malfunctions or other exceptional circumstances.

✦ SUMMARY OF RESEARCH FINDINGS

As can be seen from Table 1.2, each of the major hotel brands uses multiple simultaneous distribution channels. The most commonly available channels were voice (via the company's CRS) and electronic (through the company's corporate web site). The company that did not make a CRS number available was in the economy sector. Offering hotel rooms via the company web site is almost universal, all but one of the brands surveyed offered online reservations in this manner. It is interesting to note that this represents a considerable

Table 1.2 Channels Used By Major Hotel Brands (n = 45)

CHANNEL	NUMBER (N)	PERCENTAGE
Hotel company website	444	97%
Expedia	38	84%
Travelocity.com	35	78%
Travelweb	34	76%
WorldRes	14	31%
Voice (CRS)	44	97%

advancement when compared to surveys made only a few years ago, which found that only approximately 50 percent of the major hotel companies provided online reservations (O'Connor and Horan, 1999; Hensdill, 1998).

As shown in Table 1.2, hotel companies make less use of the other channels investigated. Approximately four-fifths of the major brands used the GDS-based intermediaries Expedia and Travelocity, three-quarters used Travelweb, and barely one-third used WorldRes. These findings are not in themselves surprising. Both Expedia and Travelocity draw their data from the GDSs, where the majority of the hotel brands represented in this study (being major hotel companies) can reasonably expect to be represented. Similarly, Travelweb draws its data from THISCO (The Hotel Industry Switching Company), and thus any of the hotel brands that use this as their switch service could be

expected to make inventory available for sale via Travelweb.

I found the chains' low usage of WorldRes surprising. With the exception of a company's own web site, using WorldRes has the lowest potential transaction cost and thus would appear to be an attractive channel for use by hotel companies. Examination of its property database reveals a large percentage of independent hotels, bed-and-breakfast inns, and small hotel chains. An unresolved question is why the major brands do not exploit this distribution channel.

✦ RATES AVAILABLE

Each of the electronic channels offered multiple rates. As can be seen from Table 1.3, each channel presented an average of five rates in response to the request, with more being offered to the customer by Travelocity than by the other channels surveyed.

Table 1.3 Number of Rates Offered to the Customer

CHANNEL	MEAN	STANDARD DEVIATION
Hotel company website	4.27	3.6
Expedia	3.66	1.4
Travelocity.com	6.07	3.3
Travelweb	5.62	3.6
WorldRes	4.58	3.8
Voice (CRS)	1.00	—

Presenting a variety of rates to the customer has both positive and negative implications. From a positive perspective, it offers choices to potential customers, allowing them to match their needs with the products being sold. On the other hand, presenting a large number of rates without adequate differentiation between products can confuse customers regarding what they are getting for their money. This is best demonstrated by an example encountered in the study, where a property offered 17 different rates for a particular date on Travelweb, with few (if any) discernible differences in the room descriptions. Clearly such a scenario would be confusing and frustrating for any customer wishing to book that property.

Mean prices. It was difficult to make a general observation about which of the several channels is consistently least expensive on average, although Expedia's rates were marginally lower than those offered by other channels and WorldRes seemed to offer consistently higher rates than did the others (see Table 1.4). Indeed, all things considered, prices across each of the channels were comparable—with the average price for the requested room being in the range of US$163. It was interesting that Expedia's mean rates were lower, because as an online travel agency, it has a high distribution cost, and it would be logical to assume that rates offered over this channel would reflect the higher costs. By the same token, since WorldRes's transaction costs are relatively low in comparison with those offered by the other channels surveyed, hotels could potentially offer cheaper rates over this channel. In other words, what I found is that when selling hotel products online, there does not appear to be a relationship between the cost of using the distribution channel and the rate offered. Illogically, the electronic channels with the highest transaction costs for the hotel seem to regularly offer the best value to the customer. As will be discussed below, hoteliers need to rethink their current practices and take action if they are to benefit from the increasing market for online hotel-room sales.

Segment breakout. The foregoing discussion was based on an overall look at hotel-room sales distribution. If the brands studied are subdivided into classifications based on their targeted market segment, a different picture emerges. As can be seen from Table 1.5, hotels at the low end of the market are far more likely to offer consistent rates across all channels used. While it could be speculated that the reason for this might be

Table 1.4 Average Rates Offered to the Customer

CHANNEL	MEAN	STANDARD DEVIATION
Hotel company website	$159	112
Expedia	$152	116
Travelocity.com	$166	134
Travelweb	$162	115
WorldRes	$181	168
Voice (CRS)	$163	117

Table 1.5 Market Sector Analysis (Lowest Rates)

CHANNEL	PERCENTAGE OF CASES WHERE A CHANNEL OFFERED THE LOWEST RATES			
	ECONOMY	MID-PRICE	LUXURY	CHI-SQUARED
All rates equal	46%	21%	28%	0.016*
Hotel company website	26%	47%	14%	0.036*
Expedia	14%	11%	41%	0.030*
Travelocity.com	3%	5%	7%	0.750*
Travelweb	9%	5%	7%	0.900*
WorldRes	0%	0%	0%	—
Voice (CRS)	3%	11%	3%	0.600*

*Indicates that the association is significant at the 95-percent confidence level.

that economy properties are more likely to have a single fixed price for their product irrespective of demand, it could also be due to a more consistent pricing strategy on the part of the hotel companies involved when addressing a relatively price-sensitive market. Furthermore it can be seen that consumers at the low ends of the market are far more likely to obtain low rates through direct (company-owned) channels. For economy brands, direct sales over the company's own web site were lowest 26 percent of the time. When coupled with the 46 percent of cases where the same rate is offered irrespective of the channel used, that means that a consumer reserving an economy room will find the cheapest rate on the hotel company's web site nearly three times out of four. With mid-price products, the chain's web site is even more likely to give the best rate, offering the lowest rate nearly half of the time.

The situation is different at the upper end of the market. Luxury-hotel companies' web sites gave the cheapest rate in less than 10 percent of cases. Furthermore, Table 1.6 shows that the company's web site quoted the highest rate in over one-third

Table 1.6 Market Sector Analysis (Highest Rates)

CHANNEL	PERCENTAGE OF CASES WHERE A CHANNEL OFFERED THE HIGHEST RATES			
	ECONOMY	MID-PRICE	LUXURY	CHI-SQUARED
All rates equal	46%	21%	28%	0.016*
Hotel company website	14%	16%	34%	0.011*
Expedia	0%	21%	7%	0.017*
Travelocity.com	3%	5%	10%	0.450*
Travelweb	0%	0%	0%	—
WorldRes	6%	0%	0%	0.240*
Voice (CRS)	31%	37%	21%	0.440*

*Indicates that the association is significant at the 95-percent confidence level.

of cases. Overall, the evidence seems to indicate that if you want to stay in up-market hotels, you should avoid booking on these hotels' web sites if you are searching for good value. Instead, the online intermediaries (in particular, Expedia) offer the highest probability of finding the best rate available for high-end properties, with an average savings of 5 percent available by booking through Expedia rather than on the company's own site.

Haggling required. It is also clear from the data that a hotel company's CRS is not the place to obtain the best rates, at least if one takes the first offer, as I did for this study. Irrespective of the market segment, there is a higher probability of being quoted the highest rate through this channel, and bookings through this route were almost never the cheapest available. This finding, however, is to a large extent driven by my methodology. Indeed, in many cases, as soon as I indicated that I did not plan to make a booking at the quoted rate, the CRS associate quoted another, lower rate. This anecdotal finding suggests that negotiation might have resulted in lower prices. (This is a longstanding CRS practice; see Lewis and Roan, 1986).

✦ DAWN OF A NEW WAY

From the above discussion, it can be seen that both the range of channels through which hotels can be booked and the complexity of such channels have grown. This study represents a first attempt at documenting hotel companies' pricing practices over electronic routes. The study revealed that the majority of hotel brands now use simultaneous, multiple electronic channels of distribution, making their rooms available to a relatively wide audience. While the use of CRS-based reservations has fallen slightly, there has been a growth in the availability of hotel companies' own web sites, and a vast majority of companies that I studied now make their rooms available for sale in this manner. The differences between this study's findings and earlier published research indicate a major expansion in hotel chains' use of the web as a direct-sales medium, perhaps accompanied by a realization of the web's benefits in comparison with other, more traditional, electronic channels of distribution.

Most companies offer multiple rates to customers over each channel. It is interesting to note, however, the large number of companies that now offer consistent pricing across all channels. Previous research found less than 10 percent of companies had consistent pricing and cited the lack of integration among the various inventory databases used to manage inventory as a possible cause. Yet over one-third of the brands I studied now offer consistent pricing across multiple channels, indicating progress in the industry's management of electronic distribution.

Although no single channel consistently offers the lowest prices, in-depth analysis does reveal a link between pricing and the market being targeted. First, the lowest prices can rarely be obtained from the CRS (absent negotiation), irrespective of market segment. As compared to the first-offered CRS price, a would-be customer can save at least 5 percent by booking over any of the electronic channels I examined. From the data it can be seen that consumers are more likely to find the lowest prices on the hotel chains' own web sites in the economy and mid-price segments than will be found from those companies' CRS or third-party web sites. So-called up-market hotel brands are, on the other hand, more likely to quote higher prices on their own web site than what they offer on other channels. Economy brands seem to be the only ones in the industry as a whole displaying a logical online pricing strategy (in terms of the relationship between the cost of using a channel and the rates offered there) and also in terms of actively managing their channels of distribution.

Implications. First, it is clear that for those with a taste for upscale products, the hotel brand's own web site is not the place to shop, as better value can be obtained in most cases through other channels. More interesting, however, is the fact that, in general, prices have become more or less equal across many of the channels investigated, and by implication, across many other electronic distribution channels as well. It is well established that time is a valuable commodity in today's society. Since the number and variety of ways that a consumer can book a hotel room has become undeniably manifold, the cost associated with searching through even a small number of the many consumer-focused channels currently available in the marketplace in an attempt to find a low price has increased. Given that this study has found that many of the rates being offered over alternative channels are more or less the same for many hotels, customers should reconsider whether all that time and energy searching for the lowest rate is actually worthwhile.

The implications for the hotelier are more pressing. My findings suggest that many hotel chains are not actively managing the room rates being offered in their portfolio of electronic distribution channels. Most companies offer multiple rates on each channel, which, as discussed earlier, can be beneficial as it gives a choice to the customer. Displaying too many rates, though,

can be counterproductive, if the customer becomes overwhelmed. Presenting a small number of tightly defined rates would be the most appropriate solution. However, most companies currently display about five rates in response to a customer inquiry, with others showing significantly more, usually with little or no apparent product differentiation. In addition, there appears to be inconsistency in terms of the rates being offered over electronic channels. In many cases, no clear or logical pricing strategy is apparent. The lowest prices are offered on channels with the highest transaction costs, and vice versa. A small number of companies offer consistent pricing irrespective of the channel being used to make the booking. Informal follow up with those companies revealed that they follow this strategy as they believe in the principle of one "correct" price for each customer. In this way, they do not have to address the issue of customer dissatisfaction as a result of a person's being quoted a lower price for a room on a different channel after having already made a booking. However, such an approach ignores the issue of the cost of processing a booking over a particular channel. As was discussed earlier, such costs vary greatly depending to a large extent on the number of intermediaries between the supplier and the customer. The greater the number of intermediaries, the greater the transaction cost and processing fees— and therefore the greater the distribution cost. This would seem to argue for having high rates on the channels that have high-cost structures and low prices on those with low-cost structures. Coupled with this matter is the fact that customers have become more knowledgeable about and comfortable with e-commerce issues in general, are more aware that distribution costs are lower in the virtual world than the bricks-and-mortar one, and thus increasingly expect to find the cheapest prices over electronic, and particularly direct electronic, routes. Put simply, when they go to a hotel company's web site, they expect to find the best value there. This study has shown that in many cases this is simply not the case, given that luxury hotels in particular tend to offer their highest rates over direct channels—and (ironically) their cheapest rates over the most expensive online intermediaries. Informal follow up to the study revealed that this may be due to the proactive approach of the online companies in contacting hotel companies on practically a daily basis and encouraging them to reduce their rates in return for better positioning on their search listings. In contrast, the rates on hotel companies' web sites go largely unmanaged, in many cases being set far in advance and not adjusted to reflect changing supply and demand.

Irrespective of its root cause, the behavior of hotel companies is driving Internet shoppers into the arms of the waiting online intermediaries, where in addition to consistently low prices, they also find wide product choice. Because of this, it's likely that many hotels are losing potential bookings to competitors as a result

of consumers' migration toward the online travel sites that offer relatively low rates from many different hotel chains. Instead of being presented with a list of a chain's properties on a company's web site, prospective guests see a much wider variety of options from the online intermediary and may be tempted to book a competitor's room (especially if price becomes an issue). Once consumers conclude that they will usually find better prices on a third-party channel, they will make Expedia or Travelocity, for example, their first port of call for future bookings—threatening brand loyalty, driving up transaction fees, increasing reservation leakage, and strengthening the third parties' power to demand "special rates" or commission overrides for a company to gain premium positioning (or even inclusion) in their search listings. Hotel companies need to take urgent action if they are not to lose control over the sale of their own product. At the very least, this means offering consistent prices over all channels, but more probably means providing customers the lowest rate over their own web site. This would decrease guests' motivation to book on alternative electronic channels, would help build web-site traffic, and should help to decrease distribution costs.

1.5 FACE RECOGNITION AND NAME RECALL: TRAINING IMPLICATIONS FOR THE HOSPITALITY INDUSTRY

VINCENT P MAGNINI AND EARL D. HONEYCUTT JR.

ABSTRACT. Hospitality corporations continually seek to implement strategies that enhance customer satisfaction and loyalty. One potential strategy that contributes to increased customer satisfaction and loyalty is training both associates and managers in techniques to recognize guests' faces and names. Psychological research has shown how face recognition and name recall can be applied in hospitality situations, in particular to create pseudorelationships with guests and to convert those to genuine relationships with loyal customers. Training employees and managers in mnemonic techniques for name recollection will almost certainly be a wise investment in creating satisfied guests.

✦ INTRODUCTION

Hospitality firms constantly maneuver to build and maintain relationships with their more profitable customers. Relationship-marketing strategies, in the form of heavily promoted loyalty programs, now constitute a significant portion of hospitality companies' strategic marketing.[1] In fact, customer-relationship management has become sophisticated in recent years through emerging data-mining capabilities.[2] Despite the advances of technology, an age-old, quintessential factor remains. In building and maintaining customer loyalty and commitment, the importance of remembering and addressing customers by name in face-to-face encounters is crucial.[3]

Emerging research increasingly confirms that customer emotions play an integral role in driving customer satisfaction and loyalty.[4] For example, widely accepted research that addressed antecedents and consequences of customer loyalty was revised to include the salient component of emotional loyalty.[5] In other words, researchers are converging on the fact that customers' affective states play a larger role than previously thought in consumers' satisfaction judgments. One study, for instance, found that luxury hotel customers desire to feel "sophisticated," midscale lodging guests like to feel "welcome," and economy hotel patrons want a feeling of "comfort."[6] Furthermore, customers of both midprice and upscale

hotel properties revealed that a key determinant of emotional loyalty is a feeling of "importance."[7] One way to bolster clients' feelings of comfort, welcome, sophistication, and importance is to address guests by their names. To illustrate the key role of face and name recall in the hospitality industry, Figure 1.1 offers selected scenarios that are routinely observed in full-service hotels.

Addressing someone by name involves the successful completion of two tasks: face recognition and name recall. Despite the apparent benefits gained by using customers' names, we believe that current hospitality literature lacks adequate coverage of this area. Therefore, the purpose of this article is to apply psychology research on the subject of face recognition and name recall to derive practical training implications for hospitality firms. To achieve this objective, this article is organized as follows: (1) pertinent face recognition literature is discussed; (2) face recognition training guidelines are offered; (3) background information regarding name recall is outlined; (4) name recall training suggestions are offered; (5) managerial implications are highlighted; and (6) questions for the future are raised.

✦ THEORETICAL FOUNDATIONS OF FACE RECOGNITION

In a person-to-person encounter, one rarely says, "I can remember your name, but I can't

Figure 1.1 Selected Examples of the Importance of Face Recognition and Name Recall in Full-Service Hotels

- Guests pass the front desk numerous times throughout their stay, but the front-desk associate cannot predict when this will happen and consequently cannot review the computerized guest folio instantaneously. Therefore, enhanced face recognition and name recall skills will aid the front-desk associate's memory of the guest's face and name from check-in.

- At check-in guests often introduce themselves to a member of the bell staff. Face and name recall training will aid in greeting and conversing with the guests as they enter and exit the hotel's lobby throughout the duration of their stay.

- The most common form of payment in a hotel restaurant is a room charge, in which case the server sees the customer's last name. Face and name recall training can aid in greeting guests on subsequent dining experiences during the guest's stay.

- Businesses and associations often book multiple meetings in a hotel's conference space (e.g., monthly, quarterly, or annually). Banquet captains trained in face and name recall can engender confidence in an often-stressed meeting planner.

remember your face." Evidently, before calling someone by name, we must first recognize his or her face. By definition, recognition occurs when an object is represented and the immediate perceptual pattern is compared with a revived percept—or image—and a judgment of likeness is passed.[8] While this universal definition is applicable for face recognition, there are nuances of face processing that make the task different from other forms of recognition.

Face recognition is a capability that humans begin to develop during infancy; for example, newborns are attracted to face-like patterns.[9] Researchers postulate that humans are born with a certain degree of face recognition ability since, within forty-three minutes of delivery, newborns track face-like patterns more than non-facelike patterns.[10] Also, newborns spend longer staring at faces rated attractive by adults than at faces rated unattractive.[11] Adult-level facial identity ability continues to develop until adolescence.

In fact, recognition of faces increases significantly between seven and eleven years of age; however, fourteen-year-olds make more errors than adults.[12]

Recognizing faces is distinct from distinguishing other objects.[13] If a picture of a face is presented upside down, recognition is hindered in comparison to distinguishing other inverted objects.[14] In experiments, recognition of familiar faces is 95 percent accurate when they are presented upright but declines to 50 to 60 percent accuracy when the identical faces are shown upside down.[15] Likewise, detection of edges is an integral part of visual identification for most objects; however, respondents were hampered from recognizing familiar faces when they were shown edge-based representations.[16] In addition, empirical evidence suggests that presenting a face in the form of a photographic negative disrupts recognition considerably more than such a reversal does for basic-level object recognition.[17]

✦ TRAINING FACE RECOGNITION

With that research background in mind, the following discusses how to improve employees' face recognition ability. In the initial encounter with a guest, the hospitality associate should be trained to take a few seconds to concentrate on the guest's face and take note of facial features. It is recommended that the associate select and mentally exaggerate one facial feature. In choosing that feature, the associate should avoid the common mistake of choosing a feature that can be easily changed, such as hairstyle, facial hair, or eyeglasses.[18] Also, facial recognition is enhanced considerably by remembering internal facial features (e.g., eyes, nose, mouth) as opposed to external features (e.g., hairline, jaw, ears).[19] A sound analogy to make when introducing this procedure is to have associates exaggerate a facial feature as if they were drawing a caricature of the individual. Studies show that most caricaturists exaggerate the same facial feature for a given person. For example, most caricatures of President Nixon exaggerated the extended bulb of his nose.[20] Thus, likening face recognition strategies to caricaturing can help hotel associates more easily understand the procedure.

The task of remembering faces is apparently more difficult for male employees to learn than it is for female associates. We say this because emerging research conducted on children supports the contention that males process faces at a global level (i.e., the face in total), while females conduct face recognition at a local level (that is, using specific features).[21] As a consequence, training programs should specifically communicate to male associates the need to overcome ther global tendency and the importance of honing in on a particular internal facial feature.

Additional complications occur when associates attempt to remember a distinctive facial feature of a person of another race. Numerous studies support the notion that recognizing a face from a person of a different race is significantly more difficult than remembering a face from one's own race.[22] Most studies indicate that each distinct race experiences similar difficulty recognizing faces of people from other races.[23] In one experiment, for instance, Caucasian subjects recognized Caucasian faces more accurately than they did Japanese faces, whereas Asian subjects recognized Japanese faces more accurately than they did Caucasian faces.[24] Researchers postulate that this gap in cross-race recognition exists because individuals typically have more experience in recognizing people of their own race.[25]

✦ THEORETICAL FOUNDATIONS OF NAME RECALL

Face recognition is the first step in guest recognition. More critical and challenging is name recall. Remembering names is not an easy task.[26] For example, it is significantly easier to remember that someone holds the occupation of a "baker" than to remember that someone's name is "Mr. Baker."[27] Remembering a name is a daunting task in part because it is the final stage in a three-stage process. First, the face must be recognized as being familiar; second, information about why the face is familiar must be recovered from memory; and third, the name of the person matching that face must be retrieved.[28]

Since remembering a person's name can be a challenge, researchers recommend using mnemonic imaging techniques to aid in the task. Mnemonic techniques are defined as strategies that can enhance learning and improve later recall of information.[29] Mnemonic imaging entails taking a word, such as a name, and creating an associative image for that word. Mnemonics experts have long advocated that using mental images or pictures to represent verbal materials aids people's memory.[30] Evidence in support of mnemonic imaging is anchored theoretically along four lines of reasoning. First, words that elicit vivid imagery are learned faster in almost all situations than are words that are abstract and arouse little imagery.[31] Second, in experiments, subjects report spontaneous use of mental pictures to learn paired-association words, and these are typically the pairs that they learn fastest.[32] Third, instructing subjects to form mental images for words greatly improves learning.[33] Fourth, pictures of objects are easier to remember than are the names of objects.[34] Because of the robust evidence in support of the usefulness of mnemonic imaging in memory and recall, the next section outlines mnemonic training strategies that can be employed by the hospitality industry.

✦ TRAINING FOR NAME RECALL

Training in name recall should be taught in combination with face recognition. That is, mnemonic visual aids should be used in concert with distinguishing facial features identified in face recognition. In a recent interview with *Fortune*, memory author Benjamin Levy described how he undertakes this process:[35]

> I morph the name into something I can visualize. What is Paul? Paul doesn't mean much.

But for me, every Paul I meet reminds me of the word "pole," like a ten-foot pole. So if I've spent a lot of time looking at Paul's ears, I would picture his ears being whacked by a ten-foot pole. The next time I see him, suddenly, almost magically, it happens: I see those ears, and they're [being] smacked with a pole! Therefore this man is Paul. He's not Steve—because there's no stove.

In addition to detailing this process, Levy also stated that concentration is an essential part of this process. In the interview with *Fortune*, Levy said that in the first twenty seconds that he meets someone, no one else in the entire world matters. By concentrating and employing mnemonic images, Levy can memorize as many as 150 first names at a corporate event.[36]

While creating an image of a facial feature is a commonly used mnemonic tactic to help commit names to memory, several of the following other methods can also be taught to hospitality associates.

One memory technique, called first-letter mnemonics, is perhaps the most popular form of mnemonics.[37] The method entails using the first letter of a word to remember that word. For example, a hospitality associate could be trained to think of an action word that starts with the same letter as the name she or he is trying to remember and then imagine the person in that action. For instance, Greg could be galloping, or Susan can be swimming. Significant empirical evidence supports the effectiveness of employing first-letter mnemonics.[38]

Another mnemonic tactic is to visualize the person's name written on his or her forehead.

President Franklin Roosevelt, an expert in name recall, employed this technique.[39]

An additional mnemonic technique is called the key-word method.[40] This method entails a two-stage process. First, the unfamiliar word is transformed into a familiar word that begets an image. Then, the two pieces of information are associated via a mental image that shows the two interacting with each other.[41] By this method, when a hospitality associate meets a customer, the associate could be trained to think of someone that she or he already knows with the same name. Then the associate could create a mental image of something that she or he has done with the person that she or he already knows and connect this image to the new person.

Finally, hospitality associates should be trained to say the customer's name throughout the conversation because repetition aids memory. For example, in an introduction, repeating a name immediately reinforces memorization.[42] When saying good-bye, using the customer's name can aid name recall when the customer returns.[43]

✦ MANAGERIAL IMPLICATIONS

Hospitality firms would benefit from implementing face recognition and name recall training programs for their service providers. Not only will associates sharpen their skills by adopting these tactics, but the training initiatives would also have the effect of reinforcing the importance of calling guests by name. Specific training sessions on this area would convey a message of importance. In terms of implementing the training, hospitality companies have several options: (1) firms can administer the training internally by adopting the recommendations outlined in this article (see Figure 1.2); (2) firms can outsource the training; or (3) firms can administer internal training but augment the sessions through commercially available face recognition and name recall training videos. If outsourcing is the method of choice, an Internet search will identify contact information for training professionals and firms that sell training videos.

While it is not possible for a hospitality associate to remember the names and faces of thousands of customers, face recognition and name recall training can enhance an associate's ability to remember a core group of "regular customers." As detailed in Figure 1.3, the following three types of customer interactions occur in the hospitality industry:[44] (1) a one-time-only encounter; (2) a pseudorelationship, where the customer interacts with the provider on a number of occasions but the service customer remains a "stranger" to the provider; and (3) a true relationship where the service provider knows the customer well enough to remember his or her name. Research indicates that true relationship customers are more highly satisfied, are more trusting of the service firm, and are more willing to spread positive word of mouth than those customers in pseudorelationships.[45] Therefore, if face and name recall training can convert a portion of pseudorelationships to true relationships, the firm would experience a larger percentage of highly satisfied, and potentially profitable, customers.

Face and name training should also be offered to hospitality supervisors and managers as a module of the modular training that nearly all hospitality corporations provide. (For example, Hyatt uses Supervisory Skill Builders that are produced by the American Hotel & Motel Association's Educational Institute.) In fact, these memory skills would be especially useful because managers and

Figure 1.2 Summary of Key Points and Name Recall Training

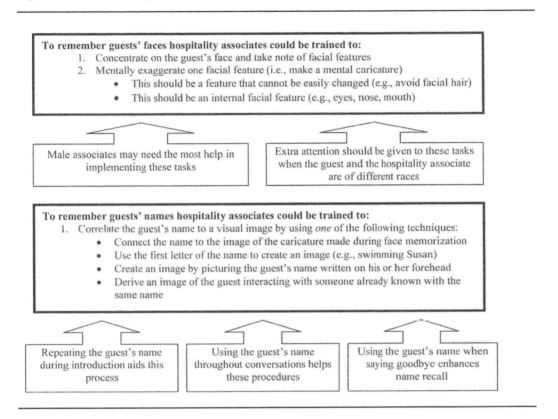

To remember guests' faces hospitality associates could be trained to:
1. Concentrate on the guest's face and take note of facial features
2. Mentally exaggerate one facial feature (i.e., make a mental caricature)
   - This should be a feature that cannot be easily changed (e.g., avoid facial hair)
   - This should be an internal facial feature (e.g., eyes, nose, mouth)

Male associates may need the most help in implementing these tasks

Extra attention should be given to these tasks when the guest and the hospitality associate are of different races

To remember guests' names hospitality associates could be trained to:
1. Correlate the guest's name to a visual image by using *one* of the following techniques:
   - Connect the name to the image of the caricature made during face memorization
   - Use the first letter of the name to create an image (e.g., swimming Susan)
   - Create an image by picturing the guest's name written on his or her forehead
   - Derive an image of the guest interacting with someone already known with the same name

Repeating the guest's name during introduction aids this process

Using the guest's name throughout conversations helps these procedures

Using the guest's name when saying goodbye enhances name recall

supervisors can employ the techniques to both greet customers and motivate employees. For example, Sam Walton's success with Wal-Mart can be attributed in part to his ability to learn the names of his subordinates. Furthermore, relationship marketing entails maintaining positive relationships with customers, employees, suppliers, and competitors.[46] Therefore, supervisors and managers can use memory skills daily to command authority and respect in interpersonal communications at myriad levels inside and outside the firm.

A benefit that face and name recall training has over other improvement initiatives is that the principal investment is the cost of training. Emerg-

ing return-on-quality literature posits that all quality initiatives must be held financially accountable and that various quality initiatives should be compared with each other because quality initiatives are not equally valid.[47] Face recognition and name recall training has an advantage over other strategic initiatives because such training does not require, for example, the purchase of new equipment for guestrooms or the daily dispensing of free amenities to guests. Accurately measuring return on investment for training is a daunting task, but a face recognition and name recall initiative has a considerable advantage over competing initiatives that require asset capital. Costs aside,

Figure 1.3 A Taxonomy of Customer Interactions for Hospitality Firms

<u>Distinctive Characteristics of an Encounter</u>

- A one-time interaction [b]
- The service provider and customer do not expect to interact with each other in the future [b]

<u>Distinctive Characteristics of a Pseudorelationship</u>

- Repeated contact between a customer and provider organization, but the customer may see a different provider each time [b]
- The customer does not get to know any individual service provider, but by having repeated contact with the same company and its procedures the customer is afforded some of the familiarity of a relationship [b]
- Those customers in pseudorelationships can identify the particular firm that they frequent, but do not know a particular individual service provider within the firm [b]

The overarching goal of a face-recognition and name-recall training program is to convert a portion of pseudorelationships into true relationships.

<u>Distinctive Characteristics of a True Relationship</u>

- Customer and provider can get to know each other as role occupants and sometimes as acquaintances or even friends [a]
- Over time the customer and the provider develop a history of shared interaction that they can draw on whenever they interact to complete a transaction [a]
- Customers can identify a particular person as their service provider even though they may not know the person's last name or even be able to recollect his or her first name without help [a]

a. B. A. Gutek, A. D. Bhappu, M. A. Liao-Troth, and B. Cherry, "Distinguishing between Service Relationships and Encounters," *Journal of Applied Psychology and Research* 84, no. 2 (1999): 218–33.
b. B. A. Gutek, B. Cherry, A. D. Bhappu, S. Schneider, and L. Woolf, "Features of Service Relationships and Encounters," *Work & Occupations* 27 (2000): 319–52.

remembering clients' names and faces becomes paramount as companies seek repeat business through loyalty programs. It is unwise for hospitality firms to send the following message: "Of course your business is important to us; you're the guest whose name I always forget."

✦ FUTURE DIRECTIONS

Modest advances have been made in understanding the primary drivers of face and name recall. This article seeks to apply those research findings to advance the hospitality human resources area. While this article expands the hospitality discipline's knowledge, the following future extensions should be considered.

Cultural training issues. Programmatic research is needed to determine how face recognition and name recall training programs should be adjusted in various cultural settings. For instance, Six Continents, Marriott, Starwood, and Accor opened a combined total of more than forty hotels in China in 2002 alone.[48] How should training programs be adapted to fit the Chinese situation? Even within the United States, approximately 60 percent of the U.S. hospitality industry's line-level employees are ethnic minorities.[49] Training effectiveness can be enhanced by adjusting programs or modules to account for cultural characteristics,[50] but further research is necessary to determine when and how the adjustments are best implemented given the broad diversity of the U.S. lodging workforce.

How much is too much? Modern computerized biometric technology has the ability to recognize faces. A number of technology companies manufacturer products that can capture people's faces and search for matches with customer images stored in a database. Such face recognition applications are increasingly employed by casinos to exclude known criminals and cheats from entering establishments. It has also been suggested that casino hotels can use face recognition technology to identify preferred customers as they arrive. Consequently, as customers approach the front desk, accommodations and amenities are already being arranged. This raises the following research questions: Is this going too far? Does this process constitute an invasion of privacy that would leave customers with an uneasy feeling? Or conversely, will clients embrace such added attention and improved level of service? In either case, it behooves hospitality operators to train their staff in name and face recognition to improve guest service.

ENDNOTES FOR SECTION 1.5

1. J. T. Bowen and S. Shoemaker, "Loyalty: A Strategic Commitment," *Cornell Hotel and Restaurant Administration Quarterly* 44, no. 5–6 (October-December 2003): 31–46.

2. V. P. Magnini, E. D. Honeycutt, and S. K. Hodge, "Data Mining for Hotel Firms: Use and Limitations," *Cornell Hotel and Restaurant Administration Quarterly* 44, no. 2 (April 2003): 94–106; and H. Min, H. Min, and A. Eman, "A Data Mining Approach to Developing the Profiles of Hotel Customers," *International Journal of Contemporary Hospitality Management* 14, no. 6 (2002): 274–85.

3. M. S. Nyman, "What Was Your Name Again? Some Tips for Remembering Names (and Avoiding This Question)," *American Salesman* 4, no. 8 (1996): 27.

4. J. Barsky and L. Nash, "Customer Satisfaction: Applying Concepts to Industry-Wide Measures," *Cornell Hotel and Restaurant Administration Quarterly* 44, no. 5–6 (October-December 2003): 173–83.

5. S. Shoemaker and J. T. Bowen, "Commentary on Loyalty: A Strategic Commitment," *Cornell Hotel and Restaurant Administration Quarterly* 44, no. 5–6 (October-December 2003): 47–52.

6. Barsky and Nash, "Customer Satisfaction."

7. J. Barsky and L. Nash, "Evoking Emotion: Affective Keys to Hotel Loyalty," *Cornell Hotel and Restaurant Administration Quarterly* 43, no. 1 (February 2002): 39–46.

8. F. C. Bartlett, *Remembering: A Study in Experimental and Social Psychology* (Cambridge: Cambridge University Press, 1964).

9. C. J. Mondloch, T. L. Lewis, D. R. Budreau, D. Maurer, J. L. Dannemiller, B. R. Stephens, and K. A. Kleiner-Gathercoal, "Face Perception during Early Infancy," *Psychological Science* 10 (1999): 419–22.

10. M. H. Johnson, S. Dziurawiec, H. Ellis, and J. Morton, "Newborns' Preferential Tracking of Face-Like Stimuli and Its Subsequent Decline," *Cognition* 40 (1991): 1–19.

11. A. Slater, G. Bremner, S. P. Johnson, P. Sherwood, R. Hayes, and E. Brown, "Newborn Infants' Preference for Attractive Faces: The Role of Internal and External Facial Features," *Infancy* 1 (2000): 265–74.

12. S. Carey, R. Diamond, and B. Woods, "Development of Face Recognition: A Maturational Component?" *Developmental Psychology* 16 (1980): 257–69.

13. B. E. Brooks, L. J. Rosielle, and E. E. Cooper, "The Priming of Face Recognitions after Metric Transformations," *Perception* 31 (2002): 297–313.

14. R. Yin, "Looking at Upside-Down Faces," *Journal of Experimental Psychology* 81 (1969): 141–45.

15. V. Bruce and A. Young, *In the Eye of the Beholder* (Oxford: Oxford University Press, 1998).

16. H. Leder, "Matching Person Identity from Facial Line Drawings," *Perception* 28 (1999): 1171–75.

17. V. Bruce and T. Valentine, "The Use of Pigmentation and Shading Information in Recognizing the Sex and Identities of Face," *Perception* 23 (1994): 803–22.

18. A. W. Young, D. C. Hays, K. H. McWeeny, B. M. Flude, and A. W. Ellis, "Matching Familiar and Unfamiliar Faces on Internal and External Features," *Perception* 14: 737–46.

19. H. D. Ellis, J. W. Shepherd, and G. M. Davies, "Identification of Familiar and Unfamiliar Faces from Internal and External Features: Some Implications for Theories of Face Recognition," *Perception* 8 (1989): 431–39.

20. Bruce and Young, *In the Eye of the Beholder.*

21. D. E. Everhart, J. L. Shucard, T. Quatrin, and D. Shucard, "Sex-Related Differences in Event-Related Potentials, Face Recognition, and Facial Affect Processing in Prepubertal Children," *Neuropsychology* 15, no. 3 (2001): 329–41.

22. D. T. Levin and B. L. Angelone, "Categorical Perception of Race," *Perception* 31 (2001): 567–78.

23. Bruce and Young, *In the Eye of the Beholder.*

24. J. R. Vokey and J. D. Read, "Familiarity, Memorability, and the Effect of Typicality on the Recognition of Faces," *Memory and Cognition* 20, no. 3 (1992): 291–313.

25. Ibid.

26. Bruce and Young, *In the Eye of the Beholder.*

27. K. H. McWeeny, A. W. Young, D. C. Hay, and A. W. Ellis, "Putting Names to Faces," *British Journal of Psychology* 78 (1987): 143–51.

28. A. W. Young, D. C. Hay, and A. W. Ellis, "The Faces that Launched a Thousand Slips: Everyday Difficulties and Errors in Recognising People," *British Journal of Psychology* 76 (1985): 495–523.

29. F. S. Bellezza, "Mnemonic Devices: Classification, Characteristics, and Criteria," *Review of Educational Research* 51, no. 2 (1981): 247–75.

30. J. R. Anderson and G. H. Bower, *Human Associative Memory* (Hillsdale, NJ: Lawrence Erlbaum, 1980).

31. Ibid.

32. Ibid.

33. Ibid.

34. Ibid.

35. J. Useem, "Your Name Is Mud, or a Pole, or a Stove," *Fortune* 146, no. 1 (July 8, 2002): 40.

36. Ibid.

37. M. M. Gruneberg and P. E. Morris, *Applied Problems in Memory* (London: Academic Press, 1979).

38. G. R. McKenzie and J. Sawyer, "Effects of Test-Like Practice and Mnemonics on Learning Graphic Facts," *Theory and Research in Social Education* 14, no. 3 (1986): 201–9.

39. K. Hallbom, *Remembering Names through NLP* (Evergreen, CO: NLP Comprehensive 1999).

40. N. K. Malhotra, "Mnemonics in Marketing: A Pedagogical Tool," *Journal of the Academy of Marketing Science* 19, no. 2 (1991): 141–49.

41. Ibid.

42. W. Lampton, "Win at the Name Game: Six Ways to Better Effectiveness," *Fund Raising Management* 10, no. 5 (1979): 42.

43. B. Levy, "Say My Name, Say My Name," *Incentive* 176, no. 9 (2002): 99–100.

44. B. A. Gutek, A. D. Bhappu, M. A. Liao-Troth, and B. Cherry, "Distinguishing between Service Relationships and Encounters," *Journal of Applied Psychology* 84, no. 2 (1999): 218–33.

45. B. A. Gutek, B. Cherry, A. D. Bhappu, S. Schneider, and L. Woolf, "Features of Service Relationships and Encounters," *Work & Occupations* 27 (2000): 319–52.

46. R. M. Morgan and S. D. Hunt, "The Commitment-Trust Theory of Relationship Marketing," *Journal of Marketing* 58 (1994): 20–38.

47. R. T. Rust, A. J. Zahorik, and T. L. Keiningham, "Return on Quality (ROQ): Making Service Quality Financially Accountable," *Journal of Marketing* 59, no. 2 (1995): 58–75.

48. Z. Coleman, "Hotel Groups Bolster Presence in China," *Wall Street Journal,* May 8, 2002, p. D10.

49. F. Andorka, "Diversity Task Forces Meet to Set the Agenda," *Hotel and Motel Management* 212, no. 4 (1997): 32–36.

50. J. B. Tracey and M. J. Tews, "Training Effectiveness: Accounting for Individual Characteristics and the Work Environment," *Cornell Hotel and Restaurant Administration Quarterly* 36, no. 6 (December 1995): 36–42.

1.6 SPAS AND THE LODGING INDUSTRY Peter C. Anderson

✦ OVERVIEW

Spas are becoming such a significant component of the service menu for resorts and full-service hotels that their absence, especially in amenity-rich resort environments, is glaringly obvious. Within the leisure industries in 2003, revenues related to spas ranked number four behind golf fees and dues ($19.7 million), cruise line revenues ($14.7 million), and health club revenues ($14.1 million). At $11.2 million, spa revenues outpaced amusement park revenues ($10.3 million), box office receipts ($9.5 million), and vacation ownership sales ($5.5 million) (Thacker, 2004; Audi

and Wright, 2004). In this section, we first examine trends that support a sea change in North Americans' attitude toward spa use. After evaluating spa demand demographics, we discuss the types of spas currently popular in the industry, development and operational considerations, the components of a spa experience, compensation issues, and trends in the spa industry.

✦ SPA DEMAND

According to the International SPA Association research, between 2002 and 2003, 11 percent of the national population over the age of 16 made one or more spa visits. This statistic shows that one in ten Americans visited a spa during that period. Additionally, of these, 41 percent were visiting spas for the first time, indicating a larger population embracing spa usage. Age demographics show that 14 percent of clients are between the ages of 16 and 24, and over 50 percent are in the 25 to 44 age bracket.

An emerging national statistic is the number of male visits to spas. Twenty-three percent of spa visits and 29 percent of spa goers were men in 2003, trending toward special gender-oriented treatments and male-only spas being opened worldwide.

Spa selection criteria are determined by a number of factors. An established and known environment—for instance, as a part of an established resort, club, or destination spa—often influences the decision, as does atmosphere, quality of treatment, and friendliness of staff. Additionally, among spa goers, nine out of ten respondents report they would return for a similar experience.

Most spa customers believe they received good value for their spa dollar. On a 10-point scale, services were given an average of 8 for value, with massage generating 8.8 on the value-for-service scale.

Spa services demonstrated the highest and heaviest demand on weekends, followed by appointments after work on weekdays. Gender demographics also play a role in spa demand, as men are more likely to go for regular weekly visits after business hours or while traveling on business. Women, however, often visit spas during regular business hours (Thacker, 2004; Audi and Wright, 2004).

The International Hotel Resort Spa Association (IHRSA) reports that branded resort spas such as Canyon Ranch are opening in the day spa market, adding new competitive pressure on the independents. Nontraditional players are also adding product supply. For example, corporations are creating in-house spa environments, hospitals are adding wellness as part of their repertoire, and medi-spas, with a primary focus on cosmetic surgery, are adding spa business as an additional profit center. Health clubs are also trying to capture a piece of the pie by adding spa practices. The rationale in this market is that time-crunched patrons can benefit from the one-stop-shopping approach to fitness and wellness, but the health club operator also uses the spa as an enticement to join the fitness center.

As the day and destination spa markets become saturated, it will become imperative for survival that each operator differentiate itself from the competition. The necessity for market segmentation to ensure clear communication with consumers will be a key to success in the maturing spa market. Another component of success will be a branding strategy that the consumer can immediately identify with respect to spa performance and the consumer's personal comfort level.

✦ HEALTH ISSUES AND SPA DEMAND

Increasingly, spa goers are looking to create prolonged wellness that integrates and renews body, mind, and spirit. To that end, Eastern and Western lifestyle issues related to medicine, philosophy, and spirituality are becoming a mainstay of many spa/wellness experiences. To best deliver this, the wellness spa (located at day, destination, or resort environments) supports guests' needs by creating an experience, not just a series of treatments. All the guest amenities, facilities, treatments, and programs must be seamlessly integrated into a personally tailored guest experience. These experiences should be targeted toward couples, parents with children, and teenagers. In the early 1990s, spas were considered a natural outgrowth of fitness facilities and focused primarily on treatments related to body wellness. As market sophistication evolved, the body-mind connection attracted consumer focus. In the beginning of the twenty-first century, spas and marketers are overtly addressing body, mind, and spirit connections in order to respond to emerging market sensibilities. Among the components one might find in a modern spa are services related to:

- Complementary and alternative medicine in mainstream lifestyles

- Traditional Western medical and Eastern lifestyle/wellness practices

- A proactive approach to overall health and the quality of one's life

Body

- Action spas are attracting a greater percentage of men who are looking for a way to unwind and keep active. Because of this trend, an aggressive array of activities—including cardio-circuit courses, squash, racketball and tennis, free and fixed weights, jogging, and bike paths, hikes, and water spots—is still a basic spa/wellness requirement.

- As part of the wellness experience, medical affiliations are sometimes available to provide information and to check blood pressure, heart conditions, bone density, and so on.

- Exceptional food can be tailored to virtually any dietary restriction or request.

- When examining which body treatments to include, note that salt glows and exfoliant treatments are approximately four times more popular than any other body treatment. These items are a mainstay in successful spa services.

- Guests must be able to upgrade their experience with add-ons such as eye-firming therapies and mineral-enhanced hydrotherapy soaks. Further, it is important to sell services in several time blocks so that guests can select services that fit their schedule and financial budget.

Body, Mind

- Educational programs at many levels include classes and clinics. These programs personally empower the guest, expand the wellness center's demand base, and encourage repeat visits. Health and wellness issues encompass cardiovascular health, holistic childrearing, the integration of Eastern and Western medical practices, indigenous spiritual practices, aging, intimacy, transition/death, vitality, strength training, cooking programs (macrobiotic, vegan, vegetarian, indigenous), women's issues, and so on. Traditionally, educational programs at spas have focused primarily on personal health issues.

- Mind-body techniques may include spiritual and cultural instruction. Examples include tai chi, visualization, progressive muscle relaxation and biofeedback, labyrinth walking, meditating and chanting, sweat lodges, and storytelling.

- Extensive yoga programs should include Hatha yoga for body control, Ashtanga yoga for cardio workout, Iyengar yoga for balance and alignment, and Kundalini yoga for breath work.

Body, Mind, Spirit

- Comprehensive touch/alternative manual therapies, including chiropractic treatment and deep tissue massage (rolfing, myofascial release, neuromuscular massage, acupressure/shiatsu, watsu, Trager massage, etc.) are a necessary component of any wellness clinic. This modality is an extension of the basic massage offered at all spas and wellness/healing centers. Practitioners who provide manual therapies should be cross-trained in the areas of subtle energy work such as reiki, chakra balancing, and chi gung. Offering alternative touch/energy therapy as a component of traditional massage has the potential to accelerate market acceptance.

- Ayurvedic treatments are popular and provide an additional link between the East-meets-West philosophy showcased in many day spas. Elements of ayurvedic treatments can be incorporated into most touch therapies.

As far back as 1993, a well-known study by David Eisenberg revealed that one-third of all patients had visited a practitioner of alternative health care in the past year, at a cost of $13.7 billion. This indicated to the medical community that the significant out-of-pocket expenses implied not only lost revenues to traditional (allopathic) doctors but also a broad dissatisfaction with mainstream medicine. A great number of people were taking the issues of health and well-being into their own control, thus setting the stage for the popularity of proactive wellness programs.

In 1997, Eisenberg updated his study. He estimated the total number of visits to alternative medical providers at 600 million, representing an expenditure of over $27.1 billion. The number of visits to alternative care physicians in 1997 was greater than the total number of visits to traditional primary care physicians in the same year. The increasing popularity of alternative wellness modalities, the aging of the population, and the strength of the economy are all factors that support the growth of this trend. As of this writing, it appears to continue to grow.

The use of at least 1 of 16 (alternative) therapies during the previous year increased from 33.8 percent in 1990 to 42.1 percent in 1997. The fastest-growing therapies were herbal medicine, massage, megavitamins, self-help groups, folk remedies, energy healing, and homeopathy. The probability of users visiting an alternative medicine practitioner increased from 36.3 percent to 46.3 percent. In both 1990 and 1997, alternative therapies were used most frequently for chronic conditions, especially back problems, anxiety, depression, and headaches. In general, it can be concluded that alternative medicine expenditure increased substantially between 1990 and 1997, and this can be attributed primarily to an increase in the proportion of the population seeking alternative therapies rather than increased visits per patient.

The most frequently reported principal medical conditions for which alternative therapies were sought are summarized in Table 1.7.

✦ SPA CLASSIFICATION

Spa development and its attendant popularity have deep historical roots and vast potential for the hospitality industry. The term *spa* was once reserved for European destination resorts where guests went to "take the waters" and restore a healthy and balanced life. However, the term now is used to describe many types of facilities and amenities in the U.S. lodging industry. At one end of the spa spectrum are dedicated desti-

Table 1.7 Most Frequently Reported Principal Medical Conditions

AILMENT	ALTERNATIVE THERAPY	
	PRIMARY	SECONDARY
Back problems	Chiropractic	Massage
Allergies	Herbal	Relaxation
Fatigue	Relaxation	Massage
Arthritis	Relaxation	Chiropractic
Headaches	Relaxation	Chiropractic
Neck problems	Chiropractic	Massage
High blood pressure	Megavitamins	Relaxation
Sprains or strains	Chiropractic	Relaxation
Insomnia	Relaxation	Herbal
Lung problems	Relaxation	Spiritual healing/herbal
Skin problems	Imagery	Energy healing
Digestive problems	Relaxation	Herbal
Depression	Relaxation	Spiritual healing
Anxiety	Relaxation	Spiritual healing

nation resort spas aimed primarily at those seeking a specialized combination regime of health, fitness, and pampering. Modalities and treatments include massages, unique treatments, custom dietary plans, lectures, and adventures that can include, but are not limited to, an array of activities ranging from nonsurgical facelifts to helicopter skiing.

Destination resorts, such as Miraval's Life-in-Balance and Canyon Ranch, with locations in the Berkshires in Massachusetts and the Arizona desert, draw demand because of their facilities and reputation. The primary reason for going to a destination resort spa is to enjoy the spa itself and its related activities. The destination itself is a demand generator.

Closely related to a destination resort spa is the amenity spa. Amenity spas provide services to resorts and full-service hotels. The primary difference between an amenity spa and a destination spa is the scope and depth of spa services. Amenity spas, while sometimes quite extensive, *support* the resort environment, whereas destination spas are the *focus* of the resort environment. In situations where a full-service, high-end hotel is located in an urban environment and has a significantly large spa component, the spa can operate as both an amenity spa (to the hotel) and a day spa (to the local community). Later in this chapter, we study the case of the Westin Los Angeles Century City's 35,000-square-foot Spa Mystique. This spa supports the needs of the hotel's convention and individual travelers while experiencing heavy local day spa use.

Middle-market hotel properties now feel obliged to add a spa as an amenity; however, due to capital and real estate restraints, often they cannot provide a full-service location. As a result, this sector has seen an explosion in poorly conceived and executed spa additions that provide the owner the opportunity to add ". . . and spa" at the end of the business name. These are often no more than the result of subcontracting a massage therapist and converting the guest room closest to the swimming pool into an exercise room. These spas seldom surprise and delight their guests and often reflect poorly on the spa industry overall. Fortunately, the sophistication of the industry is making it harder and harder for the ". . . and spas" to succeed.

As the spa industry matures, certain development trends are emerging. In 2005, the spa industry was considered the fastest-growing segment of the travel, hospitality, and leisure market, showing 26 percent growth from 2002 to 2004. Spas are no longer considered a niche industry but rather an entity unto themselves.

The spa industry is made up of the following segments, each with its own characteristics and operational opportunities:

- Destination spas
- Resort hotel spas
- Day spas
- Medical spas
- Mineral springs
- Club spas

DESTINATION SPAS

A destination spa is one whose sole purpose is to provide programs and facilities that support lifestyle improvements and enhance guest health. The services offered are professionally adminis-tered and include fitness, education, and lectures on lifestyle, nutrition, and disease prevention. Because of their healthful orientation, destination spas often provide programs that support postoperative conditions, address various addictions, and provide tools to cope with serious, prolonged illness.

The destination spa industry constitutes only 1.6 percent of the total spa industry, per the International Spa Association's Industry Study (Thacker, 2004). However, the growth in the development and use of destination spas reflects the market's trend toward wellness and health as a major component in spa menus.

RESORT SPAS/AMENITY SPAS

Resort spas are located on the grounds of vacation resorts where treatments for mind, body, and spirit are offered to complement other resort activities such as golf, tennis, horseback riding, skiing, and water sports. Healthful spa cuisine is on the menu as an option, complementing traditional offerings. In the evenings, guests can enjoy resort pastimes like dancing and live entertainment. Children's programs are also offered. According to the ISPA Spa Industry Study (Thacker, 2004), the resort spa represents 14 percent of spa locations in North America but accounts for almost 41 percent of the total industry revenue, 27 percent of all spa visits, and 26 percent of the industry's employees.

A luxury resort spa has the ambience of a secluded retreat on the grounds of a first-class resort. Set in beautiful surroundings, these resorts commonly have world-class golf courses and other excellent recreational facilities. Gourmet dining and exceptional spa therapies are not only expected but demanded.

DAY SPAS

Day spas are designed to provide a healing, beautifying, or pampering experience in a short period. Guests may book individual treatments that last as little as an hour or a package of treatments that take up to a whole day. Found throughout North America, day spas are free-standing or located in health clubs, hotels, and department stores. The day spa industry constitutes 72.2 percent of the total industry revenues, per the International Spa Association's 2004 Spa Industry Study. The large percentage of day spas and their growth pattern reflect spa goers' time crunch. Day spas can be owner-operated or chain-affiliated.

Preliminary data from ISPA's 2004 survey show that industry growth is still robust. As of midyear 2004, there was a total of 12,000 spas nationally, of which 8,700 were day spas. These numbers reflect 25 percent growth in the industry in general and 20 percent growth exclusively in this market. The total number of day spa visits in 2003 was 81.2 million. However, only 13 percent of the general population had used a spa in the prior 3-year period, indicating that the industry still has large growth potential.

MEDICAL SPAS

Medical treatments in various spa environments represent a significant trend in the scope, depth, and inclusiveness of numerous spas. Medical spa treatments can range from elective, reconstructive surgery to noninvasive Eastern modalities incorporating elements of Eastern philosophy that draw on the body-mind-spirit connection to create positive, measurable changes in the client/patient. Slightly over half (51 percent) of the medical spas in North America have a partnership with a medical doctor, and 26 percent have a doctor on staff. The remaining configurations include being located in a doctor's office or having licensed staff members. Botox and microdermabrasion are the two most popular treatments, followed by chemical peels and laser hair removal.

In North America, allopathic or Western medical procedures found in medical spas often incorporate Eastern-based treatments. Day, destination, and resort/amenity spas are adding medical treatments to their spa menus. Part of this trend is directly attributed to market demand, and part is attributed to health insurance plans that reimburse for some procedures. According to the ISPA 2004 survey, medical spas are the fastest-growing spa segment with respect to number of locations. The average annual growth in medical spas by location since 1999 is approximately 45 percent. Cumulative growth from 1999 to 2004 is 205 percent and from 2002 to 2004, 109 percent. Medical spas generated an estimated 1,900,000 visits in 2003, representing 1.39 percent of the total spa visits. However, this percentage of visits accounts for approximately 2.1 percent of the total industry revenues, reflecting the lucrative nature of this segment of the industry.

MINERAL SPRINGS SPAS

Many mineral springs spas are considered to be the original spa prototype, where guests go to "take the waters." Mineral springs spas, by definition, are located at naturally occurring mineral springs, and by number of locations represent 2.8 percent of the total spa industry, or 1.3 percent of the total industry revenues, making this one of the more modest income-producing segments of the spa industry. The popularity of mineral springs spas is reflected in a cumulative growth from 1999 to 2004 of 143 percent. Growth from 2002 to 2004 represents only 15 percent, implying that the number of sites available directly affects the growth in this segment.

CLUB SPAS

Club spas lack a lodging component, and their primary objective is to facilitate daily fitness activities. Many club spas' services complement the primary fitness component of the club by offering sports massage (deep tissue), chiropractic services, physiotherapy, and related treatments that address issues of pain management, flexibility, and mobility. By location, club spas represent 5.8 percent of the total spa industry in North America and account for approximately 3.7 percent of the industry's revenues. Growth in the club spa portion of the spa industry is the lowest of all spa segments. Between 2002 and 2004, cumulative club spa growth was only 3 percent.

✦ SPA OPERATIONS
SPAS AS AN OPERATING DEPARTMENT

Historically, spa operations were treated by management similarly to other revenue departments, like catering and restaurants. These departments were simply perceived as an amenity needed to attract guests to the hotel. As long as the department broke even, or didn't lose too much money, their ability to increase occupancy was deemed sufficient justification for their existence. However, in the late 1990s, hotel spas followed the path of other operating departments and were transformed from

support facilities to profit centers. This trend is strong and continues today.

In 1999, PKF Consulting identified only 30 hotels in the United States, of thousands that report data to the PKF, with extensive spa facilities and analyzed the financial performance of those properties and their spa departments. Dedicated destination spa resorts were not included in the analysis because of an insufficient sample.

While spas were a relatively small source of revenues for the sample properties, spa revenues grew at a relatively strong pace. In 1999, spa revenues for the subject sample represented just 3.3 percent of total sales. However, from 1998 to 1999, spa revenues grew 16.6 percent. This compares to revenue growth rates of 5.2 percent for rooms, 12.2 percent for food, and 3.2 percent for telecommunications, and a 0.3 percent decline in revenues for the beverage department.

During 1999, the spa departments in the sample of hotels averaged a departmental profit margin of 30.7 percent. However, spa department profits did grow a strong 51.3 percent from 1998 to 1999.

Spas mirror and enhance trends in the lodging industry. Drawing heavily from residential design and the use of technology, hotel designers and operators create a spa experience that:

- Complements the lodging experience
- Drives occupancy levels
- Enhances average daily rate
- Provides a distinctive marketing advantage

North American spas are rapidly becoming more segmented, pursuing market niches well outside the traditional ladies-who-lunch demographic. Adventure spas, fitness spas, children spas, family spas, and even pet spas are part of a new generation of spa facilities, spa programs—and, most importantly, spa aficionados. Spas now attract a much wider demographic that includes men, women, couples, children, teenagers, and families.

Since the early part of the twenty-first century, spas have been redirecting their menus to include stress relief and results-oriented therapies. By focusing on the social benefits of hanging out in a safe, relaxing place, they not only address current market needs but also support the development of spa programs that can be incorporated into virtually any leisure-oriented environment or level of lodging. In particular, destination spas and full-service resorts provide platforms that have both the infrastructure and the economies of scale to support cutting-edge spa treatments, sometimes also referred to as *spa modalities.*

Spas are no longer solely about frivolous self-indulgence and luxurious pampering. They are being reevaluated and repackaged with a broader emphasis on self-care, stress relief, emotional balancing, and preventative (as opposed to reactive) wellness modalities. This trend is being embraced by aging baby boomers as an adjunct to traditional health care. Because of this trend in health care, hotels and resorts have acknowledged and embraced the need for full-service spas as part of their amenities and facilities. The inclusion of a well-integrated spa can provide additional (and lucrative) sales and marketing opportunities. Conversely, the exclusion of a spa facility may disqualify a property from consideration. Ironically, many hotel guests may dismiss a property out of hand for lacking a spa not because they require the services of a spa but rather because its absence may imply other areas of the hotel are also deficient in meeting current market expectations.

Is it logical, then, that all full-service hotels and resorts without a spa should, without hesitation, incorporate one into their property? Clearly not. Numerous factors must be considered in developing or repositioning a spa, especially in chain environments where the lodging brand is already established. Because spas are capital- and labor-intensive, they must materially enhance the property's revenue stream to be considered viable. In addition to creating spa revenue, a spa facility also must extend length of stay, drive room rates, enhance shoulder and low-season demand, augment food and beverage revenues, and capture new market segments.

Successful spa operations start with a standardized level of procedures and a prioritized sensitivity to guest needs. As it is for all departments in a lodging environment (or business models in the freestanding day and medical spa world), profitability is essential. Especially in a spa environment, a dynamic balance is essential to meet the fiscal requirements of the owners and the physical needs of the guest.

A savvy spa manager continually monitors the spa and hotel operations to ensure that everything possible is being done to enhance the synergy of the two entities. Constant monitoring also provides an early warning system to the spa operator if revenues are falling or if expenses are not in line with anticipated revenues or budgeted amounts. Spotting these trends early enables the manager to take efficient, proactive steps to ensure that positive trends are enhanced and negative ones controlled. Constant monitoring sets a standard of operations, which is an excellent way to train and motivate employees. It also puts employees on notice that the spa is a well-run business with extensive attention to detail, which should discourage any actions that might not be in the best interest of the spa's reputation and profitability.

CUSTOMER SERVICE TRAINING

A spa's reputation is easily made or destroyed by its level of customer service. Guests can forgive an occasional shortcoming if the level of service is exceptional. For this reason, it is essential that all spas have an integrated quality management program that provides ongoing training to assist its employees in addressing customers' expectations. Customer service training (CST) helps ensure that guests' expectations are exceeded. In a spa environment, expectations are usually very high, and a trusting bond can be quickly established if the spa employees are sensitive to guests' needs.

The guest's arrival sequence, starting at the front desk, initiates the spa ritual that brings the spa guest to a place of trust, relaxation, and rejuvenation. CST is proactive and provides employees with the tools they need to meet or exceed guest expectations. Guest CST is a never-ending, all-inclusive process that bridges textbook training scenarios with operational realities. The traditionally high turnover of spa employees in the hospitality industry requires that CST be introduced as a part of the orientation process and reinforced regularly.

Nonproductive training time (time that does not directly produce revenue for the spa) is actually a minor expense when compared to the expenses related to employee turnover, poor service, dissatisfied customers, and, ultimately, loss of business and reputation. Budgets must include CST as a non-optional employee expense. For long-term success, CST is vital when margins are tight, business is slow, and turnover is high. There is a strong correlation between high employee turnover and low CST. Employees should know that the training program is an investment in them.

CST gives the employee the means to understand what is expected of them as a representative of the establishment and identifies what guests expect from their visit. Seeing the process from the guest's point of view helps employees meet or exceed expectations. This minimizes the need to provide discounts or compensation in cases of service delivery problems. Discounting or "comping" goods and services is a knee-jerk response to poor service and should be reserved for the last effort in service recovery; CST should stress this.

An inclusive training program is the engine behind stellar customer service and guest loyalty. CST should be seamless; while it predominately addresses the needs of the guest, the program also includes instruction on profitability and yield management, thus addressing the needs of the owner as well. In order to meet or exceed profitability goals, customer service must be delivered in a fiscally responsible manner. Employees must understand customer service in the operational context of the property in which they are employed.

Minimizing the expense of a CST program starts with the proper selection of employees. While there is no steadfast guarantee that a potential employee will work out over the long haul, first impressions, prior work experience, references, and, above all, attitude and enthusiasm are indications of whether or not it is appropriate to hire and invest the time and money in an applicant.

Management's expectations of guest service delivery should be clearly articulated and integrated into the corporate culture and reinforced daily at all levels and in all departments. Employees, no matter what their responsibility, position, or tenure, must be treated with the same level of respect and dignity that management requires for their guests. Reinforcing the tenets of customer service within the corporate culture provides the employee with the tools to do the right thing—that is, to ask, "What do I need to do to make a spa guest happy? How do I exceed their expectations?" Sometimes the little details reap the greatest rewards.

Employee empowerment is a key component in CST. As an employee's experience and skill base develops (and as management becomes comfortable with an employee's performance), levels of empowerment should be increased proportionately. Empowerment is a vote of confidence in an employee and a way to quickly resolve problems as they arise. This situation is said by spa managers to increase job satisfaction, and the employee's ownership of his or her position.

CST also requires a strong foundation in the technical skills of how a department runs. Routine procedures, appropriate lines of oral and written communication, and what is expected of each employee in the normal course of his or her shift help minimize problems. When problems do occur, a strong foundation in technical skills makes it easier for the employee to create alternative solutions for the guest.

Training draws on employees' EQ (emotional quotient) as well as their IQ (intelligence quotient). CST requires that employees draw on their ability to empathize with the guest. This starts by training employees to suspend judgment of a situation, become attentive lis-teners, and know the right questions to ask. This allows them to understand what the actual problem is. Training employees in this type of customer service delivery assists them in focusing on the salient issues and creating ways to address them.

Because CST is ongoing, employees can benefit from their peers' experiences. Vehicles to exchange this type of information can be as informal as role-playing and round-table discussions, or as structured as an employee newsletter. Incentives, acknowledgments, and rewards for excellent customer service delivery are an integral part of the training program. Successful CST supports a skilled and unified staff, which translates into profitable operations. CST is an investment in property that owners can't afford not to make.

PROVIDE VALUE, CREATE VALUE

Spa aficionados are savvy. They are looking to be indulged, pampered, and nurtured, not fleeced. Setting price points with market sensitivity can create tremendous customer loyalty. Because spas are no longer a one-time indulgence but rather a lifestyle choice, it is important to price services competitively and provide incentives for customers to return regularly.

Numerous variables are involved in the development and operation of a spa as part of a hotel or resort. Doing one's homework is essential to success. When a spa is developed or repositioned correctly, it can be a lucrative and rewarding experience. When it is not developed correctly, it can be a financial liability that haunts the spa director and jeopardizes the hotel's market position.

If spas and their programming are not an integrated part of the hotel's future development, the property may lose a significant competitive opportunity. Spa-less hotels or poorly run properties have an inherent competitive market disadvantage. Not only do they find it more difficult to penetrate the market, but they also often lose market share.

✦ HOW BIG SHOULD IT BE?
RESORT SPAS

The ratio of guest rooms to treatment rooms is based on many factors, including the anticipated return on investment to the owners, the topography of the site, the scope and theme of the spa, and the competition. In a destination resort, where the reason for the spa facilities is the reason for the trip, there should be an average of 1 treatment room for every 4 to 5 guest rooms. At the other end of the spectrum, such as a casino hotel, the spa is definitely an amenity, and 1 treatment room should be built for every 50 to 100 guest rooms.

The spas at lower-end hotel properties normally are limited in scope and are often between 3000 and 6000 square feet, whereas luxury spas at full-service, high-end resorts average between 10,000 and 35,000 square feet. These ranges vary based on each hotel's specific circumstances, including seasonality, accessibility, meeting space, fill patterns, and local demand. Each market and each lodging product must be individually evaluated to assess the appropriate ratio of treatment rooms to guest rooms.

Another matrix that measures the viability of a resort or hotel spa is the cost to build the facility. Once again, a number of factors support various outcomes in this process, including the amount of available land, the finishes of the spa, the finishes of the hotel (these should be compatible), and the need to develop a spa either vertically or horizontally. Vertical spas are most often built in environments where land is scarce or the allocated footprint for the spa is too small for one floor. Vertical construction always raises the price per square foot, as load distribution, drainage, and the weight of equipment and water must be factored into the construction design and budget. The cost to construct a resort or destination spa can range from as low as $200 per square foot to over $450 per square foot. High-land-value areas and plumbing-rich design schemes will send cost dramatically above this range.

DAY SPAS

Day spas often lack the grand infrastructure associated with resort spas, and for this reason the ratio of spa revenue to treatment room space is much closer. In terms of number of square feet, day spa revenues account for 43 percent of the total spa space and provide approximately 52 percent of the total day spa revenues. The remaining 57 percent of the day spa environment is allocated to guest flow, check-in desk, retail, back-of-the-house support, and, on some occasions, food and beverage areas.

MEDICAL SPAS

Historically, medical spas have placed less emphasis on the aesthetics of the spa experience and more on the treatment provided. Therefore, it is not surprising that 45 percent of the medical spa space provides 63 percent of all medical spa revenue. Retail sales are limited in medical spas, as outside of cosmetics and prescriptions, there are limited branding opportunities. While resort spa goers are anxious to wear a sweatshirt or ball cap that announces to the world where they last vacationed, most medical spa clients do not share the same need or enthusiasm about their recent microderm abrasion or rhinoplasty. Medical spas may require the use of pharmacies to fill patient's prescriptions, which from a business model could be considered part of their treatment-related retail sales.

TREATMENT TYPE VERSUS REVENUE

To this point, we have evaluated the economics and use patterns of spa types. The focus of most spas dictates how the space is allocated and where the income is generated. Spas should aim to have at least 50 percent of their total space—their prime real estate—produce direct revenue. Secondary real estate is the support and public areas necessary for atmosphere and supporting functions that assist in delivering the spa services. Secondary spa real estate includes areas where people can prepare for or relax from their spa treatments. These secondary areas are an important component in the spa development plan, as they allow guests to prolong their experience, which enhances the perceived value. If guests are hurried from their massage or facial out of the spa and back onto the street, the magic that is created can be abruptly snapped and the overall spa experience is compromised. Conversely, if a guest is allowed to soak and relax for hours after a body wrap is completed, emotionally speaking, the cost of the body wrap is amortized over the entire spa experience and not just for the time the client was enjoying the body wrap in the spa's prime real estate.

Combination rooms account for about 36 percent of North American spa spaces, but because of the various treatments offered in them, a revenue percentage generated from these spaces is hard to predict. Combination spaces allow the spa to address surges in demand for specific treatments and at the same time be flexible and respond to global market changes. Massage rooms account for approximately 27 percent of the total space in North American spas but 47 percent of the spa revenue. Given these factors, an operator would need a compelling reason to not include massage on the spa menu. Facial treatment areas reflect 19 percent of the total spa space and result in about 33 percent of the spa's overall revenue. Wet rooms, often the most underutilized portions of the spa, account for 7 percent of the space and revenue. Because many spa modalities involve water therapics, many spa developers and owners believe that wet rooms are essential, even if they seem underutilized. Because wet rooms are one of the most expensive components of a spa, it is essential that they be utilized to their fullest extent. Packaging wet room treatments with other spa services is one way to better utilize the space and create value for the spa.

✦ SPA TRENDS
ON-SITE INDUSTRY TRENDS

Anti-aging treatments and products are driving much of spa menu and retail development. This calls for devoting a treatment room to outpatient medical procedures. Programming and spa menu items include sun damage treatments, chemical peels for skin renewal, and other rejuvenation techniques that build on repeat procedures. Commensurately, spas are developing retail product lines so that clients can take the spa experience home and continue the wellness regime.

Gift card sales are driving new users to spas. In the friends and family sector as well as the corporate gift-giving world, day spa certificates are creating demand that is not directly user driven. Third-party purchasing brings to spas clients who may not normally have chosen the location or treatment, creating a large but indefinable market demand.

Regional specialties that relate to indigenous and climatic influences continue to create unique spa experiences based on-site-specific supply. This has excellent leverage potential for spa operators working to differentiate their product matrices in densely operated areas.

Increased stress management. It is important to position services for stress relief, especially to the male business traveler. Spa programming that requires a limited amount of special equipment and minimal changes to a property's infrastructure can do this.

Impulse appointments. "Life is uncertain, but I want a massage (reflexology appointment, yoga class, etc.) now!" This trend may result in developing adjunct programs for on-call staff resources. The as-needed portion of the program limits a hotel's payroll burden and other related fixed costs. Of course, this implies existing core programs and facilities where these programs can be developed and supported.

Shift in perspective. Self-indulgence, pampering, and luxury are being reevaluated and repackaged with a new, broader emphasis on self-care, stress relief, and emotional balancing. This is reflected in spa programming, the menu of services, food and beverage outlets, and spa-related retail. The retail positioning and spa programming components represent huge untapped revenue opportunities.

Changes in demographic use profile. Historically, the greatest segment of spa goers was women between the ages of 35 and 55. More couples and families are expected to visit the spa together as an alternative social/recreational activity. This trend

has the potential to extend business-related stays, fill business hotels on the weekend, and create demand for destinations. It is important to understand this trend when evaluating ways to increase market penetration in a down market.

Medical affiliations. For some markets, an affiliation with a medical center or group in the area can be established to provide treatments such as acupuncture, nutritional assessment, laser therapies (hair removal and wrinkle reduction), Botox injections, collagen treatments, chemical peels, laser resurfacing, body contouring, micro-derm abrasion, and vascular procedures. When creating these types of relationships, it is essential that spa owners thoroughly investigate the legal disclosure and liability implications of being an affiliated medical service provider.

Green environments. A spa can be ecologically sensitive by incorporating environmentally friendly features into the operation. By proactively supporting programs and products that are earth friendly, the spa does something good for the environment, provides a service to the community, and creates a competitive advantage and a unique selling point that may provide significant returns, especially in a highly competitive market.

GLOBAL INDUSTRY TRENDS

Trends in day, destination, and amenity spas influence each other. According to Susan Ellis (2004), president of Spa Finder, a spa marketing company, after the rise of the medical spa and broadening spa participation by men and teens, spa use is expected to become more popular in the future. Spa Finder's trends to watch for are abstracted below:

- Those personal elements that make the spa experience special will find their way into the design of personal living spaces in private homes.

- Private, gated living communities will develop around central spa facilities, much like golf and fly-in communities.

- Some spas will compete on the far outer reaches of luxury, with ever-increasing rare and proprietary products and services.

- Spas will make house calls. Legitimate spas will offer out-call services where spa technicians travel with appropriate equipment and personnel to a client's home, office, or hotel room.

- Destination spas and resorts will develop market segments focused on personal goals, everything from spiritual awareness to sexual health to detoxification.

- The spa travel segment will grow, with more clientele booking through online portals.

- Medical spas will continue to be popular and will add alternative therapies and couple traditional medical treatment with spa luxury and innovation.

- Day spas will not grow their exotic menus much more but rather focus on the traditional; destination/resort spas will be the businesses that experiment with more exotic services and products.

- Specialized cuisine developed for spa guest consumption will find its way into mainstream grocery/specialty food offerings. Restaurants may also add lines of healthy spa cuisine to their menus.

- Eco spas, those designed and operated around green principles of management, will become a growing segment of the industry.

✦ CONCLUSION

The foregoing discussion and explanation of the service and amenity potential of spas of varying types strongly suggests that they will continue to maintain a position of importance in the inventory of hotel services. Even the most modest of spa offerings can enhance a hotel guest's lodging experience. Someday basic spa services may be available at even moderately priced lodging properties.

✦ BUSINESS PROBLEM ANALYSIS

Mitch Jucha (2004), spa director, Westin Century Plaza, Los Angeles, California

✦ PROBLEM

Spa Mystique, a 35,000-square-foot spa, is not turning a profit. It is a newly built, state-of-the-art spa facility located adjacent to a 728-room full-service conference center hotel. The property is located in an affluent commercial and residential area of West Los Angeles with direct access to major surface arterials and freeways.

✦ BACKGROUND/STATUS QUO

The Westin Century Plaza, a Commercial and Convention Property

- 728 rooms
- Occupancy level: 55–58 percent average (weekends 30–40 percent average)
- Primarily business hotel catering to large groups and transient business travelers
- The largest hotel ballroom in Los Angeles
- Breeze Restaurant

- Where U.S. presidents stay in Los Angeles since President Ford began using the hotel during his term
- Was once called the West Coast White House because of President Reagan's patronage

Facilities of Spa Mystique in the Westin Century Plaza

- 35,000 square feet
- Café Mystique, state-of-the-art fitness center, Yamaguchi Salon, boutique
- Designed by Silvia Cipieli
- 28 treatment rooms
- 4 outdoor massage cabanas
- Separate entrance for members and local guests with valet
- Tranquility lounge
- Separate locker rooms for men and women
- Signature massage, facial, and body treatments
- Spa membership available

Guest Utilization Data

- 22 percent hotel guests
- 77 percent local guests
- 6 percent group guests
- 1 percent hotel employees
- Based on the guest type distribution, marketing budget was redirected to local day spa guests.
- Additional internal marketing completed to increase in-house usage.

The Problem

- Many of the decisions herein were based on an analysis of the profit and loss statement and the general ledger.

- Allowed comparisons to industry averages.
- Examination results:
  Retail sales were below average.
  Cost of sales was too high.
  Payroll was too high.
  Breakeven was roughly $150,000.
  Industry average profit would not be met unless $330,000 in revenue was produced.

✦ SOLUTIONS

After a Sales and Marketing Evaluation

- Redirected marketing efforts to local day spa guests.
- Created departmental marketing budget.
- Placed advertisements in local papers and magazines.
- Completed renewed efforts on in-house guests.
- Increased hours.
  Increased hours of operation of Sundays to include two additional bookable hours to increase revenue and meet demand.
  More recently, extended treatment hours to 8:00 each night of the week, resulting in 50 additional services per week.
  The increased hours are expected to yield $260,000 annually.
- Pursued corporate business.
  Marketed to local corporate offices by offering midweek discounts to their employees.
  Entered into a corporate membership agreement with MGM building employees.
- Modified spa menu.
  Created 25-minute services.
  Filled 30-minutes gaps and maximized utilization.

Catered to transient business travelers and group guests of hotel.

- Created treatment enhancements, which allowed price increases without treatment time increases.
- Added corporate spa memberships.
- Create a limited spa membership that utilized spa during low demand.

Evaluation of Competitors' Price Structure

- Performed competitive price survey.
- Survey determined that spa prices were below competition.
- Consequently, increased all spa prices by 20–25 percent.
- Implemented discounted pricing and promotions during low demand periods.
- Restructured package pricing.

Modified Staffing

- Rectified overstaffing of the locker room attendants and fitness attendants.
- Added spa group coordinator or spa sales coordinator position.

- Realigned technicians' schedules to eliminate overlapping shifts.
Overlapping shifts created an inefficiency in utilization of treatment rooms.
Without overlapping, treatment rooms are able to be fully utilized.
Prior to this change, maximum utilization topped out at 70 percent.

Performed Wage Audit

- Restructured spa technicians' wages because paying the technicians an hourly rate created an inverse payroll burden during low demand.
- Removed hourly pay and created a flat-rate commissionable salary structure.
- Brought pay structure in line with spa industry standards.
- Instituted system at the top of the competitive set.
- Provided an opportunity to issue annual wage increase based on performance.

After implementation of the above tactics and strategies, Spa Mystique more than doubled revenues from the previous reporting period. The changes were considered a success, and the spa is now profitable.

1.7 RESORT SPAS: HOW ARE THEY MASSAGING HOTEL REVENUES?

MELIH MADANOGLU AND SHERIE BREZINA

ABSTRACT.

PURPOSE. The purpose of this paper is to illustrate financial benefits of spa operations in resorts by developing a spa revenue contribution technique/method.

DESIGN/METHODOLOGY APPROACH. This purpose is achieved by utilizing current industry and academic literature in the fields of hospitality and resort management.

FINDINGS. The results show that a hypothetical resort with 300 rooms would achieve a spa revenue per occupied room of $40.08 which translates into additional annual revenue of more than $3,500,000.

PRACTICAL IMPLICATIONS. One of the implications of this study is that a well-run spa may contribute approximately US$28 per available room. Another practical implication is that spas are important generators of additional revenue as they may contribute, at times, over 20 percent to room revenue by using considerably less space than resort/hotel rooms do.

ORIGINALITY/VALUE. This paper derives its value from developing a specific technique to support the common notion that a well-operated spa makes a significant contribution to resort revenues.

✦ SPA INDUSTRY GROWTH

It took until the mid-1980s when some forward thinking resort operators added spas to their properties (Monteson and Singer, 2004). Yet, back in the 1980s, having a spa facility in a resort was considered a luxury since a spa was deemed more of an amenity than an independent profit-generating center for resort properties. The majority of these spas were located in upscale, independent resorts and spas were utilized as great marketing tools to attract guests to these establishments. Today, in the new millennium, the spa experience moves beyond being a luxury commodity. Resort operators are now realizing that having a spa is necessary not only to meet guest expectations but also to enable resorts to remain competitive in the leisure market (Foster and Mandelbaum, 2005). Dubow (2006) supports this view by stating that in resort hotels, spas are becoming increasingly important for achieving a healthy bottom line.

The number of spa locations grew at an average of 12 percent between 2002 and 2004 (International Spa Association, 2004). Bjorn Hanson, the head of PricewaterhouseCoopers' hospitality and leisure group, states that the growth of spas goes beyond adding new locations, as each spa is finding new ways to generate revenues. Hanson points out that between 1997 and 1999 average spa revenue increased 28.3 percent annually (Clifford, 2001). In terms of locations, the International Spa Association (ISPA) cites the existence of over 1,662 resort/hotel spas as of 2004 and Foster and Wohlberg (2006) predict that these numbers will continue to grow. In 2003, approximately 27 percent of the 136 million spa visits were made to resort/hotel spas. This figure shows the strategic importance of spas in resort settings (International Spa Association, 2004). However, it is still not known what the exact financial contribution of resort spas to resort revenue and profitability is. Therefore, this paper attempts to offer some more clarity into this issue.

The purpose of this paper is to illustrate financial benefits of spa operations in resorts. This purpose is achieved by developing a spa revenue contribution technique/method. The current industry and academic literature in the fields of hospitality and resort management is used to develop this method.

✦ RESORT SPAS FROM A MARKETING PERSPECTIVE

Spas appeal to resort guests as they provide a secluded realm where guests can escape from their busy everyday lives and stress. As hotels utilize more high technology to meet guest demand for increased efficiency and do-it-yourself solutions, such as in-room business services and kiosk check-in, Foster and Mandelbaum (2004) argue that spa treatments serve as important tools to fill the void of personalized, human attention in hotels and resorts. These authors claim that this is one of the main reasons why spa treatments became such an important revenue-generator for hotels by offering the analogy of moving from "high tech" to "high touch" in the hotel industry. Singer (2000) makes a similar point by contending that today's guest seems to be more in touch with the mind/body connection and is aware of the importance of taking time to slow down and "be in the moment." That is, as the resort guests look for balance and harmony in their lives, spa-related activities are now perceived as important components of overall well-being and healthy "mind and body maintenance."

✦ SPAS AS MAJOR PROFIT-GENERATING CENTERS

Traditionally, spa operations were perceived as amenities needed to attract guests to a given resort. That is, as long as the spa center achieved a break-even point and did not lose money, the ability of spas to increase the room occupancy was sufficient to justify their existence (Anderson, 2001). However, in recent years, hotel spas have followed the path of the other hotel operating departments and evolved from support facilities to profit centers. The findings of the 2004 Spa Industry Study reports that US spas earned an average of $172 per square foot; $52,163 per treatment room (where only treatment room revenue is included); $143 per spa visit; and $277 per client. In addition, despite accounting for 27 percent of total spa units/locations, resort spas account for an impressive 41 percent of the total spa industry revenue of $11.2 billion (International Spa Association, 2004). Collectively, all these figures illustrate how resort spas evolved in the last decade and became major revenue centers.

Anderson (2001) identified 30 hotels that had extensive spa facilities and reported that in 1999 the resort spas in his sample recorded a departmental profit margin of 30.7 percent. In 2004, larger spas at resort hotels achieved an average profit margin of 23.2 percent, compared to 14.5 percent for a typical urban hotel (Foster and Mandelbaum, 2005). A study conducted by Singer and Monteson (2005) revealed a similar figure for US spas that yielded an average profit margin of 27 percent. These figures show that resort spas are not only revenue generators but also solid contributors to resorts' bottom line.

Resort/hotel spas possess competitive and operational advantages over stand-alone spas both from revenue and expense perspectives. For instance, on the revenue side, resort spas can be either primary demand generators to a given resort or resort spas can benefit from the demand base that has already been generated by the hotel/resort property itself (Foster and Wohlberg, 2006). On the expense side, resort/hotel spas may share many of the fixed costs related to rent and marketing with the operating divisions of a resort. These features enable resort/hotel spas to operate more profitably than do stand-alone day spas.

✦ CONTRIBUTION OF A SPA TO RESORT REVENUE

The discussion thus far was related to the transformation of spas from a marketing vehicle to an independent profit-making center in resorts. The next section is intended to propose a specific method that will help quantify the contribution of spas to resorts' room revenue. In order to assess the input of a spa center to resort revenues, a scenario for two hypothetical resorts is created. The first resort operates a full-service spa facility, while the second resort is not engaged in spa operations. It is assumed that both resort hotels have the same number of rooms and all other facilities and amenities are identical.

As numerous practitioners admit, evaluating the contribution of a spa to a resort's occupancy rate and resort's revenue is a very difficult task.

However, by combining the figures reported in the previous studies, the researchers of this study propose a method that mimics the realities of this business. This method also quantifies the financial benefits a spa facility brings to a resort hotel. For the sake of simplicity, the two resorts are called "the spa resort" and "the plain resort." It is assumed that each of these resorts has 300 hotel rooms.

The first step in this analysis is to estimate the occupancy rate difference between the two resorts. Based on the discussions in previous studies, the authors of this study use a conservative approach by contending that, everything else held constant, "the spa resort" should achieve a occupancy rate that is 3 percent higher than the occupancy of "the plain resort" (see Table 1.8). This estimate of 3 percent is based on the "1997 health fitness dynamics (HFD) spa-goer study" which found that 81 percent of the people in their survey would choose one resort over another because of the existence of a spa (Monteson, 2001). Another valuable piece of information was obtained from the director of the "spa at Pinehurst," in North Carolina, USA, who reveals that the addition of

Table 1.8 Spa Contribution Calculation Method

MEASURES	SPA RESORT	PLAIN RESORT
Occupancy rate (%)	70	67[a]
ADR ($)	130[b]	127[b]
RevPAR ($)	88.90	85.09
SPOR ($)	40.07[c]	—
SPAR ($)	28.05	—
SPAR to RevPAR ratio (%)	31.5	—
Annual spa and room revenue ($)	12,806,025	9,317,355

Notes: [a]The occupancy rate figure was obtained from Smith Travel Research, the figure is 12-month moving average occupancy until January, 2006; [b]the ADR figure was obtained from Smith Travel Research, [and] the figure is 12-month average ADR until January, 2006; [c]SPOR data was obtained from HFD, [and] room revenue of 75 percent is assumed.

a spa is expected to increase the number of guests per room from 1.4 to 1.7 or 1.8 (Traugot, 2002). As a next step, the average daily rate (ADR) for US resorts in 2005 ($127) is obtained from Smith Travel Research (STR) to arrive at the forecasted RevPAR figure for both resorts. A spa premium of US$3 per occupied room for the "the spa resort" is included in order to reflect the marketing advantage a spa facility brings to a resort. It should be noted that in reality the ADR premium of spa resorts can be much higher. Case in point is the insight of the president of STR, Mark Lomanno (2005), who revealed that in looking at operating statistics at several hundred properties with and without spas in 2004, he found that resorts with full-service spas had an ADR of $228.07 versus an ADR of $154.42 for those without such amenities. It should be noted that the present study does not apply this premium since it is not known whether resorts without spas are similar in size and belong to the same price category.

The benefits of a spa can be classified as direct and indirect contributions to resort revenue. The indirect contribution of a spa is by being an important marketing tool. The findings show that the "indirect contribution" of a spa facility to the RevPAR of "the spa resort" is $3.81 ($88.90–$85.09) per available room. In order to find the spa's direct contribution, a spa revenue per occupied room (SPOR) figure of $40.07 is applied from HFD's 2004 study to the revenue column of "the spa resort." In this study, a daily spa revenue per available room (SPAR) metric is proposed in order to assess the contribution of the spa over the daily RevPAR. Then, the occupancy rate of the resort (70 percent) is multiplied by the SPOR figure ($40.08) and a SPAR of $28.05 is obtained. As a next step, the authors divide SPAR into RevPAR

to arrive at the ratio of spa revenue to room revenue. This yields a SPAR/Rev par ratio for "the spa resort" of 31.5 percent. In business terms this means that for each dollar that an available room brings to this resort, the spa center contributes an additional 31.5 cents.

The final phase of this technique compares the room and spa revenues for both resorts. The results indicate that operating a full-service spa facility creates a $3,500,000 difference in revenues for "the spa resort." It is evident that this dollar amount is significant not only in statistical but also in practical terms for both resort operators and researchers.

✦ WAYS FOR BOOSTING SPA REVENUE

The method presented in the previous section illustrated the overall contribution of resort spas to resort revenue. In order to offer more insight into how spa managers can increase their spa revenues, the authors of this study conducted an interview with a spa director of one of the leading resort spas in Southwest Florida. The director stated that resorts should first focus on guest experience to increase their sales. In that director's case, she mentioned that her resort was able to increase the incremental spending from $658 to $985 per night by packaging spa and other activities together.

The director also stated that pre-arrival process is a critical component for revenue maximization. She offered a case as an example where she used a system called "power booking" in which a spa front desk agent was calling guests two to three days prior to the spa reservation date and providing the opportunity for upgrades and additional bookings based on availability. This up-selling execution resulted in additional $500,000 spa revenue in one quarter (three months). This is a significant increase in spa revenues considering the fact that even larger resort spas usually have between 10 to 15 treatment rooms.

The spa reservation process is another critical component of increasing spa revenue and spa capture ratio. This is evidenced by the fact that the spa at the Bellagio Hotel and Casino in Las Vegas accepts spa reservations three months in advance by phone. La Costa Resort and Spa in Carlsbad, California takes this process a step further by running a dedicated web site for spa reservations where guests can pay by credit card and book their treatments. The spa director in Southwest Florida revealed that in her experience having separate spa reservations not only boosted revenue but also increased guest satisfaction.

✦ DISCUSSION AND CONCLUSION

The limitation of this study is that the spa contribution method is only an estimate based on data collected from the leading hotel and resort companies in the USA. Therefore, the findings of this study should be interpreted with some caution. However, the authors of this paper believe that this method can still be used as a "ballpark estimate" by the present and prospective resort managers who are planning to expand their current spa centers or are considering opening new spa facilities.

The present study fills an important gap in the spa industry literature by offering a clear definition for spa revenue per available room by using SPAR on a daily basis instead of adopting the aggregate dollar figure ($3,117) of Foster and Mandelbaum (2005). The following example may serve to illustrate this point: a spa operator may have difficulties in applying the aggregate figure of Foster and Mandelbaum when he/she tries to benchmark the SPAR of his/her resort with the competing properties. This is because one cannot tell whether Foster and Mandelbaum collected the SPAR information from resorts that operate on a year-round or seasonal basis. However, the daily SPAR metric proposed in the present study is both easy to understand and apply. Put in other words, a SPAR of $28 simply means that the spa operator was able to "yield" 28 dollars from each of the available hotel rooms. In addition, by dividing SPAR with RevPAR and keeping a record of this ratio for longer periods, resort managers may evaluate whether their spa revenue is in par with their resorts' room revenue.

Although some other intangible benefits such as creating repeat business, increasing guest satisfaction, and influencing the guests' intention to recommend the resort to others are not directly considered in this method, the present researchers acknowledge the fact that the future quantification of these variables is expected to further tip the scale in favor of spa resorts. Nevertheless, the spa contribution formula provides an important support to the claim that was discussed throughout this work. That is, spas are important generators of additional revenue as they may contribute, at times, more than 20 percent to room revenue by requiring significantly less space than resort/hotel rooms do.

There is also a disconnect among studies conducted by different companies. For instance, the application of the spa contribution method revealed that the ratio of spa revenue to room revenue may reach up to 30 percent. That leads one to believe that the total contribution of spa revenue to overall resort revenue should be considerably higher than the number (2.3 percent) reported by Foster and Mandelbaum (2005). This argument is based on the fact that room revenue makes up approximately 68 percent of total revenue in a typical hotel (Mandelbaum, 2004). That means that even if one uses a conservative estimate of 50 percent as room revenue to total revenue ratio in full-service resorts, the contribution of a spa facility to total resort revenue remains at a level of 10 percent or higher. Therefore, in order to obtain accurate spa revenue estimates, future studies should focus on assessing the "real" contribution of these facilities to resort revenue. This can be achieved by classifying the resorts as high spa-to-room revenue and low spa-to-room revenue resorts.

Although the spa industry has been around for many years, it still remains in its infancy as a stand-alone industry (Foster and Mandelbaum, 2005). At this juncture, the rapid growth in the popularity of resort and hotel spas, and the steady increase in departmental revenues, are very encouraging indicators which signal the long-term viability of the spa industry. Foster and Mandelbaum further state that aging population, significant amounts of disposable income, and people focused on taking better care of themselves and living more luxurious and healthier lifestyles, are some of the main reasons which spur the development of the spa industry. Zimmer and Clarke (2006) add that other factors such as the loss of job security have created a worried and time-poor population. This population is in a greater need of relaxation and its related health benefits. She points out that now people are less formal and are "younger" in mind and spirit than they were ten years ago. In addition, many of these people are concerned that their personal appearance remains youthful. Zimmer and Clarke

(2006) further contend that today's luxury traveler is seeking new life structures: authentic and life-enriching experiences—with a shift from fundamental needs, to higher needs and wants. These reasons lead these authors to believe that the demand for restorative and healing services provided by spas is likely to continue to grow exponentially in the next decade.

On the financial side, the major challenge in analyzing and interpreting spa information has been the lack of a uniform accounting system. Not having such a system in place made it extremely challenging for practitioners to compare the performance and develop benchmarks for their individual spa operations. A committee formed by the ISPA recently developed a uniform system of financial reporting to establish a standardized accounting system for the spa industry. Therefore, Foster and Mandelbaum (2005) claim that the days when financial data of fitness centers with a single massage room were being compared to financial data obtained from full-service spas are long gone. In addition, the same authors argue that as more spas embrace these accounting procedures, the establishment of industry benchmarks and spa profitability comparisons will become an easier task. Another major benefit of utilizing a standardized accounting system will enable industry consultants to conduct better feasibility studies which in turn may facilitate the process of securing funding from investors and lending institutions (Singer, 2003).

All the facts and pieces of information that were covered in this study demonstrate that the growth of the spa industry is here to stay. Hence, the authors of this study believe that educational institutions offering degrees in resort and hospitality management should revise their curricula to accommodate the dynamic growth of the spa industry. The growth of the industry is contingent upon educating and training future managers by arming them with necessary knowledge that is up-to-speed and up-to-date with the developments in the spa arena.

1.8 AS I SEE IT: A RITZ-CARLTON SPA DIRECTOR Holleigh Alexander

Let me begin by saying that I absolutely love what I do and the career path I chose. Every day is another opportunity to create exceptional personalized experiences while instilling a sense of well-being in each and every guest and employee that comes through my doors. In my opinion, there is not a better environment to be surrounded by every day.

I often wake up in the mornings excited to get to work and get the day started. Every day, the first thing I do when I arrive is personally greet each of my team members and review the day's spa appointments, health & wellness activities, Ritz Kids programs, and guest events. Then it's off to the Café on property to get my morning latte and a few goodies for my staff.

Once I've had the opportunity to connect with my team, I do a walk-through of all areas, check my emails, listen to my voice messages, and review my ongoing tasks list. Using these as a foundation, I build a detailed checklist of what needs to get done before the end of the day, such as: follow up calls and emails, meetings, guest and employee engagements, and operational details. Organization and prioritizing is a key component to setting up my day for success; it gives me the focus I need to handle any opportunity or unexpected obstacle that comes my way without feeling the pressure of chaos.

At 9:30 every morning, the Executive Team gets together for our morning line up meeting which typically lasts about 20 minutes. One of the things that is so wonderful about working for The Ritz-Carlton Hotel Company is knowing that every single day, in each and every department, at every property all over the world, we are all having the same meeting to discuss the topic of the day, which gets forwarded from our corporate offices. While these line ups bring our teams closer together by uniting all employees of our company, the main purposes of the daily meeting are to communicate important information about the day, to provide opportunities to learn and grow, to ensure brand quality, and to provide a platform for continuous improvement and innovation.

When I return from line up, I review our revenues from the previous day and then compare our budgeted revenue period and year to date to our actual revenue period and year to date and set new goals for the day, the week, and the remainder of the period that challenge my staff to recommend personalized services and activities that not only drive revenue but also build relationships that enhance the guest experience. Our primary goal as spa professionals is to create memorable experiences that promote overall well-being, sensory restoration, and peace and tranquility to the soul. With that in mind, simply taking an appointment without investing time to explore what the guest may really need is not an option.

Every day, usually midmorning, I have a one-on-one with my supervisor or key team leader to give direction, assist with getting tasks prioritized, offer support, and to follow up on any outstanding operational initiatives and/or issues that need to be addressed. We meet for about 20–30 minutes; it is so important to invest the time in developing a supervisor into a leader since they are the spa industry's future.

There are so many variables and layers to a spa's operation. We are service providers, retail sales people, concierges, locker room attendants, housekeepers, food runners, servers, shipping, receiving, day care providers, pool attendants, event managers, psychiatrists, and so on and so on. On any given day, you could find me doing any number of these duties, or working on schedules, payroll, booking appointments, or selling retail. Most days, however, you will find me reviewing budgets, heading off to a meeting, or researching new and innovative products for treatments and retail. I'm a product junky. I love learning about and trying new products to see if they actually deliver on what they promise. So I guess you could say that my favorite part of the job is, quite honestly, discovering the hottest new product and creating a new service around it.

In this industry, there are many opportunities to continually educate and train employees because of the rapidly evolving nature of the business. Success in suggestive selling, for example, is often proven through being hands on in the selling and recommendation process. Providing learning tools and constant support to my team ensures that they close a sale not only with one product or item but with multiple ones. I take the time in our departmental daily line ups in the morning and afternoon to teach the team something new. Whether it be product knowledge, treatment knowledge, or basic financial management, it's important to get staff involved in the work that affects them every day.

Around noon, I try to have lunch with at least one of my employees every day in our employee dining room, although there are times when I will have lunch with one of my vendors or sales reps in an effort to construct strategies that support driving revenue. Vendors often offer sales incentives for top sellers and participate in trunk shows to help raise awareness and gain confidence from the guest, thus generating more business. So, I believe that taking time to develop sustainable relationships with vendors is one of the most important aspects of this business.

After lunch, I'm off and running, reviewing the day's revenues up until that point. Then I create strategies to ensure we exceed the sales goals for the day and reforecast the goals for the following day, week, and period as necessary. It's also so important as the director of a revenue center to constantly watch your payroll and make the appropriate adjustments based on business levels. Wages can make or break your success as an operator in so many ways; too high of a payroll versus decreased revenue, understaffing, and overstaffing can all play a huge role in your bottom line. Too many employees without the support of revenue could result in losses; too few employees and your service suffers, which may also result in loss of revenue. It's a juggling act, but it definitely keeps things interesting.

By the middle of the day, we are so busy with spa appointments and Ritz Kids activities; the pool is jamming, and every piece of cardio and circuit training equipment in the fitness center is being used. I more often than not spend the afternoon assisting guests with any request or need they may have, assisting the spa concierge with checking appointments in and out, escorting guests to the locker room, giving tours of the facility, or helping a service provider who's running to their next appointment close a retail sale. I absolutely love the hustle and bustle of this time of day; it totally energizes me.

Every Saturday, I attend our guest welcome reception to mingle and promote spa treatments, health & wellness services, and Ritz Kids activities. It's a great opportunity to meet and greet and get to know who's staying with us.

As my day comes to a close, I like to regroup and review the day's operations. How did it go, what were the hiccups, where did we succeed, how did we fail, and what is the game plan for success tomorrow? And as I leave, making sure that I take the time to say goodnight to each member of my team and personally thank them for something they did specifically that had a positive impact on the day. I value my staff and the effort they put in for me day in and day out. They work so hard for the success of our department that as much as our guests cannot imagine a world without Ritz-Carlton, I cannot imagine my spa without this team.

REFERENCES

Anderson, J. R., and G. H. Bower. 1980. *Human Associative Memory.* Hillsdale, NJ: Lawrence Erlbaum.

Anderson, P. 2001. "The growth of spas as hotel profit centers," available at: www.hotel-online. com/Trends/PKF/Special/SpaCenters_Feb01. html (accessed March 1, 2006).

Andorka, F. 1997. "Diversity Task Forces Meet to Set the Agenda." *Hotel and Motel Management* 212(4): 32–36.

Audi, L., and B. Wright. 2004. *Compensation Workbook for the Spa Industry.* Chicago: Compensation Consulting Consortium, pp. 9, 11, 14, 64–77, 86–89.

Barsky, J., and L. Nash. 2002. "Evoking Emotion: Affective Keys to Hotel Loyalty." *Cornell Hotel and Restaurant Administration Quarterly* 43(1): 39–46.

Barsky, J., and L. Nash. 2003. "Customer Satisfaction: Applying Concepts to Industry-Wide Measures." *Cornell Hotel and Restaurant Administration Quarterly* 44(5–6): 173–183.

Bartlett, F. C. 1964. *Remembering: A Study in Experimental and Social Psychology,* Cambridge: Cambridge University Press.

Bellezza, F. S. 1981. "Mnemonic Devices: Classification, Characteristics, and Criteria." *Review of Educational Research* 51(2): 247–275.

Bowen, J. T., and S. Shoemaker. 2003. "Loyalty: A Strategic Commitment." *Cornell Hotel and Restaurant Administration Quarterly* 44(5–6): 31–46.

Brooks, B. E., L. J. Rosielle, and E. E. Cooper. 2002. "The Priming of Face Recognitions after Metric Transformations." *Perception* 31: 297–313.

Bruce, V., and A. Young. 1998. *In the Eye of the Beholder,* Oxford: Oxford University Press.

Bruce, V., and T. Valentine. 1994. "The Use of Pigmentation and Shading Information in Recognizing the Sex and Identities of Face." *Perception* 23: 803–822.

Carey, S., R. Diamond, and B. Woods. 1980. "Development of Face Recognition: A Maturational Component?" *Developmental Psychology* 16: 257–69.

Castleberry, J., and C. Hempell. 1998. "Electronic Shelf Space on the Global Distribution Network." *Hospitality & Leisure Executive Report* 5: 19–24.

Clifford, L. 2001. "Spa wars." *Fortune* 124(11): 211–213.

Coleman, Z. 2002. "Hotel Groups Bolster Presence in China." *Wall Street Journal,* May 8: D10.

Cooke, K. 2000. "Cut-price Carriers Leading the Revolution," *Financial Times of London,* VI.

Dubow, C. 2006. "America's best resort spas. Resort spas are becoming more popular. Which ones are worth the trip?" *Business Week Online,* available at: www.msnbc.msn.com/id/12647733/(accessed May 21, 2006).

Eisenberg, D. M. 1997. "Advising Patients Who Seek Alternative Medical Therapies." *Annals of Internal Medicine* 127(1): 61–69.

Eisenberg, D. M., R. C. Kessler, C. Foster, F. E. Norlock, D. R. Calkins, and T. L. Delbanco. 1993. "Unconventional Medicine in the United States—Prevalence, Costs, and Patterns of Use." *New England Journal of Medicine* 328(4): 246–52.

Ellis, H. D., J. W. Shepherd, and G. M. Davies. 1989. "Identification of Familiar and Unfamiliar Faces from Internal and External Features: Some Implications for Theories of Face Recognition." *Perception* 8: 431–439.

Ellis, S. 2004. "Top 10 Spa Trends to Watch in 2005." *Spa Finder,* December 16.

Everhart, D. E., J. L. Shucard, T. Quatrin, and D. Shucard. 2001. "Sex-Related Differences in Event-Related Potentials, Face Recognition, and Facial Affect Processing in Prepubertal Children." *Neuropsychology* 15(3): 329–341.

Forrester Research. 2001. *Web Travel Will Hold Up in an Industry Downturn.* Cambridge, MA.

Foster, A. and A. Wohlberg. 2006. "Hotel spas as independent profit centers," available at: www.hospitalitynet.org/news/4026556.html (accessed March 28, 2006).

Foster, A., and R. Mandelbaum. 2005. "Hotel spas: the new recreational vehicle for hotel profits," available at: www.pkfc.com/common/industry/october2005.aspx (accessed January 23, 2006).

Gomez.com. 2000. *State of Online Travel.* Waltham, MA: Gomez.

Gruneberg, M. M., and P. E. Morris. 1979. *Applied Problems in Memory,* London: Academic Press.

Gutek, B. A., A. D. Bhappu, M. A. Liao-Troth, and B. Cherry. 1999. "Distinguishing between Service Relationships and Encounters." *Journal of Applied Psychology* 84(2): 218–233.

Gutek, B. A., B. Cherry, A. D. Bhappu, S. Schneider, and L. Woolf. 2000. "Features of Service Relationships and Encounters." *Work & Occupations* 27: 319–352.

Hallbom, K. 1999. *Remembering Names through NLP.* Evergreen, CO: NLP Comprehensive.

Hensdill, C. 1998. "Electronic Distribution: Developing Paths of Least Resistance." *Hotels,* February: 41–46.

International Spa Association. 2004. *The ISPA 2004 Spa Industry Study.* International Spa Association, Lexington, KY.

Johnson, M. H., S. Dziurawiec, H. Ellis, and J. Morton. 1991. "Newborns' Preferential Tracking of Face-Like Stimuli and Its Subsequent Decline." *Cognition* 40: 1–19.

Joint Hospitality Industry Congress. 2000. *Leisure in the New Millennium.* London: Barclays.

Jucha, M. 2004. Private communication. Westin Century Plaza, Spa Mystique, Los Angeles.

Jupiter Media Metrix. 2001. "Online Travel Sites to Thrive in Slow Economy." New York.

Kim, Woo Goo, and Hyun Jeong Kim. 2007. "Determinants of Mid-Scale Hotel Brand Equity." *FIU Review* 25(1): 61–69.

Lampton, W. 1979. "Win at the Name Game: Six Ways to Better Effectiveness." *Fund Raising Management* 10(5): 42.

Leder, H. 1999. "Matching Person Identity from Facial Line Drawings." *Perception* 28: 1171–1175.

Levin, D. T., and B. L. Angelone. 2001. "Categorical Perception of Race." *Perception* 31: 567–578.

Levy, B. 2002. "Say My Name, Say My Name." *Incentive* 176(9): 99–100.

Lewis, R. C., and C. Roan. 1986. "Selling What You Promote." *Cornell Hotel and Restaurant Administration Quarterly* 27(1): 13–15.

Lomanno, M. 2005. "US lodging industry overview," presented at the Fifth Resort Management Conference, Phoenix, Arizona, USA.

Magnini, V. P., E. D. Honeycutt, and S. K. Hodge. 2003. "Data Mining for Hotel Firms: Use and Limitations. *Cornell Hotel and Restaurant Administration Quarterly* 44(2): 94–106.

Malhotra, N. K. 1991. "Mnemonics in Marketing: A Pedagogical Tool." *Journal of the Academy of Marketing Science* 19(2): 141–149.

Mandelbaum, R. 2004. "Other revenue is good revenue," available at: www.hotel-online.com/News/PR2004_4th/Nov04_OtherRevenue.html (accessed April 29, 2006).

McKenzie, G. R, and J. Sawyer. 1986. "Effects of Test-Like Practice and Mnemonics on Learning Graphic Facts." *Theory and Research in Social Education* 14(3): 201–209.

McWeeny, K. H., A. W. Young, D. C. Hay, and A. W. Ellis. 1987. "Putting Names to Faces." *British Journal of Psychology* 78: 143–151.

Min, H., H. Min, and A. Eman. 2002. "A Data Mining Approach to Developing the Profiles of Hotel Customers." *International Journal of Contemporary Hospitality Management* 14(6): 274–285.

Mondloch, C. J., T. L. Lewis, D. R. Budreau, D. Maurer, J. L. Dannemiller, B. R. Stephens, and K. A. Kleiner-Gathercoal. 1999. "Face Perception during Early Infancy." *Psychological Science* 10: 419–422.

Monteson, P. A. 2001. "Spas: a tangible, intangible asset to resorts," available at: www.hotelinteractive.com/index.asp?page_id=5000&article_id=1154 (accessed January 14, 2006).

Monteson, P. A., and J. Singer. 2004. "Marketing a resort-based spa." *Journal of Vacation Marketing* 10(3): 282–287.

Morgan, R. M., and S. D. Hunt. 1994. "The Commitment-Trust Theory of Relationship Marketing. *Journal of Marketing* 58: 20–38.

Murphy, J., E. Forrest, C.E. Wotring, and R. Brymer. 1996. "Hotel Management and Marketing on the Internet." *Cornell Hotel and Restaurant Administration Quarterly* 37(3): 70–82.

Muqbil, I. 1998. "Ten Hospitality Trends for the Tourism and Hospitality Industry." Travel Impact Newswire (travel-impact-newswire.com).

Nua Internet Surveys. 1998. "Online Travel Business Exploding." Dublin.

NFO Plog Research. 2000. Year 2000 Interactive Traveller Survey, Los Angeles: NFO Plog Research.

Nyman, M.S. 1996. "What Was Your Name Again? Some Tips for Remembering Names (and Avoiding This Question)." *American Salesman* 4(8): 27.

O'Connor, P., 2001. "The Changing Face of Hotel Electronic Distribution," *EIU Travel & Tourism Analyst* 5: 70–93.

O'Connor, P., and P Horan. 1999. "Failing to Make the Connection? An Analysis of Web-reservation Facilities in the Top-50 International Hotel Chains," Proceedings of the HITA Worldwide Conference (Edinburgh, Hospitality Information Technology Association).

Pastore, M. "Online Travel Market Largely Avoids Economic Slowdown," available at www.CyberAtlas.com (accessed April 23, 2001).

PhoCusWright. 2001. *Online Travel Marketplace* 2001–2003. New York: PhoCusWright.

Rust, R.T., A. J. Zahorik, and T. L. Keiningham. 1995. "Return on Quality (ROQ): Making Service Quality Financially Accountable." *Journal of Marketing* 59(2): 58–75.

Shoemaker, S., and J. T. Bowen. 2003. "Commentary on Loyalty: A Strategic Commitment. *Cornell Hotel and Restaurant Administration Quarterly* 44(5–6): 47–52.

Singer, J. 2000. "Spas ... today and tomorrow," available at: www.hfdspa.com/pr_nhe300.html (accessed 10 February, 2006).

Singer, J. 2003. "Is your spa a lazy asset?" available at: www.hfdspa.com/pr_nhe_0811.html.

Singer, J., and P. Monteson. 2005. "GHN special report. HFD'S 2003–2004 spa economics research a global perspective on resort based spas," available at: http://globalhotelnetwork.com/bob/pdf/hfdspa06.pdf (accessed 10 February, 2006).

Slater, A., G. Bremner, S. P. Johnson, P. Sherwood, R. Hayes, and E. Brown. 2000 "Newborn Infants' Preference for Attractive Faces: The Role of Internal and External Facial Features." *Infancy* 1: 265–274.

Thacker, G. 2004. *"Spa Industry Study: A Profile of the Spa Industry in the United States and Canada."* Toronto: Association Resource Centre, Inc., Research and Strategy Division, pp. 6–22, 23, 30, 34–50, 60–67.

Tracey, J. B., and M. J. Tews. 1995. "Training Effectiveness: Accounting for Individual Characteristics and the Work Environment." *Cornell Hotel and Restaurant Administration Quarterly* 36(6): 36–42.

Traugot, C. L. 2002. "Spa brings profit potential to resort. *Triangle Business Journal, available at:* www.bizjournals.com/triangle/stories/2002/05/27/focus4.html (accessed February 12, 2006).

Travel Industry Association of America. 1998. "Travel Agencies Still Preferred Source for Travel Information" (1998 press release), as viewed at www.tia.org/research/summinternet97.asp.

Travel Industry Association of America. 2001. *Travelers' Use of the Internet.* Washington, DC: TIAA.

Travel Research International. 1999. *The European Hotel Industry.* Staff Report.

Useem, J. 2002. "Your Name Is Mud, or a Pole, or a Stove." *Fortune* 146(1): 40.

Van Hoof, H., and T. Combrink. 1998. "U.S. Lodging Managers and the Internet." *Cornell Hotel and Restaurant Administration Quarterly* 39(2): 46–54.

Vokey, J. R., and J. D. Read. 1992. "Familiarity, Memorability, and the Effect of Typicality on the Recognition of Faces." *Memory and Cognition* 20(3): 291–313.

Yesawich, Pepperdine & Brown. 2000. *National Leisure Travel Monitor.* Orlando: Yesawich, Pepperdine & Brown.

Yin, R. 1969. "Looking at Upside-Down Faces." *Journal of Experimental Psychology* 81: 141–145.

Young, A. W., D. C. Hay, and A. W. Ellis. 1985. "The Faces that Launched a Thousand Slips: Everyday Difficulties and Errors in Recognising People." *British Journal of Psychology* 76: 495–523.

Young, A. W., D. C. Hays, K. H. McWeeny, B. M. Flude, and A. W. Ellis. "Matching Familiar and Unfamiliar Faces on Internal and External Features." *Perception* 14: 737–746.

Zimmer, R., and A. Clarke 2006. "Balancing mind, body and spirit: Why the current spa explosion is still the tip of the iceberg." Available at: www.hospitalitynet.org/news/4026301.html (accessed May 5, 2006).

SUGGESTED READINGS

BOOKS

Adams, L., R. H. Penner, and W. A. Rutes. 2001. *Hotel Design, Planning, and Development.* New York: W.W. Norton & Company, Inc.

Cohen, M., and G. Bodeker. 2008. *Understanding the Global Spa Industry: Spa Management.* UK: Elsevier Ltd.

D'Angelo, J. M. 2005. *Spa Business Strategies: A Plan for Success.* Thomson Delmar Learning.

Disney Institute. 2001. *Be Our Guest: Perfecting the Art of Customer Service.* New York: Disney Enterprises.

Gomes, A. J. 1985. *Hospitality in Transition.* Houston, TX: Pannell Kerr Forster.

Greenberg, P. 2004. *Hotel Secrets from the Travel Detective: Insider Tips on Getting the Best Value, Service, and Security in Accommodations from Bed-and-Breakfasts to Five-Star Resorts.* New York: Villard Books.

Hilton, C. 1984. *Be My Guest.* Englewood Cliffs, NJ: Prentice Hall.

Jarman, R. 1952. *A Bed for the Night: The Story of the Wheeling Bell Boy: E.M. Statler and His Remarkable Hotels.* New York: Harper and Row.

Marriot, J. W., and Conrad. A. Zackheim. 2001. *The Spirit to Serve Marriott's Way.* New York: HarperCollins.

Rushmore, S., D. M. Ciraldo, and J. Tarras. 2002. *Hotel Investment Handbook.* New York: West Group.

ARTICLES

Kim, Woo Goo, and Hyun Jeong Kim. 2007. "Determinants of Mid-Scale Hotel Brand Equity." *FIU Review* 25(1): 61–69.

Dev, C. S., J. R. Brown, and K. Z. Zhou. 2007. "Global Brand Expansion: How to Select a Market Entry Strategy." *Cornell Hotel and Restaurant Administration Quarterly* 48(1): 13–27.

Greger, K. R., and G. Witham. 1991. "The View from the Helm: Hotel Execs Examine the Industry." *Cornell Hotel and Restaurant Administration Quarterly* 32(3): 18–35.

Kandampully, J., and H. H. Hu. 2007. "Do Hoteliers Need to Manage Image to Retain Loyal Customers?" *International Journal of Contemporary Hospitality Management* 19(6): 435–443.

Kimes. S. E., and S. Singh. 2009. "Spa Revenue Management." *Cornell Hospitality Quarterly* 50(1): 82–95.

Lee, D. R. 1985. "How They Started: The Growth of Four Hotel Giants." *Cornell Hotel and Restaurant Administration Quarterly* May, 26(1).

Mandelbaum, R., and G. Lerner. 2008. "PKF Industry Analysis: Hotel Operators Massage More Profits from Their Spa Operations." *Cornell Hospitality Quarterly* 49(2): 99–104.

Page, G. S. 1984. "Pioneers and Leaders of the Hospitality Industry." In *Introduction to Hotel and Restaurant Management,* R. A. Brymer (ed.). Dubuque, IA: Kendall/Hung, pp. 21–29.

Severt, D., T. Aiello, S. Elswick., and C. Cyr. 2008. "Hospitality in Hospitals?" *International Journal of Contemporary Hospitality Management* 20(6): 664–678.

Staff article. 1985. "The Evolution of the Hospitality Industry." *Cornell Hotel and Restaurant Administration Quarterly* May, 26(1), 36–86.

SOURCE NOTES

Chapter 1.2, "The Hotel Development Process," by John Dew.

Chapter 1.3, "The Art and Science of Opening a Hotel," by Tom Dupar.

Chapter 1.4, "On-line Pricing: An Analysis of Hotel-company Practices," by Peter O'Connor, is reprinted from the February 2003 issue of *Cornell Hotel and Restaurant Administration Quarterly.* © Cornell University. Used by permission. All rights reserved.

Chapter 1.5, "Face Recognition and Name Recall," by Vincent P. Magnini and Earl D. Honeycutt, is reprinted from the February 2005 issue of *Cornell Hotel and Restaurant Administration Quarterly.* © Cornell University. Used by permission. All rights reserved.

Chapter 1.6, "Spas and the Lodging Industry," by Peter C. Anderson.

Chapter 1.7, "Resort Spas: How are the Massaging Hotel Revenues?," by Melih Madanoglu and Sherie Brezina, is reprinted from the 1st issue of 2008 in the *International Journal of Contemporary Hospitality Management.* © Emerald Group Publishing Limited. Used by permission. All rights reserved.

Chapter 1.8, "As I See It: A Ritz-Carlton Spa Director," by Holleigh Alexander.

CHAPTER TWO

ORGANIZATION

2.1 INTRODUCTION

✦ CLASSIC ORGANIZATION

At the beginning of the twentieth century, the classic European hotel organization model was predominant in hotels in the United States. The European structure was built around two major hotel managerial personalities: the chef and the maître d'hôtel. The chef was the chief or king of the kitchen. In many ways, he represented a feudal lord on his estate, who held sway over everything that had to do with selection and preparation of food in the hotel. This structure recognized the importance of the role that food and its preparation played in the hotels of the time.

Similarly, the maître d'hôtel was the master of all service in the hotel. It was his responsibility to manage the interaction of the hotel's staff and guests such that guests were always served promptly, properly, and in line with the hotel's policy. Even the titles *chef* and *maître d'hôtel,* translated from the French as "chief" and "master of the hotel," suggest a strong European influence. The fact that these terms are still in use today attests to a continuing influence; however, the roles have changed and evolved. In several places in this book, we consider the ways in which people, organizations, and jobs have changed in the hotel industry.

For many of the same reasons cited in the Introduction as to why the management of hotels has changed, hotel organization structures have also changed. As our knowledge of our guests and the markets they represent grew and became more precise, specialization within the hotel organizational structure increased the effectiveness with which the organization managed and delivered its services.

Hotel organization structures are not immune to the influences of the economy and business cycles, so the difficulties that befall business in general during economic downturns also affect hotel organizations. *Downsizing* and *reengineering* are terms used to describe the changes hotel companies have undergone.

Figure 2.1 Typical Hotel Organization Chart

In the early 1990s, some hotels eliminated entire levels of management or combined managerial responsibilities to flatten the organization. In the typical functional chart, such as that depicted in Figure 2.1, the executive assistant manager was often eliminated, making division heads directly responsible to the general manager (GM). Some hotels eliminated separate managers at the division level, with all department managers reporting directly to the GM. To some extent, we are witnessing these same actions being taken today as hotels are finding ways to reduce expenses in order to survive one of the greatest economic downturns since the Great Depression.

Regardless of how the restructuring looks, or the purpose for the restructuring, organizations are still being formed around the principles outlined in the mid-1980s by Stoner and Wankel (1986). They said that the organizing process involves balancing a company's needs for both stability and change. They go on to comment on "organizing" as a multistep process based on that proposed by Dale (1967):

- Organizing details all of the work that must be done to attain the organization's goals.

- Organizing divides the total work to be performed into groups of activities that can be performed by one person or one group of people.

- Organizing combines the work of an organization's members in some logical and efficient manner.

- Organizing sets up a mechanism to coordinate the work of the organization's members such that it forms a unified, harmonious whole.

- Organizing sets up a mechanism to monitor the effectiveness of the organization's efforts to achieve its goals.

In the modern hotel organization, even a restructured one, a linear line and staff structure has emerged to reflect this theoretical organizing process.

Figure 2.1 depicts a typical organization chart for a large hotel. Note that, with the exception of top managers, function rather than title identifies the departments. This is to indicate that job titles and associated duties vary from company to company, and, as noted, may be combined or eliminated to reflect current conditions. Looking at an organizational chart by function rather than by job title allows an industry-wide perspective, as the services a hotel delivers remains the same even through financial emergencies.

In addition, notice that in this chart the two major operating divisions are identified as *Rooms Division* and *Food and Beverage Division*. Again, on a company-by-company basis, individual functions may find homes in various divisions. Regardless, hotel organizations are primarily set up to deliver these two basic services to their guests: rooms, and food and beverage. This is most certainly the case in full-service hotels. The structure, however, may look different (at least from the food and beverage side) of a limited-service hotel.

What may differ in a given hotel company's organization is the placement of the other departments. The departments on this organization chart should be considered typical and illustrative of a generic hotel organization chart.

For purposes of illustration, the line and staff functions are defined as follows.

LINE FUNCTIONS

Line functions are the tasks assigned to hotel employees in organizational components that bring them into regular or semi-regular contact with guests. The line operations in a hotel organization are the Rooms Division, and the Food and Beverage Division. Obviously, some departmental functions within each line division have more or less guest contact than others. The underlying commonalty is that most line employees are hands-on participants in the assembly and delivery of the hotel's services.

For instance, under most circumstances, members of the hotel's security staff do not have regular guest contact. The housekeeping staff, on the other hand, may have somewhat more guest contact, as housekeepers are obviously major participants in the production of the hotel's services. However, in the Rooms Division, the front office staff has the vast majority of highly visible face-to-face contact with the guest.

Similarly, in the Food and Beverage Division, many of the employees of the restaurants, bars, room service, and banquet departments have a tremendous amount of face-to-face guest interaction. Like the housekeeping staff, however, only under special and irregular circumstances does the food production staff under the hotel chef interact with guests. Because of their importance in the service production process, these positions are still clearly identified as a line function.

STAFF FUNCTIONS

Staff functions are generally those behind-the-scenes activities that support the line functions. Under most circumstances, the individuals in these positions have little or no guest contact, although major components of the work are to influence the quality of a guest's stay.

In this organizational chart (see Figure 2.1), for instance, engineering is included as a staff function for those reasons. The success of the engineering function heavily influences the quality of the guest's stay and, at the same time, the engineering department supports the activities of almost every other department in the hotel.

For instance, the engineering department maintains and repairs equipment that is crucial to all of the hotel's line functions, including the food production equipment in the kitchen. Engineering staff can be called on to repair the tables and chairs in the dining room, the furniture in the lobby, and the carts the bellhops use to transport guest luggage. The engineering department, thus, can be considered a true staff department that serves and supports at any given time any or all of the other departments in the hotel.

An examination of organization charts at different hotels may show the engineering department as part of the Rooms Division. This may be because that is where engineering works best in the hotel's organization or perhaps this placement is only tradition.

This situation may also be true for other departments traditionally thought of as Rooms Division functions. Security is one example. In some organizations, housekeeping has been changed to a staff function rather than strictly rooms, for housekeeping, by definition, "keeps" the entire house.

✦ ORGANIZATIONS FOR THE MODERN ERA

Organizations, of course, are more than just boxes and charts. The most modern business organization structures have not changed much in form since the Roman Catholic Church first designed the pyramidal structure as a visual depiction of the organizational relationships with which we are so familiar today. If you think about it, the military, government, school systems, and nearly all businesses follow the same model.

What does affect organizations—not so much in their pictorial view but in the way they respond to external and internal stimuli—can be seen by analyzing several of the readings included here and those that are suggested at the end for further study.

At the time of his untimely death, Professor Eddystone C. Nebel III was the C. B. Smith Professor of Hotel Management at Purdue University. He had recently spent a sabbatical leave researching and observing 10 outstanding general managers and 53 key subordinates. During this research, Nebel gained critical insight into how hotel organizations function. In several chapters of his book *Managing Hotels Effectively: Lessons from Outstanding General Managers* (1991), Nebel weaves the insights gained from the GMs with organizational theory and then incorporates the increasingly important role that committees can play in the successful organization.

Another view of the peculiar dynamics of hotel organizations is provided by Mark Conklin in his essay on how the leadership can influence a hotel's effective organization. In his position as vice president of market management for Marriott Hotels and Resorts, he is positioned to comment knowledgeably. In this instance, he proposes a radical new view—one neither the Catholic Church nor the military might be comfortable with. It does, however, appear well suited to hospitality.

In reviewing the recent literature on hotel organizations, it seems apparent that this is a topic that has lost some research momentum and is one that can benefit from future research and interest. However, the research and opinion presented here highlight relatively current thinking about the relationship of organizational structure, interdepartmental connections, and the organization's people. Additional insights can be gained from suggested readings.

2.2 ORGANIZATIONAL DESIGN Eddystone C. Nebel III

This section reviews general management principles of organizational design, including the important but often neglected topic of a hotel's committee and meetings structure.

✦ THE ELEMENTS OF ORGANIZATIONAL STRUCTURE

If the efforts of people in organizations are to be channeled toward productive ends, structure must be given to their activities. Aldag and Stearns (1987) list five ways by which managers give structure to organizations:

1. Work specialization
2. Departmentalization
3. Patterns of authority
4. Spans of control
5. Methods of coordination

Whenever a manager decides to make an organizational change, he or she usually must take these five elements into account.

Specialization. If there is more than one way to accomplish something, management must make a conscious decision about how to divide tasks among workers. At one extreme is the case of little or no specialization, and an individual worker is responsible for all of the tasks required to complete a job. An example is the chef in a small country restaurant who singlehandedly prepares an entire meal for 20 guests. It is rewarding to have total control over a project and motivating to see the results of one's efforts. The problem, however, is that as demand for products

or services increases, it becomes more and more difficult for individuals or small groups to increase their output without changing the way they are organized.

One of management's tasks is to determine the extent to which work and jobs should be specialized. As a general rule, specialization holds out the possibility of greater worker productivity and managerial control over tasks. On the other hand, dividing complete jobs into smaller subunits tends to increase the need for coordinating the activities of numerous workers, each involved in separate, specialized tasks. Also, overspecialization can result in jobs so narrow that workers lose interest, motivation drops, error rates increase, and quality suffers.

Departmentalization. As organizations grow in size, managers are faced with the need to group certain jobs in order to ensure efficient coordination and control of activities. Most restaurants departmentalize activities, with food preparation and food service as separate functional departments. This is a logical and practical solution. Preparing and serving food is achieved through distinctly different kinds of work; both the process and the function of the two activities are different. Forming departments along functional lines is the most common method of organizing a business.

Authority. Every time managers restructure a job or group into different departments, they are faced with the question of how much decision-making authority to grant individual workers, managers, or departments. Organizations are never totally centralized or decentralized with regard to decision making; rather, they tend toward one direction or the other. A number of factors must be taken into account when deciding what pattern of authority is best for an organization. Managers must take into consideration the experience and personality of subordinates, the environment in which they work (Is it stable or rapidly changing?), the business strategy to be followed, and the management style with which they feel most comfortable.

Line executives have responsibility for business units that provide products or services to customers and account for the revenues of the business. In a hotel, the rooms and food and beverage departments account for most revenue. On the other hand, staff departments are set up because the principles of work specialization and departmentalization suggest efficiencies from such an organizational design. The personnel and engineering departments of a hotel are examples of staff units. Once set up, however, staff departments sometimes cause organizational problems.

How much authority should functional staff executives have over line executives? At one extreme, line executives could be given total authority. At the other extreme, staff executives, in their specialty areas, could be granted authority over line executives. Two intermediate examples: (1) Line executives are required to consult with staff specialists before making a decision, and (2) line and staff executives are required to make joint decisions. Whatever the situation, top executives like GMs must arbitrate line-staff disputes when they develop.

Span of Control. Span of control relates to the number of subordinates reporting to a supervisor. In the past, some management scholars advocated an "ideal" span of control of exactly seven subordinates. That simplistic view is no longer held. The ideal span of control is dependent on:

- *Task similarity*—The more similar the tasks of subordinates, the wider the span of control can be.

- *Training and professionalism*—The more trained and skilled a subordinate, the less supervision required and the greater the span of control can be.

- *Task certainty*—The more routine and predictable work tasks are, the greater the span of control can be.

- *Frequency of interaction*—If relationships require frequent interaction, the span of control must be narrow.

- *Task integration*—The more a supervisor must integrate and coordinate the tasks of subordinates, the narrower the span of control must be.

- *Physical dispersion*—The more widely dispersed subordinates are, the fewer a manager can properly supervise.

Some of these factors may work in opposite directions. For example, fast food restaurants are operationally quite similar to each other, suggesting a broad span of control. However, their physical dispersion works in the (opposite) direction of limiting span of control.

Coordination of Activities. Problems arise when organizations do not properly coordinate their activities. In simple organizations of only a few people, coordination is usually not a major concern. Problems develop, however, as organizations grow in complexity. As previously discussed, work specialization and departmentalization are organizational responses to the growth of a business. As duties are subdivided, it becomes increasingly important to coordinate the activities of individuals and groups toward common goals. The kind of coordination required depends on how tasks and activities are linked. These linkages result in different kinds of interdependence between individuals and groups.

Pooled interdependence refers to activities that can be performed with little interaction between individuals or groups. Suppose a hotel has three telephone operators. Each can usually perform the required duties independently—that is, without any interaction with the others—as can room maids and cashiers at food outlets. Because these workers need not interact among themselves, co-ordination of their activities is best accomplished by prescribing standardized rules and procedures for each to follow, by intensive individual training, and by direct supervision. The role of coordination is to ensure that each independently performed task is carried out at the same level of efficiency and quality.

Sequential interdependence occurs when one task's output is a second task's input. This is typical of production line operations where products are progressively assembled. A hotel example is the guest check-in process. The output of a front desk becomes an input to the accounting department in the form of a guest billing record or folio. A well-planned system linking the rooms department and the accounting department is vital for this activity to go smoothly. Proper coordination is ensured through detailed planning, scheduling, and standardization. Coordination also requires identification of the linkages that exist between activities.

Still greater coordination is required in cases where the output of Unit A is input for Unit B and the output of Unit B is input for Unit A. Whenever there is a high level of interaction between work units, they are said to exhibit *reciprocal interdependence.* One example is the coordination needed to host a major convention. Rooming decisions made by the front desk must be coordinated with accounting, sales, housekeeping, and reservations; function room usage requires interactions among convention services, engineering, food and beverage, and accounting. Because any one department's output and activity affect numerous other departments, mutual adjustments are required. Close coordination is only possible through direct communication and joint decision making by the units involved. While standardized plans and procedures are helpful, they cannot possibly solve all of the problems resulting from such a high degree of departmental interaction. Direct communication and group meetings are needed to ensure proper coordination when activities involve reciprocal interdependence.

✦ STATIC PRINCIPLES OF ORGANIZATIONAL DESIGN

Experience has accumulated for centuries about how to organize institutions such as government bureaucracies, the military, religions, large commercial trading companies, and, since the industrial revolution, large manufacturing concerns. This experience is distilled in a number of principles that have been identified. While these principles do not hold in all circumstances, they are important and should be understood and applied where appropriate.

Chain of Command. This principle holds that everyone in an organization should have a superior to whom he or she is responsible. A hotel's organizational chart depicts the chain of command. It should be possible for any employee to trace his or her way up the organization chart's chain of command all the way to the GM. The typical pyramid shape of an organization chart is a consequence of the chain of command and the span of control concept discussed previously. Chain of command is a powerful concept. It provides structure in an organization by setting forth a system of subordinate-superior accountability for everyone.

The chain of command affects communication within organizations for both subordinates and superiors. If a GM wants to make a change in housekeeping, chain-of-command considerations mean he or she should communicate with the rooms department manager, who in turn will speak to the director of housekeeping. The traditional chain-of-command structure in a hotel has the baker responsible to the chef and the chef responsible to the food and beverage director. Accordingly, the baker should communicate with the chef and not directly with the food and beverage director.

Too strict an adherence to this principle, however, can take away the spontaneity in an organization. Experienced hotel GMs often break this principle, but in a way that is not harmful to the hotel. The immediacy of some problems in hotels sometimes requires hotel executives to issue orders directly to subordinates two or more levels down in the organization. GMs may also want to maintain personal control over some project or aspect of the hotel and choose to bypass immediate subordinates in order to do so. This does little harm as long as everyone knows what is happening and the organizational climate is otherwise healthy and trusting.

Unity of Command. This principle states that each employee is responsible to one and only one superior—that is, each person has only one boss. Unity of command is violated quite regularly in most organizations. A safety officer who reports to the personnel director might correct a food server, whose boss is the restaurant manager, for a safety violation. The server feels as if she has two bosses and, in effect, she does. This common problem occurs as organizations grow in size and task specialization takes place. Specialists in safety (or accounting, personnel, data processing, and so on) often do have authority, in their specialty area, over workers who do not report directly to them through the chain of command. Problems can develop because of conflicting orders from more than one boss. The solution is not necessarily to eliminate specialization and staff positions but rather to ensure, by closely coordinating activities, that order rather than confusion reigns. The GM plays a key role in coordination throughout the hotel.

Delegation. Young managers often find delegation a difficult task to master. A subordinate's ability to successfully carry out an assignment depends in part on the clarity of his or her superior's delegation instructions. Delegation can range from assigning a minor task to a subordinate to granting complete responsibility for a major undertaking. It is important for both superior and subordinate to understand and agree on the level of responsibility, the freedom of action, and the amount of authority that accompanies a delegated task.

Each level of delegation is useful in different circumstances. Here are examples of orders that result in different degrees of delegation:

- Gather information for my decision.
- Set out two or three alternatives; I'll then choose.
- Make a recommendation for my approval.
- Make a decision but inform me of it before proceeding.
- Take action but inform me of it before proceeding.
- Take action on your own; it's not necessary to communicate with me regarding this matter.

The extent to which authority is delegated depends in part on the experience of the subordinate. Young, inexperienced subordinates can expect only limited delegation until they have proven themselves. The amount of authority delegated usually increases as trust between superior and subordinate is built.

It's been said that when a person becomes a manager, he or she gives up earning an honest living. Hotel managers don't usually make beds, cook food, or provide service directly to guests. Rather, their job is to see to it that the organization they manage provides proper guest services.

✦ THE HOTEL FUNCTIONAL ORGANIZATIONAL DESIGN

Individual hotels are usually organized along functional lines, with departments grouped according to the particular work activity in which they are engaged. Figure 2.2 depicts a typical organization chart for a 500-room hotel. The hotel is divided along functional lines into five administrative departments: rooms, food and beverage, accounting, sales, and personnel. The five department heads report directly to the GM. As Figure 2.2 shows, each department is subdivided into smaller organizational units. These subdivisions represent refinements of the work performed and the knowledge and skills of the people in each subunit.

The Rooms Department. The rooms department performs the lodging function of a hotel. Reservations must be accepted, guests must be hospitably received and assigned clean rooms, the status of available and occupied rooms must be kept current, guests must receive mail and phone messages promptly, security must be maintained, public spaces such as lobbies must be kept clean, and guest questions must be answered. These are some of the important functions of the rooms department. The rooms department is divided into a number of subunits, each of which performs rather specialized tasks. In many instances, these subunits are also referred to as departments. For example, the laundry department, which in a 500-room hotel is quite large, is responsible for cleaning and pressing all the hotel's linens and employee uniforms as well as guest laundry. Its function is extremely specialized. Little of the knowledge and skills required to manage a laundry operation are transferable to other areas of hotel operations.

The front office is where guests are greeted when they arrive at the hotel, where they're registered, and where they're assigned to a room. Telephone operators and other guest communications functions usually fall under the front office department. The hotel's bell staff is also part of this department. Reservations takes and tracks hotel's future bookings. The housekeeping

Figure 2.2 Typical Hotel Organization Chart

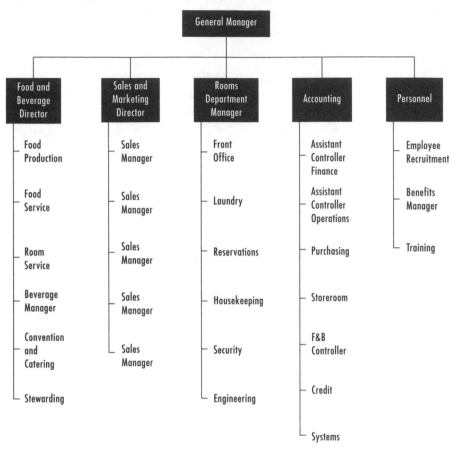

department is responsible for cleaning guest rooms and public spaces. Security is responsible for guest safety. Finally, the engineering department is responsible for the operation and maintenance of the hotel's entire physical plant, including electrical, mechanical, heating, air conditioning and ventilation, structure, and plumbing. It also performs minor repairs and renovations.

A great deal of interdependence exists between the subunits of the rooms department, thus calling for close coordination of activities. Linkages exist between the front office and the reservations department. Reservations must in-

form the front office of the number of presold rooms each day to ensure that a current inventory of rentable rooms is always available. The front office must let reservations know whenever walk-in guests (those without reservations) are registered. Linkages also exist between the front office and housekeeping. Information regarding room status must flow both ways: When a guest checks out, the front office must inform housekeeping so the room may be cleaned. Once it is cleaned, housekeeping must inform the front office so the room may be sold. These are both examples of reciprocal interdependence in which individual units provide each other with inputs. Other linkages within the rooms department are illustrative of sequential interdependence, which occurs when the output of one unit becomes the input of another. An example is housekeeping's inability to properly provision a guest room if the laundry does not supply enough clean towels or bedsheets. A less obvious example deals with the output of information from one department to another. For example, engineering cannot replace a defective light switch in a guest room if housekeeping does not report the problem. These examples illustrate the reciprocal and sequential interdependence that exists between subunits of the rooms department. Effective management under these conditions calls for standardized plans, procedures, schedules, and deadlines. Coordination between units also requires frequent direct communications between executives.

The Food and Beverage Department. The primary function of the food and beverage department is, of course, to provide food and drink to a hotel's guests. In earlier times, when an inn had only one dining room, this was a much simpler task. Today, however, providing food and drink is much more complicated. The 500-room hotel in this discussion might well have a coffee shop, a gourmet restaurant, a poolside snack bar, room service, two banquet halls, and ten separate function rooms where food and beverage may be served. It might also have a piano bar and lounge, a nightclub, and a lobby bar. This adds up to 19 food and beverage outlets, excluding room service! On a busy day (or night), it's likely that each of these outlets will be used. Often, more than one event takes place in an outlet during a 24-hour period.

There is great diversity in the activities performed by a food and beverage department and considerable variety in the skills required, so the department is comprised of a number of functional subunits where tasks are specialized. To begin with, there is the food production, or kitchen, department. In a 500-room hotel, this unit is headed by the executive chef, a person of great stature and authority in a first-class hotel. Under the executive chef are a variety of culinary specialists responsible for different aspects of food preparation. The service of food in a hotel's restaurants and food outlets is usually the responsibility of a separate department, which, in a large hotel, is headed by an assistant food and beverage director. The food service department contains the individual restaurant and outlet managers, maître d's, waiters, waitresses, and bus help. Because of the special problems associated with room service, many large hotels have a separate subunit responsible only for room service. The high value and profit margins associated with alcoholic beverages cause hotels to form a separate department with responsibility for the bars, lounges, service bars, and other alcoholic beverage outlets. Most full-service hotels do considerable convention and catering business. A convention uses small function rooms for separate meetings, larger rooms for general sessions, and even larger facilities for banquets. Catered events include local parties, wedding receptions, business meetings, and other affairs held by local groups. To provide for the unique needs of these customers, hotels often organize separate catering and convention departments that specialize in this kind of business. Finally, the job of cleaning the spaces of the food and beverage department, dish- and warewashing, and general food and beverage expediting is often assigned to a separate subunit known as the stewarding department.

Sales and Marketing. This department is quite small, making intradepartmental coordination fairly easy. Also, the department is removed from most day-to-day operational problems faced by other departments. Still, there is a division of work among sales managers, usually based on the type of customers a hotel is attempting to attract. Individual sales managers often specialize in corporate accounts, conventions, or tour and travel markets. Sales managers are sometimes further subdivided along geographical lines such as regional or national accounts. Still, the sales staff, even for a 1000-room hotel, usually does not exceed a dozen or so members. Sales managers work more or less independently in their particular market segments. Thus, problems of intradepartmental interdependence are usually not severe (Pelletier, 1988).

Personnel. A hotel's personnel department is a staff organization set up to handle a specialized function. It serves no customers, books no business, and prepares no meals, yet it plays a vital role in a hotel's efficient operation. In Figure 2.2, the personnel department is subdivided into three subfunctions: employee recruitment, benefits administration, and training. The personnel director must be an expert on labor law and able to advise managers in other departments. While these three subfunctions are related, they do not present many problems of interdependence. Instead, the personnel department's major challenge occurs as it attempts to interact with other hotel departments. Personnel may recruit, inter-

view, and screen prospective employees, but final hiring authority resides in the line departments. The same is true of promotion and disciplinary decisions, where the personnel department's input is advisory only. As a staff department, personnel's effectiveness is largely dependent on its manager's ability to form effective working relationships with other departments.

Accounting. The accounting department often combines both staff and line functions. Its traditional role is recording financial transactions, preparing and interpreting financial statements, and providing management with timely reports of operating results. Responsibilities also include payroll preparation, accounts receivable, and accounts payable. These functions are the responsibility of the assistant controller for finance. There is, however, another dimension to the accounting department that connects to operations, cost accounting, and cost control throughout the hotel. This often results in the department being called the controllers' department rather than the accounting department. The two central concerns of accounting control are rooms, food, and beverage. The accounting department's front office cashier tracks all charges to guest accounts. The night auditor reconciles all guest bills with the charges from the various hotel departments. Although these employees work at the front desk and sometimes have direct guest contact, they are members of the accounting department and report to the assistant controller for operations.

The food and beverage controller, and the food and beverage cashiers, who work in the accounting department, keep track of the revenues and expenses of the food and beverage department. Food and beverage cashiers report to the assistant controller for operations, and the food and beverage controller reports directly to the hotel controller. The food and beverage department may be responsible for food preparation and service, but the accounting department is responsible for collecting revenues! The food and beverage controller verifies the accuracy and reasonableness of all food and beverage revenues. The accounting department is responsible for tracking and preparing daily reports on the costs of the food and beverage used in the hotel. In many cases, the accounting department is also responsible for purchasing and storeroom operations. Finally, the director of systems is responsible for designing the accounting and management information systems used throughout the hotel. This discussion demonstrates the accounting department's direct involvement in day-to-day operational aspects of the hotel.

We make two final points about the accounting department. First, accounting is responsible for collecting and reporting most of a hotel's operational and financial statistics. It, therefore, plays an important hotelwide staff role as data provider for decision making and budget preparation. Second, the accounting department head is responsible not only to the hotel's GM but also to the hotel chain's financial vice president or to the hotel's owner. The reason for this dual reporting relationship is to provide the hotel corporation an independent verification of the accuracy of the financial and operating results of the hotel—that is, independent from the GM. Thus, unity of command is routinely violated in the case of hotel controllers.

✦ STRENGTHS AND WEAKNESSES OF A FUNCTIONAL ORGANIZATION

The reason for organizing a business along functional lines is to group employees who perform similar tasks or have similar skills. The strength of a hotel's functional organizational design is the resulting efficiency within individual departments or subunits. Performance of common tasks allows for work specialization, which increases overall productivity. Because functional departments perform similar tasks, workers rapidly develop specialized skills and knowledge. Training is easier because of task similarity and the many opportunities for inexperienced workers to learn from experienced workers. This helps new employees quickly learn the skills and behavioral patterns that lead to success.

A functional organization is a logical way to organize work because it fosters efficiency, teamwork, and coordination within departments. However, the functional design's most important strength is also the source of its greatest shortcoming. The success of a hotel is measured by its overall performance, not the performance of one department. A functional department's strength lies in its ability to focus on its own tasks and activities. Although this is surely important for departmental efficiency, it does not necessarily ensure the overall effectiveness of a hotel. Because they are specialized, it is sometimes difficult for functional departments to fully appreciate the relationship between their performance and the overall performance and goals of the hotel. All departments must keep hotelwide goals of customer service and profitability in mind rather than focus narrowly on their own concerns. A method must be found to coordinate the activities of individual departments and to set hotel-wide strategies and goals. Left to themselves, it is unlikely that individual departments would be capable of doing this. Specialization at the department and subdepartment levels results in the need for leadership at the top of an organization. Someone above the departments must set the overall strategic course of the hotel, set hotelwide goals, coordinate activities between departments, and arbitrate interdepartmental disputes. A hotel's functional organization demands strong leadership at the top.

While functional departments produce specialists within a narrow skill category, they do not develop executives with broad hotel exposure. Consider the heads of a hotel's marketing and food and beverage departments. These two executives might only have superficial knowledge of each other's specialty. Their education and work experience are likely so different that either would be at a loss if placed in the other's department. The director of sales might have a marketing or general business degree and spend a career in sales-related work. The food and beverage director, on the other hand, could have a culinary diploma and a hospitality degree, extensive food production and service experience, and little or no sales experience. One often finds accountants running the controller's office, engineers in charge of engineering and maintenance, individuals with degrees in personnel administration heading the personnel department, and a variety of educational backgrounds among room managers.

Managers educated in hotel administration are capable of filling most department head slots. The longer managers stay in one department, the more narrowly specialized they become. While a manager may perform well within one department, he or she may be unprepared to address problems that require a hotelwide knowledge and perspective. Narrow specialization can result in bias, mistrust, and friction between departments unless upper management takes steps to counter this. Individual departments may pursue their own narrow interests rather than broader overall goals and objectives (Dann and Hornsey, 1986). This is a particular problem for hotels because of the need for close interdepartmental cooperation in providing guest services.

✦ HOW MEETINGS HELP COORDINATE THE ACTIVITIES OF A HOTEL

There is plenty of potential for service breakdowns in hotels. A well-thought-out set of standard operating procedures and systems can decrease the chances of many routine mistakes. Still, because of the amount of reciprocal interdependence that exists between departments, close cooperation is a must. Nowhere is this more important than at the department-head level, where differences in functional specialties are most extreme (Dann and Hornsey, 1986). The vehicle often used to foster cooperation between functionally specialized departments is the executive operating committee (EOC).

The Executive Operating Committee. The EOC is made up of the GM and other hotel senior executives. There's no magic formula for EOC membership, but usually it's those executives who report directly to the GM. Thus, the EOC consists of the most senior members of a hotel's management staff: the heads of the functional departments who report directly to the GM and are responsible for the hotel's major budgetary units. A subgroup of these executives—the GM, rooms manager, sales and marketing director, food and beverage director, and controller—usually produce the hotel's occupancy, revenue, and profit forecasts for each year. These forecasts form the basis for the hotel's overall annual budget, and meeting annual budget goals determines executive bonuses.

The exact duties of an EOC vary from hotel to hotel. The duties and responsibilities of groups can be spelled out in detail or left ambiguous. A hotel's EOC can be loosely structured or highly structured. An important question GMs must answer is the amount of authority they wish to delegate to the EOC. Depending on the circumstances, one EOC might be structured to make certain group decisions, a second to play a strong though consultative role to the GM, and a third to have a weak or nonexistent decision-making role.

Quite apart from decision making, EOCs play an important communications role within hotels. This occurs by virtue of the fact that EOC members meet regularly to discuss hotel business. Any time meetings are held, communication takes place. Scott and Mitchell (1976) identify four functions of communication:

1. To provide information that helps executives in their decision making
2. To motivate by fostering a commitment to organizational objectives
3. To control by resolving ambiguities in the role, responsibilities, and duties of executives
4. To afford individuals the opportunity to express their feelings and emotions

It is important to note that all four of these functions of communication may take place during meetings. Meeting frequency, agenda, and the amount of decision making delegated to an EOC depend on a variety of factors. The more participative the GM's management style, the more likely the EOC is engaged in joint decision making. Authoritarian GMs find little need to foster a strong EOC. The greater the need for change within a hotel, the more likely it is that EOC meetings are frequent. The less experienced the hotel's department heads, the more helpful frequent EOC meetings are because they can serve as a learning and training vehicle for inexperienced managers.

Under the influence of a skilled GM, the EOC can play an important role. Some of the ways it may be useful are:

- To foster group problem solving and decision making
- To build a feeling of joint responsibility for overall hotel performance
- To help instill common attitudes and beliefs among top executives
- To foster top-down, bottom-up, and horizontal communication
- To assign duties, assess progress, and control activities
- To build interdepartmental cooperation
- To teach, coach, and build a responsive senior executive team
- To ensure acceptance of priorities and decisions by senior management

Other Hotel Committees and Meetings. Well-managed hotels address the need for coordination of activities through an elaborate structure of committees and meetings. Just like a hotel's organization chart, these committees and meetings constitute a formal part of a hotel's organizational structure. The GM usually prescribes a hotel's committee and meeting structure. Each group's responsibilities are spelled out (sometimes in great detail), regular meeting schedules are promulgated, and minutes are often taken and distributed to participants and to higher-level executives, including the GM. The committee and meeting structure of a hotel should be a well-thought-out part of its formal organizational structure.

The purposes of the committees and meetings in a hotel vary with the complexity of the hotel. They address a range of concerns including daily operations, intradepartmental and interdepartmental issues, hotelwide concerns, and financial, personnel, and marketing issues. Table 2.1 lists the regularly scheduled meetings of a typical large hotel. While not the meeting schedule for an actual hotel, it could be. It will pay dividends to review this list carefully. The meetings a hotel holds provide clues about what it takes to manage it.

One of the first things to note is the sheer number and diversity of meetings. Surely, one might say that if a hotel were to hold all of these meetings, there would be little time left over to do any work! In fact, the effective management of hotels requires frequent meetings. They are part of the work of the hotel. Table 2.1 shows an average of 249 scheduled meetings each year dealing with interdepartmental issues. Also, the GM attends 295 regularly scheduled meetings each year. In many hotels, this is the actual case.

There is no denying that meetings are time-consuming and sometimes unproductive. Still, there doesn't seem to be a better way to effectively manage a hotel (Conlin, 1989). One often finds frustrated, dissatisfied executives in hotels where there are too few meetings. These executives complain about not being kept informed of what is going on. As elementary as it may seem, it is easy for a hotel to fail to keep its managers and employees adequately informed. This shortcoming can have disastrous consequences for the attitude and morale of a hotel's staff. A second complaint relates to service breakdowns that occur as a consequence of too few meetings. Hotels are subject to frequent, usually daily, changes. Meetings must be scheduled frequently in such an environment, or their effectiveness is lost. Too few meetings results in confusion over a hotel's goals and objectives. People need to know what is important to the hotel. What does it value most? What does it stand for? What constitutes good performance? Because hotels provide many intangible services, a constant effort must be made at all levels to provide answers to these questions. Meetings are an effective means of accomplishing this vital management function (Hosansky, 1989).

Hotels are businesses that require an extraordinary degree of interdepartmental cooperation in order to provide high-quality guest service. The functional organizational design used in most hotels fosters efficiencies within each department of a hotel but is weak with respect to coordination between departments. One of the organizing strategies employed to overcome this problem is a formal meeting

Table 2.1 Typical Meetings Structure for a Major Hotel

MEETING	ATTENDANCE	FREQUENCY	PURPOSE	MEETING LENGTH
Operations	GM, department heads, front office, manager on duty, housekeeping, security, engineering, executive chef	1 to 5 times per week	Review upcoming day's activities and previous day's results	15 to 30 minutes
Staff	GM, department heads, all subdepartment managers reporting to department heads	Weekly	Review last week's performance, this week's activities, next week's plans and special projects; present performance awards	1 to 2 hours
Executive Committee	GM, department heads	1 to 4 times per month	Performance review, policy, strategy, formulation	1 to 2 hours
Sales Forecast and Marketing	GM, resident manager, front office, sales, reservations	1 to 4 times per month	Review room demand for upcoming 90 days, devise strategies to increase room-nights average rates, or both	1 to 2 hours
Department	GM as needed, department head, and all subdepartment heads, managers, and supervisors	1 to 2 times per month	Review department issues	1 hour
Subdepartment	Department head as needed, subdepartment head, all members, management, and staff	Monthly	Subdepartment, department issues	1 hour
Credit	GM, controller, sales, front office, reservations, catering and credit manager	Monthly	Review accounts receivable	1 hour
Safety	Personnel, food and beverage, housekeeping, and engineering	Monthly	Review safety program and safety record	1 hour
Energy Conservation	Chief engineer, resident manager, food and beverage, personnel, rooms, and housekeeping	Monthly	Control of energy costs	1 hour
Supervisory Staff Meeting	All management and supervisory personnel	Semi-annually	Review hotel performance, present awards, start new programs	1 hour
Annual Meeting	All hotel management and employees	Annually	Year-end review of performance and awards	1 hour
Employee Meetings	GM and selected employees from throughout the hotel	Monthly	Informal communication and discussion	1 hour
Supervisor/ Junior Manager	GM and selected first-line supervisors and junior managers	Monthly	Informal communication and discussion	1 hour

structure designed to foster interdepartmental communication and cooperation. Thus, an important part of management's organizing function is to design an effective meeting structure that compensates for and complements a hotel's functionally departmentalized organization.

2.3 AS I SEE IT: HOTEL ORGANIZATION STRUCTURE Mark Conklin

One way to represent the environment in our hotel is a chart I use at our new-hire orientation class (see Figure 2.3). I call this a *reverse organizational chart*; it is also referred to as an *organizational pyramid*—and, as you can see, the GM is on the bottom of the hierarchy.

At the top is the customer. Customers are the reason we are here. This focus on our guests creates alignment throughout the hotel. Our mission is to ensure that every guest leaves satisfied and wants to return, thus ensuring customer loyalty. One of Marriott's fundamental beliefs is "If you take good care of your employees, the employees will take good care of your customers."

Figure 2.3 Reverse Organizational Chart

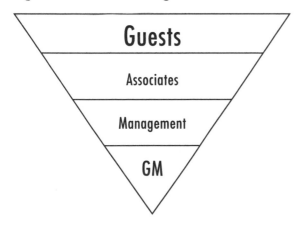

This belief is at the core of who we are and what we believe in as a company.

I say that we have two types of customers: external customers—our guests—and internal customers, who are the hotel's associates. I don't use the term *employee* but have replaced it with the word *associate*. The difference is that employees work *for* you and associates work *with* you. *Associate* implies partnership and working together, which is a subtle but powerful message. *Employee* suggests a class structure wherein someone is always organizationally inferior to someone else.

It is my belief that the front line associate is the most important person in the hotel, because he or she serves the customer. The job of the supervisors, managers, and the leadership team is to:

- Support the front line and remove the barriers to doing good work.

- Lead and help people do their jobs better.

This means managers support the front line by:

- Demonstrating concern for associates (and it must be sincere).

- Solving their problems quickly and fairly.

- Above all, treating associates with dignity, kindness, and respect.

To accomplish this, leaders must develop working relationships with associates that are based on mutual trust. Quite simply, it is my fundamental belief that our associates will not treat our customers any better than we treat them. This is the cornerstone of our culture, and the challenge is to keep this idea alive as the company grows.

As leaders, it is our job, then, to establish the direction and to create the environment where people focus on our customers. We set the tone for outstanding service, which requires a lot of coaching and leadership.

Putting the GM at the bottom of the pyramid shows that the leader actually works for the people who work with the leader. I view my role as doing whatever it takes to gain and keep customers. To create this environment, I've tried to capture the following key operating principles:

Select the Right People

- We work hard to select the right people using predictive screening tools. We look for people whose talents predispose them to provide great service and who have the highest potential to fit in with our culture.

- We involve our hourly associates in the selection process—after all, they have to work with the new people; therefore, line associates and managers take collective responsibility for the success of a newly hired associate.

Invest in Training

- Our emphasis on training is a reflection of Marriott's corporate culture. We invest in building the skills and knowledge of associates to give them the tools to succeed. We also provide them with an operational framework (standard operating procedures) that represents the foundation for our training.

Create Empowered Associates

- The foregoing combination of training and standards creates empowered associates who have the authority, accountability, and confidence to do their jobs. Years ago, we were challenged to operate our hotels with fewer managers. To accomplish this and to improve customer service, we had to have trained, empowered, and involved associates running the business.

- These systems and standards and this attention to detail help us deliver a consistent product and reliable service, which gives customers confidence and trust in our brand name.

Recognize and Promote

- Recognition in our organization takes place in many forms to create a positive environment. One of the greatest ways to show appreciation is by promotion. More than 50 percent of our managers started as hourly associates.

- Our associates like us, they trust us, and they act in our best interests. Recent company-wide associate opinion surveys indicate that 95 percent of our associates rated Marriott as an average or above average place to work. This is 15 points above the service industry norm.

Finally, it is my strong opinion that our managers should be hands-on. The hands-on manager is one who stays close to the customer and close to the associate—and hands-on managers never forget who is making them successful.

REFERENCES

Aldag, R. J., and T. M. Stearns. 1987. *Management*. Cincinnati: South-Western.

Conlin, J. 1989. "Management Strategy: Get Control!" *Successful Meetings* 38(7):37–42.

Dale, E. 1967. *Organization*. New York: American Management Association, p. 9.

Dann, D., and T. Hornsey. 1986. "Towards a Theory of Interdepartmental Conflict in Hotels." *International Journal of Hospitality Management* 5:23.

Hosansky, M. 1989. "Meetings Give You a Leg Up the Corporate Ladder." *Successful Meetings* 38(5):51–52.

Pelletier, R. 1988. "Overnight Success Takes Some Time." *HSMAI Marketing Review* 7(1):16–20.

Scott, W. G., and T. R. Mitchell. 1976. *Organization Theory: A Structural and Behavioral Analysis*. Homewood, IL: Richard D. Irwin.

Stoner, J. A. and C. Wankel. 1986. *Management*. Englewood Cliffs, NJ: Prentice-Hall, pp. 233–234.

SUGGESTED READINGS

BOOKS

Levine, K. 2004. *A Survival Guide for Hotel and Motel Professionals*. New York: Delmar Learning.

Nebel, E. C. III. 1991. *Managing Hotels Effectively: Lessons from Outstanding General Managers*. New York: Van Nostrand Reinhold.

ARTICLES

Pondy, L. R. 1967. "Organizational Conflict: Concepts and Models." *Administrative Science Quarterly* 12:296–320.

Schaffer, J. D. 1984. "Strategy, Organization Structure, and Success in the Lodging Industry." *International Journal of Hospitality Management* 3(4):159–165.

Schaffer, J. D. 1985. "A Dynamic Model of Organizational Performance in the Lodging Industry: The Role of Competitive Strategy and Organization Structure." *Proceedings*. CHRIE Conference, Seattle, WA, pp. 168–173.

SOURCE NOTES

Chapter 2.2, "Organizational Design," by E. C. Nebel III.

Chapter 2.3, "As I See It: Hotel Organization Structure" by Mark Conklin.

CHAPTER THREE

GENERAL MANAGERS: A VIEW AT THE TOP

3.1 INTRODUCTION

In most companies, an individual who has attained the title of general manager (GM), or something similar, heads the organization. Most of us in the hotel field consider this job the pinnacle of one's career. In many hotel companies, the job serves as the springboard to corporate jobs or larger and more prestigious properties.

In previous editions of this book, it was noted how surprising it is that so little has been written about hotel general managers. Little structured attention was paid to the development of their careers and the skills and strengths they bring to their jobs. Strangely, this is still the case.

A 1981 article by M. J. Arnaldo presented a statistical profile of hotel general managers. Arnaldo drew a demographic picture of his sample ($n = 194$) and commented that, although GMs changed jobs frequently, they reported a high degree of job satisfaction. He also provided an ana-

lytical framework for reporting how these GMs allocated time and importance to a number of classic managerial roles. The most important of the managerial roles ranked by the GMs were (in descending importance): leader, entrepreneur, monitor, and disseminator, with six others (figurehead, liaison, spokesman, disturbance handler, resource allocator, and negotiator) assuming less importance (see also Mintzberg, 1973).

Readers of Arnaldo's article may be struck by the similarities that echo in Nebel and Ghei's contribution here. Another useful comparison can be made by reading Arnaldo's work with that of David Ley (1978). This work, based on a small sample of seven GMs in comparable properties in one hotel company, recorded how much time the GMs allocated to the same managerial work roles (Mintzberg, 1973). The difference here was that Ley asked for a corporate office rating of each

GM's effectiveness. He compared the effectiveness ratings (highly effective, effective, and less effective) to the observed time allocations of the GMs to leadership and entrepreneurial activities. Ley concluded that in this small group, the more effective managers spent more time on entrepreneurial activities than leadership activities. In contrast, Arnaldo's much larger group of GMs devoted much more time to leadership than entrepreneurship. This should suggest to the reader some interesting questions about what sorts of activities might best prepare future GMs for that role.

This makes the Nebel and Ghei piece all the more interesting. Although the number of individuals who participated in the study was relatively small, the GMs were studied intensely. An important contribution of the study is the structural framework from which to view the job of a GM. Simply speaking, it is a hotel general manager theory that can be used to explain, predict, or control the position of GM.

A central aspect of career development among GMs is explored by Rutherford and Wiegenstein (1985), which looked for the first time at the role of mentoring as it could be measured to affect the success and satisfaction of a modern hotel GM's career.

Although the demographic, salary, and operational data in that article are out of date, the focus of the research can still be useful to those who aspire to the top job in a hotel organization. Also, because the literature on hotel GMs is so sparse, the insights gained from the managers studied in this case add flesh and tone to the work of the other authors included in this section. In the mentoring research, Rutherford and Wiegenstein conclude that there is ample evidence that seeking out and developing mentoring relationships can have a positive effect

on several aspects of a GM's career. The full reference for this article can be found in the suggested readings section at the end of this chapter.

Another view of the career and personal aspects of the GM's job is discussed by Pavesic and Brymer (1990). In a number of studies, they examined how job satisfaction and stress affect managerial careers. In a review of this technical research, the authors interpret the behavioral dimensions of the GM's career, work values, and personal challenges. Hotel careers are challenging, but as these researchers point out, they do not have to be arduous.

In the research reported by Woods, Rutherford, Schmidgall, and Sciarini (1998), they sought answers to questions regarding the importance of various operational measures, and at the same time asked GMs for suggestions about the structure of a hotel-related education. Students reading this article find solid suggestions from successful GMs, as the sample for the study was drawn from mostly upscale and luxury hotels with more than 500 rooms. Much of the financial data are out of date, but many of the conclusions are still viable (please see suggested readings for full article information).

In an interesting newer article, Beth Chung-Herrera and her colleagues study the specific skills and competencies demonstrated by successful hotel leaders. The model they develop can be useful to hotel organizations, schools, and professionals crafting the structure of successful careers.

Speaking of success, the two professionals who contribute their thoughts on the job of GM have attained that level in separate areas of the country and for different types of organizations.

Tom Underwood is the GM of the full service Marriott in Richmond, VA—a White

Lodging property. His property is a business/convention hotel, which offers different challenges for Mr. Underwood. He brings forth his "typical" day, which usually begins at 7:00 A.M. and does not usually end until 6:00 P.M. In this article, the reader will be able to see what it takes to be a GM from a different perspective.

When this article was written, Nicholas R. DiMeglio was the GM of The Ritz-Carlton Club, Aspen Highlands. Since then, Mr. DiMeglio has been promoted to the position of vice president of The Ritz-Carlton Club operations, where he now oversees multiple properties. In his article, Mr. DiMeglio provides the reader with a snapshot of Ritz-Carlton and his duties as GM of a single property.

From an academic standpoint, the Nebel and Ghei contribution, coupled with the piece by Chung-Herrera et al., can be considered the overarching theory guiding the hotel GM's job. Underwood and DiMeglio provide us with the insights and views of insiders and with clear evidence that the theory actually works in practice. This is our goal for this edition of this book: to provide the reader with the opportunity to see that there should be a connection between the book learning of the classroom and what happens in the real world.

3.2 A CONCEPTUAL FRAMEWORK OF THE HOTEL GENERAL MANAGER'S JOB EDDYSTONE C. NEBEL III AND AJAY GHEI

ABSTRACT. This article, based on the research of one of the authors into hotel general managers' effectiveness, presents the viewpoint that the job of a hotel general manager can be better understood by analyzing the influences that shape it. The two major contextual elements that influence the job are deemed to be job demands and relationship issues. They differ depending on the time frame (short-run, intermediate-run, or long-run) under consideration. These two elements give rise to specific job functions and concomitantly suggest various managerial work roles that must be performed in each job function. Finally, the importance of the communications requirement for being effective in the job is emphasized. Keywords: Job demands, relationship issues, time frame, job functions, managerial work roles, communications requirement.

Major hotels of today are diverse, multifaceted, and fast-paced businesses engaged in a wide variety of operational activities. Their organizational and operational complexity increases with size. A hotel, irrespective of whether it is an independent or part of a chain, can be managed as a separate, independent business entity. Thus, each individual hotel can, in effect, be treated as a unique profit center. While it takes more than one person to effectively manage a hotel, the executive with overall operational responsibility for this business is the general manager (GM) of the hotel. "The general manager is the key implementer of the business strategy for the property and the behavioral role model for the entire management team" (Eder and Umbreit, 1989, 333). It can thus be argued that the GM is the central management figure in the hotel business. The demands and challenges of managing hotels are reflected in the complexities of the GM's job.

This article takes a close look at the context in which GMs of major hotels work and how this context affects the nature of their job. It is based on the research of one of the authors (Nebel, 1991) into the managerial effectiveness of hotel GMs. The purpose of the research was, in part, to better understand the nature of the GM's job, and through this understanding develop a conceptual framework of it. As Dann (1990) has stated, "[T]here is now a need to . . . develop a conceptual framework for the better understanding of the actual nature of managerial work in the hospitality industry."

Ten extremely successful GMs of some of America's finest hotels agreed to participate in the study. Each of the GMs studied was an experienced, top-rated hotel executive with an average of ten years' experience in the position. One research goal was to study hotels that exhibited the fullest range of operational and managerial complexity. Thus, the smallest participating hotel was an internationally renowned luxury property of about 400 rooms, and the largest was a great convention hotel of nearly 2000 rooms. The author stayed as a guest at each hotel, observed each GM for three days as he proceeded through his normal workday,

and recorded his every activity. The research methodology followed closely that employed by Kotter (1982). It employed a combination of participant observation of GMs at work, extensive personal interviews with both the GMs and 53 of their key division heads, background surveys, and analysis of organizational and operational information from each hotel. The personal interviews extended over a number of days and took between four and six hours with each GM, and about one hour with each of their division heads. In addition, informal interviews were conducted with at least 100 other executives and employees of the ten hotels. The field research was conducted while the author was on sabbatical leave and resulted in over 700 pages of field notes, which were subjected to extensive qualitative data analysis.

From this analysis and from an exhaustive review of the literature on managerial work in hotels (Guerrier, 1987; Guerrier and Lockwood, 1991; Koepper, 1988; Ley, 1978; Shortt, 1989; Umbreit, 1986) there has emerged a view of the hotel GM's job that is given in Figure 3.1, which presents a model of the influences that shape the job. The model incorporates ideas found in the research of Kotter (1982) and Mintzberg (1973). Kotter (1982, 10–33) showed how job demands and relationship demands affect executive behavior. Mintzberg (1973, 55–99) described ten separate work roles that managers perform. Figure 3.1 reflects how the hotel context influences the various job functions and managerial work roles GMs must perform in order to be effective.

The two major contextual elements of the GM's job that affect the specific job functions and the generic managerial work roles are job demands and relationship issues. These, depending on whether they relate to the short-run, the

Figure 3.1 Influences That Shape the General Manager's Job

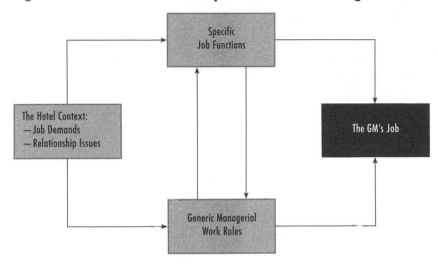

intermediate-run, or the long-run time frame, give rise to certain specific job functions. They also suggest, in general, the various managerial work roles GMs are required to perform. It is the symbiosis of these specific GM job functions and the generic managerial work roles that actually defines the GM's job. We now proceed to discuss each of the elements described in Figure 3.1.

✦ JOB DEMANDS AND RELATIONSHIP ISSUES

Table 3.1 lists key GM job demands and relationship issues according to whether they relate to a hotel's short-run, intermediate-run, or long-run time frame. The structure for this table is adapted from Kotter's study of managerial behavior (Kotter, 1982, 10–33).

Table 3.1 Key Job Demands and Relationship Issues of Hotel GMs

TIME FRAME	KEY JOB DEMANDS	KEY RELATIONSHIP ISSUES
Short Run	Day-to-day operational control of service, costs, and revenues. Intense pressure to earn profits and render high-quality service.	Intense and frequent downward, internal verbal communication and interaction with hotel subordinates.
Intermediate Run	Train and develop subordinates. Fine-tune hotel's service strategy to changing external environment. Develop and refine the organization structure.	Downward internal communication. Lateral communication with the external environment. Upward communication with corporate superiors and staff specialists or owners.
Long Run	Capital expenditure decisions in line with hotel's strategic service vision. Develop and sustain organizational stability and vitality.	Downward internal communication to further stability and vitality. Lateral communication with the external environment. Intense upward communication with corporate office or owners.

✦ THE SHORT RUN

The short-run demands on hotel GMs revolve around the daily, ongoing operational issues of providing high-quality guest service, controlling costs, and maximizing revenues. Hotel GMs bear direct responsibility for their properties and thus, like operational managers in charge of profit centers anywhere, are under tremendous pressure to produce short-run results. They must, therefore, devote a substantial amount of their time and efforts toward exercising effective operational control. An important functional characteristic of hotels is that many of their day-to-day business problems have extremely short lead times. That is to say, most service-centered problems in hotels must be solved quickly or not at all. Moreover, major hotels are both organizationally and operationally complex businesses in which numerous, highly diverse activities take place constantly as well as concomitantly.

To stay on top of this complicated short-lead-time business is unquestionably the single most challenging and demanding aspect of the GM's job. To be able to do so effectively and in a proactive manner so as to retain the ability to influence events, GMs must engage in intense verbal communication and interact frequently with subordinates. In discharging these responsibilities, a hotel GM can be said to be performing the job function of operational controller. However, the heavy workload of short-run operational demands must not take up all the time of GMs, as they must also concentrate on intermediate-run and long-run demands and issues as well.

✦ THE INTERMEDIATE RUN

In addition to their involvement in daily operational issues, effective GMs must train and develop subordinates as well as formulate plans and programs that systematically improve their operational control over the hotel. As changes take place in the external environment, GMs must adapt and fine-tune the hotel's service strategy and organizational structure on an ongoing basis to keep abreast of these changes. These initiatives represent a proactive response to the operational demands of the business; they take time to implement and constitute the bulk of intermediate-run demands faced by a hotel GM. These intermediate-run demands, then, involve putting into place a hotel's organizational structure, systems, and people who are capable of quick and effective response to external stimuli and who can simultaneously help the hotel meet its demanding daily operational commitments. Thus, in effect, the GM is fine-tuning the hotel's service strategy and refining and realigning its operating systems to ensure a smoothly functioning business.

All these efforts require intense, downward internal communication and a high degree of interaction with subordinates. In addition, intermediate-run job demands require the GM to develop communication channels and to nurture relationships that extend beyond the specific domain of the hotel. These relationships include, first, a wide-ranging network of hospitality industry and community contacts who can help the GM better understand the hotel's external environment; and, second, the GM's corporate superiors and staff specialists, whose cooperation is needed for the successful implementation of the formulated specific plans and programs for the hotel. In carrying out these responsibilities, the job function of a hotel GM can be referred to as that of organizational developer.

✦ THE LONG RUN

Two important long-run demands of a GM's job relate to the capital needs and the organizational stability of the hotel. Capital expenditure decisions are required in order to ensure the long-run viability of the hotel, and they, therefore, must be consistent with the hotel's strategic service vision. The other important long-run demand on GMs is the need to develop a degree of organizational stability and vitality that is in tune with the hotel's carefully planned and clearly defined strategic service vision.

The key relationship issues for long-run capital expenditure decisions are communications upward with corporate executives or owners and laterally with an assortment of industry and community contacts as sources for intelligence concerning the hotel's competitive operating environment. Developing organizational stability depends on ongoing programs of human resources training and development and of sequential career progression. Many of the human resource programs that foster intermediate-run goals ultimately benefit long-run organizational stability and vitality.

Organizational stability enables a hotel to consistently deliver high-quality service and effectively control day-to-day operations. Organizational stability and vitality also gives the hotel the maturity and experience required for it to rethink its basic marketing and service strategies in the event of altered market or environmental conditions. Finally, stability permits the hotel to make any required transition with minimal disruption to its regular operational practices. Key relationship issues associated with organizational stability include continual monitoring of the external environment and intensive downward communication within the hotel. In fulfilling these responsibilities, the GM's job function can be described as that of business maintainer.

✦ ROLES PLAYED BY A GENERAL MANAGER

This section is organized around Mintzberg's study (1973), in which he suggested ten generic work roles for managers. Mintzberg grouped these ten work roles into three broad categories: interpersonal, informational, and decisional. Interpersonal work roles included those of figurehead, leader, and liaison; informational work roles covered those of monitor, disseminator, and spokesperson; and decisional work roles were those of disturbance handler, entrepreneur, resource allocator, and negotiator. A brief description of these generic managerial work roles is given in Table 3.2 on the next page.

The influence of Mintzberg's work is reflected in the studies of hotel GMs by Arnaldo (1981) and Ley (1978) and that of restaurant managers by Ferguson and Berger (1984). The previous section explained how job demands and relationship issues had an impact on the job functions of GMs. It was from that discussion that we proposed the three specific GM job functions of operational controller, organizational developer, and business maintainer. Each of these three job functions requires GMs to perform various managerial work roles in order to be successful. Combining the various managerial work roles with the specific job functions helps provide a clearer understanding of the GM's job. These relationships are shown in Table 3.3 on page 97.

Although the GMs studied were observed performing each of Mintzberg's ten managerial work roles, the interpersonal roles of leader and liaison, the informational roles of monitor and

Table 3.2 General Managerial Work Roles

WORK ROLE	DESCRIPTION
Interpersonal	
Figurehead	Symbolic head of the organization. Required to perform certain legal activities and attend to social activities.
Leader	Responsible for staffing, training, direction, and motivation of subordinates.
Liaison	Develops a network outside the organization to gather information.
Informational	
Monitor	Seeks and analyzes a wide variety of outside information (from liaison role) and inside information (from leader role).
Disseminator	Transmits information received both from outside and inside the organization to other members of the organization.
Spokesperson	Transmits information about the organization to outsiders.
Decisional	
Disturbance Handler	Takes corrective action whenever organization faces unexpected, nonroutine disturbances.
Entrepreneur	Looks for ways to change the organization for the better. Seeks information externally and internally for improvement ideas. Initiates and supervises improvement projects.
Resource Allocator	Responsible for allocating all important resources of the organization, both financial and human, including how the manager schedules own time, programs work, and authorizes actions.
Negotiator	Responsible for the organization's major outside negotiations.

disseminator, and the decisional roles of disturbance handler, entrepreneur, and resource allocator were found to be of particular significance. These roles were performed regularly as GMs carried out their various job functions. We now proceed to describe the managerial work roles most often performed by GMs while discharging their three primary job functions.

✦ MANAGERIAL WORK ROLES AS OPERATIONAL CONTROLLER

The GM's work as operational controller is characterized by a high degree of involvement in the daily operations of the hotel. Because the activities of a hotel are both numerous and diverse, GMs must be constantly monitoring and disseminating

detailed information pertaining to daily operational matters. Time and again throughout the course of the working day, GMs interact with subordinates to stay on top of the numerous operational problems that occur. GMs must also be available to effectively and quickly handle disturbances that are not covered by a hotel's routine procedures or those that subordinates perceive as being beyond their scope of authority or experience. In order to effectively play this managerial work role of disturbance handler, GMs must have rapid access to reliable internal information and, in turn, be able to quickly process and disseminate this information downward in the organization. While functioning as operational controller, the GM's work role as resource allocator revolves mostly around the

Table 3.3 Combining Managerial Work Roles and Job Functions in Defining the GM's Job

TIME HORIZON	GM JOB FUNCTION	GM MANAGERIAL ROLES
Short Run	Operational Controller	• Monitor and Disseminator (of internal information) • Disturbance Handler • Resource Allocator (of own time) • Leader
Intermediate Run	Organizational Developer	• Liaison • Monitor and Disseminator (of both external and internal information) • Entrepreneur • Resource Allocator (of own time, programs, and funds) • Leader
Long Run	Business Maintainer	• Liaison • Monitor and Disseminator (of external and internal information) • Resource Allocator (of programs and funds) • Entrepreneur • Leader

allocation of his or her own time to the numerous short-run demands of the job. GMs can, of course, allocate a proportion of their hotel's financial and human resources to help solve short-run operational problems, but it is the manner in which they allocate their own scarce time that is of paramount importance when referring to the short-run operational problems of the job.

GMs perform the leader role in every contact with subordinates. Every action of a GM is analyzed and interpreted by subordinates; thus, every interaction with subordinates provides GMs with an opportunity to exercise leadership (Hales and Nightingale, 1986). That is why outstanding GMs realize they are constantly in the limelight throughout the working day. GMs also exercise leadership by deciding the operational issues on which to concentrate. Subordinates automatically look for clues regarding what GMs deem important; thus, by deciding which operational issues to focus on, GMs send an unequivocal message downward in the organization regarding what they consider important.

✦ MANAGERIAL WORK ROLES AS ORGANIZATIONAL DEVELOPER

The managerial work roles of GMs as organizational developers extend beyond the immediate confines of the hotel. GMs must monitor information about both the community and the competitive environment, and this requires them to become a liaison between the hotel and the outside world. Further, the information GMs gather from the external environment must be analyzed and disseminated to subordinates within the hotel. GMs must process both externally and internally obtained information in order to effectively play the work role of entrepreneur, the importance of which has been stressed by Ley (1978). As entrepreneurs, GMs are the developers of specific plans and programs geared to improving the operating efficiency and service strategy of the hotel. Any new plan or program imposes additional time obligations on both the GM and on subordinates. New plans and programs often involve the allocation of financial and human resources as well. Therefore, in the course of developing and implementing these specific plans and programs for the hotel, GMs play the decisional work role of resource allocator.

Finally, GMs continue in the leader work role by virtue of, first, continuing relationships with subordinates as an integral component of the job, and, second, by choosing specific plans and programs to implement. As leaders, GMs must contend with the challenge of ensuring that subordinates fully accept the plans and programs outlined for the hotel and are committed to working toward their successful implementation. This requires that GMs pay careful attention to their work roles of monitor and disseminator of information.

✦ MANAGERIAL WORK ROLES AS BUSINESS MAINTAINER

The final job function of business maintainer requires the GM to see to the long-run capital requirements and organizational stability and vitality of the hotel. In seeking capital and planning a strategy for organizational stability and vitality, the GM's work roles of liaison, monitor, and disseminator of external and internal information upward to corporate executives or owners are critical, as is the work role of allocator of scarce financial re-

sources. The resource allocator role, more often than not, requires detailed presentation of formal budget proposals that include careful financial justification. This is especially true if the GM is proposing a major directional shift in the service strategy of the hotel. As maintainer of organizational stability, the GM also plays the work role of disseminator of important information downward to subordinates. The GM must act as entrepreneur with respect to important human resource development plans and programs, and, as with all activities, continue as leader in the ongoing role of nurturing and developing managerial talent.

While GMs perform three job functions with different time horizons, it is not necessarily the case that these job functions are performed independently of each other. That is to say, it is altogether possible for GMs to perform two or even all three job functions simultaneously. It is clear from Table 3.3 that many of the Mintzbergian managerial work roles are common to more than one job function. In fact, the work roles of monitor, disseminator, resource allocator, and leader are common to all three, while those of liaison and entrepreneur are common to two of the job functions. Thus, when GMs are engaged with short-run operational concerns, they often do so in the context of longer-run considerations. For example, while responding to a short-run operational problem of slow guest check-ins—that is, functioning as operational controller—a GM may simultaneously be monitoring and evaluating the effectiveness of a front desk clerk training program—that is, functioning as organizational developer. The GM may also be formulating a long-run plan to purchase an advanced front office computer system—that is, functioning as business maintainer. The actual manner in which effective GMs perform this delicate balancing act is covered later in the text.

✦ CONCLUSION

A hotel GM's job can be better understood by examining the contextual variables that influence and help shape it. A hotel's context presents GMs with a series of job demands and relationship issues with which they must deal effectively in order to be successful. As seen, these job demands and relationship issues differ depending on the time frame under consideration. These considerations give rise to specific job functions that GMs perform through a variety of work roles.

In the short run, the GM job function was described as that of operational controller. Here, GMs are involved with the day-to-day internal operational control of their business, requiring intense and frequent downward verbal communication within the hotel. They must be adept at the managerial work roles of monitoring and disseminating a wide variety of internal information, handling nonroutine disturbances, and allocating their own scarce time to important operational issues.

In the intermediate run, the GM job function was described as that of organizational developer. Here, GMs face the challenges of developing subordinates, formulating specific plans and programs to improve their operational control of the hotel, and fine-tuning the hotel's service strategy in the context of external environmental conditions. In addition to internal downward communication, these challenges require intense lateral communication with both the hotel industry and local community sources. This helps the GM stay abreast of market and environmental trends. The GM also maintains upward communication with corporate superiors and staff specialists to ensure

their cooperation in the successful implementation of operational plans and programs. Here, GMs' work roles require them to monitor and disseminate external as well as internal information, so they act as liaison between the hotel and the outside world.

They also may initiate, as entrepreneurs would, plans and programs designed to improve the hotel's operational and organizational efficiency. This requires the allocation of their own time, as well as the financial and human resources of the hotel, to these plans and programs.

In the long run, the GM's job function was described as that of business maintainer. Here, GMs must ensure the long-term viability of the hotel through capital expenditure decisions that are consistent with the hotel's strategic service vision, and by developing a degree of organizational stability that allows the hotel to carry out its strategic plan. Intense upward communication to corporate superiors, staff specialists, and owners, as well as lateral communication with a wide variety of industry and community contacts, highlight the relationship issues of this job function. GMs are required to play the work role of liaison between the hotel and corporate office or owners as well as industry and community sources. This involves monitoring the widest variety of external and internal information and disseminating it laterally, downward, and upward. In addition, GMs play both the work roles of resource allocator of capital funds and of entrepreneur when seeing to the organizational stability of the business. All three job functions require GMs to be leaders, a work role they play through every contact with subordinates. Finally, these job functions need not and often are not performed independently of each other.

Three important conclusions about the GM's job can be drawn from this analysis:

1. By their nature, major hotels of today provide GMs with a variety of challenges that require careful attention be paid to short-run, intermediate-run, and long-run time frame issues. Thus, GMs must be able to successfully carry out three separate and different job functions. They must be effective as operational controllers, organizational developers, and business maintainers if they are to enjoy long-term success as effective GMs.

2. To be effective at all three job functions requires that GMs perform a large variety of managerial work roles. While GMs perform all ten of Mintzberg's managerial work roles, they must be particularly effective at seven of them to be successful operational controllers, organizational developers, and business maintainers. They must develop the wide variety of skills necessary to play the work roles of leader, liaison, monitor, disseminator, disturbance handler, entrepreneur, and resource allocator.

3. The importance of communications in the hotel GM's job becomes apparent from this analysis. Every job function and every managerial work role carries with it a communications requirement. GMs must be adept at gathering, analyzing, and disseminating external and internal information, and they must be able to effectively communicate laterally, downward, and upward. Without good communication skills, GMs cannot possibly be effective in any of their three job functions (Worsfold, 1989).

Today's major hotels are complex businesses engaged in a wide variety of activities. The demands of managing these businesses are reflected in the complexities of the GM's job. To be effective, hotel GMs must understand the key job demands and relationship issues hotels thrust upon them. They must perform three separate job functions that relate to different time frames. To do this, they must become adept at a number of managerial work roles, depending on the job function they are performing. Finally, hotel GMs must become accomplished communicators if they are to effectively meet the variety of challenges they face.

3.3 GROOMING FUTURE HOSPITALITY LEADERS: A COMPETENCIES MODEL BETH G. CHUNG-HERRERA, CATHY A. ENZ, AND MELENIE J. LANKAU

The ability to identify the skills and competencies required for tomorrow's industry leaders is essential for companies that hope to remain competitive. Some firms, such as Marriott International and Choice (Enz and Siguaw, 2000) have made identifying leadership competencies a priority. Identifying appropriate competencies helps senior managers in selecting, developing, and coaching future leaders, as well as mapping career paths and planning management succession. In this article, we present a leadership-competency model that is industry specific and future based. Our goal in creating this model was to provide the hospitality industry with a functional-competency model that: 1) organizations can use to develop their own model for leadership development, 2) employees can use to understand the competencies they need for advancement, 3) hospitality schools can use to design curriculum, and 4) students can use to craft career paths. We first describe the nature and use of competency models and then describe our study. We examine the critical competencies that we found to be important (and those that, surprisingly, are not as important). Last, we consider the possible uses for the industry-wide model that we have developed.

✦ COMPETENCY MODELS

A competency model is a descriptive tool that identifies the knowledge, skills, abilities, and behavior needed to perform effectively in an organization (Lucia and Lepsinger, 1999). Designed to help an organization meet its strategic objectives through building human-resources capability, competency modeling has been in existence since the 1970s, starting with the first models created by David McClelland (Mirabile, 1997, 73–77). Such models gained popularity in the late 1980s and remain in use today.

Competency models focus on behavior rather than on personality traits, because personality traits are usually hard to measure accurately (Lucia and Lepsinger, 1999; ACA's Competencies Research Team, 1996, 6–21). Expressing desirable traits in behavioral terms is essential for a competency model to be useful as a human-resources tool, because the model must not only define the competencies necessary for effective performance but also indicate how to tell when a particular competency is being demonstrated. Most competency models express traits and characteristics

in behavioral terms on the grounds that behavior is the observable manifestation of personality traits and characteristics. Competencies are deemed critical for inclusion in a model when they distinguish superior performers from poor performers.

Competency models are less specific than is the job analysis typically performed for specific positions, and models can encompass a whole family of jobs. Choice Hotels International, for example, developed competency models for each of the top four levels of its organization (i.e., senior vice president, vice president, senior director, and director). In so doing, the company found that the competencies for success of a senior vice president were similar to those needed for the other three positions.

✦ USING COMPETENCY MODELS

Competency models provide a common language for discussing capabilities and performance. The development of a competency model can help provide guidance for a host of different HR practices and ensure that those practices are consistent. Specifically, competency models can be used as a foundation from which to establish criteria for a broad array of HR systems (McLagan, 1996, 60–65; Lucia and Lepsinger, 1999). For instance, listed below are eight HR activities that can be guided or enhanced with the use of a well-developed competency model.

1. *Recruitment and selection.* Looking beyond skills to performance dimensions such as teamwork, competency models can help to establish what it takes to do well on the job. Armed with this information, companies can focus recruitment dollars on finding the greatest number of prospective employees who have the right mix of

competencies for the job in question. The content of appropriate selection instruments (e.g., structured interviews, role plays) can target the key competencies—and, hence, the whole package of needed skills and abilities. Beyond their usefulness in improving selection tools, competency models also provide candidates with a clear and realistic picture of expected behavior.

2. *Training and development.* Assessing gaps between existing employee skills and those identified by a competency model can be extremely useful in devising a long-term strategic plan for leadership training and development. Identification of the skills needed to perform effectively makes it easier to ensure that the design and delivery of training are aligned with the organization's objectives. When a competency model is used as the foundation for training objectives, individual leadership gaps can be assessed and a training plan devised to address deficiencies.

3. *Performance appraisals.* Performance-management systems can be enhanced by a competency model that provides a shared set of expectations regarding what is important and what will be monitored and measured. Competency models help managers to focus performance-appraisal discussions on critical aspects of behavior, thus providing a strategic tool for consistent and meaningful evaluation.

4. *Coaching, counseling, and mentoring.* Competency models are often used as the basis for 360-degree feedback, in which a manager receives performance information from all relevant sources (including supervisor, subordinates, self, peers, and customers, if applicable). Coaches and advisers can use the information so gathered to guide the employee in design-

ing a development plan and making critical-skill improvements. The clarity and specificity of competency models enable coaches and mentors to reinforce desired behavior and tie performance-management systems to necessary competencies.

5. *Reward systems.* A tremendous percentage of a hospitality organization's operating expenses is devoted to employee compensation. To attract, retain, and motivate employees, reward systems must be equitable and linked to desired behavior. Competency models can be extremely useful for defining the behavior that will be rewarded.

6. *Career development.* For employees who aspire to reach the next level on a career path, a competency model serves as a map. Competency models make employees aware of the behavior and skills needed to advance and achieve success, allowing them to prepare accordingly.

7. *Succession planning.* Competency models can be used to identify possible successors for critical jobs by clarifying the requirements for the job and providing a method for assessing a particular candidate's readiness. Without a clear understanding of the competencies needed by future leaders, it is difficult for a firm to measure its "bench strength"—that is, to determine whether the organization has people with those capabilities and, if it does, who they are.

8. *Change management.* Organizations can work toward an uncertain future by creating models that are based on competencies that may be necessary for future leaders, as well as competencies needed for current operations.

Competency models confer several advantages on a company. First, a competency model is useful for building an integrated framework for developing a company's human-resources system. Used consistently, such a model should lead to improved and consistent performance standards. More important, the model can be a critical guide during periods of instability and change. Moreover, making HR decisions on the basis of carefully developed competency models reduces legal challenges to those decisions. (Note: Include specific competencies in the job description to reduce legal liability, especially if the competencies will be used for performance appraisals.) Finally, well-developed competency models enhance a company's ability to communicate with its employees regarding the behavior connected with success, thereby increasing the firm's ability to achieve its business objectives (ACA's Competencies Research Team, 1996).

✦ LEADER COMPETENCIES FOR THE LODGING INDUSTRY

With point number 8 in mind, we sought to devise a future-oriented leadership-competency model for the lodging industry. We consider this endeavor to be important given the absence of an industry-focused model that works across many organizations. (Our research found no current models for hospitality leadership.) Having an industry-wide model is important because it can inform students and employees alike about the expectations for future leaders as identified by senior-level managers. Furthermore, an industry-wide model helps to paint a comprehensive picture of the critical skills needed by the entire industry, thereby assisting senior managers in hotel organizations as they devise and implement their recruitment, selection, and development systems.

Looking ahead. We focused our competency model on managerial behavior that industry executives anticipated would be needed ten years from now. We wanted a model that could be used as a prototype to guide people's aspirations in the coming years and to create future leaders. Asking leaders to focus on the future is a common approach when building competency models, although the resulting model may not identify all necessary competencies (given that one cannot see the future). (Note: Firms including PDI, DDI, and Hay Management employ forecasting techniques. We used the linkage systems method, asking participants to forecast future important behaviors; see Linkage, 1997.) The essential limitation in asking current leaders to project future competencies is that they may be unable or unwilling to define the future differently from the present. However, many thoughtful executives are able to envision and plan for a future that is not simply a reflection of the present, highlighting behavior that they see as increasingly important.

Using a number of different competency studies (Mirabile, 1985; Evarts, 1988; Zingheim, Ledford, and Shuster, 1996; Blancero, Boroski, and Dyer, 1996) as a starting point, we constructed a provisional behavioral-competency model that captured the most important dimensions of leaders' behavior across several industries. Using this preliminary model, we refined the components through hospitality managers' feedback, developing the competency model by means of the customized generic model method (Dubois, 1993). We collected managers' comments by surveying individuals from around the globe who participated in senior-level executive-education programs at Cornell University. In our pilot survey, respondents could add other competencies that they felt were becoming increasingly important and eliminate those items that they deemed inappropriate.

Based on the feedback from the pilot study, we modified the competency model to reflect hospitality-specific behavior. In this fashion, we arrived at a final competency model consisting of 8 overarching factors, 28 dimensions, and 99 specific behavioral competencies. The factors and dimensions were derived from the literature on competency models and through hospitality managers' feedback. The eight overarching factors are communication, critical thinking, implementation, industry knowledge, interpersonal skills, leadership, self-management, and strategic positioning. Each of those factors comprised up to six dimensions that captured various aspects of that factor. Leadership, for example, is composed

of the following six dimensions: developing others, embracing change, fortitude, fostering motivation, leadership versatility, and teamwork orientation. As another example, Table 3.4 shows the behavioral items and dimensions for the self-management factor.

We listed the 99 hospitality competencies (Table 3.5) in a survey that was faxed worldwide to 735 senior-level industry executives at various hotel companies. Using a five-point Likert-type scale ranging from 1 (not at all important) to 5 (extremely important), respondents were asked to rate the importance of each of the 99 competencies or skills for a senior-level manager ten years from now (see the accompanying list). A total of

Table 3.4 Self-Management: Dimensions of a Competency Factor

FACTOR	SELF-MANAGEMENT			
DIMENSIONS	**ETHICS AND INTEGRITY**	**TIME MANAGEMENT**	**SELF-DEVELOPMENT**	**FLEXIBILITY AND ADAPTABILITY**
Characteristics	Acts in an ethical manner.	Effectively handles multiple demands and competing priorities.	Deals constructively with own failures and setbacks.	Adapts to changing circumstances.
	Treats people fairly.	Manages time to ensure productivity.	Seeks feedback from others.	Works constructively under stress and pressure.
	Treats people with respect.	Spends time on the most important issues, not just the most urgent ones.	Adjusts behavior in response to feedback and experience.	Works effectively in ambiguous situations.
	Displays consistency between words and actions.		Pursues continual learning and self-development.	Views problems as opportunities and mistakes as progress.
	Considers ethical implications prior to taking action.		Demonstrates awareness of own strengths and weaknesses.	
	Protects confidential information.			

Table 3.5 99 Lodging Competencies

(1) Anticipates obstacles and develops contingency plans.

(2) Adapts to changing circumstances.

(3) Manages time to ensure productivity.

(4) Monitors progress of others and redirects efforts when necessary.

(5) Works effectively in ambiguous situations.

(6) Prepares people to understand changes.

(7) Seeks feedback from others.

(8) Works toward win-win solutions with others whenever possible.

(9) Steers conflicts away from personalities and toward issues.

(10) Provides employees access to information.

(11) Takes a stand when resolving important issues.

(12) Integrates planning efforts across work groups or functional units.

(13) Displays consistency between words and actions.

(14) Identifies measurable action steps that support the hotel's strategy and mission.

(15) Works constructively under stress and pressure.

(16) Acts in an ethical manner.

(17) Presents ideas in a convincing manner.

(18) Expresses disagreement in a tactful and sensitive manner.

(19) Treats people with respect.

(20) Considers a broad range of factors (internal, external, and trends) when solving problems and making decisions.

(21) Translates business strategies into clear objectives and tactics.

(22) Brings together different perspectives and approaches and combines them in creative ways.

(23) Summarizes and clarifies what people say to ensure understanding.

(24) Coaches others in skill development.

(25) Challenges others to make tough choices.

(26) Works to understand why others resist change instead of forcing others to accept change.

(27) Accurately identifies strengths and weaknesses in others.

(28) Stays informed about industry practices and new developments.

(29) Examines and monitors trends in the hotel business.

(30) Understands the agendas and perspectives of owners, staff members, managers, and other parties.

(31) Clarifies expectations to staff members about assignments, roles, and responsibilities.

(32) Selects leadership style most appropriate for the situation.

(33) Provides challenging assignments to facilitate development.

(34) Applies cross-functional knowledge to understand and solve problems.

(35) Expresses confidence in people's competence to do their jobs.

(36) Addresses and works through conflict.

(37) Interacts with people in a direct and open manner.

(38) Views problems as opportunities and mistakes as progress.

(39) Works to establish strong relationships with owners.

(40) Understands and harnesses individual differences to create a competitive advantage.

(41) Develops action plans to meet customer needs.

(42) Reduces redundancies in processes and procedures.

(43) Gives specific, timely, and constructive feedback.

(44) Adjusts behavior in response to feedback and experience.

(45) Models the changes expected of others.

(46) Considers alternatives before making decisions.

(47) Listens to people without interrupting.

(48) Protects confidential information.

(49) Encourages employees to use their initiative to remedy problems when they first occur.

(Continued)

Table 3.5 (*Continued*)

(50) Takes calculated risks when appropriate.

(51) Builds networks with people inside and outside the hotel.

(52) Spends time on the most important issues, not just the most urgent.

(53) Commits organizational resources for community events.

(54) Considers pros and cons of proposed solutions to problems.

(55) Develops new systems or processes for increased efficiency.

(56) Encourages others to express their views, even contrary ones.

(57) Listens carefully to input and concerns expressed by others.

(58) Deals constructively with own failures and mistakes.

(59) Handles multiple demands and competing priorities.

(60) Knows the strengths and weaknesses of competitors.

(61) Defines and sets up quality standards for employees.

(62) Gives others the authority necessary to accomplish their objectives.

(63) Adjusts leadership approach to fit other individuals.

(64) Involves others in critical decisions that affect them.

(65) Understands complex concepts and relationships.

(66) Delegates enough of own work to others.

(67) Identifies and defines problems.

(68) Determines which of many problems may become crises.

(69) Defines priorities for the staff.

(70) Confronts problems early before they become unmanageable.

(71) Works as a member of a team.

(72) Considers ethical implications prior to taking action.

(73) Gets others interested and involved in the change process.

(74) Creates needed systems and procedures to support changes.

(75) Keeps others updated with information.

(76) Considers customer needs when making decisions.

(77) Considers the effects of decisions on community well-being.

(78) Champions new ideas and initiatives.

(79) Focuses on important information without being distracted by unnecessary details.

(80) Employs a team approach to solve problems when appropriate.

(81) Understands owners' and stakeholders' values and how they perceive issues.

(82) Influences and shapes owners' and stakeholders' decisions.

(83) Recognizes and seizes strategic opportunities in the environment.

(84) Promotes respect and appreciation for diversity and individual differences.

(85) Treats people fairly.

(86) Allows others to lead under the appropriate circumstances.

(87) Pursues continual learning and self-development.

(88) Promotes quality initiatives.

(89) Deliberately allows direct reports to use their own methods for completing tasks.

(90) Demonstrates awareness of own strengths and weaknesses.

(91) Understands organizational strengths and weaknesses.

(92) Writes in an effective manner.

(93) Actively and frequently listens directly to customers.

(94) Sees how things fit in the big picture.

(95) Promotes teamwork among groups; discourages us-versus-them thinking.

(96) Inspires and motivates others.

(97) Makes sound decisions under time pressure and with limited resources.

(98) Speaks clearly and articulately in a variety of situations.

(99) Builds partnerships and alliances with community organizations.

137 industry leaders responded either online or via return fax, yielding a response rate of 18.6 percent. Participants' positions ranged from director to CEO or chair of international hotel chains and corporations. Response rates for executive-level employees are notoriously low, and our response rate for this sample was typical for this population (Agle, Mitchell, and Sonnenfeld, 1999).

✦ KEY COMPETENCIES IDENTIFIED

Competency in self-management is the overarching factor that was rated highest by our respondents, followed by knowledge of strategic positioning, implementation skill, and critical thinking. (Table 3.6 summarizes the ratings.) The self-management factor achieved a mean importance score of 4.32 out of 5. This factor consists of four behavioral dimensions, namely: (1) ethics and integrity, (2) time management, (3) flexibility and adaptability, and (4) self-development. Looking at the behavioral dimensions within each competency factor, we found that the behavior of acting ethically or with integrity was the most important to the responding senior leaders. *Post-hoc* Scheffe tests from an analysis of variance revealed that this behavioral dimension of self-management was rated significantly higher than the other three dimensions. The ethics–integrity dimension contains six specific behavioral competencies, such as "Treats people with respect," "Displays consistency between words and actions," and "Considers ethical implications prior to taking action" (see Table 3.4). The overriding importance of ethical behavior is consistent with previous competency models devised by managers outside the lodging industry. (See competency research reports by consulting firms such as Personnel Decisions

International (www.personaldecisions.com) and Center for Creative Leadership (www.ccl.org).) The other specific competencies that fall under the self-management factor are "Works constructively under stress and pressure," "Seeks feedback from others," and "Spends time on the most important issues, not just the most urgent." Overall, self-management skills encompass actions related to the personal characteristics of the leader and how she or he handles himself or herself.

Competency in strategic positioning was the overarching factor considered to be second in importance for future leaders. This factor comprises the following four dimensions: (1) awareness of customer needs, (2) commitment to quality, (3) managing stakeholders, and (4) concern for community. Examples of behaviors that fall under these dimensions include "Influences and shapes owners' and stakeholders' decisions," "Promotes quality initiatives," and "Considers customer needs when making decisions." This factor clearly captures the hospitality industry's service orientation. The senior managers whom we surveyed suggested that future lodging-industry leaders need to be vigilant in their commitment to both quality and the needs of a variety of different stakeholders, including owners, Wall Street, employees, and customers.

Implementation, critical thinking, and communication skills were also deemed "extremely important" by senior managers. Leaders of the future will need to possess a strategic orientation and approach to decision making that permits them to both plan and redesign their organizations. In addition, communicating persuasively, listening, and enabling others will be essential skills for managers hoping to reach senior leadership positions.

Table 3.6 Leadership Competency Model for the Lodging Industry

FACTOR	MEAN	DIMENSION	MEAN
Self-management	4.32	Ethics and integrity	4.58[a]
		Time management	4.28
		Flexibility and adaptability	4.22
		Self-development	4.12
Strategic positioning	4.17	Awareness of customer needs	4.39
		Commitment to quality	4.26
		Managing stakeholders	4.21
		Concern for community	3.67[b]
Implementation	4.16	Planning	4.23[c]
		Directing others	4.15
		Reengineering	4.02
Critical thinking	4.15	Strategic orientation	4.24[d]
		Decision making	4.18
		Analysis	4.17
		Risk taking and innovation	4.03
Communication	4.12	Speaking with impact	4.27
		Facilitating open communication	4.14
		Active listening	4.06
		Written communication	4.06
Interpersonal	4.09	Building networks	4.20[e]
		Managing conflict	4.07
		Embracing diversity	4.01
Leadership	4.09	Teamwork orientation	4.25[f]
		Fostering motivation	4.19
		Fortitude	4.14
		Developing others	4.02
		Embracing change	3.98
		Leadership versatility	3.97
Industry knowledge	4.09	Business and industry expertise	4.09

a. "Ethics and integrity" scored significantly higher than the other three dimensions in this factor ($p < .01$).

b. "Concern for community" scored significantly lower than the other three dimensions in this factor ($p < .01$).

c. "Planning" scored significantly higher than "Re-engineering" ($p < .05$).

d. "Strategic orientation" scored significantly higher than "Risk taking and innovation" ($p < .05$).

e. "Building networks" is significantly higher than "Embracing diversity" ($p < .05$).

f. "Teamwork orientation" scored significantly higher than did "Developing others" ($p < .05$), "Embracing change" ($p < .01$), and "Leadership versatility" ($p < .01$).

Industry knowledge, leadership, and interpersonal skill were factors that, while important, were ranked lower than the others by our respondents. The relatively low score for industry knowledge seems to suggest that the importance for leaders of industry-specific expertise is decreasing as time goes on. One reason for this is that industry expertise can be acquired by an adept leader, while the capacity for flexibility in a changing business environment can be hard to learn and often is inherent in an individual's personality and skill set. Interpersonal and leadership skills also scored lower than did other factors. We found it particularly interesting that the dimensions of developing others, embracing diversity and change, and leadership versatility were viewed as some of the least essential skills for the future.

Concern for community was a particularly low-rated dimension of strategic positioning. Scheffe *post-hoc* tests revealed that this dimension was rated significantly lower than the other three strategic-positioning dimensions. Although this dimension is not typically included in competency-modeling research, we (incorrectly) thought that it might be important to hospitality leaders because of their extensive connections with local community events and activities. This dimension consisted of three items: "Commits organizational resources for community events," "Considers the impact of decisions on community well-being," and "Builds partnerships and alliances with community organizations." Contrary to our thinking, the results revealed that those three were among the lowest-rated of all 99 items presented on the survey. When compared to other activities, a concern for and relationship with the local community in which the company operates does not seem to be a core competency needed for future hospitality leaders. On the other hand, competencies that appear to be the likely core attributes of future leaders are ethics, awareness of customer needs, time management, speaking with impact, commitment to quality, and team orientation.

✦ USING INDUSTRY-WIDE COMPETENCY MODELS

We believe that competency models can be important in building an effective human resources system. They can also help in educating future generations of leaders by guiding university faculties in designing curricula to meet the industry's future needs. An increasing number of university programs are focusing on competency building in an effort to prepare students for a specific industry (see *Journal of Management Education* 25(2)). For example, the master of management in hospitality (MMH) program at Cornell University assesses entering students against three core competencies that are deemed necessary for graduation. These competencies are leadership skills, teamwork and group process skills, and written and oral communication skills. Students are evaluated through an assessment center as they enter the MMH program and are given feedback at the end of the assessment center, as well as after each subsequent semester. If they have weaknesses in any of the three competencies, the students must make plans to improve their skills. Students' competency development is further supported by special modules offered by faculty members to enhance key skill areas. These modules contain both lecture and experiential components.

Industry-specific competency models can also help students seek out employment and career tracks that will give them ample opportunity to develop needed skills. The model presented here provides a comprehensive framework to inform future managers about what will be needed or expected to lead future lodging firms. A good competency model serves as both a roadmap and a prototype for achieving success.

Employees in lodging organizations may find this model useful as a general guide for self-development. In the absence of an institutional program to help develop a promising manager, a competency model can be used by an individual to design and plan her or his own career choices.

Last, individual lodging organizations can use this industry-wide model to build their own specific model. Once an organization has tailored the model to its specific needs, that firm can use the model in a variety of ways. For example, Choice Hotels International now uses its competency database to perform annual readiness assessments to determine managers' leadership capability. The competencies in Choice's model are the basis for the company's selection, promotion, and succession planning. Marriott employs a system-wide leadership-development initiative, called the Benchstrength Management System, which is used by current senior managers to build leadership capacity. Using the tools and measurements from this system, Marriott's senior managers are responsible for identifying potential leaders and ensuring that those individuals develop the skills and competencies needed to carry the company forward. Targeted development plans are created to assist senior managers in filling critical positions that are "stretch" assignments for high-potential managers. The Benchstrength Management System provides Marriott with a consistent approach to evaluating its leadership potential and ensures that the company focuses on core capabilities that are key to future success.

3.4 AS I SEE IT: WHAT I DO Emilio Fabico

In reflecting upon what it is I do as a manager in the hospitality industry, it is clear that there are the tasks that I must complete, and then there is all the other stuff. Throughout our careers, there are always plenty of duties that we are responsible for completing and that are important to our business. These processes are typically mandated by operational need, fiduciary responsibility, or regulatory requirement. The manner in which virtually all of these tasks are completed is typically inflexible and requires little or no creativity. It is unlikely that one's professional success will come from one's ability to perform these duties successfully.

✦ THE OTHER STUFF

The swirled, chocolaty surface of a 3 Musketeers bar is not unlike that of any other candy bar; it is the fluffy stuff inside that makes it unique. We are not sure exactly what it is, but it sure is good and differentiates it from the others. That is the other stuff. That is what I spend most of my time focusing on and constantly working to improve. That other stuff is leadership. There is a world of people smarter than me who have written books on this subject, so I certainly do not profess to have any of the answers. What I can share with you is what the zigs and zags of my career path have taught me.

✦ IF IT WEREN'T HARD, EVERYONE WOULD DO IT

It is called *leadership,* not *maintainership.* Leadership is about leading. It is being proactive rather than reactive. It's being out ahead of challenges, as opposed to chasing them. It is about truly being engaged in and passionate about your work. It is about wanting to be and working toward being the best. As I walk the resort and interact with our employees and guests, I attempt to be aware of the challenges that each of the operations is facing. What are they proud of that they should be recognized for? What barriers are preventing them from continuing to improve? What might be around the corner that we are not aware of yet? What is important to our guests? What can we do, for our guests and employees, to make us better than our competition? How can we meet our employees' developmental needs? Woven into all of these questions, and what should always be factored into the answers, are people—individuals with diverse backgrounds, varying opinions, and different needs. As a leader, I must be able to recognize those differences and respond appropriately to each of them. Being skilled at listening is just as important as leading. How can one answer without knowing the questions? In a 24/7 industry like ours, this interaction and these questions never stop.

Early in my career, when I was a shift manager, a clear line divided work time and off time. After my ten-hour day, the hotel and I went our separate ways until I was back for my next shift. In more senior leadership roles, this line is no longer as clear. Especially in the age of the BlackBerry, that line can completely disappear. Here is the part where I make a pitch for balance. That, too, is a valuable leadership skill. Without question, it's possible to be a great leader and still have balance. This is important not only to the leader, but also to those he or she leads, as they often feel compelled to follow the leader's example. This should remain a priority throughout one's career.

✦ SIX DEGREES OF SEPARATION

I have found that many of the successes or failures I face every day can be traced to one source: respect. I must respect the fact that I work for a public company and must ensure that growth and the success of the business remain at the forefront of the decisions I make and the actions I take. I must respect the talents of my direct reports. I must work to inspire, influence, and support them toward their goals. I must not micromanage them. I must also strive to identify their accomplishments and celebrate their successes. I must respect that people enjoy feeling fulfilled, so I must work to provide the tools and environment that will allow them to be successful. I must respect that our guests have choices when selecting their hotel. They have decided to entrust us with their money, time, and away-from-home experience. We have an obligation to provide them with an experience that will leave them with a lasting positive memory and influence them to return time after time. I must lead knowing that all of us want to be treated fairly and respectfully. When employees are asked why they leave their employment, the answer generally centers on lack of respect or being valued.

✦ "WHAT MAKES THE MUSKRAT GUARD HIS MUSK? COURAGE!"

Well said by the *Wizard of Oz*'s Cowardly Lion. Although courage is not always easy to find, my role requires me to have it. I must have the courage to give honest, timely, and constructive feedback to my direct reports and my peers. I must have the courage to speak up when what I have to say may not be popular or may cause others pain. I must have the courage to take risks, if the calculated outcome will benefit our operation.

✦ JUST SAY NO

On a personal level, I must be true to myself. I can recall in school knowing exactly what my professional values were and never doubting that I would always remain true to them. As the years passed, the titles got fancier and the paychecks got bigger. I found myself separating from my beliefs. After losing a job a few years ago (I didn't truly lose it; I know where it is, but someone else now has it), I came to the realization that my paycheck was like a drug. I was thinking in terms of what I could do to get more of it. I had lost sight of how fun and exciting our industry is. Don't be afraid of the zig-zagging career path. I found that it often leads where you never planned to go and teaches you what you could have never planned to learn.

And that's as I see it: what I do.

3.5 A DAY IN THE LIFE OF A HOTEL GENERAL MANAGER

Tom Underwood, General Manager, Richmond Marriott Downtown

In the hotel business, there are rarely ever 2 days that are exactly alike, or rarely does a day go as you may plan it ahead of time. As the general manager, you must be able to react and prioritize where your daily efforts are focused, and very commonly, your efforts are directed towards immediate guests' issues, fire alarms, being understaffed, etc.

In general, I always approach everything that I do in a very focused manner. Our efforts are always focused in three areas—guest satisfaction, employee satisfaction, and owner satisfaction. At Marriott hotels, we all live by Mr. Marriott's words that if you take care of the associates, they'll take care of the guests, and the guests will return, which ultimately will take care of the owners.

A "typical" day for me starts at 7 A.M. I am a fan of arriving at 7 A.M. (weekdays), because in most business/convention hotels, our guests are up, having breakfast, and departing, or starting their meetings within the 7–9 A.M. timeframe. When I arrive at 7 A.M., I immediately report to the lobby/front desk, and check in with our front office staff and manager. Immediately, I can tell if there are any issues from the night prior or that morning that I will need to be involved with. The front office has a preshift meeting at 7 A.M. each morning and they discuss the day's events, game plan, etc. I usually attend this meeting, as the front desk is really the "hub" of the hotel. After checking in with the front desk, and attending their preshift meeting, I usually do a quick walk-through of the lobby area, greeting guests, picking up trash/newspapers, making sure the lights are on and the TV's are on the correct channels, etc. I make it a point to specifically interact with all associates including the bellmen, valet parkers, front desk staff, and PBX operators.

After my tour of the lobby, I visit the restaurant. Again, the restaurant is generally at its busiest time between 7–8 A.M. I usually walk through, greet guests, and I can usually determine pretty quickly if there are issues with staffing. As I walk through, I always make it a point to pick up dirty plates and I always check the breakfast buffet for quality. I then walk through the kitchen and visit all areas quickly and speak to all associates.

I then proceed to the banquet area. I prefer to do this earlier, rather than later, in the day. I try to do a very quick walk-through of the meeting rooms that are being used that day, and also do a quick visual inspection of the room setup, the buffets, lighting, and the rooms' cleanliness. I always make a specific point to interact with our group contact if possible and give him/her my business card and assure them that I'm there all day if they need me.

After touring all of these areas, I usually stay in the lobby area through the duration of the morning rush. At approximately 8 A.M., I try to break away and visit the housekeeping department's preshift meeting. I find this more important than others, because housekeepers generally have a true appreciation for being recognized and for having the hotel's general manager stop by.

At 8:30 A.M. each morning, I attend the Daily Stand-Up meeting for our sales department. This is their version of a preshift meeting.

At this meeting, I try to make note of any appointments or site visits that the team may have for the day or the week. This meeting usually lasts 10 minutes.

At 9:00 A.M. each morning, I attend the hotel management Daily Stand-Up meeting, which is attended by at least one manager from each department. At this meeting, we address the following:

- Front office discusses occupancy, number of arrivals, number of departures, arriving VIPs, any issues from the previous night, and tonight and tomorrow's managers-on-duty (MODs)
- Director of event planning discusses in-house groups, arriving groups, their events for the day, and major movement of group attendees
- Director of sales discusses any site visits or sales appointments
- Each manager has an opportunity to discuss what is on his/her agenda for the day.

At 9:15 A.M., I generally return to my office to get organized for the day. At this time, I try to reply to any emails, review items in my mailbox, listen to any voice mails, and look at my calendar for the day. On most days, I have what we call "Department Accountability Meetings." Each day, I have 2–3 of these meetings in the 10 A.M.–noon time frame with different departments (each department has one per week). At these meetings, we review with the department-head manager: their period-to-date wages compared to budget, their period-to-date expenses compared to budget, any projects that they are working on, and employee issues and any customer issues.

After these meetings end (around noon on most days), I make a quick tour of the banquet areas to see how the groups are progressing and to see how our lunch setups look; at which point I always see if any assistance is needed. After this, I visit the lobby area, interact with all associates, visit the front entrance/exterior, then visit the front desk and check in with the front desk manager on how the day is progressing. I then visit the restaurant to see if there's any assistance needed. If the restaurant is doing well, I progress back to the kitchen area, again making the rounds and verifying that everything is under control.

At some point between 12 and 2 P.M., I visit the employee cafeteria to have lunch. Many general managers eat in the restaurant, or other areas, but I think it's very important to eat with the hourly associates, and it gives me an opportunity to interact with someone different each day at lunch. During this time, besides eating, I'm obviously noting the quality of the food and cleanliness of the area. After lunch, I generally visit the back-of-house banquet areas, corridors, and associate restroom/break room area to make sure all areas are clean and organized.

Upon completion, I try to return to my office, again to return email, voice mail, and visit the sales managers (my office is in the sales office), to see what questions they have, learn issues they're working on, and hear success stories.

Generally, in the 2–3 P.M. time frame, I always try to break away and walk the guest floor hallways from top to bottom. On busy days, I randomly pick a handful of floors. On slow days, I go to the top and walk all hallways all the way to the bottom. During this afternoon tour, I'm making notes of any wall damage, necessary repairs, and the condition of housekeeping closets. I also interact with each housekeeper, and verify that each hallway is clean. This is a very important part of the day, as this is what our paying guests see. On certain days of the week, I actually inspect rooms with our housekeeping management team. I don't do this daily, but in general, I formally inspect 10–20 rooms per week, document them, and review with the management team, as well as the housekeeper. After my building tour, I usually go to my office and email any issues that I've noted to the director of engineering and the director of housekeeping, so they can follow up on each and assign duties to their team.

Again, at this point, I check email, voice mail, and return any calls that have been left for me. On certain afternoons, I have meetings during this time. Once per week, we have a "yield meeting," in which I meet with the director of revenue management and the director of sales. We review the next 90 days' occupancy and groups and we review our pricing, restriction, and booking strategy. We review the dates that we may be oversold and determine if we should adjust rates. On another day, once per week, we have a weekly sales meeting with the sales managers. At this meeting, we review the previous weeks market share report, review any business that needs to be closed (tentatives), review our pace reports compared to previous years, and go over any other topics of interest to the team.

Generally, between 4 and 6 P.M., my time is spent walking the building, mostly the lobby areas, front entrance areas, and the front office areas. I do this because this is the time of day when we usually have a lot of foot traffic, groups on breaks, guests arriving to check in, shift change at the front desk, and the bar is opening. This is also a good time to interact with the evening associates, who are just starting their shifts. After visiting all key areas, I usually visit the housekeeping office and the banquet manager's office to see how their day went and if there are any pending issues that I can assist with or should be aware of.

Before leaving for the day, which generally is between 5:30 P.M. and 6:00 P.M., I try to make sure I've visited all operational areas. I also make a specific point to speak with the front desk manager on duty about anything special that he/she should know about—incoming groups, incoming VIP's, etc.

Once home for the evening, my phone is always on and I always answer it. In the hotel business, we are open 24 hours per day, 7 days per week, and it's important to be available for any guest issue or emergency that may occur.

3.6 A SNAPSHOT FROM A GENERAL MANAGER OF A RITZ-CARLTON CLUB AND RESORT Nicholas R. Dimeglio

✦ OVERVIEW

The Ritz-Carlton Club, Aspen Highlands is located in Aspen, Colorado at the base of Aspen Highlands ski area. The Club consists of 73 two- and three-bedroom fractional residence units, located in three separate buildings. The Ritz-Carlton Club, Aspen Highlands is the centerpiece of the Aspen Highlands Village, a mixed-use development consisting of retail, whole-ownership, a major ski-in/ski-out facility, and the Club. The Club is conveniently located 3 miles from downtown Aspen's renowned set of shops and restaurants.

While Club Members enjoy the nearby galleries, skiing, and nightlife, they feel at home with legendary Ritz-Carlton service inside the Club. Service includes twice-daily housekeeping, maintenance concierge, and a dedicated Member experience team. The property also offers Member storage, two health clubs, two outdoor heated pools, a full-service spa, Members' lounges, recreational facilities, ski valet services, Caffè Siena, and The Willow Creek Bistro.

The general manager position is responsible for leading all aspects of the operations, including Member and employee engagement, financial performance, and support and leadership within the community. The general manager also works to provide unique experiences and events to support fractional sales growth.

✦ MY DAILY CONTRIBUTIONS

As the general manager, I am responsible for energizing the Ritz-Carlton Gold Standards and ensuring that the company's philosophy is implemented to meet or exceed Member, employee, and financial expectations. This begins with daily morning line-ups in the Executive Office, in which representatives of each department discuss goals and Members in-house, and share "wow" stories.

In support of Employee Engagement, I am continually challenging the staff to improve club operations and ensure compliance with brand standards to protect brand integrity. I have also built key relationships in the local community and acted as the voice for the Ritz-Carlton Club in the Village through active participation within Aspen Highlands associations. Aspen Highlands Condominium Association Board relations is extremely important, requiring constant board member engagement, management team collaboration, and the supervision of quarterly association meetings, minutes, and action items.

As the general manager, I retain a diverse leadership team capable of enlivening Ritz-Carlton service values by utilizing employee talents and Ritz-Carlton training programs.

Ritz-Carlton service values build close relationships with Members and create Member loyalty, exceeding their expectations, and maintaining The Ritz-Carlton mystique. To be sure such values are upheld, I begin and end the day by greeting the ladies and gentlemen who operate the Club by visiting their departments.

3.7 MINI-CASE: SUNSET HOTELS AND SUITES

Shortly before the end of 2001, Mr. Andre Johnson, president of Sunset Hotels and Suites, Inc., heard through the company grapevine that several department and operational managers at the company's hotels in northern California were unhappy with their promotion prospects. Unwilling to risk losing these young managers, Johnson was contemplating how to help these men and women manage their careers, at the same time making staying with Sunset attractive and challenging.

Sunset Hotels and Suites is a growing West Coast chain with nine properties in southern California, six in the San Francisco Bay area (northern California), and five in the Seattle-Portland region. The hotels in the Bay area were the most recent acquisitions, and although fewer in number than the southern California region, boasted 20 percent more rooms and were more recently built. They also included the youngest management staff, many of who were retained from the staffs of the acquired hotels. Sunset is a privately owned company, operated as an S-corporation, with all of the corporate officers and hotel GMs holding shares of the company's stock.

Several of the unhappy managers had talked with their GMs and human resource officers about their frustrations. These included:

- Many of the GMs were young, in their thirties and forties, successful, and tending to not move.

- There are no regional managers, as Johnson prefers to run a fairly flat corporate organization.

- Several felt locked into narrow specialties (convention services, catering sales, housekeeping management, and front office) without clear prospects for cross-training to add breadth to their career.

- They were not particularly unhappy with salaries and the usual benefits, but some grumbled about the valuable stock options the GMs get, largely based on the performance of the operating managers' departments.

Johnson called a meeting of the Bay area managers at the Mark Hopkins Hotel in San Francisco (*not* a Sunset property) and invited all department managers from Sunset to be his guests for a 2-day conference. Similar meetings were announced and planned in the Pacific Northwest and southern California.

REFERENCES

ACA's Competencies Research Team. 1996. "The Role of Competencies in an Integrated HR Strategy." *ACA Journal* Summer: 6–21.

Agle, B. R., R. K. Mitchell, and J. A. Sonnenfeld. 1999. "Who Matters to CEOs? An Investigation of Stakeholder Attributes and Salience, Corporate Performance, and CEO Values." *Academy of Management Journal* 42:507–525.

Arnaldo, M. J. 1981. "Hotel General Managers: A Profile." *Cornell Hotel and Restaurant Administration Quarterly* 22(3):53–56.

Blancero, D., J. Boroski, and L. Dyer. 1996. "Key Competencies for a Transformed Human Resources Organization: Results of a Field Study." *Human Resource Management* 35(3):383–403.

Dann, D. 1990. "The Nature of Managerial Work in the Hospitality Industry." *International Journal of Hospitality Management* 9(4):319–334.

Dubois, D. 1993. *Competency-based Performance Improvement: A Strategy for Organizational Change.* Amherst, MA: HRD.

Eder, R. W., and W. T. Umbreit. 1989. "Measures of Managerial Effectiveness in the Hotel Industry." *Hospitality Research and Education Journal* 13(3): 333–341.

Enz, C. A., and J. Siguaw. 2000. "Best Practices in Human Resources." *Cornell Hotel and Restaurant Administration Quarterly* 41(1):48–61.

Evarts, H. F. 1988. "The Competency Programme of the American Management Association. *Journal of Management Development* 7(6):48–56.

Ferguson, D. H., and F. Berger. 1984. "Restaurant Managers: What Do They Actually Do?" *Cornell Hotel and Restaurant Administration Quarterly* 25(1):2 7–37.

Guerrier, Y. 1987. "Hotel Managers' Careers and Their Impact on Hotels in Britain." *International Journal of Hospitality Management* 6(3):121–130.

Guerrier, Y., and A. Lockwood. 1991. "Managers in Hospitality: A Review of Current Research." *In Progress in Tourism, Recreation, and Hospitality Management,* C. P. Cooper (Ed.), 2:151–167. London: Bellhaven.

Hales, C., and M. Nightingale. 1986. "What Are Unit Managers Supposed to Do? A Contingent Methodology for Investigating Managerial Role Requirements." *International Journal of Hospitality Management* 5(1): 3–11.

Koepper, K. 1988. "Management Effectiveness: A Hotel Industry Appraisal." *Lodging* 14(4):53–57.

Kotter, J. P. 1982. *The General Managers.* New York: Free Press.

Ley, D. A. 1978. "An Empirical Examination of Selected Work Activity Correlates of Managerial Effectiveness in the Hotel Industry Using a Structured Observation Approach." Unpublished Ph.D. dissertation, Michigan State University, East Lansing, Michigan.

Linkage, Inc. 1997. *Introduction to Competency Modeling.* Lexington, MA: Linkage.

Lucia, A. D., and R. Lepsinger. 1999. *The Art and Science of Competency Models.* San Francisco: Jossey-Bass.

McLagan, P. 1996. "Great Ideas Revisited: Competency Models." *Training and Development* 50(1): 60–65.

Mintzberg, H. 1973. *The Nature of Managerial Work.* New York: Harper and Row.

Mirabile, R. J. 1985. "A Model for Competency-based Career Development." *Personnel* April: 30–38.

————. 1997. "Everything You Wanted to Know about Competency Modeling." *Training and Development* 51(8):73–77.

Nebel, E. C., III. 1991. *Managing Hotels Effectively: Lessons from Outstanding Hotel Managers.* New York: Van Nostrand Reinhold.

Pavesic, D. V., and R. A. Brymer. 1990. "Job Satisfaction: What's Happening to the Young Managers?" *Cornell Hotel and Restaurant Administration Quarterly* 30(4): 90–96.

Shortt, G. 1989. "Work Activities of Hotel Managers in Northern Ireland: A Mintzbergian Analysis." *International Journal of Hospitality Management* 8(2):121–130.

Umbreit, W. T. 1986. "Developing Behaviorally-anchored Scales for Evaluating Job Performance of Hotel Managers." *International Journal of Hospitality Management* 5(2): 55–61.

Worsfold, P. 1989. "A Personality Profile of the Hotel Manager." *International Journal of Hospitality Management* 8(1):51–62.

Zingheim, P. K., G. E. Ledford, and J.R. Shuster. 1996. "Competencies and Competency Models: Does One Size Fit All?" *ACA Journal* Spring: 56–65.

SUGGESTED READINGS

BOOKS

Barrows, C. W., and T. Powers. 2008. *Introduction to Management in the Hospitality Industry*, 9th ed. Hoboken, NJ: John Wiley and Sons.

Buckingham, M., and C. Coffman. 1999. *First, Break All the Rules: What the World's Greatest Managers do Differently.* New York: Simon & Schuster.

Kotter, J. P. 1982. *The General Managers.* New York: Free Press.

Nebel, E. C. III. 1991. *Managing Hotels Effectively: Lessons from Outstanding Hotel Managers.* New York: Van Nostrand Reinhold.

Sund, K. J. 2007. *Dealing with Uncertainty: How Hotel Managers Perceive and Interpret Environmental Changes.* Music for Strings.

Woods, R. H., and J. Z. King. 1996. *Quality Leadership and Management in the Hospitality Industry.* East Lansing, MI: Educational Institute of the American Hotel and Motel Association.

ARTICLES

Harper, S., C. Brown, and I. Wilson. 2005. "Qualifications: A Fast-Track to Hotel General Manager?" *International Journal of Contemporary Hospitality Management* 17(1):51–64.

Ley, D. 1980. "The Effective GM: Leader or Entrepreneur?" *Cornell Hotel and Restaurant Administration Quarterly* 22(3):53–56.

Morey, R. C., and D. A. Dittman. 2003. "Evaluating a Hotel GM's Performance: A Case Study in Benchmarking." *Cornell Hotel and Restaurant Administration Quarterly* 44(5/6):53–59.

Nebel, E. C., J. S. Lee, and B. Vudajivuc. 1995. "Hotel General Manager Career Paths in the United States." *International Journal of Hospitality Management* 14(34): 252–256.

Rutherford, D. G., and J. Wiegenstein. 1985. "The Mentoring Process in Hotel General Managers' Careers." *Cornell Hotel and Restaurant Administration Quarterly* 25(4): 16–23.

Sparrowe, R. T., and P. A. Popielarz. 1995. "Getting Ahead in the Hospitality Industry: An Event Analysis of Promotions Among Hotel and Restaurant Employees." *Hospitality Research Journal* 19(3): 99–117.

Taylor, M. S., and C. A. Enz. 2002. "Voices from the Field: GM's Responses to the Events of September 11, 2001." *Cornell Hotel and Restaurant Administration Quarterly* 43(1):7–20.

Wildes, V. J. 2008. "How Can Organizational Leaders Really Lead and Serve at the Same Time?" *International Journal of Contemporary Hospitality Management* 20(1):67–78.

Woods, R. H., D. G. Rutherford, R. A. Schmidgall, and M. Sciarini. 1998. "Hotel General Managers: Focused on the Core Business." *Cornell Hotel and Restaurant Administration Quarterly* 39(6).

SOURCE NOTES

Chapter 3.2, "A Conceptual Framework of the Hotel General Manager's Job," by Eddystone C. Nebel III and Ajay Ghei.

Chapter 3.3, "Grooming Future Hospitality Leaders: A Competencies Model," by Beth G. Chung-Herrera, Cathy A. Enz, and Melenie J. Lankau, is reprinted from the June 2003 issue of *Cornell Hotel and Restaurant Administration Quarterly.*

© Cornell University. Used by permission. All rights reserved.

Chapter 3.4, "As I See It: What I Do," by Emilio Fabico.

Chapter 3.5, "A Day in the Life of a Hotel General Manager," by Tom Underwood.

Chapter 3.6, "A Snapshot from a General Manager of a Ritz-Carlton Club and Resort," by Nicholas R. DiMeglio.

OPERATIONS—ROOMS

4.1 INTRODUCTION

The student of hospitality management will find the hotel's front office referred to as the *hub,* the *nerve center,* the *brain,* or some other name suggesting centrality. As H. E. Heldenbrand stated in his classic 1944 book *Front Office Psychology,* "To the guest, the manager is largely represented by the front office, and the unseen head will be judged favorably or otherwise by the guest treatment there" (Introduction). The observations, opinions, and research presented in this section are chosen to illustrate the centrality of the front office in the modern hotel.

A theme that recurs throughout many of the readings in this section is that of communication. In an increasingly communications-oriented society and world, information—its storage, retrieval, dissemination, and evaluation—can mean a competitive edge and, to a certain extent, power. Technology has given us the Internet, cellular phones, electronic mail

(email), telephone- and computer-transmitted facsimiles (faxes), overnight delivery of letters and packages, and personal data assistants (PDAs). These all combine to generate an expectation of clear and nearly instantaneous communication and, by logical extension, fast and efficient services based on communications. This, in turn, has increased the complexity of the hotel's front office and at the same time delivered increased opportunities to serve the hotel's guests. It has, therefore, significantly changed the role of the front office and the front office manager from that described by Heldenbrand.

In 1985, Rutherford studied a national sample of front office managers (FOMs) and concluded that communication had emerged as a central issue. FOMs had added to the predictable role of department manager responsibilities as facilitators and brokers of communication in its various forms with the other hotel departments, the front office, and the hotel guests. The model that emerged from this analysis carries with it the powerful message that the FOM's job clearly revolves around communication. A major conclusion of this study was that hotel firms should consider communication skills an important criterion in considering candidates for the position of FOM.

When communication is coupled with the aforementioned complexity and guest expectations of instant availability of information and data, it is easy to see why the front office and its staff operate under considerable stress. Being the hub or nerve center of a modern hotel has, as one of its positive aspects, the fact that front office staff can be keenly aware of what is happening at virtually every level of the hotel's organizational structure. One of the negative aspects is that the front office serves as a lightning rod for guest complaints. Dealing with complaints can be one of the most difficult tasks for the front office staff to learn, especially given the frequency and sometimes the intensity of guest complaints and expectations.

Successful FOMs ideally possess demonstrated competencies in both oral and written communication to deal with these complexities and challenges. The FOM, therefore, is not only a manager and a communicator with the front office staff, the hotel departments, and the guests but also a communicator in yet another way—as a teacher and trainer.

To see how this all fits together, walk a few miles in the shoes of FOM Garry Dickover. At the time this was written, Dickover was the FOM of two hotels: Marriott's River Center and Riverwalk Hotels in San Antonio, Texas. Currently general manager of the Courtyard

Convention Center in Las Vegas, Dickover invites you to see the inside of the FOM's job and how he practices the theory of managing the front office.

The theme of active communication is carried through the piece contributed by Bill Quain and Steve LeBruto. If hotels are going to actively find the best pieces of business, then there must be good communications channels among all the organizational components that guide the guest to a purchase decision. Whether this is at the front desk, through the reservations system, or through a travel agent, it is important to recognize the most attractive pieces of business and what potential bookings may be logically refused. Yes, refusing business is a central component of successful yield management, but not always. In their words: "Yield management is usually thought of in the context of turning away undesirable business during excess demand periods. However, the real art of yield management is in learning how to turn undesirable booking requests into desirable ones." Their article helps the reader, in an interesting and entertaining way, learn to make these management decisions.

As a new addition to the fifth edition, a "futuristic" look into yield management was incorporated. Milla and Shoemaker interview a number of industry professionals in order to ascertain the current state of yield management in the hotel industry, as well as provide some insight into how yield management will progress in the near future.

Yield and revenue management are also treated in the marketing section of this book with other, in some ways contrasting, views by Chappelle. The reader who wants additional insights into these concepts is directed to the contributions by that author.

In 1993, Glenn Withiam researched and wrote "American Concierges Set Service Standards," an essay used in the second and third editions of *Hotel Management and Operations*. Withiam also wrote an earlier piece, "Keepers of the Keys: Concierges in American Hotels" (1983). The "keys" reference the practice in European hotels of hotel guests leaving their room keys with the concierge upon leaving the floor of their room. The concierge, therefore, "kept the keys" for the guest. The job today has evolved to use keys as a metaphor for the processes of gatekeeping access to hotel and community services on behalf of the guest. Concierges have a professional society, Les Clefs d'Or, which uses crossed keys as an identifying device. The concierges who are members and so certified are said to be keyed.

In his article on concierges, Dr. Mario Arnaldo of Hawaii Pacific University acknowledges Withiam's work as the heritage and underpinning of his current research. Herein, Arnaldo presents an overview of research he did on the post–9/11 American hotel concierge and guest service staff. The strict application of the title *concierge* indicates a hotel employee working at a concierge-designated desk in a hotel property. To accurately assess the contributions of these hotel professionals, Arnaldo contacted dozens of contemporary concierges and guest service staff members, who generously provided examples of their concierge experiences. The author reviews in an accessible, conversational manner the following questions: What's up with concierges these days? Who does the office work? What are the organizational departments they work in? What kind of interactions do they have with other hotel departments? What is their greatest wish?

This chapter is concluded by an article written by Oliver Meinzer, who wrote this piece when he was in the position of front office manager at a Marriott property. He has recently been promoted into the resident manager position at the Marriott Newport Beach Hotel and Spa. Nonetheless, the viewpoint Meinzer gives regarding the front office manager position is invaluable. In this article, you will take a look into the position of FOM from an industry professional's perspective.

The articles and essays presented here for your consideration represent only a fraction of the potential range of issues attendant on any modern hotel front office. The duties, obligations, and responsibilities of front office personnel change from hotel company to hotel company based on such variables as market segmentation, organizational structure, corporate philosophy, and individual leadership. A large amount of management literature exists that is not specific to the front office but nonetheless pertains to the various issues and challenges that face FOMs. The articles chosen for inclusion in this section are as specific as possible to functional aspects of front office management. Other pertinent managerial insights may be applied from other contexts once the reader has a good functional grasp of front office activities. Included in the suggested readings are textbooks that treat in great depth the functional and technical aspects of front office operations. What has been attempted here is an overview of pervasive managerial issues typical of those currently facing FOMs.

4.2 A DAY IN THE LIFE OF THE FRONT OFFICE MANAGER

Garry Dickover

It's 6:00 on a Saturday morning. The alarm clock is blaring its normal "beep, beep, beep, beep." The sun is peering through the window. Time to start another day as front office manager. It is going to be a busy day, featuring 800 arrivals and 750 departures. Plus, the hotel is 50 rooms oversold. It is going to be a fun one.

It's 7:00 A.M. The drive to work is an easy one this Saturday morning. It gives me a chance to think about one thing in particular that is on tap for today. There is a 9:00 A.M. pre-convention meeting for the group that is arriving today. There is the regular morning preshift meeting. Today I also have to review hospitality standards with the front desk staff. You would think that it would be easy to have people smile and greet the guest, use a guest's name, add a value statement about the hotel or city, and thank the guest for his or her business. I don't ask for much, but to train people to do those four things can be a challenge.

Preshift meetings are an important start to the day, but it can be a hassle getting everyone together. There are a lot of reasons why an associate can't make a preshift meeting, but attendance is important to the success of my department. It is the time I have everyone together, let them know what is going on for the day, and get a chance to share with them the standards we have set and how they can apply them to the customer. At 1:00 P.M. today I have a Safety Committee meeting, and at 4:00 I have my weekly rap session

with the telephone department. Yeah, I think to myself, it is going to be a full day.

As I arrive to work, I can see that the check-outs have already started. It is nice to see the bellmen taking care of our guests. As I scan the grounds, I make sure there is no trash on the ground, the bell carts are clean, and the valet parking staff is hustling to retrieve guest cars. I look at the windows of the entryway to the hotel to check for cleanliness. The front drive is the first and last thing a guest sees, so it has to be looking good. Today, all looks good.

It is better for me to spot-check the area before the general manager comes by and sees any problems. As the FOM, I learned the GM's route when he arrives at work, so I make sure the area is clean. (This is something they did not teach me in college, along with how to repair printers and copy machines—some things you gotta learn by doing.) This morning, things look good.

It's 7:50 A.M. I make my way to the back of the front office. My desk managers are busy getting information ready for the preshift meeting. As I walk through the area, I always make it a point to greet people as I pass and wish them a good morning. I know how important it is to give each and every associate a cheerful good morning. It sets the stage for the day. And you know, it really does make people feel good. A good department head recognizes his or her associates. The first words that come out of your mouth should be pleasant. The front office team takes the brunt of all the complaints. They don't need me to harp on them.

The preshift meeting goes smoothly. The desk managers prep the team for the day, I review the hospitality standards, and we are set. As we are about to finish, I notice some tension on the staff's faces. They know they are in for a tough day—remember, 50 rooms oversold. It is important that I don't let the team see any stress I may feel on my face. The team knows how important it is to sell out the hotel. They know that once a room is empty overnight, you never get a chance to sell that room again. They also know you have to oversell the hotel. This is the time I can reassure them that the revenue department has calculated all of the slip percentages for the big group checking in. A slip percentage is the expected variation from stated arrival and rooms pick-up percentages the group's meeting planner promised. It is important for me to develop a good relationship with the revenue department. The FOM must be active in the forecast meetings to ensure the hotel is not "sold up the river," meaning overcommitted by the sales staff.

Relationship building is an important job for the FOM. It is where trust is established—trust between you and the other departments. It is not me versus them; it's *us* trying to maximize revenue and occupancy and to continue to build loyalty. This is the time to reassure the team that if we do our jobs as we have been trained, all will be fine. We do a little cheer, and out to the desk they go! Now for a cup of coffee.

I review the plans with the desk managers for the sold-out night. This is also the time I check availability at other hotels, check the stay-over requests and no-show percentages, and check for duplicated reservations. It looks like they have it under control. I double-check the staffing during the peak periods and remind the managers to get everyone to lunch. (As simple as this sounds, sometimes we forget.) I check my watch; 30 minutes to the pre-con. Better pull out the group resume, which is our profile of the group that includes, among many other things, a historical profile of the group's room pick-ups, occupancies, and food and beverage revenues.

At 8:45 A.M., I'm off to the pre-con. I head by the desk to wave to the staff, and I stop by the telephone system, bellstand, and the concierge desk. All seems to be going smoothly. At the pre-con, we all do our formal introductions and meet the group's representatives, usually the meeting planner and members of the group's leadership. We each discuss our individual departments and the relationship we will have with the group. This is our time to sell them on how well we will do for their group. It is a successful pre-con; all the parties seem happy. I spend just a couple of minutes with the group convention manager, giving an update on the oversold situation. If we have to walk guests, it is important to let the group convention manager know about the situation. Today I said we might, but we should be in good shape. She thanks me for the update.

As I make my way back to the front office, I end up walking with the resident manager (RM). He asks me how things went last night and how our hotel is for tonight. As an FOM, it is important to know what your boss is going to ask you. Bosses are all different, but they always seem to ask the same questions. It is important to review the daily sales and occupancy report from the previous day, so you know what is going on and can share this information with the RM. I gave the RM the information he wants, always emphasizing the positives.

When I get back to my office, I have a couple of associates who want to talk to me. They are bothered by the new schedule. They wanted some specific days off and, because of the business, they did not get them. This is a delicate situation. You want to be fair to the team, but you also have to respect why your managers did what they did. The best thing to do is to listen to what your associates say and then review the situation. I have found that 80 percent of the time there is an alternative. You want to create win-win solutions. By spending time with your associates, you demonstrate to them you care about their situation; this helps build loyalty. *Remember that they don't care how much you know until they know how much you care.* Another situation resolved.

The next couple of hours I spend reviewing the previous day's information and getting caught up on email, memos, and other communications. Generally, this is the time I get a couple of phone calls from upset guests. This could be for a variety of reasons. Before check-out, some people always want to let the manager know how things went. It is important to listen to customers when they complain. It is a great way to find out what deficiencies you may have in the hotel's service processes. Most complaints are caused by a breakdown in the process. Sometimes people get upset over the smallest things. Sometimes they have a right to be upset. One example from past experience was the room being so cold that when the guest lifted the toilet seat, the water had a small sheet of ice on it. Ensuring customer satisfaction is a large part of the FOM's job. You have to own hospitality. Your team sets the stage for a guest's entire stay. It better be good!

By now it is 12:15 P.M. and time for lunch. I grab the information I need for the 1:00 P.M.

safety meeting. I will go directly to that meeting after lunch. As I make my way, I check on the desk and the house count. We are now only 29 oversold. We have had some canceled reservations, and we also had 18 early departures. Things are looking good.

At 1:00 P.M. I walk into the safety meeting. This is never an exciting meeting, but it is always important. Accidents are costly to the hotel. It is important to keep accident prevention a priority for all associates. Today we talk about the most current accidents, how they could have been prevented, and the next steps. We also discuss the implications of safety and security interests for our guests. This is important to avoid lawsuits and provide guests with a safe and secure environment. The meeting wraps up at 2:30 P.M.

As I come down the escalator, I see the check-ins are starting to arrive. I head to the bellstand to see if the bell captain is caught up. All is well. Because lines are forming, I go behind the front desk to handle a few check-ins. I always like this part of the job. It also gets a smile from the desk clerks. Before you know it, you have helped move the line. Because the desk is staying busy, it is time for me to move out and manage from the lobby. This is a great way to watch what is happening. You can view your whole front office team by being in the lobby. (You can also ensure the cleanliness of the area. This helps our friends in housekeeping.) A big part of the job in the lobby is just answering questions and giving directions. Every guest I help means one guest who did not have to go to the front desk and one more guest who did not have to stand in line. This is the fun part of the job!

At 3:50 P.M., my pager goes off. It is a reminder about my 4:00 P.M. rap sessions. I can't believe 90 minutes passed while I was in the lobby. It is a good day.

Meeting with associates allows me to take the pulse of their work situation. I do it in small groups or as a one-on-one rap. It helps build a relationship within the team and also helps identify challenges I was unaware of. I ask leading questions so that the session does not become a bitch session; this helps me control the meeting. During this meeting, I discover some equipment that is needed and that we need more uniforms for the team. It would be great to buy them all new uniforms, but I have to stay within my budget. Sometimes that is hard to do. I take notes on their comments and will pass them on to the other managers. It is important for all of the managers to be in the loop. I always keep the raps to about an hour.

By now it is 5:00 P.M., our peak check-in time. I go back out to the lobby to see how things are going. On a busy day like today, I typically spend the next couple of hours helping out in the lobby. At 5:30 P.M., the night manager on duty (MOD) comes out to meet with me. We usually work the lobby together while I tell him about the day. He tells me about the previous night. Of course, the first thing he shows me is the house count: 24 rooms oversold and 352 arrivals expected. We are in good shape. It is important to track the number of no-shows. This helps you make better decisions to maximize your revenue. The MOD is a little nervous. I tell him not to worry, we will be fine. We review the sold-out night, so we don't miss anything. He tells me he already has the walk letters (expressing our regret and outlining our promises to a guest who is walked to another hotel) out on the desk. This brings a good laugh. We have done this plenty of times, so I trust that the hotel is in good hands.

It's 7:00 P.M., and things seem to be in good shape. Time to go home. I make one more trip around to the departments in the front office to see how they are doing and wish them a good evening. Another good day!

The day described above is a typical day as a front office manager. Some days have different meetings, some days have more upset guests, some days have more upset associates, and some days are just better than others are. The thing I have learned over the years is that the job of the FOM is the same. Take care of the associates, who take care of the customers, who take care of the business. It's the same job, just different players, and I love it.

4.3   YIELD MANAGEMENT: CHOOSING THE MOST PROFITABLE RESERVATIONS   William J. Quain and Stephen M. LeBruto

✦ INTRODUCTION

Yield management, as a term, is not very exciting. However, the *results* of a well-run yield management program are certainly exciting! Properly implemented, it means that a business can make more money. The keys are to sell more and to sell more profitable items.

The first step in a yield management program is to determine who is the best customer. The best customer is the one who can spend the most money at your property purchasing profitable items. The products and services you provide are the best fit for their needs. The best customers for the property are the ones who receive the greatest benefit from your services. They are willing to pay more, buy more frequently, and remain more loyal because you are satisfying their needs.

Many operations do not know who the best customers are. However, the answer is in a property's data collection system. Guest histories, food and beverage checks, cash register receipts, and the records of strategically allied business partners contain most of the information any property needs to determine the ideal customer base. In order to properly implement a yield management project, the property must be viewed as a collection of profit centers. A profit center is a place where value is created and exchanged.

One of the techniques of yield management is to let the guest in on the secrets of the establishment. Give him or her all the information necessary to truly enjoy the experience. As part of the yield management plan, management must be willing to make experts of the guests by sharing information on how they can utilize all of the profit centers.

An important part of analyzing the potential of each profit center is to identify all the possible sources of revenue. This means analyzing both the revenue-producing outlets and the people who spend the money. Every establishment has a wide variety of revenue outlets. They can range from the sale of rooms to valet service, flower delivery, specialty drinks, cigars, and creative take-out services.

Strategic alliances with car rental agencies, cooperative advertising, couponing, and packaging of all sorts will vastly change the number of channels the guest can use to spend money in the profit centers of the enterprise.

Restaurants can increase revenues by serving take-out food, catering private parties off-premises, adjusting the menu mix, and developing reward systems for servers. Especially during hours of peak demand, restaurants can design product/price combinations that offer incentives to customers to change their demand patterns. Why accept any reservation at any time? Instead, select the most profitable reservations and use incentives to move the other reservations to non-peak or shoulder times.

Profits are the only true measure of business success. The following groups all benefit from enhanced profits:

1. **Guests**—They are one of the primary beneficiaries of increased revenues and profits. If revenues are on the rise, it can mean only one thing: You are serving the guest better. Guests are happier, more loyal, and eager to tell others about the great experience they had.

2. **Employees**—In order to achieve long-term success, employees must be involved in the profit making *and* the profit taking. Let them earn as much money as they possibly can by making more money for the property.

3. **Management**—Structured reward systems are necessary for management. These systems reflect their need for income and achievement and further the profits of the property.

4. **Shareholders and investors**—Return on investment, dependable growth, share prices, and so on are all outcomes of increased revenue. Money attracts money, and the investors will relish the long-term growth potential of their investments.

Managers face six major obstacles in their efforts to implement a yield management system. These impediments are:

1. **Lack of creativity**—Does your company do things the way they have always been done? There is a need for standardization in recipes and operating procedures; however, this sometimes spills over into other areas. Training sessions in most organizations do not stress the creative side of customer satisfaction.

2. **Lack of attention**—It is difficult to stay in focus all the time. The minute you stop paying attention, things go wrong.

3. **Monitoring the wrong signals**—We tend to monitor the easy things to measure, such as food cost and inventory. We should be looking for opportunities, not statistics.

4. **Conflict between sales and service**—When profits depend on a mutual delivery of both the sale and the service, conflict can arise. Front-of-the-house and back-of-the-house employees must work together for the common cause of serving and satisfying guests.

5. **Targeting the wrong customers**—The right customers are those who will purchase the most of your products and services. Look for the customers with the money to spend to give you a reasonable profit. Use the marketing mix variables of product price, promotions, and distribution to attract and hold the right customers.

6. **Rewarding the wrong behavior**—Many sales management policies are designed to encourage occupancy and average daily rate. Restaurants, by allowing customers to reward the waitstaff, may encourage promotion of higher-priced items. In either case, the sale may not reflect the best interests of the property. Yield management is designed to increase profit, not just gross sales.

✦ BASIC CONCEPTS OF YIELD MANAGEMENT

Yield management requires knowledge of guests' expected behavior, plus an understanding of which business is most beneficial to a hotel—but it does not necessarily require high-power computers. Three main revenue management concepts allow hotels to pick up relatively easy money, or low-hanging fruit. The three concepts are simplifying the yield management system to make it manageable; examining the rate controls to make certain they allow acceptance of the business that yields the strongest revenue return; and using length-of-stay controls to shift demand from sold-out periods to slack periods.

Group business, as it relates to the above three points, is a special case. The change needed, if any, is to think in terms of which business is best for the property on a given date. By implementing the concepts discussed here, the property should see revenue gains in the next several months.

✦ AN OLD PROFESSION

One may think of yield management as a relatively recent practice, but the lodging industry has applied yield management principles for many years. In one early instance, Marriott Corporation used yield management principles long before it installed its current sophisticated system. Back when young J. W. "Bill" Marriott was working at the family's first hotel, the Twin Bridges in Washington, D.C., the property sold rooms from a drive-up window. As Bill tells the story, the property had a flat single rate and charged extra for each additional person staying in the room. When availability got tight on some nights, Bill recalls leaning out the drive-up window to assess the cars waiting in line. If some of the cars were filled with passengers, Bill would turn away the vehicles with just a single passenger to sell his last rooms to fuller cars. That technique demonstrates the core concept of yield management.

From that simple start, yield management mechanisms have become complicated—so complicated that some managers whom we have met seem to think they cannot improve revenue unless they have access to the most sophisticated tools. Worse, the hotel manager may have created an overly complex system of discounts and packages. If the manager then insists on managing every rate or package individually, the result is a sense that the property has too many programs to track and control, and it probably does. For this reason, the first suggestion for a straightforward approach to yield management is to cluster rates into a few groupings of similar programs and then work on controlling these clusters or rate categories.

The goal of yield management is to select which business to accept and which business to turn away (when demand exceeds supply), based on the relative value of each booking. Most properties do not need more than four to six rate buckets for their transient bookings. As an example, the following gives transient rate categories that combine programs of similar value:

Level 1 Rack (no discount)
Level 2 10 to 20 percent discount
Level 3 25 to 35 percent discount
Level 4 40 to 50 percent discount
Level 5 greater than a 50 percent discount

Each level or bucket in the above hypothetical structure might comprise several room rates. Given such a structure, a manager need not agonize over whether to restrict rooms offered at a rate of $150 in hopes of getting a rate of $155. While it is given that those $5 bills would pile up, the complexity is not worth it, especially when one might be working so hard on the $5 difference that one overlooks the opportunity to earn, say, $50 more by selling at rack rate.

If a given set of discounts isn't working, the hotel should change the categories. For instance, if a hotel's business fell entirely in Level 1 and Level 2, with virtually no business in Level 3, a manager should rearrange the rate buckets. The three rate buckets could be discounts from rack rate of 10 to 15 percent, 20 to 40 percent, and greater than 40 percent—or any other arrangement that makes a meaningful division among rate categories.

The following principles apply to setting up categories to manage rates at a hotel:

1. Segment programs based on clusters of discounts representing similar values. Yield management requires risk and reward management. Rate categories are designed to enable turning down one booking request in favor of a higher-value booking projected to come later. However, risking $150 in certain revenue in hopes of achieving a $155 booking seems to make little sense if the latter is not a sure thing.

2. In deciding whether to accept a particular customer's business, take into account both the cost of opening rooms and the offsetting ancillary spending that occurs when a room is sold. To take an extreme example, the most valuable guest for a casino-hotel—the high-stakes gambler—might be paying the lowest room rate.

3. Limit the total number of transient rate categories to no more than six or so, particularly if there is no automated yield management system. The chief reason for that limit is that yield management requires forecasting demand for each rate category. Not only is it time-consuming to forecast numerous categories (with diminishing returns as the number of categories increases), but the more categories are created, the less accurate the forecasts are for each.

4. Each rate category should have a reasonable volume of activity to allow monitoring of traffic in that category. If it is found that one of the categories is rarely used, consider redistributing the rate hierarchy.

5. Group business should have a separate hierarchy of buckets to allow the operator to track pick-ups of room blocks. In addition, mixing group activity with individual booking activity clouds the historical information as you trend data by which rate categories are collected.

✦ RATE CATEGORY CONTROLS

The point of yield management is to use demand forecasts to determine how much to charge for rooms on a given day. When the hotel sells out, the ability to determine which reservations to accept or deny is lost, because all requests for the sold-out date (including those for multiple-night stays that involve the sold-out date) must be rejected. A property's yield management objective should be to sell out the hotel as close to the arrival date as possible, because the further in advance the hotel is sold out with discounted (or short-stay) business, the greater is the likelihood that high-value bookings will be turned away. This forecasting regime requires a continual process of comparing remaining demand for high-rate stays (and multiple-night stays) against remaining available inventory. Rate category controls help ensure available inventory to accommodate the projected high-rate demand.

Table 4.1 demonstrates how rate categories are controlled to increase total room revenue. The table assumes a 500-room hotel (or a hotel with 500 rooms remaining to be sold). The objective is to hold rooms open for high-rate demand without leaving a large number of rooms unsold. In this example, although the hotel would prefer to sell all 500 rooms at rack rate, the hotel's managers project that they can sell 380 (or more) rooms at rack rate. Their inventory plan is set up to maintain room availability for this forecasted high-rate demand. The managers would like to sell the remaining 120 rooms in the next rate category down (Bucket 1), but their demand forecast projects they will not be able to sell all

Table 4.1 Hypothetical Room Rate Structure

RATE BUCKETS	DISCOUNT OFF RACK RATE	AVAILABLE ROOMS (ESTIMATED)	DEMAND FORECAST
Rack (General)	None	500	380
Bucket 1	10%–20%	120	63
Bucket 2	25%–35%	57	75
Bucket 3	40%–50%	0	140

120 in that rate category. Based on current trends, however, even though they have a total of 500 rooms to sell, they won't be selling any rooms in the deep-discount category because there is sufficient demand at higher rates.

When evaluating how well a property is managing its inventory, there are two basic indicators: (1) On dates the property is selling out, it should be observed how far in advance that sellout occurs; (2) if the property is not selling out, it must be determined whether the property ever turned away business as a result of discount controls or because the property had committed too many rooms to groups—that is, if a group does not pick up its room block, did the hotel, as a result, refuse reservations from transient guests?

Full-occupancy dates frequently receive less attention from property managers than one might expect, given the revenue potential of a sellout. One reason is that some properties are too slow in closing out discounts to restrict room availability to expected high-rate business. Hotels do close the discounts, but not always soon enough. A common practice is to set threshold levels at which discounts are closed at a predetermined level (90 percent occupancy, for example). While this approach is well meant, all it succeeds in doing is preserving the last 10 percent of the hotel's inventory for high-value guests, when a proactive approach might shut down discounts earlier and gain the hotel even more high-paying guests (and revenue).

Another reason hotels often don't focus on sold-out dates is that the persons responsible for managing the hotel's inventory are also usually responsible for high-profile tasks, including forecasting daily occupancy. Thus, a revenue manager may spend more time determining whether a particular date will run an occupancy of 65 percent or 75 percent than determining how to make the most out of excess demand on a projected 100 percent occupancy date. The process of forecasting a date's occupancy is important, but so is determining how to gain the most revenue from a sold-out date.

For all the time spent in month-end analysis of occupancy levels, average rates, and market comparisons, rarely is conclusive evidence found that properties perform as well as they could. Moreover, the more often those two questions are asked (i.e., did we fill too early? and did we turn away business on days we didn't fill?), the more employees work to give the desired revenue results. As occurs in many cases, you get what you inspect, not what you expect.

✦ LENGTH-OF-STAY CONTROLS

Implementing length-of-stay controls takes the rate management decision a step further. The essence of rate category control is having one room left to sell and deciding whether to sell it to one guest for $100 today or to wait and sell it to another guest for $150. The essence of length-of-stay controls, on the other hand, is having one room left to sell at $150 and deciding whether to sell it for one night or to wait, with the prospect of selling it to another guest for four nights. In the rate category decision, the hotel can net an additional $50, while the length-of-stay decision can generate as much as $450 in additional revenue.

Managing stay lengths is complex, but mastering length-of-stay patterns may be the most rewarding of yield management functions. The most sophisticated inventory management controls requests down to granular levels of detail:

by program or rate category, by length of stay, or by day. This level of control really requires an automated system. As is the case with managing rate discounts, however, measurable revenue improvements connected to length of stay can be achieved without sophisticated automated systems, as long as the application of controls is kept fairly simple.

Just as setting rate control categories requires an understanding of demand by rate category, length-of-stay management requires an understanding of demand by various length-of-stay intervals. To make the call in the preceding example, the manager needs to know the level of demand for four-night stays before he or she turns away (or accepts) the request for a one-night stay.

The most common length-of-stay statistic used in the hospitality industry is average length of stay, which describes the average duration of a guest's hotel stay over a range of dates. One needs more effective statistics than simple average length of stay to manage stay patterns. What the revenue manager needs to know is the total number of arrivals on a given date for one night, two nights, three nights, four nights, five nights, and so forth. To illustrate the difference between those two statistics, imagine that a manager was determining whether to apply minimum-stay restrictions on a peak night. The manager could know that the average length of stay is 3.6 nights, or the manager could have specific length-of-stay information (e.g., 10 percent of the arrivals on a given date are for one-night stays, 25 percent are for two-night stays, and so on). Naturally, the manager wants to know how much of the demand will be affected if he or she were to reject all one-, two-, and three-night stays with the expectation that the hotel can be filled with people staying four or more nights. Table 4.2 shows an example of a chart with this type of information.

Most central reservation and property management systems developed in the last few years facilitate stay pattern controls, although at varying levels of sophistication. The ideal system enables a property's managers to set controls for each arrival date by discrete lengths of stay. Such a system enables the property to close availability to one-, four-, five-, and eight-night stays, for instance, but allow stays of two, three, six, seven, or nine nights (or longer). Most new systems at least allow minimum-stay controls by rate category.

Caution: One aspect of yield management systems' stay controls can become overused. Most

Table 4.2 Hypothetical Stay-Length Forecast

DAY	OCCUPANCY	ARRIVALS	ARRIVALS PER DAY LENGTH OF STAY (DAYS)				
			1	2	3	4	5
Wednesday	76%	117	7	9	21	41	39
Thursday	82%	103	8	17	21	24	33
Friday	90%	118	10	24	12	26	46
Saturday	100%	138	28	23	22	28	37
Sunday	83%	111	19	13	16	22	41
Monday	78%	86	12	13	18	21	22

systems allow managers to place a closed-to-arrival restriction on selected dates. This restriction enables a property to sell through stays arriving before the given date—that is, multiple-night stays for which the closed date is a second or subsequent night—but rejects all requests to arrive on that date. The problem hotels create for themselves by using this approach is that they end up saving space for two- and three-night stay-throughs while rejecting multiple-night stays by guests proposing to arrive on the closed night.

Obviously, the hotel does not want to lose revenue from stay-through guests to those staying for just the closed night, but having the system forbid a multiple-night stay that begins on the peak night may actually be worse than having no controls at all. In such a case, some form of minimum or other discrete length-of-stay controls is appropriate. Any property still using a flat closed-to-arrival restriction should reconsider in light of this problem.

✦ GROUPS: RATES, DATES, AND SPACE

Yield management is usually thought of in the context of turning away undesirable business during excess demand periods. However, the real art of yield management is learning how to turn undesirable booking requests into desirable ones. Thus, an important element of yield management is teaching all employees the art of saying yes.

The art of saying yes is particularly important in negotiating group business, which generally involves decisions about rates, dates, and space. *Rates* are how much the group is going to pay; *dates* are when the group is going to be staying; and *space* is how many rooms the group will use. Turning an undesirable proposal into a desirable contract involves varying these components until both the hotel's sales associate and the meeting planners have what they consider a worthwhile package. Too often, hoteliers either deny a group's request outright or focus on adjusting the group's proposed room rate to make the request appealing to the hotel. At times, the better response is to give the group the rate it requests but to change the dates of the proposed business to a time when the hotel's forecast is for empty rooms. Even less obvious is the option to ask the group to change the number of rooms it proposes to block. Committing to more rooms (and thus more overall revenue) or fewer rooms (reducing displacement) leaves the opportunity to sell to a second group interested in your property.

Applying revenue management principles to group business involves more than changing a group's proposal from undesirable to acceptable. Perhaps even more important is the ability to make a proposal that is merely acceptable into a contract that represents a great piece of business. Working within a hotel's normal acceptable boundaries, one thing that typically makes a proposed piece of business undesirable is the hotel's ability to sell that space to others at a better profit margin. That's why the most common response to an unacceptable proposal is to ask for a higher price.

Turning a mediocre proposal into an excellent piece of business might work as in the following example. Say that one group requests 200 rooms at a 350-room hotel for $80 per room, which is a $16,000 piece of business that was really not expected. The forecast shows that the total revenue without the group for that date would have been $29,000 with 290 rooms booked at an average rate of $100. The group's business will bring the hotel to 100 percent occupancy and generate a total of $31,000 in revenue (having displaced some of the forecasted transient arrivals). The revenue on the 60 extra rooms gives the hotel more than enough incentive to accept this group, with a $2,000 increase in total revenue. (Assume per-room ancillary spending offsets the variable costs on the extra rooms.)

Any good sales director is going to feel good about the $16,000 in business he or she helped bring to the hotel. Even if someone points out that the business really brought only $2,000 in additional revenue to the hotel, there still is reason to feel good about this arrangement. Another way to look at this group, however, is that it represents $16,000 in unanticipated room revenue from which the hotel is extracting only an additional $2,000 in revenue because the group has displaced higher-rate business. By manipulating the other variables and, in this case, moving this group to a date that will displace little other business, the hotel can extract maximum value from this group. Even if the hotel needed to reduce the room rate to $60 to entice the group to move to other dates, the added value would be $12,000 instead of $2,000, because the group would be displacing less (anticipated) higher-rate business. Note that the calculations for this example are for only one night, but a group would typically stay for multiple nights, thus amplifying both the benefit of moving the group and the penalty for accepting the proposal as offered.

The hotel could also propose that the group's room block be smaller—for example, in a situation where the group is attending a convention for which the dates are already fixed. This proposal is less effective from both the hotel's point of view and that of the group, but it still in-creases the value of the group. Because the forecast is that the group would displace 140 rooms that would have sold to transients at $100 each, the hotel gains back $20 in displaced revenue for every room sold to transients instead of to the group. Cutting the group's room block in half, for instance, actually nets the hotel another $2,000 in revenue. While the group has little incentive to reduce its request for rooms (unless the market is otherwise sold out), the hotel could insist that the group block fewer rooms if the group's original offer did not make up for revenues the hotel would have obtained from transients.

✦ CONCLUSION

Whether a hotel is just getting started or is ready to take the next logical step toward more sophisticated inventory controls, systems are available to support its efforts.

The concept of volume discount does not always apply in an environment where the supply is limited, as in the case of a hotel that is near to selling out. Sometimes less is more. This is a particularly important message for meeting planners who inflate their numbers, assuming this will make their business more appealing to the hotel.

Unfortunately, forces may work against taking the types of revenue-enhancing actions discussed here. One is the tendency to accept the first option that clears the hotel's minimum standards, or to accept the business but negotiate on the rate. Current sales-incentive plans are possibly another hindrance to these opportunities. Even the more progressive incentive plans that reward sales activities based on revenues rather than just room-nights can discourage behavior that benefits the hotel. This is done by encouraging the salesperson to book business that may not develop the highest revenue for the hotel, as in the example of the group that proposed to book 200 rooms.

✦ CASE STUDY: THE POWER OF INFORMATION

This case study explains how Disney uses simple information about hotel guests' stay patterns to increase revenues at their Orlando resort hotels (Quain et al., 1998). One of the highest-demand weeks of the entire year in Central Florida is the holiday week between Christmas and New Year's Day. Ironically, this strong week is followed by one of the lowest-occupancy weeks of the entire year, the first week of January. Disney's Orlando resorts typically sell out the Christmas to New Year's dates by the end of September, if not sooner. But the first week in January has been a challenge for Walt Disney World's marketers, who have developed programs and events to fill the void caused by the exit of the holiday crowd. Although Florida residents can be tempted with deep discounts to boost the occupancy for the month of January, the resorts cannot develop enough demand to fill their rooms one week following one of the biggest holidays of the year.

Disney took many creative measures to boost the resorts' occupancy that week. For example, the Walt Disney World Marathon, which was originally held during the three-day Martin Luther King Jr. holiday weekend to help ensure the race's success, was moved to the first weekend of January. The move was a win for both the race and the hotels. The Martin Luther King holiday weekend maintained its strong occupancy levels without the marathon, and the end of the first week of January received a much-needed occupancy boost from the marathoners and their families. The good news for racers, moreover, was that more of them could find a room at the Walt Disney World resorts because they no longer had to compete with vacationers for limited rooms over the King holiday weekend. Despite the marathon's success, Walt Disney World's marketers knew this was not the complete answer, and they continued to look for ways to increase hotel occupancy immediately following the holidays.

As part of the effort to increase occupancy during the first week of January, the revenue management department at Disney began studying ways to use minimum-stay controls in conjunction with New Year's Eve to preserve rooms for guests who wanted to stay beyond New Year's Day. This was in the early days of yield management, when length-of-stay controls were relatively uncommon and a new corporate culture had to be developed. Such a seemingly extreme concept drew skepticism and concern within the company. Senior managers had to be reassured that this new form of controlling inventory would not end up causing them to carry empty rooms during their busy season.

In another demonstration of how knowledge is power, the revenue management department had recently developed a report that summarized arrivals by length of stay (a concept discussed by Cross, 1997). This report demonstrated two things: First, they did indeed have demand for guests arriving late in the holiday week and staying through several days into January; second, over 35 percent of arrivals during the holidays were guests staying three or fewer nights. Disney's estimates of unconstrained demand over the holidays indicated it could easily afford to accept stays of four nights or longer only and still sell out its peak nights.

Taking a deep breath, Disney's revenue managers set a minimum-stay restriction for arrivals during the holiday week accepting reservations for four nights or longer only. This calculated decision was intended to improve revenue during the first week of January while presenting minimal risk to the normal strong revenues during the preceding holiday week. The experiment attracted attention throughout the company. When late September came and the resorts were not sold out, some people were concerned the holiday might not fill. However, the forecast predicted the resorts would not be sold out by the usual late September date under the four-night minimum stay restraint. Because of the limitation, Disney was turning away shorter-stay requests that in previous years would have been accepted (and sold out the holiday week by September), with the forecasted expectation that the resorts could book longer stays to guests calling in October, November, and even early December. Trend reports helped affirm the resorts were still on a pace that would sell out the hotels, which eased some minds in the revenue management department. (It is worth noting that guests desiring a short stay could be offered almost their pick of rooms the week after New Year's Day.)

The final results were well worth the effort and nail-biting. The hotels filled to capacity over the holidays, having sold out in late October. Occupancy for the first week of January rose 10 percentage points, almost entirely driven by guests arriving prior to New Year's Day and staying the minimum four nights. The room revenue contribution alone was worth over $1.5 million.

Disney's success in this example highlights a simple principle that many hotels miss. Disney was not paralyzed by the fact that it did not have perfect information or that it was not in a position to maximize revenue with optimal inventory controls. Instead, Disney's revenue managers made use of the information available to them to achieve a measured improvement in revenue while minimizing their risk.

✦ THE REVENUE MANAGEMENT GAME

The following game (accessible at www.goconcierge.net/gotconcierge/gotconcierge.pdf), developed by Dennis Quinn, has been used by guest speakers at Cornell University's School of Hospitality Administration to initiate discussions on the objectives of yield management. It is not an exercise in identifying who is proficient at yield management decisions. Rather, it is intended to demonstrate how capacity controls can affect a hotel's revenues and to develop an appreciation for the process throughout the organization.

OBJECTIVE

Maximize room revenue for a five-room hotel.

RULES

As each reservation request is announced (use Table 4.3), participants decide whether they wish to accept the request at the time it is made. Accepted reservations are recorded on the chart with the room rate written in each

Table 4.3 Reservation Requests

CALL NUMBER	ROOM RATE	ARRIVAL DAY	STAY LENGTH	COMMENTS
1	$ 80	Thurs	3	
2	$ 80	Tues	2	
3	$120	Fri	2	
4	$ 40	Mon	1	$40 is below your average rate goal for the week. Should you take it anyway if Monday is going to run vacant? We've seen incremental groups turned away because management warned sales to meet the monthly average rate goal. Be careful of what you ask for.
5	$120	Tues	1	
6	$ 60	Thurs	3	First, tell audience this is AAA discount (instead of telling them the rate). Point out the value of tracking rates versus source of business when managing inventory.
7	$120	Sat	1	
8	$ 60	Tues	5	
9	$ 60	Thurs	3	This is a package that includes dinner shows, meals, and recreation, which adds $110 in value to the hotel each night. Discussion: room revenue goals versus total profitability. Assign programs to rate buckets based on total value, not just room rate.
10	$ 40	Tues	5	
11	$ 80	Tues	5	
12	$120	Sat	1	
13	$100	Mon	2	
14	$ 60	Fri	2	
15	$100	Fri	2	
16	$100	Sun	7	What does it cost for you to lose this business?
17	$ 40	Sun	3	
18	$ 60	Sun	4	

date block (Table 4.4). Once a day is sold out, subsequent requests that include that day must be rejected. At the end of the game, participants add up the total revenue they generated for that week.

Hints

- Participants cannot go back and add a prior reservation once the next call is announced. The prior guest has hung up and booked with the competitor.

Table 4.4 Booking Grid for Five Room Hotel

	SUN.	MON.	TUES.	WED.	THURS.	FRI.	SAT.	TOTAL
Fill in the room rate for each accepted reservation for the appropriate number of days.								
Room 1								
Room 2								
Room 3								
Room 4								
Room 5								
Total								

- No, overbooking is not an option.

- The host should fill in a booking grid on a first-come, first-served basis, denying requests only when days are sold out. This will serve as the no-control method.

- You can let the audience know they will receive a maximum of 18 calls, if you want to help out.

- Remember, this is not a game of skill. It is a game for demonstration and discussion. The hotel's next revenue manager will not be selected based on the results of this game!

GAME DISCUSSION POINTS

Each participant should compare the difference between optimal revenue and the actual revenue achieved. (Optimal revenue in the above game is $2,360.) Divide the difference into actual revenue to show the percentage of potential improvement. For example, if a participant earned $2,000, the potential for improvement is 18 percent—that is, $(2,360 - 2,000) + 2,000 = 18$.

How much is that percentage improvement in annual room revenue worth to the hotel? How about half that improvement? How much revenue might management be leaving on the table at the hotel? For example, what would be the hotel's annual room revenue multiplied by 118 percent? How about by 109 percent?

What is the percentage occupancy of the hotel in the no-control environment? How does that make participants feel about low-occupancy months?

Did anyone score below the no-control level? What does this tell you about the need to make responsible decisions when accepting reservations?

4.4 THREE DECADES OF REVENUE MANAGEMENT: WHAT'S NEXT?

Silvia Milla and Stowe Shoemaker

ABSTRACT. This paper discusses future trends in revenue management (RM) in the hotel industry based on interviews with industry leaders. The integration of customer behaviour and preferences into marketing and pricing strategies appears to be a major future trend. Examples of this trend are the increased attention given to the analysis of total customer value both in the short and long term. Group RM is also receiving considerable attention from hoteliers. Many of the participants interviewed identified a need to improve the accuracy of forecasting, given the increased complexity of group business. To reap the benefits of these new strategies, companies will need to invest in technological as well as human support. In the past, RM has been driven by the search for technological solutions to improve RM techniques. In the future, it is foreseen that the customer will be the driving force of all RM efforts. *Journal of Revenue and Pricing Management* (2008) 7, 110–114. doi:10.1057/palgrave.rpm.5160127. Published online 4 January 2008.

✦ INTRODUCTION

Table 4.5 List of Interviewees

NAME	POSITION	COMPANY
Chris Bishop	Senior Director of Corporate Revenue Mgt	Harrah's Entertainment
Elizabeth Cambra	Corporate Director, Revenue Optimisation	Outrigger Enterprises Group
Bill Carroll	Senior Lecturer	Cornell University
Kathlen Cullen	Partner	Inspire Resources
Tim Coleman	VP Revenue Management	MGM Brands
Sharon Duffy	VP of Revenue Management	Hilton Hotels Corporation
Chris Elam	VP of Revenue Management	Hyatt Hotels Corporation
Jan Freitag	Director	Smith Travel Research
Tim Genovese	VP of Hotel Performance Support	Intercontinental Hotel Group
Carryl Helsel	Partner	Inspire Resources
Jon Higbie	Director of Revenue	Revenue Analytics
Warren Lieberman	President	Veritec Solutions
Sameer Mehra	Revenue Manager	Oberoi Hotels
Mahindroo Puneet	Corporate Director of Revenue Management & Global Distribution	Taj Hotels
John Riddel	Senior Vice-President Pricing	PROS Revenue Management
James Ruttley	VP, Client Services	IDEAS
Jimmy Suh	Managing Director	The PLC Group
November, 2007		

This paper presents an overview of the future of revenue management (RM) based on interviews conducted with industry leaders around the world. Table 4.5 provides a list of our interviewees.

Four major areas were identified as having the greatest growth potential in hotel RM:

1. Integration of customer relationship management (CRM) and RM

2. Pricing, segmentation, packaging

3. Group RM

4. Organisational structure

Below we briefly expand upon each of these areas.

✦ CRM AND RM

The integration of CRM and RM was a theme we heard repeatedly throughout our various phone calls. Yet, as stated by Tim Genovese of Intercontinental Hotel Group, 'Revenue management practices at this stage of the game do not take a great deal of relationship management into account, except for special corporate rates for volume accounts'.

However, industry experts see the integration of CRM and RM as one of the areas with the most potential for the future of RM. Puneet Mahindroo, with Taj Hotels, believes that it is becoming increasingly difficult for hotels to differentiate both their products and their pricing among their competitors. 'Amalgamating customer relationship management and revenue management will be critical for hotels to create new, more creative differentiation strategies'. John Riddel with PROS Revenue Management also illustrates this idea: 'Companies are going to need to focus more and more on total customer value and not on just the myopic perspective of one sale'.

The integration of PMS, RES, and RM systems is still a challenge for many companies as the technology systems are not all fully compatible. 'Right now, we have a number of fragmented systems in the industry that try to play along well together', says Jimmy Suh from the PLC Group. Tim Coleman of the MGM concurs: 'There are tremendous problems of integration still today in

the industry'. In the next few years, further collaboration among software vendors will need to take place in order to resolve conflicts between systems, such as having different aggregation levels in customer segmentation. Further investment in upgrading and integrating systems will also help solve the current data management problems.

The analysis of customers' buying patterns based on their lifecycles can also be an interesting area for the future of RM, especially for hotel companies that focus on long-term relationships. For example, even if three customers have spent the same amount of money over a certain number of years, the buying behaviour of a 40-year-old married businessman may differ from that of a 65-year-old leisure traveler or a single 25-year-old female. Mahindroo argues: 'There are practical realities to face. If a customer has been supporting a hotel for many years, the customer has gone through many different lifecycles. The question is how to assess which lifecycle is the most profitable. I don't yet have an answer for that question, but would like to'. Identifying the parameters by which the lifecycle can be measured and translating them into pricing solutions is a challenge. 'I would be interested in seeing a study that quantifies the lifecycle of customers', Coleman acknowledged.

✦ PRICING, SEGMENTATION, AND PACKAGING

Companies have recently started to realise the importance of pricing for revenue maximisation in addition to optimising inventory allocation. John Riddel argues that the discipline of RM should, in the future, be called price optimisation. 'You can't change rooms very fast but you can sure change the price. It gives you final control'.

At present, pricing strategies do not make a distinction between customers' frequency of stay. 'Pricing is currently a commodity type of pricing, where a customer that has stayed 100 nights is quoted the same rate as one that stays only one night over a peak time', argues Tim Genovese.

Understanding consumers' buying behaviour and price elasticity in order to be able to charge the right price to each customer will become increasingly important. 'Yield management opens and closes each rate. The key question is what should the rate be', highlights John Higbie with Revenue Analytics. Tim Coleman further illustrates this point: 'The finer we can segment our market, the better we can target and get the right product in front of the right customer in the right channel at the right price'.

There is also much discussion in the field about one-to-one pricing as a future trend. This involves the ability to price each individual customer differently. Interviewees were asked whether they saw it as a future trend. Not everyone is in agreement as to its practicality. John Riddel believes that as we continue to understand customer buying behaviour, in the future every single customer will be charged a different price. James Ruttley, on the other hand, argues that the issue is not to have a particular price for each particular customer but more to identify what segment each customer is coming from. 'Getting down to that level of detail (individual customer) wouldn't necessarily make sense', he explains. Hoteliers seem to agree with Ruttley. Some leaders foresee that customer segmentation will only have smaller market groups in the near future. Genovese points out: 'Segmentation is only going to get larger but it will be a long time before it can get as detailed

as one customer per segment'. Mahindroo also agrees: 'It (one-to-one pricing) sounds very good in theory. In reality, how can you achieve that? In the near future, we can only hope to provide customized offerings for a select group of preferred customers out of a database of a million customers'.

Tim Coleman provided a wonderful insight into one-to-one pricing when he said: 'You don't need a price for each customer. What's important is that customers feel that the price is unique to them'.

The industry agrees that dynamic packaging and pricing is a major future trend in RM. 'From a customer's perspective, it will be important that customers feel that the product, service and price they are given are based on their needs', says James Ruttley. Chris Bishop with Harrah's Entertainment explains: 'In the near future, customers will be able to use drop-down menus to choose if they want a bottle of wine in their room, use the spa or attend a show'. This will be particularly important for experience-sensitive customers, who can be offered a variety of options to choose from and charged accordingly with bundled prices. A key issue to solve is what the right price would be for each particular package to each particular customer. A distinction was made by Tim Coleman between making unique offerings to customers and making a customer feel special. The former is not necessary because it would involve getting to such a level a detail that even if technologically feasible, it would be operationally unachievable. According to Coleman, the key is to create the perception that customers are treated in a unique way, although technically it may not be the case.

✦ GROUP RM

Industry leaders were also asked to comment on the main future trends of group RM. One of the areas where group RM is likely to grow in the future is in the area of group forecasting. 'Group revenue management should get down to the same level of detail as transient yield management and group-acceptance decisions should be made based on alternative group displacement instead of only transient displacement', argues John Riddel.

Taking into account the total value of a group and not just room revenues is an area that is getting more attention in the group business. Variables should be expanded to include size, room and non-room spend, length of stay, use of function space, and so forth. Also, it is important to calculate the number of actual reserved rooms out of the total number of rooms blocked. Unbooked rooms, no shows (wash), and early check-outs in groups are a common occurrence. The later usually depends on the activities programmed by the company for the last day. 'Being able to forecast all these factors becomes critical', says Tim Coleman.

A possible current limitation in group forecasting may be technological. Systems at present are only able to take into account several variables at a time, argues John Higbie. Software vendors acknowledge that most present RM systems are not so powerful and are not fully suitable to compare the profitability of two groups as opposed to just looking at the opportunity cost of traditional transient displacement. Purveyors, however, are working on new and more complex group RM software solutions and progress will be seen in the near future.

The ability for groups to do online booking represents another challenge from a technological and a pricing perspective. Quoting small groups online is certainly more achievable than quoting large groups with different needs or groups that require more personalised attention. A problem to solve in online booking is the calculation of unconstrained demand. 'Every time a group makes an online request, it is used to calculate demand, which will necessarily increase the rates for the next group that tries to book an event during the same dates', explains Sameer Mehra with Oberoi Hotels. The convenience of the Internet, however, makes online booking an attractive option for meeting planners, and it is expected that more of it will be seen in the future.

✦ ORGANISATIONAL STRUCTURE

The RM function is undergoing critical changes in hotels. Industry leaders were asked to define the optimal organisational structure of the RM function at hotels. Some favoured the idea of having a centralised RM structure, while others argued in favour of having a local RM team.

Jimmy Suh, for example, argues that having a centralised RM team at the corporate office could be beneficial for the hotel as more skilled individuals are attracted to a single location and are able to execute strategies more effectively. They can also receive a better compensation for their work. Along the same lines, Tim Genovese contends that as the RM function increases in complexity, fewer and fewer revenue managers will be seen on properties, especially small and midsized hotels, because there will be fewer individuals with the necessary skill set that hotels can afford to have at each property. John Riddel further emphasises this point, highlighting the fact that RM in the future will need such specialised human capital that the function will have to become more and more centralised.

One advantage of having a centralised RM team is distributing the cost over several properties. With technology, remote RM is becoming increasingly more feasible. Moreover, it would help bring more revenues to all properties rather than each individual property maximising its own revenues. 'Demand can be shifted between properties, instead of steeply discounting prices in one property in order to steal demand from another property of the same chain', indicates John Riddel.

On the other hand, Bill Carroll with Cornell University is in favour of a local RM function. He argues that the nuances of the transient and group markets demand individuals who are knowledgeable about the specific area and market where the hotel is located. Having a centralised function with a single revenue manager for several hotels will deprive the RM function of a vital input, which is the knowledge of the market that being at the property provides to revenue managers.

Another point of contention about the organisational structure in a hotel is the interaction between sales and RM. This can often be a source of conflict, as the departments may work towards achieving different goals. Most interviewees view marketing and RM in hotels as having equally important roles and working side by side to understand and fully integrate CRM and RM.

Regardless of the organisational structure, argues Tim Coleman, the leadership potential of revenue managers is paramount as the role gains more and more centrality in the organisation. Another aspect highlighted by interviewees was the need to make departments accountable for their decisions. Warren Lieberman with Veritec Solutions explains: 'Performance measurement is critical for maximizing the long-term impact of a RM team. Negotiation can take place but, later on, departments should be accountable for the decisions that were made through performance measurement'.

Going a step further into the future, some industry leaders are talking about a fully integrated RM function that oversees the marketing, sales, pricing and distribution functions of a hotel. Owing to the lack of individuals trained in both areas, and particularly, the need to change people's mindsets, this integrated structure is still a long way away. The RM function, however, is evolving at a fast pace. 'The position of director of revenue management is more often seen at hotels as they recognize the importance of the position', highlights Carryl Helsel of Inspire Resources. Before this can happen, companies need to recruit and train individuals who can competently respond to the needs of the RM function. 'Right now, hotels have purchased systems that they do not have a chance of fully exploiting because of the lack of sufficiently skilled personnel', argues John Higbie. Jimmy Suh agrees: 'A huge understated initiative in the industry is the need to start attracting more talented people and not only attracting them but placing them in the position in which they could oversee the decision-making process for some of the sales and marketing strategies'.

Extracting the full potential of technology ultimately depends on the people using it. Proper utilisation of systems is still an issue in the hospitality industry, as Kathleen Cullen of Inspire Resources well illustrates:

No matter how sophisticated technology can be, a challenge of today is the lack of sophisticated users of the RMSs. Too many RMs believe that they can out-think the system. Many end up placing overrides on the RMSs without fully understanding the negative impact this is having on the system recommendations. This continues to a point of the RMS being blamed for a lack of proper recommendations.

✦ CONCLUSION

Differentiating the product and service through CRM enabled companies to take better care of customers' needs. The future of RM calls for the alignment of marketing strategies with revenue goals in a more fully integrated manner to be able to provide customers with a customised product at a price they are willing to pay. How customers will react to increased scrutiny, dynamic pricing, and a myriad of other situations is an interesting point for further investigation. It is foreseen that as much as technology has been the driver and enabler of RM in the last few decades, the customer will be the driver of RM in the years ahead.

4.5 CONCIERGE (CONE-SEE-AIR-J) Mario Arnaldo

I vividly remember my first and last contacts with a concierge.

First contact. Not knowing the correct term, I would simply have called him "the Supe," or building superintendent. We had just moved to France after enjoying a year in Somalia, East Africa. My dad used to work for the United Nations, so we literally moved to different countries and continents every 2 or 3 years. This time our home was an apartment on the seventh floor of a well-used building in the immediate outskirts of Paris. We have our own concierge? Wow! And his name is Monsieur Guy de Roquefort? I was only 14 years old, so it was easy to get impressed, or disappointed. Well, Monsieur de Roquefort's scent certainly reminded me of the cheese with his namesake. He was unshaven and less than tidy. His uniform *du jour* was an undershirt, a stick of Gauloises (French cigarettes) in one hand and a glass of cheap Beaujolais in the other. But Guy had a good heart, engaged me in titillating conversations about "cherchez les femmes" (much more rewarding than the four-hour French lessons I had in school), always fixed the toilets that wouldn't flush, and delighted in announcing every single piece of mail we received. He probably would not get within 50 feet of an employment agency. However, if I could give him a shower and a shirt, I would hire him in a heartbeat. Monsieur Guy de Roquefort's *soul* was in the right place. I still remember him, see? That was in 1964.

I fondly remember my most recent contact with a concierge.

Last contact. This article was written in 2004. Forty years later is a long stretch of time after my first contact with a concierge. Thanks to my dad's international assignments, I've used up seven passports. Thanks to my two international airline jobs, I've filled up my last passport with immigration stamps from 32 cities in 5 continents. I have enjoyed a privileged opportunity to meet and work with a multitude of professionals, but one, in particular, in Seattle, stays in my memory.

She was punctual. Polite. Charming. Endearing. Never forgot the slightest detail. Never overbearing or invasive. Made my socks roll up and down with legendary service. Went way beyond the call of duty in answering the simplest of requests. "Where can we get great fresh oysters? Where is . . . ? How do we . . . ?" It was as if my engagement and honeymoon to come were made in heaven. This was in 1997. Since then, she has faithfully written us every year during the holiday season with neat, short, handwritten, personal notes. Her envelopes are also written by hand. She does not use insensitive, computer-generated labels. She always hopes we will come back to visit her again and enjoy Seattle. She has *never* asked questions like, "Can we book a room for you?" We correspond regularly about hospitality concepts to bring reality to my hospitality students, or ideas she can bring to her in-house training programs. On two occasions, Mr. Robert Thurston, managing general partner, enthusiastically gave us permission to study his hotel as a class project, long distance from Honolulu!

That's Annie Delucchi, former concierge at the Inn at The Market, a great boutique hotel in Seattle, literally a shout away from Pike Place Market. Eight months prior to our arrival at the IATM, my fiancée and I had never met Annie. All our interactions were via email. Not even a phone call. Annie has since been promoted to executive liaison at the IATM. Know what? If my wife and I were given complimentary reservations at an-

other Seattle property, we would still go to Annie's property and pay for our rooms. You see, I'm not just a reservation record on the IATM database. I can be me, someone who has a preference for fresh oysters! My wife is not "the Mrs." She, too, can be herself. She can spend the whole day walking back and forth to Pike Place Market to select just the right bouquet of fresh flowers or just the right jewelry accessories. Annie Delucchi's *soul* is in the right place.

Wassup? During the fall 2003 semester, I was designing interactive games for my international students to enjoy as part of our weekly class discussions. One of these games was the Concierge Game. This game is the basis for the research I did on concierges for this article.

So I reviewed the Witham concierge articles, used Google to point me to a few hundred pages of articles, scoured dozens of concierge-related websites, emailed and talked to dozens of hospitality professionals, and finally interviewed concierges in Honolulu, Hawaii, to highlight six significant findings about the modern concierge. The six findings concern passion, titles, technology, Les Clefs d'Or, stars, and Aloha!

Finding #1: Passion. The concierges and guest service staff I talked to, whether they had their keys or not, are, without exception, passionate about what they do. They all have what some have called *gotta-wanna,* an almost insatiable desire to exceed customer expectations with minor regard for themselves or the time clock.

Finding #2: Titles. Got concierge? Job titles I compiled included concierge, head concierge, chef concierge, concierge supervisor, lobby concierge, guest service agent, guest services manager or supervisor, activity agent, and the more recent compcierge and technocierge, for those who assist road warriors with laptops and other electronic paraphernalia. However, whether or not properties enjoy a keyed concierge, management must openly recognize and support the need to provide concierge services. Anecdotally, seasoned concierges, no matter what they are titled, will tell you, as do Nargil, Kahn, and Peterson (2003) that "one doesn't have to be at an upscale property to provide the kind of service that will keep guests coming back." Presence of a concierge, keyed or not, is a plus when it comes to four-star and five-star ratings (*Mobil Travel Guide*) or four-diamond and five-diamond ratings (AAA). The concierges and guest service staff I met are part of front desk operations, with a designated area close to—but distinct from—the check-in area. When I visited some Honolulu hotels, the front desk areas appeared to have lulls in operation during midmorning hours, after check-out rush time, and before afternoon check-in times. In contrast, the concierge area appeared to be continuously busy whether midmorning, noon, afternoon, or early evening.

More and more organizations are answering "Yes!" to the question "Got concierge?"

A fall 2003 television series, *Life of Luxury,* with Robin Leach, featured one of the more exclusive UK concierge services, Quintessentially. Quintessentially, a membership organization affiliated with luxury facilities worldwide, essentially provides the same services the lobby-based concierge would without the restrictions of being in a facility. According to their website (www.quintessentially.com/home.php):

> Quintessentially aims to satisfy practically any last-minute whim our members may have, from front row seats at a fashion show and spur of the moment chartered yachts, to impossible

dinner reservations at some of the world's most exclusive restaurants and last-minute theatre tickets, and with 24/7 member telephone and email assistance our experts are always on hand to save you time, hassle and money. Fantastic offshoots of the Quintessentially brand include the Quintessentially magazine and the exclusive Quintessentially "Beyond Black" credit card. Quintessentially members are also continuously kept up to date with what's hot and what's not through our weekly newsletter, offering indispensable advice on the essential art and cultural events of the moment, as well as invitations to charity affairs, gala balls, shopping evenings, film premieres and exclusive after-event parties.

In the middle of finalizing this article in December 2003, my own university, Hawaii Pacific University, advertised its latest service. Guess what it was? Yep! A concierge desk to help students and other stakeholders access and utilize the services of the university.

Finding #3: Technology and the Compcierge. I predict that no amount of technology will ever replace the concierge or guest service staff. Inger Boudouris and the other concierges I interviewed or emailed agreed with this prediction. However, there is room to enjoy and take advantage of what the current technology has to offer. You don't have to look far. Check out the extensive usage of PDAs in last fall's TV series *Las Vegas* and *The Threat Matrix*. At one end of the technology spectrum, the Westin Santa Clara uses Sony's Contact-ME for remote video conferencing from the concierge's home (a three-hour round-trip commute) directly to the hotel lobby's monitor, some 80 miles away. After some weeks of emailing, I obtained permission from the Westin Santa Clara general manager and support from Clifford Planning, LLC, a premier Hawaii-based architectural firm, to conduct a 1-hour videoconference between Anna Morris and my hotel and resort management students. We had a terrific experience; this is a perfect example of the application of technology to enhance a traditional service rather than replace it.

At another level of technology, interactive software programs such as GoConcierge (GC) [http://www.goconcierge.net/home/] allows a user to manage and provide guests with information and services in a consistently impressive manner. Adam Isrow, who designed and developed this interactive web-based program, provided me a username and password and gave me an opportunity to validate and confirm for myself how user-friendly GC was. I predict the concierge's uniform will include a wireless PDA, a camera-video cell phone, a software program similar to GoConcierge, and other electronic gadgetry. Isrow said in an interview:

> I think you appropriately summarize the commonality of the concierge position with passion! These people (generally speaking) love what they do, love people, and are therefore great people to be around. I enjoyed your prediction—video cell phone and a PDA—I don't think you are too far off!

And then there's Mike Doi, a guest services coordinator, sitting in the Outrigger lobby on Waikiki Beach, with his uncanny memory for names, places, phone numbers and his reliable Rolodex. He does have a computer monitor at his desk, but like many concierges, prefers not to use it while interacting with a guest. Mike also shifts from speaking English to Japanese to pidgin and back without blinking an eyelash, on the phone and with walk-ins who step up to his desk.

Others exemplified by Dave Nishi and Sally Yates agree it would be wonderful for their properties to enjoy state-of-the-art technology, more computers, more staff, and more space. From my conversations with them, I found that both Dave and Sally are equally adamant about not letting the gadgetry come between the guest and the service provider. Know what? Dave, guest services manager at the Ohana Maile Sky Court, can't even spell *Les Clefs d'Or,* but he has over 25 years of customer service under his belt. Dave also has many years of information technology (IT) experience, but given the choice, says, "I always prefer to deal with the guests face to face. Sometimes you just can't trust your computer or PDA." Sally is one of only a handful of Les Clefs d'Or concierges in Hawaii, and she has enjoyed her position as senior concierge at the Halekulani Hotel for over 10 years. She says, "We enjoy working with our guests on a personal one-on-one basis at the desk, and sometimes the computer work takes us away from that service." One concern we discussed was maximizing eye contact with the guest, or avoiding interactions that take your eyes away from the guest.

I found these statements enjoyably revealing because (a) they were self-initiated, (b) Dave works in a three-star property and Sally in a four-star property, and (c) Dave and Sally have never met.

Finding #4: Les Clefs d'Or (LCD) USA. In the original Witham article on concierges (1983), there were about 40 members in LCD USA. Back then, many travelers didn't know whether a concierge was Mozart's second movement in D flat or the alternate entrée. In 1993, there were 200 U.S. concierges in the LCD membership, and the savvy traveler started looking for the concierge. Even in fiction, 007 (James Bond) had his hotel contacts—concierges! In 2003, there were 450 concierge members in LCD USA representing over 100,000 rooms in 250 four- and five-star properties.

Over 3400 international members from 37 countries make up the LCD worldwide. The LCD headquarters in Paris is called the Union International des Concierges d'Hôtels. Although the concierge position is predominantly male in Europe and other countries, 53 percent of U.S. concierges are female.

Concierges continuously network with one another and the communities in which they work. Concierge associations are found in many cities throughout the United States. Some only admit hotel concierges as members (LCD as well as non-LCD concierges); others include local vendors and employees from car rental agencies, tour companies, tour guides, restaurants, art galleries, and so on (maybe even university concierges! Who knows?).

Many concierge country sections also have community-based organizations. In the United States, for example, Les Clefs d'Or Foundation of the Americas (United States, Canada, Mexico, and Brazil) provides financial support and in-kind donations of goods and was founded to respond to the suffering of concierges and/or their families and significant others affected by catastrophic or life-threatening illnesses.

Charles Holzer, director of media for LCD USA and chef concierge at the RiverPlace Hotel in Portland, Oregon, explained to me:

> Each [LCD local chapter] is different in its composition, yet each association's purpose is the same: to positively enhance the guest experience through knowledge, education, mentoring, networking, and friendship. In general, local

meetings consist of an educational element, whether that is speakers from local organizations, vendors, or attractions. This could also entail bringing in members from the hospitality industry to discuss strengthening the concierge desk, enhancing revenue, or working in a more supportive manner with management.

After I interviewed Inger Boudouris by phone, we spoke and corresponded many times. In one of our discussions, this is what Inger told me about concierges:

> You know, being a concierge is being a "concierge for all seasons," because you must be able to turn around on a dime, multitasking and at the same time making important decisions while talking on the phone, et cetera! I love being a concierge because of what I call the unpredictable challenges, and it makes one's life very exciting—no day, no hour, no minute is the same. There is no time for stress because you are always in the midst of happenings. Today, it's snowing. We have a wedding ceremony in our lobby this afternoon. Afternoon tea will be served in the pub today, wedding receptions everywhere, and in the middle of all this, guests will be checking in and out—I love it!

A brief but supremely informative phone interview with Shujaat Khan, vice president of LCD USA and chef concierge at the Capitol Hilton in Washington, DC, revealed these weathered and tested beliefs:

- Time management of your skills is extremely important when you have only limited resources!

- How much do you really love people? The professional in you needs to come out, especially when you're being challenged with the unruly customer, the overdemanding VIP, or the jealous significant other!

- The successful concierge operation is always a major business revenue generator.

- How do you fix the dissatisfied? The process usually ends up being more important than the end product.

- Of paramount importance to the future concierge: exercising the best balance of ethics and the highest code of conduct.

Finding #5: Got stars? Not? Don Massagli (2002) wrote an article that at first glance appears to be a straightforward commentary applauding the assurance, confidence, and customer relations packaged in your hotel concierge. The reader should know that Massagli brings an uncommon perspective, as he is the senior vice president of Park Ridge, Illinois-based *Mobil Travel Guide* (http://www.mobiltravelguide.com/). The *Mobil Travel Guide* inspects and rates thousands of hotels and restaurants and publishes the travel guide and other travel publications. Coincidentally, I had an opportunity to interview Massagli in person; he repeated to me that concierges add a touch of distinction to any property, regardless of its star status. I predict that hotel management will pay increasingly more attention to their concierge and concierge services, whether the property has two stars or five. Jameson (Withiam, 1993) sums it up best: "[G]uests are going to ask the kind of questions that concierges routinely answer, regardless of whether the hotel has a concierge desk."

Finding #6: Aloha. (In Hawaii, Aloha means more than just "hello" or "goodbye." It also refers to a spirit that encompasses welcoming, friendly accommodation that embodies giving the gift of friendship. —Editor)

Silverman (Withiam, 1993) hit the nail on the head: "Does management create the environment to make exceeding expectations possible?" Probably not all the time. Whatever the number of stars the property has, management must continuously maintain a dynamic environment enabling all employees, whether or not they work in guest services, to exceed guests' expectations. So what is the energy source of all the legendary stories of Houdini-like concierges? My interaction with concierges in Hawaii, the "Land of Aloha," tells me that concierges are loyal and have a built-in desire to please and satisfy within legal and moral limits. The concierge in Hawaii makes it happen by practicing "service through Aloha." And when he or she doesn't have that particular desired resource (the dinner reservation, a hard-to-find gift for the significant other), he or she knows how to network out the solution through Aloha with fellow concierges.

At the time of this writing, there was no Les Clefs d'Or section in Hawaii, but there are several Les Clefs d'Or concierges on Oahu, Kapolei, and the other popular resort areas of the state. According to Pam Davis, publisher of the *Oahu Concierge* newsletter:

Our goal is to disseminate pertinent information to the hospitality industry as a whole, focusing on the latest happenings, keeping them informed on recent changes and improvements at places they might very well recommend, as well as including industry changes and promotions. As we are the only industry publication on Oahu located in one of the few cities without an official [Les Clefs d'Or] organization, we have an additional burden to try to fill that void by holding regular gatherings where industry professionals can mingle and share information, but unfortunately they are not monthly, and they rarely (due to travel complications) include those from the outer islands.

✦ LAST THOUGHTS

My research revealed Holly Stiel has probably written more about concierges than anyone else anywhere in the English-speaking and -writing world. I urge students, educators, and professionals in all service industries to browse through her website (http://www.thankyouverymuchinc.com/index.html). Any one topic she writes about could be a customer service seminar or workshop. During an interview with Holly, I was reminded of one of the quotes from her website:

> The reality is that there is no sign above the [hotel] entrance telling customers how to behave, and sometimes they behave badly. So the responsibility for appropriate behavior falls on the service provider.

And, I would argue by extrapolation, this responsibility falls specifically to guest services employees such as the concierge.

The modern concierge serves as the knowledgeable, sensitive, and efficient interface between the guest and the array of hotel and community services available to travelers. It is this exciting profession I have attempted to overview in this article.

4.6   AS I SEE IT: MANAGEMENT OF THE FRONT OFFICE

Oliver Meinzer

The following article is not based on extensive research but rather on my experience working in front office operations, as either an associate or a manager. It looks at the operation from my point of view. In this article, I write about the setup of key areas of the front office operation, namely the bellstand, the front desk, and the guest relations department. I provide some ideas about the physical setup as well as ideas about hiring the right associates and the training tools. I also provide insights into the daily tasks in all areas, what I look for as a manager, and the reasons behind certain processes and actions in the day-to-day operation.

This article should give the reader an idea about what the front office operation incorporates and what it takes to run such a department. The information can be used by the reader to understand processes better and get a good idea if working in this area is something he or she might be interested in. At the end of the chapter, I provide a timetable of a regular workday in the life of a front office manager.

✦ BELLSTAND

The bellstand and its associates are important because they are usually the first and last encounter the guest has with the hotel and its staff. Traditionally, the bell staff was considered concierge as well, as they usually had the best insider knowledge about the location and attractions, and they always had a friend or relative working there as well to get the guest a special deal. This is still the case in hotels where the bell staff has been with the property for many years. In newer properties, it is primarily the concierge who has this kind of connection. The basic duties of a bellperson include, but are not limited to, handling incoming and outgoing guest luggage, greeting arriving and departing guests as they enter or leave the hotel lobby, storage of luggage for guests, and being present in the lobby area to answer questions or assist the guests with any requests they might have. Specific tasks differ from property to property.

Depending on a property's check-in and check-out procedures, as well as the type of customer checking in or out (families on a 1-week vacation would need more time and ask more questions than a business traveler who checks in late at night and leaves early in the morning), the bell staff may spend a significant amount of time with the guest, accompanying him or her to the room and explaining the features of the hotel (including safety features like emergency exits) and its surroundings. This is a key encounter for the hotel, as the bell staff has a lot of influence on the guest, enabling the staff to steer the guest toward the hotel's outlets and amenities. This, of course, is only possible and effective if the associates are trained properly and have the necessary knowledge about the hotel offerings. A lot of hotels provide incentives for the bell staff to refer customers to the outlets, usually a dollar amount per realized reservation. The bell staff gets a lot of information from guests about their stay, experience, and encounters, and about the guests themselves. This kind of information is invaluable for the hotel. If proper reporting channels are in place (you will read more about how this information can be tracked later on in this chapter), the hotel can be proactive in addressing an incident before the guest considers it a problem. This information also helps the hotel recognize special occasions like birthdays and anniversaries. The bell staff is the hotel's eyes and ears, the ambassadors for the property. It is important to understand their significance and the influence they have on the hotel and front office operation.

The bellstand is usually located in the main entrance area, easily accessible by both guests and staff. It is usually close to a storage room where luggage and other guest items can be stored. The bellstand should have a telephone with an outside line to enable the staff to make reservations, inquire about hours of operations, and so on. A computer with access to the Internet and the property management system (PMS) allows the bell staff not only to provide the latest online information but also to access guest information like room numbers and contact information or to leave messages on guest accounts. Maps and informational material about attractions in the surrounding area help the bell staff point guests in the right direction after making recommendations about leisure activities. If no printer is attached to the computer, preprinted driving directions to popular destinations (e.g., airport, train station, landmarks) can be handed out to guests.

Luggage tags are used to label guest luggage for storage. There are usually two parts to the ticket, one for the bag/item and the second for the guest to claim the stored items later. The storage room should be big enough to handle the storage demands for the property. This room must be secured by a lockable door and access must be controlled to protect the stored items. The shelving should be arranged and labeled to reflect the numbers or letters on the luggage tags. This makes it easier for the bell staff to store and retrieve items, and it keeps the storage room organized and clean. It is important to always "tag" any stored items and ensure the customer presents their part of the tag when picking up items. Otherwise, the hotel might be held liable for lost/ missing items. The bellstand should also be equipped with plenty of luggage carts. Those carts should match the decor and category of the hotel (you probably do not want to use a wooden dolly in a five-star property). The bell staff must ensure that the carts are kept in good condition. This includes polishing the metal or brass parts as well as maintaining the carpeted area and wheels to ensure proper functionality.

Another important item for the bellstand is a so-called trip log, a simple spreadsheet where the staff marks the room numbers of check-ins and check-outs they performed. This log is a great help if you have to retrace a luggage delivery or pickup or simply as a tool to communicate which room is next. Sometimes luggage gets delivered to the wrong room (YES! This does happen), but the trip log helps the staff rectify the situation immediately.

The bellstand is a front-of-the-house area with direct guest contact. It is important that this area is kept clean and organized. The bell staff must ensure that they are wearing the proper uniform and that the uniform is in top condition. In order for the staff to attend to all guest requests and questions, it is imperative for them to have all the necessary knowledge before they start their shift. Helpful tools that ensure daily information is communicated to the front-of-the-house staff,

including a preshift meeting, where the important details for the day are being discussed, a whiteboard with information on it, or a daily newsletter in everybody's mailbox. However, it is the front office manager's responsibility that the associate either attend the preshift meeting or read the information provided on the whiteboard or newsletter to get the necessary information for their shift (as a front office manager, you can make this part of the shift and, therefore, the property's attendance policy applies).

The bell staff itself should be trained like any other front-of-the-house staff. First of all, it is important to hire the right candidates. As a front office manager, you look for applicants who are outgoing, comfortable with working in public, well groomed, and articulate, and who have a good understanding of service and a positive attitude. It is always better to interview more candidates to make sure you find the right person for the job than to go with the first decent applicant. Never compromise when it comes to hiring great staff!

Once a new bellperson is hired, proper training is key. A possible training rotation should include housekeeping (great insight into the room setup, the different room types, and locations), front desk (basic check-in and check-out procedures and basic knowledge about the property management system), the outlets (knowledge about the restaurant menu, spa offerings, etc.), loss prevention (first aid, security, and emergency procedures), as well as basic training to cover the phones—and, of course, guest contact etiquette.

Once the staff member completes the required training and is working regular shifts, regular performance checks should be implemented to ensure that his/her knowledge stays up to date. It is the front office manager's responsibility to supply the bell staff with the appropriate tools and information to perform their duties. Therefore, regular meetings are necessary to communicate any changes or additions and to collect feedback from the staff. The bell staff is at the front of the line. Their input is invaluable for the front office operation. It is important to stop everything, listen, and use their information to adjust and improve the front office operation and, ultimately, the guest experience. It has proven helpful in my workplace to cross-train other associates at the bellstand as well. Associates in loss prevention, room service, the front desk, or any other department are then able to help out at the bellstand if necessary. Sometimes, check-ins come in waves, and the current bell staff might not be able to get bags to guest rooms in a timely manner. Having the flexibility of calling associates from other departments to help out ensures guest satisfaction and is a nice change for the other associates.

Because in many cases the bellstand is located in a high-traffic area and is the first area the guest sees and interacts with, the hotel must make sure that the guest's first and last impressions are positive.

✦ FRONT DESK

The front desk or reception area is where staff-guest interaction is probably most intense. The front desk manages the room inventory as well as the check-in and check-out process and the account activities for each guest in house. The front desk assigns rooms to the arriving guests according to their preferences and requests (many properties have a staff person, called the rooms controller, who is in charge of assigning rooms to incoming individual guests and groups). This is the department with the most traffic in the front office area. The agents deal with the check-in/check-out procedures, handle cash, resolve conflicts, address reservation/billing inquiries, and perform guest services. They have to be jacks-of-all-trades because the front desk is the most important access point for information, complaints, and requests at the hotel.

The front desk is usually located in the lobby area (sometimes, in high-rise properties, the front desk is located on a higher floor), easily accessible from the main entrance door and the guest room elevators. In some properties, front desks take the form of individual islands instead of a long counter. The advantage is that the agent can access the lobby area much more quickly to greet or assist the guest. The desk is divided into several equally equipped workstations. The number of workstations depends on the size of the hotel. A good rule of thumb is 1 workstation per 100 guest rooms. Each workstation has (this again varies from property to property) a computer or property management system (PMS) terminal with a credit card reader and printer, room key encoder, telephone, reference guide with information about room location, outlet location, currency exchange, market codes, rate codes, technical support information, cash, credit card and check handling instructions, emergency procedures, and other property-related information. It is vital that this folder—an important front desk tool—is in order and up to date at all times. Other necessities for each workstation include paper and pens, area maps, key cards, key sleeves, and scissors. As with the bellstand, it is important to keep workstations clean and organized at all times, as they are all in direct view of the guest and reflect on the hotel's operation.

The primary tasks for a front desk associate are the checking in and checking out of guests. During the check-in process, the agent should verify specific information related to the guest's reservation. The information includes but is not limited to duration of stay, requested room type or room preference, room rate (it is important for the front desk agent to verify the guest's eligibility for discounted rates by checking membership cards [e.g., AAA or AARP], company IDs, government credit cards), special requests or arrangements, method of payment, and any frequent-stay membership/airline affiliation. The verification of this information is important to avoid discrepancies in the billing process and adjustments during check-out, and to ensure accuracy in room availability. Unfortunately, this process is also important because it is abused frequently, meaning that customers book the AAA discounted rate even though they are not members with the hope the front desk will not ask for their AAA ID. At that point, they usually forgot the card. In order for hotels to ensure the integrity of their rate discounted and negotiated rate programs, these discounts should not be given unless proper ID is being produced by the customer at check-in.

Discrepancies in the billing process can be time-consuming and, therefore, a significant inconvenience to the guest. It is important to verify the room rate during the check-in process (especially if a guest's room rate changes during the stay); otherwise, the front desk must adjust revenue during the check-out process, which takes extra time and affects the room revenue figures negatively. Many hotels offer a service called "Express Check-Out," in which a copy of the final bill is delivered to the room in the early morning of the guest's check-out day. This service enables the customer to use the receipt for their records and/or expense report and eliminates the need for them to stop by the front desk to check out. This is very convenient for customers, and it allows for an easy departure experience. However, if the information on the final bill is incorrect, additional time is required from the customer to rectify the situation and, therefore, the process becomes a detriment for customers. Several hotel companies are now offering to email the final bill, which makes it even more important that all the information is accurate. It is very common for customers who prefer to receive their receipt via email to not view it until they have already departed the hotel. Hence, making any correction to the folio becomes even more time-consuming. Billing discrepancies are the most common reason for guest complaints.

The verification of length of stay helps the front desk manage room inventory more accurately. Especially in a sold-out situation, the hotel depends on all guests who are supposed to check out, according to the property management system, to actually check out, as their rooms have been sold to other guests for the night. If a guest's departure date is incorrect and he or she needs to be extended, the hotel may find itself in an oversold situation. This causes a chain reaction of additional problems and costs. If a guest's actual length of stay is shorter than the property management system shows (because it was not verified during check-in) and the guest checks out earlier than expected, the hotel might have lost an opportunity to sell the room. Accuracy is, thus, very important to maximizing hotel revenue. However, there will be occasions when guests depart before the confirmed departure date. It is up to the individual property or chain if an early departure fee (usually one night-room and tax) is charged.

The correct room type and location can be essential to guest satisfaction. Selection is a matter of training and experience, as there are several aspects to consider when allocating rooms to reservations. The order of importance of the criteria may depend on local or corporate standard operating procedures.

- **Rate:** This selection criterion is pretty much self-explanatory. If there are two guests with the same room type request, you may want to assign the nicer room to the guest who pays the higher rate.

- **Length of stay:** A guest who checks in late and stays only one night might not be too concerned about the view or location of the room as long as he or she gets a good night's sleep. On the other hand, a guest staying with family or a spouse for several days will certainly have expectations regarding view and room location (the concept of proper segmentation applies here).

- **Loyalty to the hotel and company/ frequent-stay program membership level:** With competition fiercer than ever, loyalty is becoming more and more important. Almost every hotel chain has a frequent-stay program that offers various membership levels based on number of room-nights spent with the company. These membership levels have a great impact on room allocation. The hotel must ensure that the most loyal customers to the brand or chain are recognized for their repeating business. Benefits of higher membership level benefits (usually platinum or gold level) include room type and upgrade guarantees. Some programs even pena-

lize the individual property if those guarantees are not met. This shows the importance companies place on these frequent guests and the money they spend with the chain. In addition, many hotels have developed local repeat guest programs to acknowledge and reward guests who frequently stay with one specific property. These guests are not necessarily members of the hotel company's reward program.

- **Reservation guarantees:** Many corporations have introduced the concept of reservation guarantees. Examples include room type, bed type, smoking preference, or connecting rooms, guaranteed when the reservation is made and based on availability. Many companies offer monetary compensation to their guests (penalties for the hotel, as mentioned above) if the guarantees are not met at check-in.

- **VIP levels:** Hotels have individual VIP levels indicating the importance of the guest checking in—for example, a group VIP, meeting planner, corporate executive, celebrity, or a political figure. The VIP levels might include specific room assignments and check-in procedures (such as the manager on duty or general manager escorting the guest to the room) or the type of amenity for the guest.

In addition, special requests on the reservation might include information about allergies, rollaway and baby crib requests, high floor/low floor, request for a universally accessible room, and so on. Property management systems have codes that identify such requests. This helps when printing reports and when the front desk associate, during the check-in process, verifies that the requests and guarantees are met.

A method of payment must be secured either prior to check-in (e.g., for a prepaid reservation) or during the check-in process. Payment can be made in cash or by valid credit card or check; some properties also accept money orders. In most cases, a credit card imprint is made during check-in, either electronically or manually. The total amount of room and tax and an incidental amount (for phone calls, movies, room service, etc.) are authorized on the credit card to secure payment. The incidental amount varies from property to property, depending on guest room amenities and services. If a guest wishes to use cash, an equivalent amount should be collected and deposited on the guest account. Each property management system checks regularly to see if the authorized amount has been exceeded and, if so, authorizes additional funds on the guest's credit card. Any guest account without sufficient authorization appears on a credit limit exceed report, which the front desk runs regularly. Local standard operating procedures determine the next steps the front desk associate takes. Usually, the front desk tries to contact the guest via phone or text message. However, if the guest does not respond to any of the messages, the front desk might go as far as locking the guest out of his or her room. This requires the guest to stop by the front desk to get a new key issued—a good time to inquire about an alternative method of payment or to ask for an additional cash deposit.

It is important for the front desk associate to know that when guests use a debit card during check-in, the amount authorized will not be available for the guest to withdraw from the checking account until he or she checks out of the hotel and the hold is released. It should be part of the check-in procedure to inform the guest about this before taking an electronic imprint of a debit card. However, if necessary, the front desk can release holds on credit card and checking accounts immediately by contacting the appropriate bank directly. The number for the institution can be found on the back of the credit/debit card. Please note that release times might vary by financial institution. Some do it instantly; others might take 3 to 5 business days. Most front desks are equipped with a check verification system (similar to grocery stores). If a guest decides to pay by check, the front desk associate can get immediate clearance to secure payment and avoid bounced checks.

When dealing with "Method of Payment" front desk associates are frequently subject to fraud attempts. These can come in various forms; counterfeit money, stolen credit cards, and bad/stolen checks are some the most common ones. In order to prevent these, the front desk associates should be trained on detecting counterfeit money (there are markers to check the bills). Procedures should be in place to always verify the name on the credit card matches the reservation and the picture ID presented at check in. You should always make sure you get an imprint (manual or electronic) of the credit card as proof you actually have seen the card. This is equal to an electronic signature and without this, charges to the card can easily be disputed. Most hotels work with automated check verification systems to get instant approval on checks. But here again, ID verification is critical to ensure the hotel is getting the money.

Throughout the day, the front desk associate spends a significant amount of time providing guest services including directions, restaurant and activity recommendations, reservations, and rate inquiries. Therefore, it is important that all front desk associates receive detailed training in these areas. It is helpful for all new front desk associates to spend a few days in other departments (housekeeping, concierge, maybe even the restaurant) to learn about them and their mode of operation.

Working in housekeeping gives the front desk associate great knowledge about room setup, location, amenities, and views, and also an appreciation for the work the housekeeping staff does. Working with the concierge helps the front desk associate learn about the area and its attractions and activity options for the guests. With all this knowledge, the front desk associate can handle the majority of guest requests and questions, and the check-in process is faster, as the associate knows everything about the room type and location. It is helpful for the associate to visit a guest room once in a while to get refamiliarized with the room types and locations and learn about any changes made to the setup or amenity offering. Training is definitely an ongoing process. In addition, the associate should be familiar with the in-room technology, like high-speed Internet access and movie systems. This, of course, not only includes knowing how to connect to the Internet and how to order a movie but also what movies are currently showing on the hotel channel.

Most hotels these days provide an express check-out option. A copy of the guest's folio is delivered to the guest room the morning of check-out. The guest may use this as the receipt and need not have to stop by the front desk to check out (only if the billing is accurate, of course, reemphasizing the importance of verifying all information at check in). Many in-room entertainment systems also feature a video check-out option, which allows the guest to check out through the TV screen. However, this works only if sufficient funds are secured in advance to cover the balance on the account. To this day, though, many companies require their associates to present a zero balance receipt for their expense report. Therefore, there is still significant check-out traffic at the front desk.

During this process, the front desk associate verifies that all charges are correct and confirms the method of payment on the account. The guest still has the option of changing to a different method at this point. During check-out, the associate should also verify that the guest has a frequent-stay membership number on file, and if not, inquire about the guest's membership to ensure proper credit. At the end of the check-out process, the front desk associate should offer assistance with luggage and transportation and, of course, thank the guest for staying at the hotel. This is the last opportunity for the front desk to get feedback from the guest. If the guest experienced any problems during the stay, the hotel may lose the chance to rectify the situation and compensate the guest. Therefore, it is useful to inquire about the guest's experience while processing the check-out request.

The initial training of newly hired front desk associates is crucial to guest and associate satisfaction. Unless the front office manager provides the associates with the right tools from the beginning, the service encounter can become a frustrating experience for the associate and guest. Initial training should include a rotation so the associate can experience other departments, see how departments interact, and become familiar with the property, its features, and its offerings. However, training should be ongoing. It can be in the form of on-the-job training (new processes and procedures, revisiting associate actions to discuss alternative solutions for the future), a daily 15 minutes of learning (where a new topic is discussed every day), or specific job-related training classes (problem resolution, service recovery models, public speaking, interpersonal skills). Secret shoppers, organized by the front office manager, can be helpful in identifying opportunities for improvement. Using friends and family for this purpose gives them a fun night out and provides the department with valuable information about the team's performance.

Again, success starts with a good hiring process. You should look for certain characteristics when interviewing applicants for the front desk. Candidates should be very comfortable with working in the public arena. They must be able to multitask in a fast-paced environment and be able to handle a stressful conflict situation without losing their cool. As with all front-of-the-house jobs, candidates should be well polished and groomed and should possess a service-oriented personality—the willingness to go the extra mile for guests and fellow associates.

The front desk is the front-of-the-house nerve center of the hotel. You want to be sure the best associates are represented here. Selecting and training these associates is one of the main responsibilities of the front office manager. Providing them with the right tools to do their job well is key to success and guest satisfaction.

✦ GUEST RELATIONS

Guest relations are getting more and more attention these days. This attention helped many companies to develop new guest relation models focusing on the one-stop-shop guest experience—for example, the Whatever Whenever Department at Starwood's W Hotels, Marriott's At

Your Service, and Westin's Service Express. Guests can conveniently make any request or order room service by dialing a single extension; the associate who answers takes care of everything. Many companies have also implemented a customer retention database where every request is logged to better learn about guests' habits, preferences, and problems during their stay. This is invaluable information for hotels that want to anticipate guest needs and develop a clear idea about trends that might lead to potential problems. These data can be used in many ways and should be shared with every department.

SPECIFIC CUSTOMER PREFERENCES

If all requests are logged properly, the hotel has an enormous amount of information about each guest. With reference to this information, the staff can place certain items the guest usually requests in the room when he or she returns. Most systems allow the hotel to print repeat guest reports for each day that show the preferences of repeat customers, as well as incidents and requests from prior stays.

For example, the data may show that a specific guest called for extra pillows during her previous two stays at the hotel. If you tell the guest at check-in that extra pillows have already been placed in her room, you have won a customer for life. Anticipating the needs of the guests before they have to ask sets the hotel apart from the competition. The company that manages to set up a centralized database of this data for the entire chain has a significant advantage over competing brands. Consistency, though, is the key to success. Once a hotel has started this process, it must ensure consistent delivery. Otherwise, it might lose its credibility and no longer stand out in the mind of the guest.

REQUESTS AND INCIDENTS

The other important use for such a system is the analysis of the data logged through the guest's requests. It is important that all requests and issues are logged in order to make this process work. It is up to the hotel—or, more specifically, the front office manager or guest relations manager—to extract information from the system and learn from it.

Requests: Reports show the requests (e.g., towels, in-room coffee) made from which guest rooms. This information can be helpful in several ways. Towels and coffee are basic room amenities and should always be there. An increase in the number of these requests should catch the manager's eye. Reports can be narrowed by floor or even by housekeeping section to see if the performance of a particular housekeeper is the reason for those increased requests (i.e., items are not replenished when the room is cleaned). On the other hand, if the requests do not show a clear pattern, one might want to consider other reasons. For example, during the summer, people take towels to the pool, so you might experience requests for clean towels when guests get back to the room. This finding might lead the hotel to increase the number of towels in the rooms in summer. This will reduce the number of calls from the guests, reduce the time spent delivering towels, and thus free up time to take care of other guest requests faster. Similarly, an increased number of requests for mouthwash might cause the hotel to add mouthwash to the basic bathroom amenity set.

Incidents: Reports show any problems guests experience during their stay (only, of course, if the guests report them). These data help the hotel

identify topics for retraining (in case of service issues) as well as engineering-related opportunities. Again, with the reports these systems allow the hotel to produce, you can narrow the problem to specific associates (in cross-referencing with department schedules), specific rooms, or mechanical equipment such as a malfunctioning plumbing riser, hot water pump, or electrical appliances. For example, an increased amount of calls for a burned-out light bulb in a specific room might be an indicator for a broken—or dangerous—light fixture; several calls from a room indicating that the HVAC system is not working might signal a clogged filter.

If a hotel has such a reporting and tracking system in place, it is essential that every staff member is behind it and reports every issue or problem so it can be entered into the database. (The concept of "garbage in, garbage out" is relevant here.) The support for this initiative must start at the top: The general manager must give full support. This is the only way to convince everybody else to work with the system as well. This is the only way to make these systems produce accurate results that could save hotels a lot of money.

To reiterate, training the associates in the guest relations department is critical and probably more intense than other departments. The associates must be familiar with literally *everything,* as they must respond to every request and complaint. The hiring process should be similar to that at the front desk, as the characteristics of a potential guest relations associate are the same. Training should likewise include a rotation through every department to develop the insight and product knowledge that will help the staff member make the right decision. Service recovery and problem resolution training is key as well and should be a constant part in the associate development. Computer training is important too. Working with the different systems is a big part of associates' responsibilities, and the more comfortable they are with the systems, the faster they will be able to work with them. The associates in the guest relations area are the hotel's eyes and ears, but all staff and management must be aware of the importance of this area.

Working in the hospitality industry, with its crazy hours, stressful and challenging situations, weekend and holiday obligations, and so on, requires passion. If you love what you do, the rewards will come. I would not want to work in any other industry. For me, it is the greatest reward when a guest or associate thanks me for what I do.

✦ A DAY IN MY LIFE AS A FRONT OFFICE MANAGER

This is a typical schedule as I have experienced it during my time as front office manager. Of course, days are never the same in this business. However, this timetable should give the reader a sense of the challenging job of a front office manager:

7:00 A.M. Arrive in the office.

7:00–8:00 A.M. I walk all my areas and welcome my staff. Managing by walking around is a powerful tool. As a department manager, you want to be visible and accessible to your associates while you are on property (or even if you are off property). Communicating with your staff helps build team spirit and trust. It is important the staff sees that you are always willing to do what you expect

them to do. Talking to your staff shows them you are interested in their lives and you value their feedback. This is also a good opportunity to get information about problems from the previous evening and night you need to follow up with.

8:00–9:00 A.M. Checking emails and voice mails and trying to return them in a timely manner (*very* challenging).

8:20 A.M. Mr. X is at the desk complaining about his room service breakfast and wants to talk to a manager. I meet with Mr. X and take care of the issue. After the conversation, I follow up with the room service staff and the food and beverage manager to ensure the issue has been addressed. I double-check that the incident is entered into our guest relation database, so Mr. X does not experience it again when he returns.

9:00–9:15 A.M. Morning meeting with all the managers. This is the daily meeting where we discuss the previous day, the current day's events, VIPs, special guests, repeat customers, and any announcements pertaining to the overall operation (scheduled site tours, media appearances, managers out of the office, etc.).

9:15 A.M.–noon Work in the lobby with the associates. Meet and greet our regular guests and help out at the bellstand. This is what we call being the lobby ambassador. I also cover the breaks for the front desk associates to ensure proper staffing at all times. Ensuring your associates take breaks is important and the law.

10:00–10:15 A.M. Mr. Y, a repeat customer, calls inquiring about his next stay. His usual rate is not available and he does not want to pay the available rate, which is significantly higher. I negotiate with Mr.Y, and we agree on the regular rate (important if your company has a best rate guarantee); in addition, I guarantee him an upgrade for his upcoming stay.

Noon–12:30 P.M. Lunch (this is not a regular occurrence)

12:30–2:00 P.M. Catching up with emails and voice mails (between other things).

12:40–1:00 P.M. Associate X calls out for the evening shift. It will be a busy evening, so I need to find a replacement soon. Associate Y offers to stay a little longer. I call the night auditor, and he agrees to come in early. The shift is covered.

1:00–1:30 P.M. Meeting with Associate Z to go over her performance review. Regular feedback is important. You want to make sure your associates are aware of their performance. This helps them identify areas of opportunity and makes them grow. It is the responsibility of the front office manager to provide such feedback either in official reviews or in in-the-moment coaching.

1:30–2:00 P.M. I am paying my invoices. Accounting and finance knowledge is important to department managers. The department budget is your responsibility, and you have to be able to read and interpret financial statements to control your budget and secure your contribution to the bottom line.

2:00–3:00 P.M. Operations meeting. We critique the events of the past week and discuss details about the events for the coming week. This is an important way to collect information regarding check-in and check-out times, group VIPs and contacts, arrival patterns, room preferences, meeting schedules and locations, etc. Such infor-

mation is crucial to scheduling as well as preparations such as pre-keying guest rooms, setting up remote check-ins, etc.

3:00–3:30 P.M. Interview with an applicant for the front desk.

3:30–4:00 P.M. I walk all my areas, and meet and greet the associates of the evening shift. I want to make sure everybody is okay and has the tools to do their job right. I also want to make sure to hear about issues (guest or associate) early before they become serious problems.

4:00–4:15 P.M. Mrs.Y wants to talk to a manager because we do not have an upgraded room available for her. I talk to Mrs.Y and explain the sold-out situation. I compensate her with access to our VIP lounge. She is satisfied and checks into her room. A lot of times guests who are complaining and want to speak to a manager just want to be heard. Good listening skills and demeanor are important to show credibility to the guest.

4:30–5:00 P.M. Meeting with the director of room operations to discuss the sports team check-in for the next day. Proper preparation is key to success and a smooth operation.

5:00–6:30 P.M. I am in the lobby, helping my staff during the peak check-in time. Here I also have the opportunity to interact with our guests, welcome our repeat customers, and assist wherever necessary. Being in the lobby makes you accessible to your guests; talking to them, listening to them gives you a lot of information and feedback. I cannot stress enough the importance of this feedback for your operation; it is a great learning source for everybody. It also helps cover the front desk while the P.M. shift takes their breaks.

6:30–7:00 P.M. I walk all my areas one last time before I leave to make sure everything is going well and everybody is happy. I make sure all my associates know how to contact me if necessary. I stop by my office to check for emails and voice mails one last time, and then I leave for the day.

4.7 TO CHANGE OR NOT TO CHANGE: A CASE STUDY AT THE FRONT DESK NANCY SWANGER

Morgan Black has been described by the corporate office as the Miracle Worker because of the troubled properties that were turned around under Morgan's leadership. It is hoped the story at the Coug Inn will have the same happy ending; however, the Coug Inn is in a remote location, hundreds of miles from any other corporate properties.

The Coug Inn is a 150-room full-service property with several medium-sized conference rooms; it caters mostly to business travelers and visitors affiliated with the local university. The bulk of the revenue is generated between August and May, with periods when classes are not in session being extremely slow. The hotel is at full occupancy only during football weekends and commencement. Occupancy has been declining for the last year or so, with last month's RevPAR at a record low. Since arriving at the Coug Inn, Morgan has made several observations about the hotel's situation. It seems that most of the problems involve the front desk. After analyzing several previous months' comment cards and informally chatting with guests at the hotel, Morgan has sensed real dissatisfaction with the check-in process. Several common themes have emerged: The process seems to take forever, the paperwork at check-in is perceived as lengthy and hard to fill out, the front desk clerks always appear to be running around "like chickens with their heads cut off," and guests have been checked into rooms that were not clean.

After discussing the problems with the front desk manager, Morgan is in a quandary about how best to move toward a solution. The front desk manager complains that the reservations staff does not always submit the day's reservations to the front desk in a timely manner. Thus, guests arrive, and the desk clerks have no idea what rate was quoted or the room preference of the guest. This results in the guest having to refurnish information that was previously given when making the reservation. Many times, clerks are forced to leave the guest at the counter while they attempt to retrieve missing information from the reservations. Further, with over 65 percent of the housekeeping staff speaking a first language other than English, communication is difficult at best, and room status is often mistaken. The front desk manager suggests that the hotel advertise its check-in time to be from "say around 1:00 P.M. or 2:00 P.M. to 7:00 P.M." to reduce the crunch time and allow front desk clerks more time to work with each guest's check-in needs. The front desk manager further states that the new hotel in town, the Suite to Sleep Inn, has an earlier check-in time and "it seems to work okay for them" Morgan asks the front desk manager how the staff might respond to moving to a fully automated property management system. The response was not favorable; the front desk manager mumbled something about "old dogs and new tricks" and that the corporate office had not put any money into the place in years. What would make Morgan think they would put out the cash now?

In an attempt to reach a compromise, Morgan considers changing the check-in time in exchange for the front desk manager's support of the conversion to an automated system.

1. What must Morgan take into consideration before final decisions are made to adjust check-in time and install a fully automated property management system?
2. How should Morgan proceed in resolving the communication issue?
3. Who needs to be involved in the final decisions? Why?
4. How might Morgan present the case to the corporate office?

4.8 MINI-CASE: THE NEW FOM

After being transferred and promoted to front office manager of a 600-room resort hotel in Miami from a smaller property of the same chain, Jennifer Waters spent the first five or six months familiarizing herself with the hotel's markets, the area, and the resort's facilities and amenities. She also spent a significant amount of time learning the job of front office manager and concluded that it is significantly different from that of an assistant front office manager in a smaller property.

The front office staff are young, mostly students, who are in south Florida for the weather and the social amenities. Many want to become actors and are active in dinner theaters and small theater companies in the greater Miami area. For the most part, they are bright and attractive people, but they lack the professionalism that comes from a solid core of knowledge and training. Among the things that concern Jennifer as FOM are the following:

- Several members of a national association's board of directors complained of rude treatment while checking out of the hotel.
- Several times a week, after guests have checked in, they are escorted to rooms that are out of order, not clean, or already occupied.

- Four times over the last 6 weeks, cruel and demeaning practical jokes have been played on the front office assistant manager and the manager on duty during the evening.

- Guest complaints, either in person or by letter, about the hotel, its services, and its staff have more than doubled over previous years and are outpacing complimentary letters and comments by a ratio of two to one.

Jennifer believes her relations with her staff are pretty good. Her relationships, however, with other managers in the hotel are strained, particularly with housekeeping and sales.

As Jennifer seeks to understand the complexities of these problems, she decides to compile a list of their possible causes. What items might be on this list? What form could their potential solutions take?

Be sure to include rationales for the solutions and a plan that will allow her to demonstrate to top management that the analysis and solutions are likely to result in resolutions of these difficulties.

REFERENCES

Cross, R. G. 1997. "Launching the Revenue Rocket: How Revenue Management Can Work for Your Business." *Cornell Hotel and Restaurant Administration Quarterly* (April) 38(2):32–43.

Massagle, D. J. 2002. "Multitasking Concierges Provide Added Value to Properties." *Hotel and Motel Management* (August 1) 217(14):22.

Nargil, J., S. Khan, and M. Peterson. 2003. "Professional Concierges Offer Tips to Improve Guest Services." *Hotel and Motel Management* (January 13) 218(1):17.

Quain, W. J., M. Sansbury, and S. LeBruto. 1998. "Revenue Enhancement, Part 1: A Straightforward Approach for Making More Money." *Cornell Hotel and Restaurant Administration Quarterly* 39(5):44–45.

Quain, B., M. Sansbury, and D. Quinn. 1999. "Revenue Enhancement, Part 3: Picking Low-hanging Fruit—A Simple Approach to Yield Management." *Cornell Hotel and Restaurant Administration Quarterly* (40)2:76–83.

Rutherford, D. G. 1985. "The Front Office Manager: Key to Hotel Communications." *Florida International University Hospitality Review* 3(2):38–48.

Stiel, H. (no date). *Ultimate Service: A Complete Handbook to the World of the Concierge.* Englewood Cliffs, NJ: Prentice-Hall.

Witham, G. 1983. "Keeper of the Keys: Concierges in American Hotels." *Cornell Hotel and Restaurant Administration Quarterly* 24(3): 40–48.

———. 1993. "American Concierges Set Service Standards." *Cornell Hotel and Restaurant Administration Quarterly* 34(4).

SUGGESTED READINGS

BOOKS

Bardi, J. A. 2006. *Hotel Front Office Management* (4th ed.). Hoboken, NJ: John Wiley & Sons.

Bryson, M., and A. Ziminski. 1992. *The Concierge: Key to Hospitality.* New York: John Wiley and Sons.

Deveau, L. T., P. M. Deveau, N. de J. Portocarrero, and M. Escoffier. 1996. *Front Office Management and Operations.* Upper Saddle River, NJ: Prentice-Hall.

Ford, R. 2000. *Managing the Guest Experience in Hospitality.* Albany, NY: Delmar.

Giovanni, K. C. 2007. *The Concierge Manual* (3rd ed.). Wake Forest, NC: NewRoad Publishing.

Heldenbrand, H. V. 1944. *Front Office Psychology*. Chicago: American Hotel Register Company. (Editor's note: This little volume is out of print but generally is carried in hotel school libraries and some faculty offices. Many of Heldenbrand's observations are as valid today as they were in 1944.)

Kasavana, M. L. 2005. *Managing Front Desk Operations*. Lansing, MI: Educational Institute of American Hotel and Lodging Associaton.

Kildow, B. A. 2003. *Front Desk Security and Safety: An On-The-Job Guide to Handling Emergencies, Threats, and Unexpected Situations*. New York: AMACOM.

Michelli, J. 2008. *The New Gold Standard: 5 Leadership Principles for Creating a Legendary Customer Experience Courtesy of the Ritz-Carlton Hotel Company*. New York: McGraw-Hill.

Sherman, R. 2007. *Class Acts: Service and Inequality in Luxury Hotels*. Los Angeles, CA: University of California Press.

Vallen, G. K. and J. J.Vallen. 2008. *Check-In Check-Out.* (8th ed.). Upper Saddle River, NJ: Prentice Hall.

ARTICLES

Brownell, J. 1990. "Grab Hold of the Grape-vine." *Cornell Hotel and Restaurant Administration Quarterly* 31(2):78–83.

Brymer, Robert. 1991. "Employee Empowerment: A Guest-driven Leadership Strategy." *Cornell Hotel and Restaurant Administration Quarterly* 32(1):58–68.

Brunner-Sperdin, A., and M. Peters. 2009. "What Influences Guests' Emotions? The Case of High Quality Hotels." *International Journal of Tourism Research* 11(2):171-183.

Lewis, R. C. 1983. "When Guests Complain." *Cornell Hotel and Restaurant Administration Quarterly* 24(2): 23–32.

Lieberman, W. H. 1993. "Debunking the Myths of Yield Management." *Cornell Hotel and Restaurant Administration Quarterly* 34(1):34–41.

Mainzer, B. W. 2004. "Fast Forward for Hospitality Revenue Management." *Journal of Revenue and Pricing Management* 3(3):285–289.

Murthy, B. and C. S. Dev. 1993. "Average Daily Rate." In *VNR's Encyclopedia of Hospitality and Tourism*, Mahmood Kahn, Michael Olsen, and Turgut Var (eds.). New York: Van Nostrand Reinhold.

Rutherford, D. G. 1985. "The Front Office Manager: Key to Hotel Communications." *Florida International University Hospitality Review* 3(2):38–48.

Sanchez, J. F., and A. Satir. 2005. "Hotel Yield Management Using Different Reservation Modes." *International Journal of Contemporary Hospitality Management* 17(2/3):136–146.

Toh, R. S., and F. DeKay. 2002. "Hotel Room-Inventory Management: An Overbooking Model." *Cornell Hotel and Restaurant Administration Quarterly* 43(4):79–90.

Vallen, G. K. 1993. "Organizational Climate and Burnout." *Cornell Hotel and Restaurant Administration Quarterly* 34(1):54–59.

SOURCE NOTES

Chapter 4.2, "A Day in the Life of the Front Office Manager," by Garry Dickover.

Chapter 4.3, "Yield Management: Choosing the Most Profitable Reservations," by William J. Quain and Stephen M. LeBruto, is adapted from the following two articles:

Quain, B., M. Sansbury, and S. LeBruto. 1998. "Revenue Enhancement, Part 1: A Straightforward Approach to Making More Money." *Cornell Hotel and Restaurant Administration Quarterly* 39(5):42–48.

Quain, B., M. Sansbury, and D. Quinn. 1999. "Revenue Enhancement, Part 3: Picking Low-hanging

Fruit—A Simple Approach to Yield Management." *Cornell Hotel and Restaurant Administration Quarterly* 40(2):76–83.

Chapter 4.4, "Three Decades of Revenue Management: What's Next?," by Silvia Milla and Stowe Shoemaker, is reprinted from the first issue of 2008 in the *Journal of Revenue and Pricing Management.* © Palgrave Macmillan Ltd. Used by permission. All rights reserved.

Chapter 4.5, "Concierge (cone-see-air-j)," by Mario Arnaldo.

Chapter 4.6, "As I See It: Management of the Front Office," by Oliver Meinzer.

OPERATIONS: HOUSEKEEPING, ENGINEERING, AND SECURITY

5.1 INTRODUCTION

✦ HOUSEKEEPING

Some time ago, Denney was talking with a large group of housekeeping directors representing most of the major metropolitan hotels in a large northeastern city. He asked the following question: How many of you, as part of your career plan, initially considered housekeeping as a managerial role that had any attraction to you? The answer, not surprisingly, was none!

This brings up a major dilemma facing modern hotel management structures. One of the most important, most labor-intensive, and largest cost centers in the hotel is neither universally understood nor respected by the bulk of the

hotel's department managers, their employees, and, to a large extent, the hotel's guests and clients. Some encouraging signs indicate that this situation is in a state of change. Some hotel companies are experimenting with taking housekeeping out of the rooms division and making it a staff function, with the director of housekeeping reporting directly to the general manager. Others are combining housekeeping and other property management functions such as maintenance and engineering. At one firm's resorts, housekeeping directors are titled director of services and have responsibility for all nongolf recreation in addition to traditional housekeeping.

Historically, however, information on housekeeping administration for hotels has been organized around models set forth in textbooks that date back to the 1951 treatment of hospital housekeeping by LaBelle and Barton. Brigham (1955) focused her analysis of the structure of the housekeeping functions and responsibilities on the small hotel. Tucker and Schneider (1982), Schneider and Tucker (1989), and Martin and Jones (1992) provided a comprehensive inventory of the theoretical constructs, responsibilities, relationships, and techniques important to the modern housekeeper in a range of operational situations. (See the Jones contribution elsewhere in this section that updates those authors.)

Generally speaking, these works present information in a traditional structure that says the housekeeper administers four major areas of responsibility:

1. Management of people, equipment, and supplies
2. Preservation of building finishes, fabrics, and furnishings
3. Cost control
4. Recordkeeping (Tucker and Schneider, 1982, p. 38)

In analyzing the differences between the folklore and fact of the manager's job, Mintzberg (1975) concluded that substantial differences existed between the popular or academic notion of managers' jobs and their actual work.

In the last study of its type, Rutherford and Schill (1984) studied housekeepers in a similar fashion. They addressed this question: What is the relationship between what has been written about housekeeping and what housekeeping directors themselves deem important?

A survey was sent to a national sample of housekeeping executives asking them to rate on a scale of 1 to 5 the importance of 100 theoretical constructs common to the housekeeping literature. Statistical procedures (factor analysis) grouped the housekeepers' responses into eight groupings. While the traditional responsibilities of records, costs, supplies, and furnishings were still important, the issues central to the management of people were of overwhelming importance. Specifically highlighted were the following:

• Leadership
• Communication
• Strategic planning
• Hotel organizational interactions
• Departmental management
• Training

The authors concluded that new arrangements of traditional knowledge, constructs, and tactics such as those explored in their model may present future managers with windows of operational, educational, or marketing opportunity that improve competitive position or streamline the transfer of knowledge. The dissemination of this knowledge in the most efficient and effective manner is also important, for, as Mintzberg (1975) points out, "[T]he manager is challenged to find systematic ways to share his privileged knowledge."

Since 1985, very little, if any, analytic empirical research has been done on operational aspects of housekeeping and other labor-intensive hotel departments. Until there is, there will be little forward movement in the theory of housekeeping. Inspired practical experimentation on the part of housekeeping managers, however, is not lacking.

Professor Tom Jones of the University of Nevada, Las Vegas, describes how housekeeping departments are organized and staffed. He provides an overview and organizational perspective of the department, paying particular attention to the responsibilities of the various personnel within the modern housekeeping department. Professor Jones brings deep knowledge of executive housekeeping management to his writing and structures his description of the organization with a real-world, tell-it-like-it-is narrative.

As John Lagazo states in the introduction to his description of being an executive housekeeper, most people are surprised to learn that housekeeping is an important career stop for hotel managers. In one of his most recent positions (general manager of the Valley Plaza Resort in Midland, Michigan) Lagazo dealt with housekeeping every day, as it was a position that directly reported to him. John wrote this piece for the third edition, but it holds up so well. We are including it here because he captures the essence of the job of managing this complex organizational element.

In most cases, the management of the housekeeping function is no longer the province of the lead maid type. Increasingly, the expense of running the department coupled with the large numbers of employees on its staff mandates that the head of this department be well versed in all managerial skills and a sophisticated and creative leader.

✦ ENGINEERING

In a way, housekeeping, engineering, and security can all be considered guest services. In most hotels, guest services (see previous section) is a visible component that can include concierge, uniformed service, garage, and specialized recreational and leisure activities. Housekeeping, security for the hotel and its guests, and the maintenance of the hotel's engineering systems are under the best of circumstances behind the scenes and neither noticed nor experienced by guests in any but an abstract sense. They are, nonetheless, services that are critical to a safe, comfortable—and, by extrapolation, successful—guest stay at your hotel.

As stated in the first of the two articles included here (Mounts and Meinzer) on the engineering function, in the past, the chief engineer and his or her department have been metaphorically relegated to roughly the same position in the hotel's organization that they physically occupy—usually the basement or otherwise out of sight. These two articles explore the numerous indications that the importance of the engineering function can no longer be ignored or treated with less respect than any other aspect of management.

It is important that the reader recognize that the first of these articles overviews the department, explores some of the issues that affect hotel engineering, and outlines typical job functions. Part of the thrust of this article is that unlike in the past, the chief engineer is responsible for major components of the asset and the physical comfort of the guest. This would argue that the chief engineer is no different than any other department head.

The DeFranco and Sheridan article on how chief engineers (CEs) use financial information illustrates that idea. As their research demonstrates, computer technology and the use of financial information in the engineering department are vital in maintaining an efficient operation. This was not widely true even ten years ago. This research contributes to the argument that, like that of the executive housekeeper, the position of CE in the modern hotel organization mandates a leader who is more of a manager/ leader than a technician. At the same time, the CE still must manage a diverse collection of talents and skills among the engineering staff. In a fashion, this raises the question of what type of manager should a CE be? Structured research is still sparse on this topic.

The number of employees for which the CE is responsible varies widely, mainly with the size of the hotel. Fisher (1986) set the ratio for an engineering staff at 3.9 for each 100 rooms. However, much has changed since then. Other factors that can influence the diversity of human-related management for the engineering manager are market niche, sophistication of the building's design and equipment, and corporate philosophy. Therefore, if a 1000-room hotel has 40 or more people on the engineering staff, each of them presumably a highly trained, qualified, and skilled technical person, the CE's job takes on aspects of management that strongly suggests a need for refined people-related skills.

When Wasmuth and Davis studied the management of employee turnover, they found it to be relatively low in engineering departments in the majority of the hotels studied. They also found that quality of supervision was a key element in maintaining low turnover rates among these engineering departments. The most successful supervisory style had as a critical element the talent that "allowed and encouraged (the engineers) to work autonomously" (1983, p. 68).

Allowing the engineering staff to work autonomously pays tribute to both the nature of their jobs and concern for the human side of management. It also suggests that while some supervisory or management styles may be appropriate in engineering departments, others may not. Managerial style refers to the way managers manage, control, motivate, and otherwise direct subordinates. It is through managerial style that employees may or may not be encouraged and allowed to work on their own. The extent to which an atmosphere is fostered by the manager significantly affects the range of issues related to human relations, of which turnover is a prime example.

An unpublished, proprietary study of 49 hotel CE's within one hotel company sought to determine the CE's overall managerial styles. They were asked to take a standardized managerial-style inventory and fill out a short demographic questionnaire in order to determine what managerial style predominates among the self-described successful chief engineers in a major international hotel corporation.

This inventory instrument judges an individual's primary managerial style to be in one of six categories (see below), with a secondary or backup style that may be one or a combination of the others.

Managerial Styles

- *Coercive:* The "do-it-the-way-I-tell-you" manager closely controls subordinates and motivates by threats and discipline.

- *Authoritative:* The "firm but fair" manager gives subordinates clear direction and motivates by persuasion and feedback on task performance.

- *Affiliative:* The "people first, task second" manager emphasizes good personal relationships among subordinates and motivates by trying to keep people happy with fringe benefits, security, and social activities.

- *Democratic:* The "participative" manager encourages subordinate input in decision making and motivates by rewarding team effort.

- *Pacesetting:* The "do it myself" manager performs many tasks personally, expects subordinates to follow his or her example, and motivates by setting high standards and letting subordinates work on their own.

- *Coaching:* The "developmental" manager helps and encourages subordinates to improve their performance and motivates by providing opportunities for professional development. (McBer, no date)

A managerial style profile reflects both primary and secondary styles. *Primary* is the managerial behavior one uses most often, is most comfortable with, and is the style to which one normally turns under stress. The *secondary* style refers to an alternative way of managing one uses when the primary style is ineffective. Some individuals have more than one primary style, and some utilize multiple secondary styles.

The comparisons showed that each group of CEs is primarily affiliative in style, a trait that flies in the face of their reputation as crusty curmudgeons.

With "affiliative" as the primary style of this group of engineers, it was somewhat surprising that the secondary style was "democratic." Combining the "democratic" secondary style with the predominant "affiliative" style would certainly produce an organizational atmosphere where the employees would feel encouraged to be independent and autonomous.

The data developed through application of this instrument to this sample of CEs tends to support the theory that successful CEs and their departments favor management styles that put people first. At least at this juncture, it appears that the "affiliative" style works best in the milieu with people and tasks managed by the CE. This was, however, a small study of a single company and as such can only be suggestive. The data in this study do, though, provide us with a broader view of the facets of management of the modern hotel engineering function.

✦ SECURITY

It is an unfortunate fact of modern hotel management that the days of simply providing comfort, high-quality food, beverage and lodging services, and a home-away-from-home atmosphere are severely affected by the inventory of problems presented by the predatory elements of modern society. At the same time, hotel security departments are responsible for protecting the hotel's assets from loss.

Hotels are usually fairly close-mouthed about their security and its functions, duties, and personnel. On an individual basis, a good overview of security can be found in publications of the Educational Institute of the American Hotel and Motel Association (www.ei-ahla.org). Typically, however, the modern hotel security department is organized as a staff function, with the director of security reporting directly to top management. We have little data or insight about the manager of the hotel security function, as little, if any, research has been done on the subject. Anecdotally, from the editor's experience, most of the managers recently hired to fulfill this function have a security background in the military or a law enforcement career with civil authorities.

Typically, the director of security has a staff in keeping with the nature and size of the threats to a particular hotel, the size of the hotel, its location, and its managerial strategy. A director of security administers the functions of his or her department against two broad and general classifications of threats: external and internal.

External threats are generally those that present risk for the hotel and its guests due to the actions of outsiders. Internal security is a functional area that generally is concerned with reducing the threat of loss of assets; in most cases, this refers to control of highly attractive and popular consumer goods such as wine, expensive foodstuffs, furnishings, and, of course, the hotel's cash.

The responsibilities of the security manager in contending with the above threats include the following:

- Providing physical security at the perimeter of the hotel.

- Adapting policies and procedures to the building design and location.

- Utilizing electronics, modern telecommunications devices, proximity alarms, motion detectors, and closed-circuit TV to enhance the hotel's ability to eliminate threats.

Security directors participate in certain levels of administrative or operational activities that deal with policies, training, education, and human resources to avoid hiring what has become known as the high-risk employee. This is due primarily to the increasing risk hotels and other employers face from negligent hiring.

Having policies and procedures in place to deal with the management of emergencies is also a fundamental aspect of the hotel security director's job. These emergencies can take a number of forms; in recent years they have been known to include fires, hurricanes, floods, earthquakes, blackouts, robberies, bombs or bomb threats, medical and dental emergencies, and some forms of terrorism. It is a fact of modern life that the properly managed hotel, from a security standpoint must have contingency plans in place and training programs to help its employees deal with these potential threats.

A further responsibility of the security director is liaison with civil authorities. Increasingly, as the article included here points out, hotels are being held accountable for what they either knew or should have known about potential threats. The best way to keep up on this is by cultivating a good relationship with the local police.

Finally, the major responsibility of a modern hotel security director is to assist in policy development. Hotels must have policies that guide the implementation of procedures, training, and inspection to meet the inventory of potential risk. Hotels also must gather data to make sure they are aware of all facets of the risk environment. The security function must also assist the hotel in formalizing a structure that links all pertinent parts of the hotel's organization to the concept of total security for the organization, its employees, and its guests.

In the legal analysis contributed to this edition, Melissa Dallas outlines and discusses the major families of risk facing hotel managers. She also includes in her analysis current examples of how the law affects the management of hotels in the modern era. This comprehensive and detailed article has a conversational and engaging style unusual in legal treatises.

In the article included here by Abbott and Fried, the authors explore in some depth one of the trickiest risk environments that (literally) surround many hospitality operations: the parking lot. Because parking lots can be remote, poorly lighted, or not patrolled, they are increasingly sources of risk. Courts are increasingly finding that landlords have liability for third-party criminal activity, so operators are advised to be aware of this potential liability.

As if that were not enough to give one pause, the article by Beattie and Gau serves notice that there is yet another realm of risk that now affects our ability to manage hotels safely. Workplace violence—including homicide—is a growing problem for hospitality operations. The authors explore telling examples and discuss a structural theory to guide further research and the establishment of policies.

This chapter is concluded by a nice piece by Chris E. McGoey. McGoey is an internationally known author, trainer, speaker, and professional security consultant and through his experience is eminently qualified to discuss hotel security. He is an expert in the fields of security management, crime, and loss prevention. He specializes in the anticipation, recognition, and prevention of crime on most commercial property types. To make his points as pertinent as possible, he views hotel security from the standpoint of the most important

person in the equation: the hotel guest. In this particular article, McGoey does an excellent job of illustrating the existing risks and challenges facing hotel security in the present times. He gives us inside access to those areas that provide a hotel with the most security challenges, as well as how best to deter crime on a hotels' property. As McGoey states, "frequent travelers quickly find the hotels that offer adequate security amenities and return the favor by becoming loyal customers." This obviously stresses the importance of one often overlooked hotel function—security.

✦ SUMMARY

Housekeeping, engineering, and security, while not, typically, obvious functions, are nonetheless critically important to the management of any hotel. All of them are and have been evolving for the past several years into professionally managed departments responding to internal and external stimuli that can critically affect their interactive relationships with other hotel departments and, ultimately, in the delivery of hotel guest services.

A number of books dealing with these departments are listed as suggested readings. The reader seeking more in-depth information can find it in these books.

5.2 HOUSEKEEPING ORGANIZATIONS: THEIR HISTORY, PURPOSE, STRUCTURES, AND PERSONNEL Thomas Jones

✦ ORIGINS OF HOSPITALITY AND HOUSEKEEPING

By definition, *hospitality* is the cordial and generous reception and entertainment of guests or

strangers, either socially or commercially. From this definition we get the feeling of the open house and the host with open arms, of a place where people are cared for. Regardless of the reasons people go to a home away from home, the presumption is that they need to be cared for there. They need a clean and comfortable place to rest or sleep, food service, an area for socializing and meeting other people, access to stores and shops, and a secure surrounding.

Americans have often been described as a people on the move, a mobile society. Even as our country expanded, we required bed and board. Travelers in the early 1700s found hospitality similar to that in their countries of origin, even though these new accommodations might have been in roadhouses, missions, or private homes, and the housekeeping might have included no more than a bed of straw, changed weekly.

Facilities in all parts of young America were commensurate with the demand of the traveling public, and early records indicate that a choice was usually available; travelers based the decision on where they expected to find good food, overnight protection, and clean facilities. Even though the inns were crude, they were gathering places where anyone could learn the news of the day, socialize, learn the business of the area, and rest.

The business of innkeeping has become the hotel industry of today, but the main tenets remain: a clean, comfortable room, access to food and entertainment facilities, and a courteous and concerned staff who mean it when they ask, "May we be of service?"

Housekeeping departments play a vital role in today's lodging industry. People involved in housekeeping operations service guest rooms, maintain and service public and special areas, and, in many instances, operate laundries and recreational and health facilities. The people of housekeeping are also a part of the overall team of hosts and hostesses who welcome the hotel's guests. They show concern and care when something goes wrong with the guest's visit, and they are quick to initiate action that will make things right again.

Major hotel companies have been quick to recognize the value of housekeeping and other service industry workers. Good hotel management does not see housekeeping work as demeaning or menial. To the contrary, all high-quality hotel operational management personnel have, at one time or another, performed housekeeping functions; as a result, they understand the worth and value of the people who perform such functions regularly.

Students of the service industry should remember the statement made proudly by one of America's most prestigious resorts, The Greenbriar of White Sulfur Springs, West Virginia. This statement appears on a sign that is visible as one enters the resort: "Ladies and Gentlemen Being Served by Ladies and Gentlemen."

✦ THE ROOMS DEPARTMENT

FRONT DESK AND HOUSEKEEPING

The rooms department of a lodging establishment is directly and solely involved with all aspects of the sale, occupancy, and servicing of guest rooms. The department manager is usually called the resident manager, although the title is somewhat misleading in its implication that this manager lives on the premises; most do not. Synonymous titles include rooms manager, rooms director, director of rooms operations, and, simply, hotel manager (not to be confused with the general manager).

The rooms department is usually a combination of two principal operating departments: the front office and the housekeeping department. The manager in charge of the front office oversees several subdepartments: reservations, front desk, bell staff, PBX, transportation, possibly concierge, and any other form of guest reception function.

The manager in charge of housekeeping functions is most commonly known as the executive housekeeper. Depending on the size of the hotel, subdepartments within the housekeeping sphere of operations (e.g., in-house laundry, recreation department), and, in some cases, corporate policy, the person in charge of housekeeping may have any one of a number of titles, all considered synonymous with executive housekeeper. A few such titles are:

- Housekeeper
- Housekeeping manager
- Director of services
- Director of internal services
- Director of housekeeping operations

For the purposes of this article we refer to this manager as the *executive housekeeper*.

There was a time when most executive housekeepers worked under the direction of the front office manager. They were, in fact, not executives but people who had worked their way up from a maid's position, with little or no managerial training. Today, however, the size, cost, and complexity of housekeeping operations have put the executive housekeeper on an equal footing with other department managers. As a result, executive housekeepers are now seen as sharing equally in responsibility under the resident manager for the operation of rooms departments.

The hotel industry is a highly labor-intensive hospitality business. More total employees may be involved in food and beverage (F&B) operations than in any other department. Because of the diversity of F&B operations (restaurants, lounges, banquet services, and kitchen), there are plenty of managers to control the total operation. In housekeeping, however, a single department head (the executive housekeeper) is responsible for the largest staff, operating cost center, and physical area of the property.

Today's modern executive housekeeper must be a trained manager skilled in planning, organizing, staffing, directing, and controlling operations. He or she must also be skilled in employee and human relations, have a superior understanding of cost controls, and have a strong technical background in purchasing, decorating, and renovation. Last, but not least, the executive housekeeper must be an able delegator. Without strong expertise and the inclination to pass tasks to others, convey the necessary power to act, and, finally, hold others accountable for their actions, the executive housekeeper must personally perform all working functions. This writer has never yet found the person who could make 3000 beds in one day.

✦ ORGANIZATION

Housekeeping organizations are as varied as types and sizes of hotel. Except for bed-and-breakfast operations, the trend today is away from the small, 80-room mom-and-pop hotel. It is, therefore, appropriate to discuss hotels of a size that might be considered a model appropriate to the greatest variation—say, 200 or more rooms. Most hotels would have identical functions, but size might dictate that one person perform several functions in a small hotel. Obviously, the larger the facility, the greater the need for a large staff with enough individuals to fill each unique function. Consider then, the following hotel:

- A modern suburban corporate transient hotel
- 350 rooms
- Two restaurants (one 24-hour and one dinner house)
- Banquet area with 15,000 square feet of meeting space
- Room service
- Kitchen to support all food services
- Main lounge with nightly entertainment
- Banquet beverage service and service bar outlets for both restaurants and room service
- Outdoor pool and winter indoor pool with health club facilities, sauna, and steam room
- Game room (video games, pool, and table tennis)
- In-house laundry for rooms department and banquet linen
- Two company-owned gift shops.
- Front desk fully computerized with a property management system

HOTEL ORGANIZATION

Prior to investigating the housekeeping department organization, it is appropriate to visualize an organization for the entire hotel. The organization diagram in Figure 5.1 could easily be that of the model hotel just described.

Note the position of the executive housekeeper within the organization. Executive housekeepers may occupy a greater or lesser position in any organization. Some executive housekeepers report directly to the gen-

eral manager; others even hold corporate executive positions. Others report to the chief of maintenance. In this case, however, the executive housekeeper is a middle manager—a full department head, equal to the front office manager and other principal department heads within the staff. Two junior managers report to the executive housekeeper: the housekeeping manager and the laundry manager. Both the executive housekeeper and the front office manager report to the resident manager, who is a member of the property executive committee. This committee is the top policymaking body for the property under the general manager.

THE HOUSEKEEPING ORGANIZATION

Figure 5.2 describes a typical housekeeping department organization, suitable for the model hotel.

Note the utilization of the two principal assistants. The housekeeping manager is the first assistant to the executive housekeeper and is in direct charge of all guest rooms in the hotel. This emphasizes the delegation that has taken place in that the housekeeping manager is not just an assistant to the executive housekeeper but a junior manager with a functional responsibility. This part of the organization can be managed in several ways. Each individual room attendant can be scheduled independently, or attendants may be grouped into scheduled teams, with the same hours on and the same time off. In this illustration, team staffing and scheduling are presented because this approach is more efficient for daily scheduling.

The laundry is another specific function to which a junior manager is assigned. In this

Figure 5.1 Hotel Organization (Through Department Head)

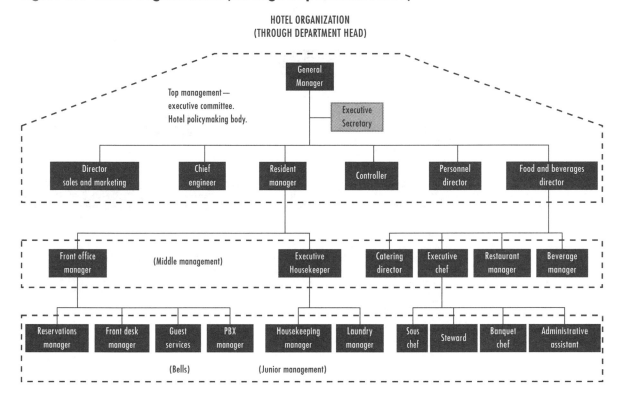

HOTEL ORGANIZATION
(THROUGH DEPARTMENT HEAD)

case, the required technical expertise is more specific. It includes knowledge of commercial laundry machinery and equipment, knowledge of piecework production, the utilization of chemicals, and their effects on an expensive inventory of linen.

Both junior managers and the executive housekeeper have line supervisors who report directly to them. (Below the management level, we recognize an hourly structure for employees who are paid by the hour at a given wage rate as opposed to being on salary.) Each supervisor has one or more hourly workers who round out the departmental organization.

Note that the organization shown in Figure 5.2 under the housekeeping manager is incomplete. The number of floor supervisors or team leaders and workers depends on the number of rooms a room attendant is expected to clean in a given 8-hour period. The national standard for rooms cleaned by one room attendant in one 8-hour period varies from 13 to 20, depending on the market mix. Hotels occupied primarily by traveling or group business transient guests are more efficient to clean because occupancy is primarily single, and such guests are up and out of their rooms early each day. Also, they are inclined to leave their rooms fairly neat. For this segment, room attendants can clean from 18 to 20 rooms per day. When the mix features more double occupancy with families on vacation, access to rooms for cleaning is more difficult and

Figure 5.2 Housekeeping Department Organization

HOUSEKEEPING DEPARTMENT
ORGANIZATION

STAFFING AND SCHEDULING CONCERNS

For our model hotel of 350 rooms, assume an 18-room workload per day. On any 100 percent occupancy day, we would need approximately 20 room attendants to clean all guest rooms. Placing these room attendants in teams of five, each working under one floor supervisor, creates a need for four supervisors. Also assume that one section housekeeping aide is assigned to each team to handle corridor cleaning, provide certain services to room attendants during the day, and to care for other public areas within the guest room portion of the hotel. Finally, assume that five laundry workers are needed in the laundry regularly, and that persons hired to relieve

cuts into the efficiency of staffing. In such cases, room attendants are not able to clean as many rooms in the same 8-hour period.

room attendants on days off can also relieve in the laundry.

The complete organization should now come into focus, except for one remaining concern. Hourly personnel cannot work seven days a week but are usually confined to a five-workday schedule. The following formula can establish the entire rooms cleaning, laundry, and relief staff requirement; increasing the staff allows for days off for regular room attendants, laundry workers, floor supervisors, and section housekeeping aides. (See the staffing guide, discussed below.)

At 100 percent occupancy on a continuous basis:

regular staff $\times$ seven days =
total staff $\times$ five day maximum
$S_1 \times 7 = S_2 \times 5$
$S_2 = S_1 \times 7 \div 5$

For the model, $S_2 = 25 \times 7 \div 5 = 35$ total working staff, all limited to a 5-day workweek. The additional ten employees can be organized into two special teams identical in composition to the regular teams and the laundry workforce. These swing teams relieve all regular and laundry personnel teams twice each week and have two days off themselves. This portion of the organization can now be scheduled to work by team units rather than as individual workers, which greatly simplifies personnel scheduling. (For further information on scheduling techniques, the reader is encouraged to read the basic text from which this article is drawn.)

The balance of the housekeeping organization is noted in the functions to be performed and, for purposes of illustration, must be scheduled individually. Specifically, personnel required for the second shift, persons required to staff the linen room and central housekeeping communications, and personnel organized under the senior housekeeping aide for public area cleaning and maintenance round out the total department staff.

The entire housekeeping department staff might, then, take on the appearance provided in the staffing guide outlined in Table 5.1.

The staffing guide is created to accurately document the need for total personnel. Every position within the department is listed, and it can be used to fill vacancies when they occur. Note teams identified by color.

This identification system shows which teams are regular teams, the one that works in the laundry, and which ones are considered swing teams. This particular staffing guide presumes that a 100 percent staff has been hired to support an occupancy averaging 85 percent or more for an extended period. Should occupancies be forecast as a lesser amount, a 100 percent staff need not be hired, and staff vacancies can be distributed over the entire team network. Fluctuations in daily occupancy are dealt with by scheduling down within each team on a fair and equitable basis. This task can be delegated to the floor supervisor, but controls must be in place that guarantee fairness to all who must be cut out of a day's work due to low occupancy.

✦ PERSONNEL AND JOBS IN THE HOUSEKEEPING DEPARTMENT

What follows is a listing of the jobs one might find in a hotel housekeeping department. The basic function and scope of responsibility are indicated for managerial positions, and for hourly jobs, titles and responsibilities are listed. Where several names or titles apply to the same function in the hourly structure, each name is noted.

Table 5.1 Department Staffing Guide

POSITION NO.	TITLE	NAME ASSIGNED
	Management Team	
1	Executive housekeeper	_____
2	Housekeeping manager	_____
3	Laundry manager	_____
	Fixed Team	
4	Linen room supervisor	_____
5	Linen room attendant	_____
6	Senior housekeeping aide (public area supervisor)	_____
7	Public area housekeeper 1 (male)	_____
8	Public area housekeeper 2 (female)	_____
9	Public area housekeeper (relief)	_____
	Evening Team	
10	Night supervisor	_____
11	Night section housekeeper	_____
12	Night housekeeping	_____
13	Night (public area) housekeeper 1 (male)	_____
14	Night (public area) housekeeper 2 (female)	_____
15	Night (public area) housekeeper (relief)	_____
	Regular Rooms Cleaning Teams:	
	Red Team	
16	Senior housekeeper (supervisor)	_____
17	Section housekeeping aide	_____
18	Section housekeeper 1	_____
19	Section housekeeper 2	_____
20	Section housekeeper 3	_____
21	Section housekeeper 4	_____
22	Section housekeeper 5	_____
	Yellow Team	
23	Senior housekeeper (supervisor)	_____
24	Section housekeeping aide	_____
25	Section housekeeper 6	_____
26	Section housekeeper 7	_____
27	Section housekeeper 8	_____
28	Section housekeeper 9	_____
29	Section housekeeper 10	_____

Brown Team

30	Senior housekeeper (supervisor)	_____
31	Section housekeeping aide	_____
32	Section housekeeper 11	_____
33	Section housekeeper 12	_____
34	Section housekeeper 13	_____
35	Section housekeeper 14	_____
36	Section housekeeper 15	_____

Green Team

37	Senior housekeeper (supervisor)	_____
38	Section housekeeping aide	_____
39	Section housekeeper 16	_____
40	Section housekeeper 17	_____
41	Section housekeeper 18	_____
42	Section housekeeper 19	_____
43	Section housekeeper 20	_____

Laundry

44	Laundry supervisor (washman)	_____
45	Laundry helper/sorter	_____
46	Laundry attendant (ironer)	_____
47	Laundry attendant (ironer)	_____
48	Laundry attendant (folder/stacker)	_____
49	Laundry attendant (folder/stacker)	_____
50	Laundry attendant (folder/stacker)	_____

Swing Team 1

51	Senior housekeeper (swing supervisor)	_____
52	Section housekeeping aide (ST-A)	_____
53	Section housekeeper A-1	_____
54	Section housekeeper A-2	_____
55	Section housekeeper A-3	_____
56	Section housekeeper A-4	_____
57	Section housekeeper A-5	_____

Swing Team 2

58	Senior housekeeper (swing supervisor)	_____
59	Section housekeeping aide (ST-B)	_____
60	Section housekeeper B-1	_____
61	Section housekeeper B-2	_____
62	Section housekeeper B-3	_____
63	Section housekeeper B-4	_____
64	Section housekeeper B-5	_____

THE EXECUTIVE HOUSEKEEPER

The executive housekeeper usually assumes complete direction, operational control, and supervision of the housekeeping, laundry, and recreation departments.

The scope of responsibility is normally broad to ensure that the incumbent has the freedom necessary to do the job. This position is now recognized as a career-enhancing step. The executive housekeeper operates the departments under his or her control in the most efficient manner possible through effective application and enforcement of company policies, the use of methods described in standard operating procedures, and the use of sound management principles. He or she is primarily responsible for the cleanliness of guest rooms and public areas assigned to the housekeeping department. He or she accomplishes tasks through proper training, motivation, and supervision of all personnel assigned to the housekeeping, laundry, and recreation departments.

THE HOUSEKEEPING MANAGER

In the model organization, the housekeeping manager assumes primary responsibility for guest room cleaning and servicing and acts as the primary assistant to the executive housekeeper.

Under the direction of the executive housekeeper, the housekeeping manager is responsible for the efficient and orderly management of guest room cleaning, servicing, and the reporting of rooms status.

He or she represents employees directly involved in rooms cleaning and is directly involved in their work schedules. He or she must react to occupancy in scheduling to keep costs under control.

THE LAUNDRY MANAGER

The laundry manager normally assumes primary responsibility for operation of the hotel's in-house commercial laundry. He or she also acts as second assistant to the executive housekeeper.

Under direction of the executive housekeeper, the laundry manager is responsible for the efficient and orderly management and operation of the hotel laundry. Through the proper use of assigned personnel, he or she provides clean linen to the house and to the banquet department according to plans and budgets.

✦ HOURLY EMPLOYEES

THE GUEST ROOM ATTENDANT (ALSO KNOWN AS THE GRA, MAID, OR SECTION HOUSEKEEPER)

The guest room attendant is primarily responsible for guest room cleaning and servicing. He or she is usually assigned a section of rooms each day, constituting a workload of a designated number of rooms to be cleaned. In general, the room attendant performs the same functions in each room assigned. The room attendant also conducts rooms checks at set times to assist in determining the reporting condition of the house: rooms occupied, rooms ready (vacant and ready to rent), and rooms on change (vacant but not yet serviced; also known as check-outs).

The room attendant also participates in general cleaning of one or more rooms each day as it is serviced in order to keep quality standards high.

Most room attendants work in compliance with standard operating procedures (SOPs) that may specify as many as 60 items that must meet a given standard in each guest room. This is not as daunting as it may sound, but the SOP system guarantees coverage where necessary.

Finally, the room attendant reloads his or her own linen cart at the end of each workday.

If so organized, the room attendant is one of several members of a housekeeping team under a floor supervisor.

THE SECTION HOUSEKEEPING AIDE (PREVIOUSLY SECTION HOUSEMAN)

The section housekeeping aide works in the guest room portion of the hotel, attending to the regular and daily cleaning of corridors, elevator cabs and landings, stairwells, service areas, floor linen rooms, vending areas, and other public spaces in the vicinity of guest rooms. The aide also helps room attendants with general cleaning, if necessary. He or she also removes soiled linen and rubbish from room attendants' carts on a regular schedule and brings supplies from storerooms to floor linen rooms when needed. The section housekeeping aide works at the direction of the floor supervisor and, when so organized, as a member of a housekeeping team.

THE FLOOR SUPERVISOR (ALSO KNOWN AS SENIOR HOUSEKEEPER OR "INSPECTRESS")

Floor supervisors are team leaders to whom several room attendants and a section housekeeping aide report. They are assigned to specific divisions of the rooms section of a property and are responsible for the quality of work performed in the several rooms sections to which their room attendants are assigned. They also are responsible for the public sectors assigned to their section housekeeping aides. They make inspections and

reports and are, in all respects, supervisors of the persons assigned to their teams. They also assist in the personnel administration of the people assigned to them.

The floor supervisor is sometimes called *inspectress,* but this may be outdated. [*Editor*: It *is* now outdated, for the term was coined to indicate a female inspector. Most operations now simply call this job *inspector,* regardless of gender.] Many floor supervisors are inspectresses just because they inspect rooms. Other inspectresses do nothing but inspect rooms and report directly to the manager on what they observe, but they have no responsibility to correct identified discrepancies because no other staff is assigned to them for work purposes. [This writer is of the opinion that persons who do nothing but inspect guest rooms, then have no employees or authority with which to take corrective action, are a superfluous use of manpower.]

THE SENIOR HOUSEKEEPING AIDE (IN THE PAST KNOWN AS HEAD HOUSEMAN)

The senior housekeeping aide is a major supervisor in the housekeeping department. He or she is usually in charge of all public areas not directly associated with guest rooms: lobbies, major public corridors, public rest rooms, offices, and other areas specifically negotiated as part of the overall housekeeping responsibility. The senior housekeeping aide is usually responsible for basic training of section housekeeping aides and for supervision of utility housekeeping aides who might perform tasks such as shampooing carpets, washing windows, or project work. The senior housekeeping aide is usually responsible for the storage and accountability of cleaning and guest supply inventories. He or she normally works as a supervisory assistant to the executive housekeeper and performs other tasks as the executive housekeeper directs.

THE NIGHT SUPERVISOR

The existence of a night supervisor presumes a second shift to which no management is regularly assigned. This situation, of course, can vary with the size and complexity of night operations. Other than as intermittently visited by housekeeping management, the night supervisor assumes total control of the department after the major rooms and hotel cleaning evolution for each day is concluded. Overseeing one or two night room attendants, a night section housekeeping aide, and several night lobby or public area personnel, the night supervisor is accountable for the balance of services performed by the housekeeping department. He or she ensures that all rooms are left cleaned and ready to rent and that guest requests for service or equipment such as cribs, bedboards, and extra linen are fulfilled. The night supervisor works closely with the hotel night manager, is usually on beeper, and makes routine inspections throughout the hotel until the department is secured each evening at the designated time. The night supervisor, like the senior housekeeping aide, is a major supervisor within the department.

THE LINEN ROOMS SUPERVISOR

The main linen room, a service area of the hotel, is the hub of housekeeping communication and activity. It might be better described as housekeeping central. The linen room supervisor, under the executive housekeeper, is the supervisor in charge of main linen room operations. His or her primary responsibility is maintaining and operating the communication link to the front desk, engineering, and each guest in need of housekeeping attention. In addition, the linen room supervisor is sometimes referred to as the chief status operator for housekeeping. Keeping up with, changing as necessary, and reporting the status of each guest room throughout the day is another major function of the linen room supervisor. He or she is the prime guest contact representative. Also, he or she oversees the activities of one or more linen room attendants who perform supply and distribution functions for items such as bedspreads, blankets, bed pads, and curtains. On the second shift, the night supervisor assumes the responsibilities of the linen room supervisor.

THE LAUNDRY SUPERVISOR

Working as a principal assistant to the laundry manager, the laundry supervisor, as the title indicates, supervises the activities of laundry attendants. Normally the laundry supervisor works as the head washperson and is in charge of all major wash equipment and chemicals. He or she also supervises the workload process and production. In our model hotel, when the laundry supervisor and team of laundry attendants is scheduled off, a swing team supervisor assumes the responsibilities of the laundry supervisor and brings his or her swing team into the laundry. Because there are two swing teams, each works in the laundry one day each week, providing the entire department with maximum flexibility and training.

THE RECREATION SUPERVISOR

In our model hotel, the recreation supervisor, under the direct supervision of the executive housekeeper, assumes responsibility for all recreation areas of the hotel. All swimming pool attendants work for the recreation supervisor and are fully Red Cross or water safety instructor qualified. (Swimming pools are properly signed to indicate "No lifeguard on duty. Swimmers enter at their own risk." This prevents the guest from abdicating responsibility for their own and their children's safety. However, all pool attendants are fully qualified to save a life.) Pool attendants, under direction of the recreation supervisor, also work in the health club, sauna, and game room, providing service to guests and maintaining cleanliness and order.

OTHER EMPLOYEES

Other employees may be found in the department, their titles indicating their activities and who they might work for. All such positions have titles appropriate to either male or female employees and are, therefore, nonsexist. Such titles are as follows:

- Utility housekeeping aide
- Linen room attendant
- Lobby housekeeping aide
- Laundry attendant
- Housekeeping trainer (a secondary job sometimes carried by a room attendant to ensure standardization of training)

✦ NEW HORIZONS IN HOUSEKEEPING

The National Executive Housekeeper's Association (NEHA) has long recognized the similarity in responsibilities of persons performing housekeeping functions in hospitals, hotels, and nursing homes. The association, therefore, draws its membership not only from hotels, retirement centers, and contract cleaning establishments but also from hospitals and nursing homes. The movement of management personnel between venues is well documented. When asked how difficult it is for a manager to make the transition in either direction, a member in hospital service once remarked, "The main function of housekeeping in both areas is to clean rooms and public areas, and to dispose of trash and rubbish. There is only one major difference, however, and that is in hospitals, we know exactly what we are walking into, and in hotels, we don't know what we may be dealing with." That was true—until the advent of the AIDS crisis.

On December 2, 1991, new rules issued by the Occupational Safety and Health Administration (OSHA) made it mandatory that employers provide to all employees who might, as a result of their job classification, come in contact with human blood or other bodily fluids, information, training, and compliance with federal precautions designed to maintain a safe workplace with regard to bloodborne pathogens (microorganisms that can cause disease in humans), especially the HIV virus and the HBV (Hepatitis B) virus.

Specifically, department managers must establish control plans to combat the threat and provide access for employees to read and understand the OSHA compliance standard. Employees such as housekeeping and laundry personnel, who as a part of their regular daily assigned duties come in contact with bodily fluids such as blood, semen, sputum, and vomit and with spent needles (sharps) discarded by diabetics or drug users, must be advised of the potential dangers. Furthermore, they must be trained and tested in how to handle such risks when they occur, and they must be offered the opportunity to be inoculated against the HBV virus at company expense. Records must be kept of all training conducted and of all exposures that occur.

✦ CONCLUSION

Housekeeping operations is no longer the exclusive territory of women, nor is it considered menial or less important than any other function in the hospitality organization. Anyone who thinks otherwise should try to imagine hotel operations without housekeeping; the picture might have general managers and presidents cleaning rooms.

Because of the large staffs involved, housekeeping operations provide junior managers outstanding opportunities to develop leadership and supervisory skills, an opportunity not always available in other departments.

This writer recalls a moment of truth several years ago when a general manager was overheard commenting to a utility aide who at the time, happened to be mopping a men's room at 1:00 A.M. The general manager said, "You know, what you are doing is just as vital and necessary as what I do every day. We just do different things and work at different skill levels. When the company thinks they can do without either one of us, they'll abolish our jobs. I don't think they will, so until they do, don't forget: Your job is just as important around here as mine is!"

5.3 ON BEING AN EXECUTIVE HOUSEKEEPER

John Lagazo

Ah yes, those were the days, sitting in our university classes, wondering where our education and futures would take us. I thought it would be quite easy—go through the management training program, become an assistant department head for a little while, move to department and then division head, then presto—general manager!

After going through the management training in my first company, I decided I wanted to stay in the rooms division—more specifically front office, so the path was laid out: hotel assistant manager, then front office manager, brief exposure in either housekeeping or reservations, then so on and so on. Never did I think I would be the executive housekeeper in arguably what are some of the finest hotels and resorts not only in the United States but in the world.

Why housekeeping? When my friends ask what I do and I say, "I'm an executive housekeeper," the first response is, "Oh, so you clean rooms?" Depending on who is asking, I either agree or say it is much, much, more. Over the years, I have had trainees or first-time assistant managers who say that housekeeping was never their initial choice, but by the time they were done, they had a different appreciation for the department.

So what is housekeeping? Is managing housekeeping just making sure the room attendants clean all the rooms every day? It is actually just a little more than that.

It is managing what usually is the largest regular staff in the hotel and the budget to pay them. It is managing supplies—whatever is in the room for the guests to use and whatever is used to clean anything and everything in the hotel, from the sidewalks to the staff areas (e.g., locker rooms, cafeteria, offices), from meeting spaces to food and beverage outlets—not to mention the guest rooms themselves.

It is managing teamwork and coordinating with all other departments in the hotel—to make sure the rooms are ready for the guests when they arrive. It is making sure that all instructions and requests from sales are carried out. Accounting must be satisfied that we are in control of dollars. It is making sure the food and beverage outlets are as clean as the guest rooms. It is making sure all of the human resources reporting requirements are met.

For the hotels that have a full-service laundry, it is managing that too—and if the hotel utilizes an off-property service (for laundry, overnight cleaning of the kitchens and public areas, uniform and guest clothes cleaning), the executive housekeeper must manage that operation as well! Even though off-property services are their own businesses, they represent the hotel; if they do not clean the linens well or are not efficient, it costs the hotel money.

Executive housekeepers must be detail-oriented and organized. Housekeeping is a 24/7 department, and it can get out of control very quickly. This means phone calls at home at 11:00 P.M. saying that your staff has not shown up or that because the boilers are down, there is no

steam for the laundry. The wildest calls I received (not too often, thank goodness) were when I worked in Hawaii. Because of the staffing challenges, I had room attendants and housepersons ferried over from a neighboring island. If the weather was bad or the boat had a mechanical problem, the phone rang around 4:00 A.M. to tell me so. I then had to figure out Plan B for cleaning rooms and the rest of the hotel that day.

Getting away from the technical side of things, being an executive housekeeper taught me a lot about managing people; I was "diversity managing" well before it became politically correct and one of the new management buzzwords. The staff is usually the most ethnically diverse, with an accompanying challenge being the level of English competency and overall education. These staff members are asked to work with hazardous chemicals in an environment with a high accident potential; they push and pull heavy weights, are exposed to bacteria, and work with dangerous equipment such as sheet and towel folders and garbage and cardboard compactors.

These people have one of the most detail-oriented jobs—a room checklist can have as many as 150 items that must be completed to proper standard.

Contrary to popular belief, this staff should also have high guest contact skills. Just because room attendants and other housekeeping staff members do not interact with guests every time they perform their duties, this does not mean they should not be skilled in guest contact. One of my former room attendants consistently told me the travel plans of one of the regular CEOs that stayed with us. She wrote down his travel dates and let us know if his wife would be with him. Because he was such a regular, we rarely had problems in accommodating him even if we were sold out, and he always had the same room with the same room attendant.

In many of the hotels, the challenge was to pull the ethnic groups together to work as a team. Housekeeping gave me a great chance to learn about different cultures—I probably would still not know what a quincinera is (a Sweet 15 birthday/debut in Latin American countries). I have eaten foods that I probably would not have otherwise and have picked up smatterings of many languages (Spanish, Creole, Tongan, Polish, Cantonese, Filipino)—which, depending on the situation, can either get me in serious trouble or give everyone a good laugh.

I learned about management styles and group dynamics, and I advise all of you who read this to learn as much about these subjects as possible. I learned about identifying the informal leaders of groups and how to influence them. I learned about individual personality styles, how to manage them, and how to get them to work together to get things done. From the people of different cultures I have worked with, I learned about the ones who avoid eye contact when you speak with them, I learned about the ones that had Old Country traditions—for instance, not respecting a female or young boss—and how to turn them around.

Housekeeping taught me how to adapt—which, on the outside, should not have been an issue because I was the boss and the staff should do as I say (traditional management). Managing people continues to change and evolve—first there was Total Quality Management, then Generation X management, and now whatever new theories are out there. To me, the bottom line is that to be a success, you must manage not only yourself but also groups of people. Manage and lead the environment (department), and you will be successful in your endeavors. Get exposure to different environments—work in city and remote resort locations—and know and understand that everywhere you go, the guest and staff makeup is different. If you are adaptable, you will also be successful.

There are some other interesting things too—for example, when I shop for home cleaning items, I know way more than I need to. Don't bother listening to commercials; send me an email or work in housekeeping and you will know why I will not buy "window cleaner with ammonia." Having managed laundry operations, I shop for clothes not only for style but for materials used and construction of the item. If you buy an item with lots of extra frills, beads, decoration, metallic buttons, and bring it to my dry cleaning store, don't be surprised if I charge you extra for what it takes to properly clean it. I may even turn you down and say I won't clean it unless you sign a damage waiver. I now know that the dry cleaning and laundry processes are murder on fabrics.

I have many great memories from housekeeping over the years:

- Using a bullhorn to conduct a morning meeting with 70 room attendants.

- Proving a Mobil inspector wrong (I had been in his room during the incident in question).

- Being the executive housekeeper at the host hotel for the Mobil five-star winners award ceremony—imagine having every room checked with a magnifying glass and white gloves!

- Having a local TV station doing a *60 Minutes*–style report on hotel cleanliness—we passed with flying colors!

Having my rooms director keep checking on me to make sure I did not get food poisoning because of food my staff would give me—I was adventurous enough to eat whatever was placed on my desk, and yes, jellyfish does have an interesting texture.

I have encountered other situations too. After a suicide in a hotel room, I could only get new staff members to go into the room because of the strong superstitious beliefs of some attendants. I have managed through both strikes and decertifications in union hotels. The celebrity stories—those alone could take up a whole book. Perhaps I could get rich from writing it!

I am glad my career path has taken me through housekeeping. At the end of the day, it really is the memories of the people I have met and friends made over the years that have made the difference. I think I would have learned the technical aspects one way or the other, but the people skills have been even more valuable. Yes, I did hold the positions of hotel assistant manager, front office assistant manager, and front office manager at various points in my career, in addition to spending time in all housekeeping management positions, including laundry/valet manager.

Where did I get all of these memories and experiences? Since leaving my alma mater in the mid-1980s, I have been at:

- Hyatt Hotels in California and Louisiana

- A Wyndham Hotel in California

- Ritz-Carlton Hotels/Resorts in California, Boston, Florida, Hawaii, and Puerto Rico (when I worked in these hotels, they were all five-star and/or five-diamond, except for Puerto Rico, which was still too new)

- Four Seasons Hotels in Boston and Chicago (both five-star, five-diamond properties)

- Short stints in St. Louis and Florida with Adams Mark and an independent four-star resort

From my current perspective as director of operations of the Madison Hotel in Washington, DC, can I say my housekeeping experience helped me? You bet! The varied experience with people, places, and management styles has prepared me for *anything* in this great hospitality business.

5.4 THE HOTEL ENGINEERING FUNCTION: ORGANIZATION, PEOPLE, AND ISSUES IN THE MODERN ERA

GLEN B. MOUNTS AND OLIVER MEINZER

✦ INTRODUCTION TO THE ENGINEERING DEPARTMENT
HISTORY OF DEPARTMENT

Historically the functions and duties of the director of engineering, his staff, and the engineering department have been relegated to the subconscious of hotel management and certainly to the hotel guests. Their place in the organization was roughly analogous to their place in the building structure: towards the bottom and basically out of sight. The only time the functions of the engineering department became noticeable was on those unhappy occasions when something went wrong with one of the building systems and guests and/or management were inconvenienced.

Consequently in the past, "out of sight, out of mind" treatment evolved for the engineering department and as a result the relative importance of that department assumed a diminished role. Also, the personnel of the engineering department were craftspeople and semi-skilled workers, usually managed by one of their own who, through longevity and perseverance, worked their way up through the ranks to supervisory status.

EVOLUTIONARY STIMULI

There is now clear evidence that this department is changing in many of the same ways that other departments of a modern hotel have had to change. The reasons for these evolutionary changes are many, but four can be highlighted here. Several of them of course are closely interconnected.

Competition. As more and more hotel organizations seek the business of ever more carefully segmented markets, many of the mechanisms of competition manifest themselves first in features of the physical plant. These can range from building design, landscaping, elevators, in-room amenities, and facilities to the latest in traditional fixtures and building systems such as plumbing; kitchen equipment; elevators; heating, ventilating and air conditioning (HVAC); and the other "behind-the-scenes" paraphernalia that make up the domain of the director of engineering.

Sophistication. Many of these building systems in today's hotels are interconnected and managed in conjunction with other departmental systems and monitored by computerized facilities. This increased sophistication has mandated more sophisticated and knowledgeable management in all departments, but perhaps the most drastic and substantive changes will be (and are) occurring in engineering.

Return on Investment. Many modern hotel plants are the result of plans and investments by a wide range of participants, including (but not necessarily always) the company owning the property and the management firm that operates the hotel. These investors have the expectation of a certain return on their investment, and subsequently expect that the management company will not only keep the hotel filled with guests but keep the property's assets in such a state that the guests will continue to want to come there. This also mandates new dimensions to the engineer's job. The combination of increased competition and sophisticated systems make for more than a traditional "repair and maintenance" approach to providing the engineering support in all areas of the hotel. To keep the hotel positively contributing to the investor's return on their money, the engineering staff has to be considered a major role player in the financial health of the organization.

Energy. The cost, use, management, and conservation of energy have added a new and singular dimension to the job of the director of engineering—one that did not exist in pre-1973 operations, simply because energy was so cheap. Since the OPEC Oil Embargo of 1973, energy prices have undergone many changes, with none making it any cheaper. Prior to that, buildings were not engineered nor managed specifically to save energy.

Since then, most hotels and most modern hotel companies have come to recognize energy as one building expense in which significant savings can be realized. If accomplished with care, and with little to no impact to the hotel guest or employee, engineering can provide delivery of hotel utilities, that is, water, electricity, natural gas services without any adverse or negative tangible effects. Hotels want to avoid, for instance, the extreme circumstances of requesting guests to take short showers while at the same time asking them to pay $180 a night for their room.

The residual effects of the embargo were twofold. Hotels that were built prior to 1973 were not constructed to be particularly energy efficient. Engineers that are managing their departments in those sorts of hotels have a more difficult job with respect to managing energy.

On the other hand, hotels that were designed and built after 1973–74 were "commissioned" prior to being opened. This implies that the buildings mechanical systems were installed and inspected in order to achieve their optimum efficiency. This, in conjunction with improvements to HVAC environmental control systems, has resulted in increasingly sophisticated systems to manage and conserve energy without adverse effects on the guests.

The first instance represents a managerial problem of "making do" for the engineering manager; the second presents the dilemma of expanding one's knowledge in a rapidly changing technological environment. It should be noted that energy remains a significant management issue for the engineer and will for the foreseeable future.

In no business system as complex as a hotel is any mechanical or electrical system the only answer. A tremendous amount of attention must be given to training of personnel to overcome wasteful habits where energy is concerned. One of the classic examples is that of the kitchen employees who turn on every appliance in the kitchen at 6:00 A.M. when maybe only 20 percent of them are used for the preparation of breakfast and most of the rest of them are not needed until close to lunch. This is representative of the sort of wasteful habits that are basically out of the control of the engineer but something that the engineer is obligated to point out to other department heads.

Those sorts of examples, in and of themselves, suggest further complications of the engineer's job. Specifically, the engineer (as opposed to the role's being relegated to the bottom of the organizational chart and the back of the house as earlier stated) now needs to have an active presence as a "total" hotel manager and needs to become adept at interacting with other department managers.

✦ PERSONNEL

MANAGER OF ENGINEERING FUNCTION

Variously referred to as the director of engineering, chief engineer, director of building operations, director of facilities, building superintendent, or some other combination of those terms, this is the individual who is responsible for the management of the building's systems and their maintenance, repair, and upkeep.

As stated earlier, in the past the director of engineering position was typically filled by people who worked their way up through the ranks from either one of the crafts or as an engineering employee specializing in one of the building

Figure 5.3 Engineering Department Organization

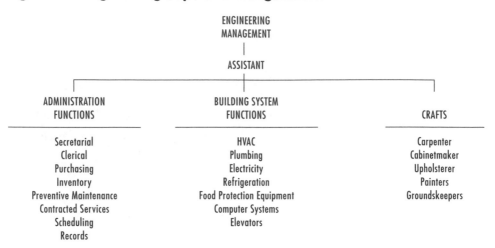

```
                          ENGINEERING
                          MANAGEMENT
                              |
                          ASSISTANT
                              |
     ┌────────────────────────┼────────────────────────┐
ADMINISTRATION           BUILDING SYSTEM
  FUNCTIONS                 FUNCTIONS                 CRAFTS
──────────────         ──────────────────         ──────────────

  Secretarial                  HVAC                  Carpenter
   Clerical                   Plumbing              Cabinetmaker
  Purchasing                 Electricity             Upholsterer
   Inventory                Refrigeration             Painters
Preventive Maintenance  Food Protection Equipment  Groundskeepers
Contracted Services        Computer Systems
  Scheduling                 Elevators
   Records
```

systems. They may have been in hotels all of their professional careers or may have come to a hotel company from engineering positions in organizations as diverse as the military, shipping lines, or manufacturing companies or as building engineers in office buildings, university settings, or hospitals.

Research evidence, however, exists that suggests this trend may be changing (Rutherford 1987). Chief engineers responding to this survey describe themselves collectively according to the data set forth in Table 5.2. Over 25 percent of those responding to this nationwide survey indicated they have a university degree. Of those,

Table 5.2 Chief Engineer Demographics

		(RAW NUMBER, IF APPLICABLE)
Average age	44.5	
Percent male	100.0%	
Percent Caucasian	92.9%	
Median salary	$35,000	
Percent university degree	27.0%	(20)
Percent of degrees in engineering	75.0%	(15)
Percent of degrees in hotel/business	25.0%	(5)
Average years at present hotel	10.9	
Average years in present position	6.3	
74 Respondents	6.15	

three-quarters were working within some area of the engineering discipline. This suggests that the sophistication of modern hotel building operations may be mandating that management possess more formal education than that required in the past. A great number of hotel companies now prefer and/or require their directors of engineering to be accredited through a third-party organization. Most notably is an accreditation through the Building Owners and Managers Institute (BOMI) or becoming certified through the American Hotel and Lodging Educational Institute as a Certified Engineering Operations Executive (CEOE).

In this study, the typical engineer was 44½ years old and had been in the hospitality business about 11 years. This suggests that this "typical engineer" has probably had significant on-the-job experience or training in his field in other industries and only recently came into the hospitality industry. After entering the hospitality industry, however, it appears that the chief engineers moved rapidly into management and have been fairly stable in their careers as evidenced by the congruence of average years in present position and average years at present hotel.

Commenting on these data one chief engineer said that in his experience more and more industry engineering managers in the larger or international hotel firms are being recruited from among those people who have had at least some college education, if not actually holding a college or university degree in engineering. He suggested that, in his company, this does not necessarily reflect a preference for academic training over practical experience but recognizes the realities of doing business in today's competitive environment. It also suggests understanding and being able to manage the sophisticated building systems that the company anticipates installing and those being developed for new hotels throughout the twenty-first century. In that comment lies one key to understanding the future of the chief engineer's job. The most successful engineers of the future will very likely be those whose training and education prepares them to think strategically, to recognize trends, and do their part to help the hotel and its owners meet and deal with the evolutionary issues discussed earlier.

OTHER DEPARTMENTAL MANAGEMENT STAFF

Referring again to Figure 5.3, depending of course on the size of the hotel and the extent and sophistication of the engineering functions in the hotel, the director of engineering may enjoy the services of a staff of junior managers, including but not limited to a chief engineer, asst. chief engineer, and supervisors. These people help carry out the administrative details of operating an increasingly complicated hotel department. Included in these would be administrative support, which may be combined with a clerical function.

Among the most important administrative functions for the engineering department are:

- Departmental accounting/reconciliation practices.

- Scheduling and payroll for staff.

- Inventory and requisition of department controllables, that is, layette bins for miscellaneous parts, building parts, and mechanical parts as required.

- Scheduling and inspecting preventive maintenance performed on all building systems and guest rooms.

- Administering contract services such as pest control, window washing, landscaping, swimming pool maintenance, grounds keeping, and various construction projects.

As the department grows in size and scope, a major administrative function involves scheduling of equipment and personnel to accomplish the tasks of the department. That is another major series of daily tasks that face administration of an engineering department. While scheduling may benefit greatly from technological advances such as microcomputers or the hotel's mainframe computer system, in a building whose systems are as complicated and interrelated as a hotel, part of the engineering function has to be prepared to react to unscheduled events ranging from overflowing toilets to stuck elevators to gas leaks and so forth.

A final administrative function involves setting the groundwork and maintaining the basis for managerial and administrative decisions that affect the long-term operation of the engineering department and, by extrapolation, the hotel itself. That is the keeping of accurate and up-to-date records regarding the various building systems and installation of capital equipment for which the engineer is responsible. In order to aid the engineering department with this ever-evolving and constantly changing environment, many new computer-based systems have been implemented to help with the scheduling of preventive maintenance for equipment in the hotel. This can range from an ice machine on a guest floor to a hot water boiler providing hot water to an entire tower. These programs not only schedule the preventive maintenance but also keep a tally on the department's progress and remind management of areas that may be falling behind. The time savings and improved productivity, not to mention having a solid PM program, is proving to be instrumental in maintaining hotels' assets for the owners.

These are the sorts of administrative details that complicate the job of any manager but may be particularly troubling to the engineer. One of the main reasons for this is that, while the engineering department is responsible for the maintenance and repair of sophisticated and complicated building systems, under most circumstances these systems or component parts of these systems are often operated by (and perhaps misused by) a wide range of people, ranging from employees to guests. Particularly in the case of guests, we have little or no control over the way in which they treat guestroom equipment and fixtures for which the engineer is responsible. Those engineers who have the luxury of a well-developed administrative staff find their job in managing the building and its systems and the attendant problems much easier if complete, accurate, and up-to-date records are available to formulate the basis for planning, purchasing, budgeting, and control. Again the implementation of often proprietary computer software systems in the engineering department is aiding, simplifying, and streamlining the access to records and PMs. By increasing productivity, these measures are allowing the director of engineering and chief engineer to focus on being more strategic and "total" hotel managers.

TECHNICAL SPECIALISTS

Typical building functions, which are the responsibility of the engineering department, are listed in Figure 5.3. Each has its own place in providing for the comfort of the guest and participating in the delivery of the hotel's services to the guests. Each has attendant complications that provide challenges for the management and staff of the engineering department.

Heating, ventilating, and air conditioning (collectively known as HVAC) are systems designed to provide control of space temperature, humidity, air contaminants, differential pressurization, and air motion to an area. Most HVAC systems are designed for human comfort and the comfort of an occupied space. Modern building HVAC systems provide for heating or cooling the air, adding or deleting moisture to or from the air to adjust for optimum relative humidity, filtering or cleaning the air, and moving the air from place to place within the hotel, providing for a number of complete changes of air in a room per hour dependent upon local codes and activities within that particular area of the hotel.

Among the complicating factors here that challenge the engineering department are that various areas of the hotel have various requirements for air. For instance, there is a different requirement in the guest room areas than there is in the kitchen area. There is a different requirement in public areas such as the lobby and areas such as bars, restaurants, or housekeeping laundry facilities. The engineers call this "providing the system with balance," and it is a major function of the individuals who are in charge of the HVAC to deliver the optimum environment to each of those various areas of the hotel and adjust the HVAC system to deliver the optimum environment to each of those various areas. In recent years, the HVAC systems serving public areas of the hotel have even been modified to enhance the guests' experience by delivering a measured and aerosolized "scent" to the air.

The plumbing system in a modern hotel has to perform a number of balancing functions also. First and foremost in the minds of management, of course, is the delivery of high-quality water service to guest room areas. Guests want high-quality water that is free from visual defects such as dirt or rust, does not carry any odors, and tastes clean and fresh. Guests also want water that is hot enough to shave, bathe, and wash with, without the danger of scalding themselves, and they also want that water in generous supply. Nothing is more frustrating to a hotel guest who is paying over $200 a night for a room to find that the hotel has run out of hot water in the middle of a morning shave or shower. At the same time, the engineering department is expected to deliver "production" hot and cold water to the kitchen areas, the housekeeping and laundry areas, and the various food service areas. Delivery of high-quality water service to the various user groups in the hotel is a major part of the engineering function, one that, of course, is only noticed when there is some obvious defect in the delivery of that particular service.

A similar case may be made for the delivery of electricity to the various areas within the hotel. As in providing high-quality plumbing services, the electrical systems of the hotel also have to be designed and maintained to serve various user groups. Again, like plumbing, there is no substitute for the lack of electricity. The engineering staff must provide the hotel with electrical service designed to meet the needs of individual departments and the needs of guests.

Refrigeration, food production equipment, and computer systems are examples of other building system functions that may be the responsibility of the engineering department to repair, maintain, replace, and/or manage. While the maintenance of many of these systems may be contracted for with outside agencies such as the supplier, the engineering department nonetheless is the first line of defense in keeping the systems operating efficiently.

In most modern hotels, the installation and service of elevator systems are generally the province of the elevator manufacturer and hotels will typically have extended maintenance agreements for the elevators. Most engineering departments will, however, closely monitor the operation of the elevator systems. In modern high-rise hotels with high-speed elevator service, the slightest problem with that service should be quickly and easily identified and reported to the contractors. It is generally the responsibility of the engineering department to monitor these services and their contracts closely and carefully.

The various crafts represented in Figure 5.3 are included to illustrate the sorts of specialized skills required in varying ways by most hotel engineering departments. Prior to 9/11 and depending upon the size of the hotel and complexity of a hotel's services, it was not uncommon to find an engineering department with a full-time staff of "specialized" engineers. This could include one or more carpenters and painters to maintain, repair, and build fixtures and furniture for the hotel's guests and staff. Similarly, if such work is not contracted out, hotels may employ an upholsterer, whose major task is to maintain a high-quality appearance of the vast collection of furniture in a typical hotel. After 9/11 many of these "specialized" positions were eliminated, and the majority of these duties were relegated to the shift engineers and or completely contracted out to a third party. Fortunately, this move proved to be successful, as it increased the engineering department's productivity, while promoting further training and experience among the other engineers. Moving forward, it has become obvious that in some cases "specializing" in only one field can limit one's progress. Certainly in the engineering discipline, for a shift engineer to be considered for promotion to a senior engineering position, they will be expected to have a working understanding of nearly all areas they may be exposed to within the engineering realm.

Upkeep of the hotel's grounds and landscaping also represent ongoing functions that require constant attention. These represent services that may be contracted to outside agencies or suppliers but are included here to suggest the range of functions for which the engineering department is responsible.

✦ ISSUES

In the previously mentioned study (Rutherford 1987), the engineers surveyed were asked to judge the relative importance of each of a list of 58 statements relating to the operation of a modern hotel engineering department. A statistical procedure was applied to rank order the statements in terms of their rated importance. The 10 most important facets of an engineer's job derived from this list are reproduced in Table 5.3 and serve as the basis for suggesting the most pressing issues facing hotel engineering managers at this time.

Table 5.3 Importance of This Item to Operation of My Department

RANK	ITEM	MEAN	SD	N
1	Knowledge of maintenance of equipment	4.760	.633	75
2	Energy conservation	4.655	.804	74
3	Energy management	4.589	.761	73
4	Responsibility for communication with employees	4.587	.680	75
5	Relations with top management	4.520	.811	73
6	Responsibility for leadership	4.514	.726	74
7	Responsibility for safety	4.486	.904	72
8	Responsibilities of an effective organizational ability	4.453	.810	75
9	Energy costs	4.444	.854	72
10	Knowledge of the types of equipment	4.370	.791	73

Scale: 1 = not at all important

Scale: 5 = of vital importance

DEPARTMENTAL MANAGEMENT

Items #4, 6, 7, and 8 suggest that the modern hotel engineers deem activities relating to management of their departments of high importance to success—communicating with employees; providing for a safe environment; being able to organize the various tasks, activities, and personnel in the department; and providing leadership—all suggest that one of the foremost issues facing the director of engineering today encompasses those which refer to managerial skills rather than the traditional view, which held the chief engineer to be more concerned with the technical aspects of his job. In years past, the chief engineer was the top of the hierarchy within the engineering discipline. This too has changed and the "chief" engineer now reports to the director of engineering. Of course, this is often based on the size and complexity of the property, but even then the "chief" engineer position often is no longer even used, and instead the director of engineering position will be used. Often with properties at or below 350 rooms the director of engineering may find themselves a multiple property manager with supervisors at each hotel reporting to them. The chief engineer position in many ways still reflects the requirements and responsibilities of being technically proficient and being a department head. The difference today is that they are needed to become more strategic and forward thinking and have more experience managing large remodeling/capitol-driven projects.

ENERGY

The fact that three energy-related items were rated in the top 10 by all responding engineers suggest that the entire realm of issues relating to energy has not yet been addressed satisfactorily by the majority of these professionals. It also suggests that energy will continue to be an issue in the foreseeable future.

With the amount of emphasis given to all energy conservation and awards, such as "Energy Star," given to hotels, it is absolutely critical that the director and chief engineer be very well versed on energy conservation methods and implementation. Often with today's economy and the volatile rate swings of all utilities, the conservation of utilities and the means with which it is done are becoming more and more important to both the management company and most certainly the owners of the property. With rates being what they are today, without having a firm grasp on utility usage, a poor producing month can escalate into a serious loss of money to the bottom line. Not only is it necessary for the engineering department to implement as many cost-saving devices as possible, it is also just as important, if not more, to educate the staff of the hotel in energy conservation and hold everyone accountable. And, of course, all these measures must work and still have no negative impact upon the guest.

RELATIONS WITH TOP MANAGEMENT

Another major dimension of the engineer's job can be seen by the importance attached to this issue. Of the other departments that the engineers were asked to rank their relationships with, only two, housekeeping and purchasing, ranked within the top 50 percent of these 58 items. Many of the directors of engineering contacted for comment agreed with top management about this ranking. They said, on a regular basis, it is becoming an increasingly important part of their job to not only report to top management but also educate top management as to the importance of the engineering function.

The days of the old school grumpy chief engineer are long gone! With the demands of top management and the degree of interaction the director of engineering now has with management, poor interpersonal skills can be a career killer as quickly as not knowing how to use a computer! Directors of engineering may not have to put on a tie on a daily basis, but their ability to communicate clearly and present themselves in a professional manner is absolutely essential.

EQUIPMENT

It should be noted that the more technical aspects of the chief engineer's job are not in any way totally ignored by the collective rankings assigned to these operational statements. That knowledge of maintenance of equipment ranked clearly first among the other statements, and knowledge of types of equipment made it into the top 10, suggests that, while the job of the chief engineer may in fact be evolving toward one of a more managerial nature, some of the tradition technical aspects of the job still play a major role in the daily discharge of an engineer's responsibility.

✦ FUTURE AND CONCLUSION

DATA FROM EMPIRICAL RESEARCH

Interpretation of the data gathered in a survey from a broad cross-section of chief engineers and subsequent follow-up conversations with selected engineers suggest that the job of the chief engineer is, in fact, evolving as suggested at the outset of this chapter.

The engineers themselves describe many incidents where they have to deal with more issues and problems related to people and departmental action and interaction than in the past when most of the issues and problems they had to face on a regular basis involved equipment and systems.

It also appears that in the future chief engineers are going to have to be more adept at inter- and intradepartmental organizational politics. To provide the hotel and its guests with high-quality services relative to the physical and environmental systems of the building, the chief engineer is going to have to compete with other department heads for scarce resources related to personnel, technology, and "operating elbow room."

Summing up, the engineering department, its management, and to a certain extent its staff and technical experts, represent an organizational function of the modern hotel that is in the process of evolutionary change. As stated at the outset, this change is driven by a number of factors. The future of successful hotel organizations will hinge to a great extent on the ability of hotel managements to recognize the importance of the contributions of the engineering department to the delivery of guest services and maintaining a high order of return on investments for the owners of the property.

5.5 THE ENGINEERING DEPARTMENT AND FINANCIAL INFORMATION AGNES LEE DEFRANCO AND SUSAN B. SHERIDAN

The engineering department is a vital part of a hotel. Energy cost alone runs anywhere from 4 to 6 percent of a property's total operation budget. Savings in energy cost can be accomplished by instituting simple steps such as modifying staff members' behavior (Dale and Kluga, 1992). How can financial data be used to continuously improve the performance of the engineering department? To answer this question, a survey was performed to collect data from hotel engineers to determine their use of financial information. It is postulated that if financial information is analyzed correctly, the engineering department can serve its profit centers better, which in turn will assist these profit centers in reducing both their cycle time and errors.

A number of studies have been done on the use of financial information by managers in profit centers of hotels, but not many were performed specifically to collect information regarding the engineering department. Malk and Schmidgall (1995) discuss the use of financial statements and information in the food and beverage department of a hotel, particularly in an effort to contain costs and maintain a profit. Turkel (1993) also advocates the development of profit and loss statements and allocating costs properly to ascertain the profitability of a food and beverage department. Malk and Schmidgall (1994) also investigate the cost percentages in the rooms division to help rooms division managers with cost containment. Quain (1992) explores the use of profit analysis by the customer segment in addition to yield management, and the topic of menu engineering to improve profits in food and beverage establishments has also been discussed (Bayou and Bennett, 1992; Dougan, 1994). However, few, if any, studies can be quoted for the engineering department.

✦ THE SURVEY

The purpose of the study was to investigate the use of financial information by hotel engineers. Therefore, questions asked included the types of financial information used, the frequency at which this information was generated, the methods used to generate the data, and the type of hardware and software used in the department. Hotel engineers were also interviewed to see how their use of financial information could improve quality in their departments by reducing cycle time and eliminating errors.

The population for this study consisted of directors of engineering in U.S. hotels that were listed in the *Hotel and Travel Index,* Spring 1994 edition. The sample was randomly selected from this index, and the selection criteria were based on the number of rooms in the property. The sample hotels all had 200 or more rooms. It was believed that hotels of this size would probably have an engineering department. The sample size was 400 hotels, and the sample hotels were located throughout the 50 states.

For the first mail-out, a cover letter and a questionnaire were sent to the general manager of each sample hotel. It was felt that if the surveys were addressed to the general managers by name, they would be more likely to read the surveys and pass them along to the directors of engineering. The initial response rate, however, was only 15 percent. In order to improve the response rate, 3 weeks after the initial mail-out, a second mail-out was sent. The second mail-out was addressed specifically to the director of engineering. Follow-up letters and questionnaires were sent to the entire sample. A total of 97 of the 400 questionnaires were eventually returned for a response rate of 24.25 percent.

✦ THE TYPICAL CHIEF ENGINEER

Of the sample, 38 percent of the respondents reported that *chief engineer* was their official title, while 36 percent held the title *director of engineering* and 7 percent *director of property operations.* The majority of the respondents (52 percent) had less than 6 years of experience with their present company and less than 3 years with their specific property (51 percent). However, when asked their years of experience within the hospitality industry, most of them (56 percent) had 6 to 15 years of experience.

The respondents also reported having substantial experience in engineering and property operations and maintenance departments. The highest response category was 9 to 18 years (39 percent), followed by 18 to 27 years (22 percent) and 0 to 9 years (16 percent).

The majority of the respondents (60 percent) worked in hotels that had 200–400 rooms, and these hotels had an average daily rate of $95.60. The largest group of respondents (32 percent) employed 7 to 9 engineering employees. Overall, the work performed was primarily done in-house and by outside contractors. Table 5.4 provides a summary of the characteristics of the respondents.

✦ HOW IMPORTANT IS FINANCIAL INFORMATION?

In order to assess how financial information can affect the performance of the engineering department, the respondents were asked to rate ten criteria. A Likert rating scale of 1 to 5 was used, with 1 being not important and 5 being very important. Table 5.5 ranks these ten criteria as perceived by the directors of engineers.

The area that received the highest mean score of 4.70/5.00 was "control costs more

Table 5.4 Profile of Respondents

	N	%
Job Title		
Chief engineer	33	38
Director of engineering	32	36
Director of property operations	6	7
Facilities manager	3	3
Others: Eleven different titles	14	16
Number of Years with Company		
0–3	31	32
3.1–6	19	20
6.1–9	11	11
9.1–12	11	11
12.1–15	13	14
15 and over	12	12
Number of Years with Property		
0–3	49	51
3.1–6	17	18
6.1–9	10	10
9.1–12	12	12
12 and over	9	9
Number of Years in the Industry		
0–3	5	5
3.1–6	9	10
6.1–9	12	13
9.1–12	23	24
12.1–15	18	19
15 and over	28	29
Number of Years with Engineering Department		
0–9	15	16
10–18	37	39
19–27	31	32
28 and over	12	13

(Continued)

Table 5.4 Profile of Respondents (*Continued*)

	N	%
Number of Rooms in Property		
200–300	29	31
301–400	28	29
401–500	16	17
501 and over	22	23
Average Daily Rate		
Less than $50	2	2
$51–$100	48	56
$101–$150	26	31
$151 and over	9	11
Number of Employees in Department		
3–6	16	17
7–9	31	32
10–12	13	14
13–15	11	11
16 and over	25	26

Table 5.5 Usefulness of Financial Information

CRITERION	RANKING	MEAN SCORE	STANDARD DEVIATION
Control cost more effectively	1	4.70	0.09
Evaluate the performance of my department	2	4.49	0.14
Plan ahead more accurately	2	4.49	0.15
Be a better manager	4	4.47	0.16
Have information for evaluation purposes	5	4.33	0.16
Be more flexible financially	6	4.00	0.19
Be more innovative	7	3.99	0.19
Staff accordingly	8	3.93	0.22
Improve communication with my staff	9	3.63	0.22
Improve motivation of my staff	10	3.55	0.23

effectively," with 80 percent of respondents rating the criterion at 5 and 14 percent at 4. This was followed very closely by "evaluate the performance of the department" and "plan ahead more effectively," both rated at 4.49. The criterion that received the lowest rating (3.55) was "improving communications with the department staff." Therefore, the majority of these managers were aware that financial information was an essential and integral part of the operations of the department.

✦ THE COMPILATION PROCESS

These data show overwhelming agreement that financial information can enable managers of the engineering department to control costs more effectively. The respondents were then asked about the compilation process. They were asked to specify the types of financial reports that are generated, the frequency at which they are generated, the number of people involved in the process, and the methods used to compile these reports.

All respondents used budgets or cost tracking in their property. Variance analysis, comparing the budgeted and actual figures, was done by 95 percent of the respondents, and 60 percent stated that a departmental income statement was prepared.

The frequency at which these reports were generated was quite varied. The respondents were asked to indicate whether the abovementioned statements were generated on a daily, weekly, biweekly, monthly, or annual basis, and to check all that applied. For the departmental income statements, monthly reporting was the norm (51 percent). This was also true for the budgeted income statement (50 percent), cost

tracking on individual accounts (40 percent), variance analysis (49 percent), and flexible budget (55 percent).

In addition to preparing these statements monthly, 22 percent of the respondents prepared daily department income statements, and 31 percent did daily cost tracking. Although budgeted income statements and variance analysis were not done daily, they were compiled weekly.

The number of people involved in preparing these statements ranged from one to ten. The responsibility, however, was generally shared between the engineering department itself and the accounting department. Half of the respondents reported that cost tracking was done by their own department and by the accounting department. Cost tracking was the analysis the engineering department performed on their own more often than they did any of the other four analyses. The accounting department, on average, performed 62 percent of the engineering department's financial work.

The majority of the respondents used computers to prepare these statements. Approximately 60 percent of the respondents used computers to compile all of the five statements. A combination of manual methods and computers was the second most commonly used method (40 percent), and no respondents reported that financial information was compiled manually only.

✦ COMPUTER TECHNOLOGY AND FINANCIAL INFORMATION

Because computers were used in compiling information, the respondents were also asked to describe the types of hardware and software used in this endeavor. Among the directors of engineering who used a computer, the IBM PC configuration was most widely used. Overall, they reported that they used custom software. For spreadsheet applications, they reported using Lotus 1-2-3 and Excel.

✦ COMMENTS FROM THE FIELD

In addition to completing the surveys, a number of engineers in a large metropolitan area in the southwestern United States were interviewed in an effort to determine, in greater depth, how they used financial information. One of the engineers stated that he used financial information now more than he used to. His role as an engineer has changed over the years, and he is currently much more of a financial planner than he used to be. He reviews all of the financial statements that relate to his department with his supervisory employees in an effort to help contain costs. This process was found to help empower employees because they could see how their performance was directly linked to the results of these statements.

Budgets were critical to all of these engineers, and they generally felt it was important to properly allocate their costs. This information was also useful because it showed if their costs (particularly repairs, maintenance, and utilities) were in line with their projections. One engineer was particularly adamant about properly accounting for his costs. In his hotel, bonuses were given on overall profitability of the hotel, and he wanted to make sure, as much as he could, that everyone received a bonus. Another engineer stated that he used financial information to help conserve and cut down on waste. He also used his financial information to be proactive in dealing with costs. The engineers believed financial information could help them in eliminating errors

such as problems in ordering inventories, or to just make sure their departments were operating as efficiently as possible, thereby reducing cycle time.

✦ CONCLUSIONS AND IMPLICATIONS

It was apparent that managers of engineering departments recognized the importance of financial information. They worked together with the accounting department to compile budgets, actual statements, and variance analyses, which were then used to evaluate the performance and success of the engineering department. Computer technology was common in their operations.

However, improvements can always be made to achieve zero defects, reduce cycle time, and enhance employee empowerment. As noted, "improve motivation of my staff" and "improve communication with my staff" were rated as the bottom two of the ten criteria given. In addition, two was the average number of people involved in the preparation of these reports. If it is not practical to have more employees share in the compilation process, the least an engineering department can do is to have more employees participate in the analysis process. When more employees are involved, motivation and communication tend to increase. This positive attitude may be passed along to other employees and guests.

Asking employees to be involved does not mean they must *do* the accounting work. Rather, those who compile the information can share with other staff members the importance of cost control and how cost savings in the engineering area can affect the bottom line, which may ultimately affect their job performance and bonuses. These discussions can be in the form of employee meetings where employees may make suggestions for improvements. Because employees encounter day-to-day problems and situations that managers may not be aware of, they may be able to offer comments and suggestions that address concerns such as staffing, cost control, and physical plant improvements. This process may help the entire department become more innovative and further empower engineering employees, reduce cycle time, and, possibly, eliminate errors.

The majority of respondents (60 percent) used computers to compile financial information. The rest used a combination of computers and manual methods. Engineering departments that do not use a computer may find that working with one may help improve their overall efficiency.

As this study has shown, computer technology and the use of financial information in engineering departments are vital in maintaining an efficient operation. According to the National Restaurant Association's 1994 Restaurant Industry Operations survey, utility expenses for restaurants increased 6.9 percent from 1992 to 1993, while repairs and maintenance increased 5.8 percent in the same period (Riehle, 1994). If not watched, these costs will probably continue to eat away the profits. It is up to the engineering department to use restaurant financial information to help contain these costs.

5.6 THE LEGAL ENVIRONMENT OF LODGING OPERATIONS

Melissa Dallas

Hotels, like other business entities, are subject to a large and continually changing body of law. However, because lodging facilities are complicated systems, the laws affecting them are more numerous and complex than those affecting most other types of businesses. Because not complying with laws can result in fines, lawsuits, and even imprisonment, it is important that managers be familiar with the many legal dangers to which hotels are subject. This does not mean they have to be lawyers, but managers should have enough legal knowledge to be aware of strategies that minimize the property's exposure to potential litigation and to train employees to minimize risks in their departments.

This chapter is a brief introduction to the legal environment in which hotels operate. We begin with a discussion of where our laws come from and how they are classified. This should give you a fundamental understanding of the legal content. Then we look at the laws and regulations that are specific to typical hotel departments. Notice the significant number of detailed references and footnotes. These are included to provide further detail for specific discussion points and to provide a source for reference.

✦ HOW LAW WORKS

The following section briefly introduces you to the law—where it comes from and how it is classified. This will help you when we turn our attention to the specifics of the law and how it applies to the lodging industry.

SOURCES OF LAW

Law comes from four sources: (1) judge-made common law (also called *case law* and *stare decisis*); (2) the Constitution; (3) legislative statutes and ordinances; and (4) administrative agencies. Each of these is discussed below.

Common law originated in England and, although decisions issued by courts in the United States have added considerably to this body of law, some decisions made several hundreds of years ago still influence present-day judicial decisions. The primary purpose of common law is to provide stability and predictability as judges rule on cases. Judges use past decisions as a precedent for deciding current cases. This decision becomes binding for lower courts in that jurisdiction and can even be used as persuasive authority for courts in other jurisdictions faced with cases having a similar pattern of facts.

Constitutional law, of course, is derived from the U.S. Constitution, which protects individuals from government excesses. When the Supreme Court, made up of nine justices, grants a *writ of certiorari,* it agrees to hear a case and then renders a decision that subsequently becomes the law of the land. On the other hand, if the Court refuses to issue a writ, the law stands as decided by a lower court.

Statutory law is made by local, state, or federal legislatures or other governing bodies. Federal and state laws are called *statutes,* and local laws are called *ordinances.* Legislatures can choose to modify or change common law by enacting statutes that codify, or spell out, a new law.

Finally, administrative law consists of regulations passed by agencies such as the Food and Drug Administration and the Occupational Safety and Health Administration. Congress approves the agencies, then authorizes them to make regulations that affect businesses as well as individuals.

CLASSIFICATIONS OF LAW

Laws generally fall into one of three major classifications: civil, criminal, or international. Most complaints filed against hotels are civil suits in which an individual has been wronged by another individual or by a corporation (which, incidentally, is a legal individual). The injured party—the plaintiff—files a lawsuit that describes the facts of the situation and asks for damages. These damages may be compensatory or punitive or both. Compensatory damages are meant to restore people to their original condition and include monetary judgments for actual damages such as back and future wages, medical costs, pain and suffering, and breach of contract. Punitive damages, on the other hand, are awarded to punish the wrongdoer. Because punitive damages in civil suits are awarded only in the case of violence, malice, or fraud, they are relatively uncommon.

Most civil cases filed against hotels involve claims of negligence. In order for plaintiffs to be successful, they must prove four elements. First, they must prove the hotel had a duty to them. Next, they must prove the hotel breached that duty. Third, they must show the breach was the reason for the incident occurring in the first place, and the hotel should have been able to foresee injuries. Finally, they must have been injured in some way so they can collect damages.

The theory of negligence requires a hotel to act reasonably to prevent foreseeable injuries to guests and visitors. To illustrate this theory, assume a front office employee did not require identification when issuing duplicate keys. A person was issued a room key by this employee, then used the key to enter a guest room and injured a guest. Here, the hotel would likely be found negligent because it breached its duty to keep guests safe, by not practicing proper key control. The intrusion and resulting injury would not have happened but for the employee issuing a duplicate key without requesting identification, and this omission resulted in injuries to the guest.

In order for someone to be criminally prosecuted, on the other hand, he or she must be charged with committing a wrong against society as a whole. Crimes require intent on the part of the defendant; if found guilty, the defendant may be charged a fine, imprisoned, or both. Crimes most often affecting hotel operations include theft, assault, and battery. Theft, of course, can relate to goods, services, or both. Assault is defined as the imminent threat of bodily harm, and battery is the actual harmful physical contact. An example of an assault is a bouncer in a nightclub wrongfully threatening a patron and running toward the patron with his arms raised. Battery is the bouncer picking up the patron and wrongfully throwing him down the steps and out the door of the club.

Although the hotel industry is becoming increasingly global, international law that is actually enforceable against an individual or a hotel company is rare. Most international laws are in the form of treaties, while others are customary laws followed by nations over time. The primary international laws applied to hotel companies are treaties that govern intellectual property such as trademarks and copyrights. The Paris Convention of 1883 affords its signatories (meaning citizens of the countries that signed the treaty) the right to file for trademark protection in any country that also signed the treaty.

Suppose, for example, a hotel chain named Paradise Lodges opened in the United States. Under the Paris Convention, the owners could file for trademark protection in other countries, thereby globally protecting the identity of Paradise Lodges. The Berne Convention of 1886 gives its signatories the right to file for copyright protection of any original literary or artistic material. Here, suppose a hotel wanted to prevent other hotel chains from using its unique jingle or song that is integral to its marketing efforts. Under the Berne Convention, the hotel could safeguard its song and prevent others from using it in their advertising campaigns.

✦ LAW AND THE LODGING INDUSTRY

Now that you have a basic understanding of how law works, we get more hotel-specific. The only way to protect a hotel company from lawsuits is to practice preventive law. This requires management to know the common legal dangers for each department and to follow the law as closely as possible.

We must first review one other concept. *Respondeat superior* is a Latin term that literally means "let the master answer." Under the theory of *respondeat superior,* employers are liable for acts of their employees if the employees are at fault and were doing work for the employer at the time of the accident or incident. The financial implication of *respondeat superior* for a hotel is obvious—the hotel pays!

FOOD AND BEVERAGE

Potential costly legal situations are present in all restaurants and bars. The most commonly litigated areas involve food safety and alcohol service.

Food Safety. Many laws governing food safety are administrative laws established by the Food and Drug Administration (FDA).[1] The FDA regulates everything from food processing[2] and labeling[3] to packaging.[4] Food and beverage sales are controlled by the Uniform Commercial Code (UCC), which lays out rules governing the sale of goods and, specifically, requires all food and beverages to be merchantable, or fit for human consumption.[5] This warranty applies whenever and wherever food or beverages are sold.[6]

In order to be protected from lawsuits, the food preparation area should be inspected regularly to ensure that no hazards exist. For example, employees should make certain that no light bulbs or food shields are broken, as glass could easily get into the food. If a server breaks a glass in an ice bin, the bin must be emptied and carefully cleaned out before it is refilled with fresh ice.

Additionally, food must be properly handled to ensure its safety. *E. coli,* bacteria often present in undercooked hamburger, can be dangerous or even deadly.[7] This threat has prompted some restaurants to cook all their hamburgers to 160 degrees to kill the bacteria.

Salmonella, bacteria that can result in severe diarrhea, fever, and abdominal cramping, is most often found in undercooked eggs, beef, and poultry, and can also be found in milk and vegetables. Cooking meats until all juices run clear and training employees to practice good handwashing techniques are imperative. Eggs pose a more difficult problem, however. In order to be perfectly safe, a restaurant would warn patrons about the possibility of salmonella before serving poached, over-easy, or over-medium eggs, hollandaise sauce, Caesar salad dressing, mayonnaise, and tiramisu. The practicality of this practice is doubtful, but perhaps a general warning on the menu would suffice.

Food and beverages must be served at safe temperatures as well. In an often discussed case involving McDonald's,[8] a 79-year-old woman, Stella Liebeck, was seriously burned when coffee spilled on her lap. After her grandson gave her the coffee he purchased from the drive-through window, he stopped so Liebeck could add cream and sugar to her drink. The entire contents of the Styrofoam cup spilled on her lap, and she received third-degree burns on over 6 percent of her body. The temperature of the coffee was initially believed to have been between 180 and 190 degrees Fahrenheit. A McDonald's quality assurance manager testified that this was the standard serving temperature range for the company's coffee. For the sake of comparison, the temperature of most home-brewed coffee usually reaches between 135 to 140 degrees.

The jury initially awarded Liebeck $200,000 in compensatory damages (reduced to $160,000 as Liebeck was found to be 20 percent at fault), and $2.7 million in punitive damages. An investigation following this verdict revealed that the actual serving temperature of the coffee was 158 degrees Fahrenheit, so the court reduced the punitive award to $480,000, or three times compensatory damages. McDonald's and Liebeck then agreed to an undisclosed settlement to close the case.[9]

The point here is that hotels need to serve safe food and beverages and to serve food and beverages safely. At the very least, customers should be advised of any known risks so they can decide for themselves whether to eat the food or drink the beverage. Food and beverages do not need to taste good under the UCC, but they must be safe![10]

Alcohol Service. Establishments that serve alcohol open themselves up to a different type of legal danger. Dram shop laws are state statutes that permit an injured third party to sue the establishment that unlawfully served the alcohol. For example, let's say a bartender at the XYZ Hotel overserved a patron. The patron then got into his car to drive home. On the way home, the intoxicated patron lost control of his car and severely injured a bicyclist. Dram shop laws permit the injured cyclist to sue the XYZ Hotel for damages. Some states that have not enacted dram shop laws permit third-party suits under their common-law theories of negligence.

Increased attention to alcohol problems has caused an increasing number of states to require their managers, servers, and bartenders to be trained in responsible alcohol service.[11] Although training does not completely protect an establishment from alcohol-related suits, it may lower punitive damages.

HOUSEKEEPING AND MAINTENANCE

Inspection and Repair. The primary legal dangers in both housekeeping and maintenance are related to negligence and involve lack of inspection and repair. Broken furniture, loose carpeting, slippery floor surfaces, potholes in parking lots, unmarked changes in elevation, snow- and ice-covered walkways, and faulty electrical cords can easily injure guests and visitors alike. In fact, injuries sustained from slips and falls are the most common type of lawsuit hotels encounter. Failure to regularly inspect rooms and public spaces for dangers may be grounds for a successful suit. Recovery for a plaintiff is even more likely if the hotel knew about a danger and did not address it.

Probably the most tragic maintenance-related cases involve injuries or even death to children. The attractive nuisance doctrine holds a property owner liable for any injuries resulting from "a potentially harmful object so inviting or interesting to a child that it would lure the child onto the property to investigate."[12] It recognizes that children, because of their age, cannot fully appreciate danger.

Lodging facilities with more than one level and those who have swimming pools must be especially diligent. Children should not be able to open windows more than a few inches, and all balconies must have railings that are close together to prevent accidental falls. Swimming pools must be maintained properly and accessible only with a room key. Signage around the pool area should be large and clearly written and require adults to accompany children at all times. Children should be entirely banned from Jacuzzis and saunas.

The best way to prevent suits in these areas is to be attentive. Both housekeepers and maintenance workers should be required to follow a regular preventive maintenance schedule. Professionals can be hired to complete periodic safety audits of hotels.

Lost and Stolen Guest Property. The housekeeping staff in hotels collects an amazing array of items left behind in guest rooms. Potential privacy problems arise if a hotel contacts guests to notify them of articles they left behind. The better way to handle this is to transfer the items to a secured area, then hold them until the guest contacts the hotel. Many states have laws that govern the finding of lost property. Generally, if the owner cannot be found in a certain period, the property may be sold in accordance with the state statute.

Stolen items pose an entirely different set of challenges. All hotels are required to provide safes for guest use. Many hotels now have in-room safes that must be programmed by the guest and are reset when the guest checks out. If guests choose not to use the safe and find some valuables missing from their room, the hotel is generally not liable.[13]

All states have enacted limiting liability statues that limit a hotel's liability for guests' property losses. These statutes vary from state to state, but in all cases, a hotel must strictly comply with the requirements to be protected.[14] Common requirements include posting the availability of the safe as well as stating the maximum amount for which the hotel is liable in case of theft.

FRONT OFFICE

Reservations and Overbooking. Every time someone phones a hotel for a reservation, he or she forms a contract with the hotel for a room. What if the hotel overbooked or if a guest stayed over and a room was not available for a guest with a reservation? Technically, the hotel breached the contract. To avoid liability, front desk agents should check area hotels for availability if they know that overbooking is likely. In the case of

a civil suit for breach of contract, the would-be guest could recover compensatory damages including payment for travel to a different hotel, the additional cost of lodging, if any, and other costs associated with the inconvenience.[15]

Due to the potential legal liability and the damage to their reputation and goodwill, some large hotel chains have completely eliminated the practice of intentional overbooking. Others continue to take the risk to ensure their hotel is completely full.

Key Control. Poor key control practices are dangerous, potentially expensive, and mostly preventable. Too often, hotel guests have been injured or even killed when a stranger entered their room using a key given to him by a front office staff member. Jury awards have been staggering, especially if the guest was raped or killed due to employee negligence and if the hotel had been put on warning for a similar event.

Good key control practices include:

- Requiring identification when issuing a replacement or additional key.

- Installing a key card system.

- Changing locks when a room key is missing (assuming the hotel does not have a key card system in place).

- Limiting the number of master keys issued to employees.

- Installing elevators that require a key to activate.

- Not having room numbers displayed anywhere on the key.

- Writing, not announcing, the assigned room number when a guest checks in.

- Not orally confirming a name and room number by telephone within earshot of a non-employee.

- Refusing to give out room information—period. The front desk agent should always phone guests to verify visitors or inquiries.

- Placing key drop boxes behind the counter on the front desk, not on top of the counter.

- Regularly inspecting room locks for damage and wear.

Although a hotel is not a complete ensurer of guest safety, it must show diligence in its duty to provide a safe environment. Employee negligence has often been the cause of violent crimes against guests, but proper training and reinforcement of acceptable key control practices can drastically reduce, if not eliminate, this type of tragedy and this type of lawsuit.

SALES

Writing sales contracts is a regular part of any salesperson's job. Contracts are written for catered events, wedding receptions, conventions, meetings, and many other purposes. If one party does not honor the contract, the other party can sue for breach, so it is essential that all sales staff receive careful and thorough training in contract writing.

Everything agreed to by the hotel and the client should be written in the contract. This practice ensures that the contract is enforceable in court and leaves no doubt as to the agreement. All the contract terms must be clear and unambiguous. It is important to note that contracts are always interpreted against the drafter, so in the case of a breach, the contract would be interpreted in favor of the client rather than the hotel.

A good rule of thumb for sales staff members to follow: The more complex the event, the more detailed the contract. No detail is too small to put in writing!

HUMAN RESOURCES

Wrongful discharge, discrimination, and Federal Labor Standards Act claims are becoming more and more commonplace. The human resource staff handles the resolution of these types of claims and many more.

Wrongful Discharge. Even in states that follow an employment-at-will doctrine, which permits an employer to terminate an employee at any time, without cause or reason, wrongful discharge suits are relatively common. Wrongful discharge claims arise when an employee is fired for reasons that are not legitimate. These wrongful discharge cases are one of two types: traditional or constructive.

Traditional wrongful discharge claims arise when an employee is unlawfully fired. An example is firing an employee for filing a workers' compensation claim, assuming the state had a statute making this discharge unlawful. Another example is firing an employee for whistle-blowing (reporting a company's illegal activities to an official).[16]

Constructive discharge occurs when an employer's actions, such as continual or severe harassment, force an employee to quit. If the hotel company is found liable, the plaintiff can receive both compensatory and punitive damages.

The wisest strategy for hotels is to develop a formal policy manual that details the possible reasons for discharge and disciplinary procedures. Employees should be thoroughly advised of these policies, and all supervisors and managers should follow the policies as closely and systematically as possible. Finally, management should document, document, and document some more!

Discrimination. Discrimination in the workplace has not always been unlawful. In fact, not until 1964 was a federal statute enacted that addressed discrimination. Since that time, other important federal statutes have been passed dealing with pregnancy, age, and disabilities. Sexual harassment suits have become commonplace recently, and they are, in effect, based on gender discrimination.

Title VII of the Civil Rights Act of 1964[17] made it illegal to discriminate against applicants or employees based on race, religion, color, national origin, or gender. The Act applies to employers with 20 or more employees, and it created the Equal Employment Opportunity Commission (EEOC) as its enforcement arm.[18]

Only in the case of business necessity or bona fide occupational qualification (BFOQ) can a hotel legally discriminate.[19] Note that the courts interpret these exceptions quite strictly, often resulting in rulings for the plaintiffs.

The Pregnancy Discrimination Act of 1978[20] made it illegal to discriminate against pregnant women unless the discrimination is a business necessity or not being pregnant is a BFOQ for the job. For example, a hotel could probably refuse to hire a woman who is seven months pregnant as a lifeguard because the pregnancy could affect her ability to act quickly to save lives.

The Age Discrimination Act of 1967 was amended in 1986[21] to make it illegal to discriminate against an applicant or an employee who is 40 years old or older. Although portraying a youthful and energetic image is important to many hotels, it is simply illegal to discriminate against an employee who is at least 40 years old as long as that employee can perform the job better than a younger employee.

The American with Disabilities Act (ADA) of 1990[22] forbids discrimination against otherwise qualified individuals on the basis of a physical or mental disability. Title I of the ADA bans discrimination in employment and applies to applicants or employees who are otherwise qualified for the position. This means the applicant or employee must be able to perform the essential elements of the job regardless of the disability. Title III bans discrimination in public accommodations (lodging facilities, for one) and commercial facilities. The ADA requires all accommodations to be reasonable[23] and to create no undue burden[24] for the business. The courts, on a case-by-case basis, determine what constitutes an undue burden.

Finally, the Civil Rights Act of 1991[25] gave plaintiffs claiming discrimination the right to a jury trial as well as possible punitive damages. The possibility of larger awards for plaintiffs has caused more employers to adopt stricter and clearer policies for selection, promotion, layoffs, and termination.

By now, most people are familiar with the plethora of sexual harassment claims that have been filed in courts. The nature of the hotel industry leaves hotels vulnerable to more claims than business in most other industries—the late and long hours of work, the privacy of hotel rooms, and the alcohol service.

Courts recognize two types of sexual harassment. The first, *quid pro quo*, literally means "this for that." *Quid pro quo*[26] claims occur when one person threatens action against another unless he or she agrees to perform a sexual act. Hostile work environment[27] claims are much more common. Here, the behavior must be sufficiently severe or pervasive, unwelcome, and not voluntary, and must affect a term, condition, or privilege of employment. Workplace behaviors found to create a hostile work environment are repeatedly sending sexually suggestive letters and notes,[28] sending risqué emails,[29] and prominently displaying nude pictures (when combined with other lewd behaviors).[30]

The best tactic for management to employ is to adopt a no-tolerance policy. This policy should be included in the employee handbook and posted conspicuously throughout the hotel. Also, employees must feel free to speak with more than one person in the event of a sexual harassment complaint, because their supervisor might be the person who is doing the harassing.

It is important to note that states and localities can adopt even stricter laws than the federal statutes. For example, some areas prohibit discrimination based on sexual orientation.[31] Others disallow discrimination based on marital status.

Federal Labor Standards Act. The Federal Labor Standards Act[32] (FLSA) mandates minimum wages, overtime pay, and equal pay for equal work, and restricts child labor.

The rate of minimum pay is established by Congress and applies to virtually all employers with annual sales of $500,000 more.[33] The FLSA, however, includes certain exceptions such as training wages[34] and tip credits.[35] Training wages at 85 percent of the minimum wage may be paid for the first 90 days to employees who are between the ages of 16 and 19 and entering the workforce for the first time. Tip credits permit employers to pay regularly tipped employees, such as servers, at a rate of pay equal to one-half of the current minimum wage. However, the combination of tips and actual wages must equal at least the current minimum wage rate. For example, if the minimum wage is $6.00 and a server receives tips averaging $3.00 per hour, the hotel could pay the employee at a rate of $3.00 per hour. If a server made only $2.00 per hour in tips, the hotel would be required to pay the server at a rate of $4.00 per hour to raise the hourly wages to the minimum $6.00 required by law. Some states or localities require a minimum wage rate higher than the federal mandate.

Overtime wages must be paid to nonexempt employees, meaning those who must be paid at least minimum wage, who work over 40 hours in one week. These wages are mandated at a rate equal to 1.5 times the regular hourly wage rate.[36] On the other hand, overtime rates need not be paid to exempt employees. The FLSA defines exempt employees as those who spend 40 percent or more of their time performing management functions or work for a seasonal amusement or recreational establishment.[37]

It is important to understand that the FLSA uses a weekly pay period to determine overtime. This is especially important to hotels who pay employees biweekly. For example, if an employee works 30 hours during the first week of the pay cycle and 50 hours during the second, the hotel must pay 10 hours of overtime for the extra hours worked during the second week of the cycle, even though the total hours worked during the pay period equaled 80.

The equal-pay-for-equal-work requirement of the FLSA requires that employers pay employees at the same rate if they perform substantially similar work that requires equal skill, effort, and responsibility.[38] Human resources must identify the core or essential elements of each position, as the courts look at these elements when comparing jobs.

Child labor laws affect many hotels, as many of the employees are young, especially during the summer season. The FLSA requires all employees to be at least 14 years old. Further, the Act restricts the number of hours that teenagers under the age of 18 can work during a 1-week period. During school days, 14- and 15-year-olds cannot work more than 18 hours per week and no more than 3 hours per day.[39] Some state laws are even stricter than the federal ones, further restricting work hours for teenagers.

Violations of the FLSA are reported to the U.S. or state department of labor and can be costly for hotels. If the violations are found to be intentional, employers may be fined up to $10,000 per offense. A second offense may result in imprisonment for up to six months.[40] Many states have even stricter penalties for noncompliance.

SECURITY

While larger hotels often hire their own security personnel, smaller properties usually either outsource this function or rely on local law enforcement officials in the case of a problem. Regardless, every employee is responsible for the security of the hotel's guests. Most jurisdictions require that lodging facilities exercise reasonable care to protect guests and patrons from reasonably foreseeable crime risks.

When deciding what preventive actions are reasonable, courts look at certain factors to determine if the hotel was put on notice. Courts consider factors such as the frequency and severity of past crimes, a recent increase in the area crime rate, and security problems posed by the facility's design. Courts also look at training and personnel activities and design modifications the hotel has undertaken in the effort to keep its guests safe.

The most common areas in which crimes are committed against guests are guest rooms and immediately outside of the property. While proper key control is vital to guest room safety, so is the regular inspection of hotel room doors and locks. In a highly publicized case, singer Connie Francis was raped at gunpoint by a man who entered her room through a sliding glass door that was easily unlocked from the outside. Francis recovered $2.5 million.[41]

Crimes can also occur in hotel parking lots. Low lighting levels support an ideal environment for crimes. If the hotel is put on warning of criminal activity, meaning it is aware of crimes that occurred on the property or in the immediate neighborhood, it should take further security precautions. These precautions might include hiring additional personnel, installing more lights, constructing a fence around the parking lot, adding a guarded gate, and adding more security monitors.

Again, all hotel employees are responsible for keeping the property as safe as possible. Employees must report any suspicious activity or person to management. Guests, too, can do their part. Placards should be conspicuously placed in guest rooms warning guests to keep their doors locked, not divulge their room number, and report any concerns to the front desk.

✦ SUMMARY

Many laws at the federal, state, and local levels affect hotel operations. It is the responsibility of management to be well informed about these laws and to take preventive measures to protect its employees, guests, and owners. Because laws often change and, in the case of a jury trial, damage awards can be quite high, it is important for management to keep abreast of the constantly evolving interpretation and application of all relevant laws. The best ways to keep current are to be active in professional associations, read trade journals regularly, and utilize the resources of legal counsel.

ENDNOTES FOR SECTION 5.6

1. Pure Food and Drug Act of 1906, 21 U.S.C. Sections 1–5, 7–15 as amended by the Federal Food, Drug and Cosmetic Act of 1938, 21 U.S.C. Section 301.

2. See Food Safety and Inspection Service, Department of Agriculture, 9 C.F.R. Chapter III establishing HACCP and other controls.

3. Nutrition Labeling and Education Act of 1990, 21 U.S.C. Section 343.

4. Fair Packaging and Labeling Act of 1966, 21 U.S.C. Sections 1451–1461.

5. U.C.C. 2–314.

6. See, for example, *Webster v. Blue Ship Tea Room*, 198 N.E.2d 309 (1964) in which the court held that the fish chowder was merchantable since bones were a natural part of fish and should be reasonably expected. See also *Evart v. Suli*, 211 Cal. App.3d 605, Cal.Rptr. 535 (1989) in which the court held that a jury could find that hamburger containing a large bone might not be merchantable. Finally, see *Kilpatrick v. Superior Court*, 8 Cal. App.4th 1717, 11 Cal.Rtpr.2d 323 (1992) in which the court decided that bacteria in oysters were "foreign" to oysters and, thus, made the food unmerchantable.

7. In 1993, more than 600 people in Washington got sick from eating Jack in the Box hamburgers contaminated with *E. coli* bacteria. Foodmaker, the parent company of Jack in the Box, set aside $100 million to cover lawsuit settlements. The largest single-case settlement was $15.6 million to the family of Brianne Kiner who lapsed into a coma for 42 days after eating a tainted burger. *The Seattle Times*, October 30, 1997. The full text of the article can be found at http://seattletimes.nwsource.com/extra/browse/html97/jack_103097.html.

8. *Liebeck v. McDonald's Restaurants, P.T.S., Inc.*, No. CV-93-02419, 1995 WL 360309 (N.M. Dist., 1994).

9. Miller, Norman & Associates, Ltd. *Electronic Newsletter*, 1(1), April 3, 1996. Can be found at: http://rrnet.com/mna/newsltr1.html.

10. The Educational Foundation of the National Restaurant Association offers both ServSafe and HACCP certification.

11. The Educational Institute of the American Hotel & Motel Association offers Controlling Alcohol Risks Effectively (CARE) certification. The Educational Foundation of the National Restaurant Association offers Bar Code certification. Also widely used is Training for Intervention Procedures (TIPS) certification. For the current laws of individual states, go to: http://www.gettips.com/.

12. From 'Lectric Law Library at: http://www.lectlaw.com/def/a090.htm.

13. See, for example, *Gooden v. Day's Inn*, 395 S.E.2d 876 (Ga. App. 1990) in which an innkeeper was not liable for the theft of a bag of money from guest's room. The court recognized that the hotel provided a safe for guests' valuables and the guest assumed the risk of theft by failing to lock up the money.

14. See, for example, *Searcy v. La Quinta Motor Inns, Inc.*, 676 So. 2d 1137 (La. App. 1996) in which the motel was liable for $4,938.95 for property stolen from a guest's room, despite a state statute limiting the motel's liability to $500. Although the motel posted notices of the statute in guestrooms, it failed to do so in the registration area as the statute required.

15. See *Vern Wells et al. v. Holiday Inns*, 522 F.Supp. 1023 (Mo., 1981) in which Vernon Wells and Robert Hughes had reservations with a Holiday Inn in San Francisco. The hotel could not honor the reservations since it was overbooked. The plaintiffs paid less to stay at another hotel, but were awarded reimbursement for their cab fares to the other hotel.

16. A number of states have enacted whistle-blowing statutes for both the public and private employment sectors: California, Connecticut, Florida, Hawaii, Illinois, Iowa, Louisiana, Maine, Michigan, Minnesota, New Hampshire, New Jersey, New York, North Carolina, North Dakota, Ohio, Rhode Island, and Tennessee.

17. Title VII of the Civil Rights Act of 1964, as amended, 42 U.S.C.A. Sections 2000e–2000e-17.

18. Title VII of the Civil Rights Act of 1964, as amended, 42 U.S.C.A. Sections 2000e ct seq., Section 705.

19. See *Wilson v. Southwest Airlines Company*, 517 F. Supp. 292 (N.D. Tex. Dallas Div. 1981) in which the court held that being female was not a BFOQ for flight attendants.

20. 42 U.S.C. 2000e(k).

21. 29 U.S.C. Sections 621–634.

22. 42 U.S.C. Sections 12102–12118.

23. 42 U.S.C. Section 12111(8). See, for example, *Martin v. PGA Tour, Inc.*, No. 9835309 (9th Cir. 2000) in which the court held that it was reasonable to permit professional golfer Casey Martin, who has a congenital disability, to drive a cart during golf competitions since doing so would not alter the nature of the sport.

24. 42 U.S.C. Section 12112(b)5(A). See, for example, *Rascon v. U.S. West* in which a U.S. West network technician suffered from posttraumatic stress disorder as a result of his service in Vietnam. The court required U.S. West to grant Rascon's leave for treatment since doing so would be a reasonable accommodation and would place no undue burden on U.S. West.

25. 42 U.S.C.A. Sections 2000e et seq. Section 105(b).

26. The first case decided under the quid pro quo theory was *Barnes v. Costle* (D.C. Cir. 1977).

27. The first sexual harassment case to reach the Supreme Court was *Mentor Savings Bank v. Vinson*, 477 U.S. 57 (1986) in which the Court defined a hostile workplace environment.

28. *Ellison v. Brady*, 924 F.2d 872 (9th Cir. 1991).

29. See, e.g., *M.V. v. Gulf Ridge Council Boy Scouts of America, Inc.*, 1988 WL 85195 (Fla. D. Ct. App. 1988), which holds that an employer can be liable if the employer knew or should have known that a supervisor was harassing an employee and failed to take any action or even investigate the claim. More recently, in *Faragher v. City of Boca Raton*, 524 U.S. 775 (1998) a court tightened the standard and held that employers would be liable only if they knew that the harassing activities were occurring. The "should have known" was eliminated. Therefore, if employers know of harassing emails or jokes being sent to employees, they would likely still be held liable.

30. *Andrews v. City of Philadelphia*, 895 F.2d 1469 (3d Cir. 1990).

31. Currently, at least 14 states have executive orders, at least 71 cities or counties have civil rights ordinances, and at least 41 cities or counties have council or mayoral proclamations banning sexual orientation discrimination in public employment.

32. Fair Labor Standards Act of 1938, as amended, 29 U.S.C. 201, et seq.

33. 29 U.S.C. 201, Section 3(s)(1)(A)(ii). 29 U.S.C. 201, Section 6(a)(1) sets the minimum wage.

34. 29 U.S.C. 201, Section 6(d)(2)(g) and Section 14(b)(1)(A).
35. 29 U.S.C. 201, Section 3(m)(1) and (2) and Section 3(t).
36. 29 U.S.C. 201, Section 7(a)(1) and Section 7(e).
37. 29 U.S.C. 201, Section 13(1) and (3).
38. 29 U.S.C. 201, Section 6(d)(1) and 29 U.S.C.A. Section 206(d).
39. 29 U.S.C. 201, Section 3(l).
40. 29 U.S.C. 201, Section 16(a).
41. *Garzelli v. Howard Johnson's Motor Lodges, Inc.*, 419 F. Supp. 1210 (N.Y. 1976).

5.7 ASPHALT JUNGLE Je'anna Abbott and Gil Fried

Because criminal activity can occur near major public facilities, developing risk-management solutions for parking facilities is now a focus of concern. Due to courts' findings of landowner liability for third-party criminal acts, eliminating or at least reducing the risk of any criminal activities must be an important component of any property's risk-management plan. Ensuring public safety within the facility itself is, of course, essential. Parking lots and adjacent areas, however, are equally important and should not be overlooked. This article discusses the landowner's potential liability for the criminal acts of third parties and describes some crime-abatement actions that can be accomplished through facility design. Of course, landowners should seek their own counsel for specific remedies that might fit their particular circumstances. For the purposes of this article, the term "landowner" will include owners, managers, tenants, and lessors.

✦ PARKING FACILITIES AND CRIME

Little in-depth analysis is available concerning criminal acts occurring in parking garages or parking lots. Crime statistics, however, clearly indicate that parking facilities are the location of much criminal behavior. A Crime Control Institute study in Minneapolis showed that many of the police departments' chronic-call locations were businesses with parking lots (Berlonghi, 1990, 259). In 1993 over six million simple assaults were reported throughout the United States, and a large percentage of those incidents occurred in parking facilities (Maguire and Pastore, 1995, 249). In 1994 parking lots and garages represented the second-most-frequent location for attempts to take property without injury and the most-frequent location for motor-vehicle thefts (Maguire and Pastore, 1996, 230). Furthermore, the same report showed 8 percent of all violent crimes, 7 percent of all rapes and sexual assaults, and 7 percent of total assaults in 1994 occurred in parking lots or garages.

Despite the risks, parking lots and garages clearly are critical to the success of major public facilities. In terms of sports events, only 5 percent of fans attending games use public transportation, while a similar number arrive on leased buses (Baim, 1994, 200). Considering the large number of professional-sports venues (both indoor and out) as well as managed college stadiums and arenas, and adding to those the number of hotels, convention centers, and similar public-access facilities, one can easily imagine that there are several million parking spaces in use by major facilities in the United States.

Security Risk. Parking facilities generally cover large areas and are open to the public. While there is plenty of activity inside a shopping mall, office building, stadium, or convention center, there is relatively little or, at times, no activity at all in the parking lot. Additionally, to make the best use of space, cars are parked fairly close together, resulting in tight, shadowy spaces between parked cars that generally are excellent hiding places for criminals. Moreover, due to the cost and availability of land, many venues rely on multi-level parking garages. Parking garages typically have poor sight lines and numerous dark corners and stairwells, making them a potential harbor for criminal activity. Patrons walking through a parking lot or a parking garage may be inattentive to such hiding places or to other individuals in the lot.

As we've just described, then, parking facilities present a significant opportunity for criminal activity. Hospitality-industry professionals, however, often rank parking lots and related facilities near the bottom of their list of risk-management concerns. For example, a 1991 survey of approximately 600 sports- and special-event professionals evaluated a variety of risk concerns (Berlonghi, 1996, 13). Few of those surveyed felt that parking-lot security was a concern. Indeed, only one in ten felt that "no parking lot security" was a problem at all (when offered that choice among a list of security issues). In other words, parking-lot security was rated lower by these events professionals than were other risk concerns such as weather conditions, insufficient budgets, one-of-a-kind or first-time events, and slippery surfaces. We wonder, however, whether those survey results indicate that parking lot–related crimes are simply underreported. Outside security firms or police often handle those crimes and may not report specific events to facility managers. It's also possible that landowners misunderstand and underestimate the magnitude of potential problems, perceiving crimes perpetrated in parking areas to be low risk. On the other hand, when specifically asked about just parking lots, "lack of security" represented the highest-rated concern by those same survey respondents.

✦ CIVIL LIABILITY

Victims of criminal misconduct are increasingly seeking compensation from the owner or manager of the property on which the criminal activity occurred (Gordon and Brill, 1996, 1–6). Such claims fall under the rules of premises liability and, typically, Gordon and Brill point out, allege a problem with the property's security system. Premise liability is founded on negligence principles. In a negligence claim, a plaintiff must prove (1) the defendant owed the plaintiff a particular standard of care, (2) the defendant deviated from that standard, and (3) the deviation caused the plaintiff's injury.

In the case of a person's injury or loss while using a parking facility, the critical question is whether the landowner had a duty to protect that individual while she was using the parking facility. A landowner normally does not have a duty to protect individuals from the criminal acts of third parties unless the acts are foreseeable. Yet if crimes on the property are likely, then a landowner has some duty to warn customers, guests, and others who may seek access to the property. A landowner incurs varying degrees of duty toward three types of people: "business invitees," licensees, and trespassers. The scope of this article is limited to the first category of individuals.

The duty owed to someone who is on the premises for a business purpose or who is providing some benefit to the landowner (i.e., a business invitee) is a high duty. The court requires a landowner to protect this person from any hidden dangers the landowner knew about, or should have known about. With respect to parking facilities, the fact that such areas may be remote does not alleviate a landowner's duty to warn a business invitee of all possible risks and, of course, to keep the facility well maintained and in good repair (see Ammon, 1993, and Maloy, 1993).

Burden of Proof. Premises liability can arise from such seemingly innocent activities as a drunk committing an unintentional battery. In one case, for example, a female spectator was walking across a parking lot after a college football game when an intoxicated man fell on her, breaking her leg [*Bearman v. University of Notre Dame, 453 N.E.2d 1196 (1983)*]. The court in this case considered whether the university had notice of the potential harm and, once the university had notice, whether it had a duty to protect its patrons. The court concluded that the university not only had notice but also owed the spectator, a business invitee, a duty of safe ingress and egress from the facility.

Another pertinent case involving a parking lot and foreseeable conduct is *Bishop v. Fair Lanes Georgia Bowling, (803 F.2d 1548, 1986).* A group of bowlers complained to the bowling alley's management of harassing behavior by the bowlers on an adjacent lane. The management took no action and, moreover, continued to serve alcohol to the harassing group despite their obvious intoxication. At 2:30 A.M. the two parties were the last to leave the facility, at which opportunity the intoxicated group attacked the other bowlers in the alley's parking lot. The *Bishop* court concluded that a jury could reasonably find that the bowling alley's managers knew or should have known of the potential for a dangerous altercation between the patrons before the altercation occurred and would, therefore, be negligent for taking no action and failing to make its premises safe for invitees.

Thus, the key point of analysis is the existence of information that puts a landowner on notice that an assault or accident is foreseeable (Miller, 1993; van der Smissen, 1990, 3). Attaching foreseeability to seemingly random accidents further expands the specter of liability should serious criminal acts occur. In other words, don't be in denial about potential liability.

The Premonition. Notice is the key requirement for proving foreseeability. For instance, in a suit stemming from a brawl during a 1980 AC/DC rock concert, the concert promoters claimed they did not have notice because "no unruly behavior had taken place in the arena, no fights had broken out, and no drinking had been observed" (McCarthy, 1995, 7). Even though the arena had no prior problems, the court nevertheless concluded that the promoter was on notice because a police officer had investigated prior AC/DC tour stops and had knowledge of various problems at other venues, which he reported to the concert promoters. The officer also knew that when the band appeared at the arena the previous year, the band had attracted a rowdy, drunk, drug-using crowd even though apparently no specific incidents of inappropriate behavior had officially been reported [*Comastro v. Village of Rosemont, 461 N.E. 2d 616 (1984)*]. Other cases have also stressed the need for landowners to act assertively to deter criminal conduct when they have information that indicates the possibility of such conduct (see, for example: *McNeal v. Days Inn of America, Inc., 498 S.E.2d 294 (Ga. 1998)*; and *Whataburger, Inc., v. Rockwell, 706 So.2d 1226 (Ala. 1997)*.

Mean Streets. If a facility's location is in an area with a significant history of assaults, muggings, and robberies, landowners may be liable if they take no steps to protect patrons from known potential dangers. That is, foreseeability issues can extend even to criminal activity in surrounding neighborhoods (Clery, 1995, 5). A classic example of such a case is *Banks v. Hyatt Corporation* [*Banks v. Hyatt Corporation, 722 F. 2d 214 (5th Circuit, 1984)*]. Hotel guest Dr. Robert Banks was robbed and shot to death as he approached the New Orleans Hyatt Hotel's front entrance. His widow and family brought a lawsuit against Hyatt, asserting that, although Banks was not actually on the hotel's property at the time of the robbery and shooting, reasonable precautions had not been taken by the hotel to protect him, and the hotel had a duty to do so. Hyatt argued that it had taken reasonable precautions to protect its guests and could not be expected to protect guests who were off the premises. Besides, the hotel contended, "Dr. Banks was guilty of contributory negligence or had at least assumed the risk by going out" (Rutherford and McConnell,

1987, 60). The jury heard testimony from both sides, including evidence that Hyatt managers were aware of numerous robberies and shootings that had previously occurred in and around the same area where Banks lost his life. Further, Hyatt employees had logged incidents, many involving weapons, in other areas around the hotel. The jury looked at the evidence of prevalent crime in the area and determined that the security precautions provided by the hotel were simply not sufficient; that the hotel did have a duty to "take reasonable care for the safety of its guests, and that the duty [extended] to adjacent areas where guests [were] likely to go and where the hotel could effectively maintain control of safety" (Rutherford and McConnell, 1987, 62). The jury awarded the Banks family $975,000.

Back to the Future. To a degree, the frequency of prior acts represents the probability that a certain risk or injury might occur (Nilson and Edington, 1982, 34–37). Yet even in the absence of prior criminal activity, landowners must take precautions to prevent reasonably foreseeable crimes. Rather than examining just the frequency of prior acts, courts are examining all the circumstances that together indicate whether a landowner should have reasonably foreseen a harm. In making this determination, the court considers the following factors (Berlonghi, 1996, 13; Gordon and Brill, 1996, 5–6):

1. The nature of the facility,
2. The facility's surrounding locale,
3. Whether the facility's records are adequately maintained,
4. The experience of the facility manager,
5. Whether the manager was aware of the criminal activity levels at the facility,

6. Security personnel's compliance with assigned patrols, and

7. The lack of customary security precautions.

Therefore, it is vital for landowners to work on the implementation of a comprehensive crime-prevention program, addressing all reasonably foreseeable criminal actions. This means that landowners should include parking-area security as a critical concern in their risk-management plans (Ammon, 1993, 117; Berlonghi, 1990, 10–11). While it is impossible to eliminate all potential suits, risk-management plans can help identify, document, and eliminate potential risks, and may reduce the prospect of being sued (van der Smissen, 1990, 3).

To determine liability, courts determine whether a property's security precautions were sufficient to prevent the criminal activity and whether patrons were warned of impending risks (allowing for the impossibility of predicting all dangerous incidents or violent behavior). When reviewing specific precautionary measures, landowners should ask the following (Clery, 1995, 5):

1. Are statistics maintained on the frequency and type of criminal activity occurring at the parking facility, and in the surrounding neighborhood (within a quarter mile)?

2. What is being done to prevent criminal behavior?

3. Do both security and non-security personnel understand and use proper security measures?

4. Is there a program in place to inform patrons and employees about security concerns?

5. Have security policies been reviewed, revised or updated, and implemented? Does such a review take place at least once a year?

6. Are there any long-range plans for enhancing security and crime-prevention initiatives?

7. What is the cost-benefit analysis of adding security measures in light of the possible harm or injury sustained by a guest, or in light of a potential jury award to a victimized patron or visitor?

Later in this paper we address common yet critical approaches to risk management (e.g., security patrols, alcohol management, crowd control). First, we discuss design factors that are often overlooked and yet can substantially affect the safety and protection that a facility can offer its guests.

ALCOHOL MANAGEMENT

For certain types of events, alcohol management is a key component of a risk management plan. Arrests or evictions at sports events often revolve around alcohol abuse.[1] Alcohol management policies can be enforced in several ways, including by preventing patrons from bringing their own alcoholic beverages into the facility. Also, in many venues, the sale of alcoholic beverages is terminated after a certain period in the competition (e.g., after the seventh inning or at the end of the third quarter).

Additional risk management strategies designed to reduce alcohol-related injuries and incidents include controlling tailgate parties and creating a designated driver program.[2] Finally, designating certain areas within the stadium or facility as alcohol-free zones may make events more attractive to families and other users[3] and reduce the likelihood that under-the-influence fans will disrupt or interfere with sober patrons.

1. B. Gilbert and L. Twyman, "Violence: Out of Hand in the Stands," *Sports Illustrated*, January 31, 1983, pp. 62–72.

2. R. E. Ammon Jr., "Alcohol and Event Management," *Crowd Management* 1, no. 4 1995,16–19.

3. R. E. Ammon Jr., "Risk and Game Management Practices in Selected Municipal Football Facilities," unpublished doctoral dissertation, University of Northern Colorado (Greeley, CO), 1993.

✦ ENVIRONMENTAL DESIGN

Environmental design refers to the process of building or renovating facilities so that their physical characteristics serve aesthetic and practical functions, including crime abatement or prevention. The use of architectural details to enhance patrons' security is spreading throughout the world (Sheard, 1995, 26–28). Litigants claiming negligent facility supervision are starting to argue that an approach such as Crime Prevention through Environmental Design (CPTED), first addressed by Jeffery (1971), could have reduced criminal activities or, had a CPTED-like system been used, it would have uncovered foreseeable hazards (Gordon and Brill, 1996, 1–6).

CPTED principles. CPTED is a relatively easy and economical way to augment security efforts if incorporated at the time of facility construction. It is possible, although somewhat more complicated to implement CPTED after the fact. The general principles of CPTED include natural surveillance, access control, and controlling the environment, all of which can be used effectively to discourage violence in parking facilities.

CPTED involves carefully selecting building features, materials, and systems to meet established passive-security and active-security requirements. Passive security refers to the physical design, such as lighting, while active security refers to the human element, such as uniformed guards, intercoms, and closed-circuit cameras.

Even though CPTED has been around for almost 30 years, many parking facilities have been designed with little or no attention to security. There are several reasons for this oversight. For one thing, little time is devoted to parking-facility design in architecture curricula and the principles of CPTED are thus not widely recognized by developers and architects. Further, since the parking lot's design is often looked at as basic if not routine, that task is generally left to the newest and least experienced person on the architectural team. Lack of planning, therefore, means that active security methods are later needed to correct problems that could have been avoided if the architectural team had incorporated CPTED principles from the start.

CPTED CONCEPTS

With respect to parking facilities, CPTED includes the following areas: lighting, natural surveillance, stair towers and elevator access controls, and restrooms.

The Light Ahead. Lighting is generally considered to be the most important security feature in parking facilities. It is a well-established fact that good lighting deters criminal activity and increases the public's perception that the facility is safe (which may increase patronage). Installing a parking-lot lighting system reduces the need for active security and reduces or eliminates car break-ins.

The basic principles of lighting design include illumination, uniformity, and glare. Illumination is simply the intensity of light falling on a surface. Uniformity refers to the ability to achieve a consistent level of lighting throughout the parking facility. (Consistent lighting can allow both patrons and security personnel to see into the far edges of parking stalls, as compared to seeing only the driving lanes well.) Glare reduces the contrast of an object against its background, making it difficult for the eye to perceive depth accurately. This condition is especially dangerous for individuals with weak or impaired vision. Glare can be minimized by the careful selection and positioning of fixtures in the parking facility. (For example, many light manufacturers design lights with glare shields, and those lights can be located above the parked cars rather than in the driving lanes to further reduce glare.)

One approach to achieving the desired quality of lighting is the Level of Service (LOS) approach developed by Mary S. Smith (1996, 2–9). Each level is represented by a grade, and this approach should be as familiar to parking-facility owners, city officials, and architects as it is to traffic engineers. The highest grade is LOS A, which denotes superior design; LOS B is above average; LOS C is average; and LOS D is the Illuminating Engineering Society of North America's minimum standard.

In addition to meeting industry standards and providing glare-free lighting, lights must be: reliable, easy to maintain, able to withstand the elements, and vandal proof.

Where good lighting is not available due to design or expense, concrete staining may be an alternative. Concrete staining is the process of dyeing walls, ceilings, and beam soffits white to increase brightness. This cost-effective method has been shown in some designs to increase the LOS by an entire grade. A top-quality concrete stain will last about ten years. A good white paint will have the same effect but requires constant maintenance. (One problem with white stain or paint, however, is that it may encourage graffiti. Fortunately, there are anti-graffiti stains that accommodate easy cleanup.)

Vision Quest. The second most critical security-design issue is natural surveillance, or the ability of individuals to observe their surroundings. Natural surveillance is easiest to achieve in open parking facilities; however, it is not impossible to achieve in parking garages. The most difficult garages in which to use natural-surveillance concepts are those garages that have numerous sloped parking areas. So today's designers are shying away from extensive ramps. Moreover, because openness increases natural surveillance, high ceilings and open exterior facades are now preferred as well. Clearly, an underground parking garage cannot allow for open facades. Yet there are underground-design schemes that incorporate natural light and ventilation, and that make it easy to hear a person in distress.

Natural surveillance also includes the manner in which employees direct people and vehicles within the parking facility. For example, it is best to direct pedestrians to designated areas where other people are likely to be walking (and criminals absent), rather than to let those guests wander through the parking facility. Likewise, concentrating entrances and exits makes supervision of those areas easier.

The Glass Tower. Since stairs, lobbies, and elevators are high-risk areas for personal injury, CPTED addresses such areas with an eye toward open design. One of the basic precepts of CPTED is to plan stairways and elevator lobbies as openly as the building codes will permit. The more visibility one has the better, including using exterior and open-air spaces. Where that option is not available due to weather or code constraints, glass may be a compromise, allowing both protection and visibility.

A Safe Place. If the facility is in a low-risk area, access control may seem unnecessary at first. Nevertheless, it is prudent to consider access control in the design stage, as the risk level may change with time. Screens and gates can be used to discourage unauthorized people from entering the parking area. If possible, the parking facility's design should guide vehicular traffic through gated pathways. Even if there is no charge for parking, an individual receiving a ticket and interacting with an attendant is given the impression of security. Moreover, measures such as those discourage criminal activity.

Location of security personnel is a critical CPTED component. Some landowners don't wish to "advertise" potential security concerns, and therefore locate their security personnel and parking-attendant booths to the rear of the facility. That thinking is backward; according to CPTED principles, landowners should locate security personnel or attendant booths at the front of the parking area, next to the primary entrance. Besides giving security employees a clear view of the property, it's a way for the owner to make a public statement about the importance of security and guests' safety.

The Hiding Place. Landowners should not include restrooms in parking-facility designs, especially in underground garages. Such restrooms present special security problems because they make excellent hiding spots for criminals. Many patrons recognize the potential danger and avoid using such facilities themselves, resulting in minimal traffic and thereby presenting a potentially dangerous condition for the patron who happens to use the restroom. Within the confines of the shopping mall, convention center, or office building is a much more appropriate place for public restrooms.

Secret Weapons. While CPTED generally encompasses passive design concepts, a few active ones are notable. Active design concepts include panic buttons, emergency phones, intercoms, sound surveillance, closed-circuit cameras, and trained guards. Parking facilities that failed to incorporate CPTED during the planning stage often find it necessary to use active techniques later. Although all of those features have obvious advantages, by themselves they are not an alternative to CPTED. Further, they tend to be expensive, and some are prone to abuse by pranksters and vandals.

✦ OTHER RISK-MANAGEMENT STRATEGIES

In addition to CPTED methods, there are other critical aspects to risk management that are well known but sometimes overlooked. We address a few of those here.

Watch It. In a survey of municipal football stadiums, 86 percent of the respondents "always" had security personnel located in the parking lot before and after the game (Ammon, 1993, 117). According to that study, only 3 percent of the respondents did not offer any security protection in parking lots. In 63 percent of the stadiums, law-enforcement authorities provided protection. Private security firms, facility employees, or a blend of employees, private security, and law-enforcement agencies provided the remaining security. There is no consensus on the number of on-duty security personnel required for given situations or even about the best security measures. Risk-management professionals agree, however, that providing adequate security is an ongoing, evolutionary process that requires consistent and detailed monitoring (Ammon, 1993, 117–120; Christiansen, 1986, 46–52; Miller, 1989, 419–437; Ross, 1985, 22–29; van der Smissen, 1990, section 23, 3).

One common measure is the use of roving security patrols. In many parking lots, such as those of malls, hotels, schools, and large stores, roving patrols can be effective and useful. Wal-Mart, for example, now employs uniformed security personnel on golf carts in some regions. Wal-Mart conducted a study on store crime and discovered that 80 percent of non-shoplifting crimes occurred outside the store. A Wal-Mart in Tampa, Florida, in particular, had been the scene of 226 car thefts, 25 purse snatchings, 32 burglaries, and 14 armed robberies prior to its implementing the golf-cart idea. Once the golf-cart program was in place, however, crime outside the Tampa store was reduced to zero (Lee, 1997, E1). Although a guard with a vehicle of some sort and the necessary security equipment (e.g., two-way radio, flashing lights) can cost about $45,000 a year, there is a strong possibility that such an investment can reduce actual risk and therefore help the store avoid costly lawsuits (or, at least, give the store's security efforts some credibility once in court). Wal-Mart, for example, was ordered to pay 75 percent of a $1.5-million award to a man shot in the head in a Wal-Mart parking lot (Lee, 1997, E1). With that in mind, $45,000 a year is a small price to pay to achieve better security and a reputation within the neighborhood and among customers as a safe place to shop.

The Crowd. Another risk-management technique used to protect patrons when entering and exiting a facility involves the use of crowd-management personnel (Ammon, Jr., 1995, 16–19). Traditionally, those individuals were used to inspect patrons' belongings for alcoholic beverages at the entrance to events (e.g., a football game or a concert). Today, those same workers are as likely to assist individuals (e.g., the elderly or disabled) as required and to direct visibly intoxicated individuals to a secure waiting room. Crowd-management personnel are now used for all sorts of public events, whether it be a rock concert, an exposition at a conference center, or a farmers' market at a shopping mall. In all cases, some training for the job is desirable. The number of security staff needed can vary based on the following factors (Berlonghi, 1996, 13):

1. The type of facility or event,
2. The number of entrances and exits,
3. The number of limited- and restricted-access areas,
4. The number of parking levels (or areas) in the facility,
5. The facility's capacity,
6. The facility's history of unruly behavior or dangerous conditions,
7. The time and length of the event (and, in some cases, the expected weather),
8. The number of spectators,

9. The demographic profile of the expected crowd,

10. Whether admission was free or paid,

11. Whether alcohol consumption is allowed or expected (see box on page 221),

12. The types of security personnel on duty (including municipal law-enforcement officers) and the level of supervisory expertise,

13. The presence and location of electronic protection devices, and

14. Specific requirements imposed by insurance carriers.

Sign of the Times. Signs are an important consideration in a risk-management and safety plan. In the parking facility itself, signs should assist patrons in moving quickly through the lot or garage to their destinations. Lost and confused guests—whether arriving or leaving—make easy targets for criminals. Landowners therefore should strive to provide clear, visible signs that are both understandable and memorable so those guests can safely move to and from their vehicles. Furthermore, signs can be used to deter criminals by announcing that regular security patrols and electronic-monitoring systems are in place.

Contract. Risk-management planning should, of course, reduce potential fiscal losses arising from the misconduct of others. Appropriate contractual provisions help to protect against such losses—in this case, when dealing with parking-security personnel retained from outside firms. Contracts with independent security vendors should contain a clause promising indemnity and setting forth what specific risk-management steps are to be taken to secure the parking areas. The contract should specify the number of security personnel to be deployed, when those workers will change shifts, what quality-control measures are to be used (e.g., spot inspections), how security personnel will handle intoxicated persons, what specific actions to take should a criminal act or personal-injury event occur, and what follow-up reporting procedures are appropriate after an injury or crime.

✦ THE SECURITY AUDIT

The design of a parking facility and the level of security needed depend on many factors. Because there is no "one size fits all" solution, a security audit is a good way to determine exactly what security a particular facility needs.

The security audit is actually quite simple. A facility might exist that originally incorporated CPTED but that has undergone many physical changes over the years. For example, imagine a convention center that started out as a simple rectangular structure. Now, picture how various asymmetrical additions could be built into the parking lots over time. Such additions now make it impossible to view large sections of the parking lot at the same time from the same vantage point. A facility such as this should undergo a security audit to identify the security lapses caused by the building expansions. Additionally, if the facility has not changed its exterior lighting system, the older system will almost certainly be insufficient to meet the current needs of the reconfigured parking areas, including being unable to light some corners at all (Gordon and Brill, 1996, 6). A security audit will show what actions need to be taken to return the level of security to where it once was.

Witness for the Defense. One aspect of crime prevention is that the sight lines of potential witnesses (patrons, employees, security personnel, and passersby) not be obstructed or hindered. For example, there should always be a clear view into and out of any cashier's cubicle. If the windows of the cubicle are covered with posters, handbills, or other advertising or personal effects, a cashier would be unlikely to witness a nearby crime, should it occur. By the same token, the posters would also hinder a potential witness's view of an attack on the cashier (Gordon and Brill, 1996, 6).

✦ HESITATE, THEN LITIGATE

Protecting facility visitors and lowering the risk of liability exposure is a primary concern of landowners. To avoid liability, many landowners are not waiting for criminal activity to occur, but are implementing risk-management plans, including for their parking-facility operations. Security patrols, crowd control, signs, alcohol management, and concise agreements with independent security providers are just some of the ways a landowner can make the parking facility safer. Using CPTED concepts is another effective method of reducing crime and liability. Today, with litigation so frequent, it seems absolutely mandatory for a landowner to take all precautions possible.

5.8 WORKPLACE VIOLENCE IN HOTELS

Mark Beattie and Jacinta Gau

Violence is the leading cause of workplace fatalities in the hospitality industry (U.S. Department of Labor, 2002). Preparation for dealing with a crisis situation is vital to management and employee training. There are two categories of workplace violence: explicit and implicit. Explicit violence is specifically directed at a hospitality employee, while implicit violence occurs in a hospitality establishment but is not directed at an employee. Managers and employees need training tools to effectively manage violence prevention, crisis management, and the aftermath of traumatic incidents. Consider the following case:

> Bruce Larson, Jr., was fatally shot in his room at the Orchard Inn in Wenatchee, Washington.

Larson, his brother, and several friends had rented rooms at the Inn during Wenatchee's 1998 Apple Blossom Festival. The group threw a party. A friend of Larson's invited a young man named Jeremy Read to the party at the Inn. At three o'clock that morning, an altercation ensued, and Read pulled out a gun and shot Larson in the chest (*Larson v. MOA Hospitality, Inc., 2003*).

Larson's estate subsequently filed suit against MOA Hospitality, Inc. (the corporation that owned the Orchard Inn), for breaching its legal duty to protect guests from harm. The estate alleged that the Inn should have known that criminal activity increases during the Apple Blossom Festival, should have taken greater steps to ensure guests' safety, and should have prevented Read from entering the property. The Washington Court of Appeals, citing its holding in *Wilbert v. Metro Park Dist. of Tacoma* (1998, 10), reasoned that "[W]hen there is no evidence that a business owner knew of the dangerous propensities of the individual responsible for the crime and there is no history of such crimes on the premises, criminal conduct is unforeseeable as a matter of law." The court entered summary judgment in favor of respondent MOA Hospitality because the record failed to establish that Orchard Inn recognized—or reasonably should have recognized—that Read posed a foreseeable threat to Larson's safety.

The linchpin of the Larson decision was foreseeability: An innkeeper has a duty to protect guests who are within a zone of foreseeable danger. Had the record indicated that the Orchard Inn knew or should have known that Read was dangerous, summary judgment would have been denied, and the case would have been put before a jury.

Would you have been ready for this situation? How well trained are you to deal with a violent situation on your property? Have your employees been adequately prepared to deal with such situations? Is your night auditor trained to be alert for potentially dangerous situations? Do your housekeepers have a procedure to follow if they discover weapons or other dangerous items in a room? Does your human resources manager know what to do for employees who are victims of domestic abuse or stalkers?

Workplace violence exists globally in all segments of industry. The European Commission defines *workplace violence* as "Incidents where persons are abused, threatened or assaulted in circumstances related to their work, involving an explicit or implicit challenge to their safety, well-being or health" (Wynn, Clarkin, Cox, and Griffiths, 1997).Violence is noted in reports from the European Agency for Safety and Health, the United States National Institute of Occupational Safety and Health (NIOSH), and the United States Department of Labor. The hospitality industry is among the top five most dangerous industries in which to work, ranking higher than police in prevalence of violence (Hoel and Einarsen, 2003).

According to Isaacs (2004, p. 13), there are four categories of perpetrator-victim relationships:

- Acts by persons who have no connection to the workplace.

- Violence directed at employees by customers.

- Violence against coworkers.

- Violence committed in the workplace by a nonworker with a connection.

Due to the constant and sometimes intense face-to-face contact in service encounters in the hotel and hospitality businesses, physical and psychological stressors are often intertwined in the conditions contributing to a violent situation (Hoel and Einarsen, 2003).

✦ MANAGING THE CRISES

Crisis management theory combines three views of workplace violence—psychological, social-political, and technical-structural—and pragmatic planning for an emergency situation is important. From each of these viewpoints, crisis situations can be assessed by examining the causes, consequences, cautions, and coping mechanisms of impending situations (Pearson and Clair, 1998). Tools for crisis management planning can then be provided in the curricula of management training programs, and hospitality employees will subsequently be prepared to deal with the aftermath of a violent situation.

The most extreme form of workplace violence is homicide. Homicide within the service sector accounted for 52 percent of all 347 workplace fatalities in that sector in 2002 (U.S. Dept. of Labor, 2004). Retail trade workers under the age of 18 were the second highest grouping of workplace fatalities between 1992 and 2000; 63 percent of those deaths were attributed to violent acts (NIOSH, 2003). Homicide is the leading cause of occupational death for women and occurs predominately in eating and drinking establishments (Levin, Hewitt, and Misner, 1996). Because statistical tracking is generalized and inconsistent, the available data are limited in scope (Hoel and Einarsen, 2003), and the limited empirical research available indicates a lack of effective training tools.

Workplace violence can devastate businesses financially, especially when litigation results from an incident. Statistics provided by Jury Verdict Research show that, "[A]ccording to the reviews of more than 3000 verdicts rendered since 1993, the median compensation awarded by juries against hotels for [sic] assaults [was] $275,000" (Donohue, 2000, 12). A study by the Liberty Mutual Research Center for Safety and Health placed the costs of nonfatal workplace violence at $84 million between 1993 and 1996 (Hashemi and Webster, 1998).

Again, training is important; many violent situations are preventable before they escalate. The Equal Employment Opportunity Commission (EEOC) enunciated these guidelines in 1965: Establish company policies, train employees, support employees' legal rights, implement investigative procedures, and punish the wrongdoer, not the victim (Donohue, 2004). These guidelines enable the hospitality manager to spot and prevent a situation before it becomes a problem. There will, however, continue to be unforeseeable events, such as those that transpired in the *Larson* case.

✦ RESEARCH FOR TRAINING PROGRAM

Data collection is central to the success of a preventive training program and vital to prevention of workplace violence. The data program logs incidents occurring within some discrete reporting period, like the data compiled by the Bureau of Labor Statistics. These incidents are coded as explicit or implicit, then narrowed into "categories of interest" to facilitate incident analysis (Rossman and Rallis, 2003, p. 321). These categories of interest reflect the four types of perpetrator-victim relationships described in Table 5.6.

Table 5.6 Categories of Interest by Incident Type

RELATIONSHIP	IMPLICIT	EXPLICIT
Criminal intent (no prior relationship)	C-I	C-E
Customer/Employee	CE-I	CE-E
Coworker	CW-I	CW-E
Nonworker Connection	NW-I	NW-E

Taxonomizing workplace violence in this manner provides the foundation for a series of category-specific case studies. These case studies focus on identifying the training tools that exist to enable the hospitality employee to identify and manage a crisis situation effectively. Case study methods are based on developing a participatory relationship between the researcher and the participants through interviews and compilation of material culture such as press coverage and police reports (Shank, 2002). A series of case studies ultimately results in what Shank (2002, 55) describes as a "cumulative case study, a single topic examined through the perspectives of many different case samplings. A single complex case is built by ordering of individual cases." Information from these case studies is coded according to standardized organizational schemes for cross-case displays. The displays are conceptually ordered to highlight the three focus areas: prevention, crisis management, and aftermath. These displays are analyzed using a case-ordered effects matrix to explain different effects that each emergent theme may have (Shank, 2002). The emergent themes point out critical areas for hospitality curricula. To explain and justify the identified emergent themes and their relevance to practice, researchers rely on "assertorial" logic, which "draws on supportive evidence to convince the reader that conditions in the new circumstances are sufficiently similar to the original research conditions for generalization to be appropriate" (Rossman and Rallis, 2003, 105). Replication of this research model in other settings adds to the reliability and generalizability of the findings. Trustworthiness is maintained through methodological rigor in the interview and fieldwork procedures.

Further research focuses on the recognition of stressors that can catalyze violent situations, as well as problems such as post-traumatic stress disorder (PTSD) that victims and witnesses may develop in the aftermath of an incident. Models used in emergency responder curricula—such as the Assaulted Staff Action Program (ASAP), used with police officers, firefighters, and emergency medical technicians—may offer useful templates to develop this curriculum component (Flannery, 1998). The hospitality industry has an obligation to provide a safe and healthy environment for its guests and employees. Huntley (2004, 1) asserts, "A workplace shooting that claims the lives of an employee and a customer would be a nightmare for any company. For a retailer dependent on public perception, it's a crisis that demands careful handling." The time has come to develop curricula that enable managers to better prepare for an incident of violence and more competently address the aftermath and ramifications. Only then will the hospitality industry be in a better situation to manage a crisis such as the following before, during, and after the event.

November 10, 2004, *Chicago Tribune:* At 2:30 A.M., Gregg P. Phillips, clad in a bullet-proof vest, used an Uzi 9mm assault rifle to fatally shoot his girlfriend, Sandra Wisniewski, at the Comfort Suites Hotel in Oak Ridge, Wisconsin. A German businessman staying in the next room was also killed, and two other people were injured. Phillips took a hostage, whom he ultimately released unharmed. Police called the rampage a "domestic violence situation." Upon surrender, Phillips asked, "How many people did I kill?" (Black, 2004).

5.9 UNDERSTANDING AND MANAGING THE RISKS AND CHALLENGES OF HOTEL SECURITY IN THE 21ST CENTURY

CHRIS E. McGOEY, CPP, CSP, CAM

What most hotel guests are still not particularly aware of when traveling for business or pleasure is that your hotel room becomes your home for the night and is your sanctuary while you sleep. It is important to give some thought about security planning. What hotel or motel are you going to select, and what room you are willing to accept? The cost of the hotel room is not always the best predictor of how safe the room will be. There are a few security rules of thumb that should apply to any hotel room you rent.

✦ HIGHER FLOORS ARE SAFER

Upper floors are generally safer from crime but worse for fire rescue. Emergency rescue is best below the fifth floor. I compromise by picking a modern fire-safe hotel and always request a room on an upper floor to reduce crime exposure. Ground floor rooms are more vulnerable to crime problems because of access and ease of escape. In a high-rise building, rooms above the fifth-floor are usually safer from crime than those below because of lesser accessibility and poorer escape routes. Also, rooms not adjacent to fire stairs are safer from room invaders because they use them for escape. Criminals do not want to be trapped on an upper floor inside a high-rise hotel. By design, high-rise buildings usually have fewer ground level access points and are easier for the hotel staff to monitor who passes through the lobby after hours. Perhaps one of the first and most famous cases of a security lapse on the part of a hotel was the case of *Garzelli v. Howard Johnson Motor Lodges* (419 F. Supp. 1210 E. D. New York, 1976).

In this case, popular singer and entertainer Connie Francis was staying at the Westbury, New York, Howard Johnson motel. She was criminally assaulted and raped by a man who entered her ground floor room through the room's sliding glass doors. From the inside the doors gave the appearance of being locked, but they could be opened from the outside without much difficulty.

On the basis of psychiatric testimony that her lucrative career as a singer was ruined because of the traumatic experience, Francis was awarded $2.5 million, and her husband, (Garzelli) $150,000. On appeal, the award to Francis was upheld, but that to her husband was reduced to $25,000. She has not successfully performed since, despite several attempted "comebacks."

The hotel violated elementary principles of security by providing sliding glass doors that could be opened from the outside. Howard Johnson's fault was a relatively slight oversight, but it led to a tragic incident that could have been prevented. Doors that seem to lock, but do not in fact do so, are an invitation to all kinds of trouble.

✦ DOOR SECURITY HARDWARE

Hotel or motel rooms should be equipped with a solid-core wood or metal door for best protection. Doors should be self-closing and self-locking. Room doors should have a deadbolt lock with at least a 1-inch throw bolt. If the lock appears worn or there are pry marks around the lock area, get another room or move to another hotel. The knob-lock should be hotel-style where you can push a button on the inside knob or turn a lever to block out all keys. This feature is designed to prevent a former guest or housekeeper from entering the room once you are safely inside. Hotels with electronic card access have the advantage of being able to disable former keycards issued to previous guests and unauthorized employees. Electronic locks also will block out most room service keys when you set the deadbolt. The room door should have a wide-angle peephole, so you can view who is at the door before opening it.

In *Kveragas v. Scottish Inns, Inc.*, (733F.2d 409 [6th Circuit, 1984]), the occupants of a room rented in the Scottish Inn in Knoxville, Tennessee, awoke to find three intruders had broken down their door, subsequently assaulted the guest,, stole $3000, and shot and wounded plaintiff Kveragas. The door that was kicked in was a hollow-core door that fit poorly into the door frame. The only lock was one inside the door knob, described as a third grade lock, and the door had a security chain that broke when the door was kicked in.

While the trial court granted summary judgment for the defendant hotel, the appeal court reversed the verdict and ordered a new trial. The evidence in this case showed that adequate locks, doors, and door hardware could probably have withstood the force used to break down the existing door.

✦ ACCESS CONTROL

Do not open your door to someone who knocks unannounced. Some criminals will pretend to be a bellman, room service, maintenance, or even hotel security to gain admittance to your room. See my web pages on *hotel room invasion* (http://www.crimedoctor.com/hotelinvasion.htm). Always call the front desk to confirm their status with the hotel and only open the door if you requested the service. Do not rely on door chains or swing bars to secure the doors while you partially open the door to speak to someone. These are unreliable security devices. Teach your children not to open the door of any hotel room without knowing the person on the other side and without your permission.

When a Ms. Boles opened her door at the La Quinta Motor Hotel, she was met by a prowler who pushed her into the room and raped her. The attacker bound and gagged Boles, threatened to return and kill her, and left her in the dark. She managed to kick the telephone receiver off the hook and to call the front desk, pleading for help.

The employees at the front desk seemed to take little interest in Boles' pleas. She talked to at least three different employees, none of whom showed any concern or sympathy with her plight. One informed her they would not be coming up to her room to help her although they had called the police. Two assistant managers and the manager stationed themselves *outside* her room listening to her screams, but no one attempted to help her.

On appeal by the hotel, the court reviewed the evidence and found abundant reason for believing the employees' callous actions in permitting Boles to remain bound in the dark and in fear for her life for 20 to 25 minutes caused psychic injuries, affirming the trial court's jury verdict.

✦ OTHER ENTRY POINTS, PARKING LOTS, AND SURROUNDING AREAS

Make sure all windows and sliding doors are secured, if they are accessible from the ground. It is a good idea to test all windows and glass doors to see if they are secure. Beware of balconies where someone can climb from one to another and enter through an open window or sliding door. If the windows or sliding doors are not securable, ask for another room or find another hotel. If your room has an adjoining door to an adjacent room, check it to see that it is secured with a deadbolt lock. If it is questionable, ask for another room.

If you are a woman traveling alone or with small children, take advantage of car valet service, if available, to avoid the parking lot. After checking in, ask the bellman or desk clerk to escort you to your room. After unlocking the room, quickly inspect the closets, under the bed, and bathroom, including behind the shower curtain, before the bellman leaves. Tip the bellman for his efforts.

Where parking facilities can be shown to have previously been the scene of criminal activity, many courts have considered this evidence of *foreseeability*, meaning the hotel should have been aware of the possibility of crime and taken measures to prevent it. Some cases have also demonstrated that hotels can be expected to act proactively to deter such conduct when they have "notice" that such conduct is possible. See, for example, *McNeal v. Days Inn of America, Inc.*, 498 S. E. 2d 294 (GA, 1998). A similar case that hinged on the issues of foreseeability and "notice" is that of *McCoy v. Gay* No. 65117, slip opin. (GA Ct. App., March 2, 1983).

It is apparently not enough to be diligent within the confines of the hotel property. The standard set by the following case is that establishments have a high degree of responsibility for guest security even on public property adjacent to their hotel.

Dr. Banks was returning from a dinner engagement to the Hyatt Hotel in New Orleans when he and his companion were accosted by two armed robbers. Dr. Banks was shot dead directly in front of the entrance to the hotel located within Poydras Plaza, an urban shopping mall that also includes the New Orleans

Superdome. When he fell, his head was 30 feet from the street curb and his feet were only 4 feet from the glass doors at the entry of the hotel. Banks' widow and children brought suit, charging the hotel with providing inadequate security and failing to warn of the danger of being assaulted at the entrance to the hotel (foreseeability, again).

A jury found negligence on the part of the hotel and awarded Banks' family $975,000, which was affirmed on appeal.

In its appellate opinion, the court said "As an innkeeper, Hyatt is potentially liable not only for dangerous physical conditions, but also for foreseeable criminal assaults by third persons. Hyatt was clearly aware that its guests faced [danger] in the immediate area surrounding the hotel, especially at the Poydras Street entrance. Hyatt did take preventive action, although the jury found, not irrationally, that Hyatt did not do enough." (*Banks v. Hyatt*, 722 F. 2d 214 p.226)

✦ OCCUPANCY CUES

Put the Do Not Disturb sign on the doorknob even when you are away; this deters room burglars (it may affect housekeeping service, however). Turn on the TV or radio just loud enough to hear through the door to give the appearance that the room is occupied. Leave one light on inside the room if you will return after dark. This helps you see upon reentry and gives the room the appearance of occupancy from the outside. Always go through the same room inspection routine every time you reenter. Women travelling alone should use caution before using the breakfast order door-knob hanger card. This card lists your name and number of persons in the room. A smart crook can knock on the door posing as room service and use your name as a ruse to gain entry.

When you find a suitable hotel that meets your safety standards and will cater to your security needs, try to stick with it or with the same hotel chain. Don't be afraid to complain to management to get the safe room you deserve.

- Always request a room on an upper floor, if possible.

- A solid door with a good deadbolt lock is best.

- Electronic card access locks help limit access.

- Make sure your door has a peephole and night latch and use it.

- Turn on the TV or radio just loud enough to hear through the door.

- Turn on a single light in the room if you plan to return after dark.

- Inspect the room's hiding places upon entering and check all locks.

- Ask the bellman for an escort and use valet parking if alone.

Although the foregoing may seem to paint a picture fraught with a lot of jeopardy and unmitigated risk, that does not have to be the case. Hotels that take these lessons to heart and incorporate well-designed policies to meet the risk have a good chance of prevailing in court should the unthinkable occur. Oftentimes, hotels so managed get to win one.

Ron Courtney and his wife Deborah were assaulted in their room during their honeymoon at the Islander Inn in Hilton Head, South Carolina. Mrs. Courtney was sexually assaulted. They sued the hotel alleging negligence and recklessness in the design, construction, maintenance, and operation of the hotel. At trial, the court held for the hotel saying that the hotel had acted reasonably to ensure the safety of guests. The case facts included the following:

- No evidence of prior assaults at the inn.

- Each guestroom doorway had a fluorescent light illuminating the hallway and observable through a viewing port in guest room door.

- There was a security awareness program for hotel employees.

- The hotel provided an extra private security guard during night hours.

- Guest room door viewing port had magnification allowing [a] wide view of hall.

- The guest room door was fire-rated steel with deadbolt, automatic door lock, and security lips to prevent picking.

- When all guest room door locks were engaged, only the manager's key would open the door.

- The hotel had a security plan utilizing both in-house and contract security.

- Specific staff members had security responsibilities.

In the appellate court's decision, the judges said: ". . . the inn, as a whole was operated reasonably . . . . obviously felt a need to protect guests . . . and measures were taken to ensure their safety . . . measures were reasonable . . . rape was truly unfortunate and horrible experience . . . defendants (the hotel) cannot be held responsible . . . For this court to hold otherwise would be equivalent to making all hotels the insurer of the guests' safety."

As the foregoing demonstrates, hotel safety and security is a growing concern among travelers throughout the world. Let's face it; traveling is stressful enough without having to worry about becoming a crime victim while away from home. One only has to look at the negative impact on hotel bookings, following a highly publicized tourist attack, to see how important the perception of security is to the traveler.

When there is a choice, frequent travelers will seek out a hotel property that has superior security amenities. Initially, savvy travelers will select a property that satisfies their criteria and balance of location, price, business facilities, and food service. However, after visiting the property, it's the security features that might determine the continued loyalty of a guest. Security, in its various aspects, therefore, could be viewed as an amenity as useful and important as the flat panel television, the well-stocked mini-bar or four different kinds of shampoo. The security-conscious guest will seek out and patronize hotels that offer the following security "amenities."

✦ DESIGN FACTORS

The first opportunity to present a positive impression about the relative safety of a hotel or motel property is at the perimeter. For maximum effectiveness, there must be an obvious and distinct design transition as you enter the property from the public street. Solid deterrent cues include significant barriers like perimeter walls, decorative fencing, landscaped terraces, and a well-defined driveway and main entrance. A strong transition sends a subliminal message to the criminal that this hotel is private property and for use by hotel guests only.

✦ LIGHTING

Good exterior lighting is designed to fill the gap between the property boundary and the hotel entrance and is the most important nighttime security feature. Public areas, when bathed in light, are both inviting to the guest and a powerful deterrent to crime. Good exterior lighting will allow you to see a potential threat at 100 feet. This minimum level of visibility gives you time to respond to the threat before being confronted by it. Exterior lighting must be even and balanced. Balanced lighting appears warm and comfortable and makes a property feel safe.

To achieve a balanced lighting effect, more fixtures are often necessary to fill the lighting gaps. Huge floodlights are not the best choice because they are not energy-efficient and tend to create glare and heavy shadows between fixtures. A surprising benefit of adding more and smaller light fixtures are that the total wattage can be reduced, which will save significant amounts of energy. Many properties have been able to pay for their entire lighting fixture upgrade in just one year, based on their energy savings alone.

✦ CURBSIDE DETERRENCE

Parking lot security is often the most overlooked area on a hotel property. Stranger-to-stranger crimes against persons are more likely to occur in the parking lot than in any other location. This is because parking lots offer the criminal the best hiding places, the fewest witnesses, and the quickest escape route. Parking lot surveillance can be relatively inexpensive, such as installing video cameras, but nothing beats a highly visible, uniformed security patrol that is capable of responding to a criminal incident and can call for help. Besides, a hotel guest would rather see a "live person" on the job who is paid to look out for their welfare.

Highly visible doormen and valet parking attendants are a great crime deterrent, especially at smaller hotel properties. Nothing instills more confidence in a hotel guest than a capable doorman who greets and makes eye contact with them as they enter the property. Criminals don't like doormen for two reasons: First, they don't want to be identified, and second, they don't want to be captured should they have to escape in a hurry. Without competent curbside security, crimes like purse snatchings, car thefts, and luggage thefts would increase substantially on most urban properties.

A doorman can monitor a property better if the number of entrances is limited, especially at night. This design philosophy gives the hotel the advantage of making the criminal feel "out of place" and, therefore, more likely to be deterred.

Access control cues must continue inside the property to be totally effective and to foster that "safe and secure feeling" within a guest. As for the criminal, access control is like peeling an onion; the more layers they penetrate . . . the more uncomfortable it should feel.

✦ INTERIOR ACCESS CONTROL

In addition to physical barriers, access control involves the use of electronic equipment, personnel, and procedures. For example, the entire hotel staff should be trained to be attentive to all persons and report suspicious activity to the manager-on-duty. Hotel guests love this high level of courtesy and staff attentiveness, while criminals hate it. Hotel criminals prefer to remain unnoticed and anonymous. Multiple staff contacts will make them feel very uncomfortable and is usually enough to make them go elsewhere to ply their trade.

The plaintiff was a registered guest at the Orlando, Florida, Howard Johnson Motor Lodge. Sometime after 9:30 P.M. she left her first floor room and went to her car to get some papers. Upon returning to her building's interior hallway, she was sexually attacked by an intruder. She alleged in her subsequent suit that the hotel allowed the building to remain open and available to anyone who entered, despite previous attacks on guests; they had no closed circuit TV monitoring and had failed to warn guests of previous attacks at that property. The jury found the defendant hotel did not meet reasonable standards for providing security, specifically (among other deficiencies) [it had] no procedures for excluding unauthorized personnel from the premises. The verdict was affirmed on appeal. *Orlando Executive Park, Inc., v. P.D.R.*, 402 So. 2d 44,2 (Florida, 1981).

In a high-rise hotel, the ground floor lobby presents another major opportunity to deter crime. The best security designs position the registration, bellman, and concierge desks in a position to view critical access points. Important access points include the front, back, and side entrances; elevator banks; lounge; and restaurant entrances. In large metropolitan hotels, extra attention needs to be paid to guest luggage, briefcases, and handbags left casually on the lobby floor.

✦ GUESTROOM SECURITY

The guest room represents the inner circle of a hotel security plan. The guest room is the sanctuary for the weary traveler where they expect to be safe. As previously established, the guest room doors and windows must be fortified to prevent forced entry, especially at the ground level. Doors must be nothing less than solid-core wood or metal, and be self-closing and self-locking. The door lock must consist of a high-quality deadbolt with at least a 1-inch bolt. The lock strike-plate must be bolted securely to the metal doorframe or by using 3-inch screws when attached to a wood doorjamb. Accessible sliding windows must have secondary security devices attached to prevent forced entry or lifting out of the frame.

Visible signs of door lock maintenance are important to travelers. Doors must be tight fitting, and the locks must be in good condition and should give a distinctive "clunk" as the deadbolt slides and locks in place. Guest room doors must be equipped with a wide-angle peephole, so a guest can see who is outside before opening the door.

A much appreciated guest amenity is the personal in-room lockbox. I especially appreciate the large ones that can secure my laptop computer. Electronic and keyless lockboxes are best, as long as they are securely anchored. Although not designed to replace the hotel safe deposit box, in-room lockboxes provide extra peace of mind when storing small valuables and personal documents.

✦ KEY CONTROL

Metal room keys are being replaced by electronically coded keycards. There is nothing more unsettling than checking into an upscale hotel and being issued a metal room key with the correct room number stamped on the key. Metal keys require a hotel to maintain an elaborate key control system with daily inventories of master key and E-Key checkout logs for the staff. The guest has no way of knowing that an adequate key control system is in place. If a room key or master key turns up missing, the affected locks must be changed. This event creates an ongoing maintenance expense for a hotel.

Metal room keys do not make the same "security statement" as coded plastic keycards. Keycards have the capability of being randomly coded at the point of registration, which reinforces the guests' perception of room security. Keycard control is computer-based and, therefore, creates the necessary audit trail automatically. Master keys can be changed in a matter of a few keystrokes and lost keycards are easily removed from the system. One of the best security features is the ability of the computer to interrogate each door lock and get a printout of everyone who accessed a particular room. This dramatically cuts down on theft from the rooms by hotel employees.

✦ PREDICTIONS

Traveler demand for hotels that promote enhanced security will increase in the coming years, especially with the added fear of terrorism. Security amenities are important to travelers, especially the elderly and women traveling alone. I predict security conscious properties will gain a competitive advantage over competing hotels that fail to recognize this important new trend.

✦ HOTEL AND MOTEL SECURITY FOR FAMILIES

Our family is at the center of our personal universe. Most people would do almost anything for the sake of their family. That includes protecting them from known dangers and harm while lodging at hotels or motels. This becomes increasing difficult, at times, because we live in an open society, where we share the same public places as the violent criminals like hotels and motels.

FAMILY SECURITY PLAN

Whenever your family walks out the front door, they leave that zone of protection that you have created. The secret to keeping your family reasonably safe once they leave home is to have a family security plan. To develop a family security plan, you must give careful thought to the public routines of each family member and think of ways to make them safer from the violent people in the world. The best way to accomplish this is to hold a family meeting to discuss this plan and play *what if* using different scenarios. For example, *what if* we need to stay overnight in a hotel? What steps should we take to make the process safer? *What if* we want to go to the swimming pool or gym? What precautions can we take to be safer in the parking lot? *What if* someone approaches to rob us while walking to our car on the street at night? What would we do and how would we react? Where would we go and who would we notify in case of emergency?

Most people have no such family plan and have not met as a family to discuss what if situations. When or if a criminal assault does occur, the family will not be prepared and will have to rely on instinct in response to the incident. What if their response instincts are wrong or their reactions inappropriate under the circumstances? We read about these all the time in the newspaper or hear about them on television, for example, where a child was walking in an unfamiliar place and was tricked into a car of a total stranger and kidnapped.

HOTELS AND MOTELS

When traveling on business or pleasure with your family, it may become necessary to stay overnight in a hotel or motel. Your hotel room becomes your home for the night and is your sanctuary while you sleep. It is important to give some thought to what hotel or motel you select and what room you are willing to accept. The cost of the hotel room is not always a good predictor of how safe the room or property will be. There are a few rules of thumb that should apply to any hotel room you rent.

ROOM SECURITY FEATURES

All of the previously discussed security features for hotel rooms are particularly important in the event the family is traveling together. Additionally, windows that can be opened should not open wide enough to allow a child to fall out. Similarly, balconies should be surrounded with child-proof barriers. Housekeeping should be contacted to cover electric outlets if necessary, and water temperature in the bath/shower should be carefully monitored.

SUPERVISE CHILDREN

Children should not be allowed to wander the hotel grounds unsupervised. Everyone at a hotel is a stranger, and it is difficult to discern who is a registered guest or who has criminal intentions. Do *not* leave a child at the pool or gym unsupervised. These are prime targets for predators.

Hotels and resorts that manage themselves as "family friendly" or offer programs and activities specifically for children have to demonstrate that their policies, particularly personnel background checks, are of utmost importance. Courts and juries do not look favorably on hotels that are lax in personnel procedures that allow child predators to be employed in areas where they are in contact with children.

A housekeeping employee, who was only given a cursory interview by the executive housekeeper, and whose references were not checked, had only been at the "family resort" 3 days before he sexually assaulted a 15-year-old guest at knifepoint. The trial jury found for the plaintiff and on appeal, the court held that the hotel, which advertised itself as a "first class family resort" was subject to a standard of reasonable care that would mean a "high degree of care" in this case. *Tobin v. Slutsky* (506 F. 2d 1097 2nd Circuit, 1974)

To recap briefly, many of the same considerations or security amenities are as important for families with children as they are for the seasoned traveler, but as pointed out in *Tobin,* courts will look very seriously at how carefully hotels will discharge their duty of care.

✦ HOTEL SECURITY ORGANIZATION AND STAFF

Most major hotels in urban areas have security staff on-site. Typically, security personnel are hired by the hotel general manager and report to the manager-on-duty (MOD) for day-to-day operations. Larger hotel chains have organized security departments with a corporate director of security, investigators, and layers of supervision with training capabilities to support the local facilities but have little to do with daily operation.

The size and organization of security staff at a hotel varies widely, depending on a variety of factors. For example, the size of the property, number of buildings, number of guest rooms, occupancy levels, convention facilities, restaurants, bars, parking structures, number of employees, crime rate in the area, and crime history inside the hotel. The type of uniform and equipment used by security staff varies as well, but typically includes a mobile radio, flashlight, and report forms. Many hotels do not authorize use of handcuffs, weapons, or arrest authority. Upscale hotels are more image conscious and like to soften the look of security officers by dressing them in suits, whereas urban facilities might go for the police-style uniform for maximum visibility at the points of access.

Hotel security is basically an entry-level position that doesn't require much education, training, or experience. Most duties are taught on the job with some training using a security manual. Basic requirements of a hotel security officer are to be at least 18 years of age, have earned a high school diploma or equivalent, have a clean criminal record, and be in good physical condition to perform the duties required. Hotel security directors are often retired law enforcement officers and provide the necessary training. Some hotels will outsource the entire security operation by contracting with a private security guard company to avoid the need to hire and supervise staff. Whatever the source of security personnel, it is important that all be properly licensed and trained to satisfy minimum state requirements.

The basic duties of hotel security personnel are to be highly visible; prevent crime, if possible; and observe and report activity that affects the safe and secure operation of the hotel. Critical duties include fire-watch floor patrols, monitoring the lobby and parking lot, and responding to calls for assistance. The best security officers communicate well, using handheld radios, writing daily activity logs, and completing detailed incident reports. Hotel security officers should have basic training in life safety, use of fire equipment and emergency evacuation procedures, responding to suspicious activities, and dealing with obnoxious guests. Large hotels should have security officers with first aid and CPR certifications. As the security staff matures, so does the depth of on-the-job scenario training and refining of response techniques, teamwork, and focus on priority areas.

✦ CONCLUSION

A hotel is a unique 24-hour environment with daily guest turnover and public access to the facility. The business of a hotel is to offer hospitality to those away from home. The best hotels make a guest feel safe by offering a combination of security amenities designed to make them feel at ease in their temporary environment. Frequent travelers quickly find the hotels that offer adequate security amenities and return the favor by becoming loyal customers.

5.10 CASE STUDY: HOUSEKEEPING, ENGINEERING, AND SECURITY

✦ INTERDISCIPLINARY SECURITY PLAN

In 2001, as a regional manager for a hotel chain that operated three urban core hotels in a large eastern city, Denise Tomes was becoming concerned that the hotels for which she was responsible were increasingly vulnerable to threats of physical harm or financial loss to guests from a variety of criminals. She knew through news and media reports that the streets of the city her hotels operate in were becoming increasingly unsafe because of aggressive panhandling, street crime, muggings, physical and sexual assaults, and automobile-related felonies.

Because her hotels total in excess of 1500 rooms and cater mainly to the convention, corporate, and free independent traveler (FIT) markets, Tomes knew that at any given time a large number of her guests were on the streets of the city and that, additionally, because of the public nature of hotels in general, it was likely that criminals could enter the hotel properties seeking victims.

These hotels were built during the late 1980s and, although regularly redecorated and remodeled to continue to appeal to the upscale market, they still reflected the architectural and security consciousness of their era in operational terms. This meant that guest room door locks were still of the standard keyed variety; elevators, fire stairs, outside hotel entrances and exits, parking structures were relatively obscure and unmonitored; and housekeeping, engineering, and guest services staff training did not, as yet, reflect the security concerns of the twenty-first century.

To help her deal with the potential problems presented by the current situation, Denise Tomes called a meeting of the heads of security, housekeeping, and engineering. She challenged them to come up with a plan to increase security for the hotels and their guests without building armed fortresses. The first task of the directors of security, housekeeping, and engineering was to set forth for Tomes an analysis of the potential risks. The second is to produce a range of alternative suggestions about how those risks might be managed through the efforts of their departments and respective staffs, combined with specific recommendations for equipment and facility upgrades. What potential risks may be present and what should be done to avoid them?

REFERENCES

Ammon, R. E., Jr. 1993. Risk and Game Management Practices in Selected Municipal Football Facilities. Unpublished doctoral dissertation, University of Northern Colorado, Greeley, CO.

Ammon, R. E. Jr. 1995. "Alcohol and Event Management." *Crowd Management* 1(4): 16–19.

Baim, D. V. 1994. *The Sports Stadium as a Municipal Investment.* Westport, CT: Greenwood, p. 200.

Bayou, M. E., and L. B. Bennett. 1992. "Profitability Analysis for Table Service Restaurants." *Cornell Hotel and Restaurant Administration Quarterly* 33(3): 49–55.

Berlonghi, A. 1990. *Special Event Risk Management Manual.* Dana Point, CA: Event Risk Management, p. 259.

———. 1996. *Special Event Security Management, Loss Prevention, and Emergency Services.* Dana Point, CA: Event Risk Management, p. 13.

Black, L. 2004. "$1 Million Bail Set for Suspect in Hotel Killings." *Chicago Tribune*, North Final Edition, November 10, page 2, section C.

Brigham, G. H. 1955. *Housekeeping for Hotels, Motels, Hospitals, Clubs, Schools.* New York: Ahrens.

Christiansen, M. L. 1986. "How to Avoid Negligence Suits: Reducing Hazards to Prevent Injuries." *Journal of Physical Education, Recreation, and Dance* 57(2): 46–52.

Clery, B. 1995. "Commercial Insurance Carriers Write Disclaimer for Crime." *Campus Watch* (1)1:5.

Dale, J. C., and T. Kluga. 1992. "Energy Conservation: More Than a Good Idea." *Cornell Hotel and Restaurant Administration Quarterly* 33(6): 30–35.

Donohue, C. H. (Ed.). 2004. "Prevent Workplace Harassment and Discrimination." *Hospitality Law* (October): 12.

———. 2000. "Study Reviews Seven Years of Hospitality Litigation." *Hospitality Law* (August): 12.

Dougan, J. 1994. "Menu Engineering with Electronic Spreadsheets." *Bottomline* 8(6): 15–17.

Fisher, R. A. 1986. "A Documentation of Factors Which Determine Staffing Levels for the Engineering Department of a Hotel Property." MPS Monograph. Ithaca, NY: *Cornell University School of Hotel Administration.*

Flannery, R. 1998. *The Assaulted Staff Action Program: Coping with the Psychological Aftermath of Violence.* Ellicott City, MD: Chevron.

Gordon, C. L., and W. Brill. 1996 "The Expanding Role of Crime Prevention through Environmental Design in Premises Liability." *NCJ Publication* No. 157-309. Washington, DC: U.S. Department of Justice, pp. 1–6.

Hashemi, L., and B. Webster. 1998. "Non-fatal Workplace Violence Workers' Compensation Claims (1993–1996)." *Journal of Occupational and Environmental Medicine* 40(6): 561–567.

Hoel, H., and S. Einarsen. 2003. *Violence at Work in Hotels, Catering, and Tourism.* Geneva, International Labor Office, Sectoral Activities Programme, WP.211.

Huntley, H. 2004. "Business Hit by Violence Must Act Quickly to Address Its Workers' Concerns." *(Washington) Tribune Business News*, November 20, p. 1.

Issacs, A. 2004. *Workplace Violence: Issues in Response.* E. Rugula, E. (Ed.). Quantico, VA: Federal Bureau of Investigation, FBI Academy.

Jeffery, C. R. 1971. *Crime Prevention Through Environmental Design.* Beverly Hills, CA: Sage.

LaBelle, A. M., and J. Barton. 1951. *Administrative Housekeeping.* New York: G.P. Putnam's Sons.

Larson v. MOA Hospitality, Inc., 2003 Wash. App. LEXIS 1872, 2003.

Lee, L. 1997. "Parking Lots Open to Crime." *Houston Chronicle*, April 27, p. E1.

Levin, P. F., J. B. Hewitt, and S. T. Misner. 1996. "Workplace Violence: Female Occupational Homicides in Metropolitan Chicago." *AAOHN Journal* 44(7): 326–331.

Maguire, K., and A. L. Pastore (Eds.). 1995. *Bureau of Justice Statistics: Sourcebook of Criminal Justice Statistics—1994.* Albany, NY: Hindelang Criminal Justice Research Center, p. 249.

———. 1996. *Bureau of Justice Statistics: Sourcebook of Criminal Justice Statistics—1995.* Albany, NY: Hindelang Criminal Justice Research Center, p. 230.

Malk, M., and R. S. Schmidgall. 1994. "Financial Analysis of the Rooms Division." *Bottomline* 8(6): 18–21.

———. 1995. "Analyzing Food Operations." *Bottomline* 10(3): 23–27.

Maloy, B. P. 1993. "Legal Obligations Related to Facilities." *Journal of Physical Education, Recreation, and Dance* (64)2: 28–30, 64.

Martin, R. J., and T. J. A. Jones. 1992. Professional Management of Housekeeping (2nd ed). New York: John Wiley & Sons.

McBer and Company. (no date). *Managerial Style Questionnaire.*

McCarthy, P. 1995. "Lessons in the Law: To What Extent Must a Venue Owner Be Held Responsible for Injuries On-site?" *Crowd Management* 1(4): 7.

Miller, A. W. 1989. "Risk Management." In *Law for Physical Educators and Coaches*, G. Nygaard and T. Boone (Eds.). Columbus, OH: Publishing Horizons, pp. 419–437.

Miller, L. K. 1993. "Crowd Control." *Journal of Physical Education, Recreation, and Dance* 64(2): 1–32, 64–65.

Mintzberg, H. 1975. "The Manager's Job: Folklore and Fact." *Harvard Business Review* (July–August): 49–61.

National Institute for Occupational Safety and Health. July 2003. "Preventing Deaths, Injuries, and Illnesses of Young Workers." Retrieved August 10, 2004, from http://www.cdc.gov/niosh.

Nilson, R. A., and C. R. Edington, 1982. "Risk Management: A Tool for Park and Recreation Administrators." *Park and Recreation* (August): 34–37.

Quain, W. J. 1992. "Analyzing Sales Mix Profitability." *Cornell Hotel and Restaurant Administration Quarterly* 33(2): 57–62.

Pearson, C., and J. Clair. 1998. "Reframing Crisis Management." *Academy of Management Review* 23(1): 59–76.

Riehle, H. 1994. "Table Service Restaurants Post Sales Gain in 1993." *Restaurants USA* 14(9):43–44.

Ross, C. 1985. "Managing Risk." *Athletic Business* (June): 22–29.

Rossman, G., and S. Rallis. 2003. *Learning in the Field: An Introduction to Qualitative Research* (2nd ed.). Thousand Oaks, CA: Sage.

Rutherford, D. G. 1987. "The Evolution of the Hotel Engineer's Job." *Cornell Hotel and Restaurant Administration Quarterly* 27(4): 72–78.

Rutherford, D. G., and J. P. McConnell. 1987. "Understanding and Managing Your Liability for Guest Safety." *Cornell Hotel and Restaurant Administration Quarterly* 27(4): 58–63.

Rutherford, D. G., and W. J. Schill. 1984. "Theoretical Constructs in Practice: Managers Rate Their Importance." *International Journal of Hospitality Management* 3(3): 101–106.

Saied, J. 1990. "Approaches to Risk Management." *Cornell Hotel and Restaurant Administration Quarterly* 31(2): 45–55.

Schneider, M., and G. Tucker. 1989. *The Professional Housekeeper* (3rd ed.). New York: Van Nostrand Reinhold.

Shank, G. 2002. *Qualitative Research: A Personal Skills Approach.* Columbus, OH: Merrill Prentice-Hall.

Sheard, R. 1995. "Architectural Influences in Crowd Management in the U.K." *Crowd Management* (2)2:4–7, 26–28.

Smith, M. S. 1996. "Crime Prevention through Environmental Design in Parking Facilities." *Research in Brief.* Washington, DC: U.S. Department of Justice, NCJ Publication No. 157–310, pp. 2–9.

Tucker, G., and M. Schneider. 1982. *Professional Housekeeping.* Boston: CBI.

Turkel, S. 1993. "Deflating F&B Results." *Bottom Line* 8(2): 8–10.

U.S. Department of Labor, Bureau of Labor Statistics. 2004. Census of Fatal Occupational Injuries, 2002. Retrieved August 13, 2004, from http://www.dol.gov.

van der Smissen, B. 1990. *Legal Liability and Risk Management for Public and Private Entities.* Cincinnati, OH: Anderson, p. 3.

Wasmuth, W. J., and S. W. Davis. 1983. "Strategies for Managing Employee Turnover." *Cornell Hotel and Restaurant Administration Quarterly* 24(2): 65–75.

Whataburger, Inc. v. Rockwell, 706 So.2d 1226 (Ala. 1997).

Wilbert v. Metro Park Dist. of Tacoma, 90 Wn. App. 304, 309; 950 P.2d 522 (1998).

Wynn, R., N. Clarkin, T. Cox, and A. Griffiths. 1997. *Guidance on the Prevention of Violence at Work.* Brussels, European Commission, DG-V, Ref. CE/VI-4/97.

SUGGESTED READINGS

BOOKS

Barth, S. 2008. *Hospitality Law: Managing Legal Issues in the Hospitality Industry* (3rd ed.). Hoboken, NJ: John Wiley and Sons.

Borsenik, F. D. and A. T. Stutts. 1997. *The Management of Maintenance and Engineering Systems in the Hospitality Industry* (4th ed.). New York: John Wiley & Sons.

Burstein, H. 2000. *Hotel and Motel Loss Prevention: A Management Perspective.* Upper Saddle River, NJ: Prentice Hall.

Cournoyer, N. G., A. G. Marshall, and K. L. Morris. 1999. *Hotel, Restaurant, and Travel Law: A Preventive Approach.* Albany, NY: Delmar.

Jones, T. J. A. 2007. *Professional Management of Housekeeping Operations.* Hoboken, NJ: John Wiley & Sons.

Maguire, W. 2008. *A General Manager's Housekeeping Inspection Program: How to Create the Reputation of the Cleanest Hotel in Town.* Scotts Valley, CA: CreateSpace.

McGoey, C. 1990. *Security Adequate . . . or Not? The Complete Guide to Premises Liability Litigation.* Middletown, RI: Aegis Books, Inc.

Newland, L. E. 1997. *Hotel Protection Management: The Innkeeper's Guide to Guest Protection and Reasonable Care.* Spokane, WA: TNZ.

Prestia, K. L. 1993. *Chocolates for the Pillows, Nightmares for the Guests.* Silver Spring, MD: Bartleby.

Raghubalan, G. 2007. *Hotel Housekeeping: Operations and Management.* New York: Oxford University Press.

Smith, H. 1993. *Hotel Security.* Springfield, IL: Charles C. Thomas.

Tarlow, P. E. 2002. *Event Risk Management and Safety.* Hoboken, NJ: John Wiley and Sons.

ARTICLES

Bean, Nelson R. 1992. "Planning for Catastrophe: The Fast Track to Recovery." *Cornell Hotel and Restaurant Administration Quarterly* 33(2): 64–69.

Dale, J. C., and T. Kluga. 1992. "Energy Conservation: More Than a Good Idea." *Cornell Hotel and Restaurant Administration Quarterly* 33(6): 30–35.

Eaton, D. E. 2004. "Beyond Room Service: Legal Consequences of Sexual Harassment of Staff by Hotel Guests." *Cornell Hotel and Restaurant Administration Quarterly* 245(4): 347-361.

Gill, M., C. Moon., P. Seaman, and V. Turbin. 2002. "Security Management and Crime in Hotels." *International Journal of Contemporary Hospitality Management* 14(2): 58–64.

Lai, J. H. K., and F. W. H. Yik. 2008. "Benchmarking Operation and Maintenance Costs of Luxury Hotels." *Journal of Facilities Management* 6(4): 279–290.

Rutherford, D. G. 1987. "The Evolution of the Hotel Engineer's Job." *Cornell Hotel and Restaurant Administration Quarterly* 27(4): 72–79.

Wilson, R. H. 2007. "Internet Hotel Reservations: The 'Terms and Conditions' Trap." *Cornell Hotel and Restaurant Administration Quarterly* 48(4): 361–371.

SOURCE NOTES

Chapter 5.2, "Housekeeping Organizations: Their History, Purpose, Structures, and Personnel," by Thomas Jones, adapted from *Housekeeping Operations* (2nd ed.). Edited by Robert Martin, Copyright © 1992. Adapted by permission of John Wiley & Sons, Inc.

Chapter 5.3, "On Being an Executive Housekeeper," by John Lagazo.

Chapter 5.4, "The Hotel Engineering Function: Organization, People, and Issues in the Modern Era," by Glen B. Mounts and Oliver Meinzer.

Chapter 5.5, "The Engineering Department and Financial Information," by Agnes Lee DeFranco and Susan B. Sheridan.

Chapter 5.6, "The Legal Environment of Lodging Operations," by Melissa Dallas.

Chapter 5.7, "Asphalt Jungle," by Je'anna Abbott and Gil Fried, is reprinted from the April 1999 issue of *Cornell Hotel and Restaurant Administration Quarterly*. © Cornell University. Used by permission. All rights reserved.

Chapter 5.8, "Workplace Violence in Hotels," by Mark Beattie and Jacinta Gau.

Chapter 5.9, "Understanding and Managing the Risks and Challenges of Hotel Security in the 21st Century," by Chris E. McGoey.

CHAPTER SIX

FOOD AND BEVERAGE DIVISION

6.1 INTRODUCTION

In discussing the ways that hotel organizations have changed, we pointed out that in earlier times food played a significant role in the organizational structure and product/service mix of hotels. It has been speculated that the preeminent role played by hotel foodservice in society became significantly diminished with the onset of Prohibition and during the 1920s. People stopped going to foodservice establishments where they couldn't "get a drink." Prohibition gave rise to competition from street restaurants that operated sub rosa as speakeasies. These restaurants were not constricted by the visible, public nature of hotel dining rooms. This diminished role was compounded in many ways by the depression years of the 1930s and the war years of the 1940s.

In general, it was difficult for most hotels' foodservice to recover from the loss of recognition that occurred during Prohibition. Recovery was further delayed by the Depression and the uncertainty and reordered national priorities that accompanied World War II.

In 1945, at the conclusion of World War II, well-documented major shifts in population and economic emphasis began to occur. Freestanding restaurants continued to compete effectively with hotel foodservice. Movement was away from downtown and central business district hotels. Motels and motor hotels were built on highway and freeway interchanges to take advantage of the mobility of the American family. Quick-service restaurants, too, affected the away-from-home eating habits of Americans. Consequently, many hotel companies felt as if the cost of providing high-quality food in the face of increased competition outweighed the benefits. The net effect was that many hotel guests and operators came to believe that hotel foodservice was little more than

246 Chapter 6 • Food and Beverage Division

a necessary evil. For many operations, this became a self-fulfilling prophecy, and hotel foodservice floundered for many years.

This situation has been reversed in recent years. Of the many factors mentioned earlier that forced organizational change (market segmentation, return on investment, demographic shifts, and so forth), it seems that return on investment has played a dominant role in this turnaround. The double-whammy issues of construction cost and return on investment expectations of people outside the hospitality industry strongly suggest that space devoted to foodservice should contribute at least its share to the profit structure of the modern hotel service system.

As a result, hotels seem to be willing to try anything to capture additional revenue, prestige, and competitive advantage. Among the tactics addressed in several of the articles and essays included in this section are partnering with restaurant companies, outsourcing a hotel's foodservice, new catering and beverage management strategies, celebrity chefs, and rethinking the entire role of hotel food and beverage.

✦ FOOD

Over 35 years ago, Allen Hubsch (1966) suggested a number of ways to revitalize hotel food and beverage service that have proved eerily prescient. Among his suggestions were:

- Hotel food and beverage facilities must become profit centers—no more a necessary evil!

- Food and beverage management calls for new and increased professionalism and less reliance on the old chef–maître d' model.

- Food and beverage outlets must become amenities that produce room-nights.

- Hotel food and beverage units must adopt street restaurant philosophies; merchandising, advertising, decor/ambience, menu, and service must compete with local competition.

- Food and beverage can be used to fill marginally profitable space in rentals, storage, or production areas.

- New food and beverage outlets can leverage existing facilities like storage and kitchens by spreading fixed costs over a wider sales base.

Hubsch's article, now considered a classic, is among the suggested readings for this section.

In support of Hubsch's ideas, Michael Riley (from the University of Surrey) reports the changes that have occurred in food and beverage management in recent years. In fact, the purpose behind this article is to answer the question "how has the function of food and beverage management changed over the years?" According to Riley, the food and beverage industry has seen changes in the process of buying food and beverage products, information technology, the cooking process, and the tastes and preferences of the guests who visit food and beverage establishments. In addition, he states that, although the old adage that hotel managers should come up from the ranks of the food and beverage department still holds today, this has changed a bit given the ever-increasing importance placed on financial and marketing skills.

As Riley puts it, "if food and beverage management has a generic heart of its own, then that must be 'catering'" (2005, p. 89). A new inclusion in this edition is written by Robyn Graff, catering/convention service manager for the Hyatt Regency Washington on Capitol Hill. In this article, Graff discusses her experiences as a corporate management trainee for Hyatt Hotels, before she proceeds to discuss her daily duties as a manager in the catering department. This article is unique in the fact that Graff offers her experiences in a training program prior to becoming a fully fledged manager. Further, she provides first-hand evidence of Riley's notion of how food and beverage is still the bedrock of hotel management.

In a major research effort that began in 1998, Laurette Dubè, Cathy Enz, Leo Renaghan, and Judy Siguaw of the Center for Hospitality Research at Cornell University studied the best practices of hotels in the U.S. lodging industry. In their words, "The goal of this research was to surface and summarize practices of use and value to the entire lodging industry" (Dubè et al., 1999, p. 7). Siguaw and Enz summarize several of the practices from that study that have been developed by hotels to achieve the "strategic charge of profitably meeting customer needs" (1999, p. 50). The authors describe how top hotels integrate the ideas of restaurant design and conceptualization with all of the variables that affect the quality of the food and the experience for the guest.

The concept of outsourcing was mentioned earlier in the context of how some hotel companies are rethinking the role of hotel food and beverage and how to maximize investments in facilities, furnishings, and equipment for foodservice outlets. According to Strate and Rappole (1997), because hotel restaurants have often been managed as a secondary function, owners and operators are questioning the conventional wisdom about how hotel food and beverage is conceived and managed. They state that this new focus on hotel foodservice results in innovative concepts and strategic alliances with well-known restaurant brands. In their article, they analyze this trend outlining historic antecedents of the practice and use the Texas firm Bristol Hotel Company as a case study.

Few would argue that, should a hotel choose to do its own foodservice, a first-class executive chef is essential to allow a hotel organization to compete effectively for food and beverage business in today's market. It is, however, fairly clear that chefs today do not have the dominant role they had a century ago. Given the importance of the food and beverage function, as established by the foregoing articles, the chef is nevertheless an integral part of the competitive strategy and a full-fledged department leader. He or she is no longer purely a technician. This individual must have developed a significant range of managerial skills (with expertise in financial analysis becoming increasingly important) to complement the technical and artistic training we have come to expect from an executive chef. The appearance of ultra-high-profile celebrity chefs adds another interesting variable to the food and beverage director's mix of challenges. If a hotel commits much of its food and beverage strategy to the talents of one famous person, it can enjoy a significant competitive advantage but also become hostage to that person's whims and personality. Many high-profile hotels in Las Vegas have "name" chef programs, and in many major population centers, top chefs have made their hotels destination venues because of their fame in the kitchen.

Patti Shock and her colleague John Stefanelli highlight the importance of the banquet and catering functions of hotel food and beverage in their piece. With the increased national attention and focus on the importance of conferences, conventions, meetings, and events of all kinds, foodservice professionals who specialize in planning and serving meals and beverages to large groups of people are increasingly important. The authors note, "Although on-premise catering is generally the second-largest source of revenue for most hotels, following sleeping rooms" and "often the highest visibility the hotel has on a local level," banquets and catering are still too often ignored by hotel school curricula. In this chapter, we partially address this lack.

Catered affairs represent a significant contribution to the profit picture of hotel food and beverage service. The efficacy of a hotel's efforts in selling and servicing the group business market may very well be the difference between profitability of the food and beverage function and some less desirable outcome. Shock and Stefanelli explore the organization, personnel, and processes of the catering department and give the reader an in-depth view of catering executives and banquet organizations. The article includes Internet addresses for additional information.

It is the revenue and visibility importance of the catering function that makes the energetic essay by Rich Benninger so intriguing. From rising at 6:00 A.M. or so, thinking today is the day he will "get everything done" in the catering and convention services office of a 5000-room resort hotel casino in Las Vegas to hitting the sack after midnight, Benninger gives the reader an insider's view of life in the fast lane of Vegas catering and convention services. As executive director of catering and convention services at the Caesar's Palace Resort Hotel and Casino, Benninger is uniquely positioned to provide these insights.

✦ BEVERAGE

In any hotel that has more than one formal bar, there is usually a separate function within the food and beverage department called *bar* or *beverage management*. Ideally, that office coordinates all matters that concern liquors, beers, and wines. The beverage manager is responsible for purchasing, receiving, storing, and issuing liquor, wine, and beer inventory, and quite obviously has the managerial responsibility to control that inventory.

Additionally, the beverage manager:

- Hires, trains, schedules, and controls all beverage and bar personnel.

- Promotes the various beverage department services.

- Coordinates the requests of other departments that require beverage services—for instance, banquet and catering, room service, chefs, and management.

- Assures that his or her department is in compliance with federal, state, and local laws and regulations.

The beverage manager administers or manages up to four types of bars.

The front or public bar is that in which the guest can, if he or she so desires, interact with the bartender and other service personnel. There are provisions for guest seating at the bar itself, which may be part of a restaurant or a separate room or area. Separate tables and stand-up areas may also be available for beverage service. A front bar may or may not incorporate entertainment.

A service bar is a hidden bar designed for use by the hotel's food and beverage service staff. It may serve one or more foodservice areas and/or room service, and it is designed specifically for efficiency and economy of service. In most cases, speed is considered the essential ingredient in service bars. Service bars typically are centrally located in the back of the house, out of guest view.

Portable bars are designed for maximum flexibility and can be used in conjunction with beverage sales associated with guest activities anywhere in the hotel or on its grounds. This may be extended in resort areas to include recreational areas.

A new facility popular in many hotels is that of the in-room bar, mini-bar, or honor bar. While sometimes the responsibility for inventory of these bars rests with room service, the beverage manager in most cases is also deeply involved in their design, marketing, and control.

In many ways, the beverage manager's job can be compared, in terms of historical stereotype, to that of the housekeeper. Often the beverage manager has worked his or her way up through the ranks of beverage server and preparer and through experience, longevity, and interest has become the beverage or bar manager. There is reason to believe that in many ways this pattern is changing. Like many other areas of hotel management, the beverage management function now faces a range of issues that are more sophisticated and complicated than traditional beverage management problems of the past. It may be that the beverage managers of the future will have to bring to their job a level of managerial, organizational, and administrative sophistication that was previously unnecessary.

The issues, responsibilities, and structural management of the hotel's beverage function are analyzed and discussed by Valentino Luciani, a past professor of beverage management at the University of Nevada, Las Vegas. Luciani's essay draws on his industry experience, research, and teaching of beverage management and provides a view of how the modern beverage manager has evolved from his or her historical counterparts.

The planning, preparation, service, and management of food and beverage in modern hotels have changed significantly since the first edition of this book was written. The essays, research, and commentary presented here are chosen to illustrate the breadth and depth of this process of change. The reader who is interested in hotel food and beverage should be able to synthesize an accurate vision of the practices and realities of this major operational division of modern hotels.

6.2 FOOD AND BEVERAGE MANAGEMENT: A REVIEW OF CHANGE

Michael Riley

Abstract.

Purpose. The paper is a reflection on the changes that have taken place in the area of food and beverage and serves as a reminder that it is still one of the most complex activities within the area of hospitality.

DESIGN/METHODOLOGY/APPROACH. The paper highlights major changes, with particular emphasis on marketing and the rising influence of design. However, the basic argument is that the changes that have taken place during the last two decades are essentially add-ons to the basic activities of the function: very little has fallen away. In other words, although technological advances, particularly in the kitchen, and the invasion of modern business techniques, such as branding and business process engineering, have brought new activities, the need for the traditional knowledge and skills remains. This makes modern food and beverage management an even more complex activity but an exciting one.

FINDINGS. The paper acknowledges the changing career patterns of those with food and beverage backgrounds but suspects that it is still the bedrock of hotel management.

PRACTICAL IMPLICATIONS. The paper defends the case for food and beverage training within hospitality management courses but acknowledges the problems associated with this.

ORIGINALITY/VALUE. The conclusion drawn is that educational decisions need a full appraisal of the functions of modern food and beverage management: which is the purpose of this paper.

The past few decades have wrought great changes on the functions of management and the way in which business is conducted. No generic function has been left untouched and it would be surprising if a specialist vocation role such as food and beverage management had escaped the march of progress—it has not. The changes in generic management that have been brought about by information technology and globalisation have created whole new ways of marketing, financing distributing and organising work. Although it is almost automatic to assume the influence of progress, in this changing milieu, it is still worth asking the question: How different is change? In other words, to assess the extent of change it is necessary to understand what change actually implies. Often, in changing situations there is a tension between the remains of the old and the new. The function of food and beverage management is an interesting case of tension between change and that which remains constant— the fine distinction between genuine change and the accommodation of the new within the traditional. What we see from the outside is an area of management where the new and the old have to live and develop together.

Although not exclusively so, food and beverage management generally sits under the hospitality management umbrella and as such reflects the changes of recent times in hospitality management. Here, change has emphasized the business aspects of profitability and marketing over the more, for want of a better word, romantic issues of food as a cultural entity and hospitality as a human propensity. In a very real sense, change has brought technological innovation and conceptual creativity. If Escoffier doesn't live here any more and instead we have celebrity chefs and global branded restaurants then all that really reflects is that society has changed and that new modes of management in the food and restaurant industry have popularised the notion of eating out to levels not previously known. This expansion has been propelled by the application of two tenets of modern marketing: specialisation and branding. Any conceptual specialisation automatically brings with it a specialisation of skill. However, once this specialism is forced to change then the skill base changes with it. This is the case with modern food and beverage management. It has broken up its original skills and knowledge base in cuisine and re-tooled with marketing and productivity knowledge on the assumption that while the old adage that a good restaurant sold itself has proved durable, it may just have outlived its time (Cooper, 1967).

Food and beverage management as an activity resides in many roles and carries various labels across different sectors of the industry: a restaurateur, a banqueting manger, a ship's purser could be food and beverage managers of one type or another. If food and beverage management has a generic heart of its own then that must be "catering"—at its simplest the cooking and serving of food. The word catering has fairly low status in the prestige hierarchy of activities yet it is not only an essential role in society but it is also a complex one requiring particular organising skills that can transform perishable materials in short time frames. Catering is about having knowledge of food and cooking and having the skills of timing and of sequencing to organise a production process within a compressed time frame. The basic process of buying, storing, costing, processing and serving food is, even without adding creative and marketing elements, a complex process. It is a process that has to be controlled and managed and what makes it so central to the notion of

food and beverage management is that it remains essentially the same in all circumstances and irrespective of size or quality be they industrial canteen, grand hotel, or smart restaurant. Whoever is in charge has to make many decisions, most of which require them to be part quantity surveyor, part cost accountant, and part cook, all rolled into one activity—and all this, despite the undoubted effects of modern changes throughout the basic process. However, in all this talk of change the question that is worth asking is has the body of knowledge required to fulfill the role of managing a food and beverage operation, in whatever guise, really changed or has it just added some more sophisticated ingredients?

The basic process has changed. The buying process, for one thing, has developed models beyond the simple price comparing market operation. In one respect, we see development along the lines of supply chain management, where the hospitality industry works with primary producers to improve quality. This development has been assisted by the use of the Internet. In another, we see the growth of horizontal integration in supply companies which supply a complete range of products, including food and beverage, on contract. Such companies have the power of economies of scale to exert a deflationary pressure on prices. It is not uncommon to find the purchasing function subcontracted to outside organizations. However, notwithstanding the purchasing model applied, there is still at the heart of the process a requirement for product knowledge. Specifications have to be drawn up and deliveries checked which makes any system dependent on human expertise.

Information technology has, for a long time, made stock management easier with stronger connections to accounting systems and forecasting systems. However, they have not replaced the need to actually physically take stock. Similarly, the use of standard recipes, with costings applied, has, with computerisation, become a budgetary control process. Again, performance against budget is determined by the willingness of cooks to actually use standard recipes. The perennial problem of food production and cost control is that it always needs vigilance by management, irrespective of the sophistication of information systems.

The cooking process too has been invaded by modern technology in the form of microwave, cook chill methods, induction ovens and many other labour-saving mechanical innovations. It has also been invaded by that emblem of modern business—outsourcing. In cooking terms this comes in the form of buying-in food instead of making it on the premises. This has a long tradition behind it but has accelerated in recent years because its transactional cost value has simply led towards subcontracting (often referred to as fabrication). The consequences of buying-in manufactured food products are, on the one hand savings in labour cost but on the other, a reduction of skill and training opportunity. The balancing act for food outlets is whether to surrender freshness and skill for bought-in products that are attractive in themselves but also save labour costs. This equation is at the heart of food and beverage management because it always has to control labour costs. What is important to the future of cuisine is that the decisions on maintaining skilled labour in each unit accumulate for the industry. The industry versus the individual establishment dimension is a crucial one for food and beverage and the most important issue is that of skill development versus de-skilling (Riley, 1981). If everybody goes in for fabricated products then cooking skills become confined to factory-like production units. In all fairness, this idea of fabrication versus freshly cooked food by skilled labour denies the grades of skill/technology combinations that lie between the two poles. The advances in cook chill and in the ability of yeasts to be reactivated after freezing have changed approaches to the preparation of food. Certainly, shift systems have declined due to the ability of technology to maintain freshly prepared food for longer periods. It is no longer necessary to start making bread in the middle of the night for breakfast—there is now a choice. Kitchens are now designed to be productive and the organisation of production has become more systematic, in that it is designed around standardised final products. This does not mean that it is time to bury the old "partie system," far from it. Over the years this system has evolved in a manner which collapsed the original division of labour into less areas of specialisation and in high standard á la carte kitchens it remain, to this day, the basis of the division of labour and productivity in the kitchen.

Notwithstanding these technological changes the real impact of change has come through the market itself. Not only are more people eating out but they are also demanding greater variety. In food and beverage management, marketing and operations share the same dilemmas. The marketing problem for food and beverage management is whether to meet the demand for variety through a market structure of specialised and possibly branded restaurants or to offer a wider choice within the restaurant menu. How much choice do we give customers? The initial dilemma here is—is wide choice attractive? If wide choice is deemed to be an attractive attribute, then another dilemma follows; that wide choice leaves open the opportunity for products and service to be provided but not consumed. For example, a large range of dishes on a menu may entice the customers to dine but if they choose narrowly then the avoidance of waste becomes a managerial objective. In these circumstances, the ideal solution would be that everything be cooked to order. The problem is that the very attractions of cuisine work against cooking to order—some dishes require long cooking times. The solutions lie in the technology of food production, storage, and regeneration. The alternative to wide choice is specialisation—offering to produce a small variety at a controlled level of quality. This would be more productive but would segment the market. In a sense the width of choice dilemma is about appeal versus productivity. One concept, which straddles both these ideas, is that of branding, whereby although the choices offered can be wide or narrow, specifying the choices within the overall concept of the brand reduces some of the uncertainty for the customer. It does not remove the issue of range of choice versus productivity but takes it into the identity of the product and by so doing handles the attractiveness issue separately from the production issues. An example would be helpful here. Compare a restaurant that has a large range of French dishes on the menu with a hamburger bar—they are different markets and the latter will be more productive than the former. Compare these extremes with a branded Bistro chain that offers choice but not as much as the French restaurant but increases its attractiveness by offering not just a range of dishes but also the reassurance of quality control through

standardisation. Similarly, an American restaurant concept might expand choice beyond the hamburger but still maintain productivity and attractiveness. In both cases, reducing uncertainty is seen as a form of attractiveness. But, this too has a sting in the tail because the more specialist the restaurant the quicker will be its redundancy (Riley, 2000a). Familiar can easily become too familiar and the system will demand more novelty.

Modern thinking says "keep it simple" even at the higher level. This was not always the case—in earlier times the great compendium of French cuisine—La Repertoire de la Cuisine based on Escoffier's *Guide to Modern Cookery* encouraged large á la carte menus. Whether French cuisine, as the fundamental corpus of knowledge for the development of skill, is relevant to modern food and beverage is a point worth debating. The value of such a corpus of knowledge, be it French or Chinese or any national based cuisine, is that it always has embedded within it a set of physical or craft skills that form the performance and motivational basis of the occupation chef or cook. While the principles of cookery can be taught outside the expensive teaching of French cuisine they are nevertheless essential for any level of cooking, even the hybrid versions of the French repertoire so beloved by celebrity chefs. Within vocational education there are serious issues of resourcing chef training that are the subject of much debate (Salleh and Riley, 1994; Baker et al., 1995). What is clear, however, is that despite the onset of technological intervention the demand for skilled chefs continues to increase. To an extent this demand is fed by the evolution of national cuisine into international cuisine. This is an ill-defined concept but nevertheless one which is easily recognisable on menus around the world. Food and beverage management used to be dominated by French cuisine and proscribed forms of table service—these were the defining skills and knowledge of the area. They stem from the hegemony of continental European of what constitutes "haute cuisine." If, in matters of taste, Europe no longer rules the roost, then all the formality and rigorous training no longer matter. Such an extreme position does not seem tenable because for one thing haute cuisine is still alive and well and for another it appears to have made a pact with our postmodernist world and become more accessible, both in terms of knowledge and price, without losing its soul. The biggest enemy of haute cuisine is not public taste but specialisation simply because of its assault on training.

At this juncture it would be appropriate to return the discussion to the notion of food and beverage management as a role and its place within hospitality management. The traditional view of food and beverage management was that the skills and knowledge it required were the defining corpus of knowledge of the hotel manager—not the sum of knowledge, not even the most valuable but definitely the part which defined the occupation as distinct from other forms of management. In other words, food and beverage management, in whatever guise it appears, is the special knowledge, the unique bit. What is more it could be said the food and beverage is the "rock 'n' roll" of hospitality management—complex, risky, creative, glamorous, dirty and messy but definitely a challenge. The [antithesis] of this view is that as most profit is made on the sale of rooms, food and beverage therefore is a subservient set of skills to those of accommodation management. In the move towards hotel management as a pure business, rooms have won

the day and this has led to the subcontracting of the food and beverage functions in hotels. To an extent this is an understandable reaction to the perennial dilemma of making any hotel restaurant profitable (Riley, 2000b). Yet this argument is not complete until the value of food and beverage, first as a contributor to hotel image, second, as constant source of business and finally, as the bedrock of cash-flow, are added in (Riley and Davis, 1992). Managing food and beverage is more complex than managing rooms and it demands a greater range of knowledge and a degree of creativity, which room management does not. It is for this reason that traditionally the career paths of hotel managers have been strewn with food and beverage experience. Yet this again is changing as financial and marketing skills come to the fore. Certainly, the modern food and beverage manager has to take on board more marketing skills and graft them on to the old skills of menu engineering based on knowledge of cuisine. Food and beverage management is a creative management activity and, to an extent, the creative end of marketing, namely the designers, have invaded this creative space. Designers and chefs have come together with entrepreneurs to innovate in the industry, adding a level of creativity to the "catering process" that lies beneath. It may well be that the need to innovate has added more to the role of food and beverage manager than it can be expected to carry and therefore subcontracting and specialisation is only natural.

In all this talk of specialisation and corporate brands, it is time to hear it for the small independents which are, after all, the majority of establishments. The romantic idea of opening a restaurant still has its appeal and people succeed and fail in a way that is still mysterious to rational thinking. If there is one message from the small business sector, it is that the feasibility study can be defied—people succeed against the odds by their drive and commitment and people fail when they should, on paper, succeed. It is, however, worth saying that the old idea of opening a restaurant motivated by romantic optimism is suffering from diminishing returns. Basic business acumen and some training are definitely an advantage. Success, however, is never permanent and restaurant and bar concepts need to be refreshed regularly as markets shift and public taste changes. Here again the influence of strategic thinking has entered the world of small restaurants, which are being encouraged to "cluster" in close proximity to form mini-destinations that can be marketed.

It is easy to undervalue the obvious and to an extent food and beverage is suffering from this trait. National cuisine, however, is now being recognised as being part of the attraction of a destination and given its rightful place in tourism destination marketing campaigns. Furthermore, the quality of experience of holidays has now to take on board the quality of food and drink

(Riley, 2000a). This is boost for the prestige of this activity.

Has the function of food and beverage management really changed? The answer is yes and no. It is an example where manual skills are closely connected to creative intellectuals skills. The chef, the accountant, the marketer, and the designer were never closer. In educational terms, what does it mean to study food and beverage management? It means having a deep understanding of food and wine and other beverages in order to be able to engineer menus, being able to cook to a degree that would facilitate designing production systems, and being able to cost and control food—an activity that looks easy but which is hard in practice. On top of this would come the skills of hospitality and the commercial skills of marketing. Whether vocational education had grasped this particular problem is a matter of conjecture. In education, food and beverage training sits very uncomfortably at the intersections between generic and vocational, education and on-job training, and public and private funding. It is this position that is a threat to skills and makes it hard to modernise.

6.3 A DAY IN THE LIFE OF A CATERING/CONVENTION SERVICES MANAGER ROBYN GRAFF

5:30 A.M. – the alarm goes off. My nerves and excitement aid the early wake-up process. I make sure that my shirt is neatly pressed, my makeup and hair make me look professional, and my metro card is in my wallet. I join about 12 other people on my apartment complex's shuttle, and head for the train. After a 30-minute

train ride, I get off at my stop and realize that I have no clue which exit to walk out of. I quickly choose to walk to the right. As I head up the escalator, I know that I have chosen the wrong exit. After a quick glance at the map, and walking a few extra blocks, I finally make it to the employee entrance of the Hyatt.

First stop … human resources. I am greeted with warm smiles, and a stack of paperwork to fill out. With my Social Security card and driver's license in hand, I start on the plethora of tax forms, the employee handbook, and a series of policies to read and sign. No more than 5 minutes after my pen hits the first paper, the director of human resources comes flying into the office, directs me to grab my purse and a form of identification and follow her. We go running through the back of the hotel, which to me was almost like a maze. Eventually, we end up on the front drive, where a very professional-looking man is waiting for us. The first thought that comes to mind is that this is the general manager, and I should introduce myself … but, there is no time! Within a matter of seconds a cab pulls up, and the three of us jump in. We pull around to the back, pick up another employee, and tell the cab driver to drive as fast as he can. As we reach our destination, I am told that we are going to have to run … and run we do! The four of us jump out of the cab, and run to the front door of an unmarked building, where upon entrance we have to go through security and show identification. It isn't until we get inside of the elevators that everyone takes a deep breath, and I am informed we are at court for an unemployment hearing. And that is how my career with Hyatt began!

Throughout my first five months with Hyatt, I participated in the Corporate Management Training Program, with a concentration in Catering. Each day during the program proved to hold a different adventure. I had to rotate through each department of the hotel; human resources, front office, housekeeping, sales, engineering, food and beverage, and catering. While every department in the hotel operates in a different

manner, there was always a morning preshift meeting, regardless of which area of the hotel I was working in. Some days I was learning the ropes at the front desk, which involved checking guests in and out of the hotel, storing luggage, and answering questions regarding the city's attractions. Other days involved managing the restaurant, making beds, fixing light bulbs, running in-room dining orders, and shadowing security.

After 5 months of training, I proved I was ready for a position in the catering department. I was promoted to catering/convention services manager, and finally had an office to call home. While each day still holds a different adventure, there is more of a daily routine that I am able to follow.

I typically arrive at the hotel by 7:30 A.M. each morning. Upon entering the employee entrance I say good morning to the security guard in the security office, and wait patiently for the elevator (which can sometimes take a while!). The elevator drops me in the main kitchen, where I say my good mornings to the restaurant servers and chefs, while the smell of "everything bagels" makes my stomach start to growl. After heading into the executive office, the first thing I do is turn on my computer, put my purse in the cabinet, and put on my name tag.

My office is conveniently located right near the coffee machine. While I check my emails, I chat with all of my coworkers while they grab their first cup of coffee for the day. Each Monday, Wednesday, and Friday morning, at 8:00 A.M., the managers in my department head into our boss's office, where we have our morning stand-up meeting. We go around the room and report what we are going to be working on that day and voice any ideas or concerns we are having. Our director then fills us in on any news he has from the corporate office and lets us know if there is anything he will need from us that day.

After stand-up, we head down to the training room for menu reading. Those present for menu reading are the catering managers, a banquet manager, chef, steward, and purchasing director. We go through all of the menus for groups that will be in-house that day and the next day. Once everyone is on the same page, we all go back to our respective departments. . . . Some days we can finish in 15 minutes; other days, it can take us an hour to get through everything.

The rest of the morning consists of touching base with clients and taking care of their needs. This can range from changing a date on a reservation to sending our menus via email, to putting together an entire program of events. By 12:30 P.M., it's time for lunch! Three or four of us head down to the cafeteria, filled with many other hungry employees. There are different lunch items every day, but I usually end my lunch with some frozen yogurt!

After lunch, it's back to the computer to respond to client emails, and work on programs. On Thursday afternoons we hold our Resume Meeting. A representative from each department is present, and the convention services managers and sales managers go over detailed information regarding their groups. The information ranges from billing, to menus, to VIPs, in order to get the hotel ready for groups that are coming in to the hotel in the upcoming week.

By 5:30 P.M. people start to filter out of the office. I take off my heels, put on comfy shoes, and grab my purse. Typically, those of us that take the metro round each other up and start our journey home. While every day is a new adventure, it never seems to get old!

6.4 BEST PRACTICES IN FOOD AND BEVERAGE MANAGEMENT

JUDY A. SIGUAW AND CATHY A. ENZ

One critical attribute of successful hotel food and beverage outlets is their ability to appropriately respond to the changing needs of the market while maintaining a profitable operation. Yet few hotel food and beverage outlets excel at this fundamental strategy. Instead, generic restaurants that provide undistinguished menu items and offer guests a poor value-for-money proposition frequently characterize hotel food service. Such hotel restaurants fail to provide menu choices, ambience, or service desired by the dining-out market (let alone their guests), and therefore they frequently operate at a loss. Indeed, some analysts have declared that hotel restaurants by their nature will lose money (Hanson, 1984).

Recently, as part of a large, comprehensive study on best practices in the United States lodging industry conducted by Cornell University's School of Hotel Administration (Dubé et al., 1999), we identified a group of best-practice food and beverage champions who had developed practices to successfully accomplish the strategic charge of profitably meeting customer needs. The champions selected via an intense screening process are The Boulders, The Breakers, Country Inns & Suites, Four Seasons & Regent Hotels & Resorts, The Greenbrier, Hyatt Arlington Hotel, The Pierre, Walt Disney World Resorts and Theme Parks, The Waldorf-Astoria, and Wyndham Hotels and Resorts (see Table 6.1). Through their best practices, this select group demonstrates the capability of executing the strategic mandate of making money while responding to the needs of their target markets through revitalized food and beverage operations.

In the following pages we first present several practices that have been used by our food and beverage champions to provide their outlets with a competitive advantage. We then examine the measures of success and report the advice our champions give others on how to prosper with hotel food and beverage service.

Table 6.1 Overview of Food and Beverage Best-Practice Champions

F&B CHAMPIONS	PRACTICE INITIATED, DEVELOPED	MEASURE OF SUCCESS
The Boulders	Food forager to improve quality of restaurant offerings	Increased food quality, decreased food cost, decreased waitstaff turnover, and increased prices, profits, and waitstaff gratuities
The Breakers	Single-theme restaurant concepts	Increased revenues
Country Inns & Suites	Cobranding of hotel and brand-name restaurant	Increased customer satisfaction, reduced hotel capital cost (from not building a hotel restaurant), increased lunch and dinner business
Four Seasons & Regent Hotels & Resorts	Single dining venue with broad cuisine choices (and two dining rooms)	Boosted capture rate of hotel guests; increased local patronage, labor cost savings
The Greenbrier	Establishing resort as a center for culinary excellence, including a culinary-apprentice program	Maintained occupancy and reputation, retained skilled kitchen staff, increased off-season business
Hyatt Arlington Hotel	Reconceptualization and redesign of dated dining room, sports bar, and lobby lounge	Doubled revenues and cover counts, received rave reviews
The Pierre	Independent consultant made responsible for food purchases (with preferred-vendor program)	Decreased food and kitchen labor costs, reduced number of vendors
The Waldorf-Astoria	Applying revenue-management practices in all F&B outlets (plus staff training)	Doubled cover counts, increased effectiveness of F&B marketing, improved customer satisfaction
Walt Disney World Resorts and Theme Parks	Restaurants designed to provide a touchable experience	Achieved high customer satisfaction and return rate
Wyndham Hotels and Resorts	Upgrade of organization's food and beverage culture	Achieved higher average checks, increased staff earnings and retention, increased total sales, wine sales, and profits

✦ THE BEST PRACTICES

The best practices adopted by our champions can be broadly categorized into three areas. One group stresses providing a high-quality F&B product to their guests (comprising practices by The Boulders, Country Inns & Suites, Four Seasons & Regent Hotels & Resorts, The Greenbrier, and Wyndham Hotels and Resorts).

A second group emphasizes the elements of restaurant concept and design in their best practices (namely, The Breakers Hotel, Hyatt Arlington Hotel, and Walt Disney World Resorts and Theme Parks). Finally, The Pierre's and The Waldorf-Astoria's best practices focused primarily on controlling costs and generating additional revenue (see Table 6.2).

Table 6.2 Food and Beverage Best-Practice Cases, Descriptions, Implementations, and Contact People

F&B CHAMPION, TITLE OF CASE	DESCRIPTION OF CASE	METHOD OF IMPLEMENTATION	CONTACT PERSON
The Boulders *Food Forager to Improve Quality in F&B*	Created position of food forager to obtain the best fresh products, allowing creativity in the kitchen.	Forager first focused on buying the highest-quality produce only within the state of Arizona, where the resort is located. Later, the forager broadened the search and expanded the number of items sought. Forager hotline keeps all F&B outlets apprised of incoming supplies. Menus are restructured around the products the forager finds.	Gray Ferguson, *food and beverage director* 602–488–9009 Fax: 602–595–4664
The Breakers *Annual Food and Beverage Staff Reorganization and Single-theme Restaurant Concepts*	Replaced formal dining and casual dining restaurants and bars with single-theme outlets to give the guest the choice of the cuisine desired rather than the choice being dictated by the guest's attire.	Transformed old-fashioned formal dining room into a modern, Florentine restaurant; casual restaurant into a top-caliber steakhouse; main bar into an oceanside restaurant; and a Victorian restaurant into a southern Italian pasta house, plus opened a French Riviera-style restaurant.	Joanne Schultz, *director of food and beverage* 561–659–8434 Fax: 561–659–8452
Country Inns and Suites *Successful Cobranding with Established Restaurant Concepts*	Developed cobranding strategy to locate Country Inns and Suites adjacent to (co-owned) T.G.I. Friday's or Italiani's.	Seeks an "A" location that provides visibility, convenience, high traffic count, and proximity to dense residential areas for the restaurant. Positions restaurant at forefront of property.	Paul Kirwin, *president* 612–212–1326 Fax: 612–212–1338

Table 6.2 *(Continued)*

F&B CHAMPION, TITLE OF CASE	DESCRIPTION OF CASE	METHOD OF IMPLEMENTATION *	CONTACT PERSON
Four Seasons and Regent *Informal Dining Venue and Alternative Cuisine*	Uses only one F&B outlet with two dining rooms. Provides cuisine choices of Alternative Cuisine, homestyle, and vegetarian options.	Single outlet allows for a focused approach for improving food quality and presentation, grasp of small details, and delivering of higher service levels because of small, qualified staff. Alternative cuisine was developed in response to a need for healthier items, homestyle cuisine was added for frequent travelers who were tired of traditional restaurant food, and vegetarian was added due to increased trend of vegetarianism among guests.	Alfons Konrad, *senior vice president, food and beverage* 416–441–4306 Fax: 416–441–4381
The Greenbrier *Programs Establishing the Resort as a Center for Culinary Excellence*	Instituting a formal culinary apprentice program, a culinary school for guests, conferences and seminars with food critics and writers, and a high school culinary training program. Also publishes *The Greenbrier Cookbook* and sends newsletters to 600,000 guests.	Established relationships with principal culinary schools in the United States. Opened formal three-year apprentice program to graduates of two-year culinary schools or individuals with equivalent experience. Successful applicants work in all areas of the hotel's kitchens and attend formal classes. Promises permanent employment to applicants from local high school.	Rod Stoner, *vice president of food and beverage* 304–536–1110 Fax: 304–536–7860
Hyatt Arlington Hotel *Redesigning and Revitalizing a Food and Beverage Outlet*	Dated dining room, sports bar, and lobby lounge were reconceptualized into Mediterranean cuisine restaurant.	Comprehensive research and analysis indicated likely success of a fusion of contemporary and Mediterranean themes. Floor-to-ceiling windows replaced one side of building, and martini bar complemented redesigned restaurant.	George Vizer, *general manager* 703–525–1234 Fax: 703–875–3298
The Pierre *F&B Cost-Plus Purchasing Agreements*	Has given financial responsibility for food purchasing to an independent consultant.	The consultant and executive chef write specifications for food products; consultant negotiates contracts with a single vendor in each food category on a percentage markup basis. Consultant audits the vendors' books annually.	Franz Klampfer, *executive chef* 212–838–2000 Fax: 212–826–0319

Table 6.2 *(Continued)*

F&B CHAMPION, TITLE OF CASE	DESCRIPTION OF CASE	METHOD OF IMPLEMENTATION	CONTACT PERSON
The Waldorf-Astoria *Revenue Maximization for the Food and Beverage Department*	Instituted revenue management for all food and beverage outlets, scheduled staff more efficiently, and repositioned outlets to attract non-hotel markets.	Each unit developed a plan to increase revenue and profitability, with a focus on reducing labor costs. Matched staffing levels with expected volume of business. Trained line staff to ensure the highest level of service.	Christophe Le Chatton, *director of food and beverage* 212–355–3000 ext. 4804 Fax: 212–872–7272
Walt Disney World *Providing a Touchable Dining Experience*	A touchable dining experience is provided via the atmosphere and the food to transport guests to another setting, another country, or another culture while they dine.	Theme restaurants are designed to be as authentic as possible in the decor, menu, beverages, and service. Line-level employees are empowered to make decisions with respect to service recovery.	Dieter Hannig, *vice president of food and beverage* 407–566–5800 Fax: 407–560–9131
Wyndham *An Integrated Approach to Food and Beverage*	Created "Best of Class" program to upgrade the food and beverage culture.	Reengineered menus and recipes; reconceptualized restaurants; modified dining rooms and introduced exhibition kitchens; upgraded tabletops and uniforms, and china, glass, silver, and specialty merchandise; developed seasonal F&B festivals and promotions; promoted F&B products within the hotels; recruited culinary talent; obtained unique product from vendors; implemented wine-by-the-glass program; developed server-training program emphasizing product knowledge and upselling; implemented waitstaff incentive programs; and reinvented room service standard operating procedures.	Patrick Colombo, *vice president of food and beverage concepts* 214–863–1000 Fax: 214–863–1665

Note: The case titles correspond to the cases written on each champion in: Laurette Dubé, Cathy A. Enz, Leo M. Renaghan, and Judy A. Siguaw, *American Lodging Excellence: The Key to Best Practices in the U.S. Lodging Industry* (Washington, DC: American Express and the American Hotel Foundation, 1999).

✦ FOCUS ON PRODUCT QUALITY

The problem for The Boulders was that the variety and quality of the produce it was obtaining were not up to the resort's high standards. As a result, the food and beverage department's culinary passion seemed to be declining along with the quality of the food ingredients. The resort's management responded by creating the position of food forager, who initially focused on buying high-quality produce locally (in Arizona). Later, though, the forager traveled farther afield and took on the additional responsibilities of purchasing spices, shellfish, cheeses, and meats. To keep the kitchen apprised of what items are coming, the forager uses a hotline to report expected delivery dates and expenditures. The Boulders' chefs then adjust menus based on the incoming items. Consequently, the food ingredients are of the highest quality, and the chefs have the chance to experiment with a continuously changing menu.

Also seeking to instill a passion for food and beverage, Wyndham Hotels and Resorts designed its "Best of Class" program, with the overall objective of making Wyndham a leader in food and beverage innovation, quality, and service. The Best of Class was a wide-ranging effort that involved both sides of the house. The chain:

1. Reengineered menus and recipes.
2. Reconceptualized its restaurants.
3. Modified dining rooms and introduced display kitchens.
4. Upgraded tabletops, waitstaff uniforms, china, glass, silver, and specialty merchandising pieces.
5. Developed seasonal food festivals and beverage promotions.
6. Promoted F&B products within the hotels.
7. Recruited outstanding culinary talent.
8. Collaborated with food vendors to obtain distinctive products and with wine vendors to upgrade wine lists and conduct tastings.
9. Implemented a wine-by-the-glass program using premium varietals with high brand awareness.
10. Developed a server training program that emphasizes product knowledge and upselling techniques.
11. Implemented incentive programs designed to motivate servers to become better educated about food and wines being served.
12. Reinvented room service procedures by providing training in proper service etiquette, modifying training videos and manuals, and upgrading equipment.
13. Revised in-house marketing materials, such as menus and in-room directories.

To deliver high-quality food and beverage products to its guests, Country Inns & Suites chose to develop a cobranding strategy with restaurant brands that are co-owned by Carlson but freestanding, primarily T.G.I. Friday's or Italiani's. This practice ensures the guest access to a high-quality, brand-name restaurant on site, but it eliminates the capital cost of building a generic restaurant in the hotel. While the core concept of locating a limited-service hotel adjacent to a restaurant is not new, Carlson's approach to the strategy is innovative, since it owns all the brands (another brand that expressly pursued a strategy of locating next to restaurants in the 1980s was Days Inns). To implement this cobranding strategy, Carlson seeks a large, "A" location that will support the restaurant, which is built at the forefront of the property for visibility. Both the restaurant and hotel benefit from this arrangement.

The goal of Four Seasons hotels is to be rated as having one of a given city's top three restaurants. To achieve this goal the chain offers a single restaurant in its hotels—but that restaurant has two dining rooms, one more formal and one less formal. Thus, with a single F&B outlet the hotel can offer two dining rooms that differ in design, but that share the same menu, chefs, line cooks, and kitchens. Compared to having multiple outlets, this approach allows its F&B staff members to provide greater attention to food quality and presentation, to focus on small details, and to deliver higher service levels via a small, highly qualified staff. In response to guests' stated desire for alternatives to a heavy, meat-based cuisine, Four Seasons has broadened its menu choices to include its trademark Alternative Cuisine, comprising a nutritionally balanced menu of alternative meals, vegetarian dishes, and homestyle preparations. Alternative Cuisine items are low in fat, cholesterol, sodium, and calories to correspond with guests' greater interest in health and fitness. Similarly, vegetarian recipes have been added to the menu in response to an increased trend toward vegetarianism among guests. Homestyle recipes, on the other hand, are just what the name implies: they have been developed from the chefs' favorite family recipes. The latter cuisine choice suits travel-weary guests who wish for a home-cooked meal.

The Greenbrier has instituted several practices to establish itself as a center for culinary excellence. The resort had to address two major problems, both of which stemmed from its remote location. First, for a time the resort was having difficulty attracting and retaining experienced culinary personnel. To end a constant cycle of recruiting and training workers and to improve the food product being offered to guests, The Greenbrier established a 3-year culinary apprenticeship program. The resort recruits candidates from principal culinary schools in the United States to complete an apprenticeship in all areas of the kitchens, as well as attend classes. Because the program runs for 3 years, the apprenticeship

has helped to stabilize the kitchen staff. Further stability comes from an agreement with the local high school by which the resort will provide permanent employment to interested students. The second problem is attracting guests during shoulder and off-season times. Continuing with its theme of culinary education, The Greenbrier established cooking classes for guests and promoted symposiums conducted by food critics and writers. The Greenbrier issues a quarterly newsletter to 600,000 guests and has published *The Greenbrier Cookbook* to further identify the resort as a culinary center—and to remain in contact with potential guests.

✦ RESTAURANT DESIGN AND CONCEPTUALIZATION

The common thread of the following cases that feature restaurant redesign is that the existing restaurants were operated in a functionally competent fashion. They had lost their competitive spark, however (or stood in danger of doing so), because of changes in guests' preferences. In response, operators took a lead from freestanding restaurants and focused tightly on customers' current wishes for theme-based casual dining.

The Breakers recognized that the public has long had an aversion to hotel restaurants, which stems from the days when hotel restaurants tried to have some of every variety of food they thought a guest might desire—none of it particularly distinguished and all of it seemingly overpriced. In response to guests' negative feelings about hotel restaurants, many hotels have dropped foodservice entirely, but this option is not open to a five-star hotel or resort. Instead, The Breakers chose to create its own strong restaurant identities through single-theme outlets that replaced the resort's existing formal- and casual-dining restaurants and bars. The practice not only helped The Breakers change the public perception of hotel restaurants but also allowed guests to choose their cuisine according to what they wanted to eat, rather than what they wanted to wear. Thus, the resort's old-fashioned formal dining room became a modern, Florentine-style gourmet restaurant. The owners converted the former casual dining room to a top-caliber steak house—with ambience to match. Perhaps most strikingly, the resort converted its main bar and lounge, which had virtually no business during the day, to a beautiful oceanside seafood restaurant. The former Victorian restaurant became a Southern Italian–style pasta house, and the Beach Club was converted to a French Riviera–style restaurant. Thus, the resort now has five restaurants that feature their own distinctive decor and ambience, without a loss in food quality.

The food and beverage outlets of the Hyatt Arlington Hotel similarly had lost their customer appeal because of their dated concept and design. After the hotel undertook a comprehensive market research study, the hotel's managers selected a restaurant theme that blends contemporary (postmodern) and Mediterranean concepts. In developing the new theme, the hotel replaced the restaurant's outer wall with floor-to-ceiling windows to transform the previously dark and unimaginative restaurant into a sun-drenched venue splashed with the Mediterranean's vivid colors. To complement the new restaurant, the hotel installed a quintessential martini bar.

Walt Disney World (WDW) Resorts and Theme Parks has long recognized the value of themes to a guest's experience—not only in its parks but also in its many restaurants. Conse-quently, WDW set out to create a "touchable" foodservice experience for the guest that combines design, decor, ambience, food, service, and entertainment in such a way as to stimulate all of the senses, not just the palate. The idea is to "offer a personal experience which is highly customized, memorable, and judged by our guests to be worth the price," remarked Dieter Hannig, vice president of F&B.

With more than 500 theme food and beverage outlets, WDW's managers realized that a restaurant's design is crucial to providing the "touchable" experience for the guest. Each restaurant is designed to be as thematically authentic as possible so that all elements of the physical facility and operations combine to transport the guest to another setting, country, or culture. The dining adventure is intended to produce the feelings, tastes, sounds, and excitement the guest would experience at the actual locale being replicated. Access to the restaurants is designed to be easy and uncomplicated. Accordingly, many restaurants are freestanding so that guests do not have to walk into hotel lobbies or down corridors. Further, line-level employees are empowered to make decisions to improve service recovery and ensure a great dining experience for the guest.

✦ CONTROLLING COSTS

Our last two champions focused on costs and revenues in the food and beverage arena. The Pierre focused on upgrading its restaurant's purchasing function—that is, setting specifications, selecting vendors, obtaining best prices, and monitoring receiving. However, The Pierre's management was concerned that controlling purchasing activities would divert the executive chef's attention from the kitchen's culinary creations. To allow the executive chef to focus on the menu the hotel delegated financial responsibility for food purchasing to an independent consultant, who worked with the chefs to develop specifications for all food products. The consultant analyzes available foodstuffs and may recommend changing specifications if a less expensive item can be substituted without comprising quality or when off-site preparation would be equally good but less expensive than preparing the food item on site. The consultant also trained kitchen employees to adhere to strict receiving standards. Most important to cost control, the consultant negotiated contracts with each vendor specifying that the vendor would earn a given percentage profit over its cost. (Some existing vendors may have blanched at this proposal, but most signed on to keep the hotel's business.) To ensure that costs are in line and that vendors are fulfilling their agreements, the consultant regularly audits inventory and cost lists from each vendor and annually audits the vendors' books to verify that the vendors are accurately stating the cost of each item.

The Waldorf-Astoria's management also believed that the revenue potential of the hotel's foodservice operations was not being achieved, but they looked beyond cost controls. Instead, the hotel took several steps to boost F&B revenue—instituting a revenue management program, implementing cost-cutting measures, training chefs to schedule employees more efficiently, and repositioning F&B outlets to attract guests from outside the hotel. The hotel created a marketing position to coordinate the marketing efforts of all food and beverage units and to help implement revenue-maximization efforts. Service recovery systems were improved. The hotel trained line employees on wines to improve their efforts in selling and serving wines. A new restaurant reservations system was introduced to improve dining-room use, cut telephone use in restaurants, and improve communication with guests. Lastly, a dining-out program, which allowed servers and kitchen employees to dine in various Waldorf-Astoria restaurants, generated many ideas for improvement and created an increased awareness of food and service quality.

✦ SUCCESS OF THE PRACTICES

The success of these practices can be gauged by various indices, depending on the practice. The food forager program at The Boulders, for instance, improved the quality of the food and lowered food costs. With new and interesting foodstuffs, the chefs have developed distinctive menus that allowed price increases—boosting average checks and profits. As a result of the increased average check, waitstaff gratuities are higher and employee turnover has been reduced. The resort also implemented menu meetings in which chefs explain their creations to servers. Chefs are once again passionate about their creations, and the meetings have created a greater rapport between the front and back of the house.

Wyndham's "Best of Class" program also re-energized the chain's F&B culture—resulting in a 15 percent increase in total sales and a 40 percent increase in wine sales. Since costs were controlled as part of the program, the hotels enjoy a 55 percent profit flow-through on the newly generated revenue. As at The Boulders, Wyndham's higher average checks have increased staff earnings and improved retention. In addition, the promotion of high-quality food has upgraded the chain's overall image.

At The Breakers the new theme restaurants have increased F&B revenue by 70 percent over the last 4 years, with much of the growth being fueled by the substantial amount of local business attracted by the new outlets. Likewise, the Hyatt Arlington Hotel has doubled cover counts and revenues since its restaurant renovation, and the restaurant receives rave reviews.

One of many reasons that guests choose to stay at The Greenbrier is its excellent culinary reputation. Thus, its reputation as a center for culinary excellence plays an important role in maintaining guestroom occupancy. The ability of Walt Disney World Resorts and Theme Parks restaurants to provide a "touchable" dining experience contributes significantly to WDW's profitability. Furthermore, both the number of return guests and percentage of satisfied customers are high—and several WDW restaurants have won awards in recent years (see sidebar).

WALT DISNEY WORLD'S F&B AWARDS: A SAMPLING

Since 1989, Walt Disney World properties have earned more than 100 food and beverage awards. Listed below is a representative sample of those honors.

- "Best Chain Overall Beverage Program Award" (2008), from *Cheers* magazine, awarded to Walt Disney World Resort.
- "DiRoNA Award of Excellence" (2007), from *DiRoNA*, awarded to Napa Rose.
- "Award of Excellence" (2004, 2005, 2006, and 2007), from *Wine Spectator* Magazine, awarded to Todd English's Bluezoo.
- "Best out of Washington State Wine Program" (2006), from *Washington Wine Restaurant Awards*, awarded to Artist Point.
- "Best Steakhouse" from *Zagat's*, awarded to Shula's Steak House.
- "Best Hotel Bar" (2004), from *Best of Citysearch*, awarded to Kimonos.
- "Award of Excellence" (1999), from *Wine Spectator* magazine, awarded to Victoria & Albert's.
- "Best Wine and Spirits Restaurant of the Year" (1999), from *Santé* magazine, awarded to California Grill.

- One of the "Top Ten Sports Bars in the Country" (1998), from *USA Today*, and one of the "Top Five Sports Bars in the Country" (1998), from *Men's Health*, both honors awarded to ESPN Club.
- "Best Kid's Menu" (1998, Readers' Choice Foodie Awards), from *Orlando Sentinel*, awarded to Chef Mickey's.
- Among the "Best New Restaurants" (1998), from *Esquire*, awarded to Citricos.
- "Best Cover" (1998), from *Restaurant Forum*, awarded to Flying Fish Cafe.
- "Restaurant Wine Award" (1995), from *Wine Enthusiast*, awarded to Artist Point.
- "Most Imaginative" (1993), from the National Restaurant Association, awarded to Grand Floridian Café.
- "America's Best Bar Menu" (1993), from *Cheers* magazine, awarded to Crew's Cup Lounge.
- "Top of the Table" (1991, first place), from *Restaurant Hospitality* magazine, one each awarded to Beaches and Cream Soda Shop and the Yacht Club Galley.

The Country Inns & Suites cobranding strategy has been a winning situation both for the hotels and for guests. For guests, having a popular brand-name restaurant adjacent to the hotel ensures that their dining needs will be satisfied. For the restaurant, the hotel guests account for 15 to 20 percent of its business. For the hotel, the proximity of a name-brand restaurant is an amenity that can encourage guests to book a room.

By using an independent consultant to negotiate with vendors and to monitor the F&B purchasing function, The Pierre was able to reduce food costs by approximately 5 percent and kitchen labor costs by 2 percent. In addition, the number of vendors used has decreased, resulting in greater efficiency for the hotel. Finally, The Waldorf-Astoria's revenue maximization strategy improved cover counts by a staggering 100 percent, while increasing wine sales and guest satisfaction.

✦ INSIGHTS

Our food and beverage champions offer the following advice and observations to managers seeking to implement similar programs:

1. The foundation for successful implementation is meeting challenges with enthusiasm and passion.
2. Some practices, such as food purchasing by an independent consultant, may not be warmly received by staff or vendors, but the commitment of upper management and a demonstration of benefits will help gain acceptance.
3. Those practices that require constant adaptation (like the food forager) will not work in a rigidly structured organization.
4. Cobranding strategies are suitable only when the hotels are partnered with restaurants that are targeting the same market segment.

5. Hotel F&B outlets' development must incorporate the guest's total experience (and focus on competing with freestanding restaurants).
6. Resources must be focused on a relentless commitment to food and beverage consistency, even when business is slow.

✦ PROFITABLE AND VITAL

Contrary to much conventional wisdom, the experience of these F&B champions shows that hotel restaurants can not only turn a profit but can contribute greatly to the hotel's overall competitive position. We note, however, that virtually all the F&B champions are operating in the upscale, deluxe, and resort segments of the lodging industry. While many hotel restaurants at all levels struggle to turn a profit, the actions of our champions indicate that focusing on guests' needs can radically reverse the downward trend of hotel restaurants. As Rod Stoner, vice president of food and beverage at The Greenbrier, pointed out, managers must stay abreast of industry trends, study the programs of other properties, and seek distinctive ideas for adaptation to their own hotels. This overview of best practices in food and beverage champions provides a starting point for what Stoner suggests. We hope that those managers seeking to revitalize or maximize the revenue potentials of their F&B operations will carefully examine the practices discussed here and will continue their progress by also investigating the practices of other properties and other industries. As a result, forward-thinking managers will be able to identify those best practices that will serve as the catalyst for improving customer satisfaction and financial performance.

6.5 STRATEGIC ALLIANCES BETWEEN HOTELS AND RESTAURANTS

ROBERT W. STRATE AND CLINTON L. RAPPOLE

Over the years hotel restaurants have often been managed as a secondary function of the hotel—that is, as a costly amenity rather than a revenue center. In part because of the high cost structure of hotel restaurants, which means high prices relative to other restaurants, they developed among potential customers a reputation for being a poor value, offering indifferent service and inferior food. Today, however, many hotel companies are rethinking how to integrate food and beverage services into lodging facilities. In the process of doing so, hotel owners and operators are asking at least four key questions about their property-level F&B service.

- What are the hotel customers' food and beverage needs and expectations?

- Which food and beverage concept best aligns with the positioning of the hotel?

- Would converting the hotel's restaurant to a brand-name restaurant concept improve the property's overall bottom line?

- Would turning to a brand-name F&B operation give the property a competitive edge?

Two results of owners' and operators' new focus on hotel food service are that (1) innovative hotel F&B concepts are being created, and (2) strategic alliances are being established between well-known brand-name hotel and restaurant companies.

The primary focus of this article is to answer the four questions stated above and provide the basic decision-making framework for matching the correct F&B concept to the target market for which the hotel has been positioned. We will identify key criteria for establishing a seamless partnership between the hotel and the restaurant. The results of such a marriage should be an improved property image overall, enhanced customer value, increased revenues, and a competitive edge. The following four main topics will be addressed:

- The value of a brand-name partner

- Existing hotel-and-restaurant alliances

- A description of Bristol Hotel Company's alliance with Good Eats Grill (including critical-decision elements)

- Future trends

✦ ALLIANCES

Developing alliances between brand-name hotel and restaurant companies is not a new business strategy, but it does seem that this approach is currently being used more frequently than ever to help companies maximize their profit potential (*Lodging,* September 1995). There are at least five reasons for this. An alliance may:

1. Create financial benefits.
2. Provide customers with greater value.
3. Improve a property's overall image.
4. Strengthen an operation's competitive position.
5. Create operational advantages.

One of the first branded restaurant concepts to operate in hotels was probably Trader Vic's, founded by Victor Bergen in 1937. By 1949 Western Hotels (which became Westin) integrated Trader Vic's into 13 hotel-based restaurants in nine countries (Witham, 1995a, 14). Other chains also hosted the restaurants and today, 60 years later, Trader Vic's still operates in such hotels as the Beverly Hilton, the Palmer House (Chicago), the Marriott Royal Garden Riverside (Bangkok), and the New Otani properties in Tokyo and Singapore. Ruth's Chris Steakhouse is another example of a popular restaurant brand operating successfully in unison with hotels, including properties operated by Hilton, Marriott, Holiday Inn, and Westin.

Despite the evidence of successful alliances between brand-name hotel and restaurant companies, most hotel companies manage their own food and beverage services, including those that also host Trader Vic's. In part that approach reflects the long industry tradition of offering travelers both food and lodging. The Marriott Corporation is a good example of a hotel company that has used this strategy of going it alone. John Randall, Marriott senior director of food and beverage concepts, states that it is Marriott's primary strategy to "completely manage our own F&B services to provide food, service, and quality consistency from property to property" (Hensdill, 1996).

The strategy of developing their own F&B concepts has not been successful for all hotel companies. This is evident from the frequent "reconcepting" found among hotel restaurants. A hotel might run a lounge one year, convert it into a brasserie the next year, and later decide to make it a grill. The end result is inconsistency in F&B service and quality, and therefore low sales and profits (Parseghian, 1996). Several factors may contribute to a general manager's believing that she or he can operate the hotel's restaurant services better than a branded restaurant company, not the least of which may be a sense of self-assurance. Some hotel general managers want to prove that they can provide a fine-dining experience whether or not a market actually exists. Others say it is because some hotel F&B operations continue to try to be all things to all people rather than providing a product that is affordable and matches customer expectations (Wolff, 1995, 24). Moreover, hotel restaurants in general have a high cost structure relative to the freestanding F&B operation down the street. Hotel restaurants have to contribute to the overall property's expenses while the restaurant next door has little capital expense and is probably just leasing square footage.

A current trend among hotels that have reevaluated their F&B operations is to replace the formal fine-dining, white-tablecloth concept with a more casual and relaxed dining experience (Allen, 1996; Liberson, 1996). Another trend indicates that more and more hotel companies are looking to establish strategic alliances with brand-name restaurant companies. Doing this has allowed hotel companies to focus on managing the hotel itself. Listed in Table 6.3 are examples of strategic alliances between hotel and restaurant companies. These examples illustrate that some of the largest hotel companies have already established strategic alliances with major restaurant chains.

✦ BRISTOL AND GOOD EATS GRILL

To comprehend fully the rationale and advantages of a hotel's decision to turn to a brand-

Table 6.3 Hotel and Restaurant Company Strategic Alliances

HOTEL COMPANIES	RESTAURANT COMPANIES
Holiday Inn Worldwide	Damon's, Denny's, Ruth's Chris Steakhouse, T.G.I. Friday's, Convenience Courts (Mrs. Fields, Little Caesars, Blimpies, Taco John's, Sara Lee)
Doubletree Hotel Corporation	New York Restaurant Group (Park Avenue Café, Mrs. Parks Café)
Marriott Hotels	Ruth's Chris Steakhouse, Studebakers, Benihana, Trader Vic's, Pizza Hut
Hilton Hotels	Trader Vic's, Benihana, Ruth's Chris Steakhouse, Damon's
Four Seasons	Bice Ristorante
Choice Hotels	Picks Food Courts, Pizza Hut
Promus Corporation	Grace Services, T.G.I. Friday's, Olive Garden, Pizza Hut
Radisson Hospitality Worldwide*	Carlson Hospitality* (T.G.I. Friday's, Country Kitchen), Damon's

*The relationship between Radisson Hospitality Worldwide and Carlson Hospitality is not an alliance per se but rather an example of a hotel company that owns and has vertically integrated both its lodging and foodservice products into one corporation.

Sources: "See Restaurant Chains Partner with Hotels to Satisfy Different Needs, Tastes," *Lodging,* September 1995, pp. 1, 8–9; "Holiday Inn Offers Assorted Food Options with New Quick Food Concept," *Hotel Business,* June 1996, p. 9; "Holiday Inn Offers Convenience Court Concept," *Nation's Restaurant News,* May 1996, p. 208; Frank H. Andorka, "High Recognition Restaurants," *Hotel & Motel Management,* November 1995, pp. 43–44; Cherie Hensdill, "Partnerships in Dining," *Hotels,* February 1996, pp. 57–60; Judy Liberson, "A Working Marriage," *Lodging,* February 1996, pp. 63–66; and Madelin Wexler, "Partnerships That Pay Off," *Hotels,* May 1995, pp. 47–50.

name restaurant for the hotel's foodservice, we analyzed the Bristol Hotel Company's decision to match two of their hotels with Good Eats Grill (Witham, 1995b, 13). Before creating the alliance with Good Eats Grill, the Bristol Hotel Company's primary F&B strategy was to use its own internally developed restaurant brands. This is a strategy that has worked well for Bristol—for example, eight outlets produced 32.4 percent F&B profit margins in 1995, and 20 out of 22 Bristol hotel-restaurants continue to use their own internally developed restaurant brands.

Despite the success of Bristol's own F&B operations, the firm decided to link two of its properties (Holiday Inns in Jackson, Mississippi, and Houston, Texas) with a franchised restau-

rant brand called Good Eats Grill—a concept developed by Gene Street, who also developed the Black Eyed Pea and Dixie House restaurant brands. We wondered why Bristol deviated from its successful formula, and so we decided to investigate why the Bristol Hotel Company elected to team with Good Eats Grill. We narrowed our focus and analysis even further by evaluating just the Houston property using interviews of the principals involved.

We asked executives from both Bristol and Good Eats Grill 70 questions in all, conducted site visits, and found additional research information in various hospitality periodicals. Additionally, Mike Feldott, of HRC Consultants, L.C., was a key adviser on restaurant brands and operations for hotels.

Product branding refers to establishing a well-known name for a given product or service whereby the particular product or service and its attributes are highly recognizable and easily recalled by consumers. The basic concept behind such so-called branding is to establish a standard on which consumers may rely to predict value (e.g., price, quality, convenience). Within the hotel industry a multitiered branding strategy has evolved among lodging companies. The following table illustrates how some hotel brands have become associated with different tiers. Note that some companies have developed products for more than one tier.

ECONOMY, LIMITED SERVICE	MIDDLE MARKET	LUXURY, FIRST CLASS	ALL SUITES
Motel 6	Holiday Inn	Four Seasons	Marriott Suites
Days Inn	Ramada Inn	Ritz-Carlton	Embassy Suites
La Quinta	Sheraton	Marriott Marquis	Residence Inns
Hampton Inn	Hilton	Beverly Hilton	Homewood Suites
Travelodge	Courtyard by Marriott	Hyatt	Bristol Suites
Sleep Inn	Radisson Guest Quarters	Westin	Clarion Suites

Source: Ron N. Nykiel, "Corporate Strategy within the Hospitality Industry," in *The Complete Travel Marketing Handbook*, ed. Andrew Vladimir (Lincolnwood, IL: NTC Business Books, 1988).

An example of the multiple-branding strategy can be illustrated by examining the different hotel brands of the Marriott Corporation. Marriott has developed Marriott Hotels, Marriott Resorts, Marriott Marquis, Courtyard by Marriott, Marriott Suites, Residence Inns, and Embassy Suites.

A somewhat similar branding strategy also exists in the restaurant industry, as shown in the following chart.

QUICK SERVICE	CASUAL, FAMILY	UPSCALE	THEME
McDonald's	Red Lobster	Ruth's Chris Steakhouse	Planet Hollywood
Taco Bell	T.G.I. Friday's	Trader Vic's	Hard Rock Café
Pizza Hut	Damon's	Del Frisco's	Benihana
Domino's	Good Eats Grill	Bice Ristorante	Lettuce Entertain You
KFC	Chili's	Palm Restaurant	Front Row Sports Grille
Church's	Olive Garden	NY Restaurant Group (Mrs. Parks)	Country Kitchen

The Country Hospitality Partnership, a subsidiary of Carlson Hospitality Worldwide, is an example of a restaurant company with a multitier branding strategy. The Country Hospitality Partnership restaurants include Country Kitchen (252 restaurants), T.G.I. Friday's (365 restaurants), Italiani's (14 restaurants), and Front Row Sports Grille (3 restaurants). Additionally, Carlson provides a good example of a hotel company that owns and has vertically integrated both the hotel and the restaurant product into one corporation. Carlson Companies, Inc., owns both Radisson Hotels Worldwide and Country Hospitality Partnership. The T.G.I. Friday's concept is being integrated into many Radisson Hotels (see: Laura Koss-Feder, "Radisson Seeks Marketing Advantages" *Hotel & Motel Management,* pp. 3, 43; Ron Ruggles, "T.G.I. Friday's Cruises into Summer," *Nation's Restaurant News,* June 1996, pp. 14, 43; and Lawrence White, "Growth Meister," *Lodging,* September 1996, pp. 52–58).

The Marriott Corporation is another example of a hospitality company that owns and integrated its own restaurant brands into its hotels. The key point is that the brand is recognizable, and this recognition equates to reliable value from the customer's perspective. This enhanced customer perception can be used by a firm to gain a competitive edge and, in turn, increase revenues and profits for the company.

Bristol Hotel Company. The Bristol Hotel Company is a 39-property chain with corporate headquarters in Dallas, Texas. In January 1995 Bristol acquired a Memphis-based hotel company, United Inns, Inc., that had 26 hotels based in six states. By the end of 1995 Bristol Hotel Company had grown from 8 to 38 properties with more than 10,000 rooms, which generated $192 million in total revenues. (Many of the properties acquired in 1995 required renovation, and many of these rooms were out of order, which negatively affected year-end 1995 financial numbers.) The revenues predicted for 1996 were around $250 million. The following key indices summarize Bristol Hotel Company's performance in 1995:

Average occupancy	64.10%
Average daily room rate	$62.67
RevPAR	$40.20
Gross operating margin	29.62%
Rooms margin	71.61%
Food, beverage margin	24.84%

Bristol primarily uses an owner-operator strategy versus management contracts in managing its hotels. As of the time of our study it owned 36 of its properties (93 percent) and managed the other three properties. Bristol's primary focus was in the full-service segment, with 35 full-service properties (89 percent) and only four limited-service properties.

Its primary target market is the mid- to upper-level corporate traveler (the source of 90 percent of the company's revenues). It also does substantial group-meeting business. Bristol is anticipating that full-service hotels will play an important role in meeting the future lodging and business demand of those two market segments. John Beckert, the chief operating officer of Bristol, considers the "full-service segment as a segment that has been somewhat abandoned, but Bristol considers the segment to be 'solid' as far as demand (anticipate 6 to 10 percent increase in demand) and a segment that allows for greater pricing power."

Table 6.4 Bristol Hotel Company Operating Strategies

STRATEGIES	IMPLEMENTATION
Unique management culture	Entrepreneurial and team-oriented
Control over hotel operations	Owner-operator focus
Assets in select geographic markets	28 properties located in Atlanta, Dallas, and Houston (fast-growing markets)
Direct sales and marketing	Focus on local market
Flexible use of brand names	*Operate under its own brand names:* Harvey Hotels, Bristol Suites, Harvey Suites *Operate under national franchise brands:* Holiday Inn, Marriott, Promus properties, Hospitality Franchise Systems brands
Emphasis on food and beverage services	Bristol's F&B profit margins (32 percent original eight and 25 percent overall) are above December 1994 national industry levels of 17.1 percent.

Source: Bristol Hotel Company 1995 Annual Report

Bristol's overall strategy is to provide customers with a first-class-hotel experience—but without being stuffy—and extraordinary overall value (price and quality). While those goals are not unusual among hotel companies, Bristol has distinguished itself in several ways. First, it has an excellent track record, established in part by achieving strong operating and financial results during the industry's recent recession.

Second, it maintains a distinct corporate culture and management style that translates into low executive-management turnover.

Third, its centralized management structure allows managers to focus on the quality of a guest's stay as the number-one priority.

The company's primary operating strategies are listed in Table 6.4.

Throughout our discussion we will analyze Bristol's six operating strategies. However, our emphasis will be on understanding why Bristol Hotel Company aligns its F&B services within their hotels in a certain fashion and how it reaches the decision to do so one way instead of another.

Table 6.5 Bristol's Own Restaurant Brands

BRAND	CONCEPT
Scoops Diner (4 units)	Theme restaurant with a 1950s concept Comfortable and casual
Remmington's (4 units)	Eclectic More upscale than a Scoops Nice hotel coffee shop
Bristol Bar and Grill (12 units)	Designed as a hotel restaurant Flexible in handling fluctuations in sales volume Self-serve Friendly and fast

Among its 39 hotels, Bristol has 22 hotel restaurant outlets and uses three internally developed restaurant brands in 20 of those properties, as shown in Table 6.5.

In addition to Bristol's own restaurant concepts and the two franchised Good Eats Grills previously mentioned, Bristol executives are considering leasing space to a branded restaurant in two of their limited-service properties.

Good Eats Grill. The Good Eats Grill Company is a privately held firm that currently has 17 restaurant outlets, of which 16 are located in Texas and another in Mississippi. Four of the 17 restaurant outlets are franchised, while the others are owned and operated by the company founder, owner, and president, Gene Street. Bristol Hotel Company is the only hotel company that is currently allied with Good Eats Grill. In 1995 Good Eats Grill's annual revenues were $23 million. Good Eats Grill is a casual, family restaurant stressing food quality and low price. A Good Eats Grill can seat 150 to 200 diners, serves lunch and dinner, has a comfortable decor and casual atmosphere, and offers excellent food quality at an affordable price. Good Eats Grill's best-selling entrees are its chicken-fried steak and vegetable plate. The approximate square footage required for a Good Eats Grill is 4,000 to 6,500 square feet (includes both front and back of the house).

The following key indices summarize Good Eats Grill's 1995 performance:

Total revenues	$23 million
Food-revenue percentage	94%
Beverage-revenue percentage	6%
Overall F&B cost percentage	28.5%
Food-cost percentage	29%
Beverage-cost percentage	22%
Average check	$8.12
Covers/year (approx.)	2.8 million

Table 6.6 summarizes the Good Eats Grill menu.

At the time of this writing, Good Eats Grill was doing business with no other hotel company besides the Bristol Hotel Company. We wondered why, and asked key people within the Good Eats Grill management why they had

Table 6.6 Good Eats Grill Menu

	MENU ITEMS	PRICE RANGE	COMMENTS
Appetizers	6	$1.99–$4.99	
Soups and salads	5	$2.19–$5.79	
Burgers and sandwiches	7	$5.29–$6.29	
Entrées	20	$5.99–$8.99	Steaks, pork chops, chicken, pasta, grilled fish Served with garden-fresh vegetables Add salad for 99 cents
Desserts	5	$2.49–$2.99	
Beverages (alcoholic and nonalcoholic)			Full service

Source: "Ride the Branding Wave," *Lodging,* September 1996, pp. 62–73.

agreed to team with Bristol Hotels. The key factors from the perspective of those managers were:

- The companies share similar proactive, team-oriented management styles.

- The firms' corporate cultures blend well.

- The projects were financially feasible.

- Bristol was looking for exactly the product that Good Eats Grill could deliver (i.e., customer value in terms of quality and price).

- Both companies wanted the deal to happen.

Good Eats Grill executives believe more hotel-and-restaurant alliances are imminent and such deals represent a trend that is here to stay. Good Eats Grill's management expects to do more restaurant-franchise deals with hotel companies as doing so offers a viable option for expanding quickly without intensive capital requirements.

Property location. For our study we selected the Holiday Inn Intercontinental, a Bristol Hotel Company property located near the Houston Intercontinental Airport. From the outside, the Good Eats Grill appears as if it is a freestanding restaurant, but in reality the restaurant is as much a part of the hotel as the lobby.

This particular Holiday Inn, a 400-room property opened in 1971, had undergone $11.5 million in renovations (of which some $1.5 million was for the conversion of the previous restaurant into a Good Eats Grill). This hotel generates approximately $7.5 million in room revenues, operates at an 85-percent occupancy level, and has an average daily rate of $60 and RevPAR of $48. Restaurant revenues are targeted to be approximately $1.5 million; food profit, 25 percent;

beverage profit, 55 to 60 percent; food cost, 28 to 29 percent; and beverage cost, 20 to 22 percent.

Property selection. During 1995, the year Bristol acquired the United Inns properties, Bristol Hotel Company executives evaluated all of their hotel-restaurant outlets and made decisions as to which restaurant concept best supported the targeted positioning of each individual hotel. Among Bristol's development strategies was a decision to use the Good Eats Grill concept in two of its properties. Just as we asked the Good Eats Grill executives, "Why Bristol?" we asked Bristol executives, "Why the decision to go with Good Eats Grill versus going with proven internally developed restaurant brands or renovating the existing restaurant?" The key element in Bristol's selection of Good Eats Grill for two new locations was in Bristol's overall assessment of which restaurant concept would be the best match for the repositioning strategies for those specific hotels.

At the Houston Holiday Inn Intercontinental, the existing restaurant, the Grand Cargo Cafe, was a typical hotel restaurant with a coffee-shop feel. The Grand Cargo Cafe had average food quality and service, low profit margins (5 percent), low sales volume, high employee turnover, little name recognition, and a below-average reputation among those customers familiar with the operation. In short, the Grand Cargo Cafe was a costly amenity for the hotel's previous owners and Bristol executives quickly determined that a change was required.

Bristol first looked at the possibility of replacing the Grand Cargo Cafe with one of Bristol's own internally developed F&B concepts (i.e., Bristol Bar & Grill, Scoops Diner, or Remmington's). After some consideration it was determined that Bristol's own concepts did not adequately complement the property's repositioning strategy. The Bristol Bar & Grill is a quick-and-friendly self-serve concept that is primarily focused on serving hotel guests (i.e., banquet guests). Such a foodservice arrangement would be inappropriate for the repositioned Holiday Inn Intercontinental, which has a large sales-volume potential comprising both walk-in diners (85 percent of the lunch trade and 40 percent for dinner) and overnight guests (15 percent at lunch and 60 percent at dinner).

Another objective in replacing the Grand Cargo Cafe was to change dramatically the perceived atmosphere of the outlet from that of a coffee shop to a substantial restaurant. Bristol's Remmington's concept, also reminiscent of a coffee shop but more upscale than Grand Cargo Cafe in price and quality, was not considered sufficiently different to achieve that goal. Moreover, Remmington's did not completely match the "casual and comfortable" atmosphere desired to complement the overall hotel repositioning strategy.

Bristol's Scoops Diner concept offered a close match to Bristol's goal of providing the customer with good overall value in a casual and comfortable atmosphere. Scoops' 1950s-theme concept, however, was developed primarily for walk-in diners rather than a hotel's overnight and meeting guests. Like Remmington's, then, the Scoops concept did not exactly fit the needs of the property's new target markets.

While hotel guests were to be a prime customer base for the Intercontinental's restaurant, the property was seen to also offer great opportunity for walk-in business. (Here are some of the key site-specific characteristics of the Holiday Inn Intercontinental that indicated a freestanding restaurant could generate substantial walk-in business: (1) the physical layout of the property—parking, entrance, signs, and size—was considered excellent; (2) the property is located close to Houston International Airport on a major highway; and (3) there was limited restaurant competition in the area despite the potential for customers from local businesses and surrounding hotels, some of which are limited-service properties.) With that in mind, Bristol executives realized that the Scoops and Remmington's concepts did not have sufficient pre-existing customer brand awareness in Houston to generate substantial walk-in traffic. In the final assessment, then, Bristol purchased the franchise rights to operate a Good Eats Grill in Houston (and at one other location).

A good match. Bristol management considers Good Eats Grill to be a competitive concept that offers a quality product, a casual environment that customers enjoy, a respected and recognizable restaurant name in the Houston area, and proven sales volume. Another key factor mentioned by Bristol executives was that the two organizations clicked, meaning that the corporate culture of each was well matched with the other. Both have an entrepreneurial base, both are flexible, and both have high-quality standards for a mid-level product at an affordable price. Shown on the next page is a table that compares the hotel, restaurant, and combined marketing strategies of the two companies (Table 6.7).

Key positioning criteria. We found that a critical factor in the selection process of a hotel's F&B brand or concept is to determine the

Table 6.7 Operating Strategies

HOTEL	RESTAURANT	COMBINED
• Primary market	• Family-style restaurant	• Appeal to corporate and family travelers
—Corporate business travelers	• Excellent food quality	• Mid- to upper-market value
—Mid- to upper-range travelers	—Fresh	• Casual and comfortable
• Secondary market	• Value	• Best overall value
—Family travelers	• Brand recognition	—Price and quality
• Brand recognition	• Casual, comfortable decor	
• First-class hotel, but not stuffy		
• Physically competitive		

customer perception that you want to create at the property and then select a restaurant theme that complements the overall property's image. Bristol COO Beckert illustrated this by saying, "At Bristol we try to identify uniqueness in our F&B concepts, which then become selling points for the property. The restaurant then goes on a short list that our sales staff use to sell rooms."

The "right" match between the hotel and the restaurant can vary from property to property. At Bristol, all 39 properties were evaluated to determine which F&B concept best fit each property, and only two locations were selected for a Good Eats Grill franchise. As we will point out later, several key factors such as conversion costs and nearby competition must be taken into consideration prior to making the final decision.

Turn up the volume. Another element related to positioning is to determine the volume and customer mix expected. For example, let's review Bristol's existing company-owned restaurant brands: Scoops, Remmington's, and Bristol Bar & Grill. Bristol management will locate a Scoops or a Remmington's in those properties

that have above-average hotel volume, and where restaurant-customer volume comprises primarily walk-in diners who are not using the hotel's other services. A Bristol Bar & Grill concept is used when the F&B market is primarily hotel guests and banquet business. The Bristol Bar & Grill is targeted specifically to serve hotel patrons with a quick-serve breakfast, convenient lunch, and buffet-style dinner. The Good Eats Grill concept, on the other hand, generally operates as a freestanding restaurant, has a proven sales volume ($1.5 to 2 million per year), offers consumer value, and has a comfortable decor that's attractive to both walk-in diners and hotel guests.

During Bristol's examination of its hotel restaurants, it was determined that a Good Eats Grill should be used when (1) it is necessary to reposition the hotel, (2) a great restaurant-volume potential exists, (3) the physical layout and location of the property can sustain a free-standing restaurant, and (4) the market mix comprises both hotel guests and walk-in customers.

Why Houston? Bristol's management felt that the Houston Holiday Inn Intercontinental needed repositioning and a recognized restaurant brand like Good Eats Grill was essential for any repositioning strategy to work. Good Eats Grill already had two successful freestanding restaurants in the Houston region. Additionally, Good Eats Grill maintained an ongoing investment in local advertising. By contrast, a Remmington's, a Scoops, or even the Grand Cargo Cafe did not have anywhere near the same level of local brand awareness and consumer acceptance.

The following list summarizes the key factors that Bristol's executives considered when selecting Houston as a location for a franchised Good Eats Grill.

- The property was being repositioned.
- Financial feasibility was evident.
- The property's existing hotel restaurants were producing low revenues.
- The physical layout of the property allowed for conversion.
- Parking, entrances, and signs would be relatively easy to provide.
- The local labor market could support the concept.
- The high-traffic location of the property (in a commercial area near the airport).
- Since there was only one freestanding restaurant within a two-mile radius, the potential for non-hotel-guest business was great.

✦ SELECTION PROCESS

A summary of the key advantages and disadvantages to consider when going with a franchised restaurant brand in your hotel follow (*Lodging,* 1995), while Figure 6.1 is a flow chart

of the basic steps to take when evaluating and choosing which franchise restaurant company to use.

Advantages

- Integral part of repositioning the hotel
- Potentially increases revenues, occupancy, profits
- Restaurant franchiser is continually assessing the menu, whereas a hotel's tendency is not to change the menu
- Franchiser is knowledgeable about the restaurant business

Disadvantages

- Franchise fee
- Requires a certain level of volume to warrant utilizing a franchise brand
- High initial investment
- Brand can lose reputation and recognition or quality levels could drop during the term of the franchise agreement
- Room service and banquet service could still require a separate kitchen operation

As previously noted, Bristol chose the Good Eats Grill concept over other restaurant companies because the Good Eats management was (1) flexible and (2) determined to minimize the bureaucracy to make the deal happen. In today's competitive market, business decisions must be made quickly and accurately or else the window of opportunity may be lost. In this particular example the basic deal was struck after two executive meetings (however, it did take the lawyers a little longer). The rest of the steps in the process caught up with the decisions that were made after those two executive meetings. Such a quick

Figure 6.1 Selection-process Flow Chart

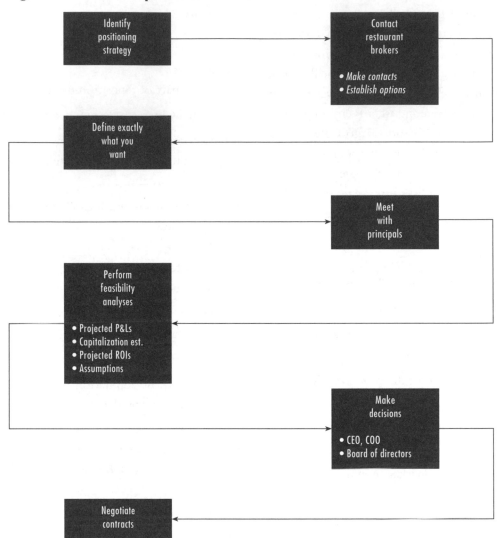

decision was possible because the two companies have similar proactive management styles, the project made financial sense for both companies, the corporate cultures blended well, and the decision-makers went with their instinct.

✦ CONTRACT RELATIONSHIPS

There are four basic types of operational options that can be established between the hotel and the F&B outlet in a hotel. Those four options are (1) internally developed restaurant brand, (2) franchised restaurant brand, (3) straight lease, and (4) management contract. Bristol's first choice (used for 20 of its 22 restaurant outlets) is to use its own internally developed restaurant brands. Bristol believes it has a proven track record in managing F&B operations profitably (*Hotel Business,* 1996).

When Bristol introduced Good Eats Grill into two of its 22 hotels with foodservice, it showed a willingness to purchase a franchised brand, provided Bristol could maintain full control of restaurant operations and products (as long as all franchise agreements were maintained). Currently Bristol is also assessing a leasing arrangement with yet another restaurant company for a couple of Bristol's Fairfield Inn properties. In those cases Bristol managers

CRITICAL ELEMENTS TO CONSIDER

Summarized below are critical elements to consider when assessing which restaurant brand concepts will best match a particular hotel property.

1. Determine the desired hotel market position and customer perception you want to create for each property. This includes knowing all about the property's competition, environment, and customers, and involves creating a unique image for your property.

2. Make sure that you objectively assess the revenue and expense potential of each operational option when examining your financial trade-offs. Such options include running your hotel company's own brand, buying and operating a franchised brand, and leasing space to a brand-name restaurant company.

3. Select a restaurant company that has a corporate culture that mirrors your hotel's corporate culture and also shares the same basic operational goals.

4. Evaluate each property on a stand-alone basis using all available facts and data. Avoid making generalizations about what will work for all properties.

5. The key criteria in identifying which properties could benefit most from a brand-name franchise-restaurant concept are:

   - Desired positioning of the hotel
   - Financial trade-offs and feasibility analyses
   - Competitive marketing analysis
   - Physical layout of the facility (parking, entrances, signs, location of kitchen)
   - The site location
   - The local labor market

6. The key criteria in selecting a particular restaurant company are:

   - Similar business goals and corporate culture
   - Initial investment cost
   - The menu offered
   - Ongoing new menu development
   - New recipes on a regular basis
   - Cooking specifications
   - Franchise fee
   - Restaurant decor
   - Training support
   - Management support
   - The ability to handle room service and banquets

7. View the hotel's restaurant outlet as a selling point that can enhance rooms sales and as a profit center that can be held accountable for achieving established profit.

seem to be indicating that it would be more profitable for them to lease out square footage in the hotels versus operating the F&B outlet themselves.

Key franchise elements. Bristol has purchased the franchise rights for its two Good Eats Grill operations. The key elements of the franchise agreement are the menu, recipes, cooking specifications, franchise fee, restaurant decor, music package, training support, and negotiated special provisions (e.g., use of Good Eats Grill recipes for banquets). Basically, Bristol purchased a turnkey operation from Good Eats Grill. Moreover, Good Eats Grill provides pre- and post-opening training support, new and updated menu development, and such regional management support as consulting, auditing, and trouble-shooting.

In exchange for the franchise and its management services Good Eats Grill receives 3.5 percent of lunch and dinner revenues as a franchise fee.

✦ MARKETING

We have already mentioned how the Bristol sales office uses the company's restaurants as a selling point to assist in booking rooms, meetings, and banquets. In addition there are three other marketing concerns that need to be considered: (1) the competition, (2) customer expectations, and (3) advertising.

Competition. The primary hotel competitors for Bristol's Houston Holiday Inn Intercontinental are a Marriott hotel (569 rooms), a Hyatt hotel (315 rooms), and a Sheraton hotel (450 rooms). As for nearby foodservice competition, Marri-

ott uses internally developed restaurant brands (Allie's American Grill and CK's) along with a Pizza Hut kiosk, while the Hyatt and Sheraton offer typical hotel restaurants. Additionally, there are some limited-service hotel properties in the area that factor into the secondary market competitive analysis.

The freestanding restaurant competition in the area is negligible. There is a Kettle Restaurant nearby, but it does not pose a strong business threat to Good Eats Grill as it has a different target market. There is a Bennigan's and T.G.I. Friday's within three miles of the Holiday Inn, but there is no other notable restaurant competition within a two-mile radius of the hotel. As it turns out, the Holiday Inn's Good Eats Grill is popular with Marriott's, Hyatt's, and Sheraton's hotel guests, and also with those hotel guests that are staying at the surrounding limited-service properties. It can be expected, then, that a guest who stays at a hotel other than the Holiday Inn, yet eats at the Good Eats Grill, may decide to stay at the Holiday Inn on return trips to Houston. The value of the strategic alliance between the hotel and the restaurant is that it establishes a unique identity for this property that sets it apart from its competition and provides a marketing edge.

Customer expectations. A primary mission-statement goal of both companies is to exceed customer expectations. With the alliance of the Holiday Inn Intercontinental and Good Eats Grill, Bristol management believes the customer is pleasantly surprised with the overall product and services that the property provides. Even though the hotel and restaurant renovations were completed in July 1996, the perceived overall value of this property to the customer generated new corporate accounts. Bristol management believes the hotel repositioning strategy in combination with the addition of the Good Eats Grill is a major reason it landed those new accounts.

Advertising. Bristol Hotel Company believes in a direct sales-and-marketing approach. The company therefore relies less on national promotion activities than many other firms. The Holiday Inn Intercontinental is no different in this regard. The hotel does some limited local advertising, but it relies primarily on a direct-sales approach along with making personal local contacts. Other than the signs around the property, there is no joint advertising or promotion done between the hotel and the restaurant. Good Eats Grill has four lighted signs on the property, and Bristol purchases no billboard ads for this property. There are two other Good Eats Grill restaurants located in Houston, and Good Eats Grill does do some radio promotion and rents billboards for those two restaurants.

✦ OPERATIONS

As a franchisee Bristol maintains total operational control of the restaurant, but Good Eats Grill recipes must be followed exactly. Unlike other Bristol properties, the restaurant has its own general manager. Bristol determined quickly that this particular property needed to establish the restaurant as a priority, but did not want the hotel general manager to get distracted from managing the rest of the hotel. Bristol therefore elevated the restaurant-manager position to that of restaurant general manager at this property. The restaurant GM reports to the hotel GM, and the result is that the property receives maximum management focus for all of its key operations.

Another distinguishing operational element at this property is the way room service and banquets are handled. The Good Eats Grill kitchen serves them. There is no separate kitchen or menu to handle room service. Bristol also uses the Good Eats Grill kitchen for banquets, and has the final say in establishing banquet menus and costs. Moreover, Bristol has the option of using Good Eats Grill menu items and recipes in preparing the banquet meals (provided that the recipes are followed exactly).

✦ FINANCE

We have shown how the correct match between a restaurant company and a hotel operator can help to reposition a hotel, increase occupancy, and increase F&B profit. We can investigate other potential financial gains by comparing a summary of the actual 1995 profit-loss statement of the Holiday Inn's original (pre-Bristol) food-service concept (Grand Cargo Cafe) with a conservatively estimated profit-loss statement of the Good Eats Grill for 1997 (its first year of full operation; see Table 6.8).

A quick comparison of those profit-loss figures shows how establishing a strategic alliance between a hotel and restaurant can improve the overall profitability of the property. Other expenses such as franchise initiation fee ($40,000–$50,000), cost of renovation ($750,000), cost of signs ($5,000), and other miscellaneous marketing costs (grand opening, flyers), must also be factored into assessing the feasibility of

Table 6.8 Profit-Loss Comparison

GRAND CARGO CAFÉ			GOOD EATS GRILL		
ACTUAL 1995	%	ITEM DESCRIPTION	%		PROJECTED 1997
831,519	70.5	Outlet revenues[1]	59.8		1,269,455
199,920	16.9	Banquet revenues	28.4		601,000
148,072	12.6	Other revenues[2]	11.8		251,430
1,179,511	100.0	Total revenues	100.0		2,121,885
405,354	34.4	Food cost	26.4		561,137
525,634	44.5	Payroll[3]	43.2		917,621
43,561	3.7	Other expenses	7.1		148,532
974,555	82.6	Total expenses	76.7		1,627,289
204,956		Profit in dollars			494,596
	17.4	Profit percentage	23.3		

[1]Outlet revenues include restaurant revenues and room service.
[2]Other revenues include banquet-room rental, house portion of the gratuity, and miscellaneous banquet fees.
[3]Including employee benefits and payroll taxes.

Source: Bristol Hotel Company.

converting or opening an operation prior to proceeding with a project like the one between Holiday Inn Intercontinental and Good Eats Grill.

Final analysis. Throughout this case study analysis, we emphasized how important the repositioning strategy was in turning around the Houston Holiday Inn Intercontinental. A quick look at key property performance indicators (Table 6.9) demonstrates the success of that repositioning strategy.

Moreover, we focused primarily on only one part of the hotel's repositioning strategy, that is, its strategic alignment with a particular restaurant concept. Other factors also contributed to the property's improved performance, including new ownership and management, an influx of cash for renovations, and its new market position. Nevertheless, the alliance between Bristol and

Good Eats Grill is seen as key to the property's turnaround. The property's previous restaurant, the Grand Cargo Cafe, was being operated as a hotel amenity rather than as a profit center. To capitalize on the restaurant's potential, the Bristol management team recognized that a new restaurant concept was needed. After objectively evaluating their options, including their own F&B concepts, the team determined that a Good Eats Grill franchise matched Bristol's restaurant needs

Table 6.9 Key Property Performance Indicators

	1996	PROJECTED 1997
Hotel occupancy	72%	85%
ADR	$49	$60
Food profit	5%	25%
Beverage profit	50%	60%

for this particular property. The Bristol experience demonstrates the importance of evaluating each property on an individual basis rather than making generalizations about what will work for all hotel properties.

In conclusion, from our perspective there is no question that now and in the future we will see more hotel and restaurant companies establishing strategic alliances. It is no longer financially feasible for a hotel restaurant to be operated as just a support function to the hotel's lodging operations. The hotel restaurant must now be viewed as a selling point to generate increased room and restaurant revenues. The hotel restaurant must be managed as its own profit center where the goal is to maximize overall property profits. For the entire property to be profitable, the restaurant concept and the hotel's market position must complement each other. Put another way, in today's competitive business environment the hotel restaurant cannot—and should not try to—be all things to all people. To achieve a competitive edge, hotel companies must consider operating a franchised restaurant brand or leasing space within the hotel to a restaurant company. Doing so may improve customer perception and value, and as a result increase the overall profitability of the property.

6.6 CONTEMPORARY HOTEL CATERING PATTI J. SHOCK AND JOHN M. STEFANELLI

Although on-premise catering is generally the second largest source of revenue for most hotels, following sleeping rooms, the on-premise catering area has been virtually ignored in the hotel school curriculum. The colleges that do offer a course in catering usually focus on hands-on classes consisting of planning, cooking, and serving a meal, which is good background but is not the role of the hotel catering department.

Catering is often the highest visibility the hotel has on a local level. Catering can create an image for the hotel, both locally and nationally.

✦ DEPARTMENT ORGANIZATION

In most hotels the director of catering reports to the director of food and beverage, with banquet managers and banquet set-up managers reporting to Catering. In other hotels you may find a director of catering and convention service reporting to the director of marketing, with the Banquet positions reporting to Food and Beverage. In the latter arrangement, Convention Service usually handles food and beverage functions for groups with 20 or more sleeping rooms with Catering selling and servicing the local social and business markets. Convention Service then does not sell; the room sales department handles that aspect. Convention Service in most hotels, however, handles all of the non-food-related logistics, including room setup, audiovisual requirements, etc. In hotels where conventions are not an important market segment, Convention Service may not exist, in which case Catering would handle all food and non-food logistics.

The director of catering assigns and oversees all functions, oversees catering sales managers, oversees all marketing efforts, interacts with clients and catering managers, coordinates with the hotel sales director, and works with the chef to update and create menus.

Under the director of catering there may be an assistant catering director who helps with marketing, oversees catering sales managers, and services one or more accounts. There may be several catering sales managers, depending on the size of the hotel. Catering sales managers maintain client contacts and service accounts. Their role is to sell and service functions. They must seek and consult with clients, plan menus, themes, room setup, and decor; negotiate prices; and coordinate with inside departments and outside vendors. There are several excellent graphic room-setup software packages available on the market.

The catering department may also employ catering sales representatives who are usually involved only with selling, leaving the servicing to others.

The banquet manager implements the director of catering's requests, oversees room captains, supervises functions in progress, staffs and schedules servers and bartenders, and coordinates all support departments. He or she is the operations director, as opposed to catering executives, who primarily sell and work with clients to plan events.

The assistant banquet manager reports to the banquet manager and supervises table settings and decor. There may be two (or more) assistants; for example, a hotel may have one for the day and one for the evening shift.

The banquet setup manager supervises the banquet setup crew; orders tables, chairs, portable bars, and other room equipment from storage; and supervises the teardown of the room after the event has concluded.

The scheduler, often referred to as the diary clerk, enters bookings in the Master Log (now usually computerized); oversees the timing of all functions and provides adequate turnover time between functions; is responsible for scheduling meeting rooms, reception areas, poolside areas, meal functions, beverage functions, other functions, and equipment requirements; keeps appropriate records to ensure against overbooking and double booking of space; and is responsible for communicating this information to relevant departments.

The maître d'hôtel is the floor manager. He or she is in charge of all service personnel and oversees all aspects of guest service during meal and beverage functions in the various function rooms on the floor.

The captain is the room manager and is in charge of service at meal functions in a specific room. Captains typically oversee all activity in the entire function room or, depending on the size of the room, in a portion of it. They also supervise the servers in their room or section of the room.

There are two types of servers, food servers and beverage servers. Food servers deliver foods, alcoholic and nonalcoholic beverages, and utensils to the table; clear tables; and attend to guest needs. Beverage servers serve alcoholic beverages, usually at receptions. Buspersons, whose primary responsibilities are to clear tables, restock side stands, and serve ice water, rolls, butter, and condiments, sometimes back up servers.

The bartender concentrates on alcoholic beverage production and service. Bartenders are often assisted by bar backs, whose primary responsibility is to initially stock and replenish the bars with liquor, ice, glassware, and other necessary supplies.

Housemen (sometimes referred to as porters) set up function rooms with risers, hardware, tables, chairs, and other necessary equipment. They report to the banquet setup manager.

Attendants "refresh" meeting rooms during breaks by emptying ashtrays when smoking is permitted, refilling water pitchers, and removing trash. Some catered functions also require coat-check attendants or restroom attendants.

The clerk (or secretary) handles routine correspondence, types contracts and banquet event orders (BEOs), handles and routes telephone messages, and distributes documents to relevant staff members and other hotel departments.

The engineering department provides necessary utility services, such as providing air conditioning/heating, setting up electrical panels for major exhibits, hanging banners, and setting up audiovisual displays.

Other miscellaneous positions include the following. A sommelier (or wine steward) is used only at fancy, upscale events. The cashier sells drink tickets to guests at cash bars. A ticket taker may be required to collect tickets from guests at the door to the function. Finally, most catering departments employ stewards to deliver the proper amount of china, glassware, and silver to function rooms.

Whatever the organizational structure, catering's favorable impact on hotel profitability is primarily due to the fact that catering has more control over the variable expenses than does the manager of a typical restaurant. In a restaurant, labor must be scheduled, heat/air conditioning must be on, and food must be kept in inventory, whether or not any guests are present in the facil-ity. In catering, a function must be booked before these items are scheduled or purchased. So there are more variable costs in catering, and more fixed costs in restaurant foodservice.

✦ THE SALES AND SERVICE PROCESS

Selling is a vital part of catering (see Figure 6.2). To sell a catering event, potential markets must be identified and cultivated. Target markets must be established. Potential markets include association meetings (local monthly meetings as well as the national annual conventions); corporate meetings, including training sessions and incentive banquets; weddings and anniversaries; bar mitzvahs; proms; garden clubs; holiday parties; reunions, both school and military; and fraternal organizations, such as the Rotary and Lions. The list is endless.

A marketing plan should be developed that clearly defines the desirable target markets, defines the demand, describes competing caterers, sets financial goals, considers other potential income that catering can generate for the hotel, and describes standardized procedures that must be used to canvass for new clients, qualify leads, make sales calls, develop contracts, and provide required products and services.

The initial contact for a function can come from the client or the catering department. In many cases, the potential client makes the first inquiry. He or she may contact you by phone, by letter, fax, email, or in person.

If the contact is by phone, be sure the person answering the phone can answer questions, or that someone knowledgeable is always available. Too often a low-paid, untrained person in the office answers the phone, and this can

Figure 6.2 Steps in Selling and Servicing a Catering Event

hamper the selling effort. The phone should always be answered within three rings. Always secure the name and phone number of the caller.

If the initial contact is by letter, email, or fax, try to answer with a phone call. Copies of the letter were most likely sent to several caterers and it is best to be the first to respond. More information is often needed, such as the budget the client has for the event or the objective of the function. This initial contact also provides the opportunity to invite the potential client to the property for lunch and a tour. Every effort should be made to get the potential client into the hotel, on your home turf.

Sometimes a letter will include a Request for Proposal (RFP), which is a written prospectus from professional meeting planners. An RFP usually indicates that the potential client is very knowledgeable about catering and is usually a sophisticated negotiator.

If potential clients stop by in person without an appointment, have someone see them as soon as possible. Offer some light refreshments to keep them occupied until someone is available. Give an accurate estimate of how long they will have to wait. Have the receptionist obtain preliminary information, such as their desired date(s) and type of function, to get them involved in the planning process right away. Also, keep a binder handy for browsing that contains testimonial letters from happy clients and photos of previous events.

A Group History File should be created whenever initial contact is made. The file should include all facets of the business relationship, from initial contact to final disposition. Standardized information includes name of contact, name of decision maker, titles, organization, types of events held, number of events held, when events are held, attendance figures, all correspondence, notes from phone conversations, contracts, credit history, potential for future business, and client preferences.

The manager responding to client inquiries must understand the hotel's capabilities. He or she especially needs knowledge of food and beverage production and service. Planning a menu for a small group is quite different from a large group. For example, soufflé for 1000 would be quite impossible.

When planning a menu, the caterer must first know the occasion or reason for the event. The style of service also depends on the occasion. It would be inappropriate to have a deli sandwich buffet for an auspicious awards banquet.

With international events, protocol must be considered in everything from decor to dietary restrictions. The World of Culture web site (http://www.webofculture.com/) provides good information on a variety of cultures.

Public space or function rooms must be forecast for space utilization, just as the hotel sales department forecasts sleeping rooms requirements.

Working well with inside departments is critical. Linens have to be requisitioned from the linen room, engineers must ensure that the room temperature is appropriate, tables must be set up, and purchasing must order the correct amounts and types of food and beverages.

Outside vendors, such as decorators, audio-visual companies, florists, printers, and photographers may be needed by the client to ensure a successful event.

Performing well is the next step. Here the emphasis shifts from sales to service. Guests must be treated with care; service must be punctual; foods, presentations, cleanliness, and ambiance must meet desired quality standards; professional attention must be paid to all details; the function host should be made to feel like a guest at the event, instead of a harassed and worried manager. Last minute requests and crises must be handled quickly and efficiently. It is imperative to be flexible.

Follow-up is vital for repeat business. Standardized procedures should be developed for thank-you calls and individualized, personal thank-you letters. Completed events should be evaluated with staff and client input. Referral business should be solicited. Appropriate souvenir gifts may be presented. And outstanding accounts should be settled.

✦ FUTURE ISSUES

Issues facing the catering department in the future include new alcohol restrictions; the demand for more menu alternatives, including low-fat, pesticide-free, generally safe, uncontaminated products; the competition from off-premise catering firms; waste disposal regulations and recycling; consumers becoming more value conscious; and service becoming a more important point of differentiation.

Subcontracting will become more common, especially for labor and food. Calling one company to provide servers is more efficient than having staff on the phone calling individual on-call workers. The independent labor contractor trains staff and does all of the payroll and paperwork.

Caterers can't afford to have all types of expertise on their staffs. With a Japanese theme, a sushi restaurant may be subcontracted. Or a local barbecue specialist, oyster roaster, or coffee service company can handle unique events. The hotel would add about 20 percent markup to the subcontractor's bill, and then add the cost of the rest of the meal prepared in-house.

In the past, menus rarely changed. Today, many menus are changed with the season. In the future it will be important to be able to distinguish between a fad and a trend. Fads, such as Nouvelle Cuisine, are short-lived. Trends, such as the demand for fresh foods and more nutritious food, are more permanent.

Probably the biggest challenge is the perception among guests that all caterers are exactly alike. Buyers may feel that there is always another caterer able to provide similar service. It is imperative for the successful caterer to differentiate their food and service from their competition. The price/value relationship will become more important as caterers attempt to rise above the competition.

There are a multitude of resources available on the web, including, for example, Room Calculator (http://www.mmaweb.com/meetings/Workshop/roomcalc.html), which will determine how many guests you can fit into a room in various configurations. Many caterers have their menus online, which are interesting to see. *Special Events Magazine* (http://www.specialevents.com/magazine/), and Event Solutions (http://www.event-solutions.com/) have timely articles that are archived online and are searchable.

A large collection of useful catering web links can be found at: http://www.unlv.edu/Tourism/Catering_and_Special_Events.html.

6.7 A DAY IN THE LIFE OF AN EXECUTIVE DIRECTOR OF CATERING SALES AND CONVENTION SERVICES Rich Benninger

Each day I wake up saying, "Today is the day I will get everything done." It is my optimist side taking control before my realist side has a chance to ruin my day. Because I ply my trade at a 5034-room hotel with over 380,000 square feet of banquet space, it is usually around 8:00 A.M. when my realist side kicks in. By this time I have been at work for an hour or more and start taking victories as soon as they come. The day is half over for the dedicated line cast members who started working at 4:00 A.M. so our thousands of guests can enjoy their morning breakfast. These employees are the backbone of catering. Their workday here will end in four more hours, and many will go to a second job.

The day will not end for the catering director until a few things are completed. The director has just one job, sort of, and is the front person for the operation. Now, please allow me to take you on a journey through a typical day in the life of a catering director. But first I must make coffee. Nobody else in the office notices that 1 ounce of coffee left in a pot does not mean "There's coffee in the pot." The following describes what I did today.

✦ BOOKING BUSINESS

Customers are the number-one component of a successful catering operation. Without customers, the grandest ballrooms, the most spectacular cuisine, and the best service are all moot points. So, every day you must work to fill the pipeline with customers. The rooms sales managers are really doing a great job. They are booking over quota and getting contracts with great food and beverage minimums. For just a moment, I fantasize that this will never end and life will always be good.

Oh no! We have just been asked why the week between Christmas and New Year's does not have any events. Transient room sales are strong, but they do not use function space. It's up to catering sales to fill in the hole. My team tells me that had sales not already done so they could easily fill space a week before or a week later, but that holiday week is going to be tough to fill. I know this is true, but the senior vice president does not care that something is tough. He wants to know what we are doing to get business. And by the way, not discount business. We start out looking for full-paying customers and if that does not work, *then* we will look at discounting.

I am excited to meet a customer for a site visit at 7:30 A.M. I am the first property she is looking at for a 2500-guest reception and concert. I just talked to her yesterday for the very first time. All our meeting space is booked, but I'm in luck; we have space in our arena. I work with the arena for about an hour to get the space and brainstorm on things we can do to book this business. The arena operations guys are great to work with. They enjoy coming to the catering office for cappuccino. I smile when I think how cheap cappuccino is and how many favors it buys from operations cast members.

We spend an hour walking our customer through her event. Her company sells very large industrial trucks, and when we tell her we can put a concrete mixer right in the middle of her reception she is all smiles. I make note to get the dimensions of the roll-up doors. We are going to be more expensive than the competition, but we provide more value. We can make this a one-stop shopping experience. I make a note to call transportation companies and gather quotes. I know the other properties will not get involved in dealing with all the outside vendors, and I use this as a selling advantage. I make a note to list this as a tentative piece of business worth $165,000 or more.

Next I make a hasty trip across property to check on a breakfast we are doing on the stage of our production show. We are lucky to have an incentive house tour our property, and we have pulled out all the stops to let this VIP group know we value their business. I am pleased with the spectacular stage sets and the look of the breakfast. I laugh with the sales manager when he apologizes for only giving us 36 hours notice on the breakfast. I assure him the financial rewards of getting large incentive bookings will more than make up for the short notice. I make a note to send each guest a thank-you note for taking the time to tour our property.

✦ FINALIZING PROGRAMS

The only time a program is truly finalized is once the customers are gone and the final bill is paid. And then just the physical stuff is over. Conversations about the really good stuff and the sometimes bad stuff can go on for years. Repeat customers are usually the best ones to have, but they tend to remember that five years ago the potato salad did not have a spoon in it when the company president went to the buffet 15 minutes before it was scheduled to open. "Let's not let that happen this year."

You spend months working to get everything planned at least 3 weeks in advance. Then you give all the information to the operating departments 2 weeks out. For some groups this works really well, and once you work out the details they only make minor changes. Other groups are not quite so tidy in their planning.

Today I had a group arrive on site, and we reviewed their banquet event orders. It would be easier to say we redid their banquet event orders (BEOs). At 9:00 A.M. we started reviewing 45 meal function BEOs. By 2:15 P.M. we had made major changes to 42 of them. I wonder aloud if they would like to change the other three just for good measure. The chefs are circling the catering office like sharks. All the food ordering is on hold until the revised BEOs are signed off on. While I'm working with the clients to refinalize, the chefs and purchasing agents are on the phone undoing all the ordering they did days ago. Purveyors are all on standby to rush product to us.

I am thankful we have excellent relationships with these wonderful people, who will now pull off miracles to get us products over the weekend.

My assistant is ready to shoot someone. Making the changes once is enough of a challenge, but now we are changing things for a second and third time in one day. I smile as I say, "Yes, I'm sure I can get you a completely new set of BEOs by 5:00 P.M." Just as I tell myself we must be done with changes, my contact calls and changes two of the remaining original three BEOs. I get no comfort from the fact that the one lone original BEO is for an event that does not happen until 5 days from now. I do, however, get great comfort from the knowledge that my clients will spend over $800,000 in the next 8 days.

✦ CREATING MENUS

I promise a major corporate client that I will write three custom menu options for their opening reception. I tell them I will do it on Saturday, and I'll fax the menus so they have them for a Monday meeting. I promise myself I will not commit to doing any more projects on Saturday. It is going to be my catch-up day, and I've been filling the day with new projects. I may have to work a few hours on Sunday to get on track for next week. The great thing about writing custom menus is every time I do one I add it to my hot menu file and just keep reusing it. I do make a notation of whom I send each one to. I would hate to send someone the same custom menu twice.

In this world of ever more sophisticated customers, the quest for new menus has taken on a life all its own. The unfortunate side of this sophisticated customer often comes with fond memories of a gourmet dinner for two at some exotic trendy restaurant. Other favorite sources of wonderful ideas are glossy cooking magazines and TV cooking shows. Now the simple task of any caterer is to figure out how to make these menus, designed to serve eight, work for hundreds or thousands. Of course, you are not alone in this situation. The culinary staff is right there with you. Please don't take it personally that many of them think you are crazy.

✦ WORKING EVENTS

Luckily for my catering department, we work at a property where we are cast in the role of salespeople. Another team of professionals handles operations. Still, I can't resist taking 10 minutes and going down to see how setup is going for a poolside reception. Somehow I spend 45 minutes at the pool, and now I'm going to have to rush to a pre-con meeting. The clients who spent the day making changes are very big customers, and the pre-con will be a big production. We have all our top executives coming by to say hello. I am anxious to see how the eight cheerleaders will do with the dance number they are performing in the center of the hollow square. I am very pleased to see the banquet and entertainment departments have everything in perfect order.

✦ LEADING AN OFFICE

One of my catering managers comes into my office and asks to talk. In 2 days she will renew her wedding vows and she is very nervous. I go into father mode and we make a list of things she has to do. I laugh when I ask her why she is nervous about having a party for 30 people when every day she books parties for hundreds of guests. I try to ease her burden of preparing some of the food herself. I suggest she just bring in the bowls she wants to use, and I'll have the kitchen fill them up with

whatever she wants. I smile when she says, "No, thank you, I make really good salads myself." I wonder does that mean our salads are not really good?

Throughout the day, my staff gives me encouragement while I am working to get all the changes made on my group. They all offer to help, and I notice the number of things I am asked to look at is very low today. I am proud of my staff and make a note to have a special breakfast at our catering meeting next week. It has been almost 2 months since we started a new format for our catering meetings, and I must say they are much better and everyone seems happier with them.

✦ BUDGETS

Yesterday we had our review for next year's budget. I must start working on a really aggressive marketing plan to make the revenue number we are after. For today, I'll just start by having a binder made so I feel like I'm making progress. I ask my assistant to run some reports, so I can take them home and look at them. I know I'll never look at them while I'm home, but if I find spare time I'll have them, just in case.

✦ MENTORING AND INDUSTRY INVOLVEMENT

I call two new interns from the university to confirm their Saturday appointments with me. I need to meet with them to determine their interests and what program they are going to follow for the 8 months they will spend with us. I hope they will want to work on the marketing plan and be active in the National Association of Catering Executives (NACE). I also have a protégé from the university, and it would be nice if all three can work together on projects. I feel pressure to provide these students with an overwhelmingly positive experience. Last year I was voted Outstanding Mentor of the Year, and now I feel a higher level of expectation.

Unfortunately, I have to cancel my NACE board of directors meeting scheduled for today. I am the president of our chapter, and I have not had time to work on the things I need for the meeting. I do not want to waste the board's time. I make a note to call our NACE intern and schedule a meeting to see what tasks I can have her handle for the board. Involvement in NACE is rewarding, but it is like a part-time job. What was I thinking when we agreed to do a fundraising dinner for 1000 in February? I'm sure it was the same thing I thought when I said I would love to teach an extension class at the university. It all seems so far away when I say yes. Somehow it all works out.

✦ ENTERTAINING

It's 5:00 P.M. and I need to leave for a cocktail party at a sister property across the street. I am joining the vice president of sales and the executive director of convention services to entertain clients. We have a cocktail party and then a 7:30 P.M. dinner and a 10:00 P.M. show. The evening is wonderful. Our clients really enjoy the special attention we give them. When 10:00 P.M. comes, I wonder if I'll stay awake at the show. My fears are unjustified.

The comedian is so funny my sides hurt from laughing. I think, what a great career. I get to have fun while I work. As the evening ends at 11:30 P.M. I confirm that I'll play golf in 2 weeks—just another sacrifice for my clients.

✦ PERSONAL LIFE

My four golden retrievers are really happy to see me. I know they have had dinner and were well cared for while I was gone, but I feed them again. It is the most wonderful thing I do each day. I take my suit off and get into sweats. It's time to go for a walk and tell them all about my day. They agree that making so many changes is just not right. We devise a plan to keep others from making my day so stressed. Then we talk about the 3-day trip we are taking to Utah the day my in-house group ends. It will be our first motor home trip, and we are all excited. It seems my golden retrievers are tired of camping in a tent. Additionally, I plan to spend time working on my online masters degree, and a motor home will be a good place to work. I try not to think too hard about my degree. It makes it hard to sleep when I think of working on my final project.

Now it's 12:30 A.M. and I need to get in bed. As I lie down, I resolve that tomorrow will be "the day I get everything done."

6.8 THE ORGANIZATION AND MANAGEMENT OF HOTEL BEVERAGE OPERATIONS Valentino Luciani

---

✦ BRIEF HISTORY OF BEVERAGES

A beverage such as a glass of wine, a beer, or a cocktail has the magic power of bringing people together. Beverages have always made an impact on the evolution of humankind. Thanks to modern technology and more advanced carbon-dating techniques, archeologists have now established with certainty that our species has been around for several hundred thousand years—a lot longer than was estimated 50 years ago. In accepting the fact that alcohol is as old as we are, it would be of great interest to discover what type of beverages were consumed over such a span of time. We can only assume that the earliest beverages were fermented cider-type concoctions made from various kinds of fruit, or brews made from grain, seeds, and anything else nature had to offer. These drinks were perhaps enriched with spices, herbs, and probably more exotic flavoring agents, some of which have been forgotten or lost over the centuries.

What is known for certain is included in recorded history, and it is relatively recent when compared to the newly established lifespan of *Homo sapiens erectus*. In recent excavations, some of the first evidence of eating food and consuming a beverage in a communal fashion is found in the Orkney Islands, close to Denmark. It was a custom then to build dwellings around a common dispenser where foods and drinks were prepared.

Egyptologists have recently published photos of wall paintings found in pharaohs' tombs. In these remarkably preserved works of art one can clearly see Egyptian workers harvesting grapes and preparing them for winemaking. The (presumably filled) wine vessels were then placed in an orderly fashion next to the tomb. The Egyptian nobles believed that these beverages made the best companions for the pharaoh's eternal travel.

Greek and Roman historians report that wine and other alcoholic beverages played a vital role in their societies. The fun-loving Romans went as far as worshiping a beverage deity: Bacchus, the god of wine. Wine and brew shops,

which are thought to have been introduced approximately 6000 years ago, could be found at every street corner of ancient Rome. In the United States, the first person on record to own a tavern and sell alcoholic beverages to patrons was Samuel Cole. His beverage business was already prospering by 1634.

Beer, which presently accounts for 51 percent of alcoholic beverage sales, carries on a fine tradition in our country. According to the diary of the *Mayflower*'s captain, the ship was not scheduled to dock on Plymouth Rock but was made to stop there mainly because it had run out of beer.

Nonalcoholic beverages such as coffee, tea, fruit juices, and, later, carbonated beverages have also made a considerable impact on our evolution and lifestyle. During the past five decades, Coca-Cola has taken the world by storm. Of the hot beverages, coffee and tea are the uncontested kings. One has to only observe the proliferation of specialty coffee shops and kiosks to begin to understand the impact of this beverage.

✦ OVERVIEW

The beverage industry grows in popularity every year. *Restaurant U.S.A.,* the official publication of the National Restaurant Association, reported in 1995 that total sales for bars and taverns neared the $11 billion mark. For the year 2005, total sales for bars and taverns were expected to exceed the threshold of $15 billion in sales. Hotels, restaurants, and resorts have for some time regarded the beverage sector as a profitable one. In a medium to large hotel, a typical beverage department can produce a profit of over 50 percent of sales. In comparison, a food department shows, at best, a profit of between 15 and 18 percent of sales. Beverage is also gradually gaining a larger share of sales. Hotel operators report that while two decades ago the sales ratio was 85–15 (85 percent food sales, 15 percent beverage sales), today the average is closer to 80–20.

Before World War II, in a small to medium-sized hotel and restaurant operation, the person in charge of the beverage department was the restaurant manager. In many properties, a lead bartender or the wine steward was given the responsibility to run the department.

Today, in a medium to large-size hotel operation, the beverage department has a distinct place in the organization chart, and the beverage manager is the person in charge of running and supervising all of the department activities. The organization chart is a diagram that shows the operation's working positions and how they interconnect. The beverage manager usually reports to the food and beverage director. In a very large hotel operation (over 2000), the F&B director reports to the vice president of food and beverage.

During the last decade, some properties have adopted a different strategy where there are separate food and beverage directors. In these properties the executive chef, who in most cases acts more as a food director than a hands-on chef, is placed in charge of the food department. He or she enjoys a higher degree of independence and reports directly to the general manager, vice president of operations, or, in some instances, directly to the hotel president. The same is true of the beverage director.

Both of these directors are considered equal in the organization chart. They strive to work together effectively and to communicate daily. They are interdependent in many ways but also are aware of the need for communication. In addition, each must establish a sound working rapport with department heads of other hotel sectors. These include front desk supervisors, executive housekeepers, human resources directors, and so forth. Typical of this case, the food manager and the beverage manager, particularly, come together at the end of the month, when the results of their efforts are included in the same profit and loss statement.

Although larger properties find this organization chart modification beneficial to the operation, the majority of hotel properties retain the traditional hierarchy, structuring the chain of command in the same fashion as for the past six or seven decades. A typical example of a classic organization chart for a beverage operation in a large hotel is shown in Figure 6.3.

Figure 6.3 Organization Chart of Beverage Department in a Medium to Large Hotel

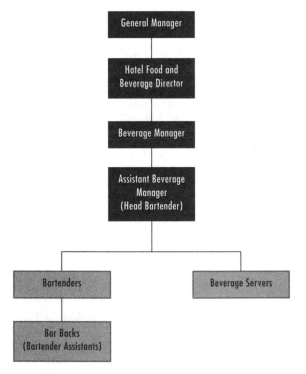

✦ SHOP TALK AND THE ACTIVE MANAGER

The bar manager or beverage director is the person who makes it all happen in relation to hotel beverages. Although specific responsibilities may vary from one hotel to another, the fundamental role of the manager is to make certain that the five basic functions of management are applied effectively. As in many other business sectors, these are planning, organizing, directing, staffing, and controlling. The wise and competent bar manager applies and adapts the fundamental principles of each of these functions to the specific needs of the operation. All five functions are determining factors in meeting the operation's ultimate objective: profitability.

It all begins with planning and continues in directing and organizing so that the staff on a daily basis diligently adheres to the established standards. Examples: checking bartenders' opening and closing duties, standardizing drink recipes, verifying that the bar par stock (established amount of beverage product) is at the proper level, scheduling, forecasting, frequently communicating with other fellow managers (in particular the catering manager and the executive steward), and so forth.

The competent bar manager always finds sufficient time to inspect the underbars (the working area behind and underneath the bar counter), the jockey boxes (the small compartment next to the ice bin), and the speed racks (where the inexpensive, or well, bottles and the more popular brand-name liquor are placed).

The above are also the areas where managers cannot place enough emphasis on how vital it is to the operation to continuously apply sanitary standards and practice the utmost cleanliness. Glassware must not only be cleaned but sanitized as well.

An important organizational and training function is the sequencing of beverage stock. This is the order in which spirits and cordials are placed on the shelves or speed rack. It also refers to the order by which the drinks are called to the bartender by the serving staff, and it must always be the same. Supervising the beverage staff and ensuring that control methods are foolproof are crucial and demanding tasks; sequencing provides part of the structural mix that helps assure consistency of product and service.

✦ MARKETING AND MERCHANDISING

Throughout the competitive hotel industry, beverage managers consider smart marketing and effective merchandising the keys to success. The marketing of the overall operation and the merchandising of the beverage product require time, experience, and commitment. To make the beverage operation attractive to different types of patrons and to convey a message of value in the service of beverages, bar managers and directors regularly brainstorm. More trendy cocktails are being created daily. Light and refreshing blush wines and sparkling wines are introduced in the preparation of new drinks. Promotional programs and attractive entertainment are featured to keep lounges full and patrons eager to return.

Conscientious beverage managers never rest on their laurels—they are always on the lookout for profitable ways to stay ahead of the competition. As the beverage sector grows and patrons' expectations increase, there are always new and challenging tasks to deal with. The following is a list of managerial tasks with which beverage managers are occupied with on an ongoing basis:

- Introducing control systems that are more effective in monitoring the operation—for example, upgrading forms for properly storing and issuing beverage products and for inventory purposes.

- Establishing ongoing training sessions.

- Evaluating beverage staff's work performance.

- Checking city and county ordinances regarding the service of alcohol and reviewing state and federal laws on handling liquor responsibly.

- Preventing bartenders from committing fraud and attempting illegal practices.

- Ensuring proper sanitary standards are applied throughout the bar outlets and the storage and the service areas.

- Making certain everyone in the department adheres to proper safety standards.

- Writing, rewriting, and updating bar working manuals and handbooks according to need.

- Evaluating the bar menu offerings and, whenever possible, replacing slow-selling liquor brands with more attractive and trendy ones.

- In particular, renewing beverage product selection of specialty beers (e.g., by featuring micro-brewed products), brandies, and cordials.

- Tracking trends. For example, a current trend is apparent in cordials or liqueurs. Beverage operators are finding that light, sweet, and pleasant-tasting cordials such as Godiva White Chocolate, Nocello, Grand Marnier, Frangelico, Drambuie, and Bailey's Irish Cream are enjoying newfound popularity. They are also seeing lots of movement in attractive new products such as Remy Red and the fabulous premium tequilas and Polish vodkas.

- Last but not least, assuring the consistency and quality of the service provided to the bar and lounge patron.

✦ HUMAN RESOURCES

Outstanding service is the result of a sound organization and diligent recruiting. Bartenders and beverage servers can be talented and willing, but if they are not provided with the necessary resources, total management support, encouragement, and guidance, their efforts will be in vain. A situation may arise where the deciding factor in the delivery of fine and consistent service depends less on personnel skills and attitude than on the role played by management.

Service is the backbone of the hospitality industry. According to Kotschevar and Luciani (1996), "with the new millennium passing by, customers' expectations are on the rise." An effective leader finds the proper ways and means to provide the employees with the tools they need to meet these expectations.

Progressive beverage managers now also use the empowerment concept. Empowerment is a management decision by which an employee is given authority to take steps outside the spectrum of his or her regular duties and make certain decisions that are normally in management's domain. According to many new beverage managers, the progressive coach approach seems to yield positive results among beverage staffs. The old disciplinarian management style is increasingly out of place in today's beverage business world.

✦ THE FUTURE OF BEVERAGE OPERATIONS

In medium to large hotel properties, like all department managers, beverage managers are required to prepare a business forecast based on historical data, hotel occupancy, and special event bookings for the forecasting period. An accurate forecast helps the manager prepare for clientele volume so that potential revenue can be maximized. It also helps greatly in effectively managing beverage stock, payroll, staff scheduling, and other expenses.

Many hotel executives agree that the first decade of the twenty-first century will be significant for the beverage industry. One peculiar prediction is that, although total hotel revenues are expected to grow considerably, the ratio of beverage sales to room sales will remain the same or decrease slightly. Because of the terrorist attacks in 2001 and the ongoing wars in the Middle East, hotel revenues have not met expectations. Beverage sales, though, have seen an increase in revenue growth. Much of this is due to vigorous promotion and merchandising, particularly of new cocktails and ambitious—even spectacular—wine sales programs. Independent bar and lounge operators also feel confident that, unless more unpredictable events take place, the rest of the decade will be challenging but prosperous.

Beverage distributing firms are also optimistic. They foresee a wider availability of beverage products not only for the hospitality industry but also in areas such as convenience stores, supermarkets, and beverage-specific retail outlets. Beverages that are expected to substantially increase in sales volume are bottled waters, bottled specialty teas, single-malt Scotch whiskys, Cognacs, aged bourbons, premium tequilas, and grappas. There is a general consensus among vendors that beer sales will remain static and that wine will experience a marginal but steady growth, particularly from new areas of production, both nationally and internationally.

It is expected that federal and state liquor laws will remain substantially unchanged, with minor exceptions. It also appears that the states will maintain the basic structure of belonging either to control or license categories. Many beverage managers are concerned about government-imposed taxes on liquor and hope they will not be increased.

Beverage managers are concerned about the continuing lowering of the blood alcohol threshold for driving under the influence (DUI) of alcohol or drugs. The lower the threshold—say, 0.08—the more careful in hiring, training, and supervising managers you have to be. Overservice of alcohol is an industry-wide problem that presents managers with a variety of challenges. It is important to have policies under which the manager and operation work, that minimize the risk to the business and to the public, while legally selling and serving beverages.

Education in beverage management is expected to extend to new horizons. Sonoma State University offers a bachelor of science degree in wine management. Through a well-planned university extension program, the University of California, Davis, is expanding on specialized short courses associated with their degree programs in enology and viticulture. The William F. Harrah College of Hotel Administration at the University of Nevada, Las Vegas, started a beverage management major commencing in the fall semester of 2001. Cornell University's School of Hotel Administration, among others, is considering expanding their professional development courses and adding courses on handling and serving alcoholic beverages with care.

✦ AS I SEE IT

While reviewing the industry's projections, it would be difficult to leave out hotel executives' most recent comments on labor issues and concerns. During the past decade, it has been frequently reported that staffing or finding the person most suitable for a particular job is becoming a tougher management function. Many managers agree that staffing responsibilities are requiring more time and effort than ever before. Part of this is attributed to labor trends. The pool of steady and loyal workers is decreasing in size. In addition, the hospitality industry is experiencing unprecedented employee turnover. A major restaurant company has recently reported to me employee turnover of nearly 200 percent for hourly employees, 60 percent for clerical and secretarial staff, and 25 percent for managerial staff. The turnover ratio of bartenders and cocktail servers was reported to be almost the same as that of typical dining room staff such as food servers and bus persons (Lattin, 1998). One can imagine the frustration of a beverage manager who, after spending considerable effort, time, and company money in coaching and training a new bartender, finds out she is planning to quit the following week.

What can be done to deal effectively with this concern? Rewards as motivators provide some positive results. Other means of providing monetary incentives so the operation can retain employees longer may also be effective.

It is strongly recommended here that the best measure management can undertake for this purpose is to provide the employee with a comfortable working environment, promote teamwork and camaraderie, and foster healthy working relationships. In short, the beverage manager is challenged to become the employer of choice for beverage professionals.

In general, the beverage future looks brighter than most other sectors of the hospitality industry. However, the managers and directors who truly will make a difference will be those who step out, participate, and make things happen. The aggressive new manager always finds ways to establish a good rapport with community leaders and is tireless in devising and developing new means of attracting additional clientele. Whenever possible, he or she makes the effort to attend beverage conventions and trade shows; uses the hotel web site to reinforce marketing strategies and list bar special drinks, promotions, and happy hour times; and never rests on his or her laurels.

The modern beverage manager is no longer just the head bartender. This professional is responsible for millions of dollars of the hotel's assets and operates in a high-energy, fast-paced, and challenging environment. It's a lot of fun, though, and rewarding, too. It is a managerial position with a solid future.

6.9 CASE STUDY: CRISIS IN THE FOOD COURT NANCY SWANGER

Morgan Black is the director of operations of an on-property food court made up of five branded quick-service restaurant concepts and one full-service casual dining outlet. The resort hotel, of which the food court is a part, attracts affluent guests who are traveling with their families. The food court is located in a common area not far from some of the resort's most popular, kid-friendly recreational activities. It also attracts local guests who are not staying at the resort, but just visiting.

One Sunday afternoon, when the hotel's 2500 rooms and suites were nearly at full occupancy, an incident occurred at the branded sandwich shop that was both bizarre and frightening to those involved.

As was typical of the property, lunchtime in the common restaurant area was busy and extended well into the afternoon as families arrived for weeklong stays. A father and son approached the counter of the sandwich shop to order a bite to eat. They were nearing the register to pay for their meal when the son suddenly collapsed and fell to the floor, hitting his head on the glass window separating the customers from the sandwich preparation area. The boy, who was wearing short pants, fell into a puddle of his own bloody feces as he hit the floor. As it all happened so suddenly, those who were witnesses said it was like the boy must have voided as he was collapsing, as there were no signs of any problem prior to the actual fall.

As one might expect, the scene caused quite a stir among guests in the area. One of the shop's employees promptly called 911 for an ambulance. Within a very short period, paramedics arrived to care for the boy. It was several minutes before he was stable enough to transport, as they could not get the bleeding to stop. Morgan, who was on property, arrived just as the boy was being transported to the local hospital for treatment.

Of course, a crowd had gathered, and talk of the tragedy was spreading rapidly throughout the property. The store was immediately closed and the area around the sandwich shop cordoned off. In trying to assess the situation, Morgan discovered the following:

1. When the young boy hit the floor, the puddle of bloody excrement splattered everywhere—even hitting other guests who were in line.
2. One of the employees, who probably reacted without thinking, began to clean up the mess with her bare hands.
3. The identities of the father and son were not known.
4. A reporter from the local newspaper was a guest at the food court that day and wanted comments on what happened.

Suggest a plan for Morgan's handling of the situation.

Points to Consider
- Involvement of the health department?
- Notification of the brand's corporate office?
- Condition of the boy?
- Clean-up process?
- Treatment of contaminated items?
- Handling affected guests and employees?
- Methods to reassure resort guests?
- When to reopen and resume business as usual?
- Implications of what happened—short and long term?
- Role of the resort's crisis team?
- Training gaps?

6.10 CASE STUDY: OUTSIDE THE BOX IN THE FOOD AND BEVERAGE DIVISION

The Corporate Food and Beverage Committee, through its executive director, has ordered each hotel in the SunRise Hospitality chain (11 medium-size, full-service hotels situated in the Southeast, South, and Southwest) to submit a plan to completely rethink one restaurant in each hotel. SunRise Hospitality specializes in catering to the upscale business traveler and, increasingly, the high-tech companies that are now moving to the South from California, the Seattle region, and the Northeast. Their average room rates are consistently in the top 15 percent of all hotels in their market areas. Historically, though, this has been a fairly conservative and risk-averse hotel company.

The corporate office wants to change this and, in the process, to involve each hotel in decision making. The executive director of F&B wants to evaluate plans from each hotel's food and beverage director that "think outside the box." Among the ideas floating around the company on the F&B directors' grapevine are the following:

- Feature menus that emphasize local or regional cuisine. The idea here is to utilize fresh ingredients and local meat, produce, and seafood, and to feature the ethnic and cultural diversity of each hotel's local market area. One goal of this plan is to make the hotel restaurant appeal to local clientele in addition to its guests.

- Outsource one restaurant to a well-established regional independent operator.

- Outsource one restaurant to a national chain.

- Hire a celebrity chef to bring prestige and favorable publicity to the hotel.

These are only a few of the possibilities. As food and beverage director, you have brought this plan to a meeting of your staff for purposes of general background discussion and ideas about how to proceed. Included in this meeting are the executive chef and chief steward, the manager and assistant manager of your formal French-service dining room, the wine steward, and the director of purchasing.

After presenting the corporate plan, you ask for ideas and comments. The chef, who is French, is absolutely devastated and seems to be treating the corporate directive as a personal insult. He walks out in a huff, threatening to pack up his knives and recipes and go back to France. The restaurant manager is interested in the corporate idea but says she has just spent the last 5 months hiring and training about half of her restaurant staff in tableside preparation and service of the French menu. She is worried that switching menus this fast may cause her operation to suffer, at least in the short term.

The wine steward considers the challenge somewhat ambiguous because, depending on what eventually is decided, he will have to choose a complementary wine list to enhance the new concept or lose his job to an outsider.

The director of purchasing is intrigued by the idea of exploring new local markets. However, he too worries that some of the options may diminish his responsibilities.

Your job as director of food and beverage is to help each department head develop a plan that will satisfy his or her concerns while following the dictates of corporate policy.

(*Note:* Additional insights into potential solutions to this case may be gained by reading the essay by C. Lee Evans in chapter 8 of this book.)

REFERENCES

Allen, R. L. 1996. "Hotel Chains 'Taking It to the Street' in Quests for Mainstream Dining Appeal." *Nation's Restaurant News* 30(17).

Baker, M., A. Cattet, and M. Riley. 1995. "Practical food and beverage training in the UK: A study of facilities and a debate on its relevance." *International Journal of Contemporary Hospitality Management* 17(5):21–24.

Cooper, D. 1967. *The Bad Food Guide.* London: Routledge & Kegan Paul.

Dubé, L., C. A. Enz, L. M. Renaghan, and J. A. Siguaw. 1999. *The Key to Best Practices in the U.S. Lodging Industry.* Ithaca, NY: Cornell University, Center for Hospitality Research.

Hanson, B. 1984. "Hotel Foodservice: Where's the Profit?" *Cornell Hotel and Restaurant Administration Quarterly* 25(2): 92–96.

Hensdill, C. 1996. "Partnerships in Dining." *Hotels* 30(2):57-60.

Kotschevar, L., and V. Luciani. 1996. *Presenting Service.* Chicago: Education Foundation of the National Restaurant Association.

Lattin, G. 1998. *The Lodging and Foodservice Industry.* East Lansing, MI: Educational Institute of the American Hotel and Motel Association.

Liberson, J. 1996a. "The Global Dinner Plate." *Lodging* 22(1):85–88.

Parseghian, P. 1996. "Branding Offers Hotels Opportunities to Increase Food Sales." *Nation's Restaurant News* 30(23):96.

Riley, M. 1981. "Declining hotel standards and the skill trap." *International Journal of Tourism Management* 2(2):95–104.

Riley, M. 1994. "Marketing eating out: the influence of social culture and innovation." *British Journal of Food* 96(10):15–19.

Riley, M. 2000a. "How can we better understand operational productivity in food and beverage management? A resource substitution framework." In R. C. Wood (Ed.), *Strategic Questions in Food and Beverage Management.* Oxford: Butterworth-Heinemann.

Riley, M. 2000b. "Can hotel restaurants ever be profitable? Short-and long-term perspectives." In R.C. Wood (Ed.), *Strategic Questions in Food and Beverage Management.* Oxford: Butterworth-Heinemann.

Riley, M., and E. Davis. 1992. "Development and innovation; the case of food and beverage management in hotels." In C. Cooper, (Ed.), *Progress in Tourism, Recreation and Hospitality Management.* London: Belhaven Press.

Salleh, H., and M. Riley. 1994. "Measuring culinary learning processes: education and experience contrasted." *International Journal of Contemporary Hospitality Management* 6(6): iii–vii.

Strate, R.W., and C. L. Rappole. 1997. "Strategic alliances between hotels and restaurants." *Cornell Hotel and Restaurant Administration Quarterly* 38(3):50–61.

Witham, G. 1995a. "Trader Vic's Wraps Up 60th Birthday Bash." *Cornell Hotel and Restaurant Administration Quarterly* 36(3):14.

———. 1995b. "Harvey: Expansion and Conversion." *Cornell Hotel and Restaurant Administration Quarterly* 36(4):13.

Wolff, C. 1995. "Hyatt Regency Columbus Blazes F&B Trails." *Lodging Hospitality* 51(9):24.

SUGGESTED READINGS

BOOKS

Birchfield, J. C., and R. T. Sparrowe. 2007. *Design and Layout of Foodservice Facilities* (3rd ed.). Hoboken, NJ: John Wiley and Sons.

Birchfiled, J. C., and J. Birchfield, Jr. 2007. *Design and Layout of Foodservice Facilities* (3rd ed.). Hoboken, NJ: John Wiley and Sons.

Bode, S. 2002. *Successful Catering: Managing the Catering Operation for Maximum Profit.* Starke, FL: Atlantic Publishing Company.

Dittmer, P. R., and J. D. Keefe III. 2005. *Principles of Food, Beverage, and Labor Cost Controls* (8th ed.). Hoboken, NJ: John Wiley and Sons.

Hansen, B., and C. Thomas. 2005. *Off-Premise Catering Management* (2nd ed.). Hoboken, NJ: John Wiley and Sons.

Katsigris, C., and C. Thomas. 2006. *The Bar and Beverage Book* (4th ed.). Hoboken, NJ: John Wiley and Sons.

Pavesic, D. V. 1999. *Restaurant Manager Handbook Series: Menu Pricing and Menu Design.* New York: Lebhar-Friedman.

Shock, P. J., and J. M. Stefanelli. 2000. *On-Premise Catering: Hotels, Convention & Conference Centers, and Clubs.* New York: John Wiley and Sons.

ARTICLES

Allen, R. L. 1996. "Hotel Chains 'Taking It to the Street' in Quests for Mainstream Dining Appeal." *Nation's Restaurant News* 30(17):124–128.

Hanson, B. August 1984. "Hotel Foodservice: Where's the Profit?" *Cornell Hotel and Restaurant Administration Quarterly* 25(2):92–96.

Hensdill, C. 1996. "Partnerships in Dining." *Hotels* 30(2):57–60.

Hubsch, A. W. 1966. "Hotel Food and Beverage Management." *Cornell Hotel and Restaurant Administration Quarterly* 7(3): 9–11, 18–19.

Parseghian, P. 1996. "Branding Offers Hotels Opportunities to Increase Food Sales." *Nation's Restaurant News* 30(23).

Wall, E. A., and L. L. Berry. 2007. "The Combined Effects of the Physical Environment and Employee Behavior on Customer Perception of Restaurant Service Quality." *Cornell Hotel and Restaurant Administration Quarterly* 48(1):59–60.

Wansink, B., G. Cordua, E. Blair, C. Payne, and S. Geiger. 2006. "Wine Promotions in Restaurants: Do Beverage Sales Contribute or Cannibalize?" *Cornell Hotel and Restaurant Administration Quarterly* 47(4):327–336.

SOURCE NOTES

Chapter 6.2, "Food and Beverage Management: A Review of Change," by Michael Riley, is reprinted from the first issue of 2005 in the *International Journal of Contemporary Hospitality Management.* © Emerald Group Publishing Limited. Used by permission. All rights reserved.

Chapter 6.3, "A Day in the Life of a Catering/Convention Services Manager," by Robyn Graff.

Chapter 6.4, "Best Practices in Food and Beverage Management," by Judy A. Siguaw and Cathy A. Enz, is reprinted from the October 1999 issue of *Cornell Hotel and Restaurant Administration Quarterly.* © Cornell University. Used by permission. All rights reserved.

Chapter 6.5, "Strategic Alliances Between Hotels and Restaurants," by Robert W. Strate and Clinton L. Rappole, is reprinted from the June 1997 issue of *Cornell Hotel and Restaurant Administration Quarterly.* © Cornell University. Used by permission. All rights reserved.

Chapter 6.6, "Contemporary Hotel Catering," by Patti J. Shock and John Stefanelli, adapted from *Hotel*

Catering, by Patti J. Shock and John Stefanelli, Copyright © (year and owner). Reprinted by permission of John Wiley & Sons, Inc.

Chapter 6.7, "A Day in the Life of an Executive Director of Catering Sales and Convention Services," by Rich Benninger.

Chapter 6.8, "The Organization and Management of Hotel Beverage Operations," by Valentino Luciani.

Chapter 6.9, "Case Study: Crisis in the Food Court," by Nancy Swanger.

MARKETING AND ASSOCIATED ACTIVITIES

7.1 INTRODUCTION

For most hotel companies, it was only during the 1980s that the word *marketing* was anything more than a euphemism for sales. Indeed, in the competitive landscape of the not too distant past, an aggressive and knowledgeable sales staff could accomplish most activities that related to putting guests in rooms. In the competitive environment of the present time, this has become impossible. Hotel companies that design and market a sophisticated inventory of hospitality services need a similarly sophisticated scheme for letting potential clientele know about their services.

For most hotel companies in the twenty-first century, true marketing has evolved to reflect this sophistication. This development also acknowledges increased sophistication on the part of guests and potential clientele. Business travelers, travel agents, and meeting planners who

represent and book group and convention business are educated and informed consumers. To serve this clientele, hotels have had to develop marketing efforts and product segmentation, first to interest the market, and second to allow people representing that market to make intelligent choices among competitors. Increasingly, individual consumers and small businesses are becoming more sophisticated in arranging their own travel plans over the Internet. This represents yet another challenge to hotel marketers: How do we market most efficiently to all groups? Good question.

Marketing has become an umbrella term that covers a number of strategic and tactical activities designed to tell the clientele the story of the hotel's services and to encourage that clientele to make choices based on how one hotel's marketing message matches their needs better than the available alternatives. In any given hotel or hotel company, marketing includes a range of sales activities, public relations, advertising in all media, design of symbols and images, and (increasingly) the departments of convention services, reservations, revenue management, and, perhaps, catering.

The article contributed to this section by Fletch Waller provides a strong argument for broadening the definition of marketing to include all operational aspects of the hotel. This article is an excellent overview of the marketing process. Waller illustrates the relationship between marketing and operations as a "continuing process" without which hotels probably cannot remain competitive.

It should be noted that research plays a major role in designing marketing strategies and tactics. The monograph presented in this edition by Bianca Grohmann and Eric Spangenberg has a research orientation at its core. It is designed to assist managers in choosing and generating data that are useful to staying successfully competitive. It is important that managers understand the range within which this data may be interpreted and applied. Successful managers and high-quality organizations are always seeking information and data that allow them to make accurate decisions and design effective marketing and managerial efforts.

These data can take a number of forms but, for the most part, deal with the characteristics of the hotel's target market segment that affect their choice of hotels. In this case, the research seeks to understand how consumers make choices among hotels based on the value of their various attributes.

Among all possible data available to a hotel, hotels often accumulate and interpret the following:

- *Geographic:* what sorts of communities are represented; what parts of the country or world; how far people travel.

- *Demographic:* age, sex, occupation, income, ethnicity, family, education.

- *Psychographic:* client's self-image, social or peer group, lifestyle, personality traits.

- *Behavioral:* whether the hotel choice is a routine or special occasion; what guest seeks in terms of quality, service, economy; user status (nonuser, ex-user, potential user, regular user, first-time user); usage rate (light, medium, heavy); loyalty (none, medium, strong, absolute).

While many of the specific details or programs implied under the marketing umbrella may be farmed out to agencies that specialize in advertising or public relations, the genesis of the hotel's strategic marketing plan must be within the hotel organization itself.

Yield management, long a practice of the airline industry, has found total acceptance by hotel marketing and reservations systems. Indeed, it has become an industry standard. The article in this section by Paul Chappelle can be read in conjunction with that by Quain and LeBruto in Section 4 for a comprehensive primer on yield management. Together, these articles explore various aspects of that practice from the viewpoint of Chappelle, a current practitioner. Chappelle lives the theory of yield and revenue management on a daily basis and provides insights about how it works in practice.

As the revenue manager for over 30 hotels, Chappelle has the experience to back up the theory.

The Sinclair essay on hotel pricing should be read in the context of the issues and suggestions raised by the contributions on yield management. But it goes beyond that. Drawing on Sinclair's deep experience in hotel operations, particularly sales, this contemporary work on pricing is up to date and useful not only from a conceptual standpoint but also from a practical one.

Shaw and Morris bring their collaborative talents in academe and industry to the essay on the organization of the sales function in hotels. Because, as noted elsewhere in this text, the potential markets for a hotel's services and the types of hotels are so numerous, sales efforts can be complicated. Shaw and Morris present this complex departmental function in a clear, straightforward, fashion that is both theoretically relevant and operationally practical.

Traditionally, the function of public relations for any organization, particularly hotels, was oriented toward the generation of favorable—usually free—publicity and the suppression or management of bad news. Louis Richmond proposes the different, and expanded, but not necessarily contrary position that public relations activities can positively enhance the hotel's sales and marketing efforts. He discusses his experiences in the case of the Seattle Sheraton Hotel and Towers. Using that example, he argues that through creative cooperative efforts with local charity, cultural, and volunteer organizations, hotels can serve the activities of those groups' fundraising efforts and simultaneously position themselves to show the arbiters of potential business how well the hotel can perform. His examples are instructive. Richmond, who is the CEO of his own very successful public relations firm in Seattle, retains the Sheraton and other hospitality concerns as clients.

From a completely different, but innovative approach, Paul Iacovino presents the function of marketing from an international perspective. As the vice president of marketing—Asia Pacific for the Four Seasons Hotels and Resorts, Iacovino has experienced many different issues that are often overlooked by an individual residing in the United States. However, as he reports, these issues are significant to those hotel companies operating oversees. As a new addition to this version of the text, Iacovino challenges the reader to anticipate the unexpected. In particular, he discusses the unexpected influences in Asia that have occurred in the past ten years, including those that are attributed to political, natural, financial, and technological causes.

All in all, the strategies, tactics, activities, personnel, and concepts described in the articles and essays in this section provide an overview that only hints at everything important to effective management of the marketing function. Marketing is perhaps the most written-about topic in hospitality literature. Because of the great diversity of opinion, it can be argued that there is no one "right" way to market, nor is any single piece of literature generally considered seminal to hotel marketing. The reader is urged to consider the references cited by contributing authors, the suggested readings, and active perusal of recent hospitality journals to achieve greater understanding of this fascinating process—and, by extension, its management.

7.2 BUILDING MARKET LEADERSHIP: MARKETING AS PROCESS   Fletch Waller

The hotel business has changed enormously over the last 30 years, embracing special niche forms of lodging (e.g., extended stay), new ways of segmenting markets (e.g., W's "fashionables"), brand proliferation and consolidation, new tools for acquiring customers (e.g., email), distribution innovations (e.g., Expedia), and globalization. These changes in markets and in ways hotels relate to and capitalize on them have put new demands on marketing.

Marketing, as addressed herein, is not the sales and marketing department; I mean marketing in its broadest sense of how hotels respond to and seize on market opportunities. Definition? Marketing is a process of creating and sustaining productive relationships with desirable customers. Its goal? To produce such relationships more effectively than competitors do.

Let's examine the definition and its implications. Marketing is:

- **. . . a process . . .** A process, a series of functions and actions for approaching and dealing with opportunities. *Marketing,* as used herein, is not a job but a way of proceeding to create and operate a hotel focused on customers and competitors, a way that incorporates all members of the hotel staff and its support.

- **. . . of creating . . .** The essence of marketing is creation: imagination, insight, willingness to change and evolve, and, yes, discard.

- **. . . and sustaining . . .** Loyalty over time and repeat customers are the key to productivity and optimal contribution margins.

- **. . . productive relationships . . .** A relationship must be two-sided, with benefits for both partners in the relationship. In the case of customers, the benefits are wants and needs consistently fulfilled and full value received; in the case of staff, professional satisfaction and operating profits sufficient to fund improvements provide attractive compensation, and provide returns on investors' or owners' capital.

- **. . . with desirable customers.** Not all customers are equally desirable; we want those who are willing to pay, growing in numbers, making multiple purchases, and whose needs we are able to fully satisfy.

And the goal?

- **. . . To produce such relationships . . .** *Production* implies inputs, outputs, and the measurement of productivity. Marketing productivity has been lagging for the last decade; the rising costs of acquiring customers must be reined in. (*Note*: If marketing efforts are a cause of customer decisions to purchase, then marketing productivity is the cost of stimulating that purchase decision relative to the value of that decision. Productivity is best measured by the cost of acquiring a customer not only as a percent of sales but also as dollars per *unit* of sale—for example, dollars per occupied room, dollars per group contract, dollars per cover.)

- **. . . more effectively than competitors do.** Marketing success is judged in relative terms, using competitors and similar hotels as benchmarks. As a creative process, especially in a field like hospitality wherein innovations are unprotected and easily copied, the benchmarks and goals are always moving targets. Besting the competition is the constant challenge.

By the end of this chapter, it will be clear that successful marketing of a hotel requires the orchestration of a wide variety of talents and skills, of which sales and marketing personnel are only a part. Chain hotels approach the process one way; independents must do so another. But in either case, market success depends on an effective integration of marketing and operations at the property level under the direction and leadership of a market-driven general manager.

In the late 1990s, rising costs of acquiring customers in U.S. hotels were masked by strong increases in the average daily rate (ADR). In 1995, marketing costs per occupied room (franchise and marketing fees, commissions, reservation costs, and property marketing and sales expenses) in full-service hotels averaged 15.3 percent of ADR. By 2000, it had risen to 15.6 percent; that three-tenths of a point increase over four years hardly alarmed people. However, of the expenses that make up the costs of acquiring customers, only commissions vary directly with rate; most of the expenses are personnel compensation and benefits, as well as purchases of ads, brochures, sales calls, web sites, global distribution system (GDS) delivery services, telephone time, and so on. These expenses grow over time, but not as a function of the price for which a room is sold.

If marketing were truly productive, we should have been seeing costs per unit dropping.

In dollar terms, full-service hotels saw marketing costs per occupied room balloon 38 percent in just 5 years, to $17.96 in 2000 from $12.99 per room-night in 1995! In higher-rated full-service hotels, acquisition costs rose to $22.71 from $15.86, a 43 percent increase. Resorts suffered a 27 percent increase, to $22.96 from $18.07 just five years earlier. By 2002, as rates and occupancies softened, marketing costs per occupied room in full-service hotels had begun to be reined in, at $17.02, but now accounted for 16.4 percent of ADR (PKF's Trend Reports, 1996, 1998, 2001, 2003.) The main culprit is distribution costs. Whatever the cause, marketing productivity must be improved.

✦ THE MARKETING PROCESS

Peter Drucker (1974) says the purpose of operating a business is to create a customer and keep him (or her). Investors in a hotel may have return on investment as their purpose, but for us operators, it is useful to conceive our purpose as being to create and keep customers. If we do this successfully, profits and capital returns flow. Our marketing process is our way of creating and keeping customers.

Every business has a marketing process, a way it "goes to market." It is the way management

Figure 7.1 The Hotel Marketing Process

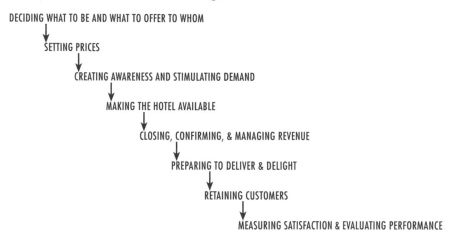

DECIDING WHAT TO BE AND WHAT TO OFFER TO WHOM

SETTING PRICES

CREATING AWARENESS AND STIMULATING DEMAND

MAKING THE HOTEL AVAILABLE

CLOSING, CONFIRMING, & MANAGING REVENUE

PREPARING TO DELIVER & DELIGHT

RETAINING CUSTOMERS

MEASURING SATISFACTION & EVALUATING PERFORMANCE

decides what they are going to do and offer, with whom they will compete, how they will attract the customers, and how they will satisfy and keep them. Most businesses, many hotels among them, do not reflect on and carefully articulate their marketing process; they just do their thing by habit and by tradition. Other businesses make concerted efforts to regularly plan and review their "going to market."

A hotel is a 24/7 business, running without stop. Typically, because of the pressure just to keep up, we do what we've done in the past, repeating our marketing process by habit. This is risky, for customers and competitors are always changing. Does a hotel need a planned and regular review of its marketing process? Considering our high fixed costs and the large leverage on profits from small changes in revenues, yes—hotels *should* take concerted and disciplined care of their marketing process. For a hotel to remain effective, it should formally review its marketing process at least once a year to be sure it is still suited to its market; if it is not, revise it to fit changing customer and competitor patterns. Further, the hotel must

measure the cost of acquiring its customers so as to steadily increase the productivity of its marketing process.

A hotel marketing process (Figure 7.1) starts with *deciding what to be and what to offer to whom*. This is not just for new hotels in pre-opening; existing hotels must adjust and fine-tune their offerings as market conditions change. The next step is to *set the price structure*. These first two steps establish the hotel's value proposition.

Next, *create awareness and stimulate demand* among the people you hope to make your customers. Then you must *make the hotel available* to them, and close the sale—that is, *commit, confirm, and manage revenue*. Flexible rate management within the pricing structure and response to short-term swings in demand and supply are necessary to create customers and optimize revenue per available room.

Now begins the transition to operations, but this is no less a part of the marketing process. In fact, this is the critical part of the process. You must *prepare the hotel staff* to meet and fully satisfy the wants and expectation of these customers you have attracted. Then you have to work to *retain those customers* and turn them into repeat loyalists. Lastly, you must *measure their satisfaction and evaluate your performance.*

Let's examine these steps and, along the way, comment on ways of improving their effectiveness and productivity.

✦ DECIDING WHAT TO BE AND WHAT TO OFFER TO WHOM

In an existing hotel, the developer and architect already may have decided many of the things it is—high-rise or resort, in the business center or on the edge of town, large rooms and baths or smallish, one restaurant or several, wood or marble, with ballroom or not, and so on. Even so, the management team must still consciously examine what they intend the hotel to be and offer to whom. The type of customer originally in mind may not be available now in enough numbers to support the hotel. Perhaps a competitor has come in and taken away a piece of the market. Perhaps the business center has shifted to another part of the city. Perhaps new customers from Korea or California have replaced the original ones from Europe and the East Coast. Even though the owner has provided a basic envelope within which to operate,

there still are options—many things the hotel team can control, many choices to be made on what to offer and to emphasize to various market segments. Is the hotel the place to be seen or the place that guards privacy? Is it better to stress family style or crisp, professional business style? Should the hotel add services, like a Japanese breakfast, to meet the needs of one particular group? Should the team put in meetings express and add more small meeting spaces to tap the short-lead-time corporate meetings market? Should it drop some services the market no longer wants to support?

The answers to what to be and offer are found by studying the *marketing situation,* which comprises three parts: (1) strengths and weaknesses, (2) the kinds and numbers of customers available in the marketplace, and (3) the other hotels with whom this hotel competes for these customers. Careful analysis yields a picture of which segments the hotel is best able to attract and serve. These become the *target markets*—the "to whoms"—and their needs and wants become the "what to be's." The key to successfully deciding what to be and offer to whom is a matter of strategic selection of, focus on, and commitment to a well-defined set of markets for whom the hotel is best suited to compete. Trying to be all things to all potential customers is a guarantee of ineffectiveness.

IMPROVEMENT TIPS

- Send prospective general managers and directors of marketing to a marketing course, one with examples or cases in market analysis.

- Assign analytic exercises to a prospective director of marketing, like coming up with three options for cutting into the small business meetings of a competitor or increasing sales of the gift shop.

✦ SETTING PRICES

Having decided what to be and offer and to whom, the next most important decision is price. Pricing is a critical decision because it determines, first, whether or not the intended customers will purchase, and second, whether they will be satisfied with the value offered and, thus, be willing to return. Third, it determines whether the hotel will be financially healthy enough to maintain itself and reward its employees so customers can once again be satisfied when they do return.

Three factors must come into consideration in pricing—the Three Cs of pricing, if you will: costs, competition, and customers' comfort zones. In F&B, costs drive pricing of menu items and beverages. Drucker (1999, 115–116) says American industry has too much cost-driven pricing, and that it needs more price-driven costing. Doesn't F&B have the opportunity to build and test menus to discover where price points should be set, and is not the chef challenged to manage ingredients and portion size to deliver the cost and margin structure desired? Yet the cost-driven practice continues.

In rooms, competition is most often the dominant factor. Costs play a role, but changes in variable cost of an occupied room are generally small and rooms' contribution margins are large, typically 65 percent or better. Moreover, hotel accounting does not measure discounts from a standard price, as do almost all other industries. So there is no visible cost in reducing price to meet competitors. Remember: Any damn fool can cut his price, and some damn fool always will. Must everyone follow? No. The key is to get in the head of the customer. The truly controlling factor is customer comfort zones, and all too often hotel management leave money on the table because they don't know what those comfort zones are. At what price does the offer attract and deliver value? That is the key question in setting prices.

Price setting requires talent and skill in data gathering and analysis, accounting and building pro formas, interpreting and drawing inferences, and decision making. Do not let salespeople set prices; do not let controllers set prices. Only one person—the GM—can pull together the inputs of sales, control, operations, reservations, and the rest, and make this crucial judgment call. Also, build at least three price scenarios and have the controller and marketing director agree on occupancy impacts. Then run a GOP pro forma on each. Out of that exercise will come a sense of the best pricing approach to take. Setting prices is the one task the GM cannot delegate, for he or she must live with and be accountable for all that results from this critical decision.

PRICING TIP

Include staffers in contact with customers in pricing discussions. A ski resort owner-operator asked me to review his proposed price schedules. I asked to have included in our meeting a senior reservation agent, a bellman, a bartender, and a front desk agent. After probing them on what they heard from customers about value, we increased four of the seven proposed room type prices, to the owner-operator's delight.

A good example of focus and targeting is Starwood's W. At risk of turning off a sizable portion of the business and leisure travel market and leaving families well behind, Starwood focuses tightly on a lifestyle segment of professional and business people, with remarkable success.

The talents required to assess the marketing situation, create a data model of the market's segments, calculate a feasible share of each, and select the targets on which to focus are comfort with data, the ability to observe and infer, creativity, patience with detail, comfort with the hypothetical, and an analytic curiosity. Usually, such analyses are uncomfortably foreign to people with backgrounds in sales, and often to operators as well. It is essential that we teach, motivate, and reward curious, careful, insightful analysis of history and market information-skills that are not natural to those typically attracted to hospitality management.

POSITIONING IN FIVE QUESTIONS

1. Who are the prospects; what do they like; how do we find them?

2. What do they now know or believe about us?

3. What, specifically, do we want them to do?

4. What do they need to come to believe so they will do that?

5. What reasons can we offer them to hold this new belief?

✦ CREATING AWARENESS AND STIMULATING DEMAND

Herein are the typical roles of the marketing department: using sales, communications, and promotions to attract the target markets. But creating awareness is not only marketing's job. Everything the public sees and hears about the hotel—its name or brand, its signs, its restaurants, the public activities of its managers, its charitable support and festivals—all create a meaning, a picture of what this hotel means and offers.

Starwood's W again offers an example: Every element of their presentation expresses the "to whom" they target. In decor, uniforms (costumes?), tone, and attitude, they focus and send a coherent message. It is critical that every department understand the target markets and agrees on the idea, the meaning the hotel intends to have for each of the target customer groups. This is called *positioning*; it's something done not to the product but to the mind of the prospect.

The team should prepare written positioning statements, including a compatible but individual positioning statement for each market segment they intend to target. These statements are the blueprint against which each ad, promotion, and sales call is tested to assure consistent messages are being sent. And those statements should be shared with all employees. When all parts of the hotel are sending a coherent and consistent message of what the name or brand means and what underlying promise is being made, the hotel establishes a clear position in the mind of the prospects—ideally, one that is attractively distinctive from competitors.

Marketers can use a variety of tools to create awareness and stimulate demand—for example, sales blitzes, telemarketing, newspaper ads, Internet sites and ads, partnership alliances, radio ads, and price promotions. The marketing mix is the range and balance of tools selected and resources devoted to each to achieve the hotel's marketing goals.

In most hotels, direct selling is still the primary marketing tool used to create awareness and stimulate demand. There are two parts of effective direct selling: sales skills and sales management. Consider one the weapon, the other the shooter.

Sales skills are not natural; enthusiasm may be natural, liking to meet people may be natural, but selling is a process that anyone can learn and that must be practiced. Make sure your salespeople are taught how to research their prospect, to listen for needs and purposes, to acknowledge that they have heard the prospect, to transform relevant features into benefits and to sell the customer's success, to anticipate objections and prepare responses, to negotiate, to ask for the order, and to thank the customer and facilitate delivery.

SALES PRODUCTIVITY TIPS

- Track competitors' group commitments so that a market's uncommitted meeting spaces for future dates are foreseen, guiding pricing.

- Don't "be fair" by treating everyone the same; motivate each salesperson individually with incentives and attention suitable to his or her own style and needs.

- Focus on team members who are below average, constantly improving the bottom, and driving average production up.

- Don't just focus on room-nights. Calculate the number of contracts needed (using your average size of group) to fill the annual room block and set goals for weekly contract production as well. This will balance the sense of importance among salespeople, whether assigned to large or small group segments.

- Don't waste sales talent on cold calling. Use a prospecting service to qualify leads; focus your selling power on prospects.

- Clean out files at least annually. Salespeople tend to hold on to prospects long after the likelihood of a booking has dwindled.

- Automate. Customer and booking management systems pay.

Sales management is quite another thing; often (usually?) the top salesperson does not make the best sales manager. The sales manager must be able to select salespeople; reinforce their training; coach, counsel and motivate them; assign them to prospects and market segments; set goals, manage compensation, review performance; and troubleshoot. He or she must also be the gatekeeper on contracts and rates, making sure that inventory of group space is optimally committed.

Compensation of salespeople need not be complicated. *First principle:* Tie compensation to goals set in terms of what you want them to do— that is, produce contracts and room-nights. Don't just set room-night goals; add measures of relationship or share of a specific customer's business.

Have salespeople suggest their own goals for the coming year; participation builds commitment. *Second:* Provide them near-term reward and reinforcement, not postponed rewards. Pay out bonuses quarterly. *Third:* Build teamwork so that one salesperson supports and encourages another. Add a team bonus multiplier to personal performance measures. *Last:* Separate performance bonuses from overall job appraisal. No one attends to suggestions for performance improvement if he or she has just received a big check for exceeding goals.

Many full-service hotels are overresourced in group sales and underweighted in transient market tools. Sales efforts should be balanced with other parts of the marketing mix—advertising, publicity, and promotions.

The range of communication options increases geometrically with proliferation of new media—cable television, news magazines and national papers, the Internet, and direct mail and telemarketing. But the eyeballs are not growing apace, meaning the audience for any one medium is steadily shrinking, putting increasing demand on measures of productivity, care in allocating resources, and creativity to get through the clutter. As audiences of prospects become increasingly expensive to reach through advertising, the tools of publicity, the Internet, and direct marketing are increasingly the media of choice.

The Internet is a demanding medium for communication; use professional help to design, maintain, and market the hotel's web site as though it were, itself, a product for which awareness must be created and demand stimulated. To draw an audience to the site and manage its visibility in search engines are skills beyond the property team. Set specific goals for the site: They might be to attract qualified prospects, to sell services, to provide customer service. Don't just have a site. And measure the experts against those goals. A passive, unmanaged, and undermarketed site is a waste of money.

Promotions can powerfully stimulate demand, but too often, price promotions are resorted to as a last-minute attempt to prop up a weak demand period. Promotions should be planned, justified on a breakeven basis, and used sparingly. Not all promotions need to be price promotions; customers invest energy and time in transactions, too: value-added promotions that offer nonmonetary savings can be used to avoid habituating consumers to buying only on sale or shopping only on price. Well-forged alliances for copromotion can increase both productivity and absolute sales volume.

The skills and talents necessary in a comprehensive effort to create awareness and stimulate demand include:

- *In sales:* Initiative, being goal-directed, listening with empathy and imagination, time management, self-confidence.

- *In sales management:* Coaching and counseling; quantitative skills (for setting booking goals and recordkeeping); priority setting, time management, and sense of urgency; leadership and problem solving; ability to manage incentive programs.

- *In communications:* Ability to write clearly; ability to select, engage, and manage professional creative talents; ability to evaluate and allocate resources among options; comfort with and appreciation of the Internet and the web.

- *In promotion:* Ability to analyze breakevens, creativity, anticipation, conceiving and selling partnerships and alliances.

- Run breakeven analyses on each ad or promotion, asking what percentage increase over normal unit sales it will take to return these dollars, using contribution margins, not revenues. Is that a reasonable expectation?

- Assign individual toll-free numbers to each ad and medium, so response to each can be tracked.

- Don't ask if your GM likes an ad; ask if the intended prospect is likely to respond to it.

- Make sure the message the audience will take away is consistent with your basic positioning: what you intend to mean and offer to that market.

✦ MAKING THE HOTEL AVAILABLE

Once a person in one of your target markets is interested in buying, how does he or she reach you? Your hotel's reservations office, the central reservation system, airline global distribution systems, corporate sales offices, and your property sales office are all parts of a distribution network. Travel agents, corporate travel managers and secretaries, meeting planners, and travelers themselves reach your hotel through this network.

Travel industry distribution channels are in chaos by virtue of the shift of travel agencies from commission to fee-for-service models, the rise of the Internet as a consumer's direct booking channel, and online third-party intermediaries like Expedia and Travelocity. Increasingly, the Internet will become your key distribution channel, but in the meantime, you must manage two parallel systems, the traditional central reservation and travel agency channels and the new electronic channels. Are the rooms you want to offer available in both systems, with helpful and up-to-date information? Are your prices sensible in each outlet? Making the hotel available is no

longer a passive stance but an active part of your marketing.

In other industries, distribution channel revolutions have brought efficiencies that benefit both consumers and suppliers. In the travel distribution revolution now underway, the consumer has benefited, but costs to hotels—the suppliers—have skyrocketed. Since 1993, full-service hotel costs of distribution (commissions, Global Distribution System fees, and reservation expenses) more than doubled, to $1377 per occupied room per year in 2002 (PKF, 2003).

Along with these channels and third-party room merchants has come pressure on prices. In the downturn of 2001–2003, this was devastating. Price comparisons are quick and easy for the consumer. Packagers and auction sites, like Priceline.com, unconsciously cultivate the destructive idea that a hotel room is a commodity, as is an airline seat. But hotels are not commodities; each differs in location, features, and benefits. A hotel team must resist the idea that a room is a room is a room, must emphasize their hotel's distinctive positioning, and must resist the urge to simply match the lowest price offered.

- Bid all groups on net price basis; do not commission meeting planning agencies.

- Analyze and understand the contribution margins achieved through each channel, not just the revenues

and average rates. Consider differential prices by channel to equalize contribution margins after variable distribution costs.

For the foreseeable future, both the traditional and Internet-based distribution systems will coexist and have to be managed. This raises a new question: What channels do you want to encourage, and what ones discourage? Conventional wisdom, in recent years, has been to make the hotel's inventory and rates available via as many channels as possible so as to capture from anywhere in the world the last drop of demand for arrival on a given day. Given their sharply differing costs, however, and the difficulty of managing a coordinated presence in these new and overlapping channels, the time may be coming for a new strategy. One possibility is to starve undesirable channels with limited information and access while being fully open and transparent to others. Another approach might be to price differentially among channels to reflect their different costs. A large Hawaiian resort group is already doing that by explaining to consumers what comparative options and costs are. Other chains advertise a guarantee that the lowest price will be found on their own web site, which is a low-cost channel for them.

Reservations, revenue, and channel management constitute the fastest-changing part of hotel management today. Channel management requires a comfort with and interest in technology and systems, and a knack for problem solving, anticipating, and risk taking (to shut down past patterns and undertake new initiatives).

✦ CLOSING, CONFIRMING, AND MANAGING REVENUE

How one commits space—a room, meeting space, ballroom, or even a restaurant table—and at what price—determines the revenues and financial health of the hotel and determines the customer's expectation of value. Revenues must be managed to optimize financial returns and customer satisfaction—that is, the customer's willingness to return.

No one department controls the tools of revenue management. They are shared among salespeople, catering and banqueting managers, front desk agents, reservation agents, and so on. To manage properly requires frequent and open conversation between managers, good forecasting, skillful selling by customer contact people, and an appreciation of each week's goals and targets for the hotel. Poor forecasting, inflexible inventory policies, and conflicting approaches by different departments with whom the customer deals can undo all the best advertising, selling, and promotion.

- Eschew seasonal price schedules and adopt pricing tiers based on forecast occupancy for the dates in question.

- Saturday has become the highest demand day of the week; make sure you are not leaving discounts on the table out of habit.

- Teach reservation agents that stay-through restrictions are not mistreating guests. A three-night stay room is a different inventory unit than a one-night stay room, and is to be rationed.

Through the same forecasting disciplines, hotel teams manage their revenues to maximize the productivity of the hotel and ensure its financial health. Revenue management tools and increasingly affordable yield systems can have a major and salutory effect on the financial health of the hotel.

Another part of revenue management is incentives for reservations upselling, conversion of callers, and average rate increases, and for front desk agents upselling. In the same way, F&B staff should be viewed as salespeople and given training on suggestive selling. Inventory policies for tier price quotes by forecast levels of occupancy, for stay-through restrictions, for same-rate substitutions and upgrading to clear demand inventory categories—all these are tools through which reservation and revenue managers optimize the RevPAR performance of the hotel.

It is in the area of revenue management that chains, especially multibrand management companies, have achieved significant advantage over independent hotels and franchisees that do not participate in cluster or regional revenue management. Decisions on pricing are still the domain of the property GM, but with a centralized expert staff collecting data and forecasting, the advice and guidance available has brought yield and RevPAR premiums to the chain member properties.

Revenue management requires attention to detail and analytic and forecasting skills, tolerance for ambiguity and comfort with change, and managing, training, leading, and motivating reservations agents. This is one of the most critical and dynamic areas of hotel management, one with which every aspiring general manager or director of sales and marketing should take pains to become familiar.

✦ PREPARING TO DELIVER AND DELIGHT

A marketer of a product can count on the factory quality-control system to deliver a consistent product for sale. When the sale is closed, the customer takes the product away and uses it. In a service business, however, the product is human behavior, and the customer uses the product in the hotel. Because we are human beings, both customers and employees, our interactions are never the same one time to the next. The job of the marketer is to help employees understand what the customer will want, need, and expect, and to sell employees on doing their job with enthusiasm.

In a full-service hotel, the conference services department embodies this preparing idea as its primary function. Conference service managers are the essential group business brokers between sales and operations. Conference services people can create loyal and repeat meeting planners; the job requires empathy, attention to detail, willingness to work unusual hours, action orientation, internal relationship building, and persuasiveness.

Preparing the hotel to fully satisfy and regularly make customers happy is as much a marketing task as attracting customers in the first place. What makes marketing hospitality services harder than marketing a tangible product is that for every market segment there must be two marketing programs, one directed externally to customers, the other internally to employees.

✦ RETAINING CUSTOMERS

The key to both financial health and market leadership is retaining a higher proportion of customers than any of your competitors. Retain more customers than others do, and over time your costs drop—because of efficiency, lower advertising and selling costs, better forecasting—and your occupancy and rates rise. Numerous studies validate the high correlation between profit leadership and customer retention.

Frequent-stay rewards are often mistaken for retention programs. They are not. Rewards can motivate returns only as long as the customer values the points or airline miles or whatever. But they do not create loyalty. They are valuable only insofar as they give employees the opportunity to come to recognize and satisfy the guest, and insofar as they give the marketing department information on who the customer is and where he or she is coming from.

Retaining customers takes more than just doing the job well. Guests and customers must come to know they are valued. Management must build relationships—the tie that binds regardless of a new hotel opening in the market or a hot promotional offer from across the street. Relationships are built on recognition and familiarity, on trust, and on appreciation. Thus, guest and customer retention must be a planned and creative activity that involves both sides of the relationship—the customers and the employees. It takes more than just smiling and trying hard. Among the talents and skills needed are analytic skills, curiosity, direct marketing planning, and management of data retrieval and direct marketing service providers.

✦ MEASURING SATISFACTION AND EVALUATING PERFORMANCE

If the purpose of the business is, in part, to keep customers, does a financial statement of rate, occupancy, revenue, expense, and profit give enough information? No. Also needed is a scorecard of customer satisfaction, of how likely customers are to return or tell others about your good hotel. That scorecard is the guest satisfaction survey. Accounting statements tell of the hotel's financial health; a guest satisfaction scorecard tells of its reputation's health. The scorecard also helps management spot changes in expectations. Customers are not the same from one visit to the next. Experience with a new hotel, perhaps even in another city, may raise a customer's standards. To measure satisfaction, one needs quantitative skills for tracking, analyzing, and reporting data, and the ability to manage the logistics of repetitive distribution, collection, and processing.

(*Note:* Many hotels rely on comment cards for tracking guest satisfaction. That may work in some situations, but if your property has a high rate of repeat customers and/or frequent business travelers, comment card data are unreliable. It is the infrequent traveler who bothers to fill out comment cards—unless there is a gripe to be expressed. Develop and use a continuing survey to get a reliable measure of guest satisfaction levels.)

The information helps management figure out what the hotel needs to be and what to offer next in order to remain competitive and keep customers. Note, now, the return to the first step of the marketing process.

✦ THE CIRCULAR MARKETING PROCESS

In other words, the marketing process isn't the straight-line, step-by-step process shown in Figure 7.1 but rather, as shown in Figure 7.2, a continuous circle around which management must go again and again as competition improves and as the customer segments in the market change. Only by

reviewing and renewing the marketing process will a hotel get ahead and continue to be the leading hotel in its market. This model of the marketing process applies to both the whole hotel and to any revenue or profit center within it. Use it like a checklist when thinking through improving the revenue and competitiveness of any operation.

✦ THE MEASURES OF MARKETING

The health of the marketing process should be measured over a longer time than a month or quarter or fiscal year, and it should be measured by more than just profit and loss data. A healthy marketing process results in:

- Rising room revenues per available room and rising F&B revenues per available seat and catering space.
- Rising market share to a share index over 100—that is, a larger share of a competitive set's

Figure 7.2 The Hotel Marketing Process

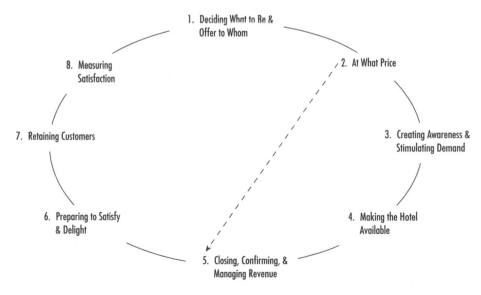

1. Deciding What to Be & Offer to Whom
2. At What Price
3. Creating Awareness & Stimulating Demand
4. Making the Hotel Available
5. Closing, Confirming, & Managing Revenue
6. Preparing to Satisfy & Delight
7. Retaining Customers
8. Measuring Satisfaction

Copyright, FCW Consulting, 1996.

occupied rooms than the hotel's share of the set's available rooms, which is its "fair share."

- Falling costs of acquiring customers, not on a percentage-of-revenue basis but as dollars per unit of sale—for example, dollars per occupied room, dollars per cover, and so on. What is the acquisition cost? The total of the advertising and business promotion budget (more often now called the marketing and sales expense), plus commissions, reservation costs, franchise fees, and marketing fees. These costs in times of inflation may not actually decline but at least should grow more slowly than do gross operating revenues.

- Rising customer satisfaction ratings.

- Increasing retention rates measured by the percentage of business from repeat customers.

- Growing top-of-mind awareness among target customer segments and, if the hotel can afford to measure it, preference by segment rising to number one among your competitive sets.

Management and owners should ask for an annual report card on the health of the marketing process—of the hotel, of a chain, of a franchise group.

✦ MANAGEMENT OF THE PROPERTY'S MARKETING PROCESS

As should by now be clear, the marketing process is larger than any one individual's job. Further, no hotel can afford the myriad talents and skills that must be orchestrated to create and sustain a healthy marketing process; a single hotel is simply not a large enough business to afford having all those talents on staff.

Franchise companies and managed chains have the mass to employ a large proportion of those talents at headquarters, but even they must call on outside services in design, database management, advertising, direct marketing, and so on. But the chains' ability to invest in new tools and hire diverse talents has led branded chains, both management companies and franchisers, to collect increasing numbers of hotels under their umbrellas. The trend toward centralizing marketing functions to serve several hotels in a region, often even hotels of different brands, is accelerating, especially with the advent of Internet-driven information sharing. The advantages are the ability to integrate multiple sources of information; to hire experts that a single hotel might not be able to afford; to share the cost of sophisticated systems for forecasting, revenue management, and customer relationship management; and to reduce the expense of marketing to individual properties.

Independents must counter such attractions with cooperative activities and aggressive local marketing. The Internet has leveled the playing field somewhat, allowing independents to be found and reviewed by consumers and travel agents in a way not possible when GDS systems were the only means of access.

✦ PROPERTY RESPONSIBILITY FOR ITS OWN MARKETING

To optimize performance, a property can neither abdicate its marketing to a chain or franchise group nor passively rely on location and presence to bring customers to the door. Each property, whether flagged or independent, must be responsible for creating and managing a marketing process tailored to its particular marketing situation—that is, its available customers; its inherent strengths, weaknesses, and employees; and its competitors. Each marketing situation is unique, even among cookie-cutter chain properties. Each has its own location, competitor, and customer dynamics.

So, given the wide range of talents and skills that must be orchestrated to create an effective marketing process, who is to lead it? Directors of sales and marketing cannot, for the process is much larger than the marketing department. Only the general manager can lead his or her marketing process; only he or she can integrate chain supports, operating departments, human resources (HR), the controller, and yes, marketing and sales.

✦ THE GM AS LEADER OF THE MARKETING PROCESS

General managers must come to see themselves as the leader of their marketing process and be comfortable in the role. This does not mean becoming expert in all tools and disciplines; it does mean seeing the whole and appreciating when to bring in what talents, when to apply what tools, and how to judge the effectiveness of the process. It means using the marketing process as an organizing concept for creating the management team and a unified viewpoint of mission and challenge.

When a hotel is led by a general manager who sees herself or himself as leader of the marketing process, when that process is thoughtfully conceived and well executed, when all employees see themselves as joint operators/marketers, that hotel becomes customer-centered, competitive, and a leader in its markets.

Few GMs are trained to do this. Many come to appreciate that location and flag are not enough; many intuitively pick up a smattering of sales, distribution, advertising, and customer re-

tention. But it is the rare GM who weaves these parts into a coherent whole and thinks through the challenge of creating and leading the marketing process. As marketing continues to develop more complex tools and as marketing productivity becomes a more pressing matter, owners, universities, and chains must address this issue of how to develop GM candidates who are comfortable with and capable of leading a comprehensive marketing process.

✦ THE MARKETING PROCESS MODEL AS A PROBLEM-SOLVING TOOL

One last word: The circular model of the marketing process is presented here mainly in terms of rooms marketing. But the model can be applied to every revenue department—to food and beverage outlets, catering, the health club, the business center, and even the laundry. The model can be used for planning, for business reviews, for presentations to lenders and owners, for troubleshooting, and as a checklist when preparing proposals for new services or facilities.

Use the model, make it part of your bag of management tools, and get your team to see their role in terms of this holistic and never-ending marketing process. If you achieve that, you will have gone far to create a customer- and competitor-focused organization, one in which employees see themselves as operators/marketers rather than just "in operations" or "in marketing" or "in HR." The few hotels that achieve and nurture a well-tuned marketing process and whose employees see themselves as integral parts of it become leaders—in market share, in customer and employee loyalty, and in financial returns to owners.

7.3 CONSUMER DECISION RULES AND IMPLICATIONS FOR HOTEL CHOICE BIANCA GROHMANN AND ERIC R. SPANGENBERG

Consumers' choices are influenced by the goals they attempt to achieve. Once a person has recognized a need, such as the need for accommodation when traveling for business or pleasure, he or she engages in an information search to identify alternatives from which to choose. Understanding how consumers evaluate competing alternatives in their purchase decision processes enables marketers in the hospitality industry to design better advertising and promotional campaigns leading to a more favorable evaluation of their offerings in travelers' eyes. This is an important step in increasing the likelihood that consumers will choose their offering as opposed to that of competitors. Given that most travelers' destinations offer several hotels, how do people choose among them? The answer to this question lies, in part, in research on consumers' attitudes and their relation to purchase intentions and subsequent purchase behavior. This chapter describes several methods consumers may use to make choices based on the evaluation of identified alternatives.

Attitude is the tendency to respond in a consistently favorable or unfavorable manner toward a target (e.g., brand or product). Important to marketers is that, if measured accurately, attitudes are predictive of behavioral intentions and relatively stable over time. Simply put, consumers generally form intentions to choose a hotel brand toward which they hold positive attitudes. Behavioral intentions, however, do not always translate into corresponding behavior. For example,

although some consumers have preferences and therefore form intentions to stay at Fairfield Inn when traveling across the country, they might end up choosing other forms of accommodation from time to time. Why would they act inconsistently with their intentions? Traveling with friends who have different attitudes and preferences, temporary price reductions of competitors, or the fact that a Fairfield Inn is not readily available in a specific area might be reasons for inconsistencies between behavioral intentions to stay at a Fairfield Inn and actual choice behavior.

Despite situational factors sometimes influencing travelers' choices, attitudes are ultimately useful in predicting actual behavior; changing or strengthening the basis of consumer attitudes may therefore increase the likelihood of consumers engaging in desired behaviors. In order to change attitudes and subsequent related behavior, marketers must understand a few basic decision rules associated with consumer attitudes. Below we introduce decision rules likely to be implemented by different segments of consumers under varying market conditions.

✦ DECISION RULES

Decision rules are strategies consumers use to choose among alternatives. Several factors can influence what decision rule consumers ultimately apply in a specific situation. Typically, the more important and less frequent a purchase decision is, the more time and effort consumers are willing to expend making that decision. Choosing a resort at which to spend a twenty-fifth wedding anniversary, for example, is a decision most consumers face only once and, therefore, are likely to take a relatively long time to make, and they are likely to be careful and thorough in evaluating alternatives. On the other hand, a salesperson traveling frequently in a familiar territory likely chooses a hotel using a routine process where far less time and consideration are given to alternatives. Further, brand-loyal customers might choose to stay with the same hotel chain whenever possible, thereby avoiding a situation where they are forced to choose among alternatives. In general, the more strongly a consumer is motivated to search and the greater the risk associated with a choice, the greater the complexity of the decision rule he or she implements.

Another important characteristic of modeling decisions is the fact that (counterintuitively and often counterattitudinally) people often do not attempt to optimize their choice. If a person's goal is optimal choice, considerably more time and effort is typically required to identify and evaluate alternatives. Therefore, consumers often choose a satisfactory (as opposed to the optimal or best possible) alternative in order to save time and effort. The use of decision rules in these instances enables people to take shortcuts in making decisions in the face of the apparently unlimited or overwhelming amounts of information available regarding all possible alternatives. Consumers usually work with a consideration set (i.e., a subset of alternatives from the entire universe of choices), so they do not have to work as hard cognitively when required to make a decision in a given product category. They then make a final decision from this reduced set of alternatives. Such decision rules are referred to as *heuristics* or rules of thumb. Employing heuristics, people save time and limit complex information processing while still making reasonable or satisfactory choices based on the few brand attributes or characteristics most important to them at the time of choice. In the context of hotel choice, brand attributes are things like location, room rates, and availability of a swimming pool, restaurant, and so forth.

Although the number of consumer decision rules is almost infinite and likely varies by consumer, basic categories and a few specific examples serve as useful tools in modeling and predicting traveler decisions. Two general categories of decision rules are (1) compensatory and (2) noncompensatory. Below we discuss how travelers make decisions using these two types of rules.

COMPENSATORY DECISION RULES

Compensatory decision rules model consumers as deriving an overall brand evaluation such that alternatives performing poorly on one attribute can *compensate* for their respective shortcomings by positive evaluations of other attributes. For example, a high-priced hotel might not be perceived positively on the dimension of room rates by some travelers; however, these same travelers might be willing to spend more money knowing they will receive better service or that the hotel is conveniently located—that is, in this example, service and location compensate for the perceived disadvantage of high room rates. The multi-attribute attitude model described in the next section is perhaps the most popular compensatory decision rule.

Multi-Attribute Attitude Model. The multi-attribute attitude model we describe herein is also referred to as a *weighted additive model* or the *Fishbein* (1975) *linear compensatory model.* In this model, people not only assess the value of each salient (or important) attribute of brand but also consider the extent to which a given alternative possesses the attributes. (*Note:* In this context, it is important to note that salience is essentially equivalent to importance. Further, the attributes salient to one market segment may be very different from those of another segment. For example, business travelers may not care at all about a spa, an airport shuttle, and room service breakfast quality, while to another market segment, these property attributes may be very important.) The evaluations of salient attributes and the beliefs that brands possess the salient attributes are included as weights in an equation determining overall brand attitude. The model is represented as:

$$A_{\text{brand A}} = \sum_{i=1}^{n} e_i b_i$$

where $A_{\text{brand A}}$ is the overall attitude toward hotel brand A, e_i is the evaluative weight associated with attribute i, b_i is the extent to which the consumer believes brand A possesses attribute i (i.e., strength of belief that i is present in brand A), and n is the number of salient attributes in consideration.

Operators and marketers typically measure important weights and strengths of beliefs using questionnaires. First, survey respondents are asked to provide evaluative weights associated with each of the attributes salient to their decision; these numbers represent each attribute's relative positive or negative associations in consumers' minds. Although scale endpoints may vary by researcher preference, our demonstration of this model assumes use of a 7-point scale on which -3 is the lowest importance rating possible, $+3$ is the highest, and a neutral importance rating is zero. An attribute that is evaluated entirely negatively by survey respondents (e.g., the availability of guest laundry) would be assigned a value of -3, whereas an attribute that is highly positive in a consumer segment's evaluation (e.g., low room rates) might be assigned a value of $+3$.

Once consumer attribute evaluations are determined, survey respondents state the extent to which they believe a brand possesses respective attributes. Again, for simplicity of demonstration, we assume that the belief strength regarding any of the attributes to be evaluated ranges between -3 (i.e., the brand definitely does not possess the attribute) and $+3$ (the brand definitely possesses the attribute). For example, if a traveler believes that Hotel X is a relatively high-priced establishment, the consumer might assign a belief value of -2 to this hotel on the attribute "low room rates," thereby indicating that Hotel X does not possess the attribute "low price" to a great extent. In other words, Hotel X performs poorly on the traveler's low room rate criterion. The hotel offering the absolute lowest price—say, Hotel Q—may be assigned a value of $+3$ on the attribute "low room rates," thereby indicating the traveler strongly believes that Hotel Q does indeed offer low room rates.

The next step in the model is multiplication of attribute evaluation (e_i) and belief strength (b_i) for each of the salient attributes. If the traveler evaluated low room rates very positively ($e_{\text{room rate}} = +3$), and Hotel X received a belief score of $b_{\text{room rate}} = -2$, we calculate Hotel X's contribution to overall attitude score relative to the attribute "low room rate" by multiplying evaluation and belief scores

$e_{\text{room rate}} \times b_{\text{room rate}} = (+3) \times (-2) = -6$. Evaluation of Hotel Q on the low room rate attribute will be more favorable—specifically, $e_{\text{room rate}} \times b_{\text{room rate}} = (+3) \times (+3) = 9$. This procedure is followed for each salient attribute for all brands in a consideration set. Other attributes, for example, could include location near the airport, availability of room service, or complementary breakfast, and the $e_{\text{attribute}} \times b_{\text{attribute}}$ products calculated for each brand and attribute.

Finally, the products of $e_i \times b_i$ for each salient attribute are summed for each brand. The resulting scores represent the relative overall attitudes held for each brand. This weighted additive model is applied to all the brands included in the survey as the consideration set, and the brand associated with the highest overall attitude score is selected as the preferred alternative.

A few considerations should be kept in mind that are important to implementation of this model. First is the notion that the model is relative in nature—that is, an overall attitude score of $+21$ for a single hotel means nothing unless it is compared to the overall attitude scores of its competitors as evaluated by survey respondents in a relevant market segment. Further, it is important to include all relevant competitors in the model. As a relative model, it may be that the market segment considers only one of five low-budget properties when traveling to a particular locale. If so, include only those five; it is not helpful to have comparisons made (explicitly or implicitly) in respondents' minds if they are not realistic (e.g., it is likely that inclusion of the Four Seasons in the consideration sets of Quality Inn customers is inappropriate). By the same token, leaving out alternatives that respondents in the market segment may truly consider can introduce error; the result

may be a finding that the property has the highest attitude score among those included on the survey, yet the model is not predictive because the survey omitted a strong competitor. Also of paramount importance is the selection of appropriate salient attribute sets. If critical, differentiating attributes are left out of the model, summated scores are not predictive of behavioral likelihood; consumers using a compensatory model in actuality are implicitly calculating scores using attributes that may have been missed by survey administrators. Thus, it is critical to select the appropriate salient attributes for inclusion in the model. Note that *appropriate* does not mean *all* attributes. Surveyors often ask about things that do not really matter to respondents. Once primed, however, respondents provide a score on attributes they may never have thought of on their own, thereby contributing falsely (positively or negatively) to overall attitude scores.

We now provide an example of the linear compensatory model, necessarily simplified with regard to number of brands under consideration and salient attributes included. Consider Charlie and Elsa Brown, a wealthy New York couple looking for a hotel to stay at while spending a weekend skiing in Vermont; the Browns represent a market segment that regularly visits this area for this purpose. Based on a discussion with friends who know the area well, the Browns identified four hotels (associated with four different brands) in the area they plan to visit. Table 7.1 shows four salient attributes the Browns consider, the importance of each attribute (e_i ranging from -3 to $+3$) and the beliefs (b_i ranging from $+3$ to -3) regarding the extent to which each of the properties possesses attribute i. (Note that there could be more or fewer salient attributes depending on the product

Table 7.1 Four Salient Attributes K Considers

ATTRIBUTE	E_I	HOTEL E B_{IE}	HOTEL F B_{IF}	HOTEL G B_{IG}	HOTEL H B_{IH}
Proximity to skiing area	+3	−1	+2	+3	+1
Low rates	−2	−1	−2	−1	+2
Fine restaurant	+1	+13	+3	+2	+1
Indoor pool	+2	0	+2	+3	+3

or service in consideration and the attributes salient to the perspective market segment.)

Using the above scores derived from survey responses, we derive an overall attitude score for each of the hotels in the Browns' consideration by computing the sums of the products of importance (e_i) multiplied by belief strength (b_i) for each attribute for each brand. For example, for Brand E:

$$\text{Attitude}_{\text{Brand E}} = \sum_{i=1}^{n} e_i b_i$$
$$= (e_{\text{proximity to skiing area}})$$
$$\times (b_{\text{proximity to skiing area E}}) + (e_{\text{low rates}})$$
$$\times (b_{\text{low rates E}}) + (e_{\text{fine restaurant}})$$
$$\times (b_{\text{fine restaurant E}})$$
$$+ (e_{\text{indoor pool}}) \times (b_{\text{indoor pool E}})$$

Note that the evaluation weights (e_i) assigned to attributes remain constant across brands, while belief strength may differ from brand to brand (indeed, *should* differ, unless brands are identical). The overall attitude toward hotels E, F, G, and H can, therefore, be calculated as follows:

$$A_{\text{Hotel E}} = (+3)(-1) + (-2)(-1)$$
$$+ (+1)(+3) + (+2)(0)$$
$$= -3 + 2 + 3 + 0 = 2$$
$$A_{\text{Hotel F}} = (+3)(+2) + (-2)(-2)$$
$$+ (+1)(+3) + (+2)(+2)$$

$$= 6 + 4 + 3 + 4 = 17$$
$$A_{\text{Hotel G}} = (+3)(+3) + (-2)(+1)$$
$$+ (+1)(-2) + (+2)(+3)$$
$$= 9 - 2 - 2 + 6 = 11$$
$$A_{\text{Hotel H}} = (+3)(+1) + (-2)(+2)$$
$$+ (+1)(+1) + (+2)(+3)$$
$$= 3 - 4 + 1 + 6 = 6$$

Thus, assuming an optimized score being sought in this instance, Hotel F, scoring highest in overall brand attitude (17), is most likely to be chosen. Hotel E, on the other hand, scored lowest on overall brand attitude (2), and is unlikely to be selected.

NONCOMPENSATORY DECISION RULES

Although many factors (e.g., high involvement, high physical, social, or economic risk) associated with a decision may lead consumers to use a compensatory decision rule, the effort is relatively complicated and often too time- and effort-intensive for people to employ for many day-to-day decisions. As suggested above, consumers may use a compensatory decision rule if they spend a lot of time on the road, for a special vacation, or for an extended stay abroad. However, they are unlikely to use such an elaborate rule when purchasing a beverage at a gas station or when they need to find inexpensive lodging in the middle of a long drive to visit friends. Thus, many decisions are made using much simpler rules. Noncompensatory decision rules tend to simplify decision making; they may lead to less than optimized results but are often employed when consumers *satisfice,* or seek an outcome that is good enough rather than optimal.

When noncompensatory decision rules are used, a brand or product cannot compensate for weak performance on one attribute by performing well on other attributes when competing alternatives are compared. For example, if consumers choose a hotel based on the single criterion attribute of low room rates, a hotel offering higher-priced accommodations with better service would not be chosen (unless rooms are not available at the hotel offering lower rates). In this case, consumers do not trade off room rates and service quality but make their decision guided solely by a property's rates.

The most commonly used noncompensatory decision rules are the *lexicographic decision rule,* the *elimination-by-aspects decision rule,* and the *conjunctive decision rule.* To demonstrate consumers' use of noncompensatory decision rules, we can use the same survey data as the compensatory decision model regarding salient attribute evaluations and brand beliefs regarding those attributes. The data, however, are used differently, as described below. For the noncompensatory rules defined below, we again consider the evaluations and beliefs regarding Hotels E, F, G, and H introduced in Table 7.1.

Lexicographic Decision Rule. When using a lexicographic decision rule, consumers select a brand according to the alternative that scores highest on a single attribute deemed most important. This is probably the way we make a lot of decisions. What is cheapest? What is most convenient? What is the best-looking alternative?

Consider the values in Table 7.1 as results of a different survey for consumers from a different market segment: Four brands of hotels are evaluated on the four attributes of proximity to skiing area, low rates, fine restaurant, and indoor pool. The importance of each of these attributes is given by e_i. Importance ratings are proximity to skiing area ($+3$), low rates (-2), fine restaurant ($+1$), and indoor pool ($+2$). Proximity to skiing area is the most important attribute in this case of hotel choice, followed by indoor pool, fine restaurant, and low rates, respectively. According to the lexicographic decision rule, proximity to skiing area is the attribute determining consumer choice in this case. Consumers have reason to believe that Hotel G is closer to the slopes ($b_{\text{proximity to skiing G}} = +3$) than are the other hotels in the consideration set, and therefore Hotel G is chosen.

Elimination by Aspects. When an elimination-by-aspects decision rule is used, attributes are again ranked according to their importance. Unlike choosing the hotel brand that performs best on a single most important attribute as with the lexicographic rule, however, elimination by aspects involves the use of cutoff values. A cutoff value is a minimal performance score a brand must have to stay in the consumer's consideration set. A consumer first looks at performance scores of brands regarding the most important attribute and eliminates all brands that do not exceed the predetermined cutoff value. We often do this with multiple attributes: "I won't pay more than $110 a night in city X, so I don't even look at properties more expensive than that, but my choice also has to have a pool." We essentially eliminate by the aspect of price first and then by whether or not the hotel has a pool.

In the example shown in Table 7.1, proximity to skiing area is the most important attribute, with an importance rating of +3. Let us assume the consumer's cutoff value is +2. That means that all of the hotel brands that have a score of at least +2 on the proximity to skiing area attribute are retained in the consideration set, while brands that do not meet this cutoff criterion are dropped from the consumer's consideration set. For this example, only Hotel F ($b_{\text{proximity to skiing area F}}$ = +2) and Hotel G ($b_{\text{proximity to skiing area}}$ = +3) meet the cutoff criterion (+2). Hotel E ($b_{\text{proximity to skiing area E}}$ = −1) and Hotel H ($b_{\text{proximity to skiing area H}}$ = +1) are not close enough to the skiing area to make the cut.

When implementing the elimination-by-aspects decision rule, the consumer replicates these steps: He or she now considers the performance of the remaining brands with respect to the attribute ranked second-highest in importance. In our example, the consumer next looks at the availability of an indoor pool at Hotels F and G. Assuming the cutoff value to be employed is +2, both brands remain in the consumer's consideration set, as the scores for indoor pool Hotel F ($b_{\text{indoor pool F}}$ = +2) and Hotel G ($b_{\text{indoor pool G}}$ = +3) both meet this criterion. At this point, the consumer has not yet found the best offering according to the elimination-by-aspects rule.

Consequently, the consumer applies the same procedure to the attribute ranked third—that is, the availability of a fine restaurant. Assuming that the consumer still uses a cutoff criterion of +2, Hotel G ($b_{\text{fine restaurant G}}$ = −1) is eliminated from the consideration set. Hotel F ($b_{\text{fine restaurant F}}$ =

+3), on the other hand, exceeds the cutoff criterion, is now the only brand left in the consumer's consideration set, and is therefore selected.

Note that using the same data set, the elimination-by-aspects decision rule leads to a different choice than the lexicographic decision rule. From a strategic standpoint, the fact that some consumers use an elimination-by-aspects decision rule should encourage hotels to improve their performance on several attributes important in consumer choice. It is not enough to be situated close to a skiing area. Other aspects of the offering might also be important in consumers' hotel selections, and performance in these areas should be monitored and, if necessary, improved. You can see, however, that it is crucial to improve services that are valued by consumers—in other words, aspects of a hotel's offering that have high importance ratings. Shortcomings in aspects that are valued highly by consumers, such as cleanliness and employee friendliness, cannot be compensated for by strong performance in areas to which consumers attach no importance (e.g., internal cost-control systems).

Conjunctive Decision Rule. When a conjunctive decision rule is employed, consumers process information by brand, as opposed to attribute by attribute, as with the lexicographic and the elimination-by-aspects decision rules. With this rule, consumers establish a cutoff criterion that must be met by alternatives in the consideration set on all salient attributes for brands to remain in consideration.

Let us assume that a consumer desires that the chosen hotel should have a score of at least +1 on all of the attributes he or she considers important. In our example, then, proximity to a skiing area, low rates, fine restaurant, and indoor pool must all rate a $+1$ on each of these dimensions to remain in the consideration set. First, the consumer evaluates Hotel E on each of these attributes. While Hotel E meets the cutoff criterion of $+1$ on fine restaurant, it falls short of the consumer's cutoff rule when it comes to proximity to skiing area, low rates, and indoor pool, and therefore is eliminated from consideration. The consumer then turns to evaluation of Hotel F, which meets the cutoff value of $+1$ on three out of four relevant attributes. It is eliminated from choice consideration, however, because of its failure to deliver on low rates. The consumer's assessment of Hotel G also leads to elimination from choice consideration because it does not meet the cutoff criterion of $+1$ on the attribute "fine restaurant." Hotel H, on the other hand, exceeds the cutoff criterion of $+1$ on all of the criteria. Thus, using a conjunctive decision rule, Hotel H is selected.

Accounting for Ties. Note that ties can frequently occur using compensatory or noncompensatory decision rules; this usually results in consumers moving to a new rule in order to break the tie. For example, if compensatory values were equal for two competitors (not shown in the examples above), a consumer might implement a lexicographic decision rule with proximity to a skiing area as the most important attribute used to pick a hotel. Or, if the conjunctive cutoff value were -1 for all attributes, both Hotels E and H in our example would stay in consideration; the consumer may then use a lexicographic decision rule based on availability of an indoor pool, resulting in Hotel H being chosen, as it is rated higher on this attribute than Hotel E.

✦ MARKETING IMPLICATIONS

Once consumer evaluations of salient attributes (e.g., availability of room service, conference facilities, wheelchair accessibility, children's programs) are determined and their beliefs regarding a hotel brand's offerings are known, managers can use this information to improve their hotel's competitive positioning in the market. The goal of any marketing strategy is to increase positive attitude toward the offering or to encourage the use of certain decision rules, thereby increasing the likelihood of being chosen by consumers.

As we have seen, when consumers use a compensatory decision rule, the overall attitude toward a hotel is determined by the sum of the products of evaluations multiplied by beliefs regarding salient attributes associated with the offering. Consequently, travelers' overall attitudes toward a hotel can be rendered more positive by strategies targeted at increasing the evaluation of an attribute in consumers' decision making, or by changing consumers' beliefs about a hotel's offerings.

Travelers' attribute evaluations can be influenced by stressing the attribute in advertising (e.g., less money spent on accommodation can be used to have more fun with the whole family by spending the savings on other activities, the availability of a business center enables business customers to save time). This strategy of influencing attribute evaluations is effective in attitude change and also relatively easy to pursue. It is, however, not a strategy always recommended for changing consumers' attitudes when they are using a compensatory model. The potential problem associated with this approach is that attribute evaluations are constant across brands in a consideration set. In our example above, travelers evaluating importance of the availability of an indoor pool

(+2) is the same for all hotel brands, E, F, G, and H. If Hotel H were successful in a marketing message in increasing the evaluation of an indoor pool with a segment of consumers, say to a rating of +3, it would increase consumers' overall attitude toward its brand. At the same time, however, consumers' overall evaluation of Hotel G would increase by the same amount, as both brands do not differ with respect to consumers' beliefs about their having a great indoor pool (i.e., both have a belief rating of +3). In the end, the attempt to increase consumers' overall attitude toward Hotel H would also benefit some of its competitors.

Thus, sometimes a more effective strategy for improving consumers' overall attitude toward a hotel's offerings is to improve consumers' brand-specific belief ratings. For example, Hotel F could strive to improve consumer belief that it offers a pleasant indoor pool by providing a picture of the pool on its website, or by stressing the availability of the indoor pool in advertisements. While consumer brand-specific beliefs are then likely to increase, Hotel F's competitors will not benefit from its strategy, and Hotel F thereby improves its competitive position.

Assuming that Hotel E cannot do anything to increase consumers' belief that it is not located in proximity of a skiing area (i.e., its location is indeed far from a skiing resort), a strategy it may employ to increase consumers' overall attitude toward the property is to add a salient attribute to the set of attributes consumers consider when making hotel choices. For example, Hotel E could provide free accommodation for children staying with their parents. It is likely that parents would consider this option important when choosing a hotel. As long as other competitors do not offer this service, Hotel E enjoys some advantage in the choices made by its target market. It is essential that when adding a new attribute, marketers consider the following: First, the attribute added must be important enough to the hotel's target market to be included in consumers' subsequent decision making (i.e., is it indeed salient?). Second, the belief that a particular hotel possesses this attribute must be stronger than the belief that any of its competitors do. This marketing strategy, often referred to as a *strategy of differentiation,* is likely to be successful when these conditions are met. Differentiation, however, is unlikely to be sustainable—that is, over time, competitors identify what added attributes successfully attract customers and copy them, thereby creating consumer belief regarding their own properties. Thus, the hotel that introduced the new salient attribute often can expect to lose its differential advantage over time unless it maintains a unique characteristic like a special location (e.g., "there is only one view property on this section of coastline") or a fabulous chef in the kitchen.

Increasing belief strength for a hotel's attributes is not always a successful strategy, assuming a compensatory model is being used. For example, consumers may find it relatively unimportant whether the hotel offers low room rates or not. In the example data in Table 7.1, the importance rating for low room rates is -2—that is, consumers in this particular target segment evaluate low room rates negatively, perhaps because they associate low rates with low quality or with small, underfurnished rooms. In this case, stressing that a particular hotel offers low rates, thereby increasing the strength of consumers' beliefs, may adversely affect consumers' overall evaluation of a property. If you compare Hotels F and H, you will see that the strong belief that Hotel H offers low rates ($b_{\text{low rates H}} = +2$) negatively affects its overall evaluation, as $(e_{\text{low rates}} \times b_{\text{low rates H}}) = (-2)(+2) = -4$. Hotel F, on the other hand, benefits from consumers not being aware of low rates, such that $(e_{\text{low rates}} \times b_{\text{low rates F}}) = (-2)(-2) = +4$.

It is important to note that importance weights associated with attributes vary across market segments. For example, while business travelers on corporate expense accounts or consumers on a once-in-a-lifetime vacation, such as a honeymoon, may attach less importance to low rates, more price-sensitive market segments usually weigh low rates more heavily in their hotel choice. It is, therefore, important for marketers to carefully define the targeted market segment(s) prior to conducting their research and applying evaluation weights and beliefs to similarly disposed consumers.

In general, it is crucial to find out what attributes targeted consumers feel are most salient to their decisions and, in response, increase performance (or perceived performance) regarding these attributes and commensurately inform market segments of this stronger position. The resultant positive attitude toward the offering should then increase the likelihood of the hotel being chosen by travelers using a compensatory decision-making model. Alternatively, as a strategic move, particularly for special niche properties, marketers may want to encourage consumers to abandon the linear compensatory model. Niche market segments may exist or may be created through marketing communications; these target markets might be better served by hotels focusing on one or more of the noncompensatory decision rules presented. For example, a segment of highly price-sensitive customers predominantly using a lexicographic decision rule with low rates as the most important attribute may constitute the primary target market for a property. In this case, travelers can be targeted by offering low prices and/or frequent-stay loyalty programs. At the same time, services deemed unnecessary or unimportant by this customer segment can be eliminated or minimized. The fact that some customer segments expect a minimal level of performance on several attributes (e.g., cleanliness, convenience, and friendly service) when they use an elimination-by-aspect or conjunctive decision rule, however, implies that focusing performance and/or marketing on a single attribute may be inadequate for some segments of travelers. A hotel would then benefit from creating a level of "at least acceptable" attributes in addition to providing stronger packages of the same attributes offered by competitors targeting the same market segment. Overall, knowing how consumers make decisions should help hotel managers to design better properties, packages, and services, and help them market those offerings to their respective target segment(s), thereby improving competitive position.

✦ COMPREHENSIVE EXERCISE

Understanding consumer decision-making rules enables you to make strategic and marketing decisions, thereby effectively targeting segments with varying goals, using multiple criteria, and following different decision rules when choosing hotel venues. This exercise gives you an opportunity to review the consumer decision-making rules discussed in this chapter and demonstrate the strategic implications of these rules for marketers in the hospitality industry.

Shannon Clarke is a chocolatier operating a small chocolate store in Knowlton, Quebec.

This year, she is planning to attend the Sixth Annual Chocolate Show in New York City. Shannon has carefully considered various transportation options and decided to travel by car. She is now considering a number of accommodation alternatives. Shannon knows very well what characteristics are salient to her regarding hotel choice. For example, low rates are significant, as Shannon has a limited budget for traveling expenses. It is also imperative that the hotel offer free parking and be located not too far from the Metropolitan Pavilion on Eighteenth Street, where the Annual Chocolate Show will take place. To keep in touch with her business while staying in New York, Shannon would also like Internet access from her room. On the other hand, she does not require the hotel to offer a nice restaurant, as she will go out on the town each night to have dinner with fellow chocolatiers. Other attributes considered in the hotel choice of small business owners attending trade shows and conventions in New York are noted in Table 7.2.

Shannon identified four hotels in an online search. The information provided online makes it easy to determine what services are offered at what rates for each of the properties. Shannon now must decide which of the four hotels she should choose. Table 7.2 shows relevant attributes, evaluation ratings, and belief ratings to be taken into consideration in Shannon's decision-making process.

Use the information provided above to answer the following questions:

1. Calculate the overall brand attitudes for all of the brands using the weighted additive/linear compensatory model.

2. According to beliefs and evaluations shown in the table, which hotel is in the best competitive position? Which hotel is in the worst competitive position?

3. Describe three strategies the hotel with the lowest overall attitude rating could use to improve consumer attitudes.

4. Which hotel would be chosen using a lexicographic decision rule if Shannon Clarke considers low rates most important?

5. Which hotel would be chosen using the conjunctive decision rule with a cutoff value of 0?

6. Given the lexicographic decision rule with "nice restaurant" as the most important attribute, what should Hotel Chelsea do? What should Hotel Lion do?

7. List salient attributes not included in the table that could be considered for hotels catering to small business owners attending conferences and trade shows in the New York area.

Table 7.2 Shannon's Salient Attributes

ATTRIBUTE	E_i	HOTEL PARK B_{iP}	HOTEL UNION B_{iU}	HOTEL CHELSEA B_{iC}	HOTEL LION B_{iL}
Low rates	+3	+2	+2	+3	−1
Location	+3	+2	+3	+2	−1
Free parking	+2	+3	+2	+1	+2
Internet access	+1	−1	+2	+1	+3
Fitness facilities	0	−1	+1	−2	+3
Nice restaurant	−1	+1	0	−2	+2

8. Using the elimination-by-aspects rule, which hotel would be chosen given a cutoff value of +2?

Answers to Practice Questions

1. The overall brand attitudes are calculated using the formula $\sum_{i=1}^{n} e_i b_i$:

$$A_{\text{Hotel Park}} = (+3)(+2) + (+3)(+2)$$
$$+ (+2)(+3) + (+1)(-1) + (0)(-1)$$
$$+ (-1)(+1) = 6 + 6 + 6 - 1$$
$$+ 0 - 1 = 16$$

$$A_{\text{Hotel Union}} = (+3)(+2) + (+3)(+3)$$
$$+ (+2)(+2) + (+1)(+2) + (0)(+1)$$
$$+ (-1)(0) = 6 + 9 + 4 + 2 + 0$$
$$+ 0 = 21$$

$$A_{\text{Hotel Chelsea}} = (+3)(+3) + (+3)(+2)$$
$$+ (+2)(+1) + (+1)(+1) + (0)(-2)$$
$$+ (-1)(-2) = 9 + 6 + 2 + 1$$
$$+ 0 + 2 = 20$$

$$A_{\text{Hotel Lion}} = (+3)(-1) + (+3)(-1)$$
$$+ (+2)(+2) + (+1)(+3) + (0)(+3)$$
$$+ (-1)(+2) = -3 - 3 + 4 + 3$$
$$+ 0 - 2 = -1$$

2. If the weighted additive/linear compensatory model is used, Hotel Union is in the best competitive position because its overall attitude rating (+21) is higher than its competitors'. Hotel Lion is in the worst competitive position because its overall attitude rating (−1) is lower than its competitors'.

3. **Strategy 1:** Hotel Lion could attempt to change the perceived relevance of some of the attributes. It could stress the importance of a good restaurant and excellent fitness facilities for a hotel in which businesspeople stay while attending a trade show or conference.

The drawback of this strategy is that some of its competitors could also benefit from it.

Strategy 2: Hotel Lion could improve its performance on some of the attributes considered important by consumers in this target segment, thereby increasing the strength of consumers' belief that it possesses these attributes. More specifically, Hotel Lion could lower rates if financially feasible, or provide better free parking.

Strategy 3: Hotel Lion could encourage consumers to consider other relevant attributes when choosing accommodations for trade show visits or conference attendance. These attributes should be associated with a strong performance by Hotel Lion and a weaker performance by other competitors. For example, Hotel Lion might introduce a shuttle service to important conference and trade show locations to make it convenient for business travelers and conference participants to reach their destination; they could also offer a coffee shop for short breaks and breakfast suited for their target segments' busy schedules, and/or introduce secretarial or other business services for travelers.

4. If a lexicographic decision rule were used, with low rates as the most important attribute, Hotel Chelsea would be chosen. It scores highest on this attribute ($b_{\text{low rate C}} = +3$).

5. Hotel Union would be chosen because it is the only hotel in the consideration set meeting the cutoff value of 0 on all salient attributes.

6. Assuming that a lexicographic rule in this instance is looking for positive belief ratings on nice restaurant (i.e., evaluation score is now positive), Hotel Chelsea must improve its restaurant offering in terms of food, beverage, and service. These changes must be fairly substantial in order to affect consumers' impressions of the restaurant. It is, thus, likely that a considerable amount of time and money will have to be spent to rethink the restaurant concept and offerings. Hotel Lion should maintain its high level of restaurant quality; it would also be possible to strengthen consumers' belief that Hotel Lion offers an excellent restaurant by increasing marketing communications. It is important to note here that understanding the consumer decision-making process is crucial in devising a successful marketing strategy: Only if a substantial (in terms of number of customers and/or profit potential) market segment is using the lexicographic decision rule based on positive evaluations of a nice restaurant in choosing a hotel does it pay to improve the restaurant (for Hotel Chelsea) or to maintain a nice restaurant offering (for Hotel Lion). If the targeted segments rely primarily on a compensatory decision rule using importance weights described in Table 7.2 above, then establishing or maintaining a nice restaurant may be counterproductive, as these consumers do not positively value that attribute ($e_i = -1$). In this case, creating a strong belief that a nice restaurant is offered decreases overall evaluations of the hotel—*and* is operationally expensive and time-consuming—that is, when targeting customers like Shannon, offering a great restaurant will not increase Hotel Lion's likelihood of being chosen. The hotel could, however, benefit from its strong performance on attributes like "nice restaurant" or "fitness facilities" not valued by the current market segment through changing its target marketing strategy. A property could, for example, target business travelers for whom exercise and fine dining are more important than low room rates or central location.

7. The following is a (nonexhaustive) list of additional attributes hotels might consider that might be salient for entrepreneurs attending trade shows and conventions: access to fax and copy machines, secretarial services, complementary breakfast, cable TV, including channels covering business topics, complementary newspaper, and shuttle service to train station or airport.

8. Using elimination by aspects (cutoff value = +2), we initially eliminate Hotel Lion and see that hotels Park, Union, and Chelsea stay in consideration based on beliefs about those brands regarding the equally important attributes of low rates and location. The next most important attribute is free parking, and we are left with hotels Park and Union in consideration after eliminating Hotel Chelsea. Finally, we eliminate Hotel Park and select Hotel Union based on the Internet access attribute (lowering the cutoff value to +1).

7.4 HOTEL PRICING Marta Sinclair and Carl R. Sinclair

✦ TRADITIONAL APPROACH

The single most important criterion of success in any business, including hotels, is profit. The purpose of this article is to discuss the importance of hotel pricing and its influence on yield or revenue management, especially in terms of profit generation, and because of inherent dangers to the industry worldwide, integrity of the established pricing structure. Historically, price has been determined by the triangular relationship of cost and demand in the context of competition (see Figure 7.3). The actual pricing structure is developed with one of these three components as the deciding factor while the other two play supplementary roles.

The traditional pricing strategy was largely cost-driven. Many hotel operators tended to favor the rule-of-thumb method. This approach, also called the $1 per $1000 rule, states that hotels should charge approximately $1 per night for every $1000 of room cost, based on an average 70 percent occupancy. Although popular in its day, the calculation of cost was commonly misunderstood (see Hanson, 1995). Another widely used quantitative method was the Hubbart Formula, developed in the late 1940s as a guideline issued by the American Hotel Association. It focused on computing an average room rate that would cover operational costs and yield a reasonable return on investment (ROI). These quantitative methods are fairly static and therefore suited for a stable economic environment. Qualitative pricing approaches, such as percentage increase of previous-year rates adjusted for inflation, payroll increases, and new cost of supplies, reflect more realistically the projected cost.

Other qualitative techniques are less exact but, by being competition-oriented, they offer more flexibility. The Pied Piper or Follow-the-Leader method uses competition as the basis for rate setting, while the Gouge 'Em approach tries to lure business away from other properties by undercutting their prices. If there is no competition to speak of, Hit or Miss fluctuation of rates tied to profitable occupancy levels could be employed. The drawback of competition-driven pricing is its sole focus on rate comparison, ignoring differences in operating expenses and customer-perceived value. An effective approach, therefore, calls for a mix of methods adjusted for different situations (see Table 7.3). The fundamental question remains: What should be the driving force in formulating a sound pricing strategy? In today's dynamic business environment, which discards the traditional view that market demand for room rates is largely inelastic, demand orientation seems to provide the best fit.

✦ CURRENT PRICING CRITERIA

"Our pricing is market-driven, not cost-based," says Scott Farrell, corporate director of distribution with Fairmont Hotels and Resorts, a Toronto-based chain of luxury properties. When the chain is setting its prices, it starts with comprehensive market research. Based on the data, the correct price for each marketplace is determined. If there is a major shift in a market, then the prices will adjust for that. However, if there is a major shift in a demand curve, then a shift of price may have no effect. It may actually leave more money on the table. For example, if the airlines go on strike, a

Figure 7.3 Three Forces of Pricing

Table 7.3 Traditional Room Rate-Setting Methods

QUANTITATIVE METHODS		QUALITATIVE METHODS	
$1 Per $1000	• Determine the cost of the property (building, furnishings and equipment). • Divide the total by number of rooms. • Divide the calculated cost per room by $1000. • Estimate at 70% average occupancy.	Gouge 'Em	• When demand is low, set rates below the market level. • When demand is high, set rates at a premium.
		Hit or Miss	• Record occupancy at each pricing level. • Analyze the collected information periodically to determine which level was most profitable. • Set the rate at the most profitable level.
Hubbart Formula	• Calculate operating expenses. • Add taxes and insurance. • Add expenses for asset depreciation. • Deduct income from sources other than room revenue. • Divide the total by number of rooms in the hotel. • Adjust the calculated room rate for estimated occupancy.	Percentage Increase	• List the rates that were charged in the previous year. • Calculate rate of inflation, payroll increase, the new cost of supplies. • Convert the increased cost into percentage increase. • Increase previous year rates by the calculated percentage increase.
		Pied Piper	• Set rates according to what other hotels in the area are asking for comparable accommodation.

Source: DeVeau, L.T., P. M. DeVeau, N. J. Portocarrero, and M. Escoffier. 1996. *Front Office Management and Operations*, pp. 83–91.

significant shift in the demand curve would result. Under such conditions, decreasing the rate by $50, for example, would only result in a $50 loss. If there is an opportunity to go after a new targeted market with a specific offer, enabling the chain to capture a greater market share, then lowering the rate serves its purpose. Generally, however, lowering rates across the board is not the preferred pricing strategy.

✦ PRICING: WHO IS IN CHARGE?

While independently owned properties make their own pricing decisions, in case of a chain it is usually corporate headquarters (HQ) that sets pricing guidelines. Often, individual properties are still responsible for the actual pricing. Because they are held accountable, they must balance corporate guidelines with their autonomy to set their prices. Caroline Shin, member of the revenue management team at Starwood Hotels and Resorts Worldwide, which operates a number of upscale brands, such as Sheraton and W Hotels, stresses the cooperative nature of this relationship. Successful pricing strategies arise from an ongoing interaction of both sides. Corporate HQ provides sophisticated tools and in-depth market analysis that would be beyond reach of individual properties. Property managers, on the other hand, offer their experience and knowledge of regional specifics that may have gone unnoticed by the corporate team. "The people who have been in the property understand the dynamics of that market, and they have developed pricing intuition," explains Shin. Some experts view intuition as a valuable part of the pricing mechanism, and even managers who are technically savvy check the numbers against their gut feeling.

✦ PRICING: SCIENCE, ART, AND INTUITION

Pricing distribution and revenue management techniques are a mix of science and art. Recent research shows that two-thirds of managers making strategic decisions under pressure and time constraints use a combination of analysis and intuition (Sinclair, 2003). The advent of modern technology, such as yield management software packages, has further strengthened this link. "Even the most sophisticated analytical model for forecasting, may it be for hotel pricing or for thermal dynamics of a nuclear plant,

still needs variables based upon assumptions," says Shin, who used to work as a nuclear engineer. The more business-savvy hotel management becomes and the more they understand the hotel dynamics and the market, the more can be gained from training them how to define their experience-based intuition and put it into numbers. In this respect, an interaction between the corporate revenue management team and individual hotels is paramount. "Every time I go out to a property, I learn something new. It only helps me when I build my analytical models to almost translate what they know into numbers," confirms Shin. The better hotels can do that, the better models they can develop. Nonetheless, inaccurate historical data remains a major limitation.

No model is ever going to be perfect, though. What seems to work best is to teach hotel managers how to use the model and to understand the direction of the pricing decisions they need to make. That is the scientific part. The art piece comes into play when they infuse the model with their knowledge and intuition. Staff training is an important part of this process. "We can't just have Ph.D.s sitting in one room coming with all these models and we just roll it out. At the same time, we can't just have people with intuitions run around and set prices," says Shin.

Revenue management teams must make sure that hotels understand how to employ the models in their daily pricing decisions. When science is applied, the revenue team can go to their experts, ask probing questions, and get solid results. Even though intuition is a part of this process, it is based only on a hypothesis that could have been triggered by a discussion with a customer, knowledge of what is happening in the marketplace, or historic trends. That is why pure intuition is not sufficient. "Managers must have reliable data to support their hunches," cautions Scott Farrell.

✦ CUSTOMER NEEDS

Customer satisfaction is a crucial part of marketing, pricing, and yield management. Any pricing strategy established by the hotel management must attract customers willing to pay the specified rate. While price is a determinator of the customer profile the hotel is looking for, it is also an indicator of the quality of services and the market segment the hotel is competing in. Therefore, yield management uses information about targeted customers' purchasing behavior and product sales to develop pricing strategy together with inventory control that delivers products that are better matched to customer needs, create greater demand, and, on that account, produce greater revenues. Lieberman (1993) states that yield management is the process of maximizing profits from the sale of perishable assets, such as hotel rooms, by controlling price and inventory and improving service through systemization. An exact definition of the target market is essential. There is a definite and firm perception in the psyche of the customer, who views the price as the value forthcoming. Therefore, the eventual satisfaction of the customer is the paramount task of the pricing mechanism. This is the make-or-break factor of the entire hotel, especially if the value expected does not match the price.

✦ ROLE OF TECHNOLOGY

While the approach to hotel pricing is still ruled by supply and demand, speed and sophistication of room-rate yield or revenue maximization is now much increased due to two technological factors: yield management software and Internet bookings.

Yield management software packages enable hotels to use a higher number of room-rate levels, or buckets, and to control inventory for rate availability in real time. Each level may consist of several room rates open under given conditions to yield a maximum profit. Traditionally, hotels used between three and five rate levels; otherwise, the adjustment became too complex for the human brain to work with. The introduction of software removed this barrier, and some hotel chains now use up to ten rate levels. This allows implementation of much narrower ranges for each bucket, thus optimizing price elasticity. This further means the software model recognizes the point at which the same number of bookings can be achieved at a higher rate.

Online monitoring of room inventory in real time facilitates the timing of the adjustment. So far, the biggest limitation is the reliability of historical data. Even in its imperfect form, the system has made a difference. However, hotel managers are fully aware that it takes years to develop brand recognition and quality but just a push of a button to damage or even destroy it, if the pricing is not set up knowledgeably. As the technology becomes more sophisticated, it will eliminate such questionable practices as overbooking, which aims at compensating for last-minute cancellations by taking in more than 100 percent reservations. Besides the question of whether overbooking is ethical and, in some countries, even illegal, better technology would definitely improve the quality of service provided by properties that engage in this practice.

Another area where technological advancement had a great impact on hotel pricing is the Internet. Its use as a booking tool has created a new level of pricing transparency and tiered competition. It also penetrated the negotiation of corporate rates. Many hotels see the effect of the Internet as both good and bad. The good side is that web site bookings are growing every day. As more customers become familiar with their favorite hotel web sites, hotel companies have started investing heavily in web site development and upkeep, which gives them several advantages. First, the cost of online bookings is lower than for bookings made through other distribution channels. Companies do not have to pay commission because the booking is direct, circumventing all intermediaries. Online booking also provides an opportunity to monitor inventory in real time without reliance on a distributor willing to share and regularly supply data. Last but not least, it generates loyal customers by making them eligible for bonus points, which they cannot earn if they use an Internet intermediary.

That is exactly where the flip side of the Internet lies. The intermediaries are getting more powerful and growing significantly in volume. Because most of them show all hotel rates on their web site, they make the information accessible to any computer user. One way to meet the challenge of more powerful intermediaries, especially if hotels need to move inventory, is to utilize auctions where the name of the hotel is not disclosed to the customer until the transaction is finalized. Such action, however, calls for extreme caution so that it does not damage a hotel's reputation or threaten its strategic partnerships. As intermediaries become bigger, rate transparency will increase to the point where it will drive the market, especially when computer literacy and Internet access become the norm.

Moreover, the Internet allows nonbranded hotels to compete more heavily with the branded hotels because they can now be displayed just as readily. Without significant advertising expense, they can compete on price. For some markets this does not matter, especially when the brand is powerful enough to charge the premium and get the business. In highly competitive markets, however, the competition creates an additional strain for the individual property. Many branded hotels must now compete with other brands through the traditional distribution channels and with nonbranded hotels on the Internet, which, in principle, lowers hotel rates. A frequently adopted strategy is to invest heavily in web site development and customer loyalty programs, assuring excellent web site functionality and that customers are rewarded for booking directly through the hotel web site rather than through the web site of a third-party intermediary. Both Fairmont and Starwood, for example, utilize their high-quality loyalty programs in this way.

Internet booking also changed the way corporate accounts are negotiated. Because many companies now require that their employees make business travel arrangements via the corporate web site, the placement of a hotel or a brand on this booking tool is of strategic importance. Being listed first in the accommodation section, for example, may bring in a higher volume of business and thus substantiate a lower negotiated rate.

✦ LONG-TERM STRATEGY FOR THE INTERNET

Because hotels cannot expect that Internet distributors will go out of business, they smartly conclude that a partnership with the devil is better than a fight with him. Besides using their own web sites, hotel companies are also making sure that the cost of their transactions goes down continuously, so they can compete even at lower rates—while maintaining a good relationship with their carefully selected online intermediaries.

There is a large number of distributors to choose from. On one end of the spectrum is, for example, Expedia, which allows participating hotels to control their rates, meaning a hotel can change its rates any time it wants. At the other end are companies, such as Hotel Reservation Network (HRN), that bind hotels contractually to a locked rate that cannot be changed. Some hotel chains do not want to partner with these distributors because they like pricing flexibility and want to make sure their rates yield as much as possible.

Adaptation to new technology has been the biggest component of change for intermediaries as well. Companies that do not have the most current technology working in real time or allowing hotels to yield rates in real time are usually not considered a suitable distribution partner for some chains. On the other hand, companies that invest in real-time technology to yield rates are ideal partners because, as the industry sees it, they work with, not against the industry by permitting hotels to raise or lower rates in real time. "They work with us," says Caroline Shin. "They give data to us very frequently so that we understand the travel pattern bookings on their web site. Then we compare it with what is happening on our web site and also what we are getting outside the Internet to make sure that our market mix is set appropriately." Pricing flexibility, compatibility with the desired hotel image, and protection of its strategic partnerships, together with cost, play important roles in selecting an intermediary.

✦ THE ROLE OF CREATIVITY IN PRICING

Creativity, either of an individual or a team, can and often does lead to innovative pricing ideas. However, its application must be specific, not just directional. It is not enough to state, "We have to do something about our occupancy level." A pricing campaign must target a number of sold rooms or generated revenue that is required in order to break even or to do better. This specific approach injects efficiency into allocating marketing money to areas where it is most effective and in periods when it is desired. If there is no task direction or overall pricing leadership, the most creative idea may book only ten room-nights instead of one hundred. It may generate more customer loyalty, but that is something the hotel may not need at the moment, although it could be an acceptable outcome in a low-season month. Pricing leadership helps team members understand the hotel's current situation and direct money and creativity to do exactly what is needed. Creativity comes up with the idea, which serves as a vehicle, but spending marketing money the smart way is a matter of experience in innovation, which turns the idea into a successful product. Creativity also plays a large part in employee satisfaction, and it lowers turnover.

In a sluggish economy, some hotels start paying attention not only to profit as the bottom line but also to revenue. This means they monitor closely the accrued cost as well as the generated revenue, thus achieving the maximum yield. Interestingly, contemporary price leadership may take different forms. It could mean, for example, elimination of smoking rooms throughout the property. Many U.S. motels are revamping rooms, ripping off cigarette-damaged furniture and carpets, and designating them as nonsmoking. This saves on maintenance and adds to overall packaging flexibility when the business is hurt by lackluster demand. This tactic means drapes, carpets, bedding, and other furnishings must be replaced less frequently; it also mitigates fire risk and enhances cleanliness and overall safety.

✦ THE ROLE OF HUMAN RESOURCES IN PRICING

Some large chains recognize that pricing is a complex issue and that they need to get better at it. There is a new focus on analyzing the culture of pricing (how it is being done) and how it can be improved. This approach is reflected even in the kinds of people chains are hiring.

Although the majority of staff involved in strategic pricing are in the hotel industry and have a background in revenue management, others are in the airline industry and have in-depth travel revenue management experience. Some chains have sought access to this experience by hiring from outside the hotel industry. This is to encourage diversification of thinking and new ways of thought—completely out of the box, as the traditional team members are joined by researchers doing a different kind of optimization analysis. The goal could be as radical as trying to

manage risk or optimize toward the railroad industry and its scheduling. On the surface, these tactics have nothing to do with revenue management per se. A lot of experience in optimizing difficult travel, however, can only be gained by bringing in people with different backgrounds in consulting or with in-depth Internet experience. In order to move pricing and revenue management to a different level of thought, a new mix of people is necessary. For this approach to work, adequate training must be in place.

In this respect, basic HR functions, such as hiring and training, have an impact on pricing. What is necessary is not only to train personnel in quantitative core skills but also in strategic thinking. For example, when a hotel does not want to take a specific piece of business, it must ask such questions as: What is the revenue? What is the rate? What am I displacing by this decision? Where do I think this will go? How does it help my RevPAR?

Hotel managers must become more analytical, so they can use all the new tools now available. When reports are created, team members must be taught how to use them. A lot of training must be provided for corporate executives, general managers, and regional revenue directors as well. They all must be trained to think more strategically and to understand analysis and the reports so that they can help their individual properties.

✦ DIVERSIFICATION: THE IMPROVEMENT OF THE PRICING PROCESS

As noted, exclusive hotel industry experience may lead to ossification because of one-sided judgment and the inability to see beyond the familiar. From this perspective, experience is both an asset and a liability. It is human nature to take for granted the way things are done after being in the same environment for a while. Therefore, hotel chains are continuously creating and refining pricing strategies to accommodate not only different market segments but also different situations a hotel may face based on occupancy levels.

Corporate HQ tries to identify these different situations and associated variables. "It is almost like a bag of goods, a bag of pricing strategies that should be tested," says Caroline Shin. Hotels are given the full menu and encouraged to try a certain strategy if they are in a specific situation. Depending on the region, an individual property may use one set of strategies more than another. In a weak economy, however, the chains have to work harder and be more flexible because the market is overflowing with demand. Adapting step by step, a hotel may apply a different strategy every week. The problem for the corporate office is to identify situations a hotel might be in and seek remedy. For example, if group bookings are low this week but competitors are full, how can the property make up the difference with transient or leisure business? The general manager may ask the corporate team, "What pricing strategies can I use in order to fill my house?" Then he or she may ask, "What else worked before for other hotels, and what may work for me based on my market specifics and market characteristics?" That way he or she can test each strategy using the provided tool and personal experience.

✦ PRICING: SUPPORT AND PROTECT

The corporate pricing structure is also in place to support and protect members of the chain in a number of areas, including pricing and partnerships. The corporate office sets guidelines for hotels in terms of pricing structure and the market segments they deal with. Fairmont Hotels and Resorts, for example, focuses on four segments: transient leisure travel, group travel, business travel, and wholesale. The corporate structure provides guidelines about how the segments fit with each other, how they cross over, and where they reside in the overall pricing structure. This information is necessary because every segment acts differently. Most market segments are dynamic and require frequent rate adjustments. One exception is the wholesale market, where pricing is still largely done the traditional way: A wholesaler provides a net rate, marks it up, and sells it to the general population. There may be a hidden cost, however, if the distribution chain includes an operator acting as a middleman between the wholesaler and the supplier.

When setting up the overall pricing structure, one starts with the retail rate, which is a bucket of premium or best available rates (BAR) charged on the open market. They usually do not carry any restrictions, such as cancellation fees, and they are fully billable. Depending on the level of occupancy, one of these rates is available on any given day when the hotel is not fully booked. It is up to the yield management system to identify which BAR to offer. All other rate types, such as discount rates and prenegotiated rates, are determined in relation to the retail rate. For instance, a corporate rate for a high-volume client will probably be set lower than the BAR rate that is estimated to sell most during the period when the contract is in place. This way the rates are nested within each other in a manner that makes economic sense.

The corporate pricing guidelines follow two main criteria: to maximize revenue and to protect key partnerships. While the hotel sales force negotiates contracts with key partners, such as longstanding corporate accounts or wholesale volume accounts, they make sure to protect these partnerships and provide them value. At the same time, they take every opportunity to maximize revenue. One cannot survive without the other, reiterates Scott Farrell. However, it is up to the hotels themselves, with guidance and additional research, to determine in their marketplace what their pricing structure should look like.

A diversified corporate team, with a mix of people with a hotel industry background and others skilled in optimization modeling, fulfills an additional function. It acts as a risk prevention mechanism, a necessary prerequisite for managing the risk inherent in pricing. Any chain with a wide variety of hotels must make sure the properties are covered in all kinds of situations. One risk containment scenario might be that the chain, in response to a changing demand curve, acquires a type of business that the brand has not catered to traditionally. Caroline Shin explains, "Sheraton did not take on airline crew business because we did not want crew members lingering in the lobby; it affected our brand image. But we thought maybe we could start taking that when our RevPAR index or occupancy slips to a certain point. So we are trying to change the standards of different market segments we are willing to take."

On the international scale, another risk management plan would be analyzing operational cost and determining whether to close down part of the hotel if market research shows occupancy will not be high enough. When PESTEL (political, economic, sociocultural, technological, environmental, legal) analysis indicates demand will drop precipitously for an extended period (because of political unrest, economic crisis, or health scare, for example), instead of hoping for the best and running a full house with a full staff, the hotel may decide to shut down floors or restaurants and save cost until the market picks up again. Selection of the appropriate strategy will depend on the market specifics and protection of the image. A property may opt to close down several floors over the weekend if it caters mostly to business clientele staying during the week. It would not, however, suspend room service, although unprofitable, if that is considered an integral part of the offered product. In a worst-case scenario, the chain may decide to sell properties in global risk areas when it determines the external circumstances make it difficult to raise occupancy on an ongoing basis.

✦ BETTER UTILIZE YOUR DISTRIBUTION CHANNELS

The Internet creates a new level of transparency as it allows the opportunity to maximize profitability. There is now a multitude of channels to choose from. Understanding the cost of each channel in relation to the value of provided service has an impact on the quality of pricing decisions. Therefore, it is necessary to determine how much revenue bookings through an Internet intermediary generate and whether or not they justify the accrued cost. There is also a tremendous risk involved. As discussed earlier, one of the key guidelines of corporate marketing is that partners be protected. Just because there is a new Internet site, this does not mean a chain can use it and advertise a lower rate, which would undermine a partnership of many years. In terms of cost, the chain must review its pricing strategy not only by market segment but also by distribution channel. "Several years ago, we would not consider the cost of distribution in our ROI. Today we do," concedes Scott Farrell.

Another challenge is to keep up with new Internet sites. The chains must reevaluate constantly and prioritize their yield so as to choose which channels to keep or drop. Fairmont Hotels and Resorts, for example, applies the 80/20 rule. They focus on the 20 percent of the online wholesalers that capture more than 80 percent of the business. As Scott Farrell puts it, "Why would I play with the other 10-12 percent? I only have so many hours in a day to manage. I may as well work with the lion's share."

✦ QUALITY ABOVE ALL?

Criteria for selecting an online distribution partner vary by price levels as well. Budget and economy properties are driven mostly by financial considerations, while upscale and luxury hotels are more concerned with compatibility. As for chains, they ask two basic questions: (1) How can the partnership increase our brand recognition or a brand reach, and (2) How much is it going to bring us in terms of revenue or profitability? Their choice has to match the brand first, and then it has to drive the revenue. If the brand is equaled with quality, online providers that project a connotation of cheapness will not be considered at all. The quality image refers not only to the hotel asset itself but also to how and where this asset is sold.

Fairmont Hotels and Resorts, as a quality brand on the luxury side, cannot compete on price. The quality of their product and the offering of the experience must be considered by the customer at the price being offered. When their hotels play with price, the corporate office watches closely. Scott Farrell explains, "If our property wanted to shift their rate by $50, I would ask why? Give me the case behind it and tell me what you are going to do to make up the additional $50 you are going to lose. If they come back to me and say they are moving their rate from $300 to $250 while driving a certain volume, I would make them go through the process of determining what incremental volume they will need to make up for the $50 in loss." In other words, pricing decisions must be driven by ROI, not only a feeling. Feelings and experience may be involved, but properties must present a strong case based on the estimated ROI and what they plan to get out of the proposed strategy. It allows them to go into the pricing change with their eyes open. They also must consider how the competition will respond. A carelessly lowered rate may lead to a price war.

✦ SPEED AND STRATEGY

The speed and immediacy of exposure via the Internet have reshaped how marketing campaigns are conducted. Having eliminated the delay of exposure to marketing collateral material, such as brochures or newspaper advertisements, hotels can conduct targeted discount mini-campaigns on their own web sites when the yield management system indicates a drop in occupancy for specific dates. In a similar manner, brand recognition can be enhanced by a carefully orchestrated online auction. The

South African hospitality group Protea (2000) was among the first in the industry using this method by offering their prospective guests the opportunity to bid on a limited number of weekend getaways at their properties that needed to boost occupancy. By setting a minimum bidding price, the integrity of the hotel image was protected. Similar auction systems, used to encourage room-night sales during slow periods, are nowadays available in the United States and Canada via several Internet intermediaries.

For chains in particular, a long-term strategy in distribution pricing is paramount. It stipulates the criteria and accepts or rejects short-term adjustments depending on what is happening in the industry, what is new in the technology, and who the new players are. In terms of corporate hierarchy, pricing is formulated and executed on three levels: (1) strategy, (2) tactics and execution, and (3) measurement. Strategy comes first, followed by tactics meant to support that strategy and their execution. Finally, the achieved outcome is measured against the set benchmarks. If the strategy is sound, it will last longer than the other two steps. Frequently, new tactics must be implemented; these drive the execution and the measurement. This requires a development of proprietary criteria for measurement and their continuous adjustment to changing conditions.

✦ PRICE ELASTICITY

Contrary to the traditional view that hotel rates are, in the long-term, generally inelastic, price elasticity is receiving a lot of attention nowadays thanks to yield management. Its goal is to take advantage of and to cover the entire spectrum of the customers' ability to purchase. Price elasticity allows hotels to capture customers who do not mind paying the high rate as well as those who are more price-conscious. This can be done in a number of ways. By using different room categories, a luxury hotel can have on the same day suites available at $500 and entry-level rooms at $200. Every room rate category has a different value proposition associated with the incremental revenue. If the variance between a standard room and a deluxe room is $75, the latter should provide an adequately greater value to the customer. The result is a clear product differentiation, which can be also achieved by stay restrictions or by the use of fencing. Examples of physical differences, or fences, are room type, view, amenities, and location. Nonphysical fences may mean different customers, transactions, or consumption characteristics. These bear many similarities to airline pricing strategies, which differentiate the product by, for example, cancellation restrictions or last-minute availability of a prenegotiated corporate rate. The result is nested pricing, allowing properties to have a very high rate available on the same day as a rate that is more attractive to the lower-end customer.

✦ NEW AREAS OF PRICING AND YIELD MANAGEMENT

Hotel pricing strategies traditionally have been limited to setting and adjusting room rates and other ongoing activities. In order to survive in the current dynamic, competitive, and even dangerous global environment, hotels and resorts are taking on other types of business, some of which are one-time projects. Organizing shows, festivals, and conferences or undergoing renovations requires a new type of core competency. Therefore, in addition to mastering current pricing strategies, hotel practitioners must acquire project management skills, such as those that are taught and practiced by the Project Management Institute (pmi.org). Mastering these skills will make hotel team members capable of maximizing yield from project-type functions the same way as they optimize revenue from room rates.

7.5 A DAY IN THE LIFE OF A REGIONAL REVENUE MANAGER

PAUL CHAPPELLE

As the sun rises, so does the stack of reports on my desk. Every morning I am greeted with the accomplishments of the day, week, month, and year before, all in the form of paper-and-ink reports roughly 2 inches thick. Each report attempts to explain the basic numbers pertinent to the smooth function and revenue generation of a hotel. Although I enjoy the development and success of the latest revenue management systems, I still prefer to do things the old-fashioned way. These reports are my comfort food for revenue management.

The first meeting of the day is the revenue maximization meeting, or revmax for short. The meeting consists of the hotel's revenue manager, general manager, director of rooms, and the entire sales and catering staff. We discuss what happened the day and night before, and we evaluate sales leads from the previous day. As a group, we decide what our approach is to each lead. We evaluate whether we will pursue the lead or refer it to a nearby hotel within the company. The revenue manager upholds any decisions made regarding the rate strategy for that day and for the next few days, which are set at that time. Any changes that need to be made are communicated throughout the day.

The next meeting of the day is the revenue management meeting. This meeting, facilitated by the revenue manager, happens once a week and is attended by the general manager, controller, director of sales and marketing, director of rooms, reservations manager, and most operations managers. In this meeting, similar to the daily revmax meeting with the sales team, we go over the numbers in much greater detail and for a much longer time. We look at the number of room-nights and rates generated through the different revenue channels, trends both good and bad, upcoming marketing strategies, and the results of past marketing strategies, and we talk about anything and everything that may affect the number of room-nights and the rate the rooms are sold at the hotel for the past year and as far out as one year.

After the leadership team has identified our opportunities, we discuss a plan for how we are going to exploit these opportunities and how we are going to measure whether what the team decided was an effective strategy. Each of these meetings is repeated in some form or another in person or over the phone for all the hotels I oversee.

✦ RESPONSIBILITIES

The daily, weekly, monthly, and yearly forecasts are the most important responsibility of a revenue manager. I am responsible for forecasting the number of rooms and the rate at which the guest will pay for a given period. I generate these forecasts based on many critical factors and some less critical. History is always a good indicator of what the future will hold for hotels. The correlation between what happened last year on this day in this month to what happens today can be between 60 percent and 80 percent.

What is going on in the area can have a huge impact on the occupancy and rate of a hotel. Local events such as festivals, races, and tournaments can all affect the number of additional persons in the city who need hotel rooms. The competition can negatively affect your hotel by running a special promotion. On the other side of the coin, the competition can and will create a positive situation for your hotel when they have abysmal service or a ramshackle product.

Other factors that may contribute to a forecast are additions to the supply of hotel rooms in the area, weather, seasonality, pickup and departure patterns of conventions, and the ever-changing local and regional economies. However, when it comes down to it, a forecast is exactly that—it is a guess of what we think may happen or what we really want to happen.

Once the forecasts are completed, they are used to project the amount of variable costs associated with running a hotel—for example, labor, or how many housekeepers, front desk clerks, and hash slingers we are going to need for a given period. Goals are set for sales and catering managers based on the forecast. The quarterly and annual forecasts are reported to the corporate offices for the purpose of forecasting the entire company's projected revenues and expenses. In turn, that information is put out to the stockholders and others with a financial stake in the company.

Forecasts and tracking of how we did compared to the forecast take up 75 percent of my time. The other 25 percent is spent exploring new opportunities for revenue growth, maintaining the various revenue channels into the hotel, managing the reservations department, acting as the liaison between the sales department and operations, and having fun.

Additional duties include exploring new revenue channels for the hotel. I have been known to visit the local competitor on a particularly busy day and offer a shuttle to our hotel and a no-line guarantee—this as the line behind the front desk stretches out the front door and halfway to the street. I am responsible for researching the demographics of the travelers coming to the area. Why are they coming? Are they traveling because of business, conventions, leisure, or are they part of a contract piece of business? How often do they come? How long do they stay? How much do they spend when they come? Where are they coming from?

The most important thing I do as a revenue manager is to ensure the different revenue channels are set up and functioning properly. These channels include the hotel brand's generic toll-free vanity number and central reservations office, the convention and visitors bureau, the local hotel's reservation and front desk, the Internet, and the global distribution system (GDS). The most critical of these channels is the Internet, which includes the brand web site. Only a few years ago it was GDS that was the most critical. In our chains, in 2004, Internet channels generated almost twice the volume of the GDS. However, the GDS is still crucial for the survival of almost every hotel. It is the system that travel agents and some of the Internet sites use to make reservations at my hotels. It contains information about rates and availability at a hotel. It must be checked daily and routinely maintained. The scary thing about the GDS is that most hotels don't know they have a problem until several months down the road. As technology grows and more and more people stop calling and start booking through their travel agents and directly over the Internet, so does the need to understand the GDS and exactly how it affects the hotel. When one of our competitors initiated a cleanup of their GDS, it resulted in several million dollars in additional revenue in six months.

Managing the reservations departments is the easy part of my job. Interacting with people is always easier than trying to interact with numbers and reports. The staff must be kept up to date on changes in the strategic goals of the hotel and changes in marketing the discount and frequent-stayer programs. I am responsible for ensuring that the training of the reservations staff and anyone else who takes reservations is consistent and current, complete with ongoing positive feedback.

It is key that a revenue manager be skilled in the art of diplomacy. As the liaison between the operations and sales departments (see Waller, 7.2), I sometimes must mediate any challenges that may occur. Part of the diplomacy is understanding each department's strategic goals and how both departments depend on each other for their own survival. The easiest and simplest approach to serving as a liaison between the two departments is facilitating frequent, open, and honest communication between all parties.

Having fun is one of my key goals in working at a hotel and in a regional capacity. It is important to maintain a balanced approach to work in a hotel. It is easy to get burned out trying to do too much. The nature of the hotel is that it is open 24 hours a day and 365 days a year. Anything that can happen to a person on any given day can happen at a hotel as well.

7.6 HOTEL SALES ORGANIZATION AND OPERATIONS

MARGARET SHAW AND SUSAN V. MORRIS

✦ SALES AND MARKETING

Sales and marketing are related concepts, and each is an art and a science. Sales flow from marketing. Marketing, well stated by Lewis et al. (1995), "is communicating to and giving target market customers what they want, when they want it, where they want it, and at a price they are willing and able to pay." The primary focus of sales is on the communication aspect of marketing. It involves direct personal selling to potential customers that you and your organization have the right product, in the right place, at the right time, and at the right price—be it a hotel, a restaurant, a casino, or contract food services.

Marketing is getting and keeping a customer, a macro approach to managing a successful business. In a broad sense, marketing is the development and delivery of a successful product, that is, the development and delivery of a satisfied customer. Hotel sales comprises finding that customer and matching his or her specific needs with the right product offering, a micro or one-on-one approach to customer satisfaction. For example, a meeting planner from Texas Instruments (TI) is planning an annual sales meeting to be held in Dallas. From a macro-perspective, this planner has selected the city and is searching for full-service lodging accommodations for 200 TI sales representatives for a five-day conference. From a micro-perspective, he or she visits several hotel alternatives and meets with the hotel sales representatives to find the best "fit." Various aspects of the meeting being planned are discussed including dates, rates, guest room accommodations, function room requirements, food and beverage services, and so forth. It is the job of the hotel sales manager to learn the specific needs and wants of the planner and "create" the right product, place, time, and price for a successful conference.

A successful conference is what the planner is really buying, not bricks and mortar. Thus, successful selling is understanding the real needs of the buyer, communicating how your product and service can best respond to those needs, and then delivering it. In another context, McDonald's Golden Arches markets fun, simplicity, good service, and a good price. McDonald's sells friendly service, good value for price paid, convenient locations, and those delicious golden chicken nuggets on which many of us grew up. Ronald McDonald is an ancillary product, a public relations endeavor, which augments and supports the idea or concept of kids and why they are special.

Public relations, advertising, and special promotions often support the selling effort. Advertisements for the Ritz-Carlton Hotel Company are directed to their business traveler clientele. Such advertisements incorporate both the selling and marketing aspects of this upscale hotel chain. The company is simultaneously selling hotel rooms to busy business executives and marketing a hotel that "remembers your needs," and is hallmarked by the vision implicit in their slogan "ladies and gentlemen serving ladies and gentlemen." A travel agent, a corporate travel manager, or a secretary, however, may have handled the actual purchase of the hotel room. Thus, the Ritz-Carlton advertisements support the sale, but they do not actually make the sale happen.

✦ SALES AND OPERATIONS

Sales is the critical link between marketing and operations. While hospitality professionals may espouse marketing, all too often it becomes ignored in the daily hustle and bustle of operations. It is the role of sales to help bridge this gap and find ways for the key customer-contact members of the hotel to keep the promise of marketing.

Selling starts by the professional sales managers prospecting, making contacts, establishing relationships with clients, uncovering their specific needs and wants. But it doesn't end there. Sales is also the host or hostess greeting restaurant patrons. Sales is the front desk clerk welcoming a guest at the local Holiday Inn or at the Waldorf-Astoria in New York City. Sales is the housekeeping staff delivering the extra set of towels requested by a guest. Sales is the sommelier in a gourmet restaurant recommending wines to complement an entrée choice. Sales is the front office cashier saying, "Thank you for staying with us. We hope you enjoyed your stay." It is amazing how a simple thank you can express appreciation for a customer's patronage and bring them back.

All client-contact personnel of a hospitality organization perform personal selling either consciously or unconsciously. This includes staff who do not regularly have guest contact, such as the credit manager. One of the authors nearly lost a $100,000 annual account when a poorly trained credit manager called the client to collect a payment that had not yet been billed. A well-trained and motivated employee who understands how a hotel works is key to successful selling. This is accomplished through the hiring and training process, and although the many facets of human resources are beyond the scope of this chapter, its importance to guest satisfaction cannot be overstated.

In this particular context, however, the hotel's human resources department can perform services on behalf of the sales department by recruiting sales associates who understand the nature of the hotel industry and its place in the broader category of the services segment of business. Services are different from products and require specialized knowledge and training to be competitive.

Because hospitality is very much a part of the services industry, it is useful to understand how services differ from products. Those characteristics that are unique to the services industry product include perishability, simultaneity, heterogeneity, and intangibility.

Perishability refers to the short shelf life of the hospitality product. If it is not sold today, the potential revenue from the sales of that product is gone. A hotel room has a 24-hour shelf life. A restaurant seat has a 2-hour shelf life. Manufactured goods have a much longer period of durability. If a television set is not sold today, it can be sold tomorrow or next week. The potential revenue from the sale of that product is not lost. But a Tuesday-night hotel room cannot be resold on Wednesday. Tuesday has come and gone. If the hotel guest room goes unsold Tuesday, the potential revenue lost from that vacant room cannot be recouped.

Simultaneity means that production and consumption occur at the same time. How can you produce a guest experience without the guest? Our customers, in a sense, are part of the assembly line. They need to be present for final production of the product offering. A vacant guest room produces nothing. Yes, the carpeting is installed; the bed is made, the bathroom plumbing works. But it all just exists until a guest arrives to use it. Simultaneous production and consumption is a unique challenge for successful operations in hospitality management. The guest needs to be present, because many of the facets of the service involve performances by hotel staff.

A related service characteristic in hospitality is heterogeneity. *Heterogeneity* refers to the variability of service delivery. Guest service agents have their moods. Customers have their moods. All have personalities of varying shapes and sizes. Hospitality is a very people-oriented business. Service personnel change from shift to shift, typically on an 8-hour schedule. Though operational manuals exist in most hospitality establishments, rarely are policies and procedures followed in an exact manner. Guests' "personalities," too, can change throughout their stay, and it may have nothing to do with how they were treated by service personnel. Dealing with heterogeneity in service operations is dealing with reality. Mistakes will happen. But more importantly, mistakes can be addressed. Often a simple apology can win back a customer regardless of who was at fault when a mistake happens.

Intangibility is a fourth major characteristic of service businesses. Some consider it the most important component to recognize. Intangibility refers to the highly intangible nature of the service product offering. Intangibility is a feeling; it is having a sense about something that one cannot fully articulate. The intangible nature of the service product cannot be prejudged. Consumers cannot really see, touch, smell, hear, or taste a service product prior to consumption. They can only anticipate. One can test drive a car before an automobile purchase is made to see what it feels like to drive. But a hospitality customer cannot test drive a hotel weekend package or a restaurant meal prior to consumption. The intangibility aspect of hospitality emphasizes that service delivery is critical to customer satisfaction. Most customers have an idea of what to expect. But, in the end, they are really not sure of what they are buying until the hospitality experience actually takes place. Finally, after the service has been consumed, the guest has only the memory of the performance.

The foregoing unique characteristics represent the foundational challenge to the hotel's sales staff: they must find a way to promise performance and experience in such a way that the hotel's operations departments can deliver on the promise. If the essence of marketing is finding and keeping a customer, then the sales promise is fundamental to that effort. Operations' most important role is the keeping of that promise to the customer—having that customer walk away with a positive and memorable experience and want to return again.

✦ MANAGEMENT OF THE SALES PROCESS

Sales management is effectively directing the personal selling efforts of a hospitality establishment. It involves managing the sales process from both an individual and team perspective. In other words, sales management addresses the logistics of sales solicitation and the development of sales account executives to enhance their sales productivity. Sales account executives need to manage their day-to-day activity, sales teams need to coordinate their efforts, and customers need to feel that they are working with a professional and well-managed organization.

There are several components to hospitality sales management. These include sales organization; sales account management; recruitment, training, and development; goal setting; and performance appraisals. Sales organization refers to departmental and individual organizational issues and inventory management. The following section focuses on the sales organization aspect of hospitality sales management.

✦ SALES ORGANIZATION

Sales organization can be viewed from three perspectives. These include departmental organization, individual planning of sales activity, and inventory management. A sales department needs to be organized, and sales managers within that organizational setup need to coordinate their efforts. Sales managers need to plan or organize their individual activities on a daily, weekly, and monthly basis. Allocating the sale of inventory to various customer segments needs to be managed, as well. These are important issues in hospitality sales management, and following is a more detailed discussion of each.

DEPARTMENTAL ORGANIZATION

Organizing a sales department means determining who is going to do what. Sales solicitation needs to take place, administrative tasks need to be completed, and managerial decisions need to be made on a regular basis. In medium- to large-size hospitality establishments, a director of sales and/or a director of marketing coordinates these efforts. In smaller operations, it is not unusual to have one individual responsible for all of the above. For most bed and breakfast operations in the United States and Canada and the small boutique hotels in Europe, for example, the owner and/or manager of the establishment typically handles sales activities.

Figure 7.4 is a sample sales organizational setup for a midsize urban hotel targeting business clientele. The sales managers in this example are organized by target market and by geographic territory. Sales manager 1 is responsible for corporate accounts located in the immediate downtown and surrounding area. Sales manager 2 is responsible for national corporate accounts. This refers to companies based in other areas that conduct business or have the potential to conduct business at the hotel. Both of these sales managers solicit group and transient business from their account base.

Sales manager 3 targets meetings and convention business from national association accounts. This business may include executive board

Figure 7.4 Organization of an Urban Hotel Sales Department

meetings, committee meetings, regional conferences, and annual conventions.

In this example, once group events have been booked they are turned over to the conference services department for service delivery. Both the sales managers and director of conference services report to the director of sales and marketing. The sales team meets weekly to discuss issues pertinent to achieving the department's sales objectives.

Weekly sales meetings are very much a part of a sales department's organizational structure, be it a sales force of two or twelve sales account executives. They are critical for effective communication within the department. At these meetings, each team member highlights his or her weekly activity with regard to new prospects uncovered, tentative bookings, verbal definites, cancellations, etc. (Verbal definites are bookings where clients have verbally committed their meeting or function to the facility but a signed contract is not yet in hand.) In other words, sales managers share with each other progress reports on various accounts they are currently working on. Thus, each team member gets an up-to-date informal report on the status of all current sales activity.

For example, one sales manager may be working on a tentative booking but considers it weak because of strong competition for this particular account. Call this Group A. Another sales manager may have a new prospect with similar space requirements interested in the same dates. Call this Group B. Assume, however, that the property has the capability of booking only Group A or Group B over the same dates because of space limitations. When these types of issues surface at sales meetings (which they frequently do), discussion will occur raising the following types of questions:

- What is the likelihood that either group will eventually book its business at the property?

- What is the estimated profitability and/or contribution margin for each group?

- Is either group a regular client?

- What is the likelihood of repeat business from either group? In other words, what is the long-term profitability for each?

- Can either group consider alternative dates? (A *very* important question.) What would incite them to move dates?

- Do convention history reports match their current space allocation requests?

These are just a sampling of questions that need to be raised and answered. It is a never-ending process in hospitality sales management to search for the best fit for both the buyer and seller.

✦ CONCLUSION

The organization of sales management is the process of directing the personal selling efforts of a hospitality establishment. It involves effectively managing the sales process from both an individual and team perspective. Sales or account managers need to manage their day-to-day activity; sales teams need to coordinate their efforts. Sales account management involves developing, maintaining, and enhancing customer relationships. Sales managers develop expertise for specific market segments, industry segments, and/or customer accounts, and common traits among successful sales account executives include self-confidence, high energy, empathy, enthusiasm, and a sense of self-worth.

This chapter introduces the foundation for hospitality sales and marketing. First and foremost, sales flow from marketing. If management doesn't have a marketing mindset, then sales efforts will be all for naught.

Marketing is giving the targeted customers what they want, when they want it, where they want it, at a price they are willing and able to pay. Sales is direct communication with potential customers letting them know we have what they want. In many respects, sales is the link between marketing and operations. Operations is essentially the delivery component of marketing and the final determination of a happy (or unhappy) customer.

Marketing begins, transcends, and ends with the consumer. Sales makes sure it happens.

The powerful world of nonprofit organizations can make or break a hotel. This is a very strong statement when you consider our public relations firm, Richmond Public Relations, represents the Seattle Sheraton Hotel and Towers, a hotel that has potential revenues of $80 million to $100 million a year in rooms, food, and beverage and employs more than 600 people. Although the fortune of large convention hotels usually rests on the approval of large associations, meeting planners, Mobil and AAA awards, and myriad corporate decisions, nonprofit organizations definitely play a role in a hotel's financial success. The time and effort that hotels allot to public relations and nonprofits can profoundly influence destination decisions of meeting planners and major associations.

◆ DONATIONS, DONATIONS

Every day the Sheraton receives three or four letters from local organizations soliciting donations of cash, rooms, and meals for benefits, auctions, and raffles. These seemingly simple requests add up to approximately 1000 requests every year. All of these organizations have nonprofit status and are doing valuable work in the community. They range from the symphony, opera, and ballet to large hospitals and universities. The smallest of preschools and local grassroots citizen activist organizations are also regular solicitors. Each of these organizations has a mission and purpose, that, if realized, could make the community a better place in which to live. Because mostly every request is valid, how does the hotel or public relations firm go about deciding which organizations to support? Each decision must be based on a benefit to the hotel.

Let me give an example of how working with the community has, indeed, benefited the hotel. One such request was a handwritten note from an elementary school student requesting a complimentary room for her school raffle. We were promised in the letter that the hotel would be mentioned in the raffle and given as much publicity as possible. This school was located 20 miles from the hotel in a small town that, on the surface, did not seem as if it could provide a lot of return benefit to the hotel. Because of the sincerity of the request, we decided to donate a room package. About four months after the donation was made, our firm received a call from someone who worked for a very large company in Seattle wanting to make room reservations. He called me rather than the hotel because he wanted me to know he was booking the Sheraton because of its donation to his child's school. Because we were the only hotel to donate a room to his child's school auction, he felt an obligation to have his guests stay at the Sheraton. Therefore, his company was moving from another hotel to ours because of a donation that, in actuality, cost about $35. The potential revenue from his account was valued in the thousands of dollars. Additionally, his company is a member of trade associations that hold numerous regional and national conventions that can also influence the direction of business to the Sheraton.

Other benefits linked to this donation were that the Sheraton's name was seen in print on more than 1000 raffle tickets, and people who attended the drawing were made aware of the Sheraton's contribution. The return on investment from this one donation was enormous in direct revenue alone and also generated an excellent amount of goodwill in the local community. All of this revenue and potential revenue was the result of one small donation!

✦ ASSOCIATIONS, NATIONAL MEETINGS

When large associations choose Seattle as the host city for their national conferences, the individual hotels bid on being the host hotel. The host hotel is in a favorable situation concerning room rate and food and beverage functions. A well-thought-out public relations program can play an important role in an association's deciding which hotel to use. Working with the sales staff, the public relations firm can obtain as much information about the association as possible and decide how they can influence the association to use the Sheraton.

A major southwestern association was in the process of deciding which hotel to use for its Seattle conference. With research, we found that this particular organization supported a major national charity that was also supported by the Sheraton. We contacted the director of the local charity organization, who, in turn, phoned his counterpart in the southwestern city. He was informed of the Sheraton's sponsorship of his nonprofit and that one of his large corporate sponsors was looking for a hotel to use in Seattle. The director of the southwestern nonprofit called his contact in the corporation and apparently did a good job of convincing him to use the Sheraton. Whether or not the decision was made directly because of this call or the combination of other sales efforts, most of the sales and marketing staff concurred that the hotel's support of the local nonprofit organization was instrumental in securing a major piece of association business. We have found that the nonprofit world will go all out to help corporations that help them. In addition, nonprofit organizations can effectively utilize this win-win model of partnership between business and nonprofits to solicit help from other companies and businesses.

✦ SOCIAL EVENTS AND FUND-RAISERS

The social catering business is fiercely competitive. Nonprofit organizations are always seeking the lowest possible rates and prices, but because of their standing in the community, they sponsor important events at hotels. The more prestigious the organization, the higher the ticket price and the greater the potential that the attendees can generate revenue for the hotel in the future by booking rooms for other events. Most members of the boards of directors of nonprofit organizations are leaders in the community and business world. Their recommendation can go a long way toward securing a favorable image for the hotel in the local market.

In dealing with social catering events for nonprofit groups, we always inform organizations that the hotel staff will work closely with them to ensure the success of their event. However, the nonprofit must clearly understand that the hotel is a *for-profit* business. We have to strike a deal that is good for the organization and, at the same time, good for the hotel. The organization is helped to understand that the more profitable the hotel, the more support can be provided for the nonprofit organization. If the hotel does not make a profit, it cannot continue to offer its support. By offering the organization special services rather than lowering the price to the point where the hotel will not make any profit, we ultimately help the organization raise even more money for their event. We have come up with many creative contributions to nonprofit organizations that not only increase their potential for raising money but also favorably highlight the services of the hotel.

One of the hotel's most popular donations to nonprofit organization auctions is a series of cooking classes for ten people that includes a kitchen tour and lunch. This item, usually set at a minimum bid of $500 to $700, enables a group of people to combine their financial resources for a potentially higher bid. The cooking classes also enable the hotel to highlight one of its chefs and give people a back-of-the-house view of the kitchen. We have tracked the success of these cooking classes and found that almost every one of the participants has booked reservations in the hotel restaurants. What is given away as a donation comes back many times over in increased business and greatly enhances the perception of the hotel's goodwill in the community.

Another innovative donation was a tour with the hotel's curator of the corporate art collection. The Sheraton, well known for its art collection, employs a professional curator. Most of the major social service organizations and nonprofit organizations show an interest in the arts, and this type of donation stands out from the overnight accommodations typically offered by other hotels.

The hotel's limousine can also play a part in the donation program. The use of the limousine always adds a prestigious quality to a gift and raises more money for the organization, while costing the hotel only a minimal labor and operating cost.

Making a major donation to social catering fundraisers that are booked in the hotel helps ensure the event will be rebooked the following year (assuming the food and service are high quality). The ability to predict annual bookings provides savings in sales staff time and marketing efforts.

When major social catering events are held in other hotels, the Sheraton also makes significant donations to show organizations it is interested in supporting their cause no matter where their event is held. Of course, the hotel remains interested in having the group book their event at the Sheraton next season. However, our agency always encourages the Sheraton to purchase a table when events are hosted in another hotel, for several reasons: to show support for the organization, to let the staff see how the event is managed at another facility, and to compare quality of service and food.

✦ HOLIDAY CARD PROGRAM

Another significant community contribution we make is our annual holiday card. Each year we select a different organization to be the beneficiary of this program. We print the Sheraton corporate holiday card and then provide the organization with an extra 10,000 cards for its own fundraising campaign. These cards are printed at no charge to the organization as long as they provide us with original artwork. The organization that is chosen is always selected so that there is a return to the hotel. The organization chosen in 1987 had previously held a major event at another hotel. We informed them that if they switched to the Sheraton, they would be the beneficiaries of the 1988 holiday card campaign.

✦ CONTROL

The hotel has certain prerequisites in making donations to nonprofit organizations.

1. The organization must be a 501(c)3 organization recognized by the Internal Revenue Service.
2. A request must be received in writing on the organization's stationery.
3. The organization must return to the hotel written notification of the donation through a raffle advertisement, program book, or announcement.
4. The donation must be in a live and not a silent auction whenever possible.
5. All responses are filed, and when a request for next year's gift arrives, we check to see if we received the recognition we required.

Different levels of donations are awarded based on the event and the amount of recognition received. The Sheraton has donated gift certificates to the dessert buffet and a dinner for 100 people in Fullers, the hotel's award-winning restaurant.

Our commitment to the community is based on the belief that each member of the organizations we support can act as a public relations spokesperson for the hotel. When businesses help organizations, their members and volunteers usually develop a loyalty to the giver. Our goal is to infiltrate the community aggressively as a good corporate citizen. At the same time, we want the community to know that we need their business. The more business they give us, the more help we can return to the community.

✦ CLASSIFICATION OF ORGANIZATIONS

The nonprofit world can be divided into six general areas, as set out below. For each classification, major examples of the many possible representative organizations are listed.

Cultural Organizations

Most of these organizations have a large and prestigious board of directors. There is a tremendous amount of potential room business and catering functions from the organizations and their board members.

- Symphony orchestras, opera companies, ballet companies, chamber music organizations, and presenting organizations, as well as campus cultural organizations
- Art museums, museums of history and industry, science museums, and craft and folk art museums
- Major, alternative, and community theater companies

Health Organizations

- Hospitals
- Medical schools
- Research centers

Educational Organizations

- Alumni associations
- University and college fundraising campaigns

- High school and PTA organizations
- Preschool and private school fundraisers

Religious Organizations
- Churches
- Synagogues
- Religious schools and camps
- Adult religious community organizations

Social Service Agencies
- United Way
- Community charity groups
- Neighborhood grassroots organizations
- Charities such as Easter Seals and March of Dimes
- Food banks
- Cystic Fibrosis Foundation
- Juvenile Diabetes Foundation
- Boy Scouts of America

Social and Fraternal Organizations
- Rotary
- Kiwanis
- Elks
- Shriners

✦ MARKETING APPROACHES

Before you approach an organization, you need to have a plan that puts you on the offensive rather than the defensive. Many times hotels find themselves responding to people asking for money rather than actually going to the organization to tell them they are there to help them.

The more creative you can be, the easier it will be for the organization to work with you. Your plan should include researching the following items:

- The members of the board of directors and their company affiliations
- The needs of the organization
- Their budget—easy to do because they are a tax-exempt organization
- Past catering functions—where they were held, prices, and number of attendees
- Housing needs of the organization and how you can help

Read newspapers about the organization and totally familiarize yourself with their goals. Make sure you meet with a major staff member and a board member. To meet with just one or the other simply means you will have to hold another meeting to review what you discussed at the last meeting. The most important overall consideration is to understand the nonprofit organization's needs and to work together with their representatives for a win-win solution.

Make sure you work out before the event how the hotel will be credited and recognized. Recognition of the hotel's contribution is often assumed, forgotten, or left to chance. The hotel can be recognized in many ways. A complimentary ad in a season's program or newsletter will go a long way in justifying your investment. If you are trying to attract the organization, it must have an audience that is part of your marketing mix. Calculate what it would cost to advertise in their program book throughout the season. Bargain with the organization for a complimentary ad for the amount of the donation you are making. Other possible returns for your donation include:

- Having the organization give the hotel complimentary tickets that can be used by the staff for entertaining clients. This strategy can be effective if concerts are sold out and your hotel is in possession of the only tickets.

- Asking the organization give you access to their mailing list. This strategy can be crucial in trying to publicize a new weekend program or the opening of a new food and beverage outlet.

- Requesting the organization commit to a two-year contract. This strategy not only makes it easier for the organization to plan ahead but helps the hotel in projecting revenues.

- Donating meeting rooms to the organization for seminars and retreats if food and beverages are ordered. Most organizations have to pay for meeting facilities.

One of the most important aspects of any donation is the follow-up. Make sure you are aware of the news created by the organization you are helping and make them feel they are part of *your* organization. If major events take place, have the hotel's general manager send a congratulatory letter. If someone has a birthday, have your pastry chef send over a birthday cake. If you can help them publicize their events in your newsletter, work with them and inform them you are giving them complimentary publicity. Work together all the time so that each organization receives something from each other, if possible, on a fairly regular basis.

✦ CASE STUDY

Our firm approached the board of directors of the Seattle Symphony in hopes that they would move a major luncheon to the Sheraton. We told them we would be happy to offer complimentary room accommodations for the conductor and his wife for the duration of the symphony season if they would help influence their women's organization to use the Sheraton for their luncheon. By hosting the conductor and his wife in the best available room, we not only built up a good relationship with the conductor but also showed the board of directors we were very interested in supporting the symphony.

By proactively informing the board of directors that the Sheraton was committed to the symphony, we, at the same time, helped them understand our need for their board members' business so that we could continue our support for them. Donating to significant cultural institutions is often a sound business decision because most members who serve on boards of large cultural organizations are the community's business leaders. They know the wisdom of a sound decision, and, indeed, continue to offer ongoing support to the Sheraton. As a result of the Sheraton donating a room to the conductor and his wife, the symphony moved the luncheon to the hotel. The hotel maintains a strong relationship with the conductor, and the symphony continues to use the Sheraton for their room, food, and beverage business. In a classic example of a win-win situation, the symphony supporters, their board of directors, and their musicians act as public relations spokespeople for the Sheraton. In many ways, the results of this strategy have ensured several hundred people working on our behalf.

✦ PRESS AND MEDIA

It is important to remember that the people in the press are also part of the community. Ultimately, donations to nonprofits will touch many press and other media people in personal ways by helping their local organizations, such as schools, hospitals, and social service and cultural organizations. They will be especially interested in publicizing events with personal impact. It is also important to realize that hotels with many events create a buzz that generates more local press activity. Organizations like to be involved in active and exciting hotels. If a certain number of events are in one hotel and twice that amount are in another hotel, the more active hotel is bound to have more requests for events.

✦ COSPONSORSHIP

Another effective way to maximize public relations in the area of nonprofit donations or charities is to cosponsor events with radio stations or newspapers. The exposure that can be provided through this medium not only places your property with other responsible companies but also helps spread the word of your company's involvement automatically through the media.

Take advantage of your local and regional radio stations to develop joint promotions. Work with the promotion director to find out how the hotel can help the station's favorite charity. Donate the ballroom or smaller meeting rooms for dances, parties, etc., with a guarantee of a no-host bar. The radio station acts as a free advertising service to draw people to the event. It is in their best interest for their advertisers to draw large audiences. Have the nonprofit organization receive an admission charge to the event so that it is up to the nonprofit organization to also try to draw a large audience. By working with the radio station and the char-

ity, the hotel not only maximizes its exposure but also increases its potential revenue.

✦ REGIONAL ORGANIZATIONS

Identify major nonprofit organizations in feeder markets and work with them in their major fundraising events. This will help increase weekend business and act as a reinforcer to advertising placed in those markets. The impact of regional organizations can be just as strong as your local organizations. If your property has a strong regional weekend market, this program can be an effective way to increase room business.

Identify corporations that have branches in feeder cities with ties to major nonprofit organizations. Any time your property can get its name across to the public in a major feeder market, you reinforce advertising dollars or actually save them. Remember, the return on investment, if carefully monitored, can be significant.

✦ CONCLUSION

The more times your hotel property is written and talked about, the more people automatically identify it with positive community activity. It is eventually in the best interest of a community to ensure the business success of your hotel when it knows you will help its favorite charities or organizations. In order to work with the community, you must educate the community to work for and with you. The best recommendation is that made by the public, and only when public relations truly works with the public can the property benefit. By putting the public in public relations, the public speaks for you and your property and results in profits through public relations.

7.8 ANTICIPATING THE UNEXPECTED: HOTEL MARKETING EVOLVES IN ASIA PACIFIC Paul Iacovino

Early in the author's previous edition of this book, there was a discussion of changes in the organization of hotels and hotel management. Changes in management approach, style, and emphasis continues today. We can anticipate that a continued evolution in hotel management will be the normal course of action, as modern business practices find their way into all areas of the operation. In no aspect of hotel management is this more pronounced then in the field of hotel marketing.

Most significant hotel marketing innovations began in North America, where the model depended less on third parties, such as travel wholesalers and travel agents. Focus has primarily been on the corporate travel function, the meeting planner, and the traveler. This direct approach was a catalyst for the growth of direct sales as an important marketing tool, in the 1950s. The growth of the direct sales organization within hotel management represented the earliest beginnings of modern marketing in the industry. Today property-based sales forces and regional sales efforts are the norm worldwide. Changes and innovations in hotel marketing continue to be initiated from North America. The proliferation of the World Wide Web as a marketing and distribution channel is the most recent example.

Anticipating that changes in hotel marketing would be transferred from North America to Europe, Asia, and other parts of the world does not take much effort. Understanding what innovations or events would accelerate the pace of the assimilation of new marketing approaches, has been more akin to reading a crystal ball or tea leaves. In Asia the third-party wholesale model of marketing and distribution still remains a strong component in the demand side of the business. Hotel companies that have been doing business in Asia for longer periods have maintained an emphasis and orientation to this model. However, this has shifted swiftly and significantly in just the past 10 years. The reasons for the changes in this particular aspect of the business and others of equal importance are many. Anticipating these changes has been and will continue to be a skill to hone as a larger number of players vie for customers in the Asian travel market.

Perhaps it is unexpected events and innovations coupled with the expansion of international brands, which have lead to the greatest changes in the Asia Pacific marketing model. In a smaller and faster-paced world, the Asia experience may hold some valuable lessons for the North American hotel manager.

Looking at the past 10 years in Asia, there have been four categories of unexpected influences on business travel and tourism. These include events categorized as political, natural, financial, and technological, specifically the World Wide Web.

Hotel marketing managers in Asia have become adept at responding to crisis and have learned to maintain a level of agility as well as a steady hand as events out of their control unfolded around them with uncanny consistency. Looking first at the "political" impacts on travel and tourism one need not go back even as far as the late 1990s for examples. In 1998 Indonesian dictator Suharto was removed from office, and tourism and most other travel to that nation came to a halt, with the fear of riots and unrest.

Two examples of political events that lead hotel management and tourism officials to rethink marketing priorities were the 2008 Summer Olympics in Beijing and political turmoil in Thailand.

China greatly limited travel visas into the country in the lead-up to the Olympics, as government officials worried about terrorism and other political threats from outside the country. What hoteliers were forced to grapple with was a sharp decline in business, leisure, and the number of meetings being held. Unfortunately for some, this decline outweighed the benefits of the Olympics themselves. China continues to challenge the tourism industry today with increasingly stringent visa restrictions for its domestic travelers planning a holiday in the new gambling Mecca of Asia—Macau SAR. In addition, the Chinese government's relaxation of restrictions on outbound international travel continues to be an attraction for travel industry marketers throughout the region. These decisions, by their very nature, are political and difficult to anticipate and counter. Hotel marketers in China quickly understood that they would need to turn the focus of their efforts to previously secondary markets or develop completely new sources of demand. While for others in the region, the potential

for the Chinese tourist to replace or augment activity from other parts of the world has presented an enormous opportunity.

Political strife in Thailand has had an enormous impact on tourist travel into that country. Although the country attracts tourists from nearly every corner of the world, it depends a great deal on travel from the United States and Japan. Both countries populations are skittish when faced with nearly any kind of travel uncertainty but, political unrest coupled with fear of terrorism, will turn the taps off fast in both of these travel-oriented nations. Travel marketers in Thailand quickly learned, as those in Indonesia and other places before them, that Americans and Japanese would not be convinced to overlook the trouble or that the unrest was confined to areas outside the path of normal tourist activities. The Thais were somewhat insulated from the disappearance of a significant source of their tourism in that the British, Australians, and Germans, a much heartier traveling population also found Thailand to be an attractive destination.

Efforts were ramped up, special offers provided and aimed at these and other markets. Marketers also looked to create new aspects of tourism. One such example is in the area of medical treatment and surgery. But, the Thai experience in 2008 ended with little option for the tourism industry, and hoteliers in particular, when the protestors took over and closed Bangkok's international airport. Nearly all travel to the country stopped with the airport out of commission. This was one occurrence that even the savviest marketer could not counter.

The most damaging of all political influence on travel and tourism facing hotel marketers and their counterparts in destination marketing is war and terrorism. Since the 9/11 attacks in the United States, the marketers in Asia have had to address varying degrees of impacts on travel. September 11, along with the outbreak of wars in Afghanistan and Iraq, impacted travel worldwide. Again as with other aspects of political influences on travel, the region looked more and more inward, developing business opportunities in previously less interesting places such as Taipei, Korea, and India. Of course, the Chinese traveler has quickly become the most sought-after guest.

Some terrorism events had a more localized impact such as the Bali bombings in 2002 and 2005, the Jakarta Marriott Hotel bombing, and most recently the November 2008 attacks on the Oberoi and Taj Palace hotels in Mumbai. These events brought travel into the destination nearly to a standstill in the short term and have had long and enduring impacts far after the events.

The Bali situation is unique today because of the fact that the same spot was targeted twice in relatively close succession. The resort marketers in this destination followed many different approaches to the significant fall-off in demand they experienced, depending on the markets their properties targeted. Many properties in the three- and four-star categories responded with significant discounts and focused on younger, more adventurous travelers. This approach proved to be successful and after a short period, demand in this segment of the market rebounded.

Operators of high-end luxury properties were faced with a different challenge than their colleagues in the three- and four-star segment. Many attempted to attract guests through the same discounting and packaging activities as their more mass-market counterparts. However, the lesson was quickly learned or reinforced that high-end travelers are not as influenced by discounts. Instead, these travelers preferred destinations that did not hold the threat of danger or the memories of sadness and tragedy. In effect, marketers that chose this approach at the outset simply discounted what little business was predisposed to come to the market in the first place.

The main key to successfully navigating the post-bombing period was the focus on markets that would pay a premium for their travel experience but, because of budget and timing of their travel, were never strong source markets for the high-end resorts. Attracting Japanese, Taiwanese, and Korean travelers predisposed to travel in groups or purchase travel through wholesale channels was a key to the success of many around these events. This strategy allowed marketers to provide discounts in selected markets without exposing the lower pricing to the wider audience of high-end travelers to Bali. The emphasis on building demand and, hence, occupancy, along with a strict commitment to maintaining pricing at pre-bombing levels proved a successful combination. Avoiding the urge to discount to the wider traveling public and a commitment to consistent pricing through all distribution channels is what the industry calls "price integrity." This has lead to important changes in hotel marketers approach to swings in demand.

In late March 2003 a new challenge to travel marketing and the entire travel and hospitality industry emerged, which begins our discussion of the second unexpected influence, "natural." The event was the outbreak of SARS in Hong Kong and Singapore. The virus spread to Canada and travel to and from Asia and Canada came to a complete stop. Hotels and resorts in many Asian locations ran nearly empty; one could walk through normally busy airports, encountering only a few hearty souls, most in protective masks. The SARS epidemic and the threat of its spread around the world was the most significant example of unexpected events impacting the travel and hospitality business as nothing has before or since.

The shortened news cycle and the Internet brought SARS into the lives of everyone worldwide. The medical community struggled to determine the cause and potential for containment of the virus, resulting in business travel and leisure travel from within the region coming to a halt as well as that from other parts of the world. The fear of SARS among the public was, to an extent, irrational. It became clear that the virus in places like Singapore, Indonesia, and Thailand had been contained. Marketers in these destinations directed resources to educate the markets about the measure taken to protect citizens and travelers from infection and to reassure businesses and leisure travel partners that these were safe places to travel.

Nothing the travel industry did to calm fear on behalf of their destinations worked. Until the "all clear" was handed down by the World Health Organization, marketing expenditures to build business and tourism travel was best kept in the bank. The wisest marketers during the SARS period were those that "kept their powder dry." Preparing marketing campaigns to launch after the WHO had lifted restrictions on a destination was the best management of advertising, promotion, and direct sales budgets.

Another lesson of the SARS period was that people needed to be completely certain that danger and risk had subsided before venturing back to the region. This proved to be a challenge made more difficult for marketers to manage,

given that the Internet and news media remained full of SARS coverage in Vietnam and China, well after the risks had subsided in other parts of Asia. To the international traveler, particularly the Japanese and North American traveler, China and Southeast Asia were one. The travel drought dragged on into the early summer. When the fear did subside, as might be expected, business travel rebounded at a faster pace then leisure travel; proof that the pursuit of profits makes a business traveler a brave warrior in today's world. But, to no one's surprise, the leisure traveler was much slower to return.

Learning from previous travel catastrophes, upscale travel marketers kept their powder dry and refrained from wild discounting in the leisure segment, again turning to distribution channels that would protect the integrity of their pricing and provide access to regional markets, which was less affected by the media coverage of SARS. It was later that year that advertising budgets were again in full swing and not until mid-2004 that travel levels returned to normal in the region.

Just a couple of years later, Bird Flu made its appearance throughout the region. The limited deaths attributed to the virus as well as its apparent containment, mostly related to the fact that the virus does not spread from human to human, gave the region its first break in the onslaught disasters that had impacted the industry since 2001. Bird Flu's arrival did serve to remind travel marketers that in a world of faster and larger aircraft and the web, they had to anticipate these events and manage each situation with a cool head and patience.

The third unexpected influence, "financial" begins with the discussion of the Asian Financial Crisis of the late 1990s. This event awoke the hotel industry in the region to the effects of economies growing with little control and more than a dash of corruption. With most Asian currencies losing significant value against the U.S. dollar, many hoteliers determined that pricing in the U.S. currency was a safe hedge against continued swings and further devaluation. Most of South East Asia moved to U.S. dollar pricing for international travelers. But, with demand plummeting along with the value of local currency, most marketers could only react to events and for the most part fell back on discounting as the major strategy to protect their business. For many, this was a strategy of survival.

As economies strengthened and regulation of banks and stock markets improved, apparent economic stability prompted most hotel companies to return to pricing in their domestic currency. And although the financial meltdown to come in 2008 ravaged the entire Asia Pacific region, currency fluctuations have played a far less significant role in this most recent downturn.

Ten years on technology is giving the hotel industry an opportunity for a more considered and stronger approach, leading to our discussion of the final unexpected influence, "technological." In 2008, the financial world, along with everything else, including the travel industry, has been turned on its head. This time, the industry has at its disposal an array of tools and strategies not available or even conceivable at the end of the 1990s. The World Wide Web, as a marketing tool, was just coming into its own at the time of the Asian Financial Crisis. Its primary use was as a tool for reaching mass audiences with discounts and special offers. But, as hoteliers address this most recent fall in demand, they have come to understand that the long-term nature of the event will set this crisis apart.

The most familiar technological advancement is Internet or web marketing. The advent of search marketing and the options to optimize search, create links to complementary sites and cross listings allow a uniquely tactical approach to advertising. A message and an offer can be directed toward large numbers of target customers through web sites. Directly communicating with past customers via email broadcasts and other web tools is more effective then postal direct mail and allows a wider reach at much lower costs.

Possibly an even more important advancement, than the Internet, is one unfamiliar to much of the public. These technological tools make up an array of yield and revenue management options that allow hotels to selectively offer rates or rooms inventory to coincide with the most profitable time at which to make an offer or sell a specific room category. Where the use of a company web site or third-party web sites such as Expedia, Travelocity, and other travel wholesale channels provides an effective way to build new business, the various yield programs utilized by hotel marketers serves in larger part to protect "share."

Protecting share and building new business are important aspects of today's hotel marketer's defense in an environment of continuing falling demand. This is a significant difference from nearly all other circumstances that have affected demand unexpectedly. Protecting share and building new sources of business are more of a "response" than a "reaction" to business downturns. This ability to take a more proactive, less defensive approach sets today's hotel marketer apart from his or her predecessors.

Advancements in these various technologies and the hotel marketer's familiarity and comfort with how to best use them, mean that marketers will continue to find new approaches to the unexpected events that affect the hospitality and travel business. Entering the second decade of the new century, marketers in Asia Pacific have the experience and are well prepared to address the next unexpected event that comes their way.

7.9 MINI-CASE: REVAMPING THE MARKETING RESEARCH DEPARTMENT

You're the new director of marketing research for the Mississippi Region Affiliated Resorts (MRAS), located along the length of the Mississippi River from Minneapolis to Memphis. This branded distribution company of 38 independently owned and operated hotels has become a major player in its regional competitive marketplace. As part of the company's strategic plan, however, it has been determined that the structure of the market is changing, and the general future direction of the hotels will be oriented toward providing sales and service to the conventions and meetings, which has become increasingly important because of the central location of the chain.

To become more competitive in this burgeoning market, the company has undertaken and encouraged an ambitious remodeling program among its members that has upgraded the furnishings, fixtures, and equipment of the hotels. The hotels are also committing to a minimum of the following capital investments:

• 60,000–square-foot ballroom

• 30,000 square feet of meeting and breakout rooms

• 15,000-square-foot registration and prefunction areas

With these upgraded facilities, the company feels it can compete effectively for the lucrative conventions and meetings market with the hard-flagged chains.

This strategy and capital investment requires a consequential change in research paradigms. As the director of marketing research, you've been requested by the company president to propose a completely revamped research department that will reflect this new strategy and be designed to help the independent member hotels market their new facilities most effectively.

Propose a model marketing research department for your firm that will produce the sorts of data that hotels in the chain can use to help compete with the national chains. Include in your proposal what new sorts of data would be most useful, where those may be found, and how they might be specifically useful to reflect the new mission.

REFERENCES

DeVeau, L. T., P. M. DeVeau, N. J. Portocarrero, and M. Escoffier. 1996. *Front Office Management and Operations*. Upper Saddle River, NJ: Prentice-Hall.

Drucker, P. F. 1974. *The Practice of Management*. New York: Harper and Row.

Drucker, P. F. 1999. *Management Challenges for the 21st Century*. New York: Harper Collins, pp. 115–116.

Fishbein, M., and I. Ajzen. 1975. *Belief, Attitude, Intention, and Behavior: An Introduction to Theory and Research*. Reading, MA: Addison-Wesley.

Hanson, B. 1995. "The $1 per $1,000 Rule." *Cornell Hotel and Management Administration Quarterly* 36(4): 7.

Lewis, R. C., R. E. Chambers, and H. E. Chacko. 1995. *Marketing Leadership in Hospitality: Foundations and Practices* (2nd ed.). New York: Van Nostrand Reinhold 3.

Lieberman, W. H. 1993. "Debunking the Myths of Yield Management," *Cornell Hotel and Restaurant Administration Quarterly* 34(1):34–41.

———. 2003. *PKF Trends Reports*. Dublin, Ireland: Pannell, Kerr Forster.

Protea Hotels Partners with SalesBid. 2000. Press Release. June 8.

Sinclair, M. 2003. "The Use of Intuition in Managerial Decision-Making: Determinants and Affective Moderators." Ph.D. dissertation. University of Queensland [Australia] Business School.

SUGGESTED READINGS

BOOKS

Astroff, M. T., and J. R. Abbey. 2006. *Convention Sales and Service*. Lansing, MI: Educational Institute of American Hotel and Lodging Association.

Kotler, P., J. T. Bowen, and J. C. Makens. 2005. *Marketing for Hospitality and Tourism*. Upper Saddle River, NJ: Prentice-Hall.

Kudrle, A. E., and M. Sandler. 1995. *Public Relations for Hospitality Managers: Communicating for Greater Profits*. New York: John Wiley and Sons.

Lewis, R. C. 1997. *Cases in Hospitality Marketing and Management*. New York: John Wiley and Sons.

Lovelock, C., and L. Wright. 2001. *Principles of Service Marketing and Management*. Upper Saddle River, NJ: Prentice-Hall.

Lovelock, C. 2007. *Services Marketing: People, Technology, Strategy*. Upper Saddle River, NJ: Prentice-Hall.

Raza, I. 2004. *Heads in Beds: Hospitality Tourism Marketing*. Upper Saddle River, NJ: Prentice Hall.

Reid, R. D., and D. C. Bojanic. 2010. *Hospitality Marketing Management*. Hoboken, NJ: John Wiley & Sons, Inc.

Sernovitz, A. 2009. *Word of Mouth Marketing: How Smart Companies Get People Talking*. New York: Kaplan Publishing.

Shaw, M., and S. V. Morris. 2000. *Hospitality Sales: A Marketing Approach*. New York: John Wiley and Sons.

Siguaw, J. A., and D. Bojanic. 2004. *Hospitality Sales: Selling Smarter*. New York: Delmar Learning.

Wharton, A. J. 2001. *Building the Cold War: Hilton International Hotels and Modern Architecture*. Chicago: University of Chicago Press.

ARTICLES

Dev, C., K. Z. Zhou, and J. Brown. 2009. "Customer Orientation or Competition Orientation: Which Marketing Strategy has a Higher Payoff for Hotel Brands?" *Cornell Hospitality Quarterly* 50(1): 19–28.

Gazzoli, G., W. G. Kim, and R. Palakurthi. 2008. "Online Distribution Strategies and Competition: Are the Global Hotel Companies Getting it Right?" *International Journal of Contemporary Hospitality Management* 20(4): 375–387

Jarvis, L. P., and E. J. Mayo. 1986. "Winning the Market Share Game." *Cornell Hotel and Restaurant Administration Quarterly* 27(3): 73–79.

Kim, J., D. C. Bojanic, and R. B. Warnick. 2009. "Price Bundling and Travel Product Pricing Practices Used by Online Channels of Distribution." *Journal of Travel Research* 47(4): 403–412.

Levitt, T. 1981. "Marketing Intangible Products and Product Intangibles." *Cornell Hotel and Restaurant Administration Quarterly* (August): 37–44.

Lieberman, W. H. 1993. "Debunking the Myths of Yield Management." *Cornell Hotel and Restaurant Administration Quarterly* 34(1): 34–41.

Nordling, C. W., and S. K. Wheeler. 1992. "Building a Market Segment Model to Improve Profits." *Cornell Hotel and Restaurant Administration Quarterly* 33(3): 29–36.

O'Connor, P. 2007. "Online Consumer Privacy: An Analysis of Hotel Company Behavior." *Cornell Hotel and Restaurant Administration Quarterly* 48(2): 183–200.

O'Neill, J. W., B. Hanson, and A. S. Mattila. 2008. "The Relationship of Sales and Marketing Expenses to Hotel Performance in the United States." *Cornell Hospitality Quarterly* 49(4): 355–363.

SOURCE NOTES

Chapter 7.2, "Building Market Leadership: Marketing as Process," by Fletch Waller.

Chapter 7.3, "Consumer Decision Rules and Implications for Hotel Choice," by Bianca Grohmann and Eric Spangenberg.

Chapter 7.4, "Hotel Pricing," by Marta Sinclair and Carl R. Sinclair.

Chapter 7.5, "A Day in the Life of a Regional Revenue Manager," by Paul Chappelle.

Chapter 7.6, "Hotel Sales Organization and Operations," by Margaret Shaw and Susan V. Morris, adapted from *Hospitality Sales: A Marketing Approach*, by Margaret Shaw and Susan V. Morris. Copyright © 2000 by John Wiley & Sons, Inc. Reprinted by permission of John Wiley & Sons, Inc.

Chapter 7.7, "Putting the Public in Public Relations: The Case of the Seattle Sheraton Hotel and Towers," by Louis B. Richmond.

Chapter 7.8, "Anticipating the Unexpected: Hotel Marketing Evolves in Asia Pacific," by Paul Iacovino.

FINANCIAL CONTROL AND INFORMATION MANAGEMENT

8.1 INTRODUCTION

This section on financial control and information management was substantially reconfigured for the third edition and expanded upon in this edition. At the suggestion of reviewers and textbook users, articles were chosen to illustrate the relationships among and between the activities that contribute to the hotel's profitability and operational success through the managerial responsibility for operational control.

As a department, financial management in a hotel—called many things, but usually *controller*—is far more important to the success of that hotel than the few readings included here would suggest. In most major hotel firms, the chief financial officer or controller ranks among the top two or three decision makers in the hotel's hierarchy. The importance of this job can

be established by the observation that many traditional hotel departments have been reorganized so that major portions of their functions are now responsible to the controller's office. The prime example of this is in the front office, where in the past the front office manager supervised the activities of the night audit staff, cashiers, and other front desk clerks. Increasingly, hotel firms are transferring the responsibility for night audits and cashiers to the accounting office, with the ultimate responsibility for these information-gathering and controlling functions resting with the hotel controller.

It should also be noted that an increasingly important department in hotels is the one responsible for the swiftly changing world of information management, or information technology

(IT). In many instances, IT is now also the responsibility of the hotel controller. This recognizes the training and the ability of hotel controllers to provide for the structured accumulation, storage, and reporting of data in forms that are most useful to the operating departments and other executives of the hotel.

In his lead article on the hotel chief financial executive, longtime contributor to this series of books Professor Ray Schmidgall, Hilton Professor with the School of Hospitality Business at Michigan State University, reviews recent research on the hotel controller and compares findings over time. This review presents a good view of the job and responsibilities of this key hotel executive. Schmidgall finds interesting differences in the groups studied over the years and provides a wider window for viewing the hotel controller as a career path in management of a modern hotel operation. In the past, students were merely instructed in the process of accounting and auditing and, for the most part, were unaware of the sort of career that can result from a flair for management, leadership, and number-crunching.

In support of this notion, Countryman, DeFranco, and Venegas address the question, "is a hotel controller a viable position for hospitality students?" In this newly added article, the authors found that this career can be very lucrative for hospitality students. A controller in the hotel industry averages close to $80,000 a year in base salary, approximately $10,000 in bonus money (this does not include the benefits, by the way), and works a little over 50 hours a week. In addition, Countryman and his coauthors note that a controller does not just sit at a desk pushing paper all day long. In fact, knowledge and use of technology and the management of human resources plays a vital role in performing this job successfully. As evident, this is a viable career option for hospitality students.

In another Schmidgall piece written with Agnes DeFranco, the critical practices of budgeting and forecasting are examined. While this is only a sampler of the critical duties of the hotel's financial function and its leadership, in today's business environment the accuracy of forecasting and budgeting may indeed be the difference between profit and loss.

If the aforementioned pieces represent the academic side of examination of the hotel's financial leadership, the article by Mike Draeger is invaluable as he is the chief financial executive who lives the theory on a daily basis. After a significant career with Four Seasons Hotels and Resorts and the Cal-Neva Lodge, he now serves as the controller for a company operating a number of casinos in Nevada. Join Mike for a look at the chief financial executive's job in his "As I See It" essay. Pay particular attention to his war story about the budgeting process—and, yes, the lessons from the embezzler.

No discussion of financial and operational control in a hotel would be complete without attention paid to the extremely important function of purchasing.

In the past, when the bulk of a hotel's purchasing revolved around food and beverage items, the executive chef, chief steward, and other department managers usually developed their own sources for the goods and services needed to effectively and efficiently run their department. In the modern context, however, with the vast and diverse needs of hotel operating and staff departments, this practice is no longer advisable. Neither is it a good idea from a control standpoint.

Most hotel companies have established a professional purchasing function. If purchasing is not a whole department, it is the responsibility of at least one highly experienced individual.

The purchasing director or manager typically is a person who knows a great deal about departmental operations in every phase of the hotel. He or she is able to discuss and analyze intelligently the needs of all department managers. This individual is an expert in the markets where hotels purchase goods and products essential to accomplishing the department, and the hotel's, mission. The purchasing director is familiar with variety, quality standards, style, and methods of packaging. Such arcane technical details as chemical composition, fabric and furnishing lifetimes, and other details too numerous to mention here are also the responsibility of the purchasing manager.

Lee Evans, who held corporate executive positions in purchasing with Station Casinos, Westin Hotels and Resorts, and at the hotel level, offers the reader real-world insights into the duties, responsibilities, and interactions of the hotel purchasing director. His essay provides rich detail and examples of how a hotel's purchasing director fulfills the purchasing requests of numerous hotel departments. Evans is currently director of purchasing for the Oasis Resort, Casa Blanca Spa and Golf Resort, and the Virgin River Hotel and Casino in Nevada.

Few people in this day and age would disagree that the management of data and information in all its forms is critical to business success. As recently as 1995, the year the second edition of this book was published, the Internet and World Wide Web were still pretty much off the radar screens of most businesses. Well . . . now it seems that the pace of technology and the means

and necessity to manage huge volumes of information are as common as any other aspect of business in the twenty-first century. In other words, "What did we ever do without it?"

That's why we are hesitant to include too many readings here about IT and information management—it will be old news in a couple of years, or maybe even a couple of months. As many of us can attest, the Smartphone that we purchased just a few months ago is now a "dinosaur" in the technology world.

The success of any hotel firm in the modern era will depend on how well it manages, controls, and utilizes the available information. This is true for current operations, but as managers develop new—currently unheard-of—sources of information in the lodging business environment, the information will have to be managed like any other asset or product component. In one of the previous editions of this book, an article about data warehousing was included. In the words of the author (Griffin, 1998), "data warehousing" represents a "central information storehouse designed to answer business questions." This usually involves a company-wide database system designed to provide information to all corporate components. In a way, information has become a commodity, and data warehouses are designed to most efficiently manage this new commodity. Well, maybe. According to the "Data Mining . . ." article included here by Magnini and his coauthors, identifying important variables in these warehouses can be a daunting task, hence the need for data mining. Their article discusses this new development.

Because this area is so volatile and developments in IT happen so swiftly, it is probably best for the student to develop broad, general outlines of what is possible rather than, in the context of this textbook, to focus on details of current technology. As we've seen, progress in even our desktop computers has been so rapid that any current writing will probably be outdated by the time this book reaches print.

The articles included in this section are designed to help the reader gain knowledge about, and appreciation for, the range and realm of activities, largely behind the scenes, that contribute to the financial and operational health of the hotel. These activities are often overlooked by those of us who focus our attention on the more public aspects of hotel management, but they are, nonetheless, critical to any hotel's success.

8.2 THE LODGING CHIEF FINANCIAL EXECUTIVE   RAYMOND S. SCHMIDGALL

Chief financial executives of lodging operations are given various titles, including controller, chief accounting officer, vice president–accounting, and chief financial officer. The most common title, at the property level, is *controller*. Who are these people? What are their skills? What responsibilities do they have? Answers to these questions and many others are provided in this chapter.

The lodging financial executive historically was viewed as a mere bookkeeper—that is, he or she prepared financial statements. Research shows that the lodging controller has evolved into a full-fledged member of the management team of a lodging property.

Considerable research has been conducted over the past 20 years of the membership of the Hospitality Financial and Technology Professionals (HFTP), formerly known as the International Association of Hospitality Accountants. The results of this research form the basis for this chapter. The HFTP was founded in 1953 for the purpose of advancing the accounting profession. Its chief publication, *The Bottomline,* is published eight times annually (bimonthly and two special

editions). The HFTP currently has over 4300 members in over 50 countries. The HFTP in 1981 established the Certified Hospitality Accountant Executive (CHAE). Since that time, more than 840 hospitality accountants have earned their CHAE. In 1994, the HFTP established the Certified Hospitality Technology Professional (CHTP), and in the past 6 years over 100 technology professionals have earned their CHTP. These two certifications bring immediate recognition to these professionals in the hospitality industry.

✦ PAST RESEARCH

Over the past 20 years, several studies have been made of HFTP members. Geller and Schmidgall conducted one of the first studies in 1984. They surveyed 1000 HFTP members, and 311 lodging financial executives completed questionnaires covering education, skills, authority, responsibilities, salaries, and involvement with committees of their properties.

Geller, Ilvento, and Schmidgall replicated this study in 1990, mailing the questionnaire to

750 members of the HFTP associated with the lodging industry.

The DeVeaus surveyed the 291 CHAEs in 1988. Their survey covered the usual demographics of age, gender, title, compensation, and education. They also addressed marital status, hours worked, and community/industry participation. This study included all CHAEs, not only those in the lodging segment of the hospitality industry.

Tse surveyed the HFTP membership in 1989, covering three specific areas as follows:

- Demographic information such as age, gender, and educational level

- Professional activities such as position title, years in profession, and buying authority

- Information about the respondents' companies

Her survey was not limited to members associated with the lodging industry, though hotels and resorts employed over 65 percent (648) of the respondents.

Damitio and Schmidgall updated Tse's 1989 study in 1996. Three hundred members associated with the lodging industry responded.

✦ PROFILE OF THE LODGING FINANCIAL EXECUTIVE

The demographic information of lodging financial executives includes age, gender, education, certification, experience, and compensation.

AGE

Three of these studies report the age distribution of respondents to their studies. The DeVeaus' respondents averaged 40 years old, and the largest group of respondents (57 percent) was between 30 and 39 years of age. Tse reported that 25 percent of her respondents were 31–35 years of age

and that two-thirds were in the 26–45 age groups. She did not report an average age; however, based on her reporting of salary by age, it appears that the average age was approximately 38. Damitio and Schmidgall reported an average age of 37, with 72 percent of the respondents between the ages of 30 and 46. Thus, the trend suggests a slight reduction of the average age as the HFTP membership expanded from 1988 through 1995. This trend can be expected to continue as HFTP's membership grows.

GENDER

The three studies covering age also included gender of respondents. DeVeau and DeVeau reported 20 percent of their respondents were female, while Tse reported 25.7 percent and Damitio and Schmidgall reported 28.7 percent. This trend of an increasing percentage of females is expected to continue, as a majority of students in both accounting and hospitality programs at colleges and universities across the United States are female.

EDUCATION

All five studies surveyed lodging financial executives with respect to their levels of education, as shown in Table 8.1. The most common degree in all studies is the four-year college degree. The DeVeaus reported 68 percent of their respondents have a bachelor's degree, while Tse reported a low of 55 percent. The DeVeau study was limited to CHAEs, while the Tse study covered members of HFTP from all hospitality segments. The DeVeaus reported only 8 percent had earned master's degrees, while later studies reveal master's recipients in double digits, increasing to 14 percent in the most recent study

Table 8.1 Level of Education

| | LEVEL OF EDUCATION | | | | | MAJOR OF COLLEGE GRADS | |
	HIGH SCHOOL	ASSOCIATE'S	BACHELOR'S	MASTER'S	OTHER	ACCOUNTING	HOSPITALITY
Geller and Schmidgall	10%[2]	11%	61%	11%	2%[2]	56%	8%
DeVeau and DeVeau	12%[1]	11%	68%	8%	1%[2]	37%	7%
Tse	22%[2]	9%	55%	13%	1%[2]	–	–
Geller et al.	7%[2]	15%	58%	13%	6%[3]	55%	17%
Damitio and Schmidgall	15%[4]	11%	58%	14%	2%[2]	–	–

[1]The DeVeaus reported 12 percent as "none" but did not include high school as a level. Presumably these CHAEs have at least a high school diploma.

[2]Tse reported 18 percent as having some college but less than an associate's degree. This 18 percent is combined with the 4 percent with high school diploma to equal the 22 percent reported above.

[3]Geller et al. states that in most cases "other" represents multiple degrees, such as two master's degrees.

[4]Damitio and Schmidgall combined 3 percent with high school diplomas with 12 percent of those with some college.

Table 8.2 Certifications of Lodging Financial Executives

	CHAE	CPA	OTHER	TOTAL
Geller and Schmidgall	8%	13%	—	21%
DeVeau and DeVeau	100%	22%	18%	140%
Tse	14%	15%	12%	43%
Geller et al.	17%	14%	12%	43%
Damitio and Schmidgall	20%	12%	20%	52%

by Damitio and Schmidgall. Increases in graduate degrees can be expected to continue in the twenty-first century.

Three studies included the major of the college graduates. The Geller et al. studies report that 55 percent and 56 percent, respectively, have degrees in accounting, while the DeVeaus report only 37 percent. Another interesting statistic is the increasing percentage of financial executives with degrees in hospitality education. Geller and his coresearchers, in their 1990 study, suggest the dramatic increase to 17 percent from only 8 percent in 1984 may be because students graduating from hospitality programs are choosing to work in accounting or because lodging companies are beginning to recognize the value of hospitality education for accounting positions.

CERTIFICATION

The DeVeau and DeVeau study focused on HFTP members holding the CHAE. In addition, they reported the highest percentage of certified public accountants (CPAs). The other studies suggest an increasing percentage of lodging financial executives earning the CHAE from 8 percent in the Geller and Schmidgall study in 1984 to 20 percent in the Damitio and Schmidgall study, conducted in 1996. In addition, the total certifications increased from 21 percent in 1984 to

52 percent in 1996, as shown in Table 8.2. By any measure, this is a dramatic increase. This increase clearly supports Schmidgall and Kasavana's conclusion regarding certifications:

". . . initials after one's name suggest excellence, failure to have earned the initials may well lead one's peers and supervisors to question not only one's knowledge but also abilities." (Schmidgall and Kasavana, 2000)

Most likely, lodging financial executives will continue to earn various certifications in the future as proofs of their excellence.

EXPERIENCE

Several studies provide limited insight into the professional work of the lodging financial executive. The DeVeaus reported that 53 percent of the CHAEs have between 10 and 15 years of work experience and that the average is 16 years.

Tse reported that a plurality (24 percent) of lodging controllers had 11 to 15 years of work experience. Geller et al. reported a median average of 10–12 years of hospitality accounting experience, while the median from the Damitio and Schmidgall study was 11–15 years. Across these four studies, the average years of experience (generally hospitality-related) is 10–15. The

Table 8.3 Compensation

	MEDIAN SALARY	BONUS
Geller and Schmidgall	$30,000–$34,999	9%–12% (median)
DeVeau and DeVeau	$49,900 (mean)	44% received benefit packages including a bonus
Tse	$30,000–$40,000	$2000–$5000 (median)
Geller et al.	$40,000–$49,999	11%–20% (median)
Damitio and Schmidgall	$45,001–$50,000	$6100 (mean)

average years added to an expected age of 21 or so at graduation with a bachelor's degree suggests that most lodging financial executives have spent most of their professional years working in the hospitality industry, as their average age in the most recent study was 37.

COMPENSATION

A major element of each study is the compensation of hospitality financial executives. Of course, over time the average pay is expected to increase. Table 8.3 addresses increasing compensation. The Geller and Schmidgall study conducted in 1984 revealed a median salary of $30,000–$34,999 and a median bonus of 9–12 percent of the controller's salary. Based on this information, the average annual bonus approximated $3400. The 1996 study by Damitio and Schmidgall reported a median salary between $45,001 and $50,000 and an average bonus of $6100. At the beginning of the twenty-first century, it appears lodging financial executives' median salaries are most likely to be greater than $50,000, as the last study was conducted five years previously.

SKILLS AND KNOWLEDGE

What skills and knowledge should the lodging financial executive have, and how have these changed over time? Geller and Schmidgall stud-

ied the technical skills and knowledge of lodging financial executives in 1984, and Geller et al. repeated the study in 1990. Table 8.4 reflects the results of these studies. The 1990 study included more skills, and the report provided results by type of controller. As expected, the percentage of respondents with technology knowledge (computers) increased, and most likely a study conducted today would result in a 100 percent response. Other areas that more than 90 percent of respondents indicated were required skills and knowledge included cash management and internal controls.

A study by Cichy and Schmidgall in 1996 focused on leadership of lodging financial executives. Financial executives not only must know the numbers but must also lead, as they supervise several employees. The 1996 Damitio and Schmidgall study revealed that the number of employees supervised by these financial executives varied from one to more than 30. Just over one-third (34 percent) manage two to five employees, while nearly another third (31 percent) manage six to ten people. Another one out of five (22 percent) manage 11 to 30 people, and 6 percent manage over 30 individuals. They found that lodging financial executives are expected to have skills and knowledge beyond the technical skills covered in the two Geller studies. The study of

Table 8.4 Technical Skills and Knowledge

SKILLS, KNOWLEDGE	CORPORATE	DIVISION OR AREA	HOTEL	OTHER	TOTAL	1984 STUDY
Taxes	89%	77%	74%	69%	75%	60%
Computers	92	96	99	95	97	70
Personnel	81	82	84	77	82	78
Cash management	100	89	94	81	91	89
Capital budgeting	87	89	87	77	85	80
Statistics	68	81	85	71	88	82
Auditing	87	96	87	72	84	†
Internal controls	92	100	100	94	97	†
FASB* rulings	28	23	14	18	18	n/a
Risk management	55	35	36	26	36	n/a

*Financial Accounting Standards Board

†In 1984, "auditing" and "internal control" were presented as a single item. Ninety-five percent of the respondents in 1984 indicated they possessed skills in those areas.

lodging financial executives covered seven keys to leadership (see Table 8.5) and 17 secrets of leadership (see Table 8.6).

Lodging financial executives strongly agreed that four of the seven listed keys to leadership were important to their own leadership style. The most important key was "trust your subordi-nates," followed by "develop a vision." Consistent with all other surveys of U.S. chief executive officers and presidents in lodging and foodservice, "be an expert" was dead last. Leaders from all segments clearly realize that being an expert is not the most essential aspect of leadership. Nevertheless, "be an expert" received a score of 4.0, indicating that respondents believe that having relevant expertise is not unimportant either. Rather, the survey results indicate that these leaders believe it is more important to surround themselves with the necessary expertise than to have the expertise themselves.

Of the 17 secrets of leadership, respondents strongly agreed or agreed that leaders in their organizations must have 14 of them. At the top of the list were dependability, credibility, responsibility, and accountability. At the bottom of the list was physical stamina, with a score of 4.4. (A score above 4.0 indicates inherent importance; in this case, the low score for physical

Table 8.5 Keys to Leadership

	MEAN LEVEL OF IMPORTANCE*
Trust your subordinates	5.4
Develop a vision	5.3
Simplify	5.2
Keep your cool	5.1
Encourage risk	4.8
Invite dissent	4.5
Be an expert	4.0

*The scale is from 1, "very unimportant," to 6, "very important."

Table 8.6 Secrets of Leadership

	MEAN LEVEL OF AGREEMENT*
In our organization/company, leaders must possess . . .	
Dependability	5.6
Credibility	5.5
Responsibility	5.5
Accountability	5.5
Self-confidence	5.3
Decisiveness	5.3
Emotional stamina	5.2
Loyalty	5.2
Desire	5.2
Stewardship	5.1
Courage	5.1
Empathy	5.1
Tenacity	5.0
Anticipation	5.0
Timing	4.9
Competitiveness	4.8
Physical stamina	4.4

*The scale is from 1, "strongly disagree," to 6, "strongly agree."

stamina is merely an indication of its relative unimportance when compared to the other secrets of leadership presented to the survey participants.)

RESPONSIBILITY AND AUTHORITY

Four of five of the studies focused on authority. Table 8.7 reveals the results of the two studies (1984 and 1990) conducted by Geller and others. The 1990 study divides the responses by type of controller. The vast majority (over 75 percent) of lodging financial executives have authority to sign checks, approve purchases, and extend credit. Tse found that only 56 percent of hospitality financial executives have authority to approve purchase decisions. Damitio and Schmidgall reported 56 percent were authorized to make purchasing decisions without the approval of others. They indicated controllers were most involved with technology purchases (90 percent) and, to lesser degrees, guest supplies (29 percent), furnishings and equipment (44 percent), security/maintenance systems (43 percent), and fire/safety/energy conservation systems (30 percent).

The expansion of authority based on the two Geller studies is the greatest for investing funds (from 2 percent to 46 percent) and to set or change prices (from 21 percent to 41 percent).

Both the Tse and the Damitio and Schmidgall studies covered hiring and firing authority. Tse found that more than 80 percent of the

Table 8.7 Extent of Authority Over Specific Functions

FUNCTIONS	TYPE OF CONTROLLER					
	DIVISION OR CORPORATE	AREA	HOTEL	OTHER	TOTAL	1983 STUDY
Invest funds	70%	46%	48%	30%	46%	2%
Sign checks	79	85	88	59	79	87
Extend credit	66	85	92	63	80	85
Set or change prices	26	62	48	28	41	21
Borrow funds	36	27	20	10	20	19
Approve purchases	83	89	94	69	86	82

Table 8.8 Controllers' Responsibilities

| | TYPE OF CONTROLLER | | | | | |
RESPONSIBILITIES	DIVISION OR CORPORATE	AREA	HOTEL	OTHER	TOTAL	1984 STUDY
Hotel security	15%	27%	25%	18%	22%	9%
Receivables	89	89	100	73	91	95
Payables	89	92	99	77	92	93
General accounting	89	92	98	80	92	91
Payroll	85	89	95	68	87	89
Night auditors	60	85	94	60	80	83
Income auditors	57	81	89	60	77	79
Cashiers	43	65	77	47	64	63
Food controls	47	77	78	44	65	53
Computers: Accounting	83	89	95	73	88	*
Computers: Front office and reservations	49	77	65	44	58	*
Purchasing	32	62	77	40	60	50
Receiving	28	54	66	36	52	50
Storage (inventory)	23	58	66	39	52	34
Tax returns	70	58	61	54	61	n/a
Risk management	51	39	37	24	36	n/a
Cash management	85	81	86	51	77	n/a
Beverage controls	49	77	81	42	67	n/a
Investments	75	39	40	27	42	n/a
Internal auditors	47	62	46	31	44	n/a

*In 1984, a single question asked controllers about their computer-system (EDP) responsibilities. Fifty-two percent of the respondents in 1984 had some responsibility for EDP.

respondents have the authority to hire and fire either in their own department or in their company. The percentage increased to 90 percent when only accounting personnel were involved. The 1996 study by Damitio and Schmidgall revealed 76 percent authority to hire and fire within their own department, while 7 percent have no authority to hire or fire.

Only the two Geller studies (1984 and 1990) covered responsibility, and the comparative results are shown in Table 8.8. Again, the 1990 study provided detail by type of controller and included areas not covered by the 1984 study.

More than 90 percent of the respondents indicated they have responsibility for such standard accounting functions as general accounting, receivables, and payables. Other major areas of responsibility shared by most controllers (75 percent or more) include payroll, night and income audits, computers in accounting, and cash management.

Table 8.9 Committee Involvement

	EXECUTIVE	COMPENSATION	STRATEGIC PLANNING
Geller and Schmidgall (1984)	82%	23%	41%
Tse (1988)	71	—	—
Geller et al. (1990)	86	75	94

There are indications that controllers are becoming increasingly involved with the operational aspects of their hotels. More than 50 percent of the respondents indicated that their responsibilities included purchasing, receiving, food and beverage controls, and storage (inventory). The number of respondents responsible for the storage function increased 18 percentage points from 1984 to 1990, from 34 percent to more than 52 percent, and a purchasing function was claimed by 60 percent of the respondents in 1990, which is 10 points greater than in 1984. Responsibility for hotel security, the least commonly shared function among the controllers, more than doubled in the last six years, growing from 9 percent in 1984 to almost 22 percent in the 1990 study.

The controllers' role in electronic data processing (EDP) and computer system management grew by leaps and bounds during the 1980s. In 1990, 88 percent of the respondents indicated responsibility for the computer systems used for accounting functions.

Additionally, 58 percent indicated responsibility for front office and reservations system computers—systems clearly not under the umbrella of traditional accounting functions. In the 1984 study, respondents were asked just one question about responsibility for EDP, and 52 percent of the controllers indicated that they had some responsibility for EDP. It's clear that, over the years, computer-oriented responsibilities have escalated sharply.

COMMITTEE INVOLVEMENT

Just how involved have lodging financial executives been on committees of their lodging businesses? Both of the studies conducted by Geller and others reported over 80 percent of the respondents were members of the executive committee, although the Tse study showed only 71 percent (see Table 8.9). The difference may be that the Tse study covered all hospitality segments employing HFTP members, while the Geller studies were restricted to the lodging industry. In addition, the involvement of financial executives from 1984 to 1990 increased significantly on both the compensation and strategic planning committees. The 1990 study by Geller and others also included involvement in training and risk management committees, and a majority (66 percent and 72 percent, respectively) of lodging financial executives revealed involvement.

A 1998 study by Woods and others surveyed general managers of large hotels (500 rooms or more). Eighty-one percent of the respondents in this study reported that either the vice president of finance or the controller of their hotel was a member of the executive committee.

✦ SUMMARY

Considerable research has been conducted over the past 20 years on lodging financial executives. These studies indicate that the most common title is controller and the average age is in the late thirties. Males are still dominant, though females are increasingly assuming the top financial position with lodging operations. The majority of these leaders have bachelor's degrees and majored in accounting. An increasing number of lodging financial executives are certified and have 10–15 years of hospitality accounting experience.

The skill set of financial executives includes both technical and leadership skills. The technical skill set includes technology, cash management, internal controls, and statistics. The most important leadership skills are trusting subordinates and developing a vision, dependability, credibility, responsibility, and accountability.

Financial executives commonly have authority to sign checks, extend credit, and approve purchases. To a lesser extent, they invest funds, may set or change prices, and borrow funds.

Their responsibilities range from managing receivables, payables, payroll, general accounting, night and income auditors, cash, and computers in accounting to hotel security, risk management, investments, and internal auditors.

Finally, financial executives commonly serve on the executive, compensation, and strategic planning, training, and risk management committees of their hotels.

8.3 CONTROLLER: A VIABLE CAREER FOR HOSPITALITY STUDENTS

CARY C. COUNTRYMAN, AGNES L. DEFRANCO, AND TANYA VENEGAS

ABSTRACT.

PURPOSE. This study seeks to develop a characteristic and financial profile of controllers in the hospitality industry. It also examines the differences in profiles between female and male controllers, as well as, hotel and club controllers.

DESIGN/METHODOLOGY/APPROACH. Data was collected as part of a biennium survey of the Hospitality Financial and Technology Professionals (HFTP) membership. The survey collects data on compensation, benefits, job characteristics, and demographics.

FINDINGS. On average, the 2004 projected salary for hospitality controllers is over $80,000. Female controllers get paid less than male controllers and while there are some minor differences between these two groups they may not be enough to explain the disparity in pay. The results of this study also suggest that the hotel industry pays better than the club industry; however, differences in these two segments may explain some of the variation in compensation.

RESEARCH LIMITATIONS/IMPLICATIONS. From the analysis, it is apparent that being a controller is a viable career path for individuals interested in working in the hospitality industry. Also, controllers have varied responsibilities, which include more than just number crunching such as technology and human resources management. However, given the salary difference between female and male controllers, the industry needs to create better pay equity between the genders so that it can attract more females into this career. ORIGINALITY/VALUE. This research aims to develop a more comprehensive profile of hospitality controllers and by so doing, help professors, counselors, students, and others be more open to the possibility of being a controller and viewing it as a career path.

✦ INTRODUCTION

When asked what career paths hospitality students would take upon graduation, a good number may say food and beverage and others may choose the rooms department. There may also be some who would like to make catering or sales and marketing their career choices, while others may choose human resources. However, only once in a while would one hear from a student in a hospitality program who would like to become a controller in a hotel, club, restaurant, or other hospitality concerns. There exists this stereotype that the career of a controller is quite dull and that there is not much human involvement on a daily basis, and as a controller, one would simply sit in front of a computer and work with piles and piles of papers and numbers.

✦ NEED FOR STUDY

In reality, controllers play a very important role both in the daily operations and strategic directions of a hospitality organization. Controllers are part of the executive committee. They are department heads who supervised their own crew. They work closely with all other departments to provide them with the proper financial picture and they assist these department heads in developing their budgets. Most importantly, they

are the right-hand confidants of the general managers. Research has shown that hotel controllers are able to exercise a significant amount of power due to their central role in the hotel's information network and in the decision-making process (Moore and Stefanelli, 1989).

While some hospitality companies may turn to the traditional business schools for their future accountants or controllers, more and more hospitality corporations are hiring hospitality students, since these students have a deeper understanding of the nuances of the hospitality business. In addition, many hospitality programs, especially those with more of a management focus, require 12–15 credit hours of accounting, cost control, and finance courses with the option of taking a minor in accounting from the business college. This track of courses is about 10 percent or in some cases, over 10 percent of the entire curriculum, and it provides students the best of both worlds—hospitality and accounting.

The career of being a controller in the hospitality industry is also a reflection of the best of both worlds. As a controller, one is still in the hospitality business, working in the same environment as his or her hospitality colleagues. However, when compared to colleagues in other operating departments such as rooms or food and beverage, the work hours of a controller are more regular. There might be an occasional weekend that a controller needs to be on property for inventory valuation or finalizing the annual budget. But, there is no shift work and one is not required to stay late because there is a big dinner function booked at the hotel, just to have to return the next morning because there is a 1,000-person breakfast meeting.

Therefore, it is pertinent that hospitality students understand that the controller career option is available to them, that it is a most viable career path, and being a controller, just like any other department head positions, can be the path towards the position of a general manager. Indeed, many controllers have taken that next step since they are intimately knowledgeable about the financial performance of each department in the hotel, club, or hospitality operation. From the financial data, one can begin to ascertain the strengths and weakness of each department.

✦ PURPOSE OF THE STUDY

The purpose of this study, therefore, is fourfold:

1. To provide a characteristic profile of a controller in the hospitality industry; specifically their place of employment, gender, age, years worked in the industry, education, and certification.
2. To provide a financial profile of a controller in the hospitality industry; specifically the annual salary and bonuses.
3. To ascertain if statistically significant differences exist between the characteristic and financial profiles of the two major segments of the hospitality industry: hotels and clubs.
4. To ascertain if statistically significant differences exist between the characteristic and financial profiles of male and female respondents.

It is the hope that, through the findings of this research, professors, counselors, and students will be more open to the possibility of being a controller and viewing it as viable career path.

✦ RESEARCH HYPOTHESES

Given the above purposes, the characteristic profile and the financial profile of a controller were determined. The data were then also tested for the following hypotheses. *H1.* There is no statistically significant difference between the characteristic profiles of hotel and club controllers. *H2.* There is no statistically significant difference between the financial profiles of hotel and club controllers. *H3.* There is no statistically significant difference between the characteristic profiles of male and female controllers. *H4.* There is no statistically significant difference between the financial profiles of male and female controllers.

✦ LITERATURE REVIEW
IN THE 1980s

Geller and Schmidgall (1984) provided one of the first profiles on hotel controllers. They discovered that hotel controllers were well educated with 72 percent of those surveyed having at least a bachelor's degree. In addition to being knowledgeable in accounting and financial matters, hotel controllers also had to possess knowledge in personnel management and electronic data processing, a forerunner to the more commonly used term of computer technology. As for professional certifications, very few had such designations. Only 13 percent of the respondents reported that they were Certified Public Accountant (CPA) and even less, 8 percent, reported that they were Certified Hospitality Accountant Executive (CHAE). Eighty-two percent of the hotel controllers were part of the executive committee of their property. Controllers at larger properties were more likely to be on a bonus plan with bonuses based on salary (59 percent) or sales (29 percent). Sometimes the bonuses were linked to performance or gross operating profit.

IN THE 1990s

A follow-up study was done by Geller et al. (1990) to see if the profile had changed and a slightly different profile of hotel controllers emerged. There was a noticeable increase in the number of hotel controllers that had majored in hospitality management. This was viewed as a favorable shift in that hotel companies recognized the value of hospitality management training and operations experience in the controller's position. There was also a significant change in the number of hotel controllers with the designation of CHAE. Instead of 8 percent in 1984, this percentage more than doubled in about five years, with 17 percent of the respondents holding the designation of CHAE.

The percentage of hotel controllers that reported having to be knowledgeable in computers rose to 96.6 percent (it was 70 percent in the 1984 study). The 1990 study goes further than the earlier study by actually breaking down this statistic a bit further and discovered that 87 percent of the respondents were responsible for the computer systems used for the accounting function and 58 percent were also responsible for the front-office computers and reservation system.

Another point that was made clearer in this later study was that the most common basis for bonuses was whether the organization met its profit objectives. An additional item that was added to the 1990 study was the career goals and

aspirations of the hotel controllers. The majority of [those] surveyed were desirous to move to a higher-level financial position (25.3 percent) or that of a general-management position (27.3 percent) with the same organization.

GENDER AND COMPENSATION

A more in-depth analysis of hotel controllers based on gender was done by Ghiselli and Chen (1997). In comparison to the two earlier studies (Geller and Schmidgall, 1984; Geller et al., 1990), almost 90 percent of the respondents held a bachelor's degree. This indicates that a bachelor's degree may have become a necessity or requirement for the hotel controller position. Professional certifications have also seen increases with 23.1 percent having the CHAE and 17.7 percent with the CPA designation. The majority of controllers (92.3 percent) had six or more years of accounting experience, which was viewed as a significant increase over previous studies. Overall, 37.2 percent of the hotel controllers had been in their current position for five or more years. However, nearly half of the female controllers had only been in their current position for less than a year, while 19.4 percent of the male controllers were in the same situation. Ghiselli and Chen were surprised at this finding because of the length of accounting experience reported by respondents. They felt this may have indicated considerable movement or turnover in the profession. Further results from this study show that there was a significant difference in the hotel controller salaries of males and females, with male salaries being higher. Some of this may be due to the high percentage of female controllers being in their current position for less than one year. However, even if the length of time in the current position, size of hotel, or type of ownership are compared at each level for male and female hotel controllers, the male controller was paid more than the female controller in a majority of circumstances. Some other interesting findings included the fact that base salaries have continued to drift upward but that there were a large number of salaries at the lower end. The authors felt this may be due to bonuses or pay incentives becoming a larger component of wage agreements. As for the necessary skills and knowledge needed by hotel controllers, in comparison to previous studies, the ranking of computer skills went down. The research attributed this to two factors:

1. In 1989 there was a surge in the popularity of the personal computer (PC); and
2. These skills may now be viewed as basic knowledge for all such positions.

MORE ON PROFESSIONAL CERTIFICATIONS

Other research has examined the value of professional designations such as the CHAE. In a survey of CHAE holders (Damitio and Schmidgall, 2001), there was some evidence to indicate that they had higher base salaries than non-holders. Asked specifically about this, almost 58 attributed some monetary value to their CHAE. The longer the respondent held the CHAE designation, the more likely were they to place higher value in it ($5,000 or more). In a related question, over 61 percent found the CHAE designation to be somewhat helpful to extremely helpful in getting or changing employment. There are also non-financial benefits to the CHAE such as acknowledging one's commitment to professionalism, identifying one who possesses technical expertise,

and representing a basic level of competency in both operations and management skills. In contrast to the CPA designation, the majority of the respondents felt the CPA was better than, or at least as valuable as, the CHAE. All of this aside, 97 percent of the respondents would encourage or strongly encourage other hospitality financial and accounting professionals to reach the CHAE designation.

THE CONTROLLERS' SKILL SET

The skills and education required to by a controller has changed over the years. Drawing evidence from several competency studies done on the accounting profession, a team of researchers have developed a list of knowledge, skills, and abilities required for all accountants (Palmer et al., 2004). One of the trends identified by these researchers is that there are "some skills that are becoming more important than some of the accounting knowledge normally included in accounting curriculum." In addition to accounting and financial knowledge, they would add communication skills, interpersonal skills, general business knowledge, problem-solving skills, information technology, personal attitudes and capabilities, and computer skills.

✦ METHODOLOGY

The data was collected as part of a biennium survey performed by the Hospitality Financial Technology Professionals (HFTP) Research Institute at the University of Houston. The survey focuses on the compensation and benefits, as well as the job characteristics and demographics of the HFTP membership. The association of HFTP is the predecessor of the International Association of Hospitality Accountants (IAHA) founded in 1952. The IAHA was the organization surveyed in many of the previous studies already citied.

Based in Austin, Texas, HFTP is the professional association for financial and technology personnel working in hotels, resorts, clubs, casinos, restaurants and other hospitality-related businesses. The association provides continuing education and networking opportunities to more than 4,000 members around the world, and produces the premiere hospitality technology shows HITEC and ONHTEC. HFTP also administers the examination and awards the certification for the CHAE and the Certified Hospitality Technology Professional (CHTP) designations.

Prior to the HFTP Research Institute doing the survey in 2002, the 2000 compensation and benefits survey was commissioned by HFTP and carried out by an independent research firm. The reported results (Hassmiller, 2000) will be referenced as part of the analysis.

In 2002, a random sample of the HFTP membership was used (Countryman and De-Franco, 2002). Eight hundred and sixty-one HFTP members were randomly selected to participate in the survey. A stratified sample was used to ensure that appropriate portions of the HFTP membership were surveyed. Those not involved directly in the hospitality industry such as educators and vendors were also excluded, even though they are members of HFTP. This survey was mailed to participants and they were asked to return the completed surveys in the postage paid envelope provided. Out of the 861 surveys mailed out, 272 were returned for a response rate of 31.7 percent.

In 2004, an online or web survey was used (Countryman et al., 2004). This allowed for the entire membership of HFTP to be surveyed or at least those that opted to receive e-mail correspondence from HFTP. Seven hundred and eighteen responded to the 3,149 e-mails sent out, this is a response rate of 22.8 percent. The e-mail directed respondents to a web survey.

In relationship to the two surveys, participants of the 2002 survey were asked to project their salary and bonus for that year since the survey was done during the middle of the year. Participants of the 2004 survey reported actual salaries and bonuses for 2002 and were asked to project them for 2004. Because of the overlap in surveys for the year 2002, therefore, only actual numbers for 2002, which were collected from the 2004 survey, were used in regards to salaries and bonuses reported in 2002.

Unlike some of the early studies mentioned in the literature review, this research chose to focus on those who just have the title of controller and does not include corporate controllers or division/area controllers. The Statistical Package for the Social Sciences (SPSS) was used for the data analysis. Means and frequencies were computed for the various profiles. T-tests and chi-square tests were used to determine if statistically significant differences existed between different profiles. T-tests were used to test for significant difference between means and chi-square tests were used for the frequencies.

✦ RESULTS

CHARACTERISTIC PROFILE

Table 8.10 provides a brief overview of the controllers who completed the survey in 2002 and 2004. As for industry segment, the two top categories are hotels and clubs. These two segments are investigated later as part of this research. Both

Table 8.10 Characteristics of Controllers-Survey Respondents

	2002	2004
Sample size	n = 146	n = 357
Industry segment (percent)		
Club	60.3	52.0
Hotel	23.3	29.4
Resort	8.2	9.0
Hotel management company	4.1	3.4
Club management company	0.7	1.7
Casino	1.4	0.8
Convention center	0.7	0.0
Restaurant	0.7	0.6
Other	0.7	3.1
Gender (percent)		
Female	52.1	46.7
Male	45.9	53.3
Age (percent)		
Under 25	0.7	0.0
25–34 years old	15.1	8.5
35–44 years old	42.5	35.7
45–54 years old	27.4	38.4
55–64 years old	11.6	16.3
Over 65 years old	0.0	1.2
Average number of years		
Hospitality experience	18	20
Accounting/finance experience	14	16
Education (percent)		
High school	2.4	2.3
Associate degree (two years)	6.2	5.0
Some college	13.7	15.9
Bachelor's degree	53.4	54.7
Some graduate	12.3	12.0
Master's degree	10.3	9.6
Certifications (percent)		
CHAE	13.0	21.80
CPA	20.5	17.10
CHTP	2.7	5.30

the 2002 and 2004 surveys were fairly evenly split between female and male controllers with there being slightly more male controllers in each survey. The differences between female and male controllers, especially in regards to salary, are also examined later in this research.

Most controllers are older than 35 years old. The average number of years of experience in finance and accounting is higher (2002: 18 years and 2004: 20 years) than the average number of years of experience in the hospitality field (2002: 14 years and 2004: 16 years). This means that many of the controllers started in other fields before moving to the hospitality industry. As for the length of time in their current position of controller, it averages 6.4 years (2004 survey). This is slightly higher than the 5.28 years reported in 2002. Overall, the 2004 respondents had an average of a little over 11 years as a controller, up from the 9.43 years reported in 2002.

Forty percent of the respondents in 2002 and 2004 worked as a controller for a different company or organization prior to their current position as controller. Other prior positions mentioned by respondents included assistant controller (2002: 16.4 percent and 2004: 18.9 percent), accounting/finance manager (2002: 8.2 percent and 2004: 10.3 percent), and staff accountant (2004: 7.3 percent). The average length of time spent in that prior position was a little over five years according to both studies.

The majority of controllers have at least a bachelor's or 4-year degree. There are also a noticeable number of controllers who have done some graduate work or earned a master's degree. Besides education, there are a higher percentage of controllers with the CHAE and CHTP designations.

In addition to those characteristics shown in Table 8.10, there were a few other interesting characteristics. Controllers spend the majority of their time (2002: 82 percent and 2004: 65 percent) working on finance and accounting issues. However, they also spend a lot of time on technology (2002: 18 percent and 2004: 13 percent). As for the lower percentages reported in 2004, the later survey was more in-depth and controllers were asked to be more specific in their time allocations. In addition to finance, accounting, and technology, controllers also deal with administrative and human resource issues (16 percent of their time according to the 2004 survey).

On average, controllers work about 48 hours a week. A little over 67 percent (2004) of them were members of the executive committee. This is up from the 59.3 percent reported in 2002. A majority of the controllers (2002: 62 percent and 2004: 59.2 percent) supervised 2–5 full-time employees, followed by 6–10 full time employees (2002: 19.7 percent and 2004: 17.7 percent). However, not all of these employees may be accounting or finance personnel. Almost 73 percent (both in the 2002 and 2004 surveys) of the respondents indicated that they were responsible for the information technology employees as well. Even though this is an additional responsibility for the controller from a supervisory perspective, most IT departments (2004: 81.5 percent) had only one full-time employee, with even [fewer] reported in 2002 (21.6 percent had no IT employees and 63.1 percent only had one full-time IT employee).

FINANCIAL PROFILE

Figure 8.1 shows the average salary for the controllers who completed the surveys. Salaries

Figure 8.1 Salaries

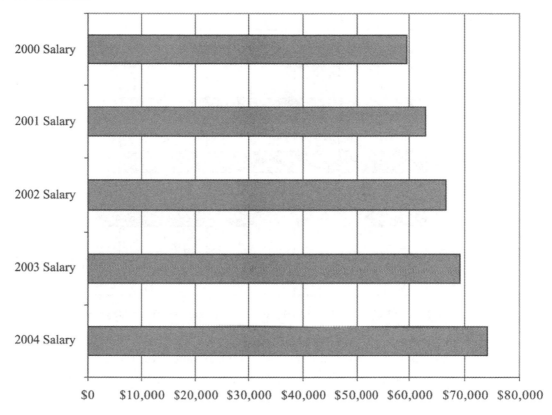

continue to rise over the years. This is consistent with the earlier profiles.

As for bonuses, several of the controllers received bonuses. Approximately 67–76 percent of the controllers received bonuses over the five years examined. Figure 8.2 shows the average bonus for each year as reported by the controllers. Criteria for bonuses include slightly more objective criteria (2002: 53.9 percent and 2004: 55.3 percent) than subjective criteria (2002: 44.74 percent and 2004: 44.3 percent). However, subjective criteria still play a significant role in the determination of bonuses. Table 8.11 shows the percentage of respondents who indicated that these various elements were used in their bonus determination.

There is some evidence that those with certifications do enjoy a slightly better total compensation package, as shown in Table 8.12. Those with a CPA appear to make the most. This may be due to the fact that the CPA designation has a longer history and is recognized in all public accounting while the CHAE is strictly for the hospitality industry. Although differences were observed, such differences were not statistically significant. This may also be due to the limited number of responses.

CLUBS vs. HOTELS

In terms of *H1* and *H2*, *t*-tests and chi-square tests were performed to determine if statistically significant difference exist between the

Figure 8.2 Bonuses

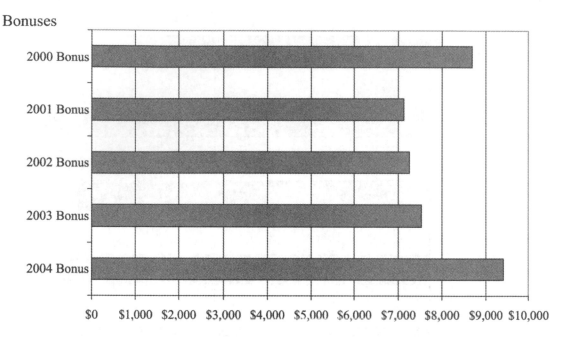

Bonuses

characteristics profiles of hotel and club controllers and between the financial profiles of hotel and club controllers. Regarding characteristics, there is statistical significance between the gender of controllers in that [in] both 2002 and 2004, there are more female controllers in the club industry than the hotel industry (2002: 58.1 percent female club controllers, 30.3 percent female hotel controllers vs. 41.9 percent male club controllers, 69.7 percent male hotel controllers; $\chi^2 = 7.392$, sig. < 0.05 and 2004: 75 percent female club controllers, 24.3 percent female hotel controllers vs. 50.5 percent male club controllers, 49.5 percent male hotel controllers; $\chi^2 = 14.221$, sig. < 0.05). In addition, there was some indication that club controllers are more

Table 8.11 Bonus Determination

	2002	2004
Profit (percent)	16.04	21.25
Holiday fund (percent)	19.89	15.45
Increased sales (percent)	1.95	2.17
Guest satisfaction (percent)	3.78	3.97
Meeting budget goals (percent)	12.73	16.30
Meeting personal goals (percent)	13.33	11.29
Board/exec. Comm. discretion (percent)	18.75	16.59
Other (percent)	13.58	7.59

Table 8.12 Certifications and Average Salary

	NONE	CHAE	CPA	CHAE AND CPA	CHTP	CHAE AND CHTP	ALL THREE
	$n = 163$	$n = 40$	$n = 35$	$n = 13$	$n = 3$	$n = 13$	$n = 1$
2004*	$70,120	$71,252	$92,000	$81,236	$70,570	$81,906	$84,000
2003	$66,471	$69,934	$76,913	$74,563	$67,593	$79,108	$78,000
2002	$63,901	$67,758	$74,211	$68,902	$66,460	$73,410	$72,400
	$n = 81$	$n = 16$	$n = 24$	$n = 2$	$n = 3$	$n = 3$	$n = 1$
2001	$59,321	$69,652	$69,326	$66,000	$68,450	$69,600	$72,000
2000	$56,312	$63,904	$66,160	$62,500	$65,267	$65,267	$68,000

Note: *Projected

likely to have the CPA designation than hotel controllers. In 2002, the difference is statistically significant at the $p < 0.05$ level and in 2004, it is statistically significant at the $p < 0.10$ level (2002: 26.1 percent of club controllers vs. 2.9 percent of hotel controllers; $\chi^2 = 8.350$, sig. < 0.05 and 2004: 19 percent of club controllers vs. 10.6 percent of hotel controllers; $\chi^2 = 3.531$, sig. < 0.10). However, other than gender and certification, there were no significant differences in age, educational level, or industry-specific certification designations among club and hotel controllers. While there was no significant difference between club and hotel controllers for the number of years of accounting/finance experience, there was a statistically significant difference in both surveys (2002 and 2004) in regard to hospitality experience. Hotel controllers had on average more years of experience in the hospitality field than club controllers (2002: hotel controllers with 18 years vs. club controllers with 11 years; $t = 4.298$, sig. < 0.001 and 2004: hotel controllers with 20 years vs. club controllers with 13 years; $t = 6.889$, sig. < 0.001).

Financially, the hotel industry pays better than the club industry as shown in Table 8.13 and

these differences are at least statistically significant at the $p < 0.10$ level, and even more so when considering just the bonuses (significant at the < 0.001 level). However, club controllers (2002: 46.30 hours and 2004: 46.11 hours) work slightly [fewer] hours per week than hotel controllers (2002: 51.25 hours and 2004: 49.86 hours).

MALE vs. FEMALE

T-tests and chi-square tests were performed on the profile data for male and female controllers in regards to H3 and H4 to determine if statistically significant differences exist between their respective characteristic profiles and financial profiles. As was already mentioned, there are more female controllers in the club industry than the hotel industry. Beyond these specific industries and consistent with the earlier findings, there are more female controllers working for club management companies and there are more male controllers working for hotel management companies and resorts. These differences are statistically different according to the 2004 survey ($\chi^2 = 28.684$, sig. < 0.001). There were not enough controllers in each of these additional categories in the 2002 survey to test for statistically significant differences, but the observed numbers are

Table 8.13 Salary Comparisons-Club Controllers vs. Hotel Controllers

	CLUB	HOTEL	T-TEST	SIG.
2004 Salary	$71,271	$76,166	−1.921	0.056*
2004 Bonus	$ 6,094	$13,912	8.718	0.001**
2003 Salary	$67,887	$72,620	−1.827	0.069*
2003 Bonus	$ 5,412	$10,215	−5.775	0.001**
2002 Salary	$64,799	$69,463	−1.827	0.069*
2002 Bonus	$ 5,036	$10,660	−6.514	0.001**
2001 Salary	$60,205	$65,758	−1.687	0.095*
2001 Bonus	$ 4,480	$12,005	−4.321	0.001**
2000 Salary	$56,622	$61,069	−1.410	0.162
2000 Bonus	$ 3,936	$16,410	−5.400	0.001**

Notes: *Significant at the 0.10 level; **Significant at the 0.05 level

consistent with the findings from the 2004 survey. As for age, there were no statistical differences found among female and male controllers. However, there were some statistical differences found in regard to education (2002: $\chi^2 = 13.065$, sig. < 0.05 and 2004: $\chi^2 = 19.660$, sig. < 0.05). It appears that more male controllers have a bachelor's (4–year college degree) or master's degree. In addition to education, more male controllers have the CHAE designation (2004: 25.4 percent female vs. 74.6 percent male; $\chi^2 = 15.206$, sig. < 0.001). Once again, because of the limited number of respondents in the 2002 survey, no statistical differences could be found. However, the numbers are consistent with 2004 results.

When the number of years of work experience in the current position or the amount of finance/accounting experience were examined, there were no statistically significant differences between females and males. If there is no difference, it is logical to deduce that there should not be a difference in compensation between male and female controllers. However, such is not the case. Table 8.14 shows the average salaries for female controllers and male controllers along with the results of the *t*-test. Male controllers do make

Table 8.14 Salary Comparisons-Female Controller vs. Male Controllers

	FEMALE	MALE	T-TEST
2004	$65,805	$80,647	−3.561*
2003	$62,514	$73,742	−4.608*
2002	$60,090	$70,636	−4.169*
2001	$57,171	$69,043	−4.580*
2000	$54,502	$64,539	−3.719*

Note: *Significant at the 0.001 level

more money than female controllers, and this was found to be statistically significant. In most cases, the male controller on average makes $10,000 more than a female controller. With the inclusion of a broader spectrum of controllers from the hospitality field and not just hotels, this provides further evidence of the results discovered by Ghiselli and Chen (1997) that male hotel controllers make more than female hotel controllers. This does not only apply to the basic salary but is also true for bonuses. Male controllers receive larger bonuses than female controllers. However, more females than males work in the club segment and vice versa for the hotel segment. As shown above there is evidence to show that the hotel segment pays more than the club segment. Despite this, further analysis within the hotel segment and the club segment separately indicates that male controllers still make more money than female controllers even within each segment.

✦ CONCLUSIONS

The purpose of this paper is to show the characteristics and financial profiles of hospitality controllers and to determine if statistically significant differences exist between controllers in the hotel and club segments and also between male and female controllers.

From Figures 8.1 and 8.2, it is apparent that being a controller is a most viable career path. The average salary in 2000 was about $60,000. Together with a bonus of over $8,500, a $68,500 compensation package is a very good number. This does not even include benefits, which can run anywhere from 25 to 40 percent of the base salary. For the 2004 projected salary, the total is over $80,000. Even though the female counterparts make less and the difference is statistically

significant, a $10,000 difference still leaves a $70,000 package. With an average benefits level of 30 percent, this makes the total over $90,000.

As the literature also suggests, controllers do more things than simply sitting at a computer. Technology and the management of human resources are important skills for controllers to master. This makes the career of a controller more varied and interesting. Therefore, students who have preconceived ideas of the monotonous life of a controller may want to give this career another serious consideration. As the results also suggest, controllers in the hospitality industry are coming from other fields or have been involved in other fields besides hospitality. Possible explanations may include a lack of supply of controllers in the hospitality field, a lack of awareness of the hospitality field until later in their career, or leaving the hospitality field for a period of time but deciding to return. Regardless, if such is the case, if one begins his or her career in the accounting department, one may attain the position of controller a lot faster as there is a need for competent individuals.

If one wants to become a controller, is the hotel industry better than the club industry or vice versa? As the results suggested, the hotel industry pays better than the club industry, especially when considering just the bonuses. However, club controllers do work slightly fewer hours per week than hotel controllers. Thus, if a student is looking for financial rewards, perhaps the hotel segment is the answer. It is also important to know that though both hotels and clubs are part of the hospitality industry, working in a hotel is not the same as working in a club. Hotels operate 24/7, whereas most clubs do not and they are usually closed on Mondays. In a hotel, one deals with an ever changing guest profile with some repeat/frequent guests while in clubs, one deals with a set of members. At the end, the student needs to understand himself or herself and know what he or she wants.

While there are some differences in the characteristic profiles of female and male controllers, these minor differences may not be enough to explain the differences in the financial profiles.

And, while the last research hypothesis is rejected, the industry needs to create better pay equity between the genders so that it can attract more hospitality students into this career. While some of the differences examined in this study may be due to the greater number of females in the club segment as compared to males in the hotel segment, further research is warranted.

8.4 BUDGETING AND FORECASTING: CURRENT PRACTICE IN THE LODGING INDUSTRY RAYMOND S. SCHMIDGALL AND AGNES L. DEFRANCO

Financial forecasts and budgets can strengthen management's control of hotel operating expenses and help determine the profitability of the property (Chamberlain, 1991, 89–90; DeMyer and Wang-Kline, 1990, 64; and Karch, 1992, 21–22). Specifically, forecasts give owners a projected level of sales, while budgets alert owners and operators alike to significant expenditures that are on the horizon or predictable shortfalls in revenues. Used together, forecasts and budgets can provide a benchmark for sales-incentive programs, executive-compensation bonuses, incentive-based management fees, and capital expenditures (Temling and Quek, 1993).

A major difference between forecasting and budgeting is that budgeting is normally viewed as a process that covers a longer period of time than forecasting. Budgeting often results in a formal, long-range plan, normally expressed in terms of dollars over time—for example, the predicted revenues and expenses of a hotel for 24 months

(Schmidgall, 1997, 369–372, 411–413). On the other hand, forecasts are generally prepared by hoteliers to establish staffing levels and may cover a period of just seven to ten days (Schmidgall, 1989, 101–2, 104–5). Long-range budgeting, therefore, is a form of strategic planning. It may entail several years' financial projections, a coordinated management policy, and a control-and-correction mechanism that allows actual results to be compared to estimates and followed by corrective steps, if necessary (Coltman, 1994).

✦ THE CURRENT STUDY

Our study serves the following purposes:

- to determine the purposes, methods, and procedures in performing an operations budget,

- to determine how an operations budget is used in budgetary control, and

- to determine the techniques used in forecasting revenues in the various operating departments in lodging properties.

Limitation. Our study used a random-sampling technique to select 600 samples that yielded 171 responses (almost 30 percent of the sample). As a result, there may be respondents who belong to the same national chain and thus represent the same set of corporate operating procedures. In addition, with the full-service and luxury segments of the hotel industry constituting more than 90 percent of our responses, the results are likely more applicable to those two groups than to limited-service hotels. Thus, although more than one-quarter of the hotel executives solicited by this study responded, it may not be useful to generalize the study's results (particularly beyond full-service hotels).

The instrument. We designed a four-part questionnaire with the assistance of a number of lodging controllers and by modifying a survey previously used in 1995 (Borchgrevink and Schmidgall, 1995). We also employed a pilot study in which other lodging controllers offered comments and allowed us to fine tune the final survey. Part I of the questionnaire included six questions that collected demographic data about the respondents and their lodging operations. Parts II and III consisted of 14 questions regarding the procedures and methods used to develop an operations budget, and about how the budget is used for financial control. Finally, the last part of the questionnaire asked respondents to provide information regarding their various operating departments' forecasting techniques.

Sampling. As mentioned, a simple random-sampling technique was used to select our study's population. Six hundred financial executives who

are associated with lodging operations were chosen from the 1997 membership list of the association of Hospitality Financial and Technology Professionals (formerly the International Association of Hospitality Accountants).

Data collection and analysis. We first sent the survey in October 1997 to each of the 600 executives, requesting them to participate in our study. To ensure a good response rate, we sent a second copy of the survey to everyone in January 1998, as a reminder. Data received were analyzed using the software package SPSS for Windows.

✦ RESULTS AND DISCUSSION

Of the 600 executives who received our survey, 171 responded, yielding a 28.5-percent response rate. The majority of the respondents held the title of hotel controller (147, or 86 percent), while the others reported such titles as assistant controller, regional controller, corporate controller, VP-controller, executive VP-CFO, and director of accounting. Respondents were mainly associated with full-service hotels (72 percent). Together with those from the luxury segment (21 percent), those executives constitute well over 90 percent of the responses. As for affiliation, the majority (62 percent) were part of a national chain, and 29 percent reported working for independent lodging properties. International chains accounted for another 7 percent, while 2 percent of the responses came from franchisees. Most of the properties reported having more than 250 rooms (71 percent) and enjoyed 1996 annual gross revenues of at least $10 million (also 71 percent). Figures 8.3 and 8.4 show the details of the lodging-property size.

Figure 8.3 Lodging Property Size, by Number of Rooms

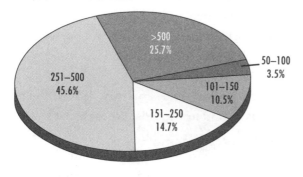

Profile of properties represented in this study.

Preparing the budget. The operations budget is an integral part of the financial operation of a lodging property, and virtually all of the respondents reported that they prepared an operations budget for the year—only three reported not preparing a budget. Moreover, almost 60 percent indicated that they set a tentative financial goal prior to developing the operations budget. The majority of those (64 percent) related that tentative financial goals were based on either sales (33 percent) or net-income (31 percent) levels. (In this case, sales equals revenues, while net income refers to the financial statement's bottom line.) Other financial executives' financial goals were based on gross operating profit, net operating profit, EBITDA, debt-service coverage, occupancy percentage, RevPAR, or some combinations of those.

We presented five possible reasons why an operations budget might be prepared, and we also offered the fill-in-the-blank answer "other." When asked to give one major reason why a budget was prepared, 45 percent selected the option that stated "It is used as a standard by which the lodging operation is managed." Another 28 percent chose the answer "It is a planning tool." About 15 percent of the respondents gave more than one reason, and their responses almost always noted a budget's value as a standard of comparison or as a planning tool.

More than 90 percent of the respondents reported that a cooperative effort among hotel departments was used to prepare the operations budget. Nevertheless 73 percent reported that the controller was the one who held the main responsibility for preparing the operations budget using the input provided by other department heads and the general manager.

Only five respondents indicated that the controller prepares the budget with little input from others. Thus, in more than three-quarters of the hotels surveyed, the controller was primarily in charge of budget preparation. In another 5 percent, the lodging units' controllers and general managers jointly prepared it, and in 12 percent of the hotels, the general manager coordinated the budget-preparation process with

Figure 8.4 Lodging Property Size, by Annual Gross Revenues (1996)

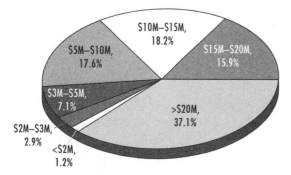

Figures in U.S. dollars (millions). Profile of properties represented in this study.

the various department heads. Other responses indicated that budget-preparation responsibility fell to an executive committee, department heads, the general manager (with input from the owner), or a budget team (for example, a team might comprise the general manager, owner, and controller).

While all but three of our 171 respondents confirmed that they prepared an operations budget for the year, less than half prepared a long-range budget (i.e., for more than a year at a time). Of those who prepared long-range budgets, more than three-quarters used a five-year time span for future planning.

Making adjustments. Only one in four of the respondents revised their budget at any point during the operating year, with the most common frequency of change being monthly (40 percent). Other responses to this question included "as needed" (21 percent), "quarterly" (16 per-cent) "semiannually" (12 percent), "bimonthly" (3 percent), and some combination of the above (4 percent).

✦ BUDGETARY CONTROL

The majority of the respondents who used budgets declared that the operations budget was used for budgetary control, with 90 percent reporting that budgets were prepared for all of the hotel's operations, versus just for selected departments. Next, we asked what level of variance between the budget (original or revised) and actual performance is permitted before corrective action is taken. The results for this question are summarized in Table 8.15. About a third of the respondents try to hold food, beverage, and labor costs within the range of 1 to 2 percent of the budgeted amounts. One-fifth of the respondents hold "other" budget items within a range of 2 to 3 percent. (The median of the responses for food and beverage costs was about 2 percent, with the

Table 8.15 Cost Tolerances between Budget and Actual Costs

	FOOD COST	BEVERAGE COST	LABOR COST	"OTHER" OPERATING COSTS
Less than 1%	11.5	14.3	8.2	8.2
1% to 1.9%	33.8	33.3	26.5	16.3
2% to 2.9%	29.0	23.1	25.9	21.1
3% to 3.9%	10.1	13.6	16.3	14.3
4% to 4.9%	6.1	4.1	12.2	17.0
5% to 5.9%	6.8	8.2	6.8	17.0
More than 5.9%	2.7	3.4	4.1	6.1
Median	2.2%	2.1%	2.6%	3.3%
Median, 7996 Study*	1.9%	1.9%	2.8%	3.7%

*R. S. Schmidgall and C. P. Borchgrevink, 1996.

medians for labor and "other" costs at about 3 percent.) Compared to responses to a similar question in a 1996 study, it appears that hotels today are slightly more tolerant in food and beverage cost variances and slightly less tolerant in allowing labor and other operating costs to deviate from the budget (Schmidgall, Borchgrevink, and Zahl-Begnum, 1996).

✦ FORECASTING TECHNIQUES

The last part of our questionnaire outlined in a grid presentation seven forecasting techniques, ranging from simple to complex (i.e., smoothing-constant method), and five principal hotel revenue-generating departments. We also allowed space so that respondents could write in other techniques. Respondents were then asked to reveal the methods they used for forecasting department revenues (see Table 8.16).

From this exercise, we find that some hoteliers used more than one technique for each department and that the methods used varied among departments. More than 40 percent of the restaurant and beverage departments, for example, appear to favor the use of "number of guests by expected spending per guest." While the chief technique applied to the rooms department was "expected units to be sold multiplied by the expected average price per unit" (reported by 73 percent of respondents), the banquet department was the high user of "last year's actual revenues adjusted subjectively" (33 percent).

Table 8.16 **Various Departments' Forecasting Techniques**

TECHNIQUES	ROOMS	ROOM SERVICE	RESTAURANT	BANQUET	BEVERAGE
Prior year's budgeted dollar amounts multiplied by 1 + X%	10%	8%	9%	10%	10%
Number of guests by expected spending per guest	7%	28%	46%	25%	41%
Expected units sold by expected average price per unit	73%	27%	27%	26%	21%
Change in advance bookings from prior year	27%	6%	4%	22%	5%
Last year's actual revenues	16%	18%	16%	19%	16%
Last year's actual revenues adjusted subjectively	20%	24%	25%	33%	29%
Average of several past years' revenues multiplied by 1 + X%	5%	6%	5%	6%	6%

Source: R. S. Schmidgall and C. P. Borchgrevink, 1996.

Accurate budgets are considered essential to profitable hotel operation. Yet obtaining reliable data is a problem. Smith and Lesure state that perhaps the greatest problem with forecasting and budgeting is the number of widely varying forecasts that are regularly published side by side, without question or support, and in some cases making all predictions vague.[1] Moreover, business projections and financial trends are often published without any explanation of the underlying assumptions. Smith and Lesure contend that perhaps the way to construct reliable forecasts and budgets is to build a statistically reliable industrywide database that can be regularly updated with and compared to new economic and financial information. Those numbers can then be used to develop a short-term outlook for the industry as a whole or various geographic and market segments.

Hoteliers' desire and need for accurate budgeting and reliable data are not new. In 1989, hoteliers reported being generally satisfied with their forecasting accuracy, and yet they desired improvement.[2] Just one year earlier, Lasky noted that budgeting was one of the factors hoteliers ignored when opening a hotel. Thus, he wrote, he was personally involved in rescuing 130 hotels and motels from bankruptcy due to this oversight.[3]

Besides the budget's role as the business plan for owners and operators, Temling and Quek discuss the importance of hotels' budgets to lenders.[4] The budget is important to this group, as it can indicate a lodging company's potential for success. It also lets the officers of financial institutions know about the financial health of the business.

As the lodging industry's competitiveness increases, so does the interest in budgeting practices, as indicated by studies that appear biennially, on average.

In 1995, 122 U.S. lodging properties were asked about their budgeting practices.[5] The areas of investigation included: budget development processes, budget reforecasting procedures, and budgetary control methods.

To further investigate the budgeting process, 140 U.S. lodging controllers were asked in 1997 about their use of forecasting and budgeting at the department level.[6] That study reported that controllers rated "proper staffing" as the main benefit of preparing forecasts and "strategic planning" as the main benefit of budgeting. That study's results also showed that a hotel's size (as measured by the number of rooms) did not significantly influence the perception of the usefulness or the practices of forecasting and budgeting.

Some years earlier, Records and Glennie provided insights to the Boca Raton Resort and Club's budgeting and business forecasting processes.[7] Forecasting business volume and scheduling the required labor to serve its customer are crucial steps in maintaining an operation's quality. Thus, using a relatively simple computer network and basic software, the Boca Raton Resort and Club ensured it could control budgets, forecasts, and labor schedules.

[1]R. A. Smith and J. D. Lesure, "Don't Shoot the Messenger—Forecasting Lodging Performance," *Cornell Hotel and Restaurant Administration Quarterly,* 37, 1 (February 1996): 80–88.

[2]R. S. Schmidgall and J. D. Ninemeier, "Budgeting Practices in Lodging and Food Service Chains: An Analysis and Comparison," *International Journal of Hospitality Management,* 8, 1 (1989): 35–41.

[3]M. Lasky, "An Rx for Hotel Health," *Lodging Hospitality,* 44, 6 (May 1988): 75–77.

[4]W. P. Temling and P. Quek, "Budget Time," *Lodging Magazine,* 19, 3 (November 1993): 21–22.

[5]C. P. Borchgrevink and R. S. Schmidgall, "Budgeting Practices of U.S. Lodging Firms," *Bottomline,* 10, 5 (August–September 1995): 13–17.

[6]A. L. DeFranco, "The Importance and Use of Financial Forecasting and Budgeting at the Departmental Level in the Hotel Industry as Perceived by Hotel Controllers,"

Hospitality Research Journal, 20, 3 (February 1997): 99–110.

[7]H. A. Records and M. F. Glennie, "Service Management and Quality Assurance: A Systems Approach," *Cornell Hotel and Restaurant Administration Quarterly,* 32, 1 (May 1991): 26–35.

✦ THE EFFECTS OF AFFILIATION, SALES, AND PROFITABILITY

To see whether a property's (1) affiliation, (2) size in terms of sales, and (3) profitability have any effect on its budgeting practices, we used the chi-square statistic. The properties' budgeting practices were reflected in the answers to eight questions that asked about the procedures and methods used to develop operations budgets and how those operations budgets were used in budgetary control.

We first classified the responses according to the properties' affiliation. A chi-square was then calculated by cross-tabulating the affiliation on one hand and the eight questions on the other. Next, the same procedure was used to classify the responses according to sales level, and then by profitability. If an effect has a probability value (p-value) or a significance level of less than 0.05, it is significant. That means, in general, the effect happens due to chance less than 5 percent of the time. As seen in Table 8.17, two of the practices were affected by property affiliation, one was affected by sales, and one was affected by profitability (see those data marked with an asterisk).

Table 8.17 Property Characteristics Correlated with Budgetary Practices

BUDGETARY PRACTICES	SELECTED PROPERTY CHARACTERISTICS		
	CHAIN VERSUS INDEPENDENT OPERATION	SIZE (SALES)	PROFITABILITY
Major reason for having an operations budget	0.009*	0.015*	0.017*
Tentative financial goal set in advance	0.018*	0.562*	0.156*
Base for the tentative financial goal	0.116*	0.292*	0.202*
Long-range operating budgets prepared	0.062*	0.008*	0.067*
Revision of operating budget	0.252*	0.914*	0.675*
Monitoring food costs	0.440*	0.516*	0.398*
Monitoring beverage costs	0.535*	0.342*	0.447*
Monitoring labor costs	0.447*	0.299*	0.416*

*Significance level is less than 0.05.

Table 8.18 The Effect of Annual Sales on Long-Range Planning

ANNUAL SALES	PERCENTAGE OF RESPONDENTS WHO PREPARED LONG-RANGE OPERATIONS BUDGETS
Less than $5 M	28%
$5 M to $10 M	28%
$10 M to $15 M	37%
$15 M to $20 M	48%
Over $20 M	74%

Note: Figures in US dollars (millions).

When the chi-square test was performed based on annual sales, a significant difference ($p < 0.05$) was found in the preparation of long-range operating budgets (Table 8.18). That is, the higher the sales level a property enjoyed, the greater the likelihood that the property prepared a long-range operations budget.

Our second set of cross-tabulations determined whether differences occur between branded lodging operations and independent properties (Table 8.16). We noted two statistical differences, namely (1) the major reason for having an operations budget and (2) whether a tentative financial goal was set in advance.

First, it appears that national-chain hotels cited different reasons for having an operations budget than did the independent properties, as shown in Table 8.19.

Hoteliers affiliated with national chains tend to have more than a single reason for creating an operations budget. In addition, it appears that national chains prepare the budget to be used for comparison purposes more often than do the independents, and that the independents prefer to use the operating budget as a planning tool (compared to the national chains).

Second, 65 percent of the chain properties responding to our questionnaire established tentative financial goals prior to developing their operations budgets compared to only 45 percent of the independent properties. This difference is most likely due to pressure from chains' corporate offices on individual properties to deliver the required "profit" to meet the chains' overall financial objective.

Table 8.19 The Effect of Affiliation on Budget Usefulness

| AFFILIATION | MAJOR REASON FOR HAVING AN OPERATIONS BUDGET | | |
	PLANNING TOOL	USE AS A STANDARD	MORE THAN ONE REASON
Chain property	26%	53%	22%
Independent property	48%	48%	5%

Note: Totals may not add up to 100 due to rounding.

Table 8.20 The Effect of Profit Margin on Budget Usefulness

| | MAJOR REASON FOR HAVING AN OPERATIONS BUDGET | | |
AFFILIATION	PLANNING TOOL	USE AS A STANDARD	MORE THAN ONE REASON
< 11%	45%	52%	4%
11% to 20%	46%	46%	9%
21% to 30%	36%	44%	20%
> 30%	10%	60%	30%

Note: Totals may not add to 100 due to rounding.

The last step of our research was to test for differences according to profitability. The profitability of each respondent was determined by dividing the net income reported by each hotel by its total sales. Respondents were then divided into four categories according to their profitability: less than 11 percent, 11 to 20 percent, 21 to 30 percent, and over 30 percent (Table 8.20). The greater the respondent's profit margin, the more likely that a single reason was cited for having an operations budget.

✦ SUMMARY AND FUTURE RESEARCH

Operations budgeting is an important part of U.S. hotels' financial planning. The majority of hoteliers set tentative financial goals prior to preparing their operations budgets. The goal for the majority of hoteliers is based on either sales or net income. Most hoteliers indicated that the major reason they used budgets at all was as a standard for comparison to actual performance figures. The second most common use was as a planning tool. At the majority of hotels, a cooperative effort among departments was used to produce the budget. In a clear majority of those

hotels, the financial executives coordinated this process. Less than half of all respondents prepared long-term operations budgets, and less than a quarter of all respondents indicated that their budgets were revised during the year.

All but two of the 171 respondents indicated that their operations budgets were used for control purposes. For all departments, the mean of the allowable deviation between the budget and actual performance ranged near 2 to 3 percent. That range is slightly tighter and smaller than the range measured in a similar study in 1996 (Schmidgall, Borchgrevink, and Zahl-Begnum, 1996).

Respondents' revenue-forecasting techniques varied by department within individual hotels. A number of respondents reported they used multiple techniques for a single department. The most commonly used technique was "expected units sold by expected average price per unit." Other techniques that were used by more than 20 percent of the respondents included "number of guests by expected spending per guest" and "last year's actual revenues adjusted subjectively."

Our research uncovered several points that deserve attention. First, virtually all hotels use an operations budget and yet less than half of the hotels budget beyond one year at a time. Future researchers might explore the reasons why more hoteliers don't prepare long-range operations budgets. Second, few hoteliers revise their budget during the year (only about one in four). Budgeting is not an exact science, so regular adjustments should be expected and planned. Third, for most hotels, the largest single cost is labor. Yet our research shows that hotels' food and beverage costs appear to be more closely controlled than are labor costs.

Future research could also focus on specific control techniques to monitor hotels' costs and to determine whether more-profitable hotels use different techniques than less-profitable hotels. Finally, further study could examine closely the forecasting techniques actually used by the operating departments. For example, in our study, the technique "last year's actual revenues adjusted subjectively" was rated high, and future research could explore exactly what "subjective" adjustments are being used.

8.5 AS I SEE IT: THE HOTEL CONTROLLER Michael J. Draeger

The controller is the manager with overall responsibility of the accounting department. This executive is credited with having his or her hand on the purse strings, an eye on the bottom line, and the ear of the general manager, all while counting the beans and balancing the books. In fulfilling this role, the controller must know the hotel operations and be familiar with what goes on in each department. As is the case with all other managerial roles, the controller must have many skills that are used daily.

Obviously, the controller is an administrator. He or she supervises the accounting functions, including payroll, payables, receivables, purchasing, and auditing. The controller wants to know that procedures are being followed and deadlines are being met. He or she questions what is happening in each hotel department. Is all the money getting to the bank, and is there enough to pay all the vendors and staff? That large group function in the ballroom is being extended 30-day credit— have their references been checked? Are purchase orders on file in the receiving department? Do the actual payroll tax deposits equal what is reported on the IRS form? Accounting affects almost every aspect of the hotel operation, and the controller is the one looked to when it comes to the proper functioning and conduct of this department.

The controller is an advisor, meaning he or she provides information and recommendations to every department in the hotel.

Regarding giving information, accounting generates more reports than any other department. Daily reports to management showing sales, labor, and purchases are a must in any business, with comparisons to budget and/or last year. The financial statements, including the balance sheet and income statement, are periodically produced in accounting. The controller is expected to be prepared to discuss these types of reports with managers and owners, and to make sense of all the numbers and percentages. A hotel holds any number of meetings where the controller discusses the financial or operational results. At these meetings, the controller is a part of the process of generating recommendations and suggestions to improve operations in areas the reports might point out. Often, a morning operations meeting finds the controller addressing labor costs that are creeping higher than appropriate given current levels of business, or the monthly manager's meeting starts with the controller giving an overview of last month's financial results and the hotel's year-to-date standing. When the owners visit the hotel, they usually attend a meeting to discuss financial results and what is being done to ensure profitability expectations are being met. The controller might even be asked to sit in on a specific department's staff meeting as its members brainstorm ways to reduce departmental costs. As others digest the information accounting provides, the controller offers advice and counsel on its significance.

The controller is also a technician. He or she must have a foundation in the debits and credits of accounting. Regardless of whether the accounting department is staffed with one person or two dozen, the controller is prepared to jump in and do the work. A tight labor market and staff turnover sometimes necessitate that the controller assist in every function. There are always balance sheet accounts to reconcile, budget variances to explain, and journal entries to post. It takes a lot to keep an accounting department functioning.

Very early in my accounting career, I began working in a small accounting department of a regional restaurant chain. Because of state laws, the restaurants could buy alcoholic beverages with cash or check only, and never on credit. To facilitate purchasing, the restaurant general manager was provided an imprest checking account for purchasing alcohol. (An imprest account is one that has a specific amount of money in it, and money is replaced with the precise amounts the checks are written for.) This account had $1000 in it, and each week the manager called the home office and had deposited into the account the amount equal to the checks written in the previous week. Then the invoices for what had been purchased were forwarded to the home office, which supported the amount of the transfer. In theory, the account balance never exceeded $1000. The bank statements were sent to the general manager of the restaurant to balance and send completed to the home office.

Because I was the new guy, I was given the task of balancing the checking account of one restaurant, which had not been balanced in over 2 years. It was well known that this restaurant's manager, an exceptional people person, wasn't good with numbers and never found time to balance that puny checking account. So I went to work ticking off the checks and deposits and trying to make the account balance to the $1000 imprest amount. There were several irregularities, and, of course, many documents (cashed checks) were missing. I worked with the bank to recreate copies and research the irregularities, of which there were many. When all was finished, I had discovered the manager had embezzled over $18,000! This manager had actually been a very astute numbers person and had found ways to divert extra funds into the account and then wrote checks to himself and others for personal use.

It was a technician who caught him. But had a technician balanced that checkbook monthly and always verified the purchases through the invoices, the embezzlement never would have happened in the first place. Procedures were wrong and not enforced, and the climate was ripe for trouble. A good bookkeeper or accountant is primarily a good technician in accounting aspects, and a good controller does not lose sight of this ability as his or her career develops.

Most successful businesses create a financial plan or budget to operate by. The more honest and detailed this plan is, the better one can gauge actual performance. Most budgets are prepared annually, with monthly detail breakdowns. The controller is a planner and is usually the one who prepares the budget—or, better yet, coordinates the hotel's efforts in preparing departmental budgets to consolidate into one master document. I worked for a company that provided major cash incentives for meeting and exceeding the annual budgeted bottom-line numbers. Budgeting was taken very seriously, and each member of management had a vested interest in all departments' performance. Budgeting is not hard to do, but it can be time-consuming.

Over the years, I became a detail-oriented and effective budgeter, although my first budget review taught me the most. My hotel and I had spent weeks and months preparing the next year's budget. All the numbers had been gone over, comparisons completed, and volumes of expense and revenue backup catalogued and bound in three-ring binders. The general manager and I flew 3000 miles, with our binders, to present the budget to our area and regional vice presidents and receive the company's stamp of approval. We were scheduled for a 5-hour review session, if that much time was needed. As the GM and I came into the review room, the vice presidents were already seated and waiting. They stated that this could be a short and productive meeting. If we would only commit to increasing our bottom line by $200,000, we could all be out of there in 5 minutes. No way! The GM and I had solid defendable numbers, and we weren't going to let months of everyone's hard honest work get blown away. Needless to say, the review lasted the entire 5 hours, our budget was ripped to shreds, and the GM and I were verbally bloodied, bruised, and beaten at the end of it all. Oh yes, our bottom line increased $350,000, and we did not make budget or our bonuses that year. A good manager should always know what the people above him are looking for and then strive or rather plan to produce it, and this includes budgeting.

Additionally, the controller is an educator. All managers have a responsibility to instruct and train others, and the controller is no exception. Obviously, the accounting staff must be proficient in their duties to perform their jobs, and the controller must ensure this is happening. However, to the majority of the hotel, what accounting does and how they do it can be quite a mystery. Controllers should demystify the role of accounting. Managers with an understanding of accounting find they have more tools to work with in the operation of their departments after they have been involved in just one year's budget process. The controller can be building public relations for accounting by using opportunities to develop others' financial awareness and expertise.

Finally, controllers should be mentors. They should be involved in the development of people.

The accounting staff should experience new challenges to keep them interested. Cross-training in other accounting or hotel positions can give staff perspective on areas not previously understood. This aids staff in developing their careers and additionally helps within the department when staff is short.

There was a time when this backfired on me, though. My accounting department had a staff of 14, and each was cross-trained to perform at least part of a job besides their own. My general cashier was responsible for counting the previous day's receipts and preparing the bank deposit. Additionally, she replenished the cash banks used in the restaurants and stores and at the front desk. She was responsible for maintaining a safe in her office that contained close to $400,000. Sadly, her father passed away and she needed to leave town for a week or so. No problem! We had someone in accounts receivable that had cross-trained in the cashiering position and was able to step in immediately. The cashiering temp completed her first week without a hitch. We left work for the weekend feeling all was well. On Monday, my cashiering temp didn't show up for work. She also didn't call. In fact, I have never seen her since. Over the weekend, she had taken advantage of procedural flaws and helped herself to $30,000 of the hotel's money and fled.

When I was able to step back and take a broad look at what had happened, I realized the problem. The accounting procedures were such that one person could steal from the safe and not be questioned. Not only was this an opportunity for a dishonest employee, but it also placed an honest employee in danger! One employee had both the combination and the key to the safe tumbler. One employee could go into the accounting offices alone on a day when the entire hotel knew the accounting department was closed. One employee could go into the cashier's office alone with a backpack and exit the office, department, and the building without anyone asking to see inside the backpack. A single employee could be in physical danger if others knew all of this and were hard up for cash. Needless to say, procedures were changed immediately and policy manuals were rewritten with haste.

The controller should be on the lookout for promising managers who show potential. Managers enjoy taking a few minutes over coffee or lunch or even just sitting in the office to talk about their objectives and goals. Often the controller can facilitate a manager's accomplishments by being a friend and being aware of the manager's professional developmental needs.

Mentoring and educating can benefit the controller in many ways—maybe, most interestingly, in his or her personal advancement and compensation. Several hotel companies evaluate and offer incentives to the back-of-the-house departments for criteria previously reserved for more service-oriented or revenue-producing departments. As a controller of an accounting department, I am measured by the service my department provides to the hotel operation—our internal customers. Accounting becomes a support department and the rest of the operation its customers. In this way, accounting offers products and services, and it works to satisfy customers. The manager and even staff can establish quantifiable objectives focused on the department's product. These become the criteria for performance evaluations, bonuses, and other incentives and rewards.

Current objectives in accounting might now include:

- Working professionally with all other departments.
- Meeting deadlines and issuing timely reports.
- Achieving superior results on internal and external audits.
- Training operational managers in the financial aspects of their departments.
- Stocking storerooms at appropriate par levels.
- Keeping the accounting offices neat, orderly, and presentable.

- Being willing to answer questions and assist with problems.

With this type of product and service attitude, there is no limit to what a department might do for its customers.

It is not easy to describe the controller's job as a daily routine. However, the position does call for skills and traits that are continually in use. Just as with all other aspects of the hotel, the scenery is always changing, guests are constantly arriving and departing, restaurants open and close, telephones ring 24 hours a day. Each day brings new challenges and opportunities, and the controller, as part of this, must embrace the many facets of the hospitality industry.

8.6 THE HOTEL PURCHASING FUNCTION   C. Lee Evans

The hotel purchasing function did not change very much from 1970 to 1990. Until the late 1980s, various tax advantages and benefits were the primary reason for the construction of U.S. hotels. Providing a substantial return on investment was not expected or required.

In our current economy, expectations of hotel profitability have changed. Profitability is now required, along with maintaining the established level of quality. This has brought about a new level of interest in the purchasing function and greater importance placed on cost savings.

The financial aspects of the hotel business changed in the 1990s. Hotels enjoyed the longest

boom in revenues and profitability over the previous 40 years.

Today, however, in the slump following the terrorist attacks of 2001, hotel managers realize that true cost savings generated in the purchasing department are dollars that drop directly to the bottom line without associated incremental cost. It is not difficult to generate arbitrary savings; the true challenge is to create cost efficiency utilizing a standard specification.

Purchasing for the hotel requires much more than obtaining three bids and circling the lowest price. The true definition of *purchasing* should be "purchasing the right product, at the right price, at the right time."

The statement sounds extremely simple, but when it is applied to the thousands of items a hotel purchases, it presents a great challenge for the purchasing manager. The hotel purchasing function supports virtually every department within the property, whether purchasing chemicals for housekeeping or stewarding, office supplies for marketing, computer supplies for accounting, or food and beverage products for the restaurant outlets.

The purchasing manager usually reports to the hotel controller or the hotel's financial control division, but I am convinced this will change. There is a need for a more operational approach to managing the purchasing function. We need to build a team that is committed to the common goal of servicing our customers and maintaining established quality standards. The reporting structure will begin to shift to operations, with the purchasing manager directly reporting to the general manager or, in larger properties, to the executive assistant/operations manager. This will help promote the philosophy of team building and support and service customers directly. As matters stand now, purchasing is viewed as a support department.

With the increasing importance of the purchasing function, the mission of the purchasing manager is to procure products and services cost-effectively that will meet or exceed the customer's expectation. The purchasing manager must continually evaluate product specifications to incorporate new products and technology. Reviewing the specific need based on the expectation of the customer helps product evaluation.

The purchasing function is changing for several reasons. In the past five to seven years, the hotel industry has undergone tremendous consolidation. With this consolidation have come economies of scale for support areas, which include marketing, accounting, purchasing, and reservation systems. Many of today's hotel companies have centralized the purchasing function to some extent. They negotiate purchasing agreements with producers and processors and distribute products and supplies through predetermined distribution channels.

✦ PURCHASING ORGANIZATION

The purchasing department can be organized into three basic areas:

- **Administrative:** This area consists of pricing, vendor selection, and the purchase of nonstocked items. Nonstocked items are products purchased for immediate use or held in storage in other departments throughout the hotel.

- **Receiving:** There are two categories of receiving: (1) hotel goods that are placed in storage in the purchasing area or are immediately issued to the requesting department or guest/group; and (2) items that have been shipped to a registered guest or expected guest/group.

- **Issuing:** Product issuing falls into two categories: (1) consumable food and beverage supplies consisting of all food items and liquor, beer, wine, and mixes to be held in the purchasing department storerooms; and (2) office supplies, printed forms, and linen. This is just a small listing of items, depending on the physical layout of the hotel.

The staffing and segregation of duties varies from hotel to hotel depending on the property size and physical layout of the back-of-the-house areas. A partial organization chart is shown in Figure 8.5. See "Sample Job Descriptions."

Figure 8.5 **Partial Hotel Organization Chart**

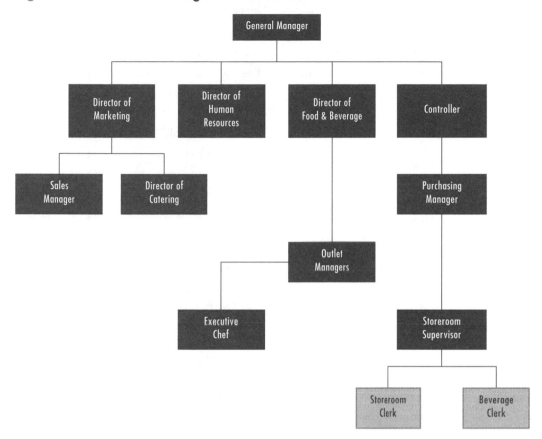

PURCHASING MANAGER

POSITION TITLE: Purchasing manager

DIVISION/DEPARTMENT: Administrative and general

REPORTS TO (TITLE): Controller

DIRECTLY SUPERVISES: Storeroom supervisor, beverage clerk, storeroom clerk

NO. OF EMPLOYEES SUPERVISED: 3

BASIC FUNCTION OF POSITION: To support the hotel department with dependable sources of materials and services, to buy competitively, to control inventories, to develop and train personnel, to implement planning to avoid emergencies, and to implement and supervise all procedures and staff in the purchasing department. EDUCATION AND EXPERIENCE OR SKILLS NEEDED: College helpful but not required. Previous buying experience a must. Food and beverage buying necessary. Accounting background needed. Extraordinary organizational skills required. Must display excellent management skills and a great deal of diplomacy.

TYPE OF GUIDANCE REQUIRED TO DIRECT THE ACTIVITIES OF THE POSITION AND MAGNITUDE OF INDEPENDENT DECISION-MAKING RESPONSIBILITY: Must have the ability to function independently within the parameters established by the controller and other upper management in the hotel. Has the authority to hire and terminate.

FUNCTIONS:

20%: Develop and monitor policies, procedures, and performance objectives for the purchasing team.

30%: Solicit competitive price quotation.

40%: Supervision of purchasing staff.

10%: Miscellaneous duties (O-G = ongoing):

> O-G: Review par stock levels.
>
> O-G: Schedule storeroom hours.
>
> O-G: Develop employees for supervision position.
>
> O-G: Maintain high levels of employee motivation.
>
> O-G: Ensure proper handling of receiving, storing, and issuing.
>
> O-G: Ensure accurate and timely preparation of daily records for purchases and issues for food and beverage forms.
>
> O-G: Visit surveyors and stay abreast of market trends.

STOREROOM SUPERVISOR

POSITION TITLE: Storeroom supervisor

DIVISION/DEPARTMENT: Purchasing

REPORTS TO (TITLE): Purchasing manager

DIRECTLY SUPERVISES: Beverage clerk, storeroom clerk

NO. OF EMPLOYEES SUPERVISED: 2

BASIC FUNCTION OF POSITION: To supervise the storeroom staff and resolve day-to-day problems in food and beverage storerooms. To assist in the procurement of all consumable food and beverage items, ensuring that they are of the right quality and right quantity. To maintain minimum investment and reduce unnecessary expenditures to maintain high sanitation standards and enforce all hotel policies relating to the food and beverage storerooms.

EDUCATION AND EXPERIENCE OR SKILLS NORMALLY NEEDED: College degree helpful but not required. One to two years' prior food and beverage background required. Must be able to read, write, and speak English fluently. Must have good organizational skills.

TYPE OF GUIDANCE REQUIRED TO DIRECT THE ACTIVITIES OF THE POSITION AND MAGNITUDE OF INDEPENDENT DECISION-MAKING RESPONSIBILITY: Must have the ability to act as administrator of the purchasing department in the absence of the purchasing manager. Must have the ability to function independently within the parameters established by the purchasing manager. Has the authority to hire and terminate.

FUNCTIONS:

50%: Supervise food and beverage clerks and provide assistance when necessary.

5%: Prepare daily food order.

5%: Prepare semiweekly food order.

5%: Maintain perpetual inventory (liquor, beer, wine).

2%: Assist purchasing manager in placing orders.

5%: Prepare weekly food bid sheet.

5%: Prepare monthly food bid sheet.

2%: Maintain accurate food and beverage vendor files.

2%: Assist in monthly inventory.

2%: Prepare monthly Food Dead Stock list (raw materials for which there is no finished product) for chef.

2%: Prepare monthly Beverage Dead Stock list for director of food and beverage.

10%: Miscellaneous duties (O-G = ongoing):

> O-G: Product quality inspection.
>
> O-G: Communication with the chef.
>
> O-G: Keep abreast of industry trends and information.
>
> O-G: Maintain accurate and organized filing system.

STOREROOM CLERK/BEVERAGE CLERK

POSITION TITLE: Storeroom clerk/beverage clerk

DIVISION/DEPARTMENT: Purchasing

REPORTS TO (TITLE): Storeroom supervisor

DIRECTLY SUPERVISES: None

NO. OF EMPLOYEES SUPERVISED: None

BASIC FUNCTION OF POSITION: To receive, store, issue, rotate, and secure merchandise as outlined in the storeroom procedures. To accurately record transactions and to follow written policies and procedures relating to purchasing and the food and beverage storerooms.

EDUCATION AND EXPERIENCE OR SKILLS NORMALLY NEEDED: Prior experience in food and beverage consumable receiving. Prior storeroom experience in issuing stock, and inventory control. Must have math aptitude and be detail oriented.

TYPE OF GUIDANCE REQUIRED TO DIRECT THE ACTIVITIES OF THE POSITION AND MAGNITUDE OF INDEPENDENT DECISION-MAKING RESPONSIBILITY: Must have the ability to function independently within the parameters established by the purchasing manager and storeroom supervisor.

FUNCTIONS:

25%: Responsible for the second thorough inspection of the product as it is being stored and rotated; ensure proper stock storage location on shelving units.

10%: Maintain high standards of sanitation and inventory organization.

10%: Participate in monthly inventory.

40%: Ensure completion of paperwork in a timely manner:

> A Form (daily record of purchases and issues of food).
>
> B Form (daily record of purchase and issues of beverage).
>
> Issue recap food.
>
> Issue recap beverage.
>
> Perpetual inventory, beverage.
>
> Perpetual inventory, paper.
>
> Food stock levels.
>
> Beverage stock levels

15%: Miscellaneous:

To complete projects in a timely manner.

✦ INTERDEPARTMENTAL RELATIONSHIPS

It is essential that the purchasing manager develop close working relationships with key managers within the hotel. These relationships should build and demonstrate trust, confidence in judgment, and integrity. Key managers include the following:

- Corporate purchasing manager
- Hotel general manager
- Executive assistant/operations manager
- Director of food and beverage
- Executive chef
- Director of housekeeping

Interaction between the purchasing manager and all other departments occurs regularly.

Spoken interaction, either by telephone or in person, is the most frequent. With the technological implementation of the Internet and email, the communication process has become more efficient. Communication can be accomplished quickly with large numbers of people.

Most day-to-day interactions of the purchasing manager involve the following key managers and issues, among others:

- **General manager/executive assistant manager:** Issues relating to quality changes and all discussions regarding capital expenditures (defined as equipment or renovation purchases exceeding $2000).

- **Director of food and beverage:** Unresolved food purchasing issues and information related to wine, liquor, and beer purchases.

- **Executive chef:** Issues relating to food purchases. This area requires close communication with respect to vendor performance, food markets, quality, and availability information.

- **Director of housekeeping:** Coordination and purchase of linens, paper goods (toilet paper, facial tissue, paper towels), uniforms, and laundry and cleaning chemicals.

A good purchasing manager bases purchasing decisions on the same criteria as all business decisions: data. One cannot be an expert on every product available. This is where purchase specifications come into play. Written specifications must be developed for all key products. These products should be tested periodically to verify that they meet or exceed specifications. Examples of testing: a monthly butcher yield test on specific meat cuts; a yearly test of terry linen by an independent laboratory.

✦ PURCHASING SOURCES

There are many sources of information about producers, processors, and manufacturers. Technical data are also available. Suppliers are the best source of information. The listings in "Purchasing Sources" are a small sample of material available to the purchasing manager. The latest and greatest means of identifying product sources has to be the Internet.

PURCHASING SOURCES

The Meat Buyers Guide (1988) by National Association of Meat Purveyors
8365-B Greensboro Drive
McLean, VA 22102
(703) 827–5754

Fresh Produce Manual (1989) by the Produce Marketing Association
P.O. Box 6036
Newark, DE 19714–6036

The Food Professional's Guide by Irena Chalmers
American Showcase, Inc., New York
Quantity Food Purchasing (2nd ed.), Lendal H. Kotschevar
John Wiley and Sons, Inc., New York

The Encyclopedia of Fish Cookery by A. J. McClane
Holt, Rinehart, and Winston, New York

The Advanced Seafood Handbook
Seafood Business Magazine
P.O. Box 908
Rockland, Maine 04841

The Packer 1990
Produce Availability & Merchandising Guide
Vance Publishing
7950 College Blvd.
Overland Park, Kansas 66210

✦ THE PURCHASING MANAGER'S DAY

7:00 A.M. Inspect the quality of food and beverage consumables as they are delivered to the hotel. This includes rejecting incorrect or inferior products and then contacting the appropriate vendor(s) to rectify issues or determine another source, if necessary. The average daily purchase cost could vary from $3000 to $50,000, depending on the size of the property and level of business.

9:00–11:00 A.M. Attend daily meeting with catering department, chef, stewarding, and banquet departments to review upcoming banquet business. Review the room setup for each scheduled function, menus, and, most importantly, the guaranteed attendance numbers.

12:00 noon. All food and beverage purchases have been received and issued. Inventory is now taken on all items in storage to determine the next day's needs. After reviewing the current levels and calculating banquet business requirements, select the vendors and place orders with suppliers, which may range in number from 1 to 25.

Spend the rest of the afternoon on purchasing nonconsumable food and beverage items, obtaining bids, and following up on outstanding purchase orders overdue for delivery.

The average workweek for the purchasing manager is 50 to 60 hours and may include weekends. For the most part, normal business hours are 7:00 A.M. to 6:00 P.M., Monday through Friday, and 7:00 A.M. to noon on Saturday.

✦ CORPORATE DIRECTION AND INTERACTION

Corporate direction and control varies with each hotel company. As a general rule, though, hotel companies that manage rather than franchise their properties are more involved in setting policies and procedures. The minimum standards of the purchasing manager vary by hotel company as well.

The corporate purchasing function is still viewed with skepticism, although not as much as in the past. Today, purchasing is a not-for-profit function, established to benefit managed properties. The idea of doing more with less applies at the corporate level as well as to the individual properties. The most efficient method of purchasing systemwide is targeting where dollars are spent and creating the most cost-efficient way to purchase high-volume expense items. Corporate hotel purchasing offices are currently working to accomplish this goal. Examples of items that could be considered for systemwide agreements between corporate and property purchasing offices are uniforms, flatware, paper goods, laundry supplies, and food products; these, too, vary by company.

✦ CASE IN POINT

The company I worked for out of college and until 1995 had its own in-house profit-driven purchasing company. This approach was not unique to this company; many of the large hotel companies had their own profit-driven purchasing arm, subsidiaries that, from a hotel owner's standpoint, could be considered double-dipping, as the owner was already paying the hotel management company a management fee. In the late 1980s and early 1990s, many hotel owners were looking for a greater return from their management company. I had the privilege and opportunities to be involved in the overthrow of the company's internal purchasing subsidiary. At that time we had been sold to foreign investors, and they were looking at every function and subsidiary in the company. With some prodding directly at the hotel company's new owner by one of the senior management, we were able to demonstrate that the days of double-dipping had to go and that the individual properties would recognize and support a corporate-level purchasing function whose only mission was to generate benefit for the properties. My boss and

I succeeded in accomplishing what was once thought could never be done because of politics.

✦ CONCLUSION

Hotel purchasing must focus on and utilize resources in the most efficient manner today. In the past, a heavy-handed approach was used to resolve issues with suppliers. As we move toward building partnerships with key vendors today, a teamwork approach provides an environment to build on the strengths of both the hotel and the vendor. This is now called *supply-chain management*.

Another key component in business today is communication, both internal and external. One of our national suppliers has the capability to link their customer service, for placing orders, with our domestic properties through a mainframe computer network linked to each property by PCs. Our hotels can place orders directly with the supplier through the network system and receive immediate confirmation from the supplier. This nationwide system allows both our properties and the corporate office to access pricing, availability, and consumption.

To succeed, we must resist the confines of our traditional paradigms. We must continually examine the ways we conduct business and strive for new and innovative approaches.

8.7 DATA MINING FOR HOTEL FIRMS: USE AND LIMITATIONS

VINCENT P. MAGNINI, EARL D. HONEYCUTT JR., AND SHARON K. HODGE

In the hotel industry, knowing your guests—where they are from, how much they spend, and when and on what they spend it—can help you formulate marketing strategies and maximize profits. Fueled by the proliferation of centralized reservation and property-management systems, hotel corporations accumulate large amounts of consumer data. This information can be organized and integrated in databases that can then be tapped to guide marketing decisions. However, identifying important variables and relationships located in these consumer-information systems can be a daunting task. The relatively new process known as data mining can be instrumental in overcoming such obstacles. (For a discussion of the use of compiled data, see Robert K. Griffin, "Data Warehousing: The Latest Strategic Weapon for the Lodging Industry?" *Cornell Hotel and Restaurant Administration Quarterly* 39, no. 4 [August 1998], pp. 28–35. For a discussion of the use of guest-history data, see Paula A. Francese and Leo M. Renaghan, "Database Marketing: Building Customer Profiles." *Cornell Hotel and Restaurant Administration Quarterly* 31, no. 1 [May 1990], pp. 60–63.) From stores of information, data mining technology extracts meaningful patterns and builds predictive customer-behavior models that aid in decision making (Kamrani, Rong, and Gonzalez, 2001, 361–377).

Data mining is a largely automated process that uses statistical analyses to sift through massive data sets to detect useful, non-obvious, and previously unknown patterns or data trends (Frawley, Piatetsky-Shapiro, and Matheus, 1992, 213–228). The emphasis is on the computer-based exploration of previously uncharted relationships (i.e., using "machine learning" methods that typically require only limited human involvement) (Peacock, 1998a). Without data mining, valuable marketing insights about customers' characteristics and purchase patterns may remain largely untapped (Shaw, Subramaniam, Tan, and Welge, 2001, 127–137). By uncovering such previously unknown relationships, managers have the potential to develop a winning marketing strategy that increases their hotel's bottom line.

Hotel managers understand the importance of adapting to the changing business environment not only to remain competitive, but merely to survive. As a result, technology has become a large and growing expense for many hotel corporations. Under such a technology framework, data mining is a valuable competitive tool being adopted by hotel corporations in an effort to create customer value. However, given the importance and complexity of data mining, senior hotel managers report a low level of understanding about data mining's capabilities, how it works, and what value this technology contributes (Dev and Olsen, 2000, 41–47). The purpose of this paper is to educate hotel managers about the benefits and application of data mining on the properties they oversee.

✦ DATA MINING VERSUS STATISTICAL MODELING

Data mining differs from traditional statistical modeling in a variety of ways. Data mining focuses on machine-driven model building, while statistical modeling stresses theory-driven hypothesis testing. Data mining techniques build models, whereas classical statistical tools are supervised by a trained researcher who possesses a preconceived notion of what to examine. With statistical *a priori* analysis, relevant associations may be overlooked. By building dependency hypotheses instead of merely verifying them, though, data mining techniques reveal important links. For example, Marriott Vacation Club International reduced the volume of direct mail it needed to reach target sales levels by correlating response rates to specific vacation offerings and specific customer characteristics (Peacock, 1998a).

Data mining also offers enormous gains in terms of performance, speed of use, and user friendliness (Le Bret, 1997). While data miners must understand statistical principles, highly specialized statistical knowledge is not necessary to study, understand, and improve decision-making processes. Data mining helps managers to spot trends more quickly.

Because researchers may ignore the assumptions and limitations of a theoretical model, traditional statistical analyses in customer-satisfaction research are often biased. Satisfaction research includes measures of the importance that customers place on product and services attributes. Typically, these measures are highly correlated, which can dramatically bias the statistical values that determine attributes' importance rankings.

Also, statistical analyses usually assume that relationships between independent and dependent variables are linear—which is often not the case. Therefore, violation of these assumptions can result in biased and misleading statistical outcomes. Data mining techniques (e.g., neural networks) overcome these limitations and outperform traditional statistical analyses in cases where such assumptions do not apply (Le Bret, 1997).

Another considerable advantage over traditional statistical models is data mining's ability to easily handle large and complex datasets (Peacock, 1998a). Data mining techniques are not hampered by large numbers of predictive variables, and that feature makes data mining useful for selecting variables, that is, identifying those within a set that are most relevant. The ability to handle large numbers of variables also makes data mining more realistic than statistical models in representing the complexity of a typical business environment.

While many analytical techniques can be classified as data mining tools, opinion has not coalesced regarding exactly which techniques should be considered part of the data mining toolkit. The tools listed in "A Data Mining Toolkit" almost certainly belong, however.

A DATA MINING TOOLKIT

- *Association rules:* Information from customer-purchase histories is used to formulate probabilistic rules for subsequent purchases.

- *Case-based reasoning:* Sets of attributes from new problems are compared with attribute sets from previously encountered problems (called cases) to find one or more boilerplate examples that provided good outcomes or solutions.

- *Decision trees:* Automatically constructed from data, these yield a sequence of step-wise rules; good for identifying important predictor variables, nonlinear relationships, and interactions among variables.

- *Descriptive statistics:* Averages, variation, counts, percentages, cross-tabs, simple correlation; used at the beginning of the data mining process to depict structure and identify potential problems in data.

- *Genetic algorithms:* Use procedures modeled on evolutionary biology (e.g., selection, mutation,

survival of the fittest) to solve prediction and classification problems or develop sets of decision rules.

- *Neural networks:* Applications that mimic the processes of the human brain; capable of learning from examples (large training sets of data) to discover patterns in data; can combine information from many predictors and work well even with correlated variables, nonlinear relationships, and missing data.

- *Query tools:* Provide summary measures such as counts, totals, and averages.

- *Regression-type models:* Ordinary least-squares regression, logistic regression, discriminant analysis; used mostly for confirmation of models built by "machine-learning" techniques.

- *Visualization tools:* Histograms, box plots, scatter diagrams; useful for condensing large amounts of data into a concise, comprehensible picture.

Looking at that toolkit, decision trees, association rules, case-based learning tools, neural networks, and genetic algorithms are categorized as machine-learning methods, while the others can be thought of as machine-assisted aids to support human learning (Peacock, 1998a).

With data mining techniques, levels of *a priori* specification can vary. In some cases, certain independent variables and dependent variables may be specified for examination, while predictor variables in other cases may be uncovered only by the data mining tool. The point remains, though, that in comparison with traditional statistical methods, data mining techniques invariably are more data driven than they are user driven.

We have observed that some hotel corporations are attempting to harness the power of information by investing in data mining technology that exploits consumer information. Hilton Corporation uses E.piphany E.4 software at its Beverly Hills headquarters, for instance (Stevens, 2001a, 35–38), and Starwood Corpora-

tion invested in Unica Corp's Affinium software (Tischelle and Maselli, 2001, 31–32). Such data mining technology allows hotel corporations to predict consumer-behavior trends, which are potentially useful for marketing applications. For example, Starwood's marketing staff can run reports and analysis on customer and occupancy data stored in a data warehouse that combines customer and transaction information from all company properties. Such information indicates where customers who visit a specific hotel live. If the data reveal that the Sheraton Fisherman's Wharf in San Francisco experiences a surge in visitors from Fort Lauderdale in April, for instance, hotel marketers can increase promotional efforts in Fort Lauderdale during the late winter months (Tischelle and Maselli, 2001, 31–32). "Examples of the Uses of Data Mining Information in Hotel Marketing" lists examples of how information gleaned from data mining can be used in a hotel corporation's marketing activities.

EXAMPLES OF THE USES OF DATA MINING INFORMATION IN HOTEL MARKETING

- Create direct-mail campaigns
- Plan seasonal promotions
- Plan the timing and placement of ad campaigns
- Create personalized advertisements

- Define which market segments are growing most rapidly
- Determine the number of rooms to reserve for wholesale customers and business travelers

✦ HARRAH'S DATA MINING SUCCESS STORY

In 1997 Harrah's hotels and casinos introduced a trademarked loyalty-card program, "Total Re-

wards," which tracks customers' purchasing activities and provides rewards that encourage spending at Harrah's properties. Rather than build glitzy properties with eye-popping attractions,

Harrah's pursued a customer-service-oriented strategy centered around data mining techniques. Harrah's used an information system called WINet to link all its properties, allowing the firm to collect and share customer information company wide. The process effectively changed the corporate culture from an every-property-for-itself mentality to a collaborative, customer-focused enterprise (Levinson, 2001).

The WINet system connects and consolidates customer information from all of the company's transaction, slot-machine, hotel-management, and reservation systems. Key pieces of information—gender, age, place of residence, and types of casino games played—help predict which customers are most likely to become frequent users. Based on this information, Harrah's designs marketing strategies to retain those customers. Customers' purchasing and gaming patterns are tracked, too, so that the company can target its customers with the most appropriate incentives. For example, customers who reside outside the local area receive complimentary hotel rooms or transportation, while drive-in customers receive food, entertainment, or cash incentives (Nickell, 2002).

Data mining techniques help to reveal data patterns and relationships that can be used to develop strong models for predicting the potential value of each customer. Given that retaining a customer is less costly than attracting a new one, building strong relationships with valued existing customers can boost profits. Having information regarding such things as the customer's birthday, anniversary, and favorite foods and drinks allows a hotel to provide excellent, tailored customer service that cements brand loyalty. Harrah's discovered that the 30 percent of its customers who spent between $100 and $500 per visit accounted for 80 percent of company revenues and generated nearly 100 percent of profits. In the first two years of its rewards program, Harrah's saw a $100-million increase in revenue from customers who visited more than one property (Nickell, 2002). As of 2001 Harrah's ranked first in the industry in profit growth (Levinson, 2001).

Because the WINet system can consistently identify which customers will be most valuable over the long term, data mining is also useful for determining when to avoid offering incentives to customers who are not lucrative. Harrah's estimates that it has saved some $20 million by withdrawing incentives from customers who are not likely to return (Levinson, 2001).

Despite Harrah's success, some remain skeptical of data mining's customer benefits and long-term financial payoffs. As an example, Susan Dobscha, co-author of "Preventing the Premature Death of Relationship Marketing," advises hotels that giant central databases "are not where customers want a relationship forged. A customer would probably prefer a lower price over, say, having their beverage choice anticipated" (Mining Hotel Data, 1998).

Another important caveat regarding data mining is that any relationship discovered must be valid to benefit a company's performance. When British Columbia Telecom tried to reward 100 of its best customers by inviting them to a Vancouver Grizzlies basketball game, for instance, it selected customers from the database comprising frequent 900-number users. After sending invitations to the printer, the marketing staff realized that those 900-number users included a large number of sex-line enthusiasts. The company avoided a serious gaffe by refining the criteria to create a list of truly loyal guests (Press, 1998, 58–61).

✦ DATA MINING APPLICATIONS FOR THE HOTEL INDUSTRY

The tasks performed by data mining can be grouped into the following five categories.

1. *Classification* arranges customers into pre-defined segments that allow the size and structure of market groups to be monitored. Also, predictive models can be built to classify activities. An illustration of such a model is one that predicts which segment's usage rate will experience the largest decrease when a particular promotion expires. Classification uses the information contained in sets of predictor variables, such as demographic and lifestyle data, to assign customers to segments.

2. *Clustering* groups customers based on domain knowledge and the database, but does not rely on predetermined group definitions. This function is beneficial because it aids hoteliers in understanding who are their customers. For example, clustering may reveal a subgroup within a predetermined segment with homogenous purchasing behavior (e.g., a subgroup of holiday shoppers within the transient segment) that can be targeted effectively through a specific ad campaign. (The idea is that the members of the subgroup will increase their number of stays or become more loyal.) On the other hand, clustering may indicate that previously determined segments are not parsimonious and should be consolidated to increase advertising efficiency. Information such as demographic characteristics, lifestyle

descriptors, and actual product purchases are typically used in clustering.

3. *Deviation* detection uncovers data anomalies, such as a sudden increase in purchases by a customer. Information of this type can prove useful if a hotel corporation wants to thank a guest for her or his recent increase in spending or offer a promotion in appreciation. Marketing managers may also attempt to draw correlations between surges in deviations with uncontrollable business-environment factors that are not represented in the database (e.g., a sharp increase in gasoline prices).

4. *Association* entails the detection of connections between records, driven by association and sequence discovery. For example, a possible detected association may be that a particular segment's average length of stay increases after a specific advertising campaign. Another association task could be employed in an effort to determine why a specific promotion was successful in one market, but ineffective elsewhere. Specific information regarding customer-purchase histories is necessary to formulate probabilistic rules pertaining to subsequent purchases.

5. *Forecasting* predicts the future value of continuous variables based on patterns and trends within the data. For instance, the forecasting function can be used to predict the future size of market segments. With forecasting one can also use data trends to project which hotel amenities are of growing importance to consumers and will be key drivers of the consumer's future perception of value.

In the hotel industry, the most common sources of data are CRSs and PMSs. Some hotel corporations also use information that resides in guest-loyalty-program databases. Hilton, for instance, analyzes data contained within its trade-marked Hilton Honors database (Stevens, 2001b, 29–30). Another potentially important source of data is the information provided by guest-satisfaction surveys.

✦ GUIDELINES FOR EFFECTIVE DATA MINING

When properly employed, data mining is a powerful and valuable marketing tool. However, simply investing in data mining technology may not guarantee success. As presented below, seven guidelines influence the effective management of data mining technology.

Guideline #1: *Match your IT priorities with an appropriate provider.* There is high demand for and low supply of data mining expertise as more companies realize the potential value of the information residing within their databases. To capitalize on this demand, a number of second-tier research firms now provide data mining services (Brandel, 2001, 67–70). However, providers offer a wide range of skill levels. The most-skilled providers can turn data into useful information. Companies that initially set clear priorities have a greater chance of reaping maximum benefits from data mining projects than do firms that are unsure of their goals (Stevens, 2001). Clear priorities include goals about what the firm would like to achieve through data mining and when it will be achieved. Without goals and objectives the hotel corporation is uncertain about what it is shopping for when seeking a data miner. It is also important to communicate these goals to prospective providers. When selecting a provider, ask the following six questions:

1. *Does the provider have experience setting up predictive models with marketing applications?* Data mining has applications other than marketing. Data mining's ability to detect patterns in data is used extensively in criminal justice and anti-terrorism efforts to anticipate illegal activity, for instance. Wall Street also employs data mining to predict moves in the financial markets. Large global corporations use data mining to gain efficiencies in purchasing and production throughout their networks. Therefore, it is not enough to have a data mining consultant, but one must find a provider that has experience in marketing. Building models to predict consumer behavior is a form of data mining that requires specific expertise. For example, a data miner with marketing-applications experience would know to replace a zip code with resident characteristics, such as median income (Brandel, 2001).

2. *Does the provider have experience in creating models within the hospitality industry?* Marketing applications of data mining are employed across diverse industries. Building predictive models for a grocery store, a furniture chain, an airline, or a hotel is different in each case. It is beneficial to find a provider that has experience in setting up models in the hotel industry. Such a provider would more clearly understand hotel-guest-segmentation processes, for example.

3. *Is the provider reputable?* Because many second-tier companies provide mining services, it is important to check the credentials and reputation of the vendor.

4. *Does the provider offer the latest technology that is appropriate?* Because of the wide range of products available, it pays to do your homework.

It is crucial to invest in the latest appropriate technology because it is extremely expensive and time consuming to switch products after one is installed—in no small part because switching products requires retraining the IT and marketing staff.

5. *Does the provider offer a product that has visual-exploration capabilities?* Cutting-edge data mining software has visual-exploration capabilities, which means that data patterns can be viewed as three-dimensional objects that can be rotated or zoomed for detailed analysis. In addition, pixel-oriented technology assigns colors to data values so that patterns and trends can be examined. Visual exploration is an immense aid to managers and marketers because it often serves as a preliminary tool in selecting the appropriate variables for data mining tasks (Shaw et al., 2001).

6. *Is the provider willing to provide a custom contract?* Contract negotiations are a critical step in initiating a successful data mining program. The contract should be as precise as possible and should abstain from nebulous clauses discussing partnership (Lacity and Hirschheim, 1995). Moreover, the vendor's standard contract should not be used, because the standard contract does not customarily include specific performance standards or penalty clauses if the vendor falls short of requirements. Worse, payment schedules in standard contracts may favor the vendor (Lacity and Hirschheim, 1995). A custom contract should be written to include service-level measures and a termination clause. The buyer should be particularly suspicious of so-called change-of-character clauses, which state that the buyer may have to pay for any changes in "functionality" throughout the life of the contract. Change-of-character clauses have caused many disputes because of the ambiguous nature of the term "functionality" (Lacity and Hirschheim, 1995).

Guideline #2: *Build segmentation and predictive models.* Building appropriate segmentation and predictive models necessitates an extensive knowledge of the hotel business. "Examples of Hotel-Guest Segments" provides examples of some of the many ways that hotel guests can be segmented (Kotler, Bowen, and Makens, 1999). Transient hotels, convention hotels, extended-stay hotels, and resort properties all segment guests differently. Furthermore, guest segmentation is distinctive for most hotel properties. Hilton's and Marriott's property-management systems segment and code markets at the property level, for instance, since each location has its own particular segments. A given property may serve a set of corporate clients, a group of government clients, and social clients (e.g., weddings and reunions). The segment categories can be strung into a large set of combinations. Furthermore, a guest could potentially fit into several categories, which poses a challenge for current data mining techniques (Shaw *et al.*, 2001). As a consequence, finding a provider that has experience creating models in the hotel industry is a major benefit. Additionally, even if the provider has hotel experience, it is critical that IT and marketing managers work closely with the provider to segment the market and build predictive data mining models.

GEOGRAPHIC
> Nations
> States
> Counties
> Cities

DEMOGRAPHIC
> Age or life-cycle stage
> Gender
> Income

PSYCHOGRAPHIC
> Social class
> Lifestyle

Personality
Behavior
Occasion of purchase decision
Occasion of use
Benefits sought
User status (e.g., potential, former, first time)
Usage rate
Loyalty status
Buyer-readiness stage

Source: P. Kotler, J. Bowen, and J. Makens, *Marketing for Hospitality and Tourism*, 2nd ed. (Upper Saddle River, NJ: Prentice-Hall, 1999).

Once a data mining model is built, confirmatory testing must be conducted to assess its predictive accuracy. For instance, a model designed to predict who will respond to a promotion should be based on a prior offering in which it is known who did or did not respond. After the model is constructed, a "holdout" group from a previous promotion can be analyzed to verify reliability. If the holdout predictions do not replicate the results of the past promotion, then the model may not be significantly predictive. To further enhance accuracy, a score can be assigned to the model based on the level of agreement between the holdout group and the entire group. Subsequent refined models can then be tested and scored. Another standard approach to model validation involves drawing two random samples from the data. The first sample is used as a calibration sample to build the model, while the second is used as a holdout sample to evaluate the model built from the calibration sample (Peacock, 1998b,

15–25). The validation process requires a knowledgeable IT professional, because when data subtleties that arise only in the sample are used to build the model, the model may be highly predictive of the sample but biased with regard to the population (Shaw et al., 2001). This is called overfitting the data. To avoid creating a biased model, the IT professional must be knowledgeable of the analytical procedure and possess a basic understanding of the hotel segment and promotional scenario from which the sample was extracted.

Guideline #3: *Collect data to support the models.* Accurate data collection is critical for successful data mining. The major obstacle to effective data mining, however, is inadequate data gathering and input (Smith, 2001, 36–37). Data problems lead to a decrease in the value of any data warehouse, in addition to diminishing the value of proposed models (Shaw et al., 2001). Problems with data are related to one or more of at least three different shortcomings.

The first possible difficulty involves missing or inaccurate data. For example, when occupation information is available for only 15 percent of a data set, it is difficult to create a profile of customer occupations. Then again, it's a problem if the data file contains occupation information for 90 percent of the population, but the accuracy of the information is poor. Hotel corporations can reduce inaccuracy of this kind by asking guests for their current occupation.

A second obstacle is poorly coded data. Databases must have standards regarding data formats, text case, and redundant codes (Stevens, 2001b). Although some software automatically formats the data properly, most do not. Problems then occur when data-input sources are added over an extended time and no one has ensured that the data entering the warehouse is properly formatted. This would occur, for instance, if, when original data mining technology was installed, predictions were made based on the reservations system and the property-management system, but then a subsequent decision was made to input data from guest-satisfaction surveys. Problems would transpire when additional data inputs are not standard or are coded improperly. For example, some models require continuous and ordinal data, while others demand categorical data fields or binary constructs (Siragusa, 2001).

A third potential problem involves using homonyms (that is, putting the same label on two or more different data elements) and synonyms (that is, using two different labels for the same data element) (Chopoorian et al., 2001, 45–51). While it may seem tautological to advise precluding this occurrence, the most common culprit is a new user on the system. It is common for hotel and IT professionals to change companies from time to time. Turnover causes coding problems when new employees bring their old labels and fail to use their new employer's framework.

Guideline #4: *Select the appropriate tools for analysis and prediction.* Numerous analytical tools can be employed to transform data into useful information. Some of the less-common analytical tools used by data mining software include regression models, factor analysis, cluster analysis, structural equation modeling, and self-organizing maps. On the other hand, the most common statistical methods used in data mining applications are decision trees, neural networks, and genetic algorithms. As previously mentioned, a decision tree is a rule-based model constructed of nodes (decision points) and branches (connections between nodes) that reach numerous outcomes based on traveling through two or more nodes. A neural network is a nonlinear predictive model that resembles a biological neural system and has the ability to learn through training. Last, a genetic algorithm is a learning-based model founded on the concept of evolution. That is, partial solutions to a scenario compete with each other, and then the best solutions are used for further problem solving (Hair et al., 1998).

Most of the statistical methods employ techniques that achieve a desired outcome. Likewise, each methodology has strengths and weaknesses, and each is appropriate for a specific scenario. Therefore, the most effective results emanate from data miners who have the expertise to select the most appropriate statistical method for a given scenario and the hotel's intended goals (Siragusa, 2001). For instance, a positive attribute of genetic algorithms is that they converge on an optimal solution, but the method is most applicable to large databases since arriving at a valid outcome may require many generations of competing solutions. Likewise, there are also pros and cons associated with neural networks. They are beneficial in analyzing complex data because of their ability to discover unusual trends, but monitoring accuracy is difficult because many intricate relationships are handled invisibly by the methodology (Hair et al., 1998).

Guideline #5: *Demand timely output.* Timeliness is critical in making marketing decisions. The length of time required to produce output varies widely among data mining packages. Before Hilton Corporation upgraded its data mining technology, for instance, the reports that managers requested from IT would take three to six weeks to arrive. "By the time they'd get the report, it was often too late to act on it," said Joanne Flinn, vice president of leisure marketing. With the new technology, managers receive reports in 30 minutes or less (Stevens, 2001b).

Guideline #6: *Refine the process.* By its nature, data mining involves knowledge that evolves over time. Never complete, data mining involves a continuous cycle of inputs and outputs based on models that must be modified and refined as conditions change in the competitive environment. Flexibility is needed to adapt the established models and processes to changes that occur (Cline, 2000). Refinement consists of three actions:

1. Chart progress toward initial goals. Use the forecasting function of data mining to regularly set new goals.
2. Compare and contrast the characteristics of the clustering output with the attributes of the classification output. When necessary, modify predictive models based on changes in the size

or structure of customers' market segments. For instance, notable variances in purchase patterns in one segment and similarities in purchase patterns among other segments may lead to refinement of the segment, usually by adding a new criterion or dimension. This action can result in the discovery of previously undetected segments with homogenous characteristics.

3. In addition to clustering and classification features of data mining, also use the associations and deviation-detection functions to assess the effects of promotions. Maintain a promotional history table in the database to use as a learning tool for future campaigns and models (Siragusa, 2001).

Guideline #7: *Hire a well-trained staff and a knowledgeable IT manager.* Information technology was initially viewed by the hotel industry as a back-office function that supports the finance and accounting areas (Cline, 2000). The industry has advanced far beyond this view during the past decade. In two sessions sponsored by the International Hotel and Restaurant Association (IH&RA), one in Singapore in 1997 and the second in Nice, France, in 1998, hotel-industry leaders pondered the role of technology. Among the conclusions reached were: "Going forward, technology will be the most competitive weapon for any hospitality company. If hospitality organizations want to compete successfully, they must do so by using technology to drive value to both the customer and to the firm" (Olsen and Connolly, 1999, 29). However, implementing such recommendations at the property level can be a difficult task.

Training is a key to effective implementation of data mining systems. Productive data mining requires two-fold proficiency among both IT managers and those who interpret the outputs.

The hotel's IT managers must also be proficient with the data mining system because the system requires continuous refinement. Just as market segments, sources of data, and property goals change, so must predictive models and analyses be modified and refined. It is an unsound policy for the IT staff to be totally dependent on the provider's recommendations for refinement and alterations. Instead, the IT staff and data mining provider should work together, with their common goal being to maximize the technology's effectiveness. The most effective data mining projects occur when IT managers and providers collaborate and share project information.

Second, adequate training must be provided to all potential users of data mining outputs. At the corporate level this includes the marketing staff, operations managers, and those developing new properties. Users at the property level include general managers, directors of sales and marketing, and the sales staff. Users must be instructed about the available reports and how to properly interpret the information. Since the information is used for decision making, it is important for users to understand the boundaries and limitations of the information.

✦ BOUNDARIES AND LIMITATIONS

Technology must serve managers' purposes, rather than dictate processes (Chudnow, 2001, 28–29). Along that line, data mining cannot capture all the information relating to what drives consumer behavior. Data mining is simply one of a number of research methods that help predict travelers' demand trends. Therefore, data mining technology

should be used in conjunction with other forecasting and research techniques. With this in mind, managers should be aware of the following four limitations of data mining technology.

Limitation #1: *Data mining analyzes only data collected from existing customers.* Data mining software generates information by analyzing data patterns derived from the company's reservation, property-management, and guest-loyalty-program systems. Patterns thus detected can help predict the actions of current guests in the system and of those with similar needs and wants. Data mining technology does not, however, provide information about market segments not found in the company's databases. Moreover, a market segment that is currently small but is on the verge of experiencing substantial growth may not be detected by data mining.

Another blind spot is the data in competitors' reservation systems. A key question in planning a marketing strategy in the hotel industry is: Who are my competitors' guests and where are they coming from? Data mining technology is unable to answer those questions.

Limitation #2: *Databases used in the mining process are often hotel-brand specific.* Just as data mining cannot analyze competitors' markets, it also creates prediction models that are brand specific. Thus, corporations that operate multiple brands often must create a data warehouse and conduct data mining for each brand. This is also true for the franchisees that may have a portfolio comprising, say, six Holiday Inns and four Marriotts.

Brand-specific marketing information is useful for the brand's corporate office to plan marketing programs, which is largely what franchisees purchase. Conversely, brand-specific marketing information may not be helpful if the hotel corporation that franchises numerous brands wants to predict customer demand based on a multiple-brand portfolio.

Limitation #3: *Data mining may not segment travelers by psychographic traits.* Segmenting consumers based on psychographic traits, such as personality and lifestyle, can be useful in the hotel industry. This is because psychology and emotion play significant roles in the hotel guest's decision process. That is, as seen in "Psychological Determinants of Demand," a traveler may select a destination for a variety of psychological reasons (Kotler et al., 1999). One limitation of data mining is that common system inputs do not account for psychological factors that influence a traveler's purchase decision.

A time-tested tool used in understanding hospitality demand trends is Stanley Plog's psychographic scale (Plog, 2001, 13–24). Many key drivers of demand identified by Plog, such as personality distribution among travelers (e.g., dependables, venturers, and centrics), are not common inputs into data mining systems. Hotels can acquire this information from customer surveys.

Limitation #4: *Data mining does not provide information about consumers' thought processes.* It is important to engage consumers in research to better understand their thinking. Information generated by data mining does not account for the fact that approximately 80 percent of human communication is nonverbal (Zaltman, 1997, 424–437). Interviews and focus groups are both useful methods for gathering information about the needs and wants of hotel guests. The insight gained from those techniques is difficult to capture in the statistical data mining outputs. That is why it is important to step back and ask what the hotel guest's inherent needs are and what the product is really about. This involves conducting in-depth conversations with guests. At times, improved insight and perspective are gained from talking with three customers for two hours rather than by surveying a thousand customers (Ohmae, 1999).

✦ CONCLUSION AND MANAGERIAL IMPLICATIONS

Data mining technology can be a useful tool for hotel corporations that want to understand and predict guest behavior. Based on information derived from data mining, hotels can make well-informed marketing decisions—including who

---

PSYCHOLOGICAL DETERMINANTS OF DEMAND

Education
Escape
Family bonding
Prestige
Relaxation
Self-discovery

Sexual opportunity
Social interaction

Source: P. Kotler, J. Bowen, and J. Makens, *Marketing for Hospitality and Tourism,* 2nd ed. (Upper Saddle River, NJ: Prentice-Hall, 1999).

---

should be contacted, to whom to offer incentives (or not), and what type of relationship to establish.

Data mining is currently used by a number of industries, including hotels, restaurants, auto manufacturers, movie-rental chains, and coffee purveyors. Firms adopt data mining to understand the data captured by scanner terminals, customer-survey responses, reservation records, and property-management transactions. This information can be melded into a single data set that is mined for nuggets of information by data mining experts who are familiar with the hotel industry.

However, data mining is no guarantee of marketing success. Hotels must first ensure that existing data are managed—and that requires investments in hardware and software systems, data mining programs, communications equipment, and skilled personnel. Affiliated properties must also understand that data mining can increase business and profits for the entire company and

should not be viewed as a threat to one location. As seen in the Harrah's example, implementing a data mining system is a complex and time-consuming process.

We advise hospitality managers to adopt a data mining system and strategy if they have not done so. Guidelines presented in this paper—including how to select and manage the data mining provider—offer guidance for implementing a viable data mining strategy. Since data mining is in its initial stages in the hotel industry, early adopters may be able to secure a faster return on investment than will property managers who lag in their decisions. Hotel corporations must also share data among properties and divisions to gain a richer and broader knowledge of the current customer base. Management must ensure that hotel employees use the data-management system to interact with customers even though it is more time-consuming than a transactional approach.

REFERENCES

Borchgrevink, C. P., and R.S. Schmidgall. 1995. "Budgeting Practices of U.S. Lodging Firms." *Bottomline* 10(5):13–17.

Brandel, M. 2001. "Spinning Data into Gold." *Computerworld* (May) 26:67–70.

Chamberlain, D. 1991. "A Written Budget Is a Valuable Tool for Tracking Your Meeting Dollars." *Successful Meetings* 40(6):89–90.

Chopoorian, J., R. Witherell, O. Khalil, and M. Ahmed. 2001. "Mind Your Business by Mining Your Data." *S.A.M. Advanced Management Journal* 66(2):45–51.

Chudnow, C. 2001. "Knowledge Management Tools." *Computer Technology Review* 21(11):28–29.

Cichy, R. F., and R. S. Schmidgall. 1996. "Leadership Qualities of Financial Executives." *Conell Hotel and Restaurant Administration Quarterly* 37(2):56–62.

Cline, R. 2000. "Hospitality 2000: The Capital." *Lodging Hospitality* 56(7):20–23.

Coltman, M. M. 1994. *Hospitality Management Accounting* (5th ed.). New York: Van Nostrand Reinhold.

Countryman, C., and A. DeFranco. 2002. "Compensation and benefits survey 2002." *The Bottomline* 17(7):11–32.

Countryman, C., A. DeFranco, and T. Venegas. 2004. "2004 compensation and benefits survey." *The Bottomline* 19(7):6–33.

Damitio, J. W., and R. S. Schmidgall. 1996. "A Profile of the Lodging Financial Executive." *Bottomline* (September):9–11.

Damitio, J. W., and R. S. Schmidgall. 2001. "The value of professional certifications for hospitality financial experts." *Cornell Hotel & Restaurant Administration Quarterly* 42(1):66–70.

DeMyer, J. P., and D. Wang-Kline. 1990. "What's On the Books? A Practical Guide to Forecasting and Budgeting." *Hotel and Resort Industry* 13(1):64.

Dev, C. S., and M. D. Olsen. 2000. "Marketing Challenges for the Next Decade." *Cornell Hotel and Restaurant Administration Quarterly* 41(1):41–47.

DeVeau, P. M., and L. T. DeVeau. 1988. "A Profile of the CHAE: Gaining Strength in Numbers." *Bottomline* (October/November):18–19.

Frawley, W., C. Piatetsky-Shapiro, and C. Matheus. 1992. "Knowledge Discovery in Databases: An Overview." *AI Magazine* (Fall):213–228.

Geller, A. N., and R. S. Schmidgall. 1984. "The Hotel Controller: More Than a Bookkeeper." *Cornell Hotel and Restaurant Administration Quarterly* 25(2):16–22.

Geller, A. N., C. L. Ilvento, and R. S. Schmidgall. 1990. "The Hotel Controller Revisited." *Cornell Hotel and Restaurant Administration Quarterly* 31(3):91–97.

Ghiselli, R. F., and B. Y. Chen. 1997. "Male and female hotel controllers in the '90s." *FIU Hospitality Review* 15(2):35–46.

Griffin, R. K. 1998. "Data Warehousing." *Cornell Hotel and Restaurant Administration Quarterly* 39(4):28–35.

Hair, J., R. Anderson, R. Tatham, and W. Black. 1998. *Multivariate Data Analysis* (5th ed.). Upper Saddle River, NJ: Prentice-Hall.

Hassmiller, B. 2000. "Compensation and benefits survey 2000." *The Bottomline* 15(7):6–25.

Kamrani, A., W. Rong, and R. Gonzalez. 2001. "A Genetic Algorithm Methodology for Data Mining and Intelligent Knowledge Acquisition." *Computers and Industrial Engineering* 40(4):361–377.

Karch, R. 1992. "Streamlining Your Hotel Cost." *Hotel and Resort Industry* 15(11):88–90.

Kotler, P., J. Bowen, and J. Makens. 1999. *Marketing for Hospitality and Tourism* (2nd ed.). Upper Saddle River, NJ: Prentice-Hall.

Lacity, P., and R. Hirschheim. 1995. *Beyond the Information Outsourcing Bandwagon*. New York: John Wiley and Sons.

Le Bret, C. 1997. "Have You Heard About Data Mining?" *Science Tribune* (October).

Levinson, M. 2001. "Harrah's Knows What You Did Last Night." *Darwin* (May).

"Mining Hotel Data." 1998. *Data Warehouse Report*, October 20.

Moore, R. W., and J. Stefanelli. 1989. "Power and the hotel controller's role." *Hospitality Education & Research Journal* 13(1):1–12.

Nickell, J. A. 2002. "Welcome to Harrah's." *Business 2.0* (April).

Ohmae, K. 1999. *The Borderless World*. New York: McKinsey and Company.

Olsen, M., and D. Connolly. 1999. "Antecedents of Technological Change in the Hospitality Industry." *Tourism Analysis* 4: 29.

Palmer, K. N., D. E. Ziegenfuss, and R. E. Pinsker. 2004. "International knowledge, skills, and abilities of auditors/accountants: evidence from recent competency studies." *Managerial Auditing Journal* 19(7):889–96.

Peacock, P. R. 1998a. "Data Mining in Marketing: Part 1." *Marketing Management* (Winter):9–18.

———. 1998b. "Data Mining in Marketing: Part 2." *Marketing Management* (Spring):15–25.

Plog, S. 2001. "Why Destination Areas Rise and Fall in Popularity." *Cornell Hotel and Restaurant Administration Quarterly* 42(3):13–24.

Press, S. 1998. "Fool's Gold?" *Sales and Marketing Management* (June):58–61.

Schmidgall, R. S. 1989. "While Forecasts Hit Targets, GMs Still Seek Better Guns." *Lodging* 15(3):101–102, 104–105.

Schmidgall, R. S., C. P. Borchgrevink, and O. H. Zahl-Begnum. 1996. "Operations Budgeting Practices of Lodging Firms in the U.S. and Scandinavia." *International Journal of Hospitality Management* 15(2):189–203.

Schmidgall, R. S. 1997. Hospitality Industry Managerial Accounting (4th ed.). East Lansing, MI: *Educational Institute of the American Hotel and Motel Association.*

Schmidgall, R. S., and M. Kasavana. 2000. "Certifications by HFTP." *Bottomline* (April/May):20–22.

Shaw, M., C. Subramaniam, G. Tan, and M. Welge. 2001. "Knowledge Management and Data Mining for Marketing." *Decision Support Systems* (May): 127–137.

Siragusa, T. J. 2001. "Implementing Data Mining for Better CRM." *Customer Inter@ction Solutions* 19(11):38–41.

Smith, M. 2001. "Refining Raw Data." *Printing Impressions* 43(9):36–37.

Stevens, L. 2001a. "CRM Analytics—CRM by the Slice—Running Analytics Is Expensive, So Companies Are Focusing on Areas with Customers." *Internetweek*, April 9, pp. 35–38.

———. 2001b. "IT Sharpens Data Mining Focus—Instead of Building Data Mining Applications with No Clear Goal, Companies Are Setting Priorities Up Front to Maximize ROI." *Internetweek*, August 6, pp. 29–30.

Temling, W. P., and P. Quek. 1993. "Budget Time." *Lodging* 19(3):21–22.

Tischelle, G., and J. Maselli. 2001. "Hotels Turn to IT to Stem Losses." *Informationweek*, December 17, pp. 31–32.

Tse, E. C., 1989. "A Profile of the IAHA Member." *Bottomline* (October/November):12–18.

Woods, R. H., D. G. Rutherford, R. S. Schmidgall, and M. Sciarini. 1998. "Hotel General Managers." *Cornell Hotel and Restaurant Administration Quarterly* 39(6):38–44.

Zaltman, G. 1997. "Rethinking Market Research: Putting People Back In." *Journal of Marketing Research* 34(4):424–437.

SUGGESTED READINGS

BOOKS

Hales, J. A. 2005. *Accounting and Financial Analysis in the Hospitality Industry.* Burlington, MA: Elsevier Buttersworth-Heinemann.

Hospitality Financial and Technology Pro. 2006. *Uniform Systems of Accounts for the Lodging Industry.* East Lansing, MI: Educational Institute of American Hotel and Lodging Association.

Jagels, M. G. 2006. *Hospitality Management Accounting* (9th ed.). Hoboken, NJ: John Wiley and Sons.

Schmidgall, R.S. 2006. *Hospitality Industry Managerial Accounting* (6th ed.).East Lansing, MI: Educational Institute of the American Hotel and Motel Association.

ARTICLES

Borchgrevink, C.P., and R.S. Schmidgall. 1995. "Budgeting Practices of U.S. Lodging Firms." *Bottomline* 10(5):13–17.

Burgess, C. 2007. "Do Hotel Managers Have Sufficient Financial Skills to Help Them Manage Their Areas?" *International Journal of Contemporary Hospitality Management* 19(3):188–200.

Choi, S. 2006. "Group Revenue Management: A Model for Evaluating Group Profitability." *Cornell Hotel and Restaurant Administration Quarterly* 47(3):260–271.

Cross, R. G., J. A. Higbie, and D. Q. Cross. 2009. "Revenue Management's Renaissance: A Rebirth of the Art and Science of Profitable Revenue Generation." *Cornell Hospitality Quarterly* 50(1):56–81.

Damitio, J. W., and R. Schmidgall. 2007. "Revisiting the Ethics of Financial Executives in the Lodging Industry." *FIU Review* 25(2):83–91.

Damitio, J. W., and R. S. Schmidgall. 1990. "Internal Auditing Practices of Major Lodging Chains." *Hospitality Research Journal* 14(2):255–268.

Dubé, L., C. A. Enz, L. M. Renaghan, and J. Siguaw. 1999. "Best Practices in the U.S. Lodging Industry—Overview, Methods, and Champions." *Cornell Hotel and Restaurant Administration Quarterly* 40(4):14–27.

Schmidgall, R. S., C. P. Borchgrevink, and O. H. Zahl-Begnum. 1996. "Operations Budgeting Practices of Lodging Firms in the U.S. and Scandinavia." *International Journal of Hospitality Management* 15(2):189–203.

Singh, A. J., and R. S. Schmidgall. 2002. "Analysis of Financial Ratios Commonly Used by US Lodging Financial Executives." *Journal of Leisure Property* 2(3): 201–213.

SOURCE NOTES

Chapter 8.2, "The Lodging Chief Financial Executive," by Raymond S. Schmidgall.

Chapter 8.3, "Controller: A Viable Career for Hospitality Students," by Cary C. Countryman, Agnes L. DeFranco, and Tanya Venegas, is reprinted from the 7th issue of 2005 in the *International Journal of Contemporary Hospitality Management*. © Emerald Group Publishing Limited. Used by permission. All rights reserved.

Chapter 8.4, "Budgeting and Forecasting: Current Practice in the Lodging Industry," by Raymond S. Schmidgall and Agnes L. DeFranco, is reprinted from the December 1998 issue of *Cornell Hotel and Restaurant Administration Quarterly*. © Cornell University. Used by permission. All rights reserved.

Chapter 8.5, "As I See It: The Hotel Controller," by Mike Draeger.

Chapter 8.6, "The Hotel Purchasing Function," by C. Lee Evans.

Chapter 8.7, "Data Mining for Hotel Firms: Use and Limitations," by Vincent P. Magnini, Earl D. Honeycutt, Jr., and Sharon K. Hodge, is reprinted from the April 2003 issue of *Cornell Hotel and Restaurant Administration Quarterly*. © Cornell University. Used by permission. All rights reserved.

CHAPTER NINE

HUMAN RESOURCES POLICY MANAGEMENT

9.1 INTRODUCTION

A pivotal moment for this section occurred in the third edition. This is when the section on human resources (HR) became a different creature than it had been in previous editions. In the past, it used to be called "The Management and Processes of Human Resources" and included several how-to articles. We now believe the reader will be better served by contemplating broad strategic policy considerations, among other issues.

A primary force for this shift in focus grew out of recent research that strongly suggests the future health of any organization will be based on human resources—that is, of course, if HR is called upon by top management for advice on legally and functionally delivering hotel services. Arguably, a well-managed HR department will offer a hotel a competitive advantage.

Among observers and participants on the hotel management scene are those who com-

pare human resources, formerly personnel management, to the weather: Everyone talks about it, but no one does anything about it. This is a problem faced by a good many managers. If an HR department is to be effective in dealing with the people they recruit, hire, and train, they need a strategic view of the future and strategies to achieve that view.

It has been said that we should be very interested in the future, for that is where we are going to spend the rest of our lives. It has also been said, "Predicting is difficult, especially about the future" (Berra, quoted in Woods, 1999). That was the premise of the lead article in this section. Kay and Moncarz brought some insight into a common question asked by many students of human resource directors; that is, "What characteristics do you look for in a potential manager?" Although the question is often stated with the purpose of determining whether or not the student sees him- or herself working for the respective organization, others listen intently with the idea that the response will provide insight into how they can become more marketable to that, and other, organizations. The results found in Kay and Moncarz's study not only pertains to the inspiring graduates of hospitality programs, but also those who have been working in the hospitality industry and are interested in becoming a top-level manager in a hotel. Not surprisingly, Kay and Moncarz found that human resource management is the most important KSA (knowledge, skill, and ability) among middle and upper-level managers in hotels. Further, the study indicated that knowledge and expertise in financial management plays a significant role in career advancement. As a result, for those who inspire to become managers in the lodging industry, this study would suggest that you should begin to hone your skills in the areas of human resources and financial management.

Perhaps one of the most challenging aspects of human resources is the issue of employee turnover. For whatever reasons, lots of employees leave hotel companies, and whenever they do, it is expensive—not only to the hotel but also to the employees. That is why Riegel's presentation of a conceptual model of turnover is an important inclusion here. This material updates research he and two colleagues did among foodservice employees, but the conceptual model holds equally well for hotel employees. It is included here because in many ways the strategic concepts of legal environment, HR professionalism, and management respect are avenues to control or reduce turnover.

In our current society filled with numerous lawsuits and increasing liability issues, the importance of the legal aspect of the human resource

department for every hotel is paramount. Our good friend, Jim Treadway (formerly president of Westin Hotels and Resorts—North America and currently president and CEO of MTM Management L.L.C.) states it best. Among the components of his "job description" is "to keep the owners out of jail," by which he means the GM must manage the business without incurring legal trouble and must avoid all possible risk of liability. The essay by Murrmann and Becker on the legal environment discusses the realms of risk facing hotels and their human resources departments. Increasingly, hotels are finding themselves at legal risk for hiring "high-risk employees." The most professional HR departments are aware of and prepared to advise their internal customers (department heads and the GM) how to employ the best people without running afoul of the ever-increasing regulatory and liability environment. See also the essay by Melissa Dallas in Section 5.6.

Reinforcing the importance of considering the HR function in a strategic light rather than an enabling one is the article included here by Tracey and Nathan. They argue that because human capital considerations are top-of-mind in research and trade publications, leadership still fails to consider HR when making strategic plans and that many firms are still mired in archaic policies and practices that threaten business activities in the business and regulatory environment. They argue their position cogently and with vigor; see if you agree with them.

An important inclusion in this edition is the perspective of HR, and functions of HR, from those who face these above-mentioned issues on a day-to-day basis. A common theme across both "Day in the Life's" is the focus on the people (i.e., employees) of the organizations. Jenny Lucas, director of education and development for Loews Hotels, describes a "normal day at the office and a "normal" day on the road. Regardless of her location, she is always focused on educating hotel managers on current issues facing the organization, as well as trends occurring in the industry. In addition, Jenny spends a good deal of time developing managers for growth and success. Likewise, Felipe Cofiño, director of human resources at the Hyatt Regency in Bethesda, Maryland, spends a good deal of his day building relationships within the hotel. He does so by walking around and speaking to the associates and managers about many issues, as well as through the scheduled one-on-one meetings with his team members.

There is no lack of research and commentary in hospitality publications, both academic and trade, that deal with human resources. Many of the articles and essays in this book could be and should be looked at with an eye toward their implications for the management of human resources in a hotel. Perhaps second only to marketing, human resources is the most written-about topic in not only the academic but also the trade press. Readers are encouraged to find publications that offer solid, practical, objective, and legally valid advice for aid in determining their individual model of how a human resources philosophy and its resultant practices should be designed. A good place to start is the list of suggested readings and references at the end of the chapter.

9.2 KNOWLEDGE, SKILLS, AND ABILITIES FOR LODGING MANAGEMENT SUCCESS CHRISTINE KAY AND ELISA MONCARZ

ABSTRACT. This study examines the effect of the following knowledge, skills, and abilities (KSAs) on managers' lodging success: human resources management, marketing, financial management, and information technology. The investigation determined that knowledge perceived as important for management success differs from actual KSAs that distinguish senior-level executives from their subordinate middle-level counterparts. The findings revealed that managers placed highest importance on and were most skilled in human resources management competencies. However, knowledge in financial management appeared to be a stronger indicator of top-level success. Underscoring the importance of financial knowledge was the finding that of all the KSAs being studied, only financial management had a significant, positive relationship with increased compensation. Moreover, financial management appeared to be a key to promotion to top-level positions. The implication of these findings is that educators, trainers, and would-be top executives should pay attention to financial management by ensuring that educational institutions and training programs provide proper coverage of financial techniques and analyses.

✦ INTRODUCTION

Today's lodging industry is more global, consolidated, and culturally diverse than ever before. Lodging professionals should be properly tooled with the knowledge, skills, and abilities (KSAs) necessary to enable them to face the industry's challenges and ensure their future success. Thus, it is timely to reexamine the requisites needed for managers to succeed in today's lodging environment.

Through the years, the consensus among industry professionals has been that human resources–related skills represent the most important element of hospitality management success.[1] Current research, however, has challenged this belief by suggesting that knowledge in such areas as finance, marketing, and information technology may be as important as or more important than human resources skills for success.[2] The implication is that the KSAs needed for managers to succeed have changed through the years and that contrary "to earlier studies, the GM of today . . . focuses on core business factors."[3] Indeed, contemporary general managers place high value on marketing, human resources, and financial management.

This research-based body of information on competencies serves as a foundation from which job descriptions, management training, and performance appraisals can be developed. Scholarly study into KSAs for hospitality management success represents a valuable resource to professionals and the lodging industry. However, research methodologies used to identify job requisites have been opinion based only—and recent opinions have been conflicting. As a result, conclusions from the studies provide limited empirical evidence for the prediction of management

success and may not represent accurate assumptions. To remedy this matter, this study is designed to compare executives' opinions on KSA requisites against actual lodging management success.

We propose that knowledge in financial management, marketing, and information technology, in addition to human resources management, constitutes a desirable attribute for management success. An investigation into the relationship between KSAs and management success will help to ensure proper identification of requisites for current and future managers. Specifically, our study examines the effect of KSAs in human resources, financial management, marketing, and information technology on lodging management advancement and success. We first investigate whether managers are competent in the KSAs that they consider most important and whether any variations in opinions or skills exist between manager groups. Our research then looks at the relative importance of KSAs on managers' advancement and monetary success. We address the following questions:

- Do KSAs perceived as important for career success differ from knowledge learned by hospitality executives?

- Do KSAs perceived as important for career success and knowledge learned by hospitality executives vary according to management level?

- Do KSAs positively correlate with lodging management success?

This study's results offer a resolution to the proposition that KSAs perceived as important for management success may differ from actual KSAs that place highly compensated managers above average performers. Any gaps found between managers' KSAs and those required for lodging success can provide direction for the future development of effective training programs for middle and upper management.

✦ DIVERGING OPINIONS ON KSA REQUISITES

As previously stated, early research on KSAs for lodging managers suggested that leadership and interpersonal skills are essential for managerial success and represented the highest-rated management skills recognized by hospitality professionals.[4] Today, however, industry opinions on successful management competencies, especially with respect to high-level executives, have deviated from original beliefs and support more contemporary schools of thought.[5] In particular, more importance is frequently being placed on marketing, financial management, and information technology knowledge.[6]

Current research into requisites for many different hospitality job titles has reported the need for increased knowledge in these new core competencies.[7] Scholars have started making separate and comprehensive investigations into such emerging KSAs as information technology, for example.[8] The implications of these more-recent studies indicate that knowledge in financial management, marketing, and information technology, in addition to the human resources–related skills, play an important role in a managers' success. Thus, the aim of our study is to test these theories regarding successful management requisites using a national group of lodging executives.

✦ THE SURVEY AND SUBJECTS

We developed a self-administered mail survey instrument to examine KSAs that were derived from a review of the hospitality literature on management competencies. A search of Purdue University's hospitality literature database produced more than fifty articles addressing KSAs and management competency, from which we compiled a voluminous list of 248 management KSAs.[9] From this list, we grouped similar KSAs together, collapsing our original list into eighty-two statements that fell under the following four domains: (1) human resources management, (2) information technology, (3) financial management, and (4) marketing. To ensure the reliability and clarity of the proposed measures, the draft instrument was tested for face and content validity by a group of subject-matter experts comprising ten industry professionals and educators. This pilot test resulted in the revision of survey statements and reduced the total list of KSAs to thirty-seven. A summary of the competency studies included in the scale development is provided in Table 9.1.

The final survey instrument consisted of two parts. Part 1 asked respondents to provide information about their professional backgrounds and organizations. In Part 2, respondents were asked to evaluate KSAs based on the level of importance for past career success and to report their current competency levels in each KSA. A 5-point importance scale ranging from *not at all important* to *extremely important* was used to measure the importance of KSAs. The self-appraisal of competency level was also measured using a 5-point rating scale.

The study universe consisted of two lodging professional groups: (1) members of the American Hotel & Lodging Association (AH&LA) and (2) alumni of Florida International University's School of Hospitality and Tourism Management

Table 9.1 Correlation Matrix for KSAs and Compensation

| CITE | SIZE | SAMPLE UNIT | | KSA DOMAIN STUDIED | | | |
		COLLECTION	ANALYSIS	HRM	FM	MKT	IT
Bart and Chen (2001)	49	Hospitality manager	Entry hospitality manager	*			
Baum(1991)	118	General manager (U.K.)	General manager trainee	*	*	*	
Birdir and Pearson (2000)	22	Research chef	Research chef	*	*	*	*
Beliter and Hoart (2000)	88	Food-services manager	Entry food-services manager				*
Breiter and Clements (1996)	301	Hospitality manager	Hospitality manager	*	*	*	*
Brownell(1994)	318	General manager	General manager	*			
Brownell(1992)	91	General manager	General manager	*			
	153	Middle manager	Middle manager	*			
Burbidge(1994)	186	Hospitality student	Entry manager	*		*	*
Cannon (1999)	103	Sales manager	Sales manager	*	*	*	*
Christou and Eaton (2000)	91	General manager	Entry hotel manager	*		*	
Chung (2000)	422	International hotel manager	Hotel personnel	*	*	*	*
Dennington et al. (1993)	9	Hospitality educator	Entry hotel manager		*		
	3	Senior hospitality manager	Entry hotel manager		*		
Feng and Pearson (1999)	133	Hospitality expatriate	Hospitality expatriate	*			
Geissler and Martin (1998)	42	Hospitality manager	Entry hotel manager	*			
Getty, Tas, and Getty (1990)	39	Hospitality manager	Entry hotel manager	*	*	*	*
Gorchels, Jambulingam, und Aurand(1999)	184	International executive	International marketing manager	*	*	*	
Hsu (1995)	121	Hospitality manager	Hospitality manager				*
Hsu and Gregory (1995)	30	Hospitality manager	Entry hospitality manager	*	*	*	
Kay and Russette (2000)	52	Hospitality manager	Entry, middle hospitality manager	*	*	*	*
Knutson and Schmidgall (2001)	234	Hospitality financial manager	Hospitality financial manager	*	*	*	
Kriegl(2000)	51	International hospitality manager	International hospitality manager	*	*		
Ladkin and Juwaheer (2000)	16	Senior hotel manager	Lodging manager	*	*	*	
Nelson and Dopson (2001)	85	Hospitality manager	Entry hospitality manager	*	*	*	*
Okeiyi, Finley, and Postel (1994)	20	Food-services manager	Entry hospitality manager	*	*	*	*
	30	Hospitality educator	Entry hospitality manager	*	*	*	*
	222	Hospitality student	Entry hospitality manager	*	*	*	*
Partlow(1990)	52	Hospitality manager	Hospitality manager	*	*	*	
	88	Hospitality educator	Hospitality manager	*	*	*	

(Continued)

Table 9.1 (*Continued*)

| CITE | SAMPLE UNIT | | | KSA DOMAIN STUDIED | | | |
	SIZE	COLLECTION	ANALYSIS	HRM	FM	MKT	IT
Perdue, Ninemeier, and Woods (2000)	114	Club manager	Club manager	*	*		
Perdue, Woods, and Ninemeier (2001)	365	Club manager	Club manager	*	*	*	
Perdue, Woods, and Ninemeier (2001)	311	Club manager	Club manager	*	*	*	
Perry, Foley, and Rumpf (1997)	53	Event manager	Event manager	*	*	*	
Siu (1998)	145	Senior hotel manager	Middle hotel manager	*	*	*	
Su, Miller, and Shanklin							
(1997/1998)	90	Hospitality manager	Entry hospitality manager	*	*	*	*
	70	Hospitality educator	Entry hospitality manager	*	*	*	*
Tas, LaBrecque, and Clayton (1996)	81	Lodging manager	Entry property manager	*			
Tan and Morgan (2001)	56	Tourism educator	Entry tourism manager	*	*	*	*
	100	Tourism manager	Entry tourism manager	*	*	*	*
Wilson, Murray, and Black (2000)	56	Catering manager	Catering manager	*	*	*	
Woods et al. (1998)	77	General manager	General manager	*	*	*	

Note: HRM = human resources management; FM = financial management; MKT = marketing; IT − information technology.

(FIU) who graduated from 1973 through 1998 and are employed in the U.S. lodging industry. We restricted participation to executives affiliated with AH&LA properties of 200 rooms or more. From the 2002 AH&LA membership list, 2,070 properties met our criteria, of which 525 were randomly selected for the study. All 360 of the qualifying FIU alumni were included.

Slightly different data-collection methodologies were employed for the two respondent groups. AH&LA properties were sent a survey packet consisting of three survey instruments. Property general managers were asked to complete one of the surveys personally and to forward the other two to a high-performing manager and a relatively low-performing manager. All of the lodging professional alumni were sent one survey to complete. From the 885 surveys mailed, 10 AH&LA and 8 FIU were returned as undeliverable. Of the 525 AH&LA mailings, a total of 57 properties (137 executives) responded, for an 11 percent response rate, and 55 of the 360 FIU alumni returned completed surveys, for a 16 percent response rate. We expected some overlap between the two groups, but we assumed that those individuals would respond just once and do so as graduates of FIU. Of the 192 responses, we were able to use 184 completed surveys for the study. The survey instrument was tested for reliability using Cronbach's alpha reliability analysis. We tested the reliability of the four perceived-importance scales and the four scales used to measure respondents' competency levels. In all, we found moderate to high reliability coefficients ranging from .80 to .89 for the eight scales. See Table 9.2 for a summary of scale reliabilities and items.

As shown in Table 9.3, responses came from thirty-three states. Approximately 75 percent of the respondents were males, mostly older than thirty-five. A high percentage (70 percent) of the industry professionals had baccalaureate or higher level degrees. Of those with degrees, more than 65 percent majored in hospitality, with business as the second most common major. Many respondents (62 percent) were experienced hospitality managers possessing more than ten years of service, and 27 percent reported more than twenty years of experience in management. The majority of managers (77 percent) were employed at medium-size properties. The study group was fairly evenly split between upper-level managers (43 percent) and middle managers (54 percent). Over half held ownership or administrative-type positions, such as general manager or vice president.

✦ ASSESSMENT OF MANAGEMENT KSAs

The upper-level executives reported human resources as the KSA in which they were most competent (mean = 4.23), followed closely by financial management (mean = 4.15; see Table 9.4). Meanwhile, they gave lower grades to their KSAs in marketing (mean = 3.72) and information technology (mean = 3.49). At the same time, these respondents' self-appraisals were in accordance with their importance rankings of those four management KSAs.[10]

Middle-level managers also reported being most competent in human resources management (mean = 4.19). However, they appraised their level of competency in financial management significantly lower than did the upper-level managers (see Table 9.5), but middle managers rated their competence in information technology higher than did the upper-level executives.[11] Moreover, unlike their vice president–type superiors, middle managers' competency levels did not correspond with the importance they placed on each KSA domain. They ranked the importance of financial management second and that of information technology third, even though they claimed the reverse regarding their levels of competence in those KSAs (referring again to Table 9.4). These findings suggest that perhaps middle-level managers are still developing their proficiencies in financial management but already have strong skills in information technology. In addition, knowledge of financial management and marketing may play a lesser role overall in this subordinate group's success, as reflected by the significantly lower importance ratings the middle managers accorded those two areas (see Table 9.5).[12]

These findings demonstrate that both manager groups placed the highest importance on and were most competent in human resources management. Likewise, the two manager types also ranked financial management second in importance for success. However, upper-level executives reported being more competent in financial management than their subordinate counterparts, suggesting that hospitality executives' KSAs vary by management level.

To better understand the importance of knowledge in human resources, financial management, and the other KSAs possessed by lodging

Table 9.2 Hospitality Knowledge, Skills, and Abilities (KSAs): Survey Scale and Items

| | COEFFICIENT ALPHA | | |
KSA DOMAIN	PERCEIVED IMPORTANCE	SELF-APPRAISAL	SURVEY SCALE ITEM
Human resources management	.89	.84	Developing positive human relations
			Motivating employees
			Training and developing employees
			Managing and supervising employees
			Recruiting, selecting, and hiring employees
			Managing employee retention and turnover
			Being a leader
			Building teams
			Managing employee grievances
			Appraising employee performance and productivity
			Having knowledge in quality assurance
Information technology	.80	.80	Using e-mail
			Using the Internet for resources and research
			Having knowledge in property management systems
			Having knowledge in reservation systems
			Having knowledge in e-commerce
			Having knowledge in operational application software
			Having knowledge in general application software
Financial management	.89	.86	Controlling costs
			Managing cash flow
			Planning and budgeting
			Having knowledge in forecasting
			Having knowledge in financial analyses
			Having knowledge in operational analyses
			Having knowledge in yield/revenue management
			Having knowledge in capital investment analyses
			Having knowledge in financial leveraging
Marketing	.86	.82	Developing product and brand strategies
			Following organizational vision and missions
			Developing promotional and public relations strategies
			Establishing measurable and achievable marketing goals
			Making deals
			Using sales techniques
			Having knowledge in marketing research
			Having knowledge in environmental scanning

Table 9.3 Respondent Profile and Property-affiliation Demographics (*N* = 184)

	n	%
Gender		
Male	136	73.9
Female	44	23.9
Age		
Younger than 35	46	23.0
35–49	81	44.0
50 and older	22	12.0
Education		
High school	33	17.9
Associates	20	10.9
Bachelor's	109	59.2
Master's	21	11.4
Hospitality management service years		
1–10	41	22.3
11–20	64	34.8
More than 20	50	27.2
Property size (number of rooms)		
1–200	9	4.9
201–500	141	76.6
More than 500	25	13.6
Management position		
Upper	79	42.9
Middle	100	54.4
Base salary (2001)		
Less than $50,000	31	16.9
$50,000–$99,999	41	22.3
$100,000 and above	27	14.7
Department		
Administrative	99	53.8
Accounting	10	5.4
Food and beverage	27	14.7
Front office	16	8.7
Rooms	13	7.1
Sales and marketing	12	6.5
Other	7	3.8

Note: Variations in total number of respondents and corresponding percentages are due to nonresponses or omissions.

Table 9.4 Manager Ranking and Mean Rating of Knowledge, Skills, and Abilities (KSAs): Perceived Importance and Self-Appraisal

KSA DOMAIN	PERCEIVED IMPORTANCE (n = 79)				SELF-APPRAISAL (n = 79)			
	RANK	RANK SCORE	M	SD	RANK	RANK SCORE	M	SD
Upper level manager								
Human resources management	1	3.68	4.36	.43	1	3.32	4.23	.41
Financial management	2	2.85	4.01	.61	2	2.96	4.15	.49
Marketing	3	1.82	3.63	.69	3	1.93	3.72	.55
Information technology	4	1.64	3.35	.82	4	1.79	3.49	.80

KSA DOMAIN	PERCEIVED IMPORTANCE (n = 99)				SELF-APPRAISAL (n = 100)			
	RANK	RANK SCORE	M	SD	RANK	RANK SCORE	M	SD
Middle-level manager								
Human resources management	1	3.43	4.23	.65	1	3.38	4.19	.50
Financial management	2	2.38	3.61	.87	3	2.28	3.72	.74
Information technology	3	2.22	3.55	.86	2	2.38	3.77	.69
Marketing	4	1.97	3.39	.84	4	1.95	3.58	.73

Note: Perceived importance scale: range is 1 = *not at all important* to 5 = *extremely important*. Self-appraisal scale: range is 1 = *low competency level* to 5 = *high competency level*. Friedman-rank tests are significant at the $p < .01$ level.

Table 9.5 Comparison of Upper and Middle Managers' Mean Importance Ratings and Self-Appraisals of Knowledge, Skills, and Abilities

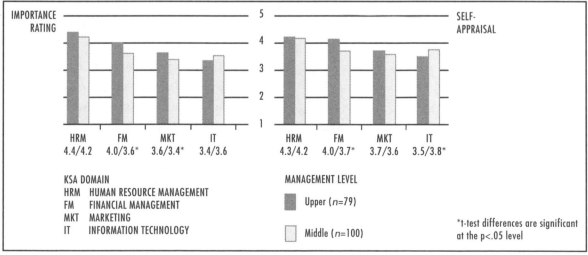

Table 9.6 Correlation Matrix for KSAs and Compensation

	1	2	3	4	5
1. Human resources management	1				
2. Financial management	.47**	1			
3. Marketing	.52**	.50**	1		
4. Information technology	.29**	.38**	.34**	1	
5. Compensation	.14	.27**	.18	−.23*	1

Note: KSAs represent respondents' self-appraisals of knowledge, skills, and abilities in respective domains; Compensation = 2001 base salary.
*Correlation is significant at the 0.05 level (two-tailed); $n=99$.
**Correlation is significant at the 0.01 level (two-tailed).

managers, we examined the correlation between managers' KSAs and monetary success (see Table 9.6). Financial management was the only KSA that had a significantly positive relationship with increased compensation ($r = .27$).[13] This result coincides in part with Chung's findings on hotel competencies, which also posited a link between hotel career success and knowledge in finance and accounting.[14] Both studies suggest perhaps a greater potential for career advancement and higher compensation levels for managers that have exceptional understanding of financial techniques and analyses.

✦ NEW INSIGHT ON MANAGEMENT KSAs

Unique to this study is a comparison between the general beliefs regarding KSAs required for lodging professionals and actual knowledge associated with lodging management success. Our study indicates that although upper-level executives placed highest importance on, and ranked themselves superior in, human resources management KSAs, financial management knowledge was found to have a stronger relationship with their monetary success than did human resources. Indeed, the correlation between financial management knowledge and increased compensation was the only significant relationship among the four KSAs that we modeled. Thus, these findings suggest that human resources management knowledge alone may not necessarily lead to success for senior-level management, as previously thought. However, these results do not mitigate the consideration that knowledge in human resources management, for example, is important and is continually employed by lodging managers. What we propose is that these other human resources–related skills perhaps represent basic requisites and are required of all managers at all levels. Moreover, competence in human resources management and especially information technology may be more beneficial for and more frequently used by entry-level and middle managers, while executives with strong competence in financial management KSAs may be in demand for senior-level positions.

Our research reveals other considerations. Increased knowledge in financial management, for instance, had no influence on either of the individual management (middle and upper) groups' monetary success but only among all managers overall. Moreover, significantly higher ($t = 9.55$; $p < .05$) compensations for upper-level executives were found, as would be expected.[15] These additional findings suggest that perhaps the relationship between increased compensation and knowledge in financial management is a function of upper-level managers' appointments and job responsibilities. That is, are managers who are appraised as having high levels of financial management knowledge promoted into upper-level positions at attractive compensation levels, or do managers develop to a higher level these financial skills after promotion?

Seeking to answer this question, we first note that compensation levels for middle- and upper-level managers typically fall within set ranges.[16] In addition, research has suggested that financial management knowledge in budget planning, operational analysis, and forecasting techniques, for example, generally is acquired within the first few years of hospitality experience, well within the tenure of middle managers.[17] These facts lead us to believe that regardless of their financial management expertise, managers' compensation depends more on their position than on their specific expertise. Our findings also suggest, however, that upper-level executives use and develop their financial management skills to a greater degree than do lower-level managers. Therefore, we believe that middle-level managers with proven abilities and knowledge in financial management may be viewed by their superiors as qualified candidates for higher-level executive positions. As a result, perhaps they have better chances of being promoted than their peers who are less conversant in financial management. This last conjecture extends beyond our study examination and thus represents a recommended research topic for further investigation and future testing.

In summary, our study results reveal that upper-level managers have significantly higher knowledge in financial management and have compensation ranges twice that of their subordinate counterparts. Consequently, middle managers aspiring to the upper ranks of management may best pursue the goal by honing their analytical skills and knowledge of financial management. Financial data analyses frequently monitored by general managers are net profit, gross operating profit, and cash flow, representing recommended areas of study for these would-be executives.[18] Hotel owners want general managers who speak the financial language and think in terms of creating value for their firms. Lodging professionals aspiring to successful careers must recognize the significance of earnings and cash flows. After all, it is the ability of a company to generate earnings and cash flows that will enable the entity to expand, pay dividends, and repay obligations.

A well-grounded understanding of margins and return on investment is also needed.[19] Financial measures such as profit margin, operating efficiency ratio, return on assets, and return on equity tell the story of business performance, and lodging professionals must manage their companies using these measures. It is the evaluation of these measures of performance that will enable managers to get a better handle on a firm's changing performance over time, to compare a company with its competitors, and to make required operational improvements. A good grasp of return on equity and the challenge of financial leverage in striking a proper balance between the benefits and the costs of debt financing will serve to evaluate how efficiently the owner's stake in the business has been used. Using this knowledge effectively can make a difference in lodging professionals' ability to advance to higher levels within their organizations.

✦ IMPLICATIONS OF STUDY

This study has implications for many stakeholders including lodging professionals, recruiters, trainers, and educators. These findings can serve to better prepare middle-level professionals for the responsibilities facing them in their future positions. Being properly equipped can increase executive recruits' potential for success, especially during the introductory period in their upper management positions. Likewise, lodging professionals should recruit entry-level managers who have graduated from hospitality programs with a strong financial management curriculum to ensure their managerial advancement and the firms' long-term profitability and growth.

Current executives also could benefit from the research findings by improving, for example, their knowledge of financial, operational, or capital investment analyses, yielding higher performance for their firms and thus generating more lucrative personal bonuses. Cash flow, earnings, and a firm's value are pivotal in achieving goals for hospitality firms.

Training programs sponsored by lodging firms can also be tailored to improve knowledge of financial skills and prepare current managers to achieve success and go up in the career ladder. In addition, the findings from this research can help recruiters in developing effective screening tools and practices, as well as assist executive trainers with future training programs. Competencies identified under this study can be incorporated into future job descriptions and performance appraisal instruments.

✦ CONCLUDING REMARKS

In conclusion, our study sheds new light on past beliefs regarding the KSA and lodging-management-success relationship. We posit that knowledge in financial management plays a significant role in managers' advancement and careers in the lodging industry. The research results reaffirm recent opinions that hospitality management requisites have changed over time, with increasing importance placed on competencies such as financial management and marketing. Our results agree with those of a recent *Cornell Quarterly* article, which suggested that the need for industry-technical expertise is decreasing even as nonindustry-specific knowledge becomes increasingly important.[20] Our results challenge the long-held beliefs and opinions of many that human resources–related skills represent the most important element of hospitality management success. Based on our findings, we propose that KSAs in such areas as human resources and information technology may represent basic skills for all managers and are perhaps most beneficial at lower levels of management. At the same time, knowledge in financial management can drive professional success to a greater degree as managers advance to higher ranks of responsibility.

We established that differences exist between executive opinion on KSAs considered important and actual competencies distinguishing senior-level executives from their subordinate middle-level managers. Therefore, we encourage the continuation of scholarly study and empirical testing of KSAs for hospitality management success. We recommend adopting management requisites from other professional fields that can be integrated into future hospitality research on lodging management success. We suggest this because a low percentage of the variance in success was explained by the four KSA predictors in this study. We also suggest an extensive investigation into a hierarchal structure of financial management competencies to establish knowledge relevancy for different management levels. Additional examination into marketing knowledge represents an intriguing topic of study, as knowledge in marketing was found to have a statistically significant influence on monetary success within the upper-level manager group. Replication studies applied to international managers would help to broaden the generalizability of research findings. Moreover, future research could be conducted to determine KSA success factors in other segments of the hospitality industry, including food service and clubs.

ENDNOTES FOR SECTION 9.2

1. See Richard F. Tas, "Teaching Future Managers," *Cornell Hotel and Restaurant Administration Quarterly*, vol. 29, no. 2 (August 1988), pp. 41–43; Judi Brownell, "Hospitality Managers' Communication Practices," *International Journal of Hospitality Management*, vol. 11, no. 2 (May 1992), pp. 111–28; David Jackson and John Humble, "Middle Managers: New Purpose, New Directions," *Journal of Management Development*, vol. 13, no. 3 (1994), pp. 15–21; Judi Brownell, "Women in Hospitality Management: General Managers' Perceptions of Factors Related to Career Development," *International Journal of Hospitality Management*, vol. 13, no. 2 (June 1994), pp. 101–17; and Deborah Breiter and Christine J. Clements, "Hospitality Management Curricula for the 21st Century," *Hospitality & Tourism Educator*, vol. 8, no. 1 (November 1996), pp. 57–60.

2. See Allan Yen-Lun Su, Judy L. Miller, and Carol Shanklin, "Perceptions of Industry Professionals and Program Administrators About Accreditation Curriculum Standards for Hospitality Programs," *Journal of Hospitality & Tourism Education*, vol. 9, no. 4 (1997/1998), pp. 36–40; and Robert H. Woods, Denny G. Rutherford, Raymond Schmidgall, and Michael Sciarini, "Hotel General Managers Focused on the Core Business," *Cornell Hotel and Restaurant Administration Quarterly*, vol. 39, no. 6 (December 1998), pp. 38–44.

3. Woods et al., "Hotel General Managers."

4. See Brownell, "Women in Hospitality Management"; Breiter and Clements, "Hospitality Management Curricula"; Esther Okeiyi, Dori Finley, and Rose Tindall Postel, "Food and Beverage Management Competencies: Educator, Industry and Student Perspectives," *Hospitality & Tourism Educator*, vol. 6, no. 4 (Fall 1994), pp. 37–40; Charles G. Partlow and Mary B. Gregoire, "Is Graduate Hospitality Education Relevant?" *Hospitality & Tourism Educator*, vol. 6, no. 3 (Summer 1994), pp. 13–16; and Richard F. Tas, Suzanne V. LaBrecque, and Howard R. Clayton, "Property-management Competencies for Management Trainees," *Cornell Hotel and Restaurant Administration Quarterly*, vol. 37, no. 3 (August 1996), pp. 90–96. For research conducted in the United Kingdom, see Tom Baum, "The U.S. and the U.K.: Comparing Expectations of Management Trainees," *Cornell Hotel and Restaurant Administration Quarterly*, vol. 32, no. 2 (August 1991), pp. 79–84. For research conducted in Taiwan, see Jui-Fong Hsu and Susan R. Gregory, "Developing Future Hotel Managers in Taiwan: From an Industry Viewpoint," *International Journal of Hospitality Management*, vol. 14, nos. 3–4 (September–December 1995), pp. 261–69.

5. James Carper, "People, Trends and Ideas," *Hotels*, vol. 28, no. 4 (April 1994), pp. 21–22.

6. See Su et al., "Perceptions of Industry Professionals," pp. 36–40; Woods et al., "Hotel General Managers," pp. 38–44; Kyoo Yup Chung, "Hotel Management Curriculum Reform Based on Required Competencies of Hotel Employees and Career Success in the Hotel Industry," *Tourism Management*, vol. 21, no. 5 (October 2000), pp. 473–87; Ardel A. Nelson and Lea Dopson, "Future of Hotel Education:

Required Skills and Knowledge for Graduates of U.S. Hospitality Programs Beyond the Year 2000—Part One," *Journal of Hospitality & Tourism Education*, vol. 13, no. 5 (2001), pp. 58–64.

7. See Linda Gorchels, Thani Jambulingam, and Timothy W. Aurand, "Executive Insights: International Marketing Managers: A Comparison of Japanese, German, and U.S. Perceptions," *Journal of International Marketing*, vol. 7, no. 1 (1999), pp. 97–105; Debra F. Cannon, "Career Dynamics of Hotel Sales and Marketing Professionals," *Journal of Hospitality & Tourism Education*, vol. 11, no. 4 (1999), pp. 40–44; Mervyn D. J. Wilson, Anna E. Murray, and Margaret A. Black, "Contract Catering: The Skills Required for the Next Millennium," *International Journal of Contemporary Hospitality Management*, vol. 12, no. 1 (2000), pp. 75–78; Christine Kay and John Russett, "Hospitality-management Competencies: Identifying Managers' Essential Skills," *Cornell Hotel and Restaurant Administration Quarterly*, vol. 41, no. 2 (April 2000), pp. 52–63; Joe Perdue, Jack Ninemeier, and Robert Woods, "Competencies Required for Club Managers," *Cornell Hotel and Restaurant Administration Quarterly*, vol. 41, no. 2 (April 2000), pp. 79–85; Kemal Birdir and Thomas E. Pearson, "Research Chefs' Competencies: A Delphi Approach," *International Journal of Contemporary Hospitality Management*, vol. 12, no. 3 (2000), pp. 205–09; and Bonnie J. Knutson and Raymond S. Schmidgall, "Challenges and Opportunities for Women: Achieving Success in Hospitality Financial Management," *Journal of Hospitality & Tourism Education*, vol. 13, nos. 3–4 (2001), pp. 45–54.

8. See Cathy H. C. Hsu, "Computer Skills Needed and Demonstrated by Hospitality Management Graduates: Perceptions of Hotel Operators" *Journal of Hospitality & Tourism Education*, vol. 7, no. 2 (Spring 1995), pp. 25–29; Wonae Cho and Daniel J. Connolly, "U.S. based Hospitality Programs: Looking to Keep Pace with Today's High-tech Industry Needs," *International Journal of Hospitality Information Technology*, vol. 1, no. 1 (1999), pp. 27–43; Deborah Breiter

and Heidi Hoart, "Competencies in Food-service Information Technology Expected by the Food-service Industry of Graduates of Hospitality Bachelor's Degree Programs in the United States," *Journal of Hospitality & Tourism Education*, vol. 12, no. 2 (August 2000), pp. 11–17; and Keith H. Mandabach, Dawn VanLeeuwen, and Priscilla Bloomquist, "Hospitality Technology Education: Student Successes in Mastering the Hidden Curriculum," *Journal of Hospitality & Tourism Education*, vol. 13, no. 1 (2001), pp. 49–56.

9. See Purdue University, Lodging, Restaurant and Tourism Index (West Lafayette, IN: Purdue, 2001). After 2003, this index became available through EBSCOhost service.

10. To determine whether managers' opinions regarding the importance of knowledge, skills, and abilities (KSAs) differ from managers' actual abilities, we used Friedman's rank test. The Friedman test is a nonparametric alternative test to a repeated measures analysis of variance. "The scores of each variable are ranked and the mean ranks of the variables are compared. The Friedman test statistic is approximately distributed as a chi-square distribution. The idea behind this statistic is that if there is no difference between groups, each subject's rankings would be random, and there would be no difference in the mean ranks across the variables." See SPSS Base 10.0 Applications Guide (Chicago: SPSS Inc., 1999), pp. 240–41.

11. A *t*-test for equality of means found significant differences between upper-level and middle-level managers' self-appraisals of KSAs in financial management ($t = 4.644$; $p < .05$) and information technology ($t = -2.475$; $p < .05$).

12. A t-test for equality of means found significant differences between upper-level and middle-level managers' importance ratings of KSAs in financial management ($t = 3.619$; $p < .05$) and marketing ($t = 2.073$; $p < .05$).

13. In addition, a multiple regression analysis revealed an r^2 of .218 ($n = 99$) and only financial management having a significantly positive effect on

management success (dependent variable measurement: 2001 base salary). The regression analysis showed that for each 1-point increase in financial management knowledge, managers can potentially earn $19,500 more annually.

14. Chung, "Hotel Management Curriculum Reform."
15. A t-test for equality of means found a significantly higher ($t = 9.55$; $p <.05$) level of compensation for upper-level managers (mean = $106,100) than for middle-level managers (mean = $52,725).
16. See American Hotel & Lodging Educational Foundation, Hospitality Compensation and Ben-

efits Survey, 2002 ed. (Washington, DC: American Hotel & Lodging Educational Foundation, 2002).
17. For discussion of level of experience required for competency development, see Charles G. Partlow, "Identification of Graduate Level Competencies in Hospitality Management," *Hospitality Research Journal,* vol. 14, no. 2 (1990), pp. 223–29. For information on managerial experience, see: Woods et al., "Hotel General Managers," p. 43.
18. Woods et al., "Hotel General Managers."
19. Carper, "People, Trends and Ideas."
20. Woods et al., "Hotel General Managers."

9.3 THE CAUSES AND CONSEQUENCES OF TURNOVER IN THE HOSPITALITY INDUSTRY Carl D. Riegel

Turnover is and has been a pervasive problem for the hospitality industry. Substantial anecdotal evidence suggests that turnover rates can reach as high as 200 or 300 percent in rank-and-file positions, and management turnover, at least at the operations level, can approach 100 percent in some organizations. While the importance of turnover as a problem for our industry was somewhat obscured by the recession of the early and mid-1990s, it has moved to the forefront with the advent of unprecedented full employment.

A low unemployment rate presents a three-pronged challenge for the industry. First, the number of workers in traditional target markets for hospitality is decreasing. This is likely to remain this way for some years to come. Second, unless the industry can present opportunities for meaningful advancement in pay and responsibility, it will continue to attract, in large measure, a transient workforce—that is, employees will view

working in the industry as something to do while they prepare to do something else or while they wait for "something better" to come along. Unfortunately, at the time of this writing, "something better" can easily be found by talented people who are not happy working in the industry. Finally, despite unprecedented efforts to change its image, the industry is frequently perceived as the employer of last resort rather than the much-touted employer of choice. Although this perception is probably not deserved, it acts to make the current labor shortage much worse for the hospitality industry than for many other fields of employment.

For service industries like hospitality, turnover is a serious problem. It makes an existing workforce shortage worse, and in some cases it can be argued that turnover is a symptom of an insidious organizational disease. More important, however, is that recent research has established a strong link between employee satisfaction and overall profitability. In this article we examine the concept of turnover in detail—what it is and why we should care. Next, we examine what many believe to be the causes of turnover, and we then turn our attention to emerging areas of concern about the real costs of employee turnover. Finally, we examine what some researchers believe will help stem excessive turnover.

✦ WHAT IS TURNOVER, AND WHY SHOULD WE BE CONCERNED?

In general, *turnover* refers to either voluntary or involuntary separation from organizations (Bluedorn, 1982). Involuntary separations (firings) can be a problem if they occur frequently, but the focus of this article is primarily on voluntary separation from organizations—that is, the process by which people quit their jobs.

Historically, hospitality organizations have perceived turnover in two ways. First, many companies are concerned that turnover costs the organization money and, because of that, unacceptable levels should be avoided. Turnover costs money for a variety of reasons, including:

1. The actual costs related to separation
2. The cost of replacing employees, such as advertising, interviewing, and moving expenses
3. Learning curve inefficiencies by new employees
4. Costs associated with the temporary disruption of the work force
5. Nonquantifiable costs due to diminished image, customer loyalties to previous employees, and so forth

Some hospitality firms take the view that turnover is not necessarily undesirable because performance and longevity have an inverse U-shaped relationship. As Figure 9.1 suggests, performance increases over the short to the

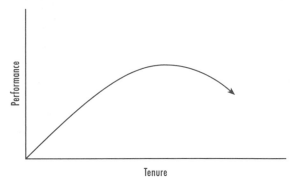

Figure 9.1 Tenure/Performance Philosophy

Source: Adapted from Staw.

intermediate term but decreases or stagnates over the long term—that is, the longer employees stay, the less likely they are to demonstrate increases in performance. More importantly, the longer they stay, the more they cost in raises and increased benefits. Firms adopting this tenure/performance position are concerned primarily with the distribution of tenure throughout the organization and more likely to concentrate on *appropriate* rates of turnover rather than *reduced* rates of turnover. For many firms holding this philosophy, turnover control strategies may be viewed as not worth the effort when pay raises are combined with anticipated future performance. The problem with both of these philosophies, as we show later in this article, is that they are limited. They view turnover as an event or phenomenon rather than a process. Thus, it is the event that managers must control rather than the process. A more expansive and probably a more effective approach does not focus on the turnover event per se; rather, it comes from a process perspective that views turnover as but one outcome of a sequential chain of events. Before we discuss this notion of phenomenon versus process, let us turn our attention to the causes of turnover.

✦ THE CAUSES OF TURNOVER

Many researchers (March and Simon, 1958; Porter and Steers, 1973; Price, 1977; McFillin, Riegel, and Enz, 1986) believe that turnover occurs as a result of a complex series of factors that influence employee attitudes and eventually affect employee behavior. Models sometimes oversimplify the processes they represent; however, a model is useful to provide a reasonable approximation of reality and is, therefore, useful in assisting us in understanding and predicting outcomes.

The model shown in Figure 9.2 uses "intent to leave" as a measure for actual departure. Intent to leave is a surrogate or stand-in measure; however, it has been well substantiated in previous research as a proxy for actual departure. As the model suggests, intent to remain in or leave an organization is a function of two related factors: the level of job satisfaction and the degree of an employee's commitment to the organization. Job satisfaction is also influenced by individual personality traits and specific job events. If the level of job satisfaction is high, then the employee's commitment to the organization tends to be strong and he or she will hold positive job attitudes and can be expected to stay on the job. On the other hand, if the level of job satisfaction is low, commitment decreases, job attitudes decline, and the employee, if given the opportunity, leaves the organization. This gives rise to new areas of concern.

Figure 9.2 Model of Turnover

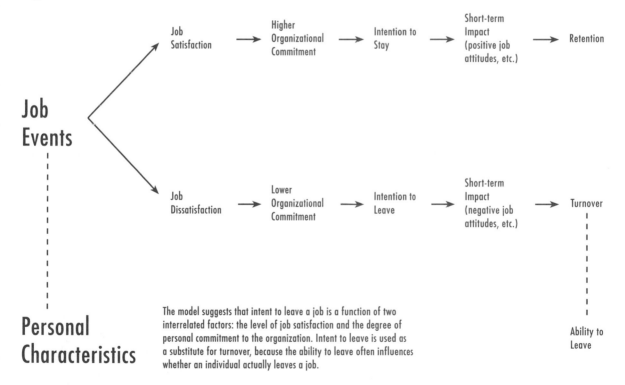

The model suggests that intent to leave a job is a function of two interrelated factors: the level of job satisfaction and the degree of personal commitment to the organization. Intent to leave is used as a substitute for turnover, because the ability to leave often influences whether an individual actually leaves a job.

Source: Adapted from McFillin, Riegel, and Enz, 1986.

✦ NEW AREAS OF CONCERN

We previously explored two of the traditional philosophies that describe how hospitality organizations view turnover. While these philosophies point out reasons for organizations to control or reduce turnover, they offer a limited perspective of the potential damage excessive turnover can have. As we discussed earlier, a more comprehensive model views turnover not as an isolated event but as a process. This process views turnover as a series of related events, and each of these events can have negative consequences for employees as well as for organizations. A closer look at Figure 9.2 demonstrates this. According to the diagram, turnover results from negative attitudes toward the organization and occurs only if an employee has the ability to leave. This means that he or she must have other job options, not need to work, or not care to work. If employees have limited or unacceptable options and do not have the ability to leave the organization, they may adopt other withdrawal behaviors such as complaining, absenteeism, poor performance, or unacceptable customer service behavior. This implies that turnover is only one choice of a variety of withdrawal behaviors available to disaffected employees, and disaffected employees can act out these behaviors either as isolated occurrences or as a set of behaviors. Furthermore, the individual choice of withdrawal behavior depends on a variety of other factors such as degree of unhappiness, perception of self-worth, and, most importantly, the ability to find acceptable alternative employment.

Given this view of turnover, companies with high rates of turnover are likely to experience a variety of negative outcomes. One way to categorize these outcomes is to look at how they affect individual employees as well as how they affect the organization in both the short and the long term. Figure 9.3 indicates that both organizations and individual employees suffer from the effects of high rates of turnover, including attendance problems, decreased cooperation, decreased work performance, and even sabotage. In the longer term, however, the effects are more systemic and potentially more devastating. For example, high rates of turnover can worsen existing turnover rates, contribute to system problems such as poor customer relations, and even eventually limit a firm's ability to develop and implement strategy. The potential dollar cost of this is incalculable but potentially enormous. A question of major importance for firms with high turnover rates is not only who leaves but also who stays. In some cases, it may be that employees who stay with an organization are not necessarily the ones the organization wants to keep and those who do leave are not necessarily the ones the organization wants to see go. In some cases, outstanding employees find the organizational environment so dissatisfying they opt to separate from the company, and those who remain are those who can adapt to a dysfunctional environment or those who have no choice but to stay.

In addition, there is evidence that excessive turnover rates can have a substantial and negative impact on profitability. Recently, a great deal of discussion has centered on customer loyalty and the importance of avoiding customer defections. Simply put, the argument goes something like this. It costs a great deal to create new customers. The costs associated with advertising, promotion, and other marketing efforts are staggering. Thus, it is wiser to try to retain existing guests than to create new ones. Furthermore, the longer

Figure 9.3 The Effects of Turnover on Hospitality Organizations

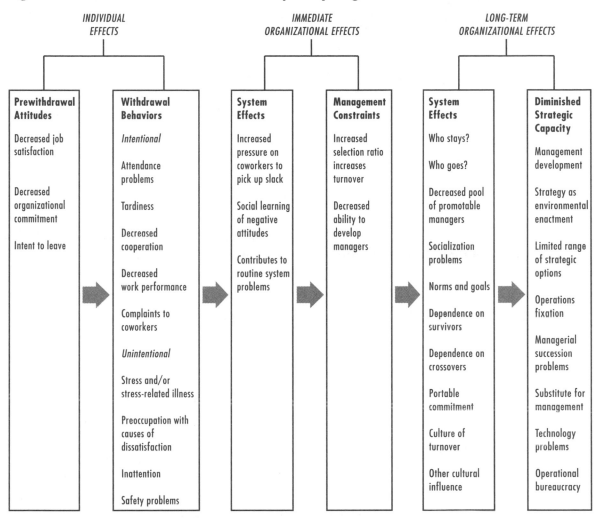

INDIVIDUAL EFFECTS · IMMEDIATE ORGANIZATIONAL EFFECTS · LONG-TERM ORGANIZATIONAL EFFECTS

Prewithdrawal Attitudes

Decreased job satisfaction

Decreased organizational commitment

Intent to leave

Withdrawal Behaviors

Intentional

Attendance problems

Tardiness

Decreased cooperation

Decreased work performance

Complaints to coworkers

Unintentional

Stress and/or stress-related illness

Preoccupation with causes of dissatisfaction

Inattention

Safety problems

System Effects

Increased pressure on coworkers to pick up slack

Social learning of negative attitudes

Contributes to routine system problems

Management Constraints

Increased selection ratio increases turnover

Decreased ability to develop managers

System Effects

Who stays?

Who goes?

Decreased pool of promotable managers

Socialization problems

Norms and goals

Dependence on survivors

Dependence on crossovers

Portable commitment

Culture of turnover

Other cultural influence

Diminished Strategic Capacity

Management development

Strategy as environmental enactment

Limited range of strategic options

Operations fixation

Managerial succession problems

Substitute for management

Technology problems

Operational bureaucracy

---

customers stay with a company, the more they are worth. Generally, they buy more, buy more frequently, and are less price-sensitive. In fact, one management writer (Reichheld, 1996) suggested that decreasing customer defections by as little as 5 points can double profits. With respect to the monetary value of customer or guest loyalty, several researchers (Heskett et al., 1984) suggested a strong relationship between employee satisfaction, customer loyalty, and profitability. They call this concept the *service-profit chain*. As Figure 9.4 illustrates, employee retention is a key driver in creating customer retention and is, therefore, a critical factor in determining profitability.

The new concerns about turnover discussed in this section strongly indicate that the conventional thinking about turnover may capture just a small portion of its devastating effects. Now let's look at ways of reducing turnover.

Figure 9.4 **The Service-Profit Chain**

Increased Profitability & Growth

Customer Loyalty

Customer Satisfaction

Perceived Service Value

Employee Retention & Productivity

Employee Satisfaction

Internal Work Quality

Source: Adapted from Heskett et al., 1994.

✦ WHAT CAN BE DONE?

A study of turnover in the hospitality industry (McFillen, Riegel, and Enz, 1986) found that hospitality employees in one organization ranked these reasons as the most likely causes for high turnover rates:

1. Treatment by superiors
2. Amount of work hours
3. Job pressure
4. Scheduling
5. Training
6. Fringe benefit packages
7. Better opportunities elsewhere
8. Physical demands of the job

A short-term strategy would be for managers to focus on these reasons—in other words, working on fair treatment of employees, creating fair and reasonable schedules, and so forth. However, these strategies do not necessarily address the causes of excessive turnover and are likely to have limited effectiveness and to be short-lived. A longer-term solution would take into account the causes of worker dissatisfaction and attempt to deal with these in a comprehensive and continuous manner.

Frederick Herzberg (1976) suggests that dissatisfaction occurs as a result of a lack of what he calls "hygiene factors" and that satisfaction occurs as a result of what he calls "motivators." While there is not necessarily any linkage in the organizational behavior literature between job satisfaction and job performance, a substantial body of theory does suggest that satisfied employees adopt prosocial and, therefore, committed behaviors toward the organization. Herzberg says hygiene factors that can cause dissatisfaction among employees include salary, working conditions, fringe benefits, and job security. While paying a fair salary or providing job security decreases dissatisfaction, it does not necessarily create satisfaction in employees. Motivators or satisfiers recognized by Herzberg include achievement, recognition, challenging work, responsibility, and advancement. These factors, if provided for by the organization, create satisfaction and therefore commitment. Thus, hospitality managers who are concerned about turnover as an insidious disease process should not only take care of the extrinsic job factors, such as job security and salary, but they also must pay a great deal of attention to providing opportunities for advancement, challenging work, and so forth.

In addition to attending to environmental factors in the organization, paying attention to the selection of employees in the first place goes a long way toward quelling dissatisfaction and, therefore, diminishing turnover. An axiom in the human resource field is that the goal of selection is not to hire the best-qualified employee but rather to hire the best employee for the particular job, the point being that it is important to match prospective employees to the organization and the position. Similarly, efforts to select employees who will be successful in a particular job as well as successful in the organizational culture enhance the likelihood of their retention. Selection is an important human resource function that is worthy of substantial effort and care.

✦ SUMMARY

Turnover is a problem of longstanding significance for the hospitality industry. The effects of high turnover rates on hospitality businesses are substantially greater than many existing philosophies suggest, and dealing with turnover as an isolated event fails to acknowledge its causes and, therefore, is likely to have limited impact as a turnover control strategy. Comprehensive approaches that attempt, on the one hand, to eliminate sources of dissatisfaction and, on the other hand, to promote employee satisfaction and retention have greater potential to strengthen commitment and, therefore, encourage a wide variety of prosocial behaviors that will strengthen organizational effectiveness, eliminate withdrawal behaviors (of which turnover is one), and, ultimately, contribute to guest loyalty and profitability.

9.4 CURRENT ISSUES IN HOSPITALITY EMPLOYMENT LAW

SUZANNE K. MURRMANN AND CHERYLYNN BECKER

Fairness in the workplace is a significant issue affecting the productivity, loyalty, and commitment employees have to their organizations. The treatment an employee receives from his or her supervisor affects the worker's motivation to provide excellent service to customers, ultimately affecting the bottomline profits of the organization. Many factors influence workplace justice. These include the voluntary human resource management policies that organizations put into place to provide fair and equal employee treatment. In addition, a significant number of federal and state laws and regulations protect employees from various forms of discrimination, provide employees with certain rights, and specify actions employers must take when hiring and managing their workforce. Such laws may vary in their wording and coverage from state to state. However, they generally mirror law at the federal level. These laws, which significantly affect the human resource function in hospitality organizations, fall under four general categories:

- Those governing equal employment and opportunity and nondiscrimination
- Those governing compensation and working hours
- Those governing the health and safety of workers
- Those governing labor relations and collective bargaining (Jackson and Schuler, 2000)

The judicial process is a dynamic one. Continual changes occur in laws and regulations due to amendments to existing laws, enactment of new laws, and interpretations made by courts and regulatory agencies. It is mandatory for managers to keep up to date with the status of laws that affect their HR activities. Even with appropriate legal counsel, day-to-day activities of supervisors and managers are often where organizations run into legal problems. Therefore, it is necessary that managers be aware of their legal obligations.

Because space does not permit a full discussion of all relevant employment laws, the following text concentrates on federal laws that have seen significant changes in the last decade as well as those that are forecasted to change significantly in the next several years (Flynn, 2000; Goldberg, 1998). They include sexual harassment and employer liability under Title VII of the Civil Rights Act, the Americans with Disabilities Act, the Family and Medical Leave Act, and the Immigration Reform and Control Act. A discussion of these laws and implications for hospitality managers follows.

✦ SEXUAL HARASSMENT

In general, *sexual harassment* is defined as unwelcome sexual conduct in the workplace that is a term or condition of employment. Complaints of sexual harassment fall under two categories: quid pro quo and hostile work environment. Quid pro quo harassment is said to occur when submission to or rejection of unwelcome sexual conduct by an individual is used as a basis for employment decisions affecting an employee. In other words, when a supervisor demands sexual favors from his or her subordinate and either promises an employment benefit, such as a raise or promotion, or threatens the employee with loss of such benefits, quid pro quo harassment exists. Such activities may be subtle or overt, and the employee must show that he or she belongs to a protected group, was subject to unwelcome harassment that was based on his or her gender, and that acceptance or refusal resulted or could result in tangible changes to the working conditions.

While quid pro quo harassment implies an exchange of sexual favors for work benefits, *hostile work environment harassment* refers to the overall working environment in which employees function. Hostile work environment harassment is conduct that unreasonably interferes with the ability of an employee to perform his or her job properly or creates an intimidating, hostile, or offensive working environment. This may be so even if it does not lead to tangible or economic job consequences. As in quid pro quo harassment, the activities or conduct in question are unwelcome by the employee and are based on gender. The employee must also show that they are sufficiently pervasive and severe as to have caused an abusive working environment and that the employer is liable for these activities. Typical examples of this type of harassment include unwelcome physical touching; whistling, leering, improper gestures, or offensive remarks; unwelcome comments about appearance; sexual jokes; and the use of sexually explicit derogatory or otherwise offensive language.

Sexual harassment in the workplace continues to be an important discrimination issue, particularly with recent Supreme Court rulings (Goldberg, 1998). Two of particular note, *Burlington Industries v. Ellerth* and *Faragher v. Boca Raton,*[1] have significantly shaped the obligations of hospitality managers. In them, the Court clearly articulated the liability of employers for the actions of their harassing supervisors. First, in cases in which an employee has suffered tangible, detrimental employment actions, such as demotion, termination, or loss of benefits, the employer is strictly liable regardless of fault. Strict liability is premised on the fact that the supervisors are acting for the employer (company), and regardless of whether or not the employer can show it has an antidiscrimination policy, final responsibility rests with the company. In cases, however, where the employee has suffered no loss of tangible job benefits, the employer can avoid liability by showing that reasonable care was taken to prevent and promptly correct any sexually harassing behavior. Documentation that the harassed employee subsequently failed to take advantage of any preventive or corrective opportunities provided by the employer further minimizes the likelihood of employer liability for harassment charges.

For hospitality managers to protect themselves against charges of sexual harassment, they need to focus on three major areas: (1) implementation and dissemination of antiharassment and complaint policies, (2) training of personnel, and (3) complaint investigation.

Though the Court has not specifically ruled that companies must have policies specifically targeted to sexual harassment, many human resource management professionals feel employers can more easily demonstrate their "reasonable duty of care" by developing separate antiharassment policies. Such policies should explicitly define sexual harassment, both in terms of quid pro quo and hostile environment harassment, and give specific examples of inappropriate conduct. Though this point seems obvious, the policy should also unambiguously prohibit such conduct. It should also indicate protection for employees from retaliation for reporting harassment. Numerous studies have shown that employees are often afraid to report inappropriate activities because of fear of retaliation by their supervisors. Managers should develop and include in their policy multiple avenues for filing harassment complaints. One such avenue would be to start with the employee's immediate supervisor; however, an additional route would be to bypass the supervisor and complain to an individual outside of the supervisor's direct chain of command. Assurance of prompt and thorough investigations and privacy are equally important components of an antiharassment policy.

As necessary as a well-developed and well-written policy is, it is also important that the policy be disseminated in such a way that all personnel in the hospitality organization are aware of it. Merely including it in an employee handbook may not be sufficient. Antiharassment policies should be posted in locations regularly visited by employees as well as discussed with new employees. This is especially important in an industry where a significant part of the labor pool is composed of employees who do not read and speak English as their primary language. The company should also attempt to keep written acknowledgment that each employee understands the policy.

Periodic training in what constitutes sexual harassment is essential for the prevention of misconduct in the workplace and the defense of the employer against liability in court. The purpose of such training is to make supervisors and employees aware of conduct that constitutes harassment and provide them with mechanisms for effectively dealing with it. Training must be tailored to the individual workplace and take into account the diversity of the workforce; however, a number of key components should be common to training in this area. Though all employees should attend training, separate sessions should be held for supervisors and managers to instruct them in their obligations to subordinates and their responsibilities for investigating harassment complaints. The language and the customs of employees should always be taken into account when developing training materials, particularly when such activities as role-playing are used. Training in the hospitality industry should take into account the interaction of employees with third parties such as customers and outside vendors. Managers must be aware that the employer has an additional duty of care in the area of customer harassment of employees, and they should be trained to delicately but effectively deal with such situations. Finally, care must be taken to select an appropriate resource for carrying out training. This may be an in-house trainer or an outside individual or firm. In any case, the individual selected should have recognized expertise in the area of sexual harassment.

The final area of concern for managers is prompt investigation of harassment complaints. The employer who fails to document fair investigation of employee complaints will more than likely be found liable for harassment. All complaints should be investigated as swiftly as possible by an unbiased investigator who is sensitive to the privacy concerns of the complainant. If, during the course of the investigation, there is sufficient reason to believe the complainant and the accused should be separated, the complainant should not be assigned to a lesser job. Such action could be seen as retaliation for filing a complaint. Relevant material and information should be obtained, in private, from the accused and additional witnesses. Based on this, immediate and appropriate corrective action should be taken by doing whatever is necessary to end the harassment, to make the employee whole by restoring lost employment benefits or opportunities, and to prevent the misconduct from recurring. If appropriate, disciplinary action should be taken against the offending supervisor or employee, ranging from reprimand to discharge. Generally, the corrective action should reflect the severity of the conduct. Document the findings and subsequent steps taken, if any, and place this documentation in a confidential investigation file. The Equal Employment Opportunity Commission policy guidance on sexual harassment suggests that follow-up inquiries be made to ensure that harassment is not resumed and that the employee does not suffer retaliation. Finally, use what was learned from these investigations to streamline or customize future training and policy restatements in this area to more closely align with specific company needs.

✦ AMERICANS WITH DISABILITIES ACT

The Americans with Disabilities Act of 1990 (ADA) prohibits an employer from discriminating against a qualified individual with a disability with respect to job application procedures, hiring, advancement, discharge, compensation, training, and other "terms, conditions, and privileges of employment." The act has undergone almost a decade of interpretation by the courts, which continue to refine and define its coverage and the responsibilities of hospitality managers. As noted by many professionals in human resource management, these rulings at times leave as many unresolved questions as they answer concerning employer responsibilities.

Under the ADA, a qualified individual is defined as "an individual with a disability who, with or without reasonable accommodation, can perform the essential function of the employment position that such individual holds or desires."[2] There are two questions the manager must ask when determining whether an individual is qualified. First, does the individual satisfy the prerequisites for the position, such as the appropriate educational background, employment experience, skills, or licenses? Second, can he or she perform the "essential functions" of the position with or without reasonable accommodation? The former is answered by comparing the qualifications of the individual to job-related requirements and production standards traditional to the industry—for example, number of rooms cleaned per day. When identifying requirements, employers should use those used for other employees in the position and not those selected to intentionally exclude the disabled person. The latter question may be answered by defining the fundamental job duties of a position in a well-constructed written job description. Factors suggested for identifying essential functions include the amount of time spent performing the function, the number of

employees available to perform the task, the work experience of past incumbents and present employees in the position, and the consequence of not performing the function. For instance, several courts have found attendance to be an essential function of the job because the inability to maintain regular attendance creates an undue hardship upon an employer.[3]

A disability is defined under the Act as (1) "a physical or mental impairment that substantially limits one or more of the major life activities of such individual," (2) "a record of such an impairment," or (3) "being regarded as having such an impairment."[4] Impairments may include physiological disorders or conditions, cosmetic disfigurements, and anatomical loss affecting one or more major body systems. Before 1998, it was generally accepted that for an impairment to be covered under the definition of a disability, it needed to be a permanent condition that, if uncorrected, substantially limited a major life activity such as walking, seeing, hearing, or speaking. Several Supreme Court rulings have limited this definition, stating that "an individual's corrections, medications, and even subconscious mechanisms for coping with an impairment are to be considered when assessing whether that individual is disabled" and covered under the ADA (Sherwyn, Eigen, and Klausner, 2000). These rulings, though limiting the definition of a disability in one respect, in no way clarify the issue of what is considered a disability, nor may they actually limit the number of individuals claiming discrimination if managers continue to perceive individuals impaired even with corrective devices.

Traditional human resource functions and employment decisions can be considered discriminatory under the ADA. These include such activities as recruiting, advertising, and the processing of applications for employment, hiring, updating, promotion, termination, compensation, job assignment, and the like. In other words, the ADA mirrors, to a great extent, the rights of protected groups under Title VII of the Civil Rights Act. Hospitality managers should be aware of a number of issues unique to disability law. An employer risks violating the ADA by asking about medical conditions and disabilities in a preemployment situation. Questions at this point should be job-related, with inquiry limited to the applicant's ability to perform the essential functions of the job as described in the written job description. Preemployment medical examinations and tests, with the exception of testing for illegal drug use, are also seen as discriminatory in the hospitality industry. The ADA also prohibits disparate treatment discrimination—that is, limiting and segregating employees in a way that affects their opportunities because of a disability. A hospitality employer that demonstrated a pattern of hiring disabled job applicants for back-of-the-house, non-customer-contact positions, though such applicants were able to perform effectively in customer contact positions, would be demonstrating potentially discriminatory behavior. The use of employment tests or other selection criteria that are not job-related to screen out disabled applicants is prohibited under the ADA. For example, if an employer requires an interview that is job-related and consistent with business necessity as part of the application process, it would not be legal to reject a hearing-impaired applicant solely because he or she could not be interviewed.[5] Finally, failure to reasonably accommodate disabilities

of either job applicants or employees constitutes discrimination under the ADA.

Accommodation for individuals with disabilities is at the core of the ADA. By law, *reasonable accommodation* mandates employers to accommodate qualified individuals who can perform the essential functions of a job, unless this causes significant difficulty or expense—that is, undue hardship.[6] Accommodations can be modifications or adjustments (1) in the job application or testing process that allow a qualified applicant with a disability to be considered for a position equally with other applicants, (2) in the workplace or in the manner or method in which the job is performed that allow the employee to perform the job, or (3) that enable the disabled employee to enjoy the benefits and privileges of the job equally to those without disabilities. Types of accommodations may include but are not necessarily limited to the following:

1. Modifications of existing facilities (ramps and entrances, bathroom facilities, workstations, etc.)
2. Job restructuring
3. Modified work schedules
4. Reassignment to vacant positions
5. Acquisition and modification of equipment or devices
6. Adjustment or modification of examinations or training materials
7. Provision of qualified readers and interpreters (for preemployment activities, etc.)

The EEOC has issued guidelines for employers to follow for compliance. Hospitality managers should follow these procedures. Using the interactive process outlined in the following guidelines should increase the likelihood of employees viewing a manager as reasonable and concerned about their needs.

1. Notify employees and job applicants of the employer's obligation under the Act to make reasonable accommodations.
2. Wait for a request for a reasonable accommodation by a qualified individual with a disability.
3. Analyze the particular job to determine its purpose and essential functions. Communicate to the employee your understanding of the essential functions of the job and the abilities needed to perform them.
4. Consult with the disabled individual to ascertain the precise job-related limitations imposed by the disability and how those limitations can be overcome.
5. With the disabled individual's assistance, identify potential accommodations and assess the effectiveness of each in enabling the individual to perform the essential functions of the job.
6. Consider the disabled individual's accommodation preferences and select and implement the accommodation most appropriate for both the employee and employer. This is a final decision that should be made by the manager.

Given the relative youth of the ADA, it is anticipated that interpretation of even the most basic areas of the law—for example, the definition of a disability—will continue to evolve. There are, however, certain steps that many feel to be appropriate for managers (Sovereign, 1999). Facilities should be made as accessible as possible. This is particularly true of the hospitality industry, given its public accommodation requirement. Because the concept of reasonable accommodation is based on a clear understanding of the essential functions of the job, well-written job descriptions are extremely important in managing liability

associated with the ADA. With the exception of drug testing, all preemployment medical inquiries and examinations should be eliminated. Always attempt to accommodate a qualified disabled individual. A case of undue hardship can be made after accommodation is researched. Finally, in organizations that are large enough to support service staff, an individual should be designated as the ADA resource for other managers and used when accommodations are requested.

✦ FAMILY AND MEDICAL LEAVE ACT OF 1993

All hospitality employers with 50 or more employees are covered by the Family and Medical Leave Act of 1993 (FMLA). The FMLA was passed in an attempt to balance the demands of the workplace with the family and medical needs of employees. Employers both in and outside of the hospitality industry expressed grave concerns over the impact of the law on workplace productivity and employer compliance. Many of these fears proved unfounded; many, however, were not. Compliance with the law has proved cumbersome, given its technical recordkeeping nature. Since the enactment of this act, the Department of Labor (DOL), which oversees the FMLA, has seen thousands of complaints filed and has changed the guidelines and directives to comply with dozens of court rulings.

The FMLA allows employees up to 12 weeks of unpaid leave during any 12-month period to deal with family and medical issues. Companies that employ 50 or more people (within a 75-mile radius), including part-time and temporary workers, during each of 20 or more calendar workweeks in a year are covered. In order for an employee to be eligible for leave, he or she must have worked at least 1,250 hours for the employer. An eligible employee may take unpaid leave for the following reasons:

- The birth of a child

- The placement of a child with the employee for adoption or foster care

- A serious health condition of a spouse, child, or parent

- The employee's own serious health condition

The DOL regulations define *serious health condition* as any illness, injury, impairment, or physical or mental condition that involves:

- Any period of incapacity or treatment involving inpatient care in a hospital, hospice, or residential mental care facility

- Any period of incapacity requiring absences from work, school, or other regular daily activities of more than three calendar days that also involves continuing treatment by a health care provider. (*Continuing treatment* means either treatment two or more times by a health care provider or one treatment that results in a regimen of continuing treatment. A *regimen of continuing treatment* includes only those treatments that cannot be initiated without a visit to a health care provider, such as taking prescription drugs. It does not include taking over-the-counter medication, nor does it include therapy such as bed rest, drinking fluids, and exercise.)

- Continuing treatment by a health care provider for any period of incapacity because of pregnancy or for prenatal care, or for a chronic or long-term health condition that is incurable or so serious that, if not treated, would likely result in a period of incapacity of more than three calendar days

As a general rule, ailments such as the common cold, the flu, earaches, upset stomach, minor ulcers, headaches other than migraine, routine dental or orthodontia problems, and periodontal diseases are not serious health conditions unless complications arise.

Employers covered by the FMLA must post notice of the act and their obligations as well as provide additional information to employees concerning their entitlements and obligations through standard mechanisms such as employee handbooks and manuals. An employee requesting leave is required to give 30 days notice to his or her employer, if possible. If such notice is not possible, the employee must provide "such notice as is practical" so that the employer has an opportunity to plan for the employee's absence. As little as one to two days' notice (or less) may be sufficient in emergency situations. Employers may require a medical certification, such as a doctor's statement, from a health care provider to support leave requests. Additional opinions concerning the employee's condition and periodic reports from the employee on leave regarding his or her status and intent to return may also be required. During the time of the leave, the employer must continue existing health care benefits.

Leave can be taken intermittently or on a schedule that reduces the typical number of hours per workday or workweek when medically necessary. Incremental leave may be taken in increments as short as one hour.

Under the FMLA, the employer is obligated to place the employee, once returned from leave, in the same position he or she left. If this is not possible, the employee must be placed in a position equivalent in pay, benefits, and other terms and conditions of employment. Based on rulings to date, "equivalent" appears to be construed as "identical" by the DOL.

A number of significant compliance issues cause difficulty for human resource professionals and employment law attorneys. Because of their technical nature, they are not discussed here. However, several issues are worthy of note because they affect hospitality managers and supervisors in general.

While attendance has been successfully defended by several employers under the ADA as an essential function of a job, FMLA leave absences cannot be used in discipline and termination decisions. Therefore, it is particularly important in intermittent leave situations to record the reasons for absences. Supervisors should be encouraged to document "verbatim reasons" for absences. This information allows a manager to conduct an "FMLA audit" of employees who may be undergoing disciplinary action for excessive absenteeism.

Though the FMLA does allow for managers to require medical certification from employers for leave purposes, as well as second opinions, overuse of such information could open up liability under the ADA (Shea, 2000). Managers must be wary of asking for more medical information than is necessary for the purposes of granting FMLA leave. Medical certification is a useful tool to employ if there is doubt about the existence or extent of an employee's health condition. However, it is not necessary as long as the absence has been noted as FMLA leave.

A "serious" health condition under the act may include many "minor" illnesses and conditions of short duration. Absences of less than three days may also be considered legitimate reasons for leave. This is due to the interpretation of the FMLA-specific wording. Indeed, many experts in the area agree that regulations have gone beyond the intent of the legislation in terms of interpreting what a serious illness should be. Managers should be aware that, at this point, a liberal interpretation must be placed on this definition.

✦ IMMIGRATION REFORM AND CONTROL ACT OF 1986

In 1986, Congress enacted the Immigration Reform and Control Act (IRCA) in response to significant increases in undocumented immigration and vocal concerns from unhappy voters. This law was an attempt to control undocumented immigration in a number of ways, including the imposition of sanctions on employers for knowingly hiring undocumented workers. In addition, the law provided for amnesty for undocumented immigrants who could demonstrate a record of continuous residence in the United States for a designated period. These regulations, along with increased support for border patrol activities, were thought to significantly diminish the attractiveness of U.S. jobs for undocumented workers, thereby protecting jobs and wages for legal workers in the United States.

Critics of the IRCA argued that it would encourage employers to engage in greater discrimination against U.S. citizens and legal aliens based on their appearance and cultural background, and safeguards against such discrimination were included in its content. However, several studies to date have shown that even with these safeguards in place, a pattern of discriminating against individuals based on physical appearance or accent exists

(Phillips and Massey, 1999). Such discrimination includes the denial of jobs as well as paying lower wages to undocumented workers. This decrease in pay, below legal minimum, is thought to take place to compensate for the risk involved in being sanctioned under the act.

The IRCA requires employers to verify the employment eligibility of all employees hired by and working for the organization and to complete and maintain eligibility paperwork. This paperwork, commonly referred to as *I-9 forms,* must be maintained on all employees, U.S. citizens as well as aliens authorized to work in the country. The Immigration and Naturalization Service (INS) is charged with enforcing the IRCA. However, any number of other federal agencies, including the EEOC, the Justice Department, and the Department of Labor, may request a review of the eligibility documentation records of a company. Employers must verify an employee's or applicant's identity and eligibility to work by requesting proof of both within three days of hire. Documents that can be used to verify identity include a state driver's license, state or school I.D. card, and a voter's registration card. Eligibility to work may be established using a number of documents including a Social Security card, birth certificate issued by a U.S. state, county, or municipal authority, or an unexpired INS employment authorization. Some documents, such as a U.S. passport, establish both identity and work eligibility. A complete list of all appropriate documents is provided on the back page of the I-9 form.

As mentioned earlier, the Act contains antidiscrimination provisions that are in addition to and do not change discrimination under Title VII of the Civil Rights Act. The IRCA bans discrimination against legal aliens or people intending to become U.S. citizens. An alien has employment rights equal to a U.S. citizen, unless citizenship is a bona fide occupational qualification. If an alien is authorized to work in the United States, an employer cannot give preference to a U.S. citizen who is less qualified.

Employers have several responsibilities under the law:

1. Employers cannot request more or different documents than are required under the provisions of the law. Though it is often easier for managers to require specific, approved documentation such as a driver's license or Social Security card, they must accept any qualified document from the I-9 list if it appears to be valid.

2. Employers cannot knowingly use, attempt to use, possess, obtain, accept, or receive any forged, counterfeit, altered, or falsely made documents. It is often extremely difficult to identify counterfeit documents. However, managers should closely scrutinize the documentation of all applicants for obvious falsification—for example, multiple individuals with the same or similar Social Security numbers.

3. Employers cannot backdate or otherwise falsely make I-9 forms appear as if they are or have been in compliance with the IRCA. Individuals responsible for hiring on an ongoing basis should perform eligibility verification. Paperwork should be kept up to date.

4. Employers must have new employees complete Section 1 of the employment verification I-9 at the time of the hire by filling in the correct information, signing, and dating the form.

5. Employers are responsible for reviewing and ensuring that the employees fully and properly complete Section 1 of the employment verification I-9. Applicants who do not fully complete this section should not be hired.

6. Employers must examine the original documents(s) (the only exception is a certified copy of a birth certificate) presented by the employee and then fully complete Section 2 of the employment verification I-9.

7. Employers must keep the employment verification I-9 for three years after the date employment begins or one year after the person's employment is terminated, whichever is later.

In order to avoid penalties under the IRCA, hospitality managers should use the following checklist:

- Verify employment status of every person hired.

- Employ only U.S. citizens and aliens authorized to work in the United States.

- Verify employees' status within three days of their being hired to work.

- Inform each new job applicant, either orally or in writing, that you hire only U.S. citizens and aliens lawfully authorized to work in the United States and that you require all new employees to complete the designated verification for I-9.

- Examine documentation presented by new employees, record the information on the I-9, and sign. Retain these documents for three years.

- Do not ask for proof of citizenship or authorization to work before deciding to hire the applicant.

- Do not refuse to offer employment to anyone on the basis of foreign accent or appearance.

- Do not discharge present employees based on foreign appearance or language.

The above discussion of these key issues only scratches the surface of the legal challenges facing hotel HR managers. When you consider that the 535 members of Congress and the members of 50 state legislatures are constantly proposing laws that result in regulation, it is easy to see why HR managers can face daunting tasks in assisting the organization and its managers in staying out of legal trouble.

ENDNOTES FOR SECTION 9.4

1. *Burlington Industries v. Ellerth*: 524 U.S. 742; 118 S. Crt. 2257 (1998); *Faragher v. Boca Raton*: 524 U.S. 775, 118 S. Crt. 2275 (1998).
2. 42 U.S.C. §1211(8).
3. *Tyndall v. National Education Centers*: 31 F. 3rd 209 (4th Cir. 1994); *Earl v. Mervyns Inc.*: No. 99–4264 (11th Cir. 2000).
4. 42 U.S.C. §12102(2).
5. 29 CFR Part 1630, Appendix § 1630.15(a).

6. Undue hardship is assessed by reviewing the nature and cost of the accommodations needed; the financial resources of the employer; the size of the company and the number of its facilities; the financial resources of the facility itself; and the effect of the accommodation on the expenses or operations of the facility, on other employees' ability to do their jobs, and on the facility's ability to conduct business (ADA Sec. 101[10], 42 U.S.C. 12111[10]; EEOC Sec. 1630.2[p]).

9.5 THE STRATEGIC AND OPERATIONAL ROLES OF HUMAN RESOURCES—AN EMERGING MODEL J. Bruce Tracey and Arthur E. Nathan

Effective human-resources management is one of the most important considerations in creating and maintaining a competitive advantage for a hotel (or, for that matter, any hospitality organization). Indeed, human-capital considerations top the list of current managerial concerns in the hospitality industry (Enz, 2001, 38–45). Despite the industry's concern with human resources, however, the HR function is oddly disconnected from the line function. That disconnect is evident on two primary levels. First, we argue that many business leaders fail to fully consider HR influences when making long-term plans. While most executives acknowledge the importance of HR for implementing strategic plans—"making it happen"—we have seen few who formally incorporate HR concerns when developing a strategic direction. While the predominant framework requires consideration of HR strengths and weaknesses during the strategy-formulation process, HR is primarily viewed as an "enabling" function, responsible for implementing "the plan," and thus largely ignored during the initial planning stages.

Second, we argue that many HR departments fail to execute even the most basic functions effectively. Many firms' policies and practices are archaic, inflexible, and do not directly benefit those who are most keenly affected by HR actions. Based on those concerns, we advocate the need for a new model of HR—one that should be used as a guide for developing vision, values, and goals, and one that creates a more effective and

efficient function for attracting, developing, and retaining quality employees.

To explain our model, we will first discuss the manner in which HR can contribute to the strategic-planning process. We then present data that demonstrate the link between HR practices and systems on important business objectives. Finally, we offer some ideas that may change the prevailing paradigm and the operational role of HR in hospitality organizations.

✦ HR AND STRATEGIC PLANNING

Our observations are that HR suffers from a negative image in many hospitality organizations and that, sadly, it has earned that negative image. The following views of HR may be familiar: HR is basically an employee-advocate function and represents the "soft" side of the business; HR is a cost center since it does not generate revenue; HR serves as an administrative-support office and organizes the company picnic; and HR is responsible for implementing strategy, not developing strategy. We could go on, but the point is made: human resources gets much lip service but no respect.

One of the reasons for this negative image may be the narrow application of the strategic-planning process taken by many business leaders. Too often, the human-resources function is left out of key planning steps. The following comment illustrates our point. A successful hospitality executive and colleague of ours maintains that his primary function is to determine the vision and direction of the firm, and then it's up to HR and other departments to "make it happen." This statement summarizes his views:

> HR as a function does not *per se* have a dedicated role in the strategic-planning process. Corporate strategic planning begins with an external assessment of opportunities and threats and an internal assessment of firm strengths and weaknesses. This process is not driven by a function or discipline formula, but rather by an evaluation designed to determine the relative importance and veracity of assumptions management has made about the industry and the firm. Management combines its fact-based knowledge with its assumptions and beliefs about the business it is evaluating. Strategic planning, at its core, is the process by which the veracity of these assumptions and the relative importance each has to the overall outcome are revealed. Functional executives confound and corrupt the initial stages of the planning process by becoming caught up in interdisciplinary issues that should be subservient to the strategy process they aspire to influence. As such, the CEO is forced to pull the process of formulating strategy away from these executives and rely more heavily on his or her own judgment or a formal strategy group of executives without discipline responsibilities.[1]

In this leader's view, HR plays a subservient and reactionary role in the business-planning process. While this is only one individual's perspective, we've encountered many who share similar views. We contend that HR considerations must be taken into account not only during strategy implementation, but also during the process of developing that strategy. Indeed, the prevailing models of business planning support this contention.

Several approaches can be used to predict a firm's competitive position and develop strategic plans. The traditional SWOT model (i.e., strength, weakness, opportunity, and threat) is based on a matching process such that a firms strategic direction is based on the fit between external conditions (i.e., opportunities and threats) and internal capabilities (i.e., strengths and weaknesses). Based on this assessment of fit, leaders can then take actions intended to achieve a sustained level of competitiveness—for instance, by using internal strengths to exploit external opportunities and taking advantage of opportunities to motivate change and fix internal weaknesses. Another popular framework, VRIO analysis, extends the SWOT model and maintains that competitive advantage is gained by identifying and exploiting the rare, distinctive competencies of the firm (Barney, 1997). The VRIO explanation considers a firm's resources—understood in terms of value, rarity, imitability, and organization—as keys to long-term effectiveness. In simplified terms, value is characterized by the firm's internal resources that can be used to respond to external threats; rarity is associated with the scarcity of such resources in the external environment; imitability is based on the ability of competitors to acquire, duplicate, or substitute valued resources; and organization is associated with the firm's structure and systems that are used to extract the greatest degree of value from a given resource.

These and other models (e.g., portfolio assessments, competitor ranking) that can be used to analyze strategic positions and develop plans have at least one thing in common: the human element is central to an analysis of internal strengths, resources, and capabilities. Technology, in contrast, is quite imitable and thus should not be considered as a source of competitive advantage. Human capabilities, and the social context in which such capabilities are applied, are difficult and perhaps impossible to copy or transfer to settings outside the focal context. While access to capital, relative market share, brand image, and service quality are all essential to a hospitality business, such concerns would be largely irrelevant if the appropriate human resources were unavailable. Therefore, while HR may not be the most important consideration during the strategic-planning process, this factor cannot be ignored when developing long-range plans.

✦ EVIDENCE FOR THE STRATEGIC IMPORTANCE OF HR

Despite HR's apparent image problem, it remains an essential function. Much has been written about the critical role of HR for achieving business goals and objectives, and there is a growing literature that shows HR policies, practices, and systems are related to a variety of financial and operational success indicators.[2] Indeed, there is some rather compelling evidence that the proper alignment between HR systems and business strategy will enhance a firm's performance.[3] We will complement this literature by presenting two hospitality-specific examples that support the strategic importance of HR for not only implementing long-range plans, but also developing such plans.

Example 1: Compensation and turnover. The 2000 Lodging Compensation and Benefits Survey, conducted by Realtime Hotel Reports (now part of Smith Travel Research) and sponsored

by the American Hotel Foundation, provides direct evidence for the need to consider HR factors throughout the strategic-planning process. In addition to compensation levels and benefits offered by over 2000 hotels, the survey also gathered information about employee turnover. Turnover is a key concern to many hospitality employers. It can be quite costly (Hinkin and Tracey, 2000, 14–21) and has been shown to be related to many important outcomes, including profitability (Simons and Hinkin, 2001, 65–69). As such, understanding HR policies and practices that can contribute to turnover can lead to more insightful strategic and operational decision-making.

An analysis of the relationship between compensation level and total annual employee turnover (Table 9.7) yielded statistically significant results for the following positions.[4]

While the magnitude of the correlations demonstrates that a great deal of variance in the compensation-turnover relationship remains unexplained, the data suggest that compensation

Table 9.7 **Analysis of the Relationship between Compensation Level and Total Annual Employee Turnover**

POSITION	N	X
General manager	363	−0.24
Director of sales and marketing	172	−0.20
Sales manager	145	−0.19
Reservations manager	94	−0.19
Controller	125	−0.19
Front-office manager	220	−0.17
Restaurant manager	109	−0.17
Chief engineer	252	−0.11
Executive housekeeper	311	−0.10

does have an effect on intentions to stay or leave—a finding supported by related research (Simons and Enz, 1995, 20–27).

Example 2: Training, turnover, and sales. The second example is based on an analysis of training, employee turnover, and sales data gathered from a privately held restaurant company that currently owns and operates approximately 115 restaurants and franchises an additional 70 throughout the United States. Complete data for 96 corporate-owned stores were gathered over a 12-month period beginning in January 2001. The primary proposition was that investments in training and employee turnover would be significant predictors of net sales. The training variable was expressed as the number of hours per month dedicated to skill-based programs (e.g., new employee training) and development-based programs (e.g., interpersonal customer service) for line staff. Employee turnover was also measured on a monthly basis (i.e., number of new hires divided by the total number of employees at the end of the month), as was net sales.

After accounting for store-specific effects (e.g., location, size) and time effects, the results from regression analyses of the panel data showed that both training and turnover accounted for significant variance in store sales.[5] These results suggest that if sales are influenced by training and employee turnover, then long-range plans for growth must consider the consequences of HR decisions regarding employee development and retention.

These two examples demonstrate the effects that HR can have on strategic and operational goals. Although researchers and practitioners have yet to fully understand the process by which the various HR policies, practices, and systems might influence long-range effectiveness, the data presented here reinforce the need to consider HR throughout the planning process. However, it's not enough simply to incorporate HR influences more broadly—the HR function must also be reconsidered. We contend that a holistic and collaborative approach to HR is required, one in which the HR function is closely integrated within the strategic and operational elements of the firm. Thus, HR plays a critical role in designing structures, facilitating change, and evaluating progress. This objective requires that firms embrace a new model of HR to achieve and sustain a competitive advantage.

✦ A NEW MODEL FOR HUMAN RESOURCES

The traditional role of HR is more appropriately termed "personnel." In this role, personnel professionals were responsible for recruiting and hiring, compensation- and benefit-program design, negotiating and administering collective-bargaining agreements, policy development, personnel recordkeeping, and serving as a conduit for employee views and concerns. Over the years, personnel was renamed human resources, and its role in the organization (in addition to its existing functions) became one of integrating people, policies, and cultures. To meet the needs of this role, HR practitioners' responsibilities were expanded to include communications, training, safety, employee relations, and recognition and reward programs. Along with those additional responsibilities the HR department became responsible for the organization's legal compliance in the ever-expanding area of employment law.

The expansion of the HR function resulted from changes in the way businesses were managed. One such change was the explosion of mergers and acquisitions in the hotel and restaurant industry. In the past 20 years, mergers and acquisitions have tested HR practitioners' ability to be flexible, detail oriented, and expeditious in both their support of other business functions and in the decisions they make related to HR issues. These increases in responsibility, occurring alongside changes in the business, transformed HR professionals from generalists to specialists. This metamorphosis also fostered the perception—often promoted by HR—that only "specialists" could handle such complicated issues. The HR model that emerged was one based on the centralization of knowledge, responsibility, authority, accountability, and control within the HR department.

Even as all this was taking place, however, business practices were changing. As a colleague of ours succinctly put it:

As organizations began to realize that different businesses needed and could afford different types of HR programs and benefits, even within the same corporation, HR began to decentralize, replicating the centralized HR structure at division and even business-unit levels. This had the advantage of supporting differentiated HR for each business, but its redundancies cost a lot of money and the specialist jobs got smaller (i.e., they supported smaller groups of employees) and thus attracted less capable or experienced people.[6]

Added to the complexity of this decentralized approach is the fact that business leaders are under extreme pressure to reduce expenses, increase productivity and revenues, and realign their organizations to become focused on core issues. In the last five years, these changes have led to enormous pressures being placed on businesses to reevaluate the HR function, its role and responsibilities, and how these integrate with the rest of the organization. High-performing organizations today are looking for ways to transfer authority, responsibility, and accountability for HR-related transactions and decisions to line managers and, in some instances, employees. The ramifications of this are enormous. Ironically, we see the most resistance to this change often coming from HR itself.

✦ A DECENTRALIZED FOUNDATION

The underlying premise of our model is that all decision-making authority, responsibility, and accountability should be vested in the person who supervises the employee. Thus, decisions related to hiring, promotion or demotion, training, work actions,[7] pay, and scheduling can and should be made by the immediate supervisor of the affected employee. In many cases actions of this kind do require additional approvals from the company's upper echelons. However, the farther away from the source that these decisions are actually made, the less likely it is that real-time and relevant information about the decision and its outcome will be available for the decision maker. It is also important to note that the time it takes to complete the decision-making process is extended in direct proportion to the distance it has to travel through an organization's bureaucracy.

One key construct in our proposed HR model is that HR practitioners will no longer make operational decisions, but rather act as consultants to other business functions by designing, developing, and delivering programs that give line managers the tools and training they need to effectively perform their responsibilities. The following scenarios represent common decisions made by HR practitioners.

Scenario 1: An employee resigns and the manager needs to fill the vacancy. The process will probably include deciding whether the open position can and should be filled, locating and interviewing applicants, determining whom to hire and how much to pay that person, assigning a start date, conducting training, and determining whether to retain the new employee. In the real world the immediate supervisor will know the most about everything relating to those issues and be in the best position to make the most appropriate and timely decisions. The need for direct HR intervention should be minimal.

Scenario 2: A service employee is not performing up to expectations in spite of being trained and supervised. The organization has documented policies and practices relating to progressive discipline and the issuance of notification to the employee. The supervisor should have full authority to determine the need, timing, wording, and level of notice to be given. While it's practical to assume that this type of decision might require some additional approvals, the managers directly related to the employee's performance are best suited to understanding the issues and nuances involved.

In these situations, usually there are policies and processes that require the involvement of the HR department. Yet in most organizations these decisions are best made in a timely manner by the individuals who know the most about

the issues. HR specialists should be involved in this decision-making process, but final decisions would ultimately be made by individuals outside of the HR function.

Our model has drawbacks, perhaps, but some of that relates to the fact that HR information is not always shared with line managers. One drawback is line managers' potential ignorance of the fine points of HR practice and law. The centralization of the HR function occurred in part because there was a belief that the legal and organizational issues involved in making HR decisions were so complicated that it would not be prudent to trust non-HR supervisors to make them.

Moreover, the decentralized model's redundancies could be costly. Under the new HR model the power to make decisions is entrusted to line managers. In this model it is the role of the HR practitioners to assist companies in training managers how to make and implement business decisions and then entrust them with the authority to do so. If such decision-making power is not distributed to line managers, they will not gain the necessary skills to be able to effectively perform their duties. In contrast, if line managers are supported in the HR function, the necessary information will be spread throughout the organization.

The examples in Table 9.8 illustrate how HR practitioners can use the constructs of this new model.

The responsibilities identified in Table 9.8 follow the functions that are traditionally found in HR departments. Organizations with centralized HR functions adopt these "traditional practices" on the theory that they are specialized and should only be conducted by those who are trained and skilled. That approach presupposes that being in HR is the only way to gain that expertise, and

Table 9.8 Examples of the New HR Model in Operation

TRADITIONAL PRACTICE	SUGGESTED PRACTICE UNDER THE NEW MODEL
Recruitment HR departments have become gatekeepers for whom and how many to hire.	As part of the strategic planning and budgeting process, departments should be responsible for determining and justifying staffing levels. Once identified, decisions on whether to fill positions, and with whom, should be left to the department. The role of HR should be to establish suggested sources for obtaining applicants (both internal and external), designing methods for communicating with applicants using those sources, and developing an applicant tracking system. HR should also assist line managers in developing appropriate interviewing methods and materials, train the managers to use them, and monitor the process for legal and policy compliance. Information technology now exists to provide managers with self-service capabilities to find and track applicants. At Bellagio, for example, HR designed a self-service system for applicants, which eliminated the need for data input by HR staff and allowed applicants (both internal and external) to update and monitor their application information and status. These systems are always available and can help reduce the workload of the HR staff.
Compensation HR departments control both the design and administration of the compensation program.	Salary administration can be managed by line departments through technology, such as the web-based models developed by Melonís HR Solutions group, that provides managers with the data and analytical tools that they need. This gives the responsibility and accountability for these decisions to the departments; HR's role is to provide advice and establish proper control mechanisms to prevent the inexpert (non-specialist) manager from making inappropriate decisions. In this role, HR facilitates the gathering of competitive data and then provides it directly to line managers so they can do their own payroll modeling.
Job Training New hires attend an orientation conducted by HR, and then they are given some form of on-the-job training.	All new employees attend a general company orientation that is designed by HR and presented by fellow employees. This will give the new hires a peer perspective and help them to develop relationships with other employees. Department and job training should be conducted by a trained trainer from the new employee's department or job. This trainer should have the added responsibility of evaluating the new employee's performance and conducting any retraining that may be required. HR's role should be helping to create the training materials, training the trainers, and implementing a tracking system to allow managers to monitor course attendance and related performance. Park Place Entertainment, for instance, has developed this type of employee development system. The HR department has developed scripts and protocols that serve as templates for all training and development efforts. Line managers are primarily responsible for content, giving them more control over the job- and department-specific training needs. An example of this decentralized approach to development is PricewaterhouseCoopers, which has developed online knowledge management systems that give consultants access to problem solutions that have been identified from prior projects and that may have relevance for current client needs. This type of real-time learning enhances the quality and efficiency of project work.

(Continued)

Table 9.8 (*Continued*)

TRADITIONAL PRACTICE	SUGGESTED PRACTICE UNDER THE NEW MODEL
Record Maintenance Managers fill out work-action documents (e.g., wage and job changes, disciplinary notices, and performance reviews) and submit them to HR. These are then checked for accuracy and keyed into a database, and the originals are placed in file folders. Employees also submit information that initiates actions such as vacation requests, address changes, and other general requests. These are routed through MR in a similar manner as the management documents.	Using self-service technology, managers and employees fill out and submit transaction data directly to HR or the database, where they are ultimately stored and used. Starwood's online "executive dashboard," for example, provides the corporate office with continuous information about a wide range of property-level data that are directly related to strategic goals—from employee and guest satisfaction data to occupancy and rate information. In addition, operations managers have direct access to the data, thus freeing HR from the responsibility of facilitating access requests and generating reports. HR should learn about technology and actively participate in the development of these self-service tools, and then train managers how to use them. Many organizations today are outsourcing HR, payroll, and benefits administration, and are using Internet connectivity to facilitate transactions and maintain access to their data. Many are also adopting shared-service approaches that are designed to bring more functionality and service capabilities to line managers and employees.
Management Policies Most companies have handbooks and policy manuals that strictly define legal concerns and consistent policies and processes. These materials are often printed and distributed in hopes that employees will keep them in an accessible place and read them when needed. They seek to cover every conceivable circumstance with carefully written rules, policies, and practices.	Replace company-wide rules with concepts that are consistent with local and departmental concerns. Involve line managers in the process of determining these concepts to ensure that they are applicable to the department's needs and concerns. Base the concepts on values and principles rather than rules. Policies and practices should focus on being fair rather than merely consistent. Workers in the 21st century expect to be treated as individuals, and when presented properly these practices have greater acceptance than those that treat everyone identically in every circumstance. Practices of this kind will be easiest for managers to understand, use, defend, and enforce. For example, Le Parker Meridien in New York City has a long history of focusing on values—from "frank and fearless feedback" to "happy but never satisfied"—which are the primary drivers for individual behavior and set standards for accountability and performance. HR should also monitor competitive practices and provide this information to managers. In some cases, this benchmarking information is also available online.
Organizational Structure Most companies have a hierarchical design in which decisions are made at the top and then implemented at the bottom of the supervisory structure. While empowerment as a practice has been widely debated, most organizations still maintain practices where authority is vested at the highest levels of this hierarchy.	Companies such as Winegardner & Hammons are flattening their organizational structures and giving line managers the flexibility and authority to make decisions. In other organizations, such as The Boulders in Carefree, Arizona, self-managed work teams are obviating the need for supervisory interventions and allowing trained employees to set the tone and monitor the behavior of their teams. Within both structures, decisions are made in context, with a focus on what is most relevant and important to those involved.

further, that this expertise is more important than understanding the operational nuances that exist at the line level. We suggest that HR expertise can be gained by those at the line level more easily than can the nuances of departmental activity be understood by those in HR. The key to transferring these responsibilities to the line level is training the supervisors in how best to perform these duties, providing them with the tools and technology to effectively and efficiently carry out these responsibilities, supporting them with advice, and monitoring their performance. This means that the role of HR changes from gatekeeper and decision maker to trainer and supporter.

Additionally, management should put in place strategies that reinforce the performance of managers who adopt and successfully handle these duties. Indeed, that should be tied to their reviews and total compensation. This is consistent with the goals of (a) the organization to have better-trained and -performing managers, and (b) most HR professionals to be more of an internal consultant and strategic partner than mere arbiters of proper practice. This new construct allows the line managers to achieve new competencies and control, while giving HR professionals the chance to become more of what they want to be—and should be. The organization benefits from using this new model, because decisions are made more quickly and appropriately, allowing the business to be more focused on its core responsibilities of production and service.

✦ ENABLING TECHNOLOGY

Public and private companies alike are driven to make effective decisions and to improve performance through expense control and revenue improvement. Over the past 20 years, tools have been developed to help organizations achieve these goals. This trend began when financial departments discovered online analytical processing (OLAP) tools that allowed them to collate and query information from all of the disparate files in their databases and develop queries therefrom. This ad hoc interactive querying capability allowed them to conduct complex multidimensional analyses and more rapidly discern issues that needed to be addressed. This practice provided a means for organizations to control expenses more effectively and thus improve their bottom lines.

The next challenge involved improving revenues beyond the normal realm of sales and marketing. Those same OLAP tools, when applied to complex and disparate customer databases, allowed companies to target their efforts and dollars in ways that maximized revenue opportunities. Today, customer-relationship-management (CRM) systems are helping these companies to better use their resources to satisfy their customers and increase revenues. Much has been written about these practices. For example:

> The new cross-departmental imperative for companies in virtually all industries is to empower decision makers to obtain quick answers to their business questions by immediately acquiring the information they need. The effective sharing, distillation, and analysis of information among such an array of departments—customer relationship, sales, product planning, marketing, and finance, for example—coalesces into an enterprise-wide intelligence that is greater than the sum of its informational parts (Liautaud and Hammond, 2001, 5).

As these practices become perfected, organizations will look for additional ways to improve performance, and we suggest that HR is the next area to which these might be applied. Adding employee-activity data to the practice of interactive and multidimensional analyses will help organizations to truly get the most out of their human resources. To gain this capability, human-resources departments in highly successful organizations "will understand how to use systems and software to solve business problems and will exploit technologies to achieve their business goals" (Boyett, Boyett, Henson, and Spirgi-Hebert, 2001, 28). The decision makers in this instance are the line managers, and the decisions are related to the management of their employees; giving line managers the use of a system like this will increase their access to data and give them the ability to make better decisions. This technology will assist them in converting those data into intelligence. It is expensive to store and maintain all of these data, and "until it is put in the hands of business users and brings real value to these business users, the value obtained from that information does not compensate for the cost of maintaining that data" (Liautaud and Hammond, 2001, 38). While the initial capital investments required to develop and implement decision-support technology may be high, the operational savings[8] and improved decision quality more than justify the investment.

The appropriate use of technology is critical to the successful transfer of responsibility from HR to the line managers and departments. The use of business-intelligence technology and tools will enhance line managers' skills and decision-making capabilities by giving them the same view that was once reserved for HR staff. Again, the key to this will be the training and support provided by the HR staff.

✦ SOME ADDITIONAL THOUGHTS

We would be remiss if we didn't offer some thoughts related to the tragic events of September 11, 2001, which occurred during the conceptualization and writing of early drafts of this original manuscript. The pressure on management to react to the terrorist acts and their effect on the hospitality industry has been intense. The range of responses to the plunge in business levels was varied and is not germane to our discussion. What is important to note is that swift, intelligent, and decisive actions were required in the wake of the attack. That supports the need to adopt new roles for HR and line managers.

A company's ability to adapt to changing conditions depends not only on its policies, but also on the tools that it provides to those responsible for deciding and implementing its strategies. HR departments worked with their management teams to define the strategies to address issues relevant to the attacks and then helped to implement them. Line managers needed accurate information about business and staffing levels, staff skills and abilities, and financial-modeling capabilities. Having HR and line managers in possession of and trained to use the most effective tools available will ensure the organization's capacity to meet its needs. This enlightened division of responsibilities will result in the most orderly and informed execution of each group's tasks, and promote teamwork.

It seems to us that the best part of a line manager's job is having the ability to make decisions that are most critical for a department's success. Conversely, the things that managers dislike have to do with the HR department's always telling them what to do. In truth, there are probably times when it would be convenient to pass certain responsibilities to HR, so that line managers don't have to make those decisions or would at least have someone to point to as the culprits. In the end, however, the role of a manager is about responsibility and accountability, and the adage that "the buck stops here" seems to have been written with that in mind. The following requirements will help line managers feel most comfortable in this role:

a. They have some say in the development of a company's policies and practices;

b. The company provides them with the tools and training to perform at this level;

c. There is a clear definition of HR's and line managers' responsibilities;

d. They are recognized and rewarded for good performance relative to these issues; and

e. There are programs in place to help when mistakes are made.

If it is true that our future success both at the business level and as HR practitioners lies in the adoption of new ideas and technologies, and that leaner, more focused organizations are the ones that succeed, it is imperative that this transition to a new HR model occur. To assure that the transition is smooth, we will need to learn from others' errors as well as our own mistakes, and we will need the steadfast support of the organization in maintaining this new set of roles and responsibilities.

ENDNOTES FOR SECTION 9.5

1. Statement made by the CEO and chairman of a medium-size management company of mid-price hotels.

2. For example, Paauwe and Richardson reviewed nine studies that yielded 22 significant empirical relationships between various HR policies, practices, and procedures, and several measures of firm performance. See J. Paauwe and R. Richardson, "Strategic Human Resource Management and Performance," *International Journal of Human Resource Management*, Introduction to the Special Issue, Vol. 8, No. 3, pp. 257–262.

3. Youndt, Snell, Dean, and Lepak, for instance, found that different types of organizational strategy moderated the relationship between two types of HR systems and firm performance. Specifically, Youndt et al. found that a "human capital enhancing" HR system (e.g., selectivity in hiring) was most effective in organizations that incorporated a quality-based strategy (versus other strategies). They also found that an "administrative" HR system (e.g., policies and procedures training) was most effective in organizations that employed a cost-based strategy. Thus, this study provided convincing evidence that organizational effectiveness is contingent on the proper alignment of HR systems and overall business strategy. See M. A. Youndt, S. A. Snell, J. W. Dean, and D. P. Lepak, "Human-Resources Management, Manufacturing Strategy, and Firm Performance," *Academy of Management Journal*, Vol. 39, No. 4, pp. 836–866.

4. All significant at p .05.

5. Overall $F = 44.32$, $df1 = 123$, $df2 = 1085$; $R2 = 0.82$, $p < .01$; standardized beta weights for training and turnover were 0.031 and 0.032, respectively, $p < .01$. These and related results were presented by J. Bruce Tracey and Michael J. Tews at the 2002 Meeting of the Society for Industrial and Organizational Psychology, Toronto, Canada.

6. As related by Andrew Geller, principal, organizational development, Unifi Network, a former subsidiary of PricewaterhouseCoopers LLP, Teaneck, New Jersey, April 26, 2001.

7. These are defined as disciplinary actions, commendations, granting of leaves, and the completion of related paperwork.

8. Alanna Klaussen, senior analyst with Radiant Systems, Inc., has demonstrated that a 2-percent to 10-percent savings in payroll expenses can be realized by adopting decision-support technology.

9.6 A DAY IN THE LIFE OF A DIRECTOR OF EDUCATION AND DEVELOPMENT JENNIFER LUCAS, LOEWS HOTELS

Having worked in the Food & Beverage division in hotels for years I was worried about moving off property and into a corporate role. Every day in a hotel is different—between the guests, employee situations, and new problems to solve, there is never a dull moment. What would it be like to sit behind a desk for a whole day? In operations it was usually a luxury to spend more than an hour in my office at my desk—and typically that was late at night or early in the morning. Even with my move into the regional training manager role, I was juggling three properties so training on property was just as hectic as operations. How would someone who thrives on being in the mix of the action survive in a totally foreign environment? The answer is—easily! As the corporate director of education and development, I have the best of both worlds. It's not easy to describe a "normal" day because, just like being a hotel, every day is different.

✦ A "NORMAL" DAY IN THE OFFICE

9 A.M.—It's time for our morning meeting. Just as if we were on property this is our preshift. We cover all the same elements that are shared in each of our hotels—including our brandwide topic of the day and reading a real story of one of our team members making a difference in a guest's experience. A quick review of everyone's schedule and projects for the day and we're off. I myself have several meetings and conference calls throughout the day, plus a couple of projects nearing completion.

Education and Development encompasses much more than just training. Training is part of it and we write curriculum used for both our hourly team member and management classes. With a class to roll out next week, I review the latest version of the lesson plan—couple more tweaks to make and we'll be set. I meet with the corporate training manager working on the project to discuss the changes. We are ready to schedule a conference call with our training managers in the field to review the lesson plan and exercises so they are prepared to start delivering the class on property. Before the call they will receive all the materials to read, so any questions can be answered on the call. With our heavy focus on building a brand, consistent content and delivery are more important than ever. In this case, we are working on a short refresher for our team members, so we won't personally be facilitating this class. Our leadership and management classes are typically facilitated by one of the three of us on the Home Office team.

Ready to turn my attention to the next task, I prepare for a conference call with our secret shop provider. A component of our responsibility that takes up a good deal of time and focus is documenting, updating, measuring, and reporting our operating and brand standards across the company. Ensuring the information is accurate and available for all is critical. The purpose of this particular call is to review recent updates and discuss several observations from recent property visits. The shoppers work with our standards and are trained together to ensure consistency in the scoring. They go into each hotel anonymously and stay as a guest; assessing all departments and comparing performance to standards. This in depth "snapshot" of a single guest experience allows us ensure that our hotels are adhering to standards.

The call ends and I am pulling together information for my next meeting when the phone rings. On the phone is the HR director from one of the properties looking to see who might be ready in the company to be an executive housekeeper. All of our managers are in our talent bank so I pull up information on possible candidates who are willing to relocate, reviewing our list of high-potentials first. In our talent bank I have access to all past experience, education, languages, performance, readiness, and other information useful in finding the best candidate. At first glance we have a couple of options, so I let the HR director know I will be back in touch. I make a call to a general manager to talk to her about the possibility of discussing the opportunity with their assistant executive housekeeper. The general manager is supportive of the move, and I send out a note to the candidate to set up a time to discuss the opportunity with them. One of the benefits of being in a smaller hotel company is this personal level of communication.

I gather several reports and my notes and head to a meeting. The executive vice president, director of operations, and I are discussing recent trends seen in several hotels service scores. After reviewing shop reports, reading current guest satisfaction survey comments, and conducting research with several managers at various properties (including the food & beverage director and training managers), I have a sense of why we are seeing this current trend and the actions the hotel is taking to correct the trend. We decide to monitor the scores closely for a couple more weeks to let the action plans take effect.

Switching gears again, I head to a pre-opening meeting for our newest hotel. Coordinating an opening includes a very intense training plan, which begins over a year before the property hires the first team member. With 6 months to go, we're getting closer to opening and we are meeting today to review the project timeline and verify that all the different Home Office disciplines are on track. In a couple of months, our team will be traveling to the new location frequently to train our newest team members on the Loews culture and standards.

Back in the office again, I turn to email. It's the time of year when everyone is entering their goals into our performance management system, so there are several questions from managers in the field about their goals and the software. I see that the assistant executive housekeeper has responded and is available. Several new shop reports have been posted. The vice president of HR, my boss, is available tomorrow to review our recommendations for updating and revamping several team member recognition programs. The conference call information and new workshop have been sent to the training managers and my meeting rooms and schedule for an upcoming trip are confirmed. In a couple more hours, with email questions answered, a phone call made to the manager curious about the opportunity, and preparations made for the meeting with my boss in the morning, I'll head home for the night.

✦ A "NORMAL" DAY ON THE ROAD

Having arrived last night and checked on the location of the workshop in the morning, I know exactly where I am going when I head out of my room. It's 7 A.M. and, while the workshop does not begin until 8:30 A.M., I want to be sure everything is set up long before the first person walks in the room. The training manager has already delivered all the workbooks to the room and I start preparing flipcharts, pull up the PowerPoint, test all the equipment, and am ready to go. The participants in the workshop are a great mix of managers new to Loews and those recently promoted. The HR director and general manager come to kick off the workshop with a brief introduction. We will be in class for a half-day as they have a project to work on in small groups before we continue tomorrow.

At lunch I join the training manager and HR director in the team member cafeteria. We have a busy afternoon with several career development sessions—each lasting about 45 minutes. I review the participants' profile covering their career history and credentials as well as the data from their pre-selection behavioral interview. The sessions include their manager and the HR director. We share their top five strengths from the behavioral interview and discuss ways to leverage those talents in their role. We use that review to lead into a discussion about their career goals and what they need to do to prepare for those future opportunities. The participant will follow up our meeting by submitting a development action plan.

Career Development sessions wrap up at 3 P.M., and I have the first of several roundtables with team members. This session is with seven team members all hired within the last 90-days. We are meeting to discuss their on boarding and training. Feedback from these sessions allows us to ensure we are setting our new hires up for a long successful career with us. We are able to provide immediate feedback to the training manager and Department Heads and continuously improve our training practices.

Next, after a quick conversation with the training manager to review tomorrow's schedule, I meet with the managers in our high potential program. Since we are about half way through this year's program, I am looking forward to an update on the projects we selected together 4 months ago. This hotel happens to have four participants and each has the opportunity to review their portfolio and discuss their key projects.

At 6:30 P.M., after hearing all about the great progress each manager is making on their leadership and educational initiatives, I join the HRD director and general manager for dinner. The general manager wants to know how service has been and asks about the guest room, the arrival experience last night, and for any feedback that I have thus far. We also talk about the class earlier in the day and some of the ideas and comments shared during the workshop. I invite him to stop in tomorrow when the group will be presenting what they have been working on this afternoon.

By 9 P.M. I am back in my guest room, time to respond to email and then prepare for a full day of teaching tomorrow. Long day today, but it's all worthwhile when you love what you do. As I said, there is never a dull moment—whether in the office or on the road in a hotel.

9.7 A DAY IN THE LIFE OF A DIRECTOR OF HUMAN RESOURCES

Felipe G. Cofiño

You're FIRED, Hired, Trained, Coached, Recognized, Disciplined, Promoted, and Eligible for Benefits, these are just a few of the areas of responsibilities that occupy a director of human resources day.

I remember my first day working at a hotel. I was 20 years old, and I had just put on my front desk uniform and was walking from the locker room up three floors to the front desk, which took maybe 3–5 minutes. In that time, I had at least 10 people stop me in the hall to say "hello," "welcome," "you must be new," or "do you need any help getting to your department?" My first reaction was who are you people and why are you being so nice? Over time I realized, these people are happy, I mean really happy and engaging.

Now here I am, 19 years later, and I am still with the same company. I have worked at eight different Hyatt Hotels in the DC area. Many of my friends and family, as well as other professionals ask, why have you stayed with the same company for that long? My answer is plain and simple, the people. If I had to describe our culture in one word, I would say Family! The people and the culture is what makes my job exciting and different everyday.

My typical morning begins with my human resources team walking into the office and having our brief morning chat. My human resources team consists of an assistant director of human resources, a recruitment manager, and a human resources generalist. Then after a quick check of my emails I attend an 8:30 A.M. Huddle meeting in our associate dining room. In this meeting a representative from each department comes and communicates what is happening in their areas that day. I then go get my daily Grande Vanilla Cappuccino and walk around the hotel to say good morning to everyone. One of the benefits of walking around is that there are many associates and managers who may not make it down to see us in human resources because they are busy. By walking by to see them, they are able to communicate any questions or concerns to me that I can either address right then and there or I research the issue and get back to them. One of the other benefits of walking around and speaking to the associates and managers is that it builds relationships. I then return to the human resources office for our daily stand-up meeting. This is a 5–10-minute meeting to communicate what was said in the huddle meeting and to discuss what we are working on in human resources that day. After standup, we turn on some music in the office and get to work.

I can never anticipate what the day will bring, which makes each day very interesting. I usually go back to checking emails, which never stop coming. When I have time in the morning, I like to do some research on innovative and creative ideas to improve employee relations, guest service, or training. It is very easy to do what you have traditionally done in the past because it is familiar and you do not have to re-create the wheel. However, innovation and creativity only help a person to be an effective leader, manager or trainer.

Usually by 10 A.M., I make it up to the general manager's office for my daily update. I spend time updating him on any associate concerns, upcoming training, and any HR-related projects. In turn, he asks me questions he has about compliance, policy- or legal-related issues. During this time we also discuss hotelwide concerns or improvement ideas. The general manager depends on the human resources director to provide him guidance when it comes to issues with the Executive Committee, individual managers, or hotelwide associate issues.

I then return to my office to complete some work. Whether it be a project from Corporate, one from my general manager, or a human resources project, I like to dedicate a portion of each day focusing on a specific project. Then I focus on my team by conducting one-on-one sessions. Each person has a different day for their one-on-one with me and they typically are relaxed sessions with very open dialog. During these sessions we discuss items they are working on as well as discussing their professional development. In these meetings we set goals and deadlines for the items discussed.

At this point in the day, I go to the associate dining room for lunch and then after lunch there is usually a meeting I need to attend. Depending on the day, it could be the Managing Committee meeting for the executives of the hotel, a staff meeting for all managers, a departmental meeting, a Safety Committee meeting, a service improvement meeting or a Green Team meeting for the environmental initiatives. These are just a few of the meetings that take place on a consistent basis. Other committee meetings that come up throughout the year are Make-A-Wish committee, Associate Awards Banquet committee, Associate Dining Room Committee, and the Diversity Council.

In the afternoons is when I usually have interviews, counseling sessions, or training sessions scheduled. It is also a time when there tends to be webinars and conference calls being held. After I am done with this part of the day, I go for a walk around the hotel to touch base with the associates that have come in for the P.M. shift. Then I end up by the front desk area where we conduct our PM Huddle meeting with a representative from each department. At the conclusion of huddle, I return to the office to check emails, follow up with the associates I spoke to that day and wrap up and work for the day. I always end my day by thanking my human resources team for all of their hard work.

Now, it would not be fair if I did not share some of the unique things that happen on a fairly regular basis that add the extra excitement to my day. On any given day we could have an associate get terminated for stealing, a fire, an applicant coming in for an interview drunk, a flood in the ballroom, a guest hitting the parking attendant with her purse, an associate complaining about another associate taking off their shoe or an associate claiming discrimination against their manager. These are just a few of the examples of what keeps each day different and exciting for a director of human resources.

REFERENCES

Barney, J. B. 1997. *Gaining and Sustaining Competitive Advantage.* Reading, MA: Addison-Wesley.

Baum, T. 1991. "The U.S. and the U.K.: Comparing Expectations of Management Trainees." *Cornell Hotel and Restaurant Administration Quarterly* 32(2): 79–84.

Birdir, K., and T. E. Pearson. 2000. "Research Chefs' Competencies: A Delphi Approach." *International Journal of Contemporary Hospitality Management* 12(3): 205–209.

Bluedorn, A. C. 1982. "Theories of Turnover: Causes, Effects and Meaning." *In Research in Sociology of Organizations*, S. E. Bacharach and E. J. Lawler (eds.). Greenwich, CT: JAI Press, pp. 75–128.

Boyett, J. H., J. T. Boyett, R. Henson, and H. Spirgi-Hebert. 2001. *HR in the New Economy: Trends and Leading Practices in Human Resources Management.* Pleasanton, CA: PeopleSoft, p. 28.

Breiter, D., and C. J. Clements. 1996. "Hospitality Management Curricula for the 21st Century." *Hospitality & Tourism Educator* 8(1): 57–60.

Breiter, D., and H. Hoart. 2000. "Competencies in Food-service Information Technology Expected by the Food-service Industry of Graduates of Hospitality Bachelor's Degree Programs in the United States." *Journal of Hospitality & Tourism Education* 12(2): 11–17.

Brownell, J. 1992. "Hospitality Managers' Communication Practices." *International Journal of Hospitality Management* 11(2): 111–128.

Brownell, J. 1994. "Women in Hospitality Management: General Managers' Perceptions of Factors Related to Career Development." *International Journal of Hospitality Management* 13(2): 1017–1017.

Cannon, D. F. 1999. "Career Dynamics of Hotel Sales and Marketing Professionals." *Journal of Hospitality & Tourism Education* 11(4): 40–44.

Carper, J. 1994. "People, Trends and Ideas." *Hotels* 28(4): 21–22.

Cho, W., and D. J. Connolly. 1999. "U.S.-based Hospitality Programs: Looking to Keep Pace with Today's High-tech Industry Needs." *International Journal of Hospitality Information Technology* 1(1): 27–43.

Chung, K. Y. 2000. "Hotel Management Curriculum Reform Based on Required Competencies of Hotel Employees and Career Success in the Hotel Industry." *Tourism Management* 21(5): 473–487.

Chung-Herrera, B., C. Enz, and M. Lankau. 2003. "Grooming Future Hospitality Leaders: A Competencies Mode." *Cornell Hotel and Restaurant Administration Quarterly* 44(3): 17–25.

Enz, C. A. 2001. "What Keeps You Up at Night? Key Issues of Concern for Lodging Managers." *Cornell Hotel and Restaurant Administration Quarterly* 42(2): 38–45.

Flynn, G. 2000. "Predictions About the Future of Employment Law." *Workforce* 79(1): 78–80.

Goldberg, A. C. 1998. "Top Employment Law Issues for 1999." *HR Focus* 75(12): 1–3.

Gorchels, L., T. Jambulingam, and T. W. Aurand. 1999. "Executive Insights: International Marketing Managers: A Comparison of Japanese, German, and U.S. Perceptions." *Journal of International Marketing* 7(1): 97–105.

Herzberg, F. 1976. *The Managerial Choice: To Be Efficient and To Be Human.* Homewood, IL: Dow Jones–Irwin.

Heskett, J. L., T. O. Jones, G. W. Loveman, W. E. Sasser, and L. A. Schlessinger. 1984. "Putting the Service-Profit Chain to Work." *Harvard Business Review* (March–April).

Hinkin, T. R., and J. B. Tracey. 2000. "The Cost of Turnover: Putting a Price on the Learning Curve." *Cornell Hotel and Restaurant Administration Quarterly* 41(3): 14–21.

Hsu, C. H. C. 1995. "Computer Skills Needed and Demonstrated by Hospitality Management Graduates: Perceptions of Hotel Operators." *Journal of Hospitality & Tourism Education* 7(2): 25–29.

Hsu, J. F., and S. R. Gregory. "Developing Future Hotel Managers in Taiwan: From an Industry Viewpoint." *International Journal of Hospitality Management* 14(3–4): 261–269.

Jackson, D., and John Humble. "Middle Managers: New Purpose, New Directions." *Journal of Management Development* 13(3):15–21.

Jackson, S. E., and R. S. Schuler. 2000. *Managing Human Resources: A Partnership Perspective.* Cincinnati, OH: South-Western College Publishing.

Kay, C., and J. Russett. 2000. "Hospitality-management Competencies: Identifying Managers' Essential Skills." *Cornell Hotel and Restaurant Administration Quarterly* 41(2): 52–63.

Knutson, B. J., and R. S. Schmidgall. 2001. "Challenges and Opportunities for Women: Achieving Success in Hospitality Financial Management." *Journal of Hospitality & Tourism Education* 13(3–4): 45–54.

Liautaud, B. with M. Hammond. 2001. *e-Business Intelligence: Turning Information into Knowledge into Profit.* New York: McGraw-Hill, p. 5.

Mandabach, K. H., D. VanLeeuwen, and P. Bloomquist. 2001. "Hospitality Technology Education: Student Successes in Mastering the Hidden Curriculum." *Journal of Hospitality & Tourism Education* 13(1): 49–56.

March, J. G., and H. Simon. 1958. *Organizations.* New York: John Wiley.

McFillen, J. M., C. D. Riegel, and C. A. Enz. 1986. "Why Restaurant Managers Quit (and How to Keep Them)." *Cornell Hotel and Restaurant Administration Quarterly* 27(3): 36–43.

Nelson, A. A., and L. Dopson. 2001. "Future of Hotel Education: Required Skills and Knowledge for Graduates of U.S. Hospitality Programs Beyond the Year 2000-Part One." *Journal of Hospitality & Tourism Education* 13(5): 58–64.

Okeiyi, E., D. Finley, and R. T. Postel. 1994. "Food and Beverage Management Competencies: Educator,

Industry and Student Perspectives." *Hospitality & Tourism Educator* 6(4): 37–40.

Partlow, C. G., and M. B. Gregoire. 1994. "Is Graduate Hospitality Education Relevant?" *Hospitality & Tourism Educator* 6(3): 13–16.

Perdue, J., J. Ninemeier, and R. Woods. 2000. "Competencies Required for Club Managers." *Cornell Hotel and Restaurant Administration Quarterly* 41(2): 79–85.

Phillips, J. A., and D. S. Massey. 1999. "The New Labor Market: Immigrants and Wages after IRCA." *Demography* 36(2): 233–246.

Porter, L. W., and R. W. Steers. 1973. "Organizational Work and Personal Factors in Employee Turnover and Absenteeism." *Psychological Bulletin* 80: 151–176.

Price, J. L. 1977. *The Study of Turnover.* Ames: University of Iowa Press.

Reichheld, F. F. 1996. "Learning from Customer Defections." *Harvard Business Review* 74(2): 56–67.

Shea, R. E. 2000. "The Dirty Dozen." *HR Magazine* 45(1): 52–56.

Sherwyn, D., Z. J. Eigen, and A. A. Klausner. 2000. "Interpreting the ADA and Civil Rights Law." *Cornell Hotel and Restaurant Administration Quarterly* 41(1): 85–93.

Simons, T., and C. A. Enz. 1995. "Motivating Hotel Employees: Beyond the Carrot and the Stick." *Cornell Hotel and Restaurant Administration Quarterly* 36(1): 20–27.

Simons, T., and T. R. Hinkin. 2001. "The Effects of Employee Turnover on Hotel Profits." *Cornell Hotel and Restaurant Administration Quarterly* 42(4): 65–69.

Sovereign, K. L. 1999. *Personnel Law* (4th ed.). Upper Saddle River, NJ: Prentice-Hall.

Su, A. Y. L., J. L. Miller, and C. Shanklin. 1997–1998. "Perceptions of Industry Professionals and Program Administrators About Accreditation Curriculum Standards for Hospitality Programs." *Journal of Hospitality & Tourism Education* 9(4): 36–40.

Tas, R. F. 1988. "Teaching Future Managers." *Cornell Hotel and Restaurant Administration Quarterly* 29(2): 41–43.

Tas, R. F., S. V. LaBrecque, and H. R. Clayton. 1996. "Property-management Competencies for Management Trainees." *Cornell Hotel and Restaurant Administration Quarterly* 37(3): 90–96.

Wilson, M. D. J., A. E. Murray, and M. A. Black. 2000. "Contract Catering: The Skills Required for the Next Millennium." *International Journal of Contemporary Hospitality Management* 12(1): 75–78.

Woods, R. H., D. G. Rutherford, R. Schmidgall, and M. Sciarini. 1998. "Hotel General Managers Focused on the Core Business." *Cornell Hotel and Restaurant Administration Quarterly* 39(6): 38–44.

SUGGESTED READINGS

BOOKS

Armstrong, S. 2008. *The Essential HR Handbook: A Quick and Handy Resource for Any Manager or HR Professional.* Franklin Lakes, NJ: Career Press.

Hayes, D. K., and J. D. Ninemeier. 2009. *Human Resources Management in the Hospitality Industry.* New Jersey: John Wiley and Sons.

Sovereign, K. L. 1999. *Personnel Law*, (4th ed.). Upper Saddle River, NJ: Prentice-Hall.

Smith, S., and R. Mazin. 2004. *HR Answer Book: An Indispensable Guide for Managers and Human Resources Professionals.* New York: AMACOM.

Tesone, D. 2008. *Handbook of Hospitality Human Resources Management.* Burlington, MA: Buttersworth-Heinemann.

Ulrich, D., M. R. Losey, and G. Lake (Eds.) 1997. *Tomorrow's HR Management.* New York: John Wiley and Sons.

Woods, Robert H. 2006. *Managing Hospitality Human Resources* (4th ed.). East Lansing, MI: Educational Institute of American Hotel and Motel Association.

ARTICLES

Carbery, R., T. N. Garavan, F. O'Brien, and J. McDonnell. 2003. "Predicting Hotel Managers' Turnover Cognitions." *Journal of Managerial Psychology* 18(7/8): 649–679.

Head, J., and R. Lucas. 2004. "Employee Relations in the Non-Union Hotel Industry: A Case of 'Determined Opportunism'." *Personnel Review* 33(5–6):693–710.

Kline, S., and K. Harris. 2008. "ROI is MIA: Why are Hoteliers Failing to Demand the ROI of Training?" *Internationals Journal of Contemporary Hospitality Management* 20(1):45–59.

Knicely, H. V. 1997. "The Future of Human Resources: Superhuman Resource Leadership in the Twenty-first Century." *In Tomorrow's HR Management*, D. Ulrich, M. R. Losey, and G. Lake (Eds.). New York: John Wiley and Sons, pp. 111–118.

Tracey, J. B. 2004. "Human Resources Roundtable 2003: Current Issues and Future Developments." *Cornell Hotel and Restaurant Administration Quarterly* 45(4):373–379.

Sherwyn, D., Z. J. Eigen, and A. A. Klausner. 2000. "Interpreting the ADA and Civil Rights Law." *Cornell Hotel and Restaurant Administration Quarterly* 41(1):85–93.

Walsh, K. W., and M. S. Taylor. 2007. "Developing In-House Careers and Retaining Management Talent: What Hospitality Professionals Want from Their Jobs." *Cornell Hotel and Restaurant Administration Quarterly* 48(2):163–182.

Woods, R. H. 2000. "Predicting Is Difficult, Especially About the Future: The Future of Human Resources in Hospitality Management." In *Hotel Management and Operations*, Denney G. Rutherford (Ed.). New York: John Wiley and Sons, pp. 459–469.

SOURCE NOTES

Chapter 9.2, "Knowledge, Skills, and Abilities for Lodging Management Success," by Christine Kay and Elisa Moncarz, is reprinted from the August 2004 issue of *Cornell Hotel and Restaurant Administration Quarterly*. © Cornell University. Used by permission. All rights reserved.

Chapter 9.3, "The Causes and Consequences of Turnover in the Hospitality Industry," by Carl D. Riegel.

Chapter 9.4, "Current Issues in Hospitality Employment Law," by Suzanne K. Murrmann and Cherylynn Becker.

Chapter 9.5, "The Strategic and Operational Roles of Human Resources—An Emerging Model," by J. Bruce Tracey and Arthur E. Nathan, is reprinted from the August 2002 issue of *Cornell Hotel and Restaurant Administration* Quarterly. © Cornell University. Used by permission. All rights reserved.

Chapter 9.6, "A Day in the Life of a Director of Education and Development" by Jennifer Lucas.

Chapter 9.7, "A Day in the Life of a Director of Human Resources," by Felipe G. Cofiño.

INDEX